The Jews Were Expendable

THE JEWS WERE EXPENDABLE,

Free World Diplomacy and the Holocaust

MONTY NOAM PENKOWER

WITHDRAWI

University of Illinois Press
URBANA AND CHICAGO

©1983 by the Board of Trustees of the University of Illinois.
Manufactured in the United States of America.

This book is printed on acid-free paper.

Library of Congress Cataloging in Publication Data

Penkower, Monty Noam, 1942-
   The Jews were expendable.

   Bibliography: p.
   Includes index.
   1. Holocaust, Jewish (1939–1945) 2. World War,
1939–1945—Diplomatic history. I. Title.
D810.J4P44 1983   940.53'15'03924   82-17490
ISBN 0-252-00747-6

To Yael

He who finds a wife finds good
and obtains the favor of the Lord.

Proverbs 18:22

Preface

SIX CENTURIES AFTER Dante Alighieri penned his tortured portrait of hell in 33 cantos, Adolf Hitler resolved to translate this vision of the *Divine Comedy* into reality. With regard to European Jewry, the German *Führer* succeeded fully. His mechanized kingdom of death actually created hell on earth in ways surpassing at times even the Florentine poet's fevered imagination. "Evil, more than good, suggests infinity," concluded the survivor Elie Wiesel after numbly leafing through photograph albums devoted to the Holocaust. Once the Third Reich posited the quintessence of its *Weltanschauung* on a unique, murderous hatred of all "non-Aryans"—read Jews, whose very birth constituted in its eyes guilt expiated by death alone—the Nazi progression into the inhuman knew no limits.[1] As a consequence, all earlier boundaries between the real and the fantastic blurred for the Jewish centers of Europe, which vanished along with six million innocent human beings in the ashes of Ponary, Belzec, Janowska, Auschwitz-Birkenau.

This volume seeks to fathom how and why the nations outside of Hitler's Fortress Europe abdicated moral responsibility and thus became accomplices to history's most monstrous crime. Raul Hilberg's magisterial opus focused on the German perpetrators and their collaborators, while Philip Friedman and Lucy Dawidowicz contributed much to an understanding of the victims' diverse responses. Aspects of the bystanders' conduct have been rewardingly explored by others, although these works lack, at the same time, a broad perspective.[2]

Thinking the subject at hand too vast and complex for inclusion between the covers of one book, I offer the reader nine essays on the diplomacy of the Holocaust. These in-depth case studies examine particular events, yet their separate conclusions, when taken together, possess an underlying unity. The paradigmatic topics chosen analyze the confluence of disbelief, indifference, antisemitism, and, above all, political expediency that obtained in Western counsels during Jewry's bleakest travail. Failure to act, as well as determined policy to frustrate possibilities of rescue, doomed a powerless people—lacking the ground of an autonomous state under its feet—to the diabolic realization of the "Final Solution." Against this prevailing decay of conscience, a few courageous Jews and Gentiles who sought to answer the summons of the hour could accomplish little.

The first two essays focus on the struggle during World War II for an Allied Jewish fighting force and on the "illegal" immigration of Jewish refugees to the national home in Palestine. These issues appeared paramount for many concerned about Jewry's fate under the swastika before the tragedy's true dimensions were realized beyond the borders of occupied Europe. The third chapter explores the unveiling in the free world of Germany's Final Solution, as well as the immediate reactions that followed. Chapter 4, which was originally published in *Prologue* (fall, 1981), examines the Bermuda conference and its aftermath once the Anglo-American Alliance officially acknowledged the relentless annihilation of European Jewry. The creation of the U.S. War Refugee Board is described in Chapter 5, incorporating previous contributions to special issues of the *Annals of the American Academy of Political and Social Science* (July, 1980) and *American Jewish History* (March, 1981). Chapter 6 concentrates on various efforts to rescue Jews from the Balkans, while Auschwitz-Birkenau and the martyrdom of Hungarian Jewry—the Holocaust in microcosm—are the subjects of Chapter 7. The final stage in the destruction of the Jews of Europe, set against the backdrop of a Wagnerian *Götterdämmerung* that engulfed the Third Reich, is viewed in Chapters 8 and 9 from two distinct perspectives: the confrontation between the World Jewish Congress and the International Red Cross, a study that first saw print in *Jewish Social Studies* (summer-fall, 1979), and the overtures to *Reichsführer* SS Heinrich Himmler by the Sternbuchs of Montreux and Hilel Storch of Stockholm. The epilogue, an earlier version of which appeared in *Midstream* (April, 1981), presents an overview of the Holocaust and its implications for human survival.

While taking account of the recent explosion in studies devoted to the Holocaust, this book is based primarily on the unpublished record. A number of individuals deserve particular thanks in this regard. In the United States: the National Archives, Kathy NiCastro and John Taylor; Federal Records Center, James Miller and James Hasting; Zionist Archives and Library, Sylvia Landress and Esther Togman; American Jewish Joint Distribution Committee Archives, Rose Klepfisz; American Jewish Committee Archives, Ruth Rauch; American Jewish Historical Society, Dr. Nathan Kaganoff; World Jewish Congress Archives, Jay Ticker; YIVO Archives, Marek Web; Agudas Israel of America Archives, Rabbi Moshe Kolodny; American Jewish Archives, Fannie Zelcer; Bund Archives, Hillel Kempinski; and the staffs of the Library of Congress Manuscript Division, Franklin D. Roosevelt Library, Jewish Labor Committee Archives, and the Hadassah Archives. In England: the Institute of Jewish Affairs, Dr. Elizabeth Eppler; and the staffs of the Public Record Office and the Board of Deputies of British Jews Archives. In Israel: the Central Zionist Archives, Dr. Michael Heymann; Yad Vashem Archives, Hadassah Modlinger; Weizmann Archives, Louise Calef; Hagana Archives, Joseph Kopilov and the late Shaul Avigur; Metsudat Ze'ev, Pesach Gani; Moreshet Archives, Shmuel Frankel; and the staffs of the Ben Gurion Archives and the Histadrut Archives.

A special appreciative mention is due others for opening hitherto closed archives and answering detailed correspondence: Dr. Gerhart M. Riegner (the World Jewish Congress MSS, and private MSS); Hilel Storch (private MSS); the late Irving Bunim (Va'ad HaHatsala MSS); Rabbi Morris Sherer (Agudas Israel of America MSS.); Victor Goodman (Harry Goodman MSS); Eli Sternbuch (HIJEFS MSS); Abraham Sternbuch (Isaac Sternbuch MSS); M. R. Springer (Agudas Israel of London MSS); Dr. Julius Kühl (private MSS); Dr. Reuven Hecht (private MSS); Julian Amery (Leopold Amery MSS); the late Dr. Emanuel Neumann (private MSS); Eliezer Lipsky (Louis Lipsky MSS); Dr. Israel Goldstein (private MSS); the late Rabbi Isador Breslau (private MSS); and Prof. Wilhelm Carlgren (Swedish Foreign Ministry documents, Stockholm). A copy from Chava Vagman-Eshkoli of her M.A. thesis supplied much relevant information, while Dr. Dalya Ofer lent me a copy of her valuable dissertation. I also want to thank those who graciously consented to lengthy interviews.

In wrestling with this inquiry over a number of seasons, I became especially mindful of Fustel de Coulange's trenchant observation that "years of analysis are required for one day of synthesis." Some very special people helped make both exercises possible. The faith that Richard L. Wentworth, Director and Editor of the University of Illinois Press, placed in the project proved invaluable. Professors Michael Popkin of Touro College and Richard Polenberg of Cornell University read the entire manuscript, and their prodding definitely sharpened its quality. Bonnie Depp's editorial skills contributed much to this book. I also gratefully acknowledge CUNY Professor Henry Feingold's review of Chapters 4 and 8: Dr. Joseph Lowin's close examination of Chapters 1 and 4; the observations of the Hebrew University's Professor Yehuda Bauer on Chapter 8 and his responses to specific questions; and Leah Hamoui's comments on the Epilogue. My wonderful mother-in-law, Leah Baruchi (formerly Leah Stampfer Goodman) of Jerusalem, provided gracious hospitality, as did Johnny and the late Frieda Miller of London. Fellowships awarded by the Memorial Foundation for Jewish Culture and the National Foundation for Jewish Culture, as well as grants from the Eleanor Roosevelt Foundation and Dr. Julius Kühl, helped defray travel and photocopying expenses.

A rare family's interest calls for a concluding note of deep appreciation. My dear parents, Rabbi Murry S. and Mrs. Lillian S. Penkower, have helped immeasurably with searching critiques of the chapters and with their constant encouragement. Dr. Jordan S. Penkower saw to books, articles, photocopying and a host of other matters while engaged in his own research and teaching duties as a member of Bar-Ilan University's Bible faculty; he is a much cherished brother. My children, Avram Yair, Talya Chana, Yonina Rivka, Ayelet Sara, and Ariel Yaakov, their insistent interruptions notwithstanding, make life a more joyous celebration. Finally, incomparable Yael, my *eshet chayil,* even found time to file documents and to arrange the bibliography with the use of her combined skills as a reference librarian and a graduate student of Jewish history. The dedication is but a small token of my love and gratitude.

Contents

The Jews Were Expendable

The Struggle for an Allied
Jewish Fighting Force

TWO DAYS BEFORE Adolf Hitler issued the decisive order that was to inaugurate history's bloodiest conflagration, the first victims of the *Führer's* blueprint for global conquest offered their services unconditionally to the future Allied cause. On August 29, 1939, immediately after his return to London from the twenty-first Zionist congress in Geneva, Chaim Weizmann pledged to Britain's Neville Chamberlain the fullest active support of Jews in Palestine and throughout the world "in this hour of supreme crisis." President of the World Zionist Organization (WZO) and the Jewish Agency, Weizmann did not gloss over the agency's recent political differences with the Mandatory power in the Promised Land, but he concluded the official communiqué with an appeal that these give way "before the greater and more pressing necessities of the time."[1]

Weizmann actually could entertain little hope that the policy of His Majesty's Government (HMG) toward the Zionist cause might take a turn for the better with the outbreak of World War II. Only the previous February Jewish delegates to a conference in London's St. James Palace had been informed by Colonial Secretary Malcolm MacDonald that considerations of imperial strategy required the sacrifice of Zionism in the event of war: the Moslem world might endanger British interests in the Middle East, northern Africa, and India, and since the weaker Jews perforce wished a British victory, they had to approve political concessions to the Arab position in Palestine. The subsequent White Paper of May, limiting Jewish immigration to 75,000 for the next five years and thereafter with Arab consent, bore the stamp of these arguments. It also suggested Albion's decision to conclude all commitments to the Jewish national home promised by Lord Balfour's cabinet in November, 1917.[2]

Nor did the official Zionist leadership, with the exception of Jewish Agency Executive chairman David Ben Gurion, advocate on the eve of world war armed revolt to counter the White Paper. As early as March Ben Gurion had pressed for active resistance to British policy, and then went on to reorganize the Hagana and create within that underground military organization a special unit under his control to check Arab nationalism, participate in unauthorized Jewish immigration to Palestine, and make enforcement of the White Paper difficult for the British. At the Zionist congress he spoke of governing "as if we were the State in Eretz Israel." But Weizmann's preference for a staff diplomatic fight within the Allied camp carried the day. Given the internal weakness of the Yishuv (the Jewish community in Palestine), the untapped potential of five million Jews in the United States, and the desperate plight facing European Jewry, this conclusion appeared inevitable.[3]

Not surprisingly, Britain's prime minister replied to Weizmann's letter in noncommittal fashion. Expressing his warm appreciation for the contents and spirit of the communication, Chamberlain noted "with pleasure" the Jewish Agency's promise of "wholehearted cooperation" regarding manpower, technical ability, and sundry resources. "You will not expect me to say more at this stage," he ended, "than that your public-spirited assurances are welcome and will be kept in mind."[4]

The following day, upon hearing that Great Britain had declared war against Germany in accordance with her treaty obligations to Poland, the Jewish Agency Executive and the Va'ad Leumi (National Council) rallied to the Allied standard. The two Jewish organizations jointly announced a census of all people in the Yishuv between the ages of 18 and 50 for economic and military purposes to serve the Jewish homeland and to aid the British Army in Palestine. Shortly thereafter Ben Gurion met the commanders of Hagana and insisted: "We must help the British in their war against Hitler as if there were no White Paper; we must resist the White Paper as if there were no war."[5]

The Zionist executive, in taking this step, already knew that British military circles in the Middle East, as opposed to London, had strong reservations about accepting military assistance from the Jews. One War Department official informed Moshe Shertok (later Sharett), chief of the agency's political department, that the offer of 20,000-40,000 Palestinian Jews to defend Palestine was indeed welcome but raised the primary difficulty of military equipment. Chief of the Imperial Staff Edmund Ironside expressed strong sympathy for the agency's two-pronged proposal of mobilization for Palestine's defense and a unit of volunteers from Jewry in the free world to serve wherever needed, even speaking of a Jewish presence of ten million in Palestine and the adjacent countries as a real positive force in the world of the future. But General A. P. Wavell, commander of British forces in the Middle East, candidly told Shertok that he opposed the formation of a Jewish army owing to its inevitable clash with the Arabs of the area. With no immediate likelihood of Italy joining Germany at the front, General Officer Commanding Michael Barker confidently dismissed the need of a large army in Palestine. The formation, however, of a specifically Jewish force there, he concluded along the imperial line taken at the London conference, would immediately lead to a widespread Arab revolt.[6]

The undaunted Agency Executive pressed on with its recruitment program, confident that the exigencies of war would prove the intrinsic worth of its case and halt the White Paper's implementation. Over 136,000 men and women from a total Jewish population of slightly less than half a million registered for service. Sixty thousand Jewish recruits (as against 63 Arabs) quickly made up shortages in British Army technical units operating in Palestine.

Negotiations with Barker's assistants regarding "Palestinian" units went along concurrently on the mutual understanding that these would be, in effect if not in name, Jewish units. The agency thought that the government might also wish to enlist Arabs on a separate basis, but doubted that the Palestinian Arabs, having spent the last three years in armed revolt against the Mandatory authorities, would rally in large numbers to the Union Jack. This cooperation ceased, however, with Barker's sudden announcement that the Palestinian units under discussion would have to be mixed on the basis of numerical parity between Arabs and Jews. His proposals indicated that the White Paper would govern war mobilization in Palestine as well, forcing the Jewish national home, as Shertok put it in early October, "into the position of any diaspora community." In the agency's view the composition of such units would also invite mutual sabotage and recrimination between the two peoples in Palestine, thereby harming an *ésprit de corps* and the attainment of even a minimum level of efficiency by the unit as a whole.[7]

Quickly realizing that political considerations were their major stumbling block, the Zionist authorities began a diplomatic offensive in London to obtain an Allied Jewish fighting force. Receiving little tangible support for the idea from Foreign Secretary Lord Halifax, Weizmann found a ready ear in Winston S. Churchill, his long-time acquaintance who had just been appointed First Lord of the Admiralty. In a brief conversation on September 19 Churchill had assured the WZO president that he would arm the Palestinian Jews registered for national service, convinced that this would allow British troops to leave Palestine for the western front and lead the Arabs to "come to terms" with the Jews. Encouraged, Weizmann began to urge on various British government departments the development of the industrial and scientific potentialities of Jewish Palestine, especially as the Mediterranean route was still open. The agency also advanced the name of Orde Wingate, former commander of the Hagana's "special night squads" during the Arab revolt (and its current confidential advisor on military strategy), to take command of the training of Jewish officers for the future military unit.[8]

The recruitment of Jews in the free world in tandem with the Yishuv's effort proceeded apace elsewhere in Europe and across the Atlantic. Nahum Goldmann, representing the agency at the League of Nations in Geneva, obtained the approval in principle of French Colonial Minister Georges Mandel for raising 10,000 American Jewish volunteers in order to create a Jewish legion within the French Army; Czech and Polish Jewish refugees in Europe could join this corps as well. "It will be the recognition of a Jewish Government before a Jewish State is constituted," Goldmann excitedly wrote World Jewish Congress president Stephen Wise, living in New York.[9] The Zionist Organization of America (ZOA), asked by Ben Gurion a day after the war began to offer a Jewish legion to the British as it had done during World War I, had already received Secretary of State Cordell Hull's opinion that such recruitment would violate U.S. neutrality laws. But many Americans could leave the country to enlist, the British ambassador informed a ZOA delegation, and he promised to advise them of HMG's policy regarding an oath of allegiance to King George VI for the duration of the war without forfeiting their citizenship.[10]

The British Cabinet appeared disinclined to alter its prewar position, however. In cables to the colonial secretary, Palestine High Commissioner Harold MacMichael discounted the Jewish war effort as self-seeking, and he soon informed Ben Gurion and Shertok that HMG would implement the immigration and land clauses of the White Paper despite the war and the agency's recruitment drive.[11] Shertok hurried to warn his colleagues in London, where MacDonald personally confirmed this position and intimated that he thought the Jews were seizing the opportunity of the war to achieve their "relentlessly pursued" end. At a meeting of the Cabinet in mid-October the colonial secretary checked Churchill's support of Wingate's memorandum for the large enlistment of Palestine's Jews by raising alarms about renewed Arab-Jewish conflict. Churchill's wishing "an outlet for the more adventurous spirits" among Jews and Arabs, along with his assertion in Cabinet that the White Paper could not be regarded as a satisfactory solution for the Middle East, was not sufficient to move MacDonald. The colonial secretary, main architect of the White Paper, again leaned on his high commissioner's evaluation that "no reliance" could be placed on an Arab or Jewish force for purposes of Palestine's internal security.[12]

At that very moment the British authorities in Palestine also attempted to break the power of the Hagana. Forty-three participants in a secret officers' training course, including 24-year-old Moshe Dayan, were surprised with arms in their possession by a British patrol and received harsh sentences. The Mandatory had worked openly with the Hagana to

suppress the Arab rebellion, and Palestine's history clearly indicated the
Jewish need for arms in self-defense against the Arabs, yet the British
authorities now purported to be shocked at the existence of this military
organization. Systematic searches for Jewish arms should be undertaken,
General Barker proposed to his superiors, and if the Hagana and similar
organizations would not hand over their weapons, the government should
drastically reduce the strength of the Jewish police and discharge those
who had joined British military units. MacDonald gave no comfort to
Shertok in the matter, while a confidential Colonial Office memorandum
dismissed the effect of potential Jewish propaganda on American opinion as carrying "little weight." General Ironside took a sharply different
view, cabling Barker to reduce the "stupid sentence" on the 43. "Fancy,"
the chief of the imperial staff told Weizmann, "they had condemned one
of Wingate's lads to life imprisonment; he ought to have been given the
D.S.O." The Jewish army would come despite the Colonial Office, he
went on, and "besides, if it is to be a better world after the war, the Jews
must get Palestine."[13]

The Jewish Agency Executive in London arrived at a final decision on
the Jewish fighting force in the middle of November. Following Wingate's advice, it proposed a Jewish force for Palestine's defense, a Jewish
division composed of volunteers from abroad and a Palestinian nucleus,
and a cadre of 500 officers to be trained in Britain for the 15,000-man
division. Ironside's aide, Colonel MacLeod, promised to sound out his
chief on the division proposal, adding that the general planned to use
Palestine as an industrial base for HMG's armies in the east in case the
eastern Mediterranean were cut off. A week later he informed Shertok of
Ironside's insistence that the Jewish offer be unconditional as to place of
service and that the negotiations be kept secret. This stipulation nullified
the argument of Lewis Namier, eminent British historian and close
Weizmann associate, that widespread publicity of a Jewish offer would
counter MacDonald's obstructive tactics, but the agency had no real
choice. Weizmann wrote to the chief of the imperial staff on December 1,
transmitting the agency's confidential memorandum for the Jewish division and officers' cadre (no mention made of a Palestine defense force). A
positive reply under MacLeod's signature arrived three days later.[14]

Matters inched forward, however, as Wingate had predicted, and nothing conclusive transpired by the end of 1939. "M.M. [Malcolm MacDon-
ald] stands by his betrayal... the White Paper policy is to continue,"
wrote Ben Gurion, on his way home, to a member of the Hagana executive. Wavell cautioned Weizmann, about to depart for the United States
at the end of December, that a Jewish force might incite the Arabs of
Egypt and Iraq. It would be difficult to fit the "rather isolated pieces" of
Jewish effort into the current British war program, Foreign Secretary

Halifax declared to the Zionist spokesman, and implementation of the White Paper should be expedited. To make the agency's position even more difficult, the French minister of war turned down the establishment of Jewish units under the tricolor, while U.S. Ambassador William Bullitt in Paris informed Goldmann that the American neutrality laws foreclosed any such help from across the ocean. The Agency Executive turned down HMG's request for the enlistment of trench diggers (Pioneer Corps) for the western front as a "Palestinian" unit, Ben Gurion explaining to Barker in the course of a stormy interview that the Jews wished to be accorded the same honorable recognition given any other nation: only thus could they play their proper part in the war. Left to themselves, the British raised the unit in part from the unemployed; the group, mostly Jews, later aided in the Allied retreat from St. Malo harbor and then in important battles in Eritrea.[15]

No progress on the issue of the Jewish division occurred so long as the Chamberlain government retained residence at 10 Downing Street. Churchill's support for arming the Jews as the empire's "only loyal friends" in Palestine, a theme he repeated at a Cabinet meeting on February 12, 1940, failed to convince MacDonald, Halifax, and the secretary of war. While not approving a systematic search for underground weapons in the Yishuv's possession, the Cabinet concluded that harsher sentences would be meted out against all members of illegally armed organizations. The British authorities in the Middle East, at the same time, pressed for firm implementation of the White Paper to safeguard the Mandatory's military security in the area. The Palestine Land Regulations of March followed, despite a stiff debate in Commons on a censure motion against the government, and the fact, as Jewish communities across Europe emphasized in protest, that Jewry's position was "one of distress and misery unheard of since the Middle Ages." The arms searches and trials continued in Palestine; on June 14 Barker's successor indicated to the Jewish communal bodies that large-scale searches for unlicensed arms would begin in the face of the leadership's refusal to hand them over.[16]

Churchill took over the reins of British power after the Nazi invasion of the Lowlands and the fall of France in May, 1940; together with Italy's entry into the war as an Axis belligerent a month later, this saved the volatile situation for the Yishuv. The new colonial secretary, Lord Lloyd, and Secretary of War Anthony Eden at first opposed a Jewish force on the grounds of British security in the Middle East, but Churchill pressed both to free 11 battalions of regular British troops in Palestine and to arm and organize the Jews in their own defense. Weizmann's official request of Churchill to mobilize the full resources of the Jewish people in Palestine and elsewhere, including the raising in Palestine of "several divisions," an air force squadron, and a military intelligence unit, fell on sympathetic ears. In June Lloyd agreed to larger enlistments of Jewish Palestinians and their formation into distinctive Jewish units. With the appointment of a new British military commander over Palestine, the arms seizures came to a halt. While the plan for a Jewish division remained on the *tapis,* Ben Gurion urged Lloyd in early July and Weizmann again wrote Churchill a month later to arm the Jews of Palestine in self-defense. American Zionists exerted themselves to enlist advocates in Washington for the idea. The prime minister's influence proved decisive, and Eden informed Parliament on August 6 of the Cabinet's decision to recruit separate Arab and Jewish units as battalions of the veteran Royal Kentish Fusiliers (the "Buffs").[17]

In the ensuing months the agency's quiet negotiations with the Cabinet and the War Office brought the Jewish division to the edge of realization. At a luncheon with Weizmann Churchill approved of large-scale Palestinian Jewish recruitment, training the division's officers in the Middle East, and Jewish military units from outside Palestine for service anywhere at Britain's request. Wingate's suggestion for the "desert units" to operate behind enemy lines also received the prime minister's support. "The Walls of Jericho have fallen, fallen!," exulted Weizmann confidante Blanche Dugdale following the Zionist leader's successful meeting with Eden, Lloyd, and a Foreign Office representative on September 13. A month later Lloyd informed Weizmann about the Cabinet's acceptance of the program in principle: 10,000 Jews, no more than 3,000 from Palestine, could be recruited as Jewish units into the British Army and trained in the United Kingdom. Brigadier L. A. Hawes, chosen as commander of the Jewish division on December 31, moved vigorously to clinch the matter. A first draft for a public announcement was drawn up, with Weizmann and Namier almost arriving at final arrangements with Eden and new Chief of the Imperial General Staff John Dill by early February, 1941.[18]

But the sudden death of Lord Lloyd, recognized patron of the Jewish division, spelled the demise of the project. His successor, the anti-Zionist Lord Moyne, chose to accept the advice of Britain's military and political representatives in the Middle East, who looked askance at the idea of any Jewish force. Such officials took no comfort in the fact that Jews constituted over 72 percent of the roughly 9,000 recruits from Palestine up to the beginning of 1941, and they insisted that at least the constitutional clauses of the White Paper be carried out without delay as a *quid pro quo.*[19]

Moyne, Eden (now heading the Foreign Office), and the new secretary of war sought Wavell's views. He favored implementation of the White Paper and opposed the Jewish contingent on the grounds of Arab hostility and especially the shortage of military equipment. The prime minister brushed aside Wavell's fears of the Arabs, recalling that he had recently got the Jewish refugee survivors aboard the *Patria* admitted into Palestine despite the general's worries on that score, "and not a dog barked." Yet, wishing Wavell to approve HMG's strategy regarding the defense of Greece against the German onslaught, he told Moyne in early March to inform Weizmann that lack of equipment alone required postponing the plan for six months. Never to know that Churchill gave up the military program temporarily in exchange for no implementation of the White Paper's constitutional clause, Weizmann called the decision a "sore blow." Repulsed, he again set out for the United States seeking new political leverage with which to strengthen the Zionist cause.[20]

The Jewish Agency could not move the Cabinet. The pro-Nazi revolt in Iraq; the Hagana's help in Britain's invasion of Vichy Syria; the conspiracy of army officers Anwar el-Sadat, Gamal Adbul Nasser, and the Egyptian chief of staff and the Muslim Brotherhood to support Adolf Hitler in return for their country's independence from British rule—all did not count in the balance. Nothing transpired regarding a Jewish force until Weizmann came back to London in August, where he received Moyne's letter announcing the need to leave the matter in "cold storage" for another three months. Equipment scarcity (a defense suggested earlier to Eden by British Minister Resident, Middle East, Oliver Lyttleton) and the new factor of Russia's entry on the Allied side precluded a favorable decision at this time, advised the colonial secretary. Weizmann's letter to Churchill on September 10, particularly noting the keenness of America's Jewish citizens to support Great Britain if only given the Jewish fighting force, failed to bear fruit. Dismissing the fighting value of a Jewish force, the war secretary warned Moyne of its "most serious" effect on the Arabs and particularly on Saudi Arabian monarch Abdul Aziz Ibn Saud. Moyne himself doubted Palestine's capacity to solve the Jewish problem, as well as the wisdom of employing British arms to "force" three million Jews into Palestine (the figure given him at the time by Weizmann and Ben Gurion).[21]

A definite reply from Moyne—not Churchill—in mid-October, citing the previous reservations against the Jewish division, dashed the agency's hopes of September, 1940, for good. Rather than endorse "most alarming" talk from Ben Gurion and Weizmann of securing three million Jews and sovereignty in Palestine, the colonial secretary told a parliamentary pro-Zionist delegation of Victor Cazalet, Josiah Wedgwood, and Percival Harris that the "best course was to keep things as steady as possible for the present." On November 9, 1941, Weizmann informed the public for the first time both about HMG's concealment of the distinctive service given on various fronts by 10,000 Jewish recruits under the anonymous rubric "Palestinians" and about Britain's failure to live up to its promise of the Jewish division. Newspaper editorials and a heated debate in the House of Lords decried the government's decision as continued appeasement of the unreliable Arabs. (At that same moment Hitler confidentally assured former mufti of Jerusalem Haj Amin el-Husseini that he would continue the war "until the complete destruction of the Judeo-Bolshevik rule had been accomplished," and appointed his foreign guest to lead the Arab forces against Palestinian Jewry as soon as the *Wehrmacht* reached the southern Caucasus.) But Churchill could do nothing more than promise, in a public letter to the London *Jewish Chronicle* on the occasion of its centenary, that on the day of Allied victory the sufferings of the Jews and their part in the struggle against the German *Führer* would not be forgotten.[22] The first phase of the Jewish Agency's effort had ended in complete failure.

II

The inability after two years to secure HMG's approval for a Jewish force led the agency's leadership to view the United States as its new political center of gravity. Already in March, 1941, Ben Gurion had proposed a two-fold program of action to the Agency Executive regarding the future of Palestine: strengthen the Hagana to form a Jewish army, and demand Jewish rule in Palestine after the war as a means of bringing millions of Jews to the national homeland with all speed. HMG's continuation of the White Paper, despite the presence of some strong pro-Zionists in the War Cabinet, led the Agency Executive chairman to despair of a change from the British. He knew, at the same time, that American Zionist pressure had helped persuade London in May and June to strengthen Jewish self-defense in Palestine. Accordingly, Ben Gurion suggested in a memorandum that autumn to Weizmann and others at agency headquarters in 77 Great Russell Street that it would be easier to win public opinion in America for such a "radical and maximum solution" than in England. Much more disinterested in Palestine than the Mandatory, and therefore able to take a more objective view, the United States also possessed the largest Jewish community in the world. That great mass of Jews, Ben Gurion argued on the basis of previous visits to America, supported the Yishuv's effort in principle. The general American public, he thought, could also be won over to support the establishment of "Palestine as a Jewish Commonwealth immediately after the war." He would leave for the United States to undertake this mission.[23]

Ben Gurion's novel thesis that the achievement of a maximalist Zionist program depended upon capturing American public opinion had been adopted much earlier by his arch rival, Vladimir Jabotinsky. The president of the Revisionist New Zionist Organization had called a truce in his movement's armed struggle with the British immediately after the German invasion of Poland. On September 4, 1939, the former lieutenant in the Jewish 38th Battalion of Royal Fusiliers, which fought under Allenby to capture Palestine from the Turks, wrote to Neville Chamberlain: extend the precedent of the World War I Jewish Legion and create a Jewish army prior to the establishment of Palestine as a Jewish state. When Colonial Secretary MacDonald refused to consider his request that HMG give tacit or open encouragement to Jewish immigration to Palestine beyond the White Paper quotas, the Revisionists' charismatic leader decided to bring his appeal to the American people.

Jews and non-Jews began to answer Jabotinsky's call, first made publicly in June, 1940, at New York's Manhattan Center, for a Jewish army of 100,000 to rally to England's side against Hitler. Important contacts were established with the aid of influential Americans like Mr. and Mrs. John Gunther and British Colonel John Patterson, former commander of the World War I Jewish Legion. A memorandum explaining that such a project, by "placing the Jewish people on the map," would diminish the "inevitable pressure" of Europe's Jews escaping "zones of distress," went to various statesmen that summer. But Jabotinsky died suddenly in early August, 1940, and the New Zionist Organization's ship floundered in search of a helmsman.[24]

Members of an Irgun Tsva'i Leumi delegation to the United States moved to fill the vacuum. Reaching these shores in 1939–40, the small band had decided to fight the White Paper and secure the full boundaries of historic Palestine with a more aggressive style of propaganda than their mentor Jabotinsky desired. Led by the dynamic Hillel Kook (alias Peter Bergson), the young group vainly appealed to United Palestine Appeal chairman Abba Hillel Silver to take the reins from those supporting what they termed the "Weizmann spirit" of defeatist anglophilism; Stephen Wise, chairman of the umbrella-type Emergency Committee for Zionist Affairs (ECZA), received a request for substantial funds so that the militant Irgun could continue to combat Arab terrorism in Palestine. Upon Weizmann's public admission of the agency's failure to attain a limited Jewish division, the "Bergson boys" then organized the nonsectarian Committee for a Jewish Army to raise a combined force of 200,000 Palestinian and "stateless" Jews for Allied service in Palestine and its environs. Their opening drive in Washington, D.C., on December 4, 1941, with special messages of support from Secretary of War Henry Stimson, Senators Claude Pepper, Edwin Johnson, and Guy Gillette, and other notables, drew much coverage and inspired *PM*'s editorial advice to employ U.S. Lend Lease equipment for the projected Jewish army.[25]

The committee's slogan—"Jews Fight for the Right to Fight"—had particular power, coming exactly on the eve of America's entry into the war. Thousands of sympathizers, including many Jews far removed from Zionism, joined the fledgling group and its national chairman, the celebrated Dutch author Pierre Van Paassen. Americans perferred to think in large terms, and a Jewish army of 200,000, whatever its logistic problems, possessed greater attraction for many than the agency's call for a Jewish division numbering 20,000-40,000. For the first time, as Kook gauged the revolutionary step years later, Jews appeared on the front pages with a dramatic appeal instead of in the back covers listing religious services and obituaries. Senators Johnson and Elbert Thomas proved especially effective in voicing the committee's position in Washington, while Captain Jeremiah Halpern and Lord Strabolgi gained numerous supporters in Parliament and captured the front pages of the London *Jewish Chronicle*.[26]

Ben Gurion and Weizmann, for their part, concentrated on winning over the White House and influential Jewish organizations in the first months of 1942, and on uniting American Zionists behind a public manifesto for Jewish statehood and a Jewish army for Palestine. Certain members of the ECZA sought to co-opt the Committee for a Jewish Army's resourceful leadership, but in Ben Gurion's eyes the covert association of the committee's organizers with the independent Irgun in Palestine made any partnership impossible. Ultimately, the first comprehensive conference of the country's established Zionist organizations took place at the Biltmore Hotel in New York on May 9-11, 1942, where they agreed upon the establishment of Palestine as a Jewish commonwealth in the new world order. Until the realization of that achievement, the Biltmore resolutions proclaimed, the Jewish Agency should control immigration and development, and the Jews of Palestine should be given a "Jewish military force fighting under its own flag and under the high command of the United Nations."[27]

While the idea of a Jewish army made headway in the United States, the British felt compelled to cooperate with the Yishuv in an effort to halt Field Marshal Erwin Rommel's advance on the gates of Alexandria. During the summer of 1940, and again a year later, the British had received valuable help from the Jews of Palestine in underground operations to meet the danger of a Nazi invasion in the Middle East. Intelligence work, sabotage, "Arabist" agents, and the training of Hagana members for a radio network for Palestine in case of a German takeover had all received British sanction during those months of crisis. The rule of Arab-Jewish parity in the Buffs had also been discarded in mid-1941 when the British Army required additional Jewish enlistment. In early 1942 the British, enjoying the flush of a recent victory in the western

desert, approved of a Hagana plan for guerrilla activities in northern
Palestine in case of a German conquest of the country. The Palmach,
the mobile striking force organized by the Hagana command in May,
1941, after Rommel first reached Egypt's borders, received the command's assignment to execute this plan.[28]

Still, the agency's request that HMG immediately mobilize all available Jewish manpower to defend Palestine against Rommel's Afrika
Korps met with a limited response. Ben Gurion cabled British Minister
Resident, Middle East, Richard Casey on April 15 that the 10,000 Jews
now dispersed in the single defense companies of the Buffs should be
prepared for war service at the battalion level; another 10,000 should be
similarly mobilized, together with a 6,000-men supernumerary police
force; and an additional 40,000–50,000 should be equipped for home
guard duty. Field Marshal Dill, then in Washington, approved Ben
Gurion's proposals, and so cabled London. Shertok wrote to General
Claude Auchinleck, British commander-in-chief for the entire region, in
like vein two days later, adding ominously that "an even swifter destruction" would overtake the Jews of Palestine if the Nazis overran the
country than had fallen on "hundreds of thousands [sic]" of their fellow
Jews who had perished to date in Hitler's Europe. Weizmann carried the
plea to the sympathetic U.S. Under Secretary of State Sumner Welles
and also wrote to Ambassador John Winant in England. After the fall
of Tobruk to the Germans on June 21, he again wrote to Churchill
calling for a large fighting force of Jews in Palestine. But Auchinleck's
immediate need for all available weapons, the bulk coming from the
United States, to be rushed to the front at El Alamein, frustrated the
agency's desperate hopes.[29]

The agency also failed to obtain Wingate's services as the leader of a
large Jewish military force in Palestine at this eleventh hour. Receiving
encouragement from Under Secretary Welles, Weizmann drafted a request on July 2 to President Franklin D. Roosevelt with the aid of
Supreme Court Justice Felix Frankfurter and New Dealer Ben Cohen
for mustering the original division figure of 40,000 armed young men to
defend their national home. The following day Weizmann lunched with
Secretary of the Treasury Henry Morgenthau, Jr., and suggested that
Wingate be flown back from India to head the division. Morganthau
immediately got Roosevelt to contact General Dill on the matter; both
Dill and American Chief of Staff George Marshall expressed themselves
to Weizmann in favor of Wingate if the force were formed.

On July 7 the president received Weizmann (but expressly not Ben
Gurion, as Frankfurter had requested), only to tell the chief architect of
the Balfour Declaration that he wished to wait about ten days before
issuing a statement regarding the Jewish force. The British feared that

the Egyptian Army might turn against them, he explained. "You might as well try and appease a rattlesnake," Weizmann retorted. The president's thoughts, smacking of what Weizmann termed Britain's traditional placating of the Arabs, dissatisfied the WZO leader. But Roosevelt insisted to Morgenthau that the first consideration was to make sure the British kept Cairo and Alexandria from falling. If this were done, and if 50,000 rifles and 10,000 machineguns could then be gotten to the Jews, Wingate would be his choice to lead them.[30]

Churchill, too, favored Wingate's appointment, but did not get his way. Dill's transmission of Weizmann's request quickly stirred the prime minister to urge this move. The Jews, now in direct danger, should be given a chance, he wrote to Colonial Secretary Lord Cranborne on July 5. It might even be necessary, he added, to "make an example of anti-Semitic officers and others in high places" in the Middle East. Refusing to admit the validity of this charge, Cranborne warned the prime minister that the open drive for a Jewish army, which he viewed as a step toward a Jewish state, went against HMG's announced policy and was likely to lead to "serious trouble." In the end, the British military authorities refused to free Wingate from commando preparations in India against the Japanese forces holding Burma.

Churchill had to content himself once again with a message of faith to the beleaguered Jews. A demonstration in Madison Square Garden, convened on July 21, 1942, to protest the Nazi massacre of Jewry, heard the prime minister's message of special tribute to the Jewish war effort in Palestine. Official British silence on this contribution had been broken for the first time, but the Jewish division had still not come to pass. Wingate lost his last hope of again leading the Jews in battle; he would die two years later in an air crash in the Burma jungle.[31]

The British authorities finally made some concessions to the mounting pressure for a Jewish military force, but these hardly met the agency's demands. At Cranborne's urging the secretary for war announced in Parliament on August 6 HMG's decision to create a Palestine Regiment consisting of separate Jewish and Arab battalions for general service in the Middle East, to expand the supernumerary police force to a maximum of 2,000, and to complete the establishment of a Jewish rural special police by enrolling 2,500 additional recruits with all necessary training and arms. The colonial and war secretaries took this limited step specifically to check "extreme Zionists" like Shertok who sought, according to the secretaries' confidential Cabinet memoranda, to use the Jewish army as "a valuable bargaining counter at the peace table" or to achieve a Jewish state by force after the war. Accordingly, the battalions would not depart from the Buffs' static mission of guarding military installations without modern weapons or new training. The 1,500 new

men of the supernumerary police force also received inferior training
and equipment within the framework of the temporary village police. In
sum, the battalions, strengthened by over 4,600 new recruits from June
to the end of September, 1942, made only small progress to the goal of a
Jewish fighting unit.[32]

Following HMG's major victory at El Alamein (October 23–November
4, 1942), the British reverted to their traditional position of no military cooperation with the Yishuv. Receiving no further support from
HMG, the Palmach had to go back underground. The Jewish Agency
got nowhere with requests for the transfer of Jewish volunteers in other
units of the British Army to the Palestine Regiment and for a distinctive
name and badge for the Jewish battalions; the Royal Fusiliers' 38th,
39th, and 40th Jewish battalions had been designated "The Judeans"
with the Menorah as their badge in World War I. The demand for the
recruitment of 5,000 men as a Jewish home guard in urban districts also
met with failure. Shertok insisted that the Jewish battalions did not wish
to remain "hewers of wood and drawers of water" while European Jewry
was being decimated in Germany's "Final Solution"—but to no avail.
British intransigence grated further at a time when the overwhelming
majority of the Jewish political parties in Palestine, urged on by Ben
Gurion, voted to accept the Biltmore resolutions for Jewish political independence. HMG minimized the Yishuv's industrial potential, discouraged Jewish recruitment, and slighted the agency out of fear that it
might be establishing an *imperium in imperio,* charged Shertok in a
frank discussion with the Colonial Office at the very end of December.
The suspicions remained, and real cooperation did not emerge.[33]

Whitehall also increased its efforts in the United States that fall against
the cause of an independent Jewish military contingent. The State Department, which had attempted in July to secure a statement for the
Middle East favoring the postwar principles of the Atlantic Charter in
an effort to woo the Arabs away from Nazi propaganda, received Foreign Office confidential reports with which to meet the continuing pressure for a Jewish force. Similar material arrived in the hands of Reform
Jews, who firmly objected to the concept of Jewish nationalism, and at
the office of the mayor of New York, claiming the country's largest Jewish
urban population. The State Department's suggestion that a delegation
of Bergson's Committee for a Jewish Army be received by the Foreign
and Colonial offices to allay American public sentiment was peremptorily
quashed. At most, the British Cabinet decided to have the secretary of
war announce in Commons on December 15, 1942, that the defensive
role of the Jewish battalions might be different if and when "equipment
and circumstances" permitted.[34]

At the very moment that the Anglo-American Alliance first acknowl-

edged Hitler's plan to kill all of European Jewry, the Jews of Palestine
had the bitter lot of fighting "nameless and scattered." Almost 20,000
Palestinian Jewish recruits were serving in the British armed forces by
the end of 1942, with over 7,000 in internal defense and 1,000 in various
Allied armies. Another 60,000 could be found meeting direct British
needs in factories, camps, and workshops and in Army transport. Laboratories of the Hebrew University, the Daniel Sieff Research Institute,
and the Haifa Technical Institute contributed precision instruments and
valuable chemical products to the Allied forces. British Army orders for
Jewish goods totaled close to £14 million between 1941 and 1942. The
Jewish Agency, and particularly the Yishuv-operated RAF Intelligence
Center in Haifa, forwarded important information from refugees about
current conditions in Nazi-occupied Europe to HMG's military branches.
With Weizmann's approval, the agency's electronics expert played a vital
role in raiding the German radar installation at Dieppe. The record of
support by Palestine's Arab population for the Allied cause hardly ap-
proximated this British-censored record of performance, while the governments of Iraq, Syria, and Egypt favored the Nazi invader, and the
former mufti of Jerusalem used the Axis airwaves to herald the Third
Reich in the Moslem world and recruited thousands from the Balkans
into Moslem *Wehrmacht* units.[35]

"The Arabs are an excuse, not a reason," thundered Lord Wedgwood
in calling on America to accept the Mandate, arm the loyal Jews to fight
for their freedom, and do away with British appeasement in Palestine.
Yet HMG saw fit to appoint as its minister resident, Middle East, Walter Moyne, saboteur of the Jewish division a year earlier. He now
responded in Parliament to Wedgwood's "treasonable appeal" by com-
paring Zionist "aggression and domination" in Palestine to the Nazi
spirit. And the demand for a distinctive Jewish fighting force, which
could strike a blow against Hitler and avenge the more than two million
Jews already dead in the unyielding onslaught of the Holocaust, continued to go unanswered.[36]

III

With the danger of Rommel's invasion over, the British administration
in Palestine did all it could in the first half of 1943 to weaken the
Yishuv's recruitment effort. The Jewish Agency's campaign of economic
and moral pressure to increase enlistment, and thus that Zionist body's
prestige, encouraged some to attain this end by physical coercion. Although Jewish institutions in Palestine condemned isolated acts of violence, the Mandatory government used these activities as an excuse to
forbid the agency's issue of any document or badge showing fulfillment

of public duty. Viewing this regulation in terms of HMG's effort to
smear its methods as "organized terror" and to halt recruitment of Jews
into the British Army, the agency announced that all directives of its
recruitment department remained binding. Immediately thereafter a company from one of the Jewish battalions was sent abroad, negating a
British promise of September, 1940, to avoid such an action.

In April, 1943, the Jewish Agency was also denied access to the Sara-
fand training camp, and British detectives, seeking evidence for the existence of a secret military organization and coercion to obtain Jews for
HMG's forces, ransacked the Yishuv's recruitment center in Tel Aviv.
The agency responded by closing all its recruitment offices. Although
these quarters were opened two months later after the British realized
that enlistment could occur only with the agency's cooperation, the Mandatory power offered no apologies. Jewish recruitment never regained its
previous momentum. The British further weakened Jewish military
strength by shipping out the second Palestinian battalion in early July
without assurances that it would be used for actual duty.[37]

Such maneuvers reflected British fears of a Jewish revolt, suspicions
that also drove the War Cabinet to try to dampen Zionist agitation
through a diplomatic offensive with Washington. Anxious about reports
of impending Arab-Jewish conflict over Palestine and its potentially
adverse effect on the Allied campaign in North Africa, the State Department found the Foreign Office receptive to issuing a joint Anglo-
American statement on Palestine. That declaration, maintaining in effect
the White Paper policy until the war's end, contained a specific injunc-
tion at Whitehall's request against any solution for Palestine based on
armed force. The British Middle East military and political authorities,
having met earlier in Cairo to discuss the subject, recommended that all
hidden weapons in Palestine be seized and Mandatory strength increased
by one infantry division, including armor. By also bringing the British
police force up to full strength, a British gendarmerie would thus be
created in the Promised Land.[38]

The Cabinet's deliberations in June and July concerning the joint
Anglo-American statement best illustrate its members' worry that militant Jewish designs for Palestine threatened the security interests of the
empire. British Minister Resident, Middle East, Richard Casey informed
the Cabinet that the loyalty to the nominal government of the 40,000
Jews in police formations "could not be relied upon," and that the 15
percent of the Jewish Agency's budget marked for "internal security"
went in fact to the organization, training, and equipment of the Hagana's
estimated 80,000 members. "It appears that the Zionist movement in
Palestine has fallen under the control of reckless fanatics," observed
Deputy Prime Minister Clement Attlee. The Colonial and Foreign Office

secretaries strongly favored the joint declaration to "avoid an explosion" in the Middle East. Minister of Aircraft Production Stafford Cripps, proponent of a bi-nationalist solution for Palestine, suggested a conference of leading Jews to discuss the general position of Jewry in the postwar world, and thereby "remove the hysterical mood" persisting among Jews for their own state in the Holy Land.

Minister of Production Oliver Lyttleton proved especially adamant. As British minister resident, Middle East, he had provided the War Office in August, 1941, with the rationale of equipment scarcity as the answer to Weizmann's request for a Jewish fighting force. Now Lyttleton refused to have HMG "surrender to Jewish chauvinism," which he considered inimical to "our imperial interest." (The minister and colleagues did not know that Egypt's King Farouk, who informed the Third Reich of his continued hope for an Axis victory, had recently been involved in negotiations via the ex-mufti to be spirited to the German lines.) "We must remain in effective occupation of Palestine for a long time," the Cabinet minister concluded, much as a British chiefs of staff memorandum stressed that "a peaceful and secure" Palestine "is and must remain of utmost importance to the British Empire and Commonwealth" in achieving HMG's strategic needs in the entire area.[39]

Only Minister for India Leopold Amery and Winston Churchill markedly supported the Yishuv as Britain's only reliable ally in the Middle East and, hence, the agency's demand for a Jewish state. Owing to Churchill's insistence, the War Cabinet decided not to approve the seizure of illegal Jewish arms in Palestine. Otherwise, the joint declaration appeared headed for issue. At the last minute, in August, pressure from various American Jewish quarters halted its promulgation.[40]

What the two governments failed to achieve behind closed doors, the British authorities in Palestine attempted to secure by a public arms trial that same month. Determined to sully the name of Zionism in American public opinion particularly and to end the contraband sale of British arms into Jewish hands, the Mandatory tried two members of the Hagana, Eliyahu Syrkin and Eliyahu Reichlin, for illegally transferring 105,000 rounds of ammunition and 300 rifles from British stores in Egypt to Haifa. An earlier trial of two British deserters, engaged in selling stolen goods and arms to Arabs and Jews alike, had heard their attorney slander the Jewish soldiers then fighting with the British Eighth Army in North Africa. The court heard no mention of the widespread Arab trafficking in arms throughout the Middle East, mass desertion from the Palestinian Arab units, or the refusal of HMG's Transjordanian Force to take up arms against Rashid Ali's pro-Nazi revolt in Iraq. Only in such a circumstance, Ben Gurion riposted, did HMG permit Jewish soldiers to be listed as other than "Palestinians." The British went further at the

Syrkin-Reichlin trial, staged in the presence of the invited American press, aiming to discredit the Histadrut and the Jewish Agency.

The prosecutor sought to portray the Hagana as a secret organization whose real purpose, described as "stealing Allied arms," was "a cancer" in the body of the democracies' war effort. Golda Meyerson (later Meir), called to the stand, confronted HMG by publicly revealing for the first time the "secret" of past British cooperation with the Hagana and Palmach. After 60 sessions that stretched the credibility of the prosecution's witnesses, Reichlin received seven years in jail and Syrkin ten. Even more ominous was the seven-year sentence given by the military court to Avraham Sacharov, a member of Hagana's secret acquisitions unit (Rechesh) and known as "Weizmann's bodyguard," for possessing two rifle bullets without a permit. Shortly afterward a magistrate's court sentenced one Arab in Hebron to six months' imprisonment for possessing a British rifle and 86 rounds of ammunition.[41]

A large-scale arms search at Hulda and a particularly forceful one at Ramat HaKovesh that fall left no doubt that the British authorities sought to liquidate the Hagana. The thin cover of searching for deserters from the Polish Army then in Palestine—with the use of hundreds of soldiers and a magnetic mine detector—uncovered some weapons in the first settlement, none in the second. Shertok met High Commissioner MacMichael on November 17 and warned that "our arms are intended to be used for defense, and any attempt to take them away from us will touch the Yishuv to the quick." "Extreme acts" might follow, he added, resulting in much bloodshed on both sides. This grave warning and protests by Zionists in Washington and London had the desired effect. The last thing HMG wanted was to provoke a Jewish revolt throughout Palestine; MacMichael convinced the military to halt the anti-Hagana actions. The Hagana emerged from this crisis with its power intact, and the open tension of the past few months subsided.[42]

The British realized that they also had to compromise on the question of the Jewish flag. Palestinian Jews serving in British transport units managed from the beginning to mark the Star of David on their trucks, but those in the Palestinian regiments had to don the neutral badge of an olive branch surrounded by the word "Palestine" in English, Arabic, and Hebrew. While military authorities in Palestine refused as early as January, 1941, to allow the raising of any flag other than the Union Jack, on different occasions and especially on Jewish holidays the blue-and-white flag with the blue Star of David flew over Jewish camps and military gatherings together with HMG's standard. The announcement from British headquarters in Cairo opposing any further hoisting of the Jewish banner, however, followed by the local commander's suggestion of a blue standard with a white Star of David in its place, stirred the second Jewish battalion to spontaneous revolt. Unfurling their individual flag alongside the Union Jack in a hall of worship to celebrate the Jewish New Year, the battalion's third unit was supported the following day by all the other Jewish sections in the Bengazi area in remonstrating against the discriminatory order. Some time after this attempt to restore Jewish pride in place of "Palestinian" anonymity, the British removed the punishment meted out to the battalion for its insubordination, and provided some up-to-date equipment and combat training. HMG thus acknowledged for the first time, albeit in a limited fashion, the Yishuv's insistence that the emerging Jewish nation on the soil of the Holy Land be recognized as a fellow member in the war against Hitlerism.[43]

Precisely at this juncture the Jewish Agency renewed its demand for a separate fighting force. Shertok's last request, in January, 1943, for a division or, as a first step, a brigade group based upon the 22,000 Palestinian Jews then serving in the British Army, had been turned down by the secretary of war. But by now the front had receded from the Middle East, and with the Allied invasions of Sicily and Italy, such a military group could fight in Europe free from British and Arab fears about its appearance in Palestine and the Middle East. In addition, it would be difficult, as Shertok wrote a colleague during the arms trials, to deny the Yishuv its "holy task" in the campaign to conquer the Jewish "Valley of Slaughter" and to save the remnants of its people. Those serving in the British Army, in particular, did not want it said that only the heroic resistance movements of the Warsaw ghetto and elsewhere in Hitler's Europe could take up arms to the death as Jews.

The time seemed most propitious for a successful conclusion to the long campaign. Passing through Cairo on his way back to Burma, Wingate told Jewish Agency representatives in Cairo that during the Quebec conference in August he had pressed on FDR, Churchill, and the Anglo-American chiefs of staff the need for a Jewish army. Zionist officials in London had also heard rumors that a special Cabinet committee would favor an extensive Jewish state in partitioned Palestine after the war. Churchill confirmed this at a private luncheon with Weizmann on October 25, and promised to fulfill Balfour's inheritance and "establish the Jews in the position where they belong."[44]

Weizmann picked up the thread the following month, but more than half a year passed without any results. On November 23, 1943, he and Namier met with British War Secretary James Grigg, who promised to transmit their request to the Cabinet. Lengthy negotiations ensued. The British chiefs of staff cabled the the War Office their fears of Jewish designs, and warned that the partition of Palestine recommended by a special Cabinet committee would so jeopardize British security interests in the Middle East as to require: three divisions in Palestine alone; two to three divisions in Syria, Iraq, and Lebanon; two in Egypt; two-thirds of a division in Libya; two fighter squadrons; seven fighter bomber squadrons; and two PT boat squadrons after the war. In early 1944 the U.S. War Department put an end to congressional resolutions favoring Palestine as a Jewish state after the end of hostilities on the ground that Moslem unrest could yet hamper the Allied war effort. Given this perspective, the department decided not to press the British even concerning a Jewish force for the liberation of Europe itself. The resumption of active warfare in Palestine against the Mandatory administration by the Irgun and the Stern group during these same months increased the anxiety of the British and American military, and thus threatened further to demolish the agency's quest for this particular objective.[45]

Grigg dug in his heels against all entreaties from Weizmann and Shertok. Weizmann sat down with the secretary for war in March, 1944, and in a letter at month's end asked that the Allies, who had failed to save Jewry, include in the invasion of Europe a "force of free, fighting Jews ... to uphold the honour of their people, avenge its martyrs, and help to liberate the survivors"; the existing Jewish Palestinian units should be grouped into a division or a brigade group, with new Jewish recruits to come from Palestine, liberated Italy and North Africa, and other countries. Shertok reiterated the demand in early April, but it took until June 21 for Weizmann to receive Grigg's evasive reply: he had submitted his own judgment to the War Cabinet, where the matter now rested. In fact, Grigg remained suspicious that the Hagana intended to train at Britain's expense either to resist an anti-Zionist Mandatory policy after the war, or to present HMG with the *fait accompli* of a Jewish state when Britain's main effort would be directed to the defeat of Japan. Accordingly, he recommended to his Cabinet colleagues that they turn down a Jewish force of any size.[46]

As a last resort, Weizmann turned to the one individual in whom he had placed his faith since the 1917 pledge of Arthur Balfour. On July 4, 1944, he addressed a personal communication to Churchill. Recalling Britain's promise four years earlier of an Allied Jewish fighting force and noting the war service of Palestinian Jewry's volunteers, now numbering 24,000, the Zionist leader requested that these men form a division of their own and be permitted to carry the flag with the Star of David onto the battlefield of Europe. Grigg replied three days later, informing Weizmann that negotiations were taking place on the "limited plan" with the general officer commanding, Middle East, and expressing doubts that "your cracking the whip" would "make the horse move any faster." The elder Zionist statesman did not respond, for in the interim he had fallen into a deep depression over the Foreign Office's refusal to take up Adolf Eichmann's offer of negotiations for the possible rescue of Hungarian Jewry, the last sizable remnant of the Jewish people in Europe.

In his chief's absence, Shertok sharply cut off Grigg's reprimand. The Jewish Agency expected no favorable reaction from the supreme British military in the Middle East, he retorted by official letter. "Why should they, with their narrow perspective, forego battalions doing vital work in their command and trouble themselves with problems of replacement." Only the "highest political authorities" could consider fulfilling a promise once given and "the moral obligation to let at least a few thousand Jews fight as Jews at a time when millions of their people are doomed to death."[47]

Unknown to the Zionists, the catastrophe of Hungarian Jewry had deeply moved the prime minister, and he resolved to do something concrete for the Jewish people. Shocked at seeing a cable on June 27 about the gassing of some 400,000 Hungarian Jews in Auschwitz-Birkenau, and noting its suggestion to bomb the death centers, railway lines to the camps, and government buildings in Budapest, Churchill empowered Foreign Secretary Eden to act on his behalf in favor of the bombing proposals. Two days after receiving this telegram, he reminded Eden of his determination not to break Balfour's word to the Zionists. What the Jewish people were currently enduring in Europe, Churchill told his Cabinet on July 3, made "a strong case" for sympathetic consideration of projects regarding the Yishuv after the war. (The prime minister evidently had in mind the proposal for a Jewish state, then pending before the Cabinet committee.)

As for Grigg's objections even to a brigade group, Churchill thought Weizmann's suggestion of forming a small force within the British Army from already existing Jewish units to be both capable of execution and morally proper. "I like the idea of the Jews trying to get at the murderers of their fellow countrymen in Central Europe," he argued in a memorandum to Grigg on July 12. "It is with the Germans that they have their quarrel.... I cannot conceive why this martyred race scattered about the world and suffering as no other race has done at this juncture should be denied the satisfaction of having a flag." When Grigg sought a stipulation that the brigade group be available for general service in any area, Churchill reiterated his agreement with the agency's insistence on the European theater.[48] That same month the prime minister also gave his support to the agency's plan for 100 Jewish men from Palestine to be parachuted into the Balkans, where they could join 31 others currently engaged in a British–Jewish Agency project of anti-Nazi sabotage, Jewish resistance, and rescue.[49]

Churchill's decisive intervention paved the way in August for the realization of the agency's limited objective. He replied to Weizmann with the assurance of his personal attention and sympathy in the matter of a Jewish fighting force. The War Office would shortly be in a position to discuss actual proposals; in the meantime, he wished particulars about the flag before embarking on "this contentious ground." Weizmann answered that very day, sending a sketch of the symbol for Jewry the world over: two horizontal blue stripes on a white background with a blue Star of David in the center. At the same time the prime minister acceded to a request from Grigg and Colonial Secretary Oliver Stanley that the brigade not be brought back intact to Palestine after service in Europe, so as not to create "wide disturbances."

On August 17, 1944, Grigg informed Weizmann about the Cabinet's approval of the Jewish brigade group. The infantry brigade and ultimately the entire force would be transferred to Italy, "so that you may be granted your heart's desire—the chance to fight the Germans." In a series of meetings that followed, at which a greatly excited Shertok led the agency delegation, the British limited recruitment to Palestine, to Great Britain, and to Jewish refugees imprisoned in Mauritius for challenging the White Paper quotas. Against the pressure applied by its military command in Cairo, HMG finally agreed to establish the brigade primarily from existing Jewish units.[50]

The appearance of the Jewish flag on the European front remained a final obstacle, but Churchill also saw this through. Confronted by the War Office's strenuous opposition to the idea, Churchill asked U.S. Treasury Secretary Morgenthau, then in London, for his views on the subject. Morgenthau, champion of Weizmann's plea in the summer of 1942 for a fighting force under Wingate's command, also objected: the banner would provide another justification for Hitler's determination to kill all the Jews of Europe. But the statesman who, as Weizmann had written him on August 5, helped the Jews raise the flag in Palestine a quarter of a century previously, remained unconvinced. Seeking Roosevelt's reaction, Churchill informed his closest war ally that, "after much pressure from Weizmann," he had set up what in the United States would be called a "regimental combat team." The step would give great satisfaction to the Jews, and "surely the Jews, of all races, have the right to strike at the Germans as a recognized body" under their own standard. This would be "a message to go all over the world," he cabled FDR. On hearing that the American president raised no objections to the Jewish brigade as suggested, the Cabinet agreed on September 4 to the entire proposal.[51]

The Jewish Brigade became a reality at the end of September, 1944. The War Office noted the Cabinet's decision in a public communiqué on the 19th, but Churchill chose to feature the news during his war survey in the House of Commons nine days later. Vast numbers of Jews were serving with the Anglo-American forces on all fronts, he pointed out, "but it seems to me indeed appropriate that a special Jewish unit, a unit of that race which has suffered indescribable torments from the Nazis, should be represented as a distinct formation among the forces gathered for their final overthrow." The prime minister was certain that its members "will not only take part in the struggle but also in the occupation which will follow."[52]

Although some members of the Agency Executive doubted the sincerity of British intentions, it officially expressed deep gratification with this acknowledgment of Jewish services rendered to the Allied war effort and of "the Jewish desire for national recognition." Suspicions lingered that service in the brigade would come too late for actual combat but as a future occupation force in Europe. The probability of this contact with the German people horrified some of the executive, who also worried that HMG planned such duties precisely to weaken the Yishuv's military strength just when Palestine's future would be decided. Yet the political success achieved far outweighed these fears in the end. Weizmann thanked Churchill for all his help in bringing about the project's consummation, and for his "unwavering sympathy and encouragement in all our struggles." "We shall do our utmost to vindicate your faith and vision," Ben Gurion wired the prime minister on behalf of Palestinian Jewry. The Anglo-American press overwhelmingly applauded HMG's decision, as did Parliament. The only opposition came from a handful of Jewish anti-Zionists, the ex-mufti, some Arab leaders, and from the Nazi propaganda machine, which warned that the move would only strengthen Germany's will to resist her enemies to the utmost. The struggle for an Allied Jewish fighting force had come to an end.[53]

CONCLUSION

The Jewish Brigade owed its creation, in the first instance, to the Jewish Agency. With justice could Shertok cable the American Zionist Emergency Committee, successor to ECZA, "this Agency's achievement from beginning to end." Certainly his untiring activities on behalf of a Jewish force, opposed at times by different political factions in the Yishuv, entitled him to first patrimony. Weizmann's diplomatic pressure in London, and notably his strong influence on England's prime minister, played the other chief role. Ben Gurion's crusade to capture Palestinian and American Jewry for an independent Jewish army and state meant much to its success. The agency's major champions in Great Britain, Wingate, Wedgwood, and Cazalet, used every opportunity to castigate their government's unwillingness to establish such a force. And the Yishuv's significant effort on behalf of the Allied cause, especially when compared with that of the Arabs, could not fail to make some mark.[54]

The Committee for a Jewish Army, the only organization committed full-time to the idea in question, did yeoman work in galvanizing public opinion for the Jewish combat force. Its full-page newspaper advertisements, stirring stage productions like Ben Hecht's "We Will Never Die," and subsequent activity as the Emergency Committee to Save the Jewish People of Europe and then the Hebrew Committee of National Liberation all made a deep impression in the United States and Great Britain. Indeed, Palestinian Jewry's true military contribution first came to light with Van Paassen's *The Forgotten Ally,* a 1943 bestseller in both countries which he had written while chairing the Committee for a Jewish Army. The committee's resolute activities reached the point where the established Zionist groups, upon failing to co-opt its leadership, attempted to discredit in government circles Peter Bergson and the other mavericks of the Irgun delegation. Ambassador Halifax and the Colonial Office wished to silence Bergson by drafting him into the British Army, a plot his supporters in Congress foiled at the last moment. The committee's ability to capture the public imagination certainly allowed the prime minister to assert in Cabinet that this cause enjoyed great support on both sides of the Atlantic. And in a way its founders never intended, the organization's large-scale, aggressively put demands made it easier for Churchill and his colonial and foreign secretaries to deal with the established Jewish Agency, its smaller requests for a Jewish division and then a brigade, and with the more moderate Weizmann.[55]

Churchill's deep sympathy for the concept of an allied Jewish force overcame the major forces of opposition and gave this proposal some real form at last. Without the prime minister's support, evident at every crucial stage since September, 1939, the Jewish Brigade would never have gotten by the careerists in London and the Middle East. The U.S. War and State departments also rejected the idea, and a report in mid-1943 from Roosevelt's personal emissary to the Middle East, which did much to shape government opinion, omitted any mention of the Yishuv's war record. The president never made the public commitment to the Jewish force that he had promised Weizmann in July, 1942, and his "platonic interest," to quote the Jewish Socialist leader Harold Laski, did not strengthen its cause until the prime minister pressed FDR in August, 1944. Churchill justified the Jewish Brigade on military grounds, on the basis of his firm views supporting a large Jewish state in Palestine, and on the conviction that the scourge of the Holocaust called for a redemptive response from HMG to let the Jews of the Promised Land confront the murderers of their people in battle. Its subsequent record drew the prime minister's public praise. The triumph belonged to him above all.[56]

The brigade did meet the demands of the Zionist leadership to some extent. It tore aside the mask of anonymity that the British had imposed on the Jewish volunteers from Palestine. Fighting under its own flag,

Jewish officers, and commanding officer (Brigadier Ernest F. Benjamin), the force of some 5,000 participated on the Adriatic front with distinction in early 1945. The effort "redeemed our honor in our own eyes and in the eyes of others," asserted Shertok after the war. The climax came when a contingent of the brigade, each man sporting its blue-white-blue shoulder flash bearing a yellow Star of David and the words "Jewish Brigade Group" with the equivalent Hebrew initials "Chativa Yehudit Lochemet" (Chayil), marched through London under the Jewish flag in the Allied victory march on June 8, 1946. At last the yellow star could be worn with pride, replacing the yellow badge of shame that had marked Jewry's millions for martyrdom in World War II. The brigade, the first outside Jewish group to come in contact with the casualties of the Holocaust, served as "a living bridge" after the armistice to bring these scarred remnants of European Jewry to Palestine, in defiance of British immigration quotas. Finally, the excellent military training its members received in the last months of the war proved invaluable to the Yishuv's armed struggle against HMG until the creation of the State of Israel three years later.[57]

But the Zionists' rare and limited victory failed to achieve the political significance for which they had grappled with HMG on the diplomatic front these past five years. The British had radically altered their view of Palestinian Jewry since Malcolm MacDonald first dismissed the Yishuv's strength during the conference that gave birth to the White Paper. Nor did that statement of policy serve, as London had first expected, to bring about Arab loyalty during the war. Yet precisely its new realization of increased, militant Jewish power in Palestine—even Wavell admitted that the Jews, left to themselves, would defeat the Arabs—led an anxious Middle East command to insist that the White Paper be maintained throughout World War II and to oppose a Jewish state thereafter. Palestinian Jewry, as a consequence, was damned for having either too little power or too much. The British and the Yishuv, even in time of shared crisis, treated each other with distrust. As soon as the military authorities in Palestine had no need for the agency and the Yishuv's military value, this cooperation ceased. Discrimination against the Jewish volunteers of Palestine continued in the case of the brigade as well, the British disallowing any recruitment among Italian Jewry or physically fit Holocaust survivors to help the brigade attain its full strength of 6,000, and insisting on the unit's dispersion before its soldiers returned home. This last condition recalled the fate of the Jewish Legion after the last world war.

The assassination of Lord Moyne, Churchill's close friend, by the Stern group on November 6, 1944, raised serious doubts even in the prime minister's mind, and sharpened HMG's antagonism to Zionist aspirations. This hostility also sowed the dragon's teeth of Jewish civil conflict in Palestine: the Stern group, followed by the Irgun, refused to accept the Jewish Agency's actual truce with HMG during the war; the Hagana mounted a *saison* of retaliation against the dissident "terrorists." World War II ended, as it had begun, with the White Paper in force, and the doors to their one available large refuge firmly bolted against the Jews.[58]

At the root of the difficulty lay the different assumptions of the two contending forces regarding their individual positions in Palestine. Because British colonial practice traditionally viewed all HMG's subjects as an integral part of the empire, it followed, in the words of the Foreign Office, that "the right of racial minorities to be recruited into units other than the normal forces of the state" could not be tolerated. The British had recruited "since time immemorial" on the basis of territorial domicile, opposing "racial prejudice" as "alien to our national feelings and instincts." The Yishuv insisted, *per contra,* on an equal partnership in the Mandate's implementation, thus incurring the continued hostility of the administration in Palestine. And ultimately of greatest significance, as Weizmann told MacMichael's successor in October, 1944, the Jewish community there did believe that the biblical mandate pre-dated Britain's right to govern its Promised Land.[59] Thus the agency's demand to fight as Jews during World War II, rather than as "Palestinians" for defensive duty alone. The two opposing stances were, fundamentally, irreconcilable.

In the end, the tragedy of Jewish statelessness had forced the Yishuv to serve as Great Britain's nameless ally during World War II. Its final contribution of more than 31,000 soldiers to the British Army and multifold activities in other areas counted for little in the international diplomatic arena, the Arabs' sorry military record notwithstanding. HMG, MacMichael fully understood at the outbreak of hostilities, could take the Yishuv's support for granted: as long as no threat confronted the Jewish national home, the British needed no large combat force from Palestine; when Rommel drew near, Jewish recruitment logically climbed without a fighting force of its own. Still, in consequence of Britain's anti-Zionist policy, as Churchill charged, HMG had to maintain more than 20,000 troops in Palestine during the war.[60]

Having expressed the faith in August, 1940, that "moral factors as well as purely material ones" would bear on victory, Ben Gurion understandably castigated four years later the empty expressions of sympathy toward defenseless European Jewry from the self-professed guardians of democracy, who "stood aside and let it bleed to death." The people who, more than any other, had the strongest reasons for fighting in united fashion under its own flag against the Nazi moloch never received Allied approval to do so. In this respect the Jews were *sui generis,* unlike the Poles, Czechs, and other victims of the Third Reich's determination to carve out

Lebensraum for the thousand-year greater Germany of the future.[61]

The Yishuv's role in the Allied victory, therefore, met with the same official silence that muffled the last cries of its European brothers and sisters before being throttled by the SS *Einsatzgruppen,* their collaborators, and the crematoria. At a time when Jewry was fighting for its very life, only one combatant accorded the Jews recognition as openly engaged in conflict with Nazism. Adolf Hitler carried this conviction until his suicide in a Berlin bunker on April 30, 1945, having concluded his political testament for signature at 4 A.M. the previous day: "Above all I charge the leaders of the nation and those under them to scrupulous observance of the laws of race and to merciless opposition to the universal poisoner of all peoples, international Jewry." As a result, Europe became a Jewish graveyard rather than a battlefield commensurate with the honor of the Jewish people.[62] The Yishuv saw no choice but to take up arms for Jewish sovereign independence after the war. The time had come, it concluded, to end the curse of anonymity and to bring the stateless survivors of the Holocaust home.

The *Patria* and the *Atlantic*

AS THE SUN ROSE over Mt. Carmel's olive groves on November 25, 1940, the eyes of Palestinian Jewry focused upon the 12,000-ton French liner *Patria,* anchored in Haifa Bay. Five days earlier High Commissioner Harold MacMichael had announced that the more than 1,700 Jewish refugees from Nazi Europe who had "illegally" entered Palestine's waters on two steamers at the beginning of the month would be deported to a British colony, where they would be confined for the duration of World War II but not admitted to the Promised Land thereafter. Similar action, he added, would be taken against all others openly flouting the immigration laws of His Majesty's Government, so as not to "affect adversely" the country's position and "prove a serious menace to British interests in the Middle East." For the first time in its 20-year history the Mandatory power would deport Jews from Palestine. After the former passengers of the *Pacific* and *Milos* had already been transferred to the specially chartered ship for an undisclosed voyage, the Royal Navy had escorted the *Atlantic* and its human cargo of 1,829 into the harbor on the 24th. That same evening British forces had been moving some of these new arrivals to the *Patria,* with the remainder scheduled for the morrow. Rumors abounded that sailing would take place within 24 hours.[1]

The Jewish Agency and other official Zionist bodies in Palestine had proven unable to weaken MacMichael's resolve. In contrast to similar past incidents, all contact with the refugees had been forbidden. Newspapers that printed accounts faced shut-down or censorship. The chief secretary, admitting that the refugees (rather than "fifth columnists") qualified as trained pioneers or had relatives in the country, frankly told agency political department head Moshe Shertok (later Sharett) of the government's anxiety that their entry would stimulate other such trips and ultimately nullify the restrictive White Paper of 1939. Although illegals could be deducted from allotment quotas and admitted under that very immigration policy, the high commissioner refused to receive a delegation from the Jewish Elected Assembly. MacMichael had just granted asylum to 170 Polish Gentiles and their families, but Henrietta Szold, director of Youth Aliya, could not even obtain the release from the *Patria* of those 77 known candidates slated for her program. The dispatch of some food and smuggled messages of support, along with a one-day stoppage of labor in conjunction with a hunger strike by the refugees, were all that Palestinian Jewry accomplished.[2]

Nor did the Jewish Agency office in London appear capable of averting the unprecedented decree. World Zionist Organization president Chaim Weizmann, already angered by Colonial Office delays in establishing an Allied Jewish fighting force, heard Colonial Secretary Lord Lloyd privately assert that the three illegal ships were being followed by another contingent of about 1,800 refugees presently at sea. This action, Lloyd explained on November 14, might be a prelude to wider and more systematic efforts by the Gestapo, now in control of Rumanian ports, for two ends: rid the Greater Reich of Jews and embarrass HMG by using *agents provocateurs* in Palestine and stirring up pro-Arab propaganda. Weizmann wired Shertok and Jewish Agency Executive chairman David Ben Gurion, then in New York, to "prevent rise of feeling which may complicate situation." Prepared to agree under certain conditions to the proposed island of Mauritius, he sought with limited hopes to get those now at Haifa landed. A rumor on November 22 that Secretary of Labor Ernest Bevin had gotten Prime Minister Winston Churchill to order Lloyd not to send the ships away brought the Zionist spokesman welcome comfort.[3] It would be no small matter for HMG to repudiate the high commissioner's radio announcement, however, and, unknown to Weizmann, the recent arrivals on the *Atlantic* were steadily being transferred to the jammed gunwales of the *Patria*.

American Zionist organizations, for their part, had remonstrated to the press and taken some diplomatic steps. Immediately upon receiving a secret message via Syria, Stephen Wise of the Emergency Committee for Zionist Affairs (ECZA) had telephoned the totally unaware British embassy with a warning that any expulsion would have a terrible effect in the United States. Ben Gurion cabled Weizmann his entire agreement with the need to avoid giving the British "any possible embarrassment," but urged that those in Haifa be disembarked immediately and released upon verification of their *bona fides;* if Lloyd's information were correct, further transports should be intercepted by the British prior to their entering the Mediterranean and be brought to safety elsewhere. MacMichael's "shocking" action evoked the public outcry of various groups, while Poalei Zion got American Federation of Labor president William Green to cable Minister Bevin in favor of letting the refugees aboard the *Patria* enter Palestine on humanitarian grounds, at least for the war's duration.

Ben Gurion, currently finding resistance in these circles to his wish that American Jewish youth join the contemplated fighting unit, pressed the ECZA to take increased public action and to present a protest to the British ambassador. In Washington Louis D. Brandeis, Felix Frankfurter, and Benjamin V. Cohen, asked for their opinions on the morning of the 25th, strongly felt that Ben Gurion's suggested tactics would embarrass the pro-British administration of President Franklin D. Roosevelt and hamper its current attempt to secure congressional approval of Lend Lease supplies to Britain.[4] The appointment had already been made for the following day at noon, however, and it would stand.

The Zionists' desperate efforts meant little, for the British War Cabinet accepted MacMichael's recommendation that the *Patria* and *Atlantic* passengers be diverted to the Indian Ocean island. Lloyd's insistence on the need to "create a better atmosphere" in the Middle East because of Moslem unrest and military operations in the Balkans, a fear shared by the British chiefs of staff, accounted for his anxiety over a Jewish fighting force and illicit immigration to Palestine. He warned Churchill on November 21 that landing the refugees in Haifa Bay would be seen as "a surrender to Jewish agitation and more and more shiploads would come," with an "altogether deplorable political effect" on the entire region.

The prime minister, a firm opponent of the White Paper, found more congenial Bevin's plea and particularly the advice of his own private secretary, John Martin. Dismissing a suggestion to ship the refugees to more hospitable Trinidad—"surely we cannot contemplate a British Dachau on the doorstep of America"—Martin, former secretary to the 1937 Peel Commission, recommended the establishment of a Jewish state larger than the commission's partition proposal, along with an Arab federation to include Transjordan and Syria and part of Palestine. On the 22nd he relayed to the Colonial Office Churchill's argument that "the proposal to send the refugees overseas should be called off." Concurrently, however, Churchill informed Lloyd that the deportation, once announced, "must proceed"; the future exiles should not, at the same time, be "caged up" in Mauritius for the duration of the war. Two days later MacMichael wired his superior: "If all goes well, they should be all aboard on November 26 and sail November 27."[5]

The warm rays of that crisp November 25 morning did little to lighten the deep depression that weighed on the *Patria* transport. The refugees' protest on the 18th to the high commissioner, expressing their firm Zionist commitment, a willingness to join the Jewish Palestinian units in the British Army, and the conviction that exile now would be "a crueler fate" than their earlier expulsion from Germany, had still received no response. While information circulated that departure for Mauritius would be at 4:30 P.M., 120 of the *Atlantic* people began to enter the large hold. Over 200 British soldiers on board sent these new arrivals straight to the showers to prevent any infectious disease and ordered the original two shiploads to come on deck for police inspection between 8 and 10 A.M.

A few members of the *Patria*'s central committee made the rounds even before 7 A.M., urging everyone to evacuate their cabins within an hour. The motor could be heard warming up and the three smokestacks belched black. Shortly before 9 A.M. almost all the passengers had reached the deck, where their attention was diverted by three boys from Germany who dove in swim trunks to the frigid waters 15 meters below and started making for shore. As a navy patrol chased these young stalwarts, five others followed suit. Two shots in the air rang out from their pursuers.

Suddenly, a huge explosion rocked the entire vessel. In the first instant many believed the ship's captain, who asserted that an enemy attack was responsible, and they began seeking shelter downstairs. Yet the *Patria* began to list to starboard, and the British gave orders to don lifejackets. The holds flooded rapidly. Careening "lifts," luggage, and heavy beams pressed scores in the ship's bowels to death and trapped desperate swimmers in a watery grave.[6]

In seven minutes the boat capsized, steadily sinking. Sirens broke loose around the harbor, and dozens of rowboats and launches rushed to the rescue. Britisher, Jew, and Arab cooperated without stint, while port engineers bored large holes into the liner's side to gain some access inside. One heroic British soldier gave up his life in freeing trapped souls who had escaped the Nazi menace. The immediate survivors received shelter in a nearby custom house shed; over one hundred injured ended up in the government and Hadassah hospitals. Within 15 minutes on that Monday morning, only the port side of the *Patria* showed above water.[7]

High above the apocalyptic scene, a lonely figure stood stunned. From a vantage point on Mt. Carmel, Shaul Meyerov (later Avigur) witnessed the incredible sinking of the *Patria* and decided that the moment had come to leave Haifa without delay. The man ultimately in charge of the act of sabotage, as well as the entire program of *Aliya Bet* ("illegal" immigration), joined an associate and took the first taxi available to Tel Aviv. While the motor continued running, Meyerov burst into the home of Berl Katznelson and related the shocking turn of events. The editor of the Labor newspaper *Davar,* engrossed in his writing, hardly uttered a word. Hurt, Meyerov continued on to his Jerusalem apartment. The next morning he took seriously ill and fell to bed. Where had the operation gone wrong, he tortured himself, and what now?[8]

II

The *Patria* tragedy had its genesis more than two and a half years earlier when Adolf Hitler realized the dream expressed on the first page of *Mein Kampf:* the annexation of Austria, his birthplace, to the German

Reich. The *Anschluss* of March 13, 1938, as the European director of the American Jewish Joint Distribution Committee (JDC) had observed at the time, shocked Austrian Jewry into accepting during the space of five days all the oppressions its far more affluent co-religionists in Germany had undergone during the past five years. The unparalleled mass arrests, brutal attacks, closing of all Jewish institutions, and the heartless destruction of economic life initiated a wave of suicides and a panicked, unanimous search for emigration at the earliest opportunity.[9]

While President Roosevelt had Secretary of State Hull call for an international conference at Evian-les-Bains to consider the needs of all German and Austrian refugees, the immediate fate of some 185,000 terrorized Austrian Jews passed into the hands of *Untersturmführer* Adolf Eichmann. The 32-year-old colorless bureaucrat attached to the SD's Intelligence Department, by then recognized in the party's highest circles as an expert on Jewish matters, convoked a few leading Zionists at the main offices of the Gestapo on the early morning of March 25. Attired in the black uniform of the SS, he interrogated them at length and impressed his audience with some Hebrew and Yiddish words, his knowledge of their activities, and a (false) story of his birth in Sarona near Tel Aviv. At the conclusion of the appointment Eichmann declared that Zionist work in Vienna would be reactivated under a central organization. Instructed to solve the so-called "Jewish problem" in Austria completely in the "quickest and most efficient" way, he warned those present that he would use all measures to execute these orders.[10]

This encounter at the Hotel Metropol had an immediate effect. Aloys Rothenberg was appointed to the office in charge of transports to Palestine (abbreviated Pal Amt), while the Gestapo released Joseph Loewenherz from prison in order to run the Israelitische Kultusgemeinde (Jewish community office) and to obtain emigration permits for all other countries. Within three weeks an estimated 40,000–50,000 people had been registered for emigration with the newly opened Kultusgemeinde. Gestapo pressure stepped up during the next four months with the introduction of the Nuremberg racial laws, mass deportations to Dachau, expulsions from the Burgenland provinces, and ruthless "Aryanization" of Jewish property. The community, wrote a Jewish Agency visitor, quickly realized that it was "living not only in a fool's paradise, but in a veritable hell." Despite the reigning confusion and flux, he concluded somberly, "the policy may aim at a complete annihilation of Austrian Jewry."[11]

The British government, however, entrusted by the League of Nations with facilitating the growth of a Jewish national home in Palestine, was at that very moment intent on closing the obvious refuge. While gradually retreating from its July, 1937, offer of Jewish statehood in a partitioned Palestine, the Colonial Office informed the new high commissioner, Harold MacMichael, on March 10 that only 2,000 capitalists (each having £1,000) and 1,000 workers could enter the Holy Land between April and September, 1938; a mere 200 certificates would be allotted for dependent relatives other than wives and children. Moshe Shertok appealed in the name of the Jewish Agency that at least the last named category should be relaxed in view of the "catastrophic conditions" of Austrian Jewry, but his protest went wanting. Sixteen immigration certificates for Palestine lay at the disposal of the entire Austrian Jewish community the day that delirious crowds greeted the *Führer* to celebrate their "homecoming" into the Reich, and the prospects for a sudden augmentation appeared slim. The increasing violence of the Palestinian Arab rebellion and HMG's deep-felt anxiety that the friendship of the surrounding Arab countries would be lost if the Mandatory created a Jewish state, just when Germany and Italy rattled sabres in Europe, led Malcom MacDonald, the new colonial secretary, to warn Chaim Weizmann frankly that "the experiment might prove fatal."[12]

The Jewish Agency, still hopeful of some *modus vivendi* with the British government, refused to sanction a policy of clandestine immigration to the Promised Land. A first attempt, under the auspices of the Polish HeChalutz youth movement, to disembark 350 Jewish "illegals" on the *Velos* had succeeded in June, 1934, but the failure of a second trip hardened the agency's attitude. A meeting of its executive with the Palestine Office in Warsaw in February, 1935, found general agreement that this activity should be stopped immediately, Shertok insisting that the agency could only operate in an authorized manner. In a public session of the British Peel Commission on December 8, 1936, the political department's chief explained that the agency "definitely opposed" illicit immigration because "it is not selective." Some leaders of the United Kibbutz organization and the Hagana armed force did support HeChalutz's secret effort, but Ben Gurion decisively disapproved any action that might jeopardize HMG's partition offer. The agency's emigration department refused to cover any expenses, not even for the 65 HeChalutz members who quietly landed on Palestine's shore from the *Poseidon* in January, 1938. Finally, the Hagana high command decided that summer to establish the *Mossad* (institution) *LeAliya Bet* on its own, under the direction of Shaul Meyerov. The Vienna office, which until then focused on getting youngsters into agricultural centers as preparation for sanctioned immigration to Palestine, would have to work quickly in the unprecedented crisis.[13]

In the face of the official Zionist position, the Revisionist New Zionist Organization (NZO) took the lead in attempting to end Austrian Jewry's nightmare. Unhampered by agency discipline and wishing to counter the discrimination practiced against its *Betar* youth in obtaining legal certificates, the NZO executive announced at its 1935 congress in Vienna its intention to send one and a half million Jews to the Holy Land in ten years. It hesitated, at the same time, to assume responsibility for a trial shipment in a small boat from Athens to Palestine. Only the successful *"Af Al Pi"* (in spite of) run with 16 from Vienna to the Promised Land in early 1937 brought the combined cooperation of the NZO executive, the Israelitische Kultusgemeinde, and the Austrian police to the point where two more transports of *Betarim* left for Palestine before March, 1938.

Willy Perl, their organizer, asked Eichmann at the end of the month to support further efforts. The then little-known German *Untersturmführer* let a week pass before deciding against the proposal: the Nazis did not wish a "central station for criminals in Palestine." The Jews, he asserted, "will be atomized." Throwing caution to the winds, Perl and an associate traveled to Berlin and received permission from the Reich Economic Ministry to obtain the foreign exchange necessary to buy ships and thus "cleanse" Vienna of its Jews. The first transport under Eichmann's regime, 386 participants of all classes and Zionist parties, gathered at the south railroad station in June, 1938. Surrounded by Eichmann and other Nazi officials, Dr. Perl solemnly reminded the group that, returning at last to the homeland where Roman bands had driven out their ancestors, they represented "the pioneers of a proud Jewish future." The minor-key strains of "Hatikva" (the Zionist anthem) spontaneously welled up to fill the air, and the train pulled out for its rendezvous with the successful boat trip to Palestine.[14]

The Gestapo's willingness to further illegal immigration to Palestine had been established, but its wish for a large-scale emigration program focused Eichmann's attention on Loewenherz and his contacts with established Jewish relief organizations in New York and London. While hoping that the forthcoming international refugee conference at Evian would meet the Jewish plight in Germany and Austria, the Joint Distribution Committee got permission from Berlin to maintain soup kitchens and to transfer funds at the special rate granted it earlier for German Jewry. Loewenherz obtained a grant of $100,000 in June, followed by another $210,000 in September, from the JDC and the British Council for German Jewry exclusively for emigration. With Eichmann's approval, sums from this account were withdrawn only when the Nazi authorities gave equivalent payments from confiscated Jewish property. The head of the Kultusgemeinde then sold the foreign currency to wealthy prospective emigrants at four to five times its value, the difference to be used for relief and financing the exit of the poor. The unrelenting pressure of Gestapo arrests, coupled with swindles from false travel agencies and discriminatory taxes on all seeking to leave the country, convinced Loewenherz and Rothenberg that only Eichmann could effectively carry through a systemized "policy of *sauve qui peut.*"[15] A special procedure would have to be established to achieve this end quickly.

As a result of the Loewenherz-Rothenberg initiative and the failure of the Evian conference, Eichmann established the Vienna Central Office for Jewish Emigration in August, 1938. A month earlier HMG's representative had publicly announced at Evian-les-Bains that the British empire had no place for large-scale settlement of Jewish refugees; other governments followed the American decision to maintain rigid immigration quotas. While the conference resolved not to finance "involuntary emigration" and the British got Athens to instruct its missions not to issue Jews any transit visas through Greece, 100,000 registered in Vienna for emigration (15,000 to Palestine). Processed on an assembly-line basis in the Central Office, each applicant entered the confiscated Rothschild Palace, passed in front of all the interested authorities, and left the same day with pockets almost empty and a short-term Austrian passport, every page marked by a red "J" (Jude) and carrying the ultimate foreboding stamp: "You must leave the country within a fortnight. Otherwise, you will go to a concentration camp." By the end of the year and with the added pressure of a brutal Austrian *Kristallnacht,* over 60,000 had left Vienna under the novel process that Eichmann had instituted.[16]

Eichmann's efficiency brought him promotion to *Hauptsturmführer* and inspired Goering's order on January 24, 1939, that Chief of Security Police Reinhard Heydrich direct the newly established Reich Central Office for Jewish Emigration. The Vienna example of forced expulsion, with Heydrich announcing to his subordinates in early February that some 100,000 Jews had "left" Austria's borders, now became "the ultimate aim" of greater Germany. Offices under Eichmann's supervision, following the Vienna model, were soon set up in Berlin and, four months after the Nazis occupied the remainder of Czechoslovakia, in Prague. A story in the *Pariser Tageblatt* about "Bloodhound Eichmann, a new foe of Jewry," infuriated the Nazis' rising star on Jewish affairs, but he did everything to earn the title. In February Eichmann demanded 500 registrations daily from Austria for emigration, threatening to curtail the release of prisoners from concentration camps Dachau and Buchenwald if the quota were not met; these individuals had a week to leave the country.[17]

Determined to make his experimental showcase in Austria *Judenrein* at an even faster pace, Eichmann decided to take control over all emigration matters in early 1939. He closed down Jewish "travel agencies" and appointed 57-year-old Berthold Storfer to coordinate and speed up the process. Storfer, a successful businessman originally from Bukovina who had represented Austrian Jewry at Evian with Loewenherz and the celebrated physician Prof. Heinrich Neumann on Gestapo orders, had promised Eichmann that he could accomplish this task in the most efficient way. As for the Vienna Mossad, though successful in getting

386 German and Austrian Jews to Palestine via Yugoslavia and Italy right after *Kristallnacht* aboard the *Attrato,* it had suffered a severe setback when Goebbels's *Der Angriff* publicized the sailing of another of the "ghost ship's" runs; HMG subsequently pressured the Yugoslav government to halt this traffic. Eichmann's threats forced the group's Palestinian emissary, Moshe Averbuch (later Agami), to leave for neutral Switzerland, while Storfer's competition with Mossad contacts on the Greek shipping market drove prices of the few available boats sky high.[18]

Even as Eichmann tightened the screws on Austrian Jewry and Europe slid to the precipice of war, Britain's decision to end Lord Balfour's pledge of November, 1917, through the White Paper quotas raised second thoughts for some in the Jewish Agency Executive. Whitehall took strong diplomatic steps to check continuing illegal traffic over the Danube and the Black Sea to Palestine, a step privately applauded by King George VI, and Colonial Secretary MacDonald announced in July that all immigration certificates would be suspended for six months. *Kristallnacht,* the White Paper, and the free world's indifference to the crisis confronting Europe's Jews brought Ben Gurion into the camp of the *Aliya Bet* stalwarts, including laborite leaders Berl Katznelson and Yitschak Tabenkin and Hagana chiefs Eliyahu Golomb and Israel Galili. Just prior to the May, 1939, announcement, Ben Gurion convinced the Agency Executive to support *Aliya Bet* as part of a future struggle with the Mandatory power. But the executive, Ben Gurion's own Mapai political committee, and the Mossad's Meyerov all opposed his risky plan for disembarking *Colorado*'s 377 passengers by armed force at the end of July; the boat's capture by the British ended a possible split over "*Aliya Gimmel.*"[19]

Many in the world Zionist leadership had yet to adjust to Ben Gurion's sharp conversion, and the moderates succeeded in muting most public support for nonsanctioned immigration during the twenty-first Zionist congress in mid-August. With the shadows of impending war hovering over those assembled in Geneva's Grand Theatre, Chaim Weizmann set the tone by urging the continuation of "peaceful reconciliation" alongside a political battle against the White Paper in the years ahead. Zionist Organization of America president Solomon Goldman employed his Reform rabbinical training to assert that Jewish tradition regarded the scholar Yochanan Ben Zakai a greater hero than the warrior Bar Kochba; he also brought Justice Brandeis's message that the Yishuv's strength consisted in "constructive work." Abba Hillel Silver, United Palestine Appeal chairman and another Reform spiritual leader, went further on August 19, expressing his worry about the possibility of making any colossal blunder "at a time when circumstances do not warrant our taking such action." Until the political overthrow of the White Paper, he counseled those present to follow Dr. Weizmann's program of securing as much legal immigration to Palestine as possible.[20]

Silver's address threw those Mossad agents present at the gathering into dark despair, but again they found their champion in Berl Katznelson. Sensing that Silver represented the future leadership in the movement's increasingly important American branch, the man whose *Davar* offices' second floor also housed the Mossad's center of operations made a supreme effort to sway his audience the next morning. Following a reminder to Goldman not to delete Judah Maccabee and Bar Kochba from the heroes of Jewish history, the venerated labor ideologue lashed out against Silver's speech as "a stab in the back" of the refugees wandering on the seas. The hands extended by Palestine's Jewish youth to their people on the unauthorized *Velos,* he exhorted in Yiddish, represented links in the chain that extended from Nachmanides's prayer for the sea and Yehuda HaLevi's poetry, with their burning desire to return to the land promised Jews in the Bible. All immigration to Palestine and the Jew's right to life were the very essence of legality, he concluded: "The Jewish immigrant goes out in the advance ranks of the battle against the Mandatory, and we all have the duty to enlist in his army."[21]

Volley upon volley of applause greeted Katznelson's remarks, but the political commission deemed these openly stated views somewhat impolitic. As the delegates took hurried leave of one another, Weizmann pledged full support to the future Allied cause. The final resolutions included a vague reaffirmation of the "unalienable right of the Jewish people, exercised without interruption throughout the centuries of the Dispersion, to return to Palestine, where the only real and permanent solution of the problem of Jewish homelessness is to be found."[22]

The draftsmen of the White Paper thought otherwise, and moved to halt Jewish immigration to the Holy Land in the beginning six months of the war. The first shots fired by the British after Hitler invaded Poland were aimed at 1,159 Polish refugees aboard the Mossad's *Tiger Hill;* two Jewish men fell their victims that September 2, 1939. HMG persisted in warning "transit countries" against facilitating *Aliya Bet,* while Weizmann's request for 20,000 Polish children to enter Palestine on humanitarian grounds received a firm negative, despite the White Paper allowance. Given the entry of over 11,000 "illegals" in the last half-year quota period, Colonial Office Permanent Undersecretary of State John Shuckburgh, who believed that Jews "hate all gentiles," expressed the hope to his associates that "some of the sources of supply may dry up" as a result of the outbreak of hostilities. No certificates would be issued for the next six months; even those interned in the Atlit camp near Haifa, Colonial Secretary MacDonald privately asserted in October, should be

sent "back to mainland Europe after the war." To Shertok's pleas the
following month for a new quota in view of Polish Jewry's catastrophic
fate, MacDonald suggested that possible Nazi spies (a charge Whitehall
doubted in fact) and Palestine's large unemployment rate militated
against a change in policy.[23]

London's unyielding attitude did not let up. Following a discussion at
the Foreign Office in December of increased illegal immigration, one official attached to the Western Department observed: "The only hope is
that all the German Jews will be stuck at the mouths of the Danube for
lack of ships to take them." For further effect, a joint memorandum from
the Colonial and Foreign offices to European countries on January 17,
1940, stressed that unauthorized Jewish immigration to Palestine "is not
primarily a refugee movement" but a politically motivated effort, abetted
by the Gestapo, to upset the British position in Palestine and consequently the Middle East. One month later an official spokesman emphasized to the House of Lords that "the situation in which these Jews find
themselves appears to be the result of an attempt to escape from the con-
sequences of the well-known and deliberate policy of the German government, and His Majesty's Government cannot accept responsibility for it."
Despite the objections raised by Lord of the Admiralty Winston Churchill, the Cabinet simultaneously enacted the White Paper provision considerably limiting land purchase by Jews in Palestine.[24]

Britain's stance, notwithstanding the Nazi deportation of thousands of
Jews to the Lublin district, moved the American Zionist establishment
to support *Aliya Bet*. Hagana chieftain Eliyahu Golomb, on a special
mission to the United States, obtained $25,000 from Hadassah and
$10,000 each from the Zionist Organization of America and Poalei Zion.
These funds aided the Vienna Mossad's last major effort, the transfer of
2,000 Jews from Vienna, the Old Reich, Danzig, and the Protectorate,
via Bratislava, to the port of Kladovo in Yugoslavia for passage to
Palestine. Hadassah refused, however, to support a plan of Recha Freier
(the originator of Youth Aliya) to ship young refugees from Germany to
Palestine, since it would run independently of agency supervision.[25] For
the same reason, these organizations supplied no funds to help a Revisionist "*Af Al Pi*" transport of over 2,000 Jews stranded in river boats
on the frozen Danube at Sulina, Rumania. That entire group, organized
primarily by the NZO and Dr. Perl of Vienna, had received vital aid
from NZO representative Reuven Hecht of Basle and the Irgun-directed
American Friends of a Jewish Palestine. It reached the Promised Land
under the direction of Eri Jabotinsky, son of the Revisionists' president,
aboard the *Sakariya* on February 13, 1940.[26]

Eichmann considered the "progress" too slow, however, and he chose
Storfer to hasten emigration from the entire Third Reich. This "com-

mercial advisor" had been present the previous October when Eichmann dumped 1,000 Slovakian Jews on the barren plateau in Nisko, Poland, and cynically told them build a "homeland": 350 survived. While Eichmann went on as chief of Heydrich's RSHA department IV-B-4 to take charge of expelling the Jews from all German territory, Storfer joined with the Jewish sports organization Makabi in Austria to form a Committee for Jewish Overseas Transports. Visting Bucharest at the end of February, 1940, he reported to the press that 8,000 Austrian and Czech Jews faced deportation to the Lublin "reservation" if no transit visas could be obtained.[27]

In March Eichmann ordered the Jewish communities of Vienna, Berlin, and Prague to place all their emigration activities under Storfer, now to head the Division of Overseas Transport and supervise one final, large emigration "shipment" from the Reich. The Pal Amt offices in Vienna and Berlin had refused to cooperate with Gestapo pressure on Jews to cable their American relatives for $200 per person, a sum paid to the Swiss Bank Corporation in New York and then credited to a Geneva bank account, which enabled these desperate individuals to proceed to boats in Slovakia or Yugoslavia for the unauthorized voyage to Palestine. Zionist offices considered the ships involved unsafe, and demanded that certain unscrupulous crew members be dismissed. The conflict saw Rothenberg of the Vienna Pal Amt emigrate that same month, and HeChalutz director in Germany Efraim Frank receive an order from Eichmann to leave Berlin immediately; Storfer, in the meanwhile, failed to arrive at a *modus vivendi* with the agents of the Mossad. Jewish Agency circles even suspected Eichmann's appointee of being a Gestapo agent, operating along with German travel offices to smuggle emissaries and "ill-fitted" refugees into Palestine, get hold of American dollars, and turn *Aliya Bet* into "a very ugly commercial affair."[28]

The JDC, the most substantial of the Jewish relief organizations worldwide, sought not to become involved in these activities. Prior to the start of World War II, the "Joint" had taken the position that it could not finance illegal transports for fear of jeopardizing its nonpolitical program of international relief. Funds covered provisions to stranded refugees and bribes to Latin American officials, in line with the organization's humanitarian tradition, but the executive board turned down requests for *Aliya Bet* proper. This attitude continued after September, 1939: unlike the official Zionist bodies, the JDC forwarded $10,000 to aid the Revisionist ship on the Danube in January, 1940, and also sent substantial sums for the upkeep of the ill-fated Mossad convoy trapped at Kladovo.[29]

The JDC central office could not, however, remain untouched by the agony of European Jewry, especially when appeals reached New York headquarters from those daily threatened with Eichmann's zeal. Storfer had convinced the SS lieutenant-colonel that several hundred Jews from Prague and Vienna, detained since December, 1939, at Bratislava, could be transported to Palestine over the Danube and through the Black Sea with funds from sources including frozen bank accounts of once wealthy Czech Jews. The exorbitant fares to be paid by the refugees, he noted, would also cover the transfer of *Volkdeutsche* from Bessarabia on these boats' return trip to the Reich. Storfer pledged some $52,000 to move 1,400 Jews out of these two cities, and thus received the necessary foreign exchange through official Nazi quarters. Large advances, in turn, came to Storfer's hands from the Jewish community centers of Danzig and the three cities whose transport bureaus had fallen under his control and who wished to increase unsanctioned transports substantially. He next moved to secure Danube boats and bigger vessels in Athens for the two legs of the journey, while each anxious central office looked to the JDC to cover its appropriation.[30]

Aware of Eichmann's designs, the Joint retreated from principle and contributed the necessary funds. European director Morris Troper was chiefly responsible for postponing the deportations of Viennese Jewry the previous November by threatening to stop the transfer of currency to the Kultusgemeinde; a month later he confirmed to Loewenherz the JDC's support, and indicated its agreement to finance a shipment to Palestine of 800 to 1,000 people. Eichmann's continued coercion in the first half of 1940 to speed up emigration, Loewenherz's inability to get many Jews out via Siberia and Yokahama to the United States, the fall of France, and the effect on the Mediterranean traffic of Italy's entry into the war were all facts the JDC could not ignore. Mossad suspicions concerning Storfer's activity held the Joint back for a time. Finally, Troper met in Budapest during June with the Jewish leaders involved and, while having no confidence at all in Storfer, gave the undertaking his approval. The community heads convened in Berlin on July 4, and accepted Storfer's assurance that "all would proceed normally in complete safety."[31]

The odyssey of the Storfer transport began in the early morning hours of September 4, 1940. A first group, comprised of 470 HeChalutz and other Zionist organization members who had left Germany for Vienna in August, 432 who had been waiting for exit from Bratislava since December, 1939, and 84 Jews from Vienna, boarded the *Uranus* during the evening of September 3. From the Protectorate came 652 Jews whose departure for Palestine had been frustrated by Storfer's tactics since March; they left Prague for Vienna on the 2nd and entered the *Melk* at Bratislava along with 50 Viennese Jews the next day. The passengers aboard the *Helios* consisted of 329 HeChalutz and Makabi members from Prague and 300 Viennese refugees, both groups having been detained in two buildings in Bratislava since December, 1939, together with 525 Danzig refugees who had been waiting over a year after first registering for *Aliya Bet*. About 600 passengers, many just released from the Dachau and Buchenwald concentration camps on condition that they leave the Reich at once, came to the *Schoenbrunn* directly from Vienna.

Embarkation took place after nightfall so as not to attract any crowds. In the pitch darkness a member of the Danzig group fell into the Danube and drowned; his hysterical wife and two children did not receive permission to come ashore. With the trip beginning under a crossed star, the four Danube river boats pushed off.[32]

After a week without incident the ships arrived in Tulcea, a Rumanian port at the mouth of the Danube opening to the Black Sea. Despite Storfer's promises that all would go well, poor food, unsanitary conditions, and considerable overcrowding led to attempts at suicide, several deaths, and shattered nerves. The passengers' despair increased upon passing the forlorn Mossad-sponsored group at Kladovo, who could do no more than wave blue-white Zionist flags at the convoy. Their subsequent sighting of the decrepit paddle steamer *Pentcho,* then anchored midstream with 511 Revisionist-sponsored Jewish illegals between Rusczuk (Bulgaria) and Giurgiu (Rumania) for want of entry to any Danubian port, provoked further strain.[33]

The *Atlantic, Pacific,* and *Canisbay* greeted weary eyes as the four boats sailed into Tulcea on September 11, but another three weeks would pass before the voyagers could begin the second stage to their goal. Storfer's brother-in-law, in charge of his affairs at the port, insisted at first that all the voyagers cram into the first two boats. Fearing deaths from disease within 24 hours, the refugees refused. With no financial help from Storfer, who arrived later, they began repairs on the three vessels while forced to consume some private provisions that had been reserved for the long trip on the Black Sea. Pressure from the British consulate in Burcharest on the crews involved further delayed the vessels' departure.

The *Canisbay* even began to sink after the *Melk* passengers had come on board. While the Tulcea fire department pumped out water from the ship, 400 of the group had to spend 17 days in rat-infested wheat silos. With the machineguns of a Rumanian army squad trained on their backs, the distraught travelers returned to the boat, now renamed the *Milos.* Having limited food supplies and possessing bogus visas for Peru and Paraguay, the voyagers aboard the three wheat freighters left Tulcea on October 7 for Sulina and the Black Sea. The Panamanian flag fluttered above as the ships of the Reederi Avgerinos Athens line set their course for Palestine.[34]

The *Pacific,* carrying the *Uranus* group in a trying voyage, reached

Haifa three weeks later. Serving as organizer was HeChalutz's Efraim Frank, whom Jewish representatives had persuaded Eichmann to name as supervisor for the large emigration scheme. Its jammed cargo had to take turns sleeping and coming on deck for fresh air; the group had one paraffin stove and no drinking water. On the way a Bulgarian warship forced the 500-ton ship to enter Varna, where other refugees came aboard. With no coal left after a stop in the Cretan islands and five days' distance from the goal, beds, lifeboats, and any spare wood went to stoke the engines. Fourteen died on this last leg of the voyage. At 4:30 A.M. on November 1, the first view of Mt. Carmel appeared on the horizon. Shouts of joy, sobs, and warm embracing mingled with a fervent rendition of the Zionist anthem "Hatikva": "... to be a free nation in our land, the land of Zion and Jerusalem." Wrote one refugee among the 1,061 passengers: "We have arrived at a safe shore."[35] The next day would be the twenty-third anniversary of the Balfour Declaration.

The *Milos* underwent a similar voyage. Having only six sailors, no navigational instruments, and no one to take over his duties on the bridge, the Greek captain miraculously made his way eastward. After an uneventful trip the boat reached Istanbul. The authorities refused it entry, however, and the group proceeded to a small port on the edge of the Dardanelles. Receiving the same reception, they moved on to the isle of Lesbos. A cable to Piraeus for desperately needed provisions brought no results, notwithstanding Storfer's earlier assurances; the passengers eventually received help from the JDC through the Jewish community in Athens. The packed 400-ton vessel left the Cretan harbor of Iraklion just at the start of the Greek-Italian war, and with its last coal supply reached Cyprus. Having replenished their provisions, 702 aboard the typhoid-ridden *Milos* entered Palestinian waters some days later. One *hora* circle after another broke out on deck, with young and old singing "David, King of Israel, lives and endures!" In the early afternoon of November 6 the anchor dropped near the Haifa breakwater.[36]

HMG's true intentions in transferring the transports to the *Patria* soon became clear, however, and the Hagana decided to prevent the expulsion of fellow Jews from Palestine. In the face of British censorship, it posted leaflets in city and village, calling on the Yishuv to "do all in its power" to halt the deportation of those aboard. Realizing that every official attempt to prevent the ship's departure had failed, the Hagana high command hoped to so damage the *Patria* as to force the ship to stay in port for repairs; in the interim, the refugees' condition might arouse British public opinion and persuade the War Cabinet to rescind the order. Since the matter involved a political decision, Meyerov, a member of the command who had been chosen to oversee the operation, approached Moshe Shertok for approval. The agency's chief political officer, concluding that only extraordinary action could check the Mandatory's relentless effort to carry out the White Paper just when Jewry's very existence was at stake in Europe, gave the signal to proceed.[37]

Making careful plans to carry out the mission while avoiding any danger to life, those responsible thought their task accomplished by the morning of November 24. A first plan to damage the *Patria*'s rudder and propeller by attaching a large wooden barrel filled with explosives to its stern fell through, and on the night of the 18th, 27-year-old Munya Mardor agreed to explore the possibility of smuggling a mine onto the *Patria* itself. Establishing contact with the refugees' central committee on November 22, Mardor brought Hans Wendel, the committee's HeChalutz representative, several detonators connected to a fuse. An alarm clock fitted with a pocket flashlight battery would activate the small charge of two kilograms at 9 P.M. and cause a leak far removed from where the immigrants slept or met together. Yet when Wendel removed the safety catch, the bomb did not go off. The now live explosive stayed on board until the morning of the 24th, when Mardor brought his contact a new control device timed for 9 A.M. the following day. At that hour, the two agreed, the ship's passengers would be on deck for regular inspection, and swimmers should mount a diversion by diving into the sea. The Hagana emissary, in his first and only opportunity to press the refugee's hand, took his leave: "*Shalom, LeHitraot*" Peace and *Au revoir*.[38]

At that same time the 1,400-ton *Atlantic,* carrying the original *Helios* and *Schoenbrunn* transports, steamed into the bay. A grave shortage of coal had forced the ship to wait in Iraklion longer than the *Milos,* where the Greek-Italian hostilities caught it on October 28. Only with aid from the Jewish communities in Crete and Athens (and the JDC), as well as by seizing the vessel from a rebellious crew who sabotaged the coal supply, could the passengers leave Crete after almost two weeks. Stripping the boat of all available wood, the "strange metal skeleton" limped into Cyprus with the aid of British tugs. The overjoyed refugees, some exhibiting symptoms of typhoid, paid scant attention to a warning in the local press that they would be "compelled to go even further in their odyssey," rather than receive permission to weep at the Western (Wailing) Wall. Escorted by a British man-of-war, they left Limassol on November 23. Their two-and-a-half month grueling trip having taken the lives of 12, the weary travelers made Palestine 24 hours later.[39]

The devastating explosion the next morning aboard the *Patria,* set off by Wendel exactly as agreed with Mardor, galvanized a swift relief effort on the Yishuv's part. The agency sent its legal advisor, Bernard Joseph, immediately to Haifa, where the Jewish community lost no time in bringing food and clothing for the survivors. The refugees, practically all naked in a large customs shed, stood trembling with fear under British rifles. Many soldiers had tears running down their cheeks. One gray-haired lady, hugging a small child, repeated over and over: "Endlich in Palestina, endlich in Palestina."[40]

III

In a state of shock, Palestinian Jewry found some comfort in assuming that the illegals had at last found permanent shelter. Even as Shertok attended the funeral on November 26 of the first group of victims (including Wendel) and met some of the "human wrecks" in the government hospital, the British interned most of the *Patria* and *Atlantic* refugees in the Atlit camp nearby. The problem of their final destination appeared solved, thus justifying the mysterious disaster. (Almost all in the Yishuv thought that the immigrants, acting alone out of sheer desperation, had sabotaged the liner.)[41] But the tragedy had not yet reached its conclusion.

Much to his amazement, Shertok found the high commissioner as adamant as ever against admitting the anguished refugees. The facts on which the original decision had been based had not changed, he told the Jewish Agency spokesman two days after the *Patria*'s sinking. The survivors would be taken care of in "a good place" elsewhere. Shertok pleaded for mercy on humanitarian grounds, especially as the Jews had already reached the country of their hopes and had been kept in the harbor as "a constant irritation" before the eyes of the Yishuv for over three weeks; the unwarranted "harsh sentence" of the Palestine government not to admit them even after the war "had made the blood of tens of thousands boil," and quite conceivably could have led to an attempt to prevent the boat's departure. The argument reverted to the basic difference of attitude between the Yishuv and the Mandatory over the right of Jewish immigration, HMG's representative pointed out. Doing his best to maintain diplomatic form, the agency spokesman concluded his remonstrance: "You are subjecting our people to the most terrible provocation." The high commissioner did not reply. Was the matter now before the London authorities? Shertok asked in taking his leave. "The decision was there and would be acted upon," MacMichael repeated.[42]

While the gulf between Mandatory and Yishuv widened in Palestine, the American Zionists had registered their official protest with HMG in Washington. Unaware of the *Patria*'s fate because of strict British censorship, a delegation headed by Stephen Wise kept the ECZA's appointment for noon at the British embassy on November 26. Expressing their "deep distress and indignation" at the unprecedented decision to deport those on the *Patria,* the four representatives rejected the imputation of "illegality" as applied to Jews fleeing from Nazi brutality "to the one spot on earth which they may call home." Taking serious exception to the White Paper policy, they added that expulsion might well harm the American good will that they all sought for the extension of maximum aid to Britain during the war. HMG's representative countered with his government's worries about Nazi agents and Arab anxieties. Hoping that the group—"as friends"—would properly present this view before the public, another Britisher present intimated that the Foreign Office might correct the impression presented in the American press, particularly about the barring of these refugees from Palestine after the war.[43]

News of the *Patria*'s fate, which reached the delegation shortly after leaving the embassy, checked the release of its prepared statement to the press. The earlier opposition to such action on the part of Messrs. Brandeis, Frankfurter, and Cohen, the concurrence of other leading American Zionists, and Weizmann's cable advising caution all worked against strong public protest. Informed the next morning of the sinking of the French liner, Justice Brandeis felt that "whether by an act of God or an act of man," it had disposed of the matter for the time being. Open protest, he argued, might have an adverse effect, especially on the Roosevelt administration and its struggle with Congress over foreign policy. What to do if the British still deported the *Patria* survivors was a premature question, in Brandeis's mind, and represented a case "probably unlikely to arise."[44]

Brandeis's optimistic assessment was hardly shared in London Zionist headquarters, where Weizmann had a sharper picture of diplomatic realities. Informed by Colonial Secretary Lloyd of the explosion, the World Zionist Organization (WZO) president rejoined that he might have to resign his post and transfer the Jewish Agency to the United States. The Colonial Office blocked entree to Churchill, so Weizmann argued his case before other members of the War Cabinet, warning Lord Privy Seal Clement Attlee and Secretary for Air Production Archibald Sinclair that he would fight against the deportation to Mauritius until he was sent to a concentration camp as well. Technically, the refugees were "illegals," he admitted to Foreign Secretary Halifax on the afternoon of November 27, but would HMG have applied the rigid policy had the *Patria* passengers been of British origin? Making no dent, Weizmann attempted a last appeal and asked for "Christian justice," which, reputedly unlike "Mosaic justice," was to temper the law with mercy. The words stung the devout official. Abruptly ending their talk, he promised to get back to Weizmann before long.[45]

That same evening the Cabinet decided in special session to admit the *Patria* survivors, with any other such transports diverted to Mauritius or elsewhere. General Wavell, British commander-in-chief in the Middle East, quickly protested that the decision would fan Arab hostilities and thus jeopardize British military interests throughout the region, including the loss of the Basra-Baghdad-Haifa route. But Churchill, who personally dismissed the "typical" pro-Arabism of HMG's officers in that area, influenced his colleagues to override these objections. The decision on the *Patria* group stood as "an exceptional act of mercy," they concluded on December 2.

The prime minister cabled the general the same day his personal view that "it would be an act of inhumanity unworthy of the British name to force them to reembark." As for the Arabs: "If their attachment to our cause is so slender as to be determined by a mere act of charity of this kind, it is clear that our policy of conciliating them has not borne much fruit so far. What I think would influence them much more would be any kind of British military success." "Patria Mori," concluded a doubtful but resigned Wavell in reply.[46]

Some activists in the Hagana, deeply shaken over the *Patria* disaster, wished to lead the Yishuv in halting any future deportations. The high command's independent inquiry revealed that the small bomb had torn a 3 x 2 meter hole in the *Patria*'s side by blowing away several plates (whose rivets were badly rusted), rather than the expected one plate in a vessel whose coat of paint gave it a deceptively sturdy appearance.[47] With grappling hooks hoisting more corpses from the sunken ship every hour, a Hagana black-bordered proclamation in the name of "Mishmar HaYishuv" called on Palestinian Jewry to resist the deportation of the refugees by all means in their power: "Let not their right be less than the right of one who went to the scaffold and the rope was removed from his neck." Following HMG's announcement on December 4 that the *Atlantic* group faced expulsion, Mardor and others suggested that large crowds passively block all roads from Atlit to the Haifa port; Hagana units would be prepared to battle the British. Israel Galili, replacing Meyerov as command representative in Haifa, supported these views. When, however, the despairing Jewish national institutions would allow only peaceful demonstrations in the vicinity of the port at the time of embarkation, the Hagana bowed to discipline and left the Mauritius-bound detainees in MacMichael's hands.[48]

The penultimate act in the drama began in the early hours of December 9, 1940. The *Patria* survivors had been locked in separate huts the previous evening, and buses rolled into the Atlit camp carrying scores of British police. Told to be ready for departure at 4 A.M., the representatives of the *Atlantic* transport decided to resist passively by shedding their clothes and refusing to leave their barbed-wire encased quarters. Some soldiers and armed policemen, incensed by this determination, indiscriminately wielded truncheons on defenseless Jews. After six hours it was over.[49]

As the high commissioner savored his triumph, 1,581 Jewish escapees from Hitler embarked on two big Dutch liners for Mauritius (this, not-withstanding HMG's consistent argument that an Allied shipping short-age precluded the rescue of Jews from Hitler's grasp). To divert the Yishuv toward underground shelters, the government had sounded air attack sirens, a fact unknown to the demoralized refugees at the time. They arrived at their destination the day after Christmas. Twenty-two died of typhoid, first contracted before leaving Haifa, MacMichael refus-ing to wait for the customary 10-12-day incubation stage to pass; another 19 perished because of the early privations of the sea voyage.[50] Fortun-ately, the remaining illegals could not foresee that more than four and a half years would pass before the iron gates of the prison at Beau Bassin would swing open to freedom.

IV

For the first time since the start of World War II, the *Patria* and *Atlantic* tragedies brought the division between the militant and moderate wings of the Yishuv's political establishment out into the open. An article on December 2 in *HaPoel HaTsa'ir,* the Mapai labor party's weekly news-paper, attacked the "malicious hand" that caused the explosion and con-sequent death of Jewish refugees. One week later, immediately after the deportation to Mauritius, Berl Katznelson mercilessly castigated at a Histadrut gathering those who opposed active resistance to the British order. His words disturbed Joseph Sprinzak, who warned agency trea-surer Eliezer Kaplan that civil war might be in the offing. Indeed, two members of the Hagana, acting on what they understood to be the orders of their superior, retaliated a few days later by entering the offices of the Mapai paper's editor to slap him in the face. Symbolic punishment against this pair was subsequently meted out by the high command.[51]

The activist position did not waver. For such elements in labor and Hagana circles, as Israel Galili put it, the Palestine administration's "malicious hand" ultimately caused the death of more than 250 on the *Patria*. Those overseeing the sabotage would certainly not have gone ahead had the terrible results been foreseen, declared Golomb at a Mapai committee debate; the *Patria* victims represented "sacrifices" in the strug-gle for the right of Jews to immigrate to their homeland at a time when HMG aimed to check the Yishuv's future hopes. Writing years later to Mardor, Meyerov saw no alternative: responsibility for the grim result fell on the "enemy regime," the "despicable and cruel" administration and its representatives; he held this view until his death. As for the refu-gees' resistance at Atlit, Golomb viewed it to be the "one shining light" in the "dark day" when the Yishuv's political organizations decided not to link arms with these brothers and sisters in tragic need.[52]

The moderates took a pronouncedly different perspective. The politically motivated White Paper, argued Pinchas Lubianker (later Lavon), could not be changed during the war, and resistance to it should therefore be postponed. None had the right to endanger others without their consent and then call them "martyrs," Sprinzak, David Remez, and Yitschak Lofban insisted; Eliezer Kaplan added that such methods would only threaten the Palestinian Jewish community with severe British reprisals. Newspaper editor Herzl Rosenbloom of *Yediot Acharonot* branded Hagana's use of refugees in the fight against the British as "cowardice," and only a wide table kept him safe from Golomb's threatening fists during a heated private conference. Making regular visits in subsequent years to the Haifa cemetery where the *Patria* victims lay, Rosenbloom never altered these convictions.[53]

The dramatic chain of events had its profoundest effect on Moshe Shertok. Staggered by the "most pitiful sight" of a ship that large lying "prostrate and helpless"—and so close to shore—the individual who officially sanctioned the sabotage of the *Patria* thought MacMichael's intransigence incomprehensible. The agency had submitted information to the authorities proving that the majority of the refugees aboard the two ships were decent people, and any who could not prove their reliability could have been detained under arrest. The high commissioner's fear that admitting these Jews to Palestine within the White Paper framework would further strain HMG's relations with the Arabs of Iraq was "ridiculous," given the current open animosity of the Iraqis toward England. And the "organized brutality" against the *Atlantic* group Shertok thought "shattering," especially at a time when the Jewish people everywhere was "fighting desperately for its existence." It constituted an "act of terror," he privately wrote at the time, "that has added a black chapter to the history of Jewish suffering, and a shameful page in the history of British rule in the world."[54]

Both Shertok's deepening anxiety and militancy received their clearest expression in a confidential letter he sent to Weizmann eight days after the deportation from Atlit. Circumventing British censorship through a trusted messenger, the individual who was in effect the Yishuv's foreign minister seized the rare opportunity to pour out his innermost feelings in a communication also distinguished by its length and the author's preference to write the WZO president in Hebrew. After describing in detail the "heart-rending drama such as we have never seen before," the man known to favor the art of diplomatic balance raged: "Our blood boils when we listen to the baseness meted out to us—half a million Jews in Palestine, of whom over 6000 are serving in H.M. Forces, because we did not bend our backs to be beaten, or remain silent when our brothers and sisters are being baited." MacMichael, overlooking entirely the human nature of the Jew, had brought shame upon himself and his subordinates: he had to go.

As for the future, "unless enormous changes are made we are threatened with renewed misfortunes, and who can tell where we shall end up?" Separated from the few centers of Jewry whose voice could still be heard, "we are likely to be completely hemmed in by a despotic and brutal authority" operating under the cloak of war, while "counsels of despair may find an echo in many hearts, and our impotent anger find expression in an outburst which will bring misfortune upon us." Despite the agency's unique military contribution, the Palestine government sought to undermine its authority and destroy the foundations and hopes of Zionism by every means. A change had to be secured, and in good time, "lest we be too late and find a new situation crystallized for a number of years to come."[55]

Most remarkable of all, the letter suggests that Shertok began to harbor some reservations about the perspective of Weizmann, a British citizen centered in London, on Anglo-Zionist relations. The author, a Palestinian in daily contact with his country's realities, chose not to tell the WZO head the truth about the sinking of the *Patria*. Rather, the letter related that the agency had supplied provisions for the *Patria*'s departure, with Shertok and Henrietta Szold planning to bid the people farewell on board and to convey assurances of the Yishuv's determination to do everything possible to bring them back to Palestine: "But it seems that there were people in our midst who did not accept the verdict," and the catastrophe came.

Without revealing his decisive role, Shertok inadvertently revealed his reason for assuming the ultimate responsibility for the risk to the *Patria*'s passengers. Acquiescence in mass deportations of Jews from Palestine, he wrote, would represent one of the "accumulated facts" that "are taken into account ... first and foremost by the forces of oppression; they provide a basis for estimating our power to defend ourselves in the future. They exercise, therefore, a direct influence on our political fate." As for the *Atlantic* people remaining in Palestine, the writer dwelt on this subject because "it is possible that we did not succeed in convincing you sufficiently of the extent to which the matter ... has affected us" even after London had reversed the original *Patria* decision. His suspicion contained some merit: a Palestinian colleague at 77 Great Russell St., Berl Locker, lost confidence in Weizmann when the WZO president refused to press for landing this group immediately in the Promised Land.[56]

Shertok never changed his views. The memory of the "dear" *Patria* casualties "troubled and will continue to trouble my conscience forever," wrote the future premier and foreign minister of the State of Israel to Munya Mardor well after the event, but "I have never regretted the approval that was given then." He had to participate in numerous official decisions before and after May 14, 1948, he reminded a New York correspondent, in which similar risks were taken in the political battle of "a nation defending its life." "*Post factum,* we saw the martyred dead of the *Patria* as sacrifices of the great struggle for the rights of our people to return to their land and to establish there from the ruins their state."[57]

The dual tragedy proved to be a turning point for Berl Katznelson as well. The morning after the *Patria* explosion he entered Meyerov's flat. Moved and agitated, he apologized once and then again for not responding to the Hagana official's information the previous day. "Shaul," he exclaimed, "realize that the day of *Patria* is for us like the day of Tel Chai." To the influential editor of *Davar,* the defense of Tel Chai in 1920, the 1938 settlement of Chanita, and especially *Aliya Bet* served as the classic examples of the Yishuv's vow: "We shall not surrender!" Katznelson called MacMichael's spiteful insistence on closing the gates of Palestine forever to the *Patria, Atlantic,* and other illegals a "new policy" that constituted an "act of murder" for these refugees and a "cruel mockery" of the entire Yishuv.[58]

The time had come, Katznelson concluded, to proclaim Zionism's final goal: a Jewish state in Palestine. Since even Churchill and some other old pro-Zionists in the War Cabinet had signed the expulsion decree, the Yishuv had no choice but to unfurl its own banner. In a world in which Jews faced "complete isolation" and steady "decline," only a self-governing commonwealth could realize the personification of the Zionist movement—*aliya* to the Promised Land. Katznelson, who (like Meyerov) had adamantly opposed the limited Peel offer in 1937 of a Jewish state in Palestine on practical grounds and had refrained since then from proclaiming an *Endziel,* now became the first spokesman of the Zionist establishment since the war had begun to call for Jewish sovereignty. Two addresses, delivered soon after the *Atlantic* tragedy and published in *Davar,* called for the transformation of "millions of stateless and homeless Jews into an independent nation" in Palestine. Katznelson also joined with the NZO's Binyamin Lubotski to draft a declaration that insisted upon free Jewish immigration and land settlement within the "historic boundaries" of the Holy Land. Golomb and Eri Jabotinsky also affixed their signatures to the historic manifesto on December 20, and left it to their respective parties to ratify the declaration.[59]

The events in Haifa, which he deemed "a Zionist activity," also stirred David Ben Gurion. Cut off from Palestine, the Jewish Agency Executive chairman decided to press the American Zionists at this critical hour to adopt a public stance and end, as he put it to the Hadassah national board, "the danger of mental inertia" then facing the movement. Although he had publicly spoken a day before the explosion in warm praise of Britain's heroic resistance to Hitler's *Blitz,* Ben Gurion envisaged a state established with the help of world Jewry as the only alternative to HMG's White Paper. Five million Jews could be absorbed in western Palestine after the war, in his opinion, provided such a state existed. The creation of a Jewish army could convince England, with America's support, to reverse her present policy.[60]

The *Patria*'s fate moved Ben Gurion to call together the American Zionist leadership in New York on December 5, 1940. For a full afternoon at the Winthrop Hotel he exhorted the group of seven to affirm a Jewish state and army, establish permanent contacts between the two really significant Jewish communities left on the globe at the time, and activate the masses (especially Jewish youth) to this credo. He received strong encouragement from Abba Hillel Silver and Nahum Goldmann, while Stephen Wise continued to accept Brandeis's view that during the war against Hitler anything "that might add a featherweight to Britain's burden must be avoided." When the ECZA, however, hesitated to move against Brandeis's opinion, even when a cryptic cable arrived about the deportation from Atlit, Ben Gurion challenged the justice's argument and proposed to simply emulate the British: "oppose Hitler and fight stupidity and justice" in the manner of the Anglo press and critics like Lord Wedgwood in Parliament.

The sinking of the 100-ton *Salvador* in the Sea of Marmora on December 12, with a loss of 231 Jewish illegals fleeing Bulgarian territory, strengthened this position. To Ben Gurion's great surprise, former ZOA president Morris Rothenberg moved to his side. Speaker after speaker followed in like course. By a large majority, the umbrella organization then resolved to take public action against the White Paper.

Encouraged, Ben Gurion minced no words in bringing his message to the administrative committee of the ZOA in early January, 1941. Using as his text Roosevelt's recent announcement that the United State had to serve as "the arsenal for democracy" rather than conduct "business as usual," he insisted that American Jewry had to become the champion of the Jewish people. The Yishuv, acting from an "inner faith," regarded itself as a nation in the making. American Jews must join their people in Palestine in destroying the "treacherous" White Paper, he declared. Only a Jewish commonwealth in Palestine could welcome "millions" of a "ruined European Jewry" after the war. Ben Gurion and Weizmann had privately spoken in Jerusalem and London since September, 1939, of the need for a Jewish state, but the disasters in Haifa and Atlit propelled Ben Gurion to announce this political objective from a public forum at last. The unequivocal declaration by Katznelson, the only man Ben Gurion revered and loved, certainly had its impact as well. The essence of Ben Gurion's address found its way into the ZOA's *New Palestine* two weeks later.[61]

Ben Gurion's eloquent charge had broken the "policy of timidity" in American Zionist ranks, and at a UPA national conference for Palestine, held on January 25-26, 1941, in the nation's capital, an impressive convocation of American Jewry came out openly for a Jewish state. Two thousand delegates at the Hotel Willard declared their deep conviction that only by "large-scale colonization" after the war of "large masses of Jews from Central and Eastern Europe in Palestine, with the aim of its reconstitution as a Jewish Commonwealth, can the Jewish problem be permanently solved." For the first time since the start of World War II, a precise goal had been stated forthrightly by a large Zionist gathering. Rightly could the *New Palestine* editorialize that the conference "marked the opening of a new era in American Zionism."[62]

Especially noteworthy, the conference heard Abba Hillel Silver's call to rebuild "Israel's national life in Israel's historic national home." Although Jews stood loyally on Britain's side in this global conflict, the war Hitler had declared against their people five years earlier "is a war of extermination," emphasized the speaker. Accordingly, Jews would staunchly oppose the "disastrous appeasement policy" of the White Paper. The change augured significantly for the future of American Zionism, since the UPA chairman had (like Katznelson) opposed HMG's offer of Jewish statehood in 1937, and had optimistically assumed that the White Paper represented only a temporary deviance from traditional British policy. The 47-year-old Cleveland rabbi who had tilted with Katznelson over *Aliya Bet* at the 1939 congress now concluded, in opposition to Stephen Wise, that criticism of the White Paper could no longer be withheld, even at the risk of embarrassing Roosevelt's administration: silence only meant deserting the Holy Land and betraying Zionism. Had not Palestine taken 280,000 of Europe's Jewish refugees since the *Führer* had come to power, more than half of the total and nearly twice the number admitted by the United States? Endorsing Ben Gurion's projection of Palestine's capability to absorb five million Jews after the war, the future herald of the movement in the United States declared that the Zionist aim was a Jewish commonwealth (preferably within the British empire, as Ben Gurion then desired).[63]

This growing militancy of the movement in the United States would continue with the arrival that month of Bernard Joseph. The Agency Executive member who had presided over the Yishuv's relief effort for the *Patria* survivors gave his audiences a full picture at last of the tragedy from start to finish, within the context of MacMichael's personal determination to throttle the Jewish national home, whether regarding land settlement, military recruitment, or political and economic progress. Joseph soon gave Under Secretary of State Sumner Welles a firsthand account of the refugees who had reached Haifa Bay and of the agency's frustrating negotiations for a military force, and played an important role in converting the Jewish Secretary of the Treasury, Henry

Morgenthau, Jr., to the Zionist cause. The Secretary, who had trouble locating Mauritius on the big globe in his office, was visibly moved by Joseph's personal account of the fate of the *Patria* and *Atlantic* passengers. The 35-minute interview in turn paved the way for Morgenthau's future contacts with Emanuel Neumann, Silver's closest associate, and left Weizmann convinced in a subsequent meeting that Morgenthau had "all the zeal of a neophyte" who had to be restrained. Joseph returned to Palestine four months later, convinced that the United States was ripe for "very strong activity."[64]

The sinking of the *Patria* also affected the more radical resistance movements, which the anxious Shertok had characterized as "counsels of despair." The current split between the Irgun and Stern groups over Vladimir Jabotinsky's pro-British orientation since the war began may well have sparked Irgun chief David Raziel's plan to cripple the *Patria* and thereby strengthen his organization's divided ranks. His immediate resignation from the Irgun in early December and his enthusiastic response, on his return to command soon afterward, regarding a British plan to destroy the Iraqi oil fields can also be seen in this light. For Raziel, the expedition also afforded the chance to assassinate the ex-mufti of Jerusalem, then living in Baghdad. Raziel's death during that mission in June, 1941, was a blow from which the Irgun did not recover for two and a half years. His Sternist opponents actually intended no action against the *Patria,* but an impressionable 13-year-old had viewed the explosion through binoculars from the terrace of his home. The terrible scene burned a mark deep in Eliyahu Hakim, one that brought him to the ranks of the Stern group, where he participated in two plots to assassinate MacMichael and ultimately joined Eliyahu Bet Tsouri in the successful attempt against the life of Churchill's minister of state for the Middle East, former Colonial Secretary Lord Moyne.[65]

As for the *Atlantic* deportees, they remained behind bars in Mauritius for a long time. Despite Churchill's insistence in early November, 1940, that Jewish refugees sent to that island be "decently treated," the Colonial Office accepted the position that conditions "should be sufficiently punitive to continue to act as a deterrent to other Jews in Europe." Very strict discipline, a pharaonic separation of men and women for one and a half years, and epidemics of typhoid and malaria all took their toll. The group's attachment to the Yishuv deepened, nonetheless: it established a branch of the WZO, brought the Zionist *shekel,* and attended classes in Hebrew and related subjects. More than 200 men enlisted in the Allied forces, and 56 joined the Jewish Brigade.[66]

The harrowing journey's final act was not played out until after the war. As early as March, 1941, Lewis Namier of the Jewish Agency's London office asked Colonial Secretary Moyne to allow the group admission under the White Paper quota, but two years passed before HMG confidentially informed the agency that the original ban to admit it after the war had been lifted. In early 1944 Shertok urged the Colonial Office to free the detainees immediately, for surely they had by then "expiated their sin" of "fleeing from a death-trap in Europe" to Palestine; Colonial Secretary Oliver Stanley merely agreed to let the refugees be informed of the earlier decision. A suggestion in March from the American War Refugee Board's director to Secretary Hull that the "widespread suffering" of the refugees be alleviated by their entry into the United States bore no fruit. Only in February, 1945, did the House of Commons hear of the War Cabinet's decision to return the detainees to their original destination "when the necessary arrangements can be made." Bernard Joseph, on behalf of the Jewish Agency, ultimately welcomed the returning 1,310 Jews on August 26, 1945. One hundred twenty-four of their comrades were left behind on Mauritius in the local cemetery.[67]

CONCLUSION

Millions of Jews trapped in Hitler's Europe and confronted by the White Paper never witnessed the dawn of freedom. Even as the deportation to Mauritius got underway, the Foreign Office sought to have the Turkish government join in halting the journey of the *Salvador*'s survivors to Palestine. The day that the *Atlantic* group entered the prison at Beau Bassin, the Colonial Office suspended the legal immigration quota to Palestine for the next three months; its decision overrode Churchill's urging that HMG recall promises to Zionists and be guided by "general considerations of humanity towards those fleeing from the cruelest forms of persecution." (The *Patria* survivors were only released in August, 1941.) This restriction continued to September, 1941, while the British authorities rejected entry into Palestine for Jews fleeing from pogroms in Bucharest and Baghdad. Although the 200-ton *Struma* exploded outside Turkish waters on February 24, 1942, with a loss of 768 Rumanian Jews, Moyne defeated Churchill's argument to free 800 illegals from the *Darien* interned in Atlit by warning the War Cabinet about "security grounds" and "encouragement to the very undesirable trade in illegal immigration into Palestine." Three months later the Cabinet ruled against taking any steps to "facilitate the arrival of 'refugees' into Palestine," a position repeated that December to check the emigration of 4,500 Bulgarian Jews to the Promised Land.[68]

HMG's implacable attitude continued in the last years of the war, although the extent of Germany's "Final Solution" had been acknowledged by the Allies since December, 1942. Alleged Nazi spies, Arab hostility, and shortages of housing and food all served throughout 1943 as excuses for government representatives in Parliament to defend Palestine's bolted doors. Certificates were doled out gradually, so as to postpone any fundamental ruling on immigration beyond the White Paper quota. Even when HMG informed the Jewish Agency in July, 1943, of its willingness to open Palestine to all Jews who managed to reach Istanbul, London held back that information from the Turkish authorities for almost a full year, thereby considerably slowing down the rescue process. As late as December, 1944, with well over five million Jews already having perished in the Holocaust, MacMichael's recently appointed successor sought to have the Soviet government close the Rumanian and Bulgarian frontiers under its control on the ground that the "Jewish migration from South East Europe is getting out of hand"; Lord Gort made certain that visas would no longer be granted to any Jew arriving in Turkey from Axis-held territory. The new high commissioner had little cause for worry, however, since even after deducting some 12,000 illegals who arrived during the war, HMG still had 23,000 unused permits under the White Paper when V-E day dawned.[69]

The *Patria* and *Atlantic* tragedies, consequently, brought no change to the unique plight of Europe's Jews throughout World War II. With the Mandatory power continuing to darken the strongest beacon of hope for an agonized Jewry, Josiah Wedgwood felt justified in rising before the House of Lords after the *Struma* sank to ask the colonial secretary "whether he does not think that the blood of these people is on our hands?" The Gestapo lost interest in promoting forced Jewish emigration after the fall of 1940. Considering the fate of their last transport, Eichmann and his superiors could entertain no doubts that the British would not tolerate any illegal ships to Palestine. That fact made the Nazi obsession to resolve the "Jewish question" forever even more urgent: the Jews of the General-government in Poland had been "ghettoized"; the idea of Madagascar as a large-scale emigration depot had fallen through; and the invasion of Soviet Russia, with its millions of satanically viewed Jews/Bolsheviks, was on the *tapis*. In the cruelest of ironies, the earlier Central Offices for Jewish Emigration soon became transformed under Eichmann's ruthless control to central offices for Jewish deportation, and millions of victims were transported "east"—not to the Promised Land but to places like Chelmno, Treblinka, and Auschwitz-Birkenau.[70]

With the Jews alone in a world of sealed borders and scattered like chaff before the wind, Zionists the world over and their sympathizers understood that only the establishment soon of their own state in Palestine could end almost 2,000 years of exile. The *Patria* and *Atlantic* tragedies were a turning point in this sense for Shertok, Katznelson, Ben Gurion, Silver, and other such leaders. A more activist American Zionist movement reaffirmed the UPA conference declaration of January, 1941, by resolving 16 months later at New York City's Biltmore Hotel to support a Jewish commonwealth, military force, and the agency's control of immigration into Palestine to end Jewish "homelessness." A majority of the Yishuv's political parties shortly followed suit.[71]

Since British spokesmen persisted to the war's end in declaring it "untrue" that Jews could be dealt with as "a quite distinct body of persons from their fellow citizens who have been deported or displaced," the battle lines between a modern-day David and Goliath were drawn. Seared by the Holocaust, Jewry staunchly rejected a colonial secretary's myopic condemnation of the "illegals"—in February, 1945—for not having gone through the proper "formalities" to enter Palestine. Meyerov, who refused to halt such transports in mid-1944 when the *Mekfure* exploded in the Black Sea with a loss of almost 300 Rumanian Jews, would continue in command of *Aliya Bet* operations.[72] Berl Katznelson did not live to see this development: the first substantial transport of unauthorized immigrants after May, 1945, bore the labor ideologue's name. But the thirst of the Final Solution's pitifully small remnant for return to the ancestral homeland would serve, just as he had prophesied at the Zionist congress of August, 1939, as a most crucial weapon in the war for Jewish independence that loomed on the horizon.

The "Final Solution" Unveiled

IN THE FINAL WEEK of July, 1942, word from an unimpeachable German source reached the West of an official Nazi decision to murder every Jew on European soil. Edgar Salin, professor of economics and sociology at the University of Basle, removed a secret dispatch from the "drop" in his garden and read: "In the East camps are being prepared where all the Jews of Europe and a great part of the Russian prisoners of war will be exterminated by gas. Please relay this information immediately to Churchill and Roosevelt personally. If the B.B.C. comes out every day with a warning against lighting the gas ovens, then perhaps they may not be put into operation, for the criminals are doing everything to prevent the German people from finding out what they are planning to do and will certainly carry out."[1]

Like others in the free world, the internationally known Salin had heard earlier about the massacre of Jews under the swastika. Accounts of the mass killings in Kamenets Podolsk and Transnistria during 1941 appeared in the world press. In a lengthy diplomatic note on January 6, 1942, Russian Foreign Minister Vyacheslav Molotov briefly mentioned the particular cruelties suffered by the innocent Jewish population during vast executions in Russia. A two-page spread with pictures the next month in *Life,* pointing to the "methodical massacre" of Polish Jewry by starvation, epidemics, machinegunning, and drowning, concluded that "the Jews of Poland are literally dying out." Quoting Hungarian officers who had returned from the Soviet front, the Hungarian representative of the American Jewish Joint Distribution Committee (JDC) reported on March 13, 1942, that 240,000 Jews had been killed by the Gestapo in the Ukraine. The Dutch government-in-exile confirmed on April 5 that 10,000 Dutch Jews had died in poison gas experiments at Mauthausen; press bulletins continually told of slaughter in the Baltic countries and White Russia.[2]

The news became even worse when, on June 2, the BBC broadcast the gist of a detailed Bund report from Poland about "the physical extermination of the Jewish population on Polish soil." Prime Minister Wladislaw Sikorski of the Polish government-in-exile in London sounded the general alarm on June 10 over the same airwaves; the Polish National Council, at the instigation of its two Jewish members Szmul Zygielbojm and Ignacy Schwartzbart, issued a call for help to all the Allied governments that day and again on July 8. Zygielbojm, the Jewish Bundist representative on the council, confirmed his beleaguered comrades' figure (greatly underestimated) of 700,000 murdered in Poland, and beseeched the world over British radio on June 25 and again on July 2 to act without delay against "the planned extermination of a whole nation by means of shot, shell, starvation and gas." The Anglo press, Jewish Palestinian newspapers, the London *Jewish Chronicle,* and the Jewish Telegraphic Agency (JTA) carried these and other reports throughout July.[3]

On July 21, 1942, the British and American chiefs of state sent messages to a rally at Madison Square Garden, co-sponsored by the American Jewish Congress under its president Stephen Wise, the Jewish Labor Committee, and B'nai Brith, which warned that all perpetrators of these atrocities would face definite retribution after the Allied victory. Independently, the Anglo-American Alliance had received supplementary reports of systematic mass murder from numerous sources. On July 27 the JTA transmitted the first news about widespread deportations from Warsaw, begun five days earlier, aiming at annihilation.[4]

The message in Salin's hand differed radically, however, from even such factual acknowledgments. This report, which spoke of a calculated plan by the Third Reich's leadership to destroy all of European Jewry, had come from Lt. Colonel Artur Sommer, a liaison officer of the *Wehrmacht* to Admiral Canaris's counterespionage division. As part of his country's delegation to the Swiss-German negotiations beginning in September, 1940, Sommer had renewed contact with his academic mentor and friend, Professor Salin. Staunchly anti-Nazi, Sommer gave the Swiss savant vital knowledge for the Allied cause about German armaments and strategy, including the precise date of the invasion of Russia several weeks prior to the event. On special occasions Sommer requested Salin to forward what he regarded as crucial information to Churchill and Roosevelt. That rare time had come again.[5]

Moving quickly, Salin dialed Chaim Pozner (later Pazner) of the Jewish Agency's Palestine Office in Geneva: "I have some very good news. Come immediately." A Polish fugitive from the Gestapo in Danzig who had completed his Ph.D. in economics under Salin's direction in December, 1939, the 43-year-old Pozner had long established a close relationship with his caller of that day. Salin, a converted Jew *né* Salinger who turned against the Hitler regime over its blatant antisemitic policy, knew from Pozner about his link to V. C. Farrell, head of English intelligence in Switzerland. In exchange for Pozner's information (anonymously received from Sommer via Salin) and the promise that he alone be forwarded such reports, Farrell, officially serving as head of Britain's Passport Control Office in the country, eased Pozner's negotiations over immigration certificates to the Promised Land. Farrell also supplied material about the fate of Jews in Lodz and Lublin, which promptly made its way to Pozner's superiors. The date of Operation Barbarossa, for example, and pictures revealing the *Einsatzgruppen* mass executions of Jews and Russian prisoners of war were also passed on to British intelligence.

What "very good news," their code for actually the reverse, did Salin wish to convey now? In any event, their meeting would have to wait two or three days, Pozner replied. Pressing matters relating to Jews in Belgium and France had to be cleared away first.[6]

On the afternoon of July 30 Pozner arrived at Salin's home and received the shock of his life. Pogroms, massive destruction—yes. But a design to murder the entire Jewish people? And how could he respond to the totally novel circumstances, especially given his long-standing "gentlemen's agreement" with Farrell of silence? Confronted with the anguished realization that, as he burst out to Salin, "My people are burning!," Pozner resolved to notify at least one representative each of the Jewish Agency and Swiss Jewry. Aside from informing Farrell, word also had to be gotten somehow to the American government. The two men agreed to think the matter over independently and so arrive at a mutual line of action for the next morning.[7]

Even before sunrise a joint *demarche* had been set in motion. Ensconced in a local hotel, Pozner dashed off a guarded cable in Hebrew code to Chaim Barlas, director of the Jewish Agency center in Istanbul, and made an appointment with Benjamin Sagalowitz of Zurich for noon the next day. The press secretary of the Federation of Swiss Jewish Communities, Pozner reasoned, would then pass on the startling report to a few influential people. Later that evening Salin called to say that he indeed had a contact with a highly placed American in Switzerland, and would decide by 9 A.M. the best procedure to follow.

Unable to sleep, Koval-born Pozner recalled several letters received in 1941 and 1942 from his two brothers and friends like Yochanan Morgenstern of Warsaw, Frumka Plotnicka of Bendzin, and Herschel Springer of Sosnowiec. This correspondence had included coded references to events more serious than had befallen "Familie Przytyk," a pogrom in March, 1936, that marked the Jews of that small town and all of Poland defenseless before the courts, and to the communal fate of those like "Chaver Ussishkin" (director of the Jewish National Fund who had died in Palestine several months earlier). Salin's secret informant, moreover, had always been proven reliable; no reason existed to question his report suddenly at this stage. But how, Pozner agonized, was he to handle

Farrell while also transmitting the message to the American officials and some Jewish organizations?[8]

Salin's confidential information passed into a slightly wider circle on July 31. The Jewish Agency representative called off his meeting with Sagalowitz when 9 A.M. went by with no word from Salin, but a while later he received the hoped-for news. The professor telephoned him to come to his home, where Pozner heard that the anonymous American would indeed meet with Salin and pass on a message to his "big boss" in Washington. Having obtained this assurance, Pozner traveled to see Sagalowitz that afternoon.

Just before departing for Zurich, he intentionally rang up Farrell's office after the Britisher had left for his customary week-end vacation in the mountains. On Farrell's return, Pozner explained that he could hardly leave word on the matter at hand with Farrell's secretary, and he pointed to the extraordinary circumstances as justification for confiding in "only one reliable Jew": Barlas in Istanbul. Faced with the *fait accompli,* a stunned Farrell gave in; he later told Pozner that Winston Churchill had received the message. As for the Americans, Salin soon heard from Thomas H. McKittrick, president of the Bank for International Settlements (BIZ) in Basle since 1940, that he had the news relayed to Franklin Roosevelt via the American minister's direct telephone line from Berne to 1600 Pennsylvania Ave.[9]

In Zurich Dr. Sagalowitz had not been caught totally unaware by Pozner's information. A German acquaintance, Dr. Eduard Schulte,[10] had just told him of a program discussed in Hitler's general headquarters to build huge crematoria to annihilate all of Europe's Jews with prussic acid in the autumn. This prominent Gentile industrialist, an executive in a firm employing more than 30,000 workers, was so horrified on hearing this that he left Berlin and crossed over to Lausanne to convey the incredible story to a Jew named Koppelman, the legal representative of a powerful Swiss industrialist. Schulte then told his story to Sagalowitz as well. Having risked his life to relieve his conscience, Schulte—who has hitherto eluded the searchlight of history—asked Sagalowitz only to preserve his anonymity when spreading the news further. Immediate reprisals, the German suggested, might check the reported plan. To Sagalowitz, the coincidental arrival now of Pozner's message, which he never shared with anyone, made it imperative that this direct contact be taken seriously. Accordingly, Sagalowitz called Gerhart M. Riegner, director of the World Jewish Congress (WJC) office in Geneva, to tell him that he had "learned things of grave importance which must be discussed immediately."[11]

Riegner met his good friend Sagalowitz in Lausanne on August 1, the country's national Independence Day. From his ideal listening post in neutral Switzerland, the 30-year-old Berlin refugee had regularly informed his New York superiors since the invasion of Poland about German atrocities in Europe. Five months earlier, for example, he and Jewish Agency director in Geneva Richard Lichtheim had submitted a memorandum to sympathetic Papal Nuncio Philippe Bernardini in Berne that provided a country-by-country summary of Nazi deportations and killings. Riegner followed this up with information to WJC headquarters in New York that 50,000 Jews had been deported from the Old Reich in the past year to Lodz, Riga, and Minsk; the greatest part of the 70,000 Jews in the Czech Protectorate were sent to Theresienstadt and some to Lublin; 10,000 in Croatia had been placed in camps for hard labor; all those interned in Compiègne had been deported from France to eastern Europe, with those over 55 years old transferred to concentration camps in Drancy. The subsequent Bund cable from Poland, together with the brutal mass deportations begun on July 16 in France and Holland, appeared most ominous, therefore, in light of Sagalowitz's account just at hand.[12]

It took an unbelieving Riegner a week to be convinced about the authenticity of this newest revelation. At Riegner's request, Sagalowitz introduced him to Koppelman. Two other Swiss business contacts of the anonymous German industrialist vouched for his reliability. (Independently, Sagalowitz also double-checked with Pozner about the Salin-Sommer connection.) Although the Schulte information conveyed by Sagalowitz had at first struck Riegner himself as "fantastic," the WJC employee had his own knowledge of Deutsche efficiency and of sustained Nazi brutalities as early as 1932–33 in Germany, before he fled to Paris and Geneva for work and study in the field of law. Rabid antisemitic pronouncements at the League of Nations, where Riegner had represented the congress with Nahum Goldmann during the 1930s, and Hitler's consistent "prophecies" of the destruction of European Jewry in the event of world war had made an indelible impression.

Most significantly, Sagalowitz's anonymous news "suddenly made sensible" all that had transpired earlier. The terrible facts from dozens of reports about deportation to places shrouded in mystery, along with further accounts of death from starvation and execution, now tied together into one schema. The idea of a "total plan" fused the known with what had not heretofore been understood. With this vital link supplied, the pieces to the puzzle of German designs against European Jewry as a whole fell into place at last.[13]

To plan appropriate action, the WJC employee sought the advice of Paul Guggenheim, his friend and senior associate in congress affairs since World War II began. The professor of international law at the local Graduate Institute of International Studies, returning from a vacation in response to Riegner's handwritten letter, took a typical Swiss position of caution. WJC offices in Washington and London should be notified immediately by cable, he agreed. But as for the industrialist's suggestion of reprisals, let the two governments draw up their own proposals. He also insisted that since Riegner could not vouch absolutely for the reported rumor, the telegram should end with an expression of doubt. Together, the two Jews agreed on a message to WJC president Stephen Wise:[14]

RECEIVED ALARMING REPORT THAT IN FUHRER'S HEADQUARTERS PLAN DISCUSSED AND UNDER CONSIDERATION ALL JEWS IN COUNTRIES OCCUPIED OR CONTROLLED GERMANY NUMBER $3\frac{1}{2}$ TO 4 MILLION SHOULD AFTER DEPORTATION AND CONCENTRATION IN EAST AT ONE BLOW EXTERMINATED TO RESOLVE ONCE FOR ALL JEWISH QUESTION IN EUROPE STOP ACTION REPORTED PLANNED FOR AUTUMN METHODS UNDER DISCUSSION INCLUDING PRUSSIC ACID STOP WE TRANSMIT INFORMATION WITH ALL NECESSARY RESERVATION AS EXACTITUDE CANNOT BE CONFIRMED STOP INFORMANT STATED TO HAVE CLOSE CONNECTIONS WITH HIGHEST GERMAN AUTHORITIES AND HIS REPORTS GENERALLY RELIABLE
RIEGNER

Riegner brought his findings to the American and British consular authorities in Geneva on the morning of Saturday, August 8. In the absence of Consul Paul Squire, who had previously given the WJC secretary use of State Department cable facilities to inform his New York associates, Howard Elting, Jr., took down Riegner's story and his cable to Wise. When the vice-consul remarked the the news "seemed fantastic" Riegner pointed out that recent mass deportation across Europe suggested "it was always conceivable that such a diabolical plan was actually being considered by Hitler as a corollary." "So serious and alarming" did Riegner view the report, Elting recorded, that he felt it his duty to ask that the American and other governments be informed at once, that they attempt by every means to verify its contents, and that Stephen Wise be notified. Riegner then proceeded to his friend, British Consul H. Livingston; as he could not be located, two associates took down the request. The identical telegram was presented except that the addressee, chairman of the WJC's British section and Member of Parliament Sidney Silverman, was asked to "INFORM AND CONSULT NEW YORK." Riegner left both consulates uncertain whether either would dispatch the precious message.[15]

While Riegner waited "in utmost despair" for word from colleagues in New York and London, the State Department decided not to transmit his cable to Wise. Official disbelief in its contents, especially in view of the hesitation expressed therein, was understandable. Yet department members who had maintained a harsh visa policy since September, 1939, owing to some antisemitism and a fear of alien espionage, would also advise against complying with Riegner's request.[16] Overruling one subordinate's suggestion to send the cable (designated an "unreliable war rumor") to Wise, director of the European Division Elbridge Durbrow stressed "the impossibility of our being of any assistance"—even if the "fantastic" allegation were true. At the same time, the usually sympathetic Under Secretary of State Sumner Welles received an appeal dated August 11 from the JDC's Paul Baerwald to intervene with the Vichy government against the recent deportations taking place in unoccupied France. Six days later a reply carrying Welles's initialed approval informed the U.S. minister in Berne, Leland Harrison, that the Riegner message had not been passed on to its intended destination.

State recommended to Harrison that no further reports be transmitted by "third parties," and that future dispatches be limited to information involving "definite American interest." Riegner only received word on August 24 that the State Department was "disinclined to deliver the message in question in view of the apparently unsubstantiated character of the information which forms its main theme." He was simultaneously asked by Consul Squire, however, to inform him if and when corroboratory evidence came to hand.[17]

The British Foreign Office response proved better for Riegner's cause. Authorities who persisted in denying the Jewish people a distinct nationality, whether as regards a condemnation of Nazi crimes or the formation of an Allied Jewish fighting force, had additional grounds to treat the telegram that arrived on August 10 with the greatest reserve. Thus a first comment observed three days later that although numerous reports of massacres against Jews in Poland had been received, other sources had not furnished confirmation of this message. Facts could not be obtained about Riegner himself, not even from the Jewish Agency in London. Still, the acting head of Whitehall's Central Department felt compelled to express doubt on the 15th that the unverified dispatch could be held up much longer, "although I fear it may provoke embarrassing repercussions." The listed recipient, after all, was an M.P. from Liverpool. Two days later Parliamentary Under Secretary Richard K. Law forwarded the cable to Silverman, adding: "we have no information bearing on or confirming this story."[18]

Convening immediately thereafter in its offices at 55 New Cavendish St., the WJC's executive branch in London pondered the next step. Although they knew Riegner, a Ph.D. in jurisprudence, to be a very circumspect individual with good contacts among German refugees in Switzerland, Law's comment suggested caution. Political Secretary Alexander Easterman, chief foreign correspondent of the *Daily Herald* in London during the 1930s, well realized that Fleet Street consistently dismissed reports of German brutalities as exaggerated "Jewish propaganda." Joining the WJC in December, 1941, he and colleague Noah Barou had vainly sought to have a conference of nine Allied governments, meeting the next month in St. James Palace, specifically include Nazi anti-Jewish persecutions among war crimes punishable after V-E day.[19]

The WJC's British section had continued efforts to breach the wall of diplomatic silence with a press conference on June 29, 1942, where Silverman estimated the number of Jewish dead at over one million. Drs. Schwartzbart and Ernest Frischer of the Polish and Czech State Councils respectively stressed that Germany was determinedly implementing Hitler's proclaimed aim to destroy the entire Jewish people, and they called for immediate reprisals as the only way to halt the calculated mass killings. Procrastination among the major Western counsels was still the order of the day, however, even after Zygielbojm saw to the publication on both sides of the Atlantic of a ghastly account by three grave-diggers who had escaped from the death center at Chelmno.[20]

Silverman therefore quoted Riegner's cable on August 24, together with a concluding observation that "FOREIGN OFFICE HAS NO INFORMATION BEARING ON OR CONFIRMING STORY," for Western Union dispatch to Wise's congress office at 330 W. 42nd St. in New York. As to further action, he privately agreed with Easterman that additional information should be gotten from Whitehall before releasing the story to the press. "It would be a first-class blunder to go off at half-cock," the busy lawyer cautioned the section's political secretary on the 28th: "After all, a few days' careful thinking or planning will not impede the little practical [sic] we shall be able to do, until this devil has passed on into history."[21]

Additional information reaching Jewish representatives in Geneva strengthened the reliability of the controversial telegram. A memorandum from Dr. Julius Kühl of the Polish legation in Berne dated August 15, giving the testimony of two reliable Gentile witnesses, came to the attention of Richard Lichtheim. The first, a young man named Turski who reached Switzerland in early July, told about the mass pogroms in Lemberg (Lwow) and the inciting of the Polish people against the Jews there. The other refugee, who arrived the day before from Poland, added that the corpses of Jews taken from the Warsaw ghetto were "being used to supply fat and their bones for fertilizer." Hardly a Jew was to be found in all of eastern Poland, he added, including occupied Russia; the deportation of West European Jews to "the east" and even Theresienstadt ultimately means their death. Similar letters by Polish Jews, as well as accounts from the Bratislava Jewish underground (via paid couriers), also reached HeChalutz representative Nathan Schwalb and the JDC's Saly Mayer. Yet, wired an astonished Pozner to Barlas on August 29, *one month* had already passed with not a word from Palestine since his first cable about "Tochnia Haschmedski" (Pozner's guarded code for plan of destruction). The Yishuv had to be stirred immediately to action, he insisted.[22]

Other related reports were common knowledge in London and Washington diplomatic circles. Consul Squire received eyewitness descriptions from the YMCA's Donald Lowrie, now in Switzerland, about the deportations from southern France to Poland, and the fact that 15,000 others were scheduled to suffer the same fate. Squire sent on these reports via Berne to the State Department. The department also received a memorandum, forwarded on August 26 to State and the White House directly from London, by Frischer of the Czech State Council that dramatically argued for action against the unprecedented "organized wholesale dying" of European Jewry.[23]

On September 1 Riegner received a wire from Silverman that his message had reached the WJC in London. Not able to explain the interminable delay, he could at least take satisfaction that his instinctive request to have the Britisher contact New York had proven correct. Whitehall's green light now bypassed State's earlier suppression of the cable to Wise. What response would be forthcoming from across the Atlantic? Riegner wondered anxiously.[24]

Silverman's telegram of August 24, which cleared Liverpool four days later, arrived at Western Union in New York early on the 29th and reached WJC headquarters that afternoon. About to close up the deserted office, an associate dialed Rabbi Wise's study in New York's Free Synagogue to read him the contents.[25] Only a few days earlier the WJC president had joined three other American Jewish leaders in warning Secretary of State Cordell Hull that recent forced deportations from France, like "monstrous outrages" against the Jewish people elsewhere under German rule, accorded "with the announced policy of the Nazis to exterminate the Jews of Europe." He now convened some congress colleagues, who were understandably "overwhelmed" and uncertain how to respond to the telegram's "shattering effect." It was decided to cable Riegner that his message had arrived and have Wise immediately contact Welles for help.[26]

On September 2 Wise dictated a letter to the under secretary of state. Pointing out that he and his associates "have been reduced to consternation" by this cable, the Jewish leader requested the hitherto responsive Welles that the "conservative and equable" Riegner be approached to substantiate the "appalling rumor." If further information could be thus obtained, perhaps the administration and Welles's department would then be requested by the WJC to "take such action as may seem wisest." Could the under secretary ring up Wise before departing tomorrow for his Labor Day vacation, the writer asked, and also consider whether the matter did not merit Roosevelt's personal attention?[27]

Welles lost no time in answering the urgent plea. Armed with a briefing from Ray Atherton of the Division of European Affairs, he telephoned Wise the following afternoon and relayed the department's understanding that Jewish refugees, like the prisoners of war in German hands, were being sent to labor installations on behalf of the Nazi war machine. "Fine," Wise replied. "May we feel reassured?" "Who can tell, seeing that you are dealing with that madman?" his caller retorted. The under secretary, instrumental that same day in bringing about Secretary Hull's formal protest to Vichy against the deportations occurring in unoccupied France, ended the conversation with a promise that the department would seek verification of the Riegner cable. Wise agreed not to take any further action until corroboration was forthcoming.[28]

The same day another cable, arriving in the hands of Agudas Israel World Organization president Jacob Rosenheim, provided circumstantial confirmation of the Riegner report. A message from Isaac Sternbuch in Switzerland, circumventing State censorship through Julius Kühl's approved use of the Polish diplomatic pouch, announced that about 100,000 Jews had recently been killed during the German destruction of the Warsaw ghetto; "soap and artificial fertilizer" were being produced from their bodies. (Zygielbojm's speeches of August 22 and September 1 in London had already spoken of an entire people's systematic murder by gas chambers on Polish soil.) Rosenheim cabled this startling information to Roosevelt on September 4, and had Polish ambassador in Washington Jan Ciechanowski bring the message to his British counterpart and to Atherton in State. While the latter explained that the American authorities "would not take a stand" before authenticating this and earlier news received in August (Riegner's cable), Rosenheim asked the Union of Orthodox Rabbis in the United States and Canada to call a meeting of major American Jewish organizations the very same day, per Sternbuch's request. The hurriedly assembled group, informed of the Riegner message by Wise and of the Sternbuch cable by Rosenheim, did not reach any decision on a plan of action.[29]

Wise called a second gathering of the group for September 6, with B'nai Brith and the Jewish Labor Committee as co-signers. Wide-ranging proposals for action included a direct appeal from Roosevelt to the German government to stop the massacres; the intervention of neutrals, along with the sending of food to the Polish ghettos; protests by congressmen and important church and lay figures; editorial comment; and the American government's warning the Third Reich of reprisals against German aliens in the United State if the murders continued. Expressing doubt whether the Agudas Israel cable deserved credence and worried over rising antisemitism in the country, Wise mentioned that Welles had expressly requested no publicity until receiving verification from abroad. "If the Polish Jews will be annihilated," the Jewish Labor Committee's

Jacob Pat shot back, "I don't care what is going to happen to the Jews here and to you and to your government!" The heated deliberations still producing no consensus, a smaller group met three days later. It was finally agreed that no action be taken before Wise went over the matter with Welles on the latter's return from vacation.[30]

The tormented WJC president knew little rest as he privately sought to move government officials in Washington. He asked Felix Frankfurter to consider passing on copies of the two cables to "the Chief . . . the foremost and finest figure in the political world today." The Jewish Supreme Court justice, who with Eleanor Roosevelt received a copy the same day of the Sternbuch cable via James McDonald, did so; he subsequently informed Wise that Roosevelt echoed the assurances given Welles earlier by the State Department. But what of the president's masked reference, made before a White House press conference one month earlier, to the fear that the defeat of the occupational regime might result in the "extermination of certain populations"? FDR could not appeal to Germany in any case, Wise believed, because Hitler would hardly do anything for this arch enemy.[31] Instead, the ailing Reform rabbi sought the intervention of Pope Pius XII, pressed the suggestion of feeding the Jews in Poland along the Greek relief example, and showed the dreaded telegrams to understanding souls like Vice-President Henry Wallace, Assistant Secretary of State Dean Acheson, and Secretary of the Treasury Henry Morgenthau, Jr. He continued to get the official impression that deportations from the Warsaw ghetto meant forced labor on the new Russo-Polish frontier, although the Jewish Telegraphic Agency quoted an anonymous Geneva source on September 9 that "unconfirmed alarming information" (in view of continued mass deportations) reaching Switzerland stated that the Gestapo was demanding the annihilation of all Jews in Poland "as an element detrimental to the security of Germany's interests in Eastern Europe." An American Christian leader then visiting Geneva had also, at Wise's request, confirmed from Guggenheim that "deportation" meant certain death.[32]

When the skeptical Welles returned to Washington, he asked Wise, then accompanied by WJC administrative committee head Nahum Goldmann, to maintain public silence for a few weeks. The Vatican, most unimpeachable source, would be tapped for substantiation in the interim, he assured the distraught pair. An uncertain Wise accepted what he privately termed "the great responsibility," lest he lose the WJC's only sympathetic audience in the State Department and thus all contact with Riegner.[33]

The congress's London office, completely in the dark about Wise's harsh dilemma, moved on its own to confirm Riegner's cable. After a five-point proposal for urgent action sped off to the WJC president in New York, Silverman assured Law's private secretary on September 9 that Riegner was entirely trustworthy. He also asked for permission to talk with Wise by telephone, sought advice on releasing the message in question, and wondered if Vatican pressure could be brought to bear against Germany. While awaiting the Foreign Office's reply, a congress delegation to John Winant heard the genuinely moved American ambassador oppose any publicity until further inquiry had been made. Czech president Eduard Beneš strongly endorsed this position, warning that the report might actually be a Nazi maneuver to evoke Allied reaction and so give the Germans an excuse to extend the outrages. Surprised at having been unaware of the report's substance, Beneš promised to have his intelligence sources investigate thoroughly.

Only Ivan Maisky regarded the telegram as "substantially to be relied upon," and strongly urged on Easterman publicity and the idea of reprisals as perhaps having a deterrent effect against the Nazi design. The Russian government, the Soviet ambassador confided to his former journalist acquaintance that September 14, could not help in saving Jews directly because it was engaged in a supreme effort to win the war and destroy the Germans. Moscow would readily join in a firm declaration against the massacres by the major Allied powers, in Maisky's opinion, but he doubted the readiness of London and Washington to take this step.[34]

Interoffice Whitehall reactions seemed to confirm some of Maisky's judgments. The Foreign Office applauded General Sikorski's statement to the World Jewish Congress that the St. James conference had purposely excluded anti-Jewish crimes since the Jews were considered nationals of their respective states; it tied the congress's concern about a specific declaration against the annihilation of Jewry to Zionist calls for a Jewish state in then British Mandatory Palestine. Considerable efforts were made to defer suggested parliamentary questions about atrocities against Jews in Poland.

At the end of August the Central Department's W. Denis Allen went so far as to suggest that Germans, who knew better than anyone "the trouble that can be caused by minorities," were determined "as far as possible" that no minorities be left "to cause trouble in those parts of Poland which are to be incorporated into the Reich." In urging that the Foreign Office not publicize Riegner's "wild story," the same official insisted, as had the State Department, that "the German policy seems to be rather to eliminate 'useless mouths' but to use able bodied Jews as slave labor." "The facts are quite bad enough," minuted Frank Roberts regarding the Sternbuch telegram, "without the addition of such an old story as the use of bodies for the manufacture of soap." Accordingly, telephone facilities to reach WJC colleagues in New York were denied Silverman, he was finally told. Organizations could release the facts on their own responsibility, yet the parliamentary private secretary to Foreign Secretary

Anthony Eden quickly cautioned the Liverpool M.P. that any such action might "irritate" the Nazis and so provoke greater excesses.[35]

Mounting information, however, that Wise received from abroad began to chip away at the wall of diplomatic inaction. Richard Lichtheim considered the news reaching Switzerland "so terrible," he later confessed to his superiors, that he first hesitated to send the Polish legation's August 15 memorandum on to agency offices in Jerusalem, London, and New York. He had finally done so on the 30th after being convinced by coded postcards and additional messages from Poland that the report was "quite in line" with Hitler's avowed declaration that no European Jews would survive the war. Wise and Goldmann brought this dispatch to Welles and to British Ambassador Halifax on September 23 for referral to his government.[36]

On September 26 Welles used that memorandum to have Myron Taylor, the president's personal representative to the Vatican, ask the cardinal secretary of state for any corroborating information. Only the previous day Taylor had pressed Luigi Cardinal Maglioni to have the pope speak out against the "inhuman treatment of refugees and hostages and especially of the Jews" in the occupied territories. The Holy See replied two weeks later, limiting itself to an informal and unsigned statement that "up to the present time it has not been possible to verify the accuracy of reports reaching St. Peter's about severe measures taken against non-Aryans."[37]

Continuing to operate on his own, Riegner handed Squire two additional memoranda on September 25 to confirm his earlier August 8 report. The first, originating from Sommer, told of two factories in which Jewish corpses reaching German frontiers on trains from Belgium, Holland, and France were being processed into soap, glue, and lubricants. A new and cheaper procedure in the killing process consisted of injecting air into veins; the informant added that the "utility value" of a corpse had been set by Nazi physicians at 50 reichsmarks. The second memorandum, two coded letters written by I. Domb outside the Warsaw ghetto in early September, which had recently reached Isaac Sternbuch through his brother Eli, had provided a basis as well for Sternbuch's earlier cable to Agudas Israel in New York. Squire forwarded these to State three days later.[38]

Lichtheim and Riegner entertained no doubts as to the possible realization of the Nazis' ultimate goal. Already in a letter dated August 27, the despondent Jewish Agency spokesman had estimated that a maximum of one to two million Jews would survive in Europe, provided that the situation in Hungary, Rumania, and Italy did not change for the worse. "We are attending the last stage of the realization of the Nazi-aim i.e. the extermination of European Jews," Riegner wrote Wise a month later. Additional news about the recent gassing of French and Polish

Jews was broadcast by Thomas Mann over the BBC on September 27.

Hitler himself confirmed the inconceivable in a speech three days later at the Berlin Sports Palace. Recalling his statement to the Reichstag on January 30, 1939, that Jewry would be destroyed in another world war, he now warned: "at one time the Jews of Germany laughed about my prophecies. I do not know whether they are still laughing or whether they have already lost all desire to laugh. But right now I can only repeat: they will stop laughing everywhere, and I shall be right also in that prophecy."[39]

Having read WJC and other related reports during the past few weeks, a worried Under Secretary Welles finally cut the Gordian knot of official bureaucracy and silence. Wise had informed him on October 5 that Riegner and Lichtheim feared to send corroborating materials through open cables or mail; the under secretary also had received no word as yet from the government's representatives to the Vatican. Later on that same day he ordered Minister Harrison to receive either Jewish representative and forward the evidence immediately for his personal attention.[40]

Welles's directive, forwarded by Squire to the WJC's secretary in Geneva three days later, arrived at a most propitious moment. On October 1 Riegner had surreptitiously entered a hospital ward to hear a Baltic Jew's eyewitness account of the massacre of Latvian Jewry. For three hours Gabriel Zivian, recently arrived in Switzerland from Germany, described the harrowing end of Riga's 32,000 Jews by the *Einsatzgruppen* mobile killing units during the last half of 1941. Lithuania's 150,000 Jews, he added, had reportedly perished in similar fashion. A week later still fresher testimony came into Riegner's hands from a Polish Jew named Lieber, a simple mechanic who described his deportation from Belgium in mid-August and subsequent escape from the region near Stalingrad with the aid of a German officer. From a German military source Riegner also learned that the Lodz ghetto had been "cleaned out" except for those Jews working for the *Wehrmacht,* while Nazi talk of the safety of Theresienstadt was "mere propaganda." Finally, industrialist Schulte just returned with additional information: the German secretary of state for economics, Herman (actually Herbert) Backe, had proposed "to exterminate the Jews found in the German alimentary space" in view of supply difficulties. At the end of July he had obtained Hitler's signature on an order to carry out the quick deportation and subsequent annihilation in eastern Europe of some four million Jews.[41]

Harrison obtained these shattering reports from Riegner and Lichtheim in his office on October 22. The minister had been highly skeptical when sending Riegner's August cable to Secretary Hull, attributing it to "war rumor inspired by fear and what is commonly understood to be the actually miserable condition of these refugees who face decimation as a result of physical maltreatment, persecution, and scarcely endurable privations, malnutrition and disease." On October 6 he had assured State of his certainty that Jews were being "systematically evacuated" from western and eastern Europe and "sent eastward to an unknown fate." Now he received a joint note detailing the German policy of "constant and deliberate annihilation of all European Jewish communities," which showed the figures to be "quite in accord" with Hitler's last public address in Berlin.

The *aide-mémoire* of the two Jewish representatives called for a broad Allied response. It pleaded for new approaches to the Vatican; public denunciations of the crimes; and special commissions that, according Jews the status of other persecuted nations, should investigate the facts. Friendly representations should be made to the governments of Italy and Hungary expressing the hope that they would not follow the ruthless German plan of murder, as well as immediate stern warnings given to Vichy France and the Rumanian government to halt their deportations of Jews.[42]

The American minister took well over a half-hour to read the 30-page document silently. Without a trace of emotion, he raised questions about each page. Harrison also received from his callers a sealed envelope with Schulte's name alone enclosed, provided them by Sagalowitz at their insistence just prior to the morning appointment. To strengthen their case at this crucial interview, Riegner also noted that Professor Guggenheim had heard from a high official of the International Committee of the Red Cross (ICRC) about a German order to annihilate all of Europe's Jews. When Harrison pressed for the individual's identity, Reigner, despite Guggenheim's wary insistence that the name be kept confidential, complied with the name of Carl J. Burckhardt.

In Riegner's view, Schulte, risking his life to aid Jewry, had made a reasonable request in asking only that anonymity be kept forever. Burckhardt, on the other hand, had nothing to lose personally. The committee on which he served, moreover, had done pitifully little to aid Jewry in its greatest hour of need. Would Guggenheim submit an affidavit to this effect, the American minister inquired? Definitely, Riegner answered, without a moment's hesitation.[43]

A thorough investigation that followed convinced Harrison. After two days he sent off the Riegner-Lichtheim *aide-mémoire* and a report of the conversation to Welles. An affidavit from Guggenheim, taken down on October 29 by Squire at his superior's request, emphasized that Hitler's order demanded the "extermination" (*Ausrottung*) of all Jews under his control by December 31, 1942. Guggenheim's source, under the impression that this order was "in the process of being executed," had heard from two German officials (acting independently) who were attached to the ministries of foreign affairs and war in Berlin. In addition, the sympathetic Albrecht von Kessel of the German consulate general in Geneva implored the Swiss personality since September not to intervene further in specific cases, since such efforts henceforth would be "entirely useless and futile." Another Swiss citizen, living in Belgrade, who had always interceded in favor of Jews, had confirmed to Guggenheim's informant the existence of Hitler's directive. Squire also took down Zivian's sworn statement that day and vouched for its reliability. Harrison dispatched both documents to Welles directly.[44]

The two Jews had accomplished a difficult task well, but some Jewish Agency officials persisted in doubting the reports from Geneva. Chaim Barlas in Istanbul questioned Lichtheim's dispatch of August 30, particularly since former Polish Parliament member Alfred (Abraham) Silberschein expressed a far more cautious approach a month later. The director of the RELICO relief organization in Geneva, skeptical in early August on first hearing of Pozner's news, had written to Barlas on September 20 that while Warsaw lacked "200 souls," "Mr. Grushinski [Hebrew code for deportation] visited in another city." Barlas viewed the figure given by Silberschein, rather than the apparent misprint of 200,000, as sufficient to challenge Lichteim's memorandum.

The Jewish Agency Executive's Isaac Gruenbaum in Jerusalem, another refugee from Poland, also expressed his shock and disbelief, and sent three cables seeking confirmation on October 6 to Geneva, Istanbul, and Sweden's chief rabbi, the aged Zionist Marcus Ehrenpreis. Lichtheim lost no time in his response, providing summaries of Riegner's latest information. "No force" could stop Hitler or his SS, he advised, but Allied warnings might yet prove helpful in the semi-independent states of Rumania, Hungary, Italy, and Bulgaria. The other agency centers failed to confirm the August 30 memorandum, however. Finally, following a discussion on September 25, the executive allocated a total of £50 for cables to inform Jewish organizations abroad. The Jewish Yishuv of Palestine had received no word as yet from its leaders.[45]

By then Wise could entertain little reason for hope. The Interior Department's Secretary Harold Ickes, deeply moved by Wise's and Goldmann's description of the Riegner and Sternbuch cables, promised to take up once again their idea of opening the Virgin Islands as a haven to Jewish refugees; other government officials privately endorsed the movement of 5,000 children from France and the dispatch of monthly food packages costing $12,000 to the Polish ghettos. These were palliatives, however.[46] Government authorities in Washington and London announced the formation of a United Nations Commission for the Investigation of War Crimes, Roosevelt limiting his promise to postwar punishment of the "ringleaders." Yet aside from the fact that the historic announcement continued to hide the unique plight of Jewry under the term "civilian populations," what if some of the Allied powers chose to view those dispersed by the Nazis as no longer their individual responsibility? Even more to the point, such a step did not confront what Goldmann termed "the big question of massacres" just when news bulletins from abroad spoke of Minsk and Vitebsk as "completely" *Judenrein,* the murder of more than 30,000 Yugoslav Jews, thousands of Lodz Jews poisoned by gas, and continued mass deportations from France, Holland, and Belgium.[47]

A personal report on the morning of October 20, 1942, from Roosevelt's emissary to the Vatican further strengthened Wise's worst fears. With the approval of the president and Secretary Hull, Myron Taylor confidentially indicated to Wise, his son, and Goldmann the substance of impressions resulting from his recent trip abroad. Conversations with reliable sources convinced Taylor that the atrocities in France, Poland and Yugoslavia "are confirmed as generally reported." He had left two supporting documents with Roosevelt and would urge on the chief executive and the secretary of state, as he had the pope, a further statement condemning Nazi inhumanity. Welfare agencies were not now permitted, and he doubted if they would receive approval, to do anything active in Poland until some change occurred in the European war situation, "which affects the Nazi plan of extermination of many and the removal of others from given territories."[48]

Even as Wise grappled with Taylor's devastating conclusions, the Board of Deputies of British Jews felt compelled to take a stand against the Nazi atrocities. The board, originated in 1760 to represent British Jewry, had not accepted appeals from the Orthodox Agudas Israel or the WJC's British section for united action. Functioning together on international affairs with the long-established Anglo-Jewish Association as the Joint Foreign Committee, it had presented Richard Law on October 1 with Lichtheim's September cables, and pressed for a joint Anglo-American declaration specifically denouncing the mass slaughter. At that time the delegation had suggested evacuation to neutral countries and Palestine, ICRC aid to the Jews, and a separate Jewish council to advise the Allies regarding postwar relief and reconstruction. But the parliamentary under secretary had not been very encouraging at a time when the BBC was reporting the death of Jews by gas and when the *Manchester Guardian* estimated that, exclusive of occupied Russia, almost two million Jews had been destroyed in Nazi-occupied Europe; the respected newspaper warned that "the same fate is awaiting 4,500,000 more Jews in Europe if Hitler remains unchecked.[49]

On October 20 a crowd of 10,000 met in London's Albert Hall under the board's aegis to record its horror at the "deliberate policy of extermination." While messages to the assembly from Beneš and Sikorski spoke of full retribution, the archbishop of Canterbury, in the chair, called for all possible Allied rescue efforts. Disregarding the opposition of two War Cabinet ministers, Churchill sent a personal note denouncing the "systematic cruelties" to which the Jewish people "have been exposed under the Nazi regime" and which "have placed an indelible stain upon all who perpetrate and instigate them."[50]

That these barbarities were, indeed, systematic the American consul in Geneva heard from Carl Burckhardt on November 7. The "authoritative Swiss personality of Geneva international circles," whom Professor Guggenheim persistently referred to in oblique fashion in his affidavit, had been the former League of Nations high commissioner to Danzig and was currently vice-president of the ICRC and Guggenheim's academic colleague. In the course of an interview Burckhardt informed Squire off the record that he had heard of an order signed by Hitler early in 1941 that Germany "must be *judenfrei*" before the end of 1942. Knowledge of this directive had come from two "very well informed" Germans. "He then made it clear," Squire wrote to Harrison, that "since there is no place to send these Jews and since the territory must be cleared of this race, it is obvious what the net result would be." The usually cautious Burckhardt, who still continued to oppose the WJC's demand that his organization abandon its neutrality regarding the Holocaust, had thus provided Squire the conclusive piece of documentation to substantiate Riegner's original cable. On the same day, various pro-Nazi periodicals, in response to publicity in the West against the mass killings, carried a laudatory article with photographs on labor camp Auschwitz I. Without notifying Riegner, the American consul sent the record of Burckhardt's statement to Harrison two days later.[51]

While this information secretly made its way to Welles's own hands, the leaders of Poalei Zion in New York had decided to arouse "the consciousness and conscience of the Anglo-Saxon world"[52] to the unique Jewish plight in Europe.

Since the end of July a Belgian refugee had been desperately urging his colleagues on the WJC executive to mount a militant campaign against the destruction "in cold blood" of European Jewry. Aside from diplomatic *demarches* and publicity to break "the conspiracy of silence" surrounding the mass slaughter, A. Leon Kubowitzki (later Aryeh Kubovy) followed Zygielbojm, Schwartzbart, and Frischer in asking for a reprisal policy. The Allies should warn the Nazis that for atrocities against Jews, German towns and villages would be bombed. Wise (and some others of the executive) sharply objected to this course of action, stating that since the American people had not yet "completely thrown themselves" into the global conflict, the WJC could not ask them to take a special warlike step on behalf of the Jews.

Kubowitzki essayed other avenues. He pleaded with influential enter-
tainer Eddie Cantor to halt his call for United Jewish Appeal funds and
publicly advocate adequate retaliation before "the complete physical extermination" of European Jewry became a reality—to no avail. Leading
Orthodox rabbis, many having escaped from Poland and Lithuania earlier via Siberia, strongly opposed as provocative his idea for protest
meetings and a march on Washington; faith and the "tested methods" of
past centuries would deal effectively with what they considered to be the
latest reincarnation of Haman. A meeting of Anglo-Jewish journalists in
mid-August, convened by Kubowitzki to transmit the substance of reports received by the WJC from Europe, refused to believe that such
horrors were occurring in the twentieth century.[53]

A week later, however, a copy of the Bund cable about the annihilation of Jews in Poland arrived in New York, and Kubowitzki's Poalei
Zion comrades of the *Jewish Frontier* editorial board could no longer
evade the evidence. Skeptical and yet not wholly rejecting it as "the ma-
cabre fantasy of a lunatic sadist," the board decided to relegate the Bund
report to small type on the back pages of the magazine's September
issue. Not long thereafter the Poalei Zion executive heard from Wise of
Riegner's message. The American members of a subcommittee, gathering in mid-September to decide on a response, continued to oppose "any
commitment in risky projects." They did agree on certain steps, including a special issue of the *Jewish Frontier* to publicize the mass slaughter.
This number, devoted entirely to Jewry's catastrophe, should be sent to
all having intellectual or political importance in American life, along
with a letter asking for their reaction. No issue appeared for October,
while Hayim Greenberg and his staff on the labor Zionist monthly concentrated on collecting the available facts.[54]

On November 19 Greenberg sent a report entitled "Jews under the
Axis, 1939–1942" across the country. In publicizing the first documentary evidence of Hitler's policy to destroy an entire people, the editorial
board warned its readers that "the holocaust that has overtaken the Jews
of Europe" was being speeded on its way to completion. A collection of
reports on Germany, Poland, Czechoslovakia, France, Rumania, Lithuania, Yugoslavia, and Holland substantiated Hitler's September 30 address
and numerous other Nazi declarations. The coldly factual presentation,
credited primarily to the materials of the American Jewish Congress, the
WJC, and the Institute of Jewish Affairs (all under Wise's leadership),
revealed beyond question that only the Jews had no place in the Nazi
plan for the New Order. The U.S. Office of War Information praised
"the splendid job," while the *New York Post* editorialized: "If anything
can stir the humanitarian feelings of a world brutalized by 10 years of
German Fascism, this will do it." With the naked brutality of the Final
Solution finally disclosed between the covers of a magazine, the West

had to confront the fate of one people, in Greenberg's characterization, as "a unique problem of life and death in the literal sense, as a problem whose solution cannot be postponed to the day of victory."[55]

The first official statement on the dimensions of the Holocaust came from the Jewish Agency Executive in Jerusalem. By the beginning of the month the executive had received a cable from Alfred Silberschein dated October 8 that essentially confirmed Lichtheim's August 30 memorandum about mass slaughter in Poland. This telegram, also based on the report from Kühl of Aleksander Ladós's consular staff, received far more attention than the earlier document, but the arrival in Haifa on November 16 of 78 Jews from Axis-held Europe under a first exchange agreement with Germany brought eyewitness testimony of a broad spectrum not heard previously. The survivors spoke of widespread massacre; gassing at Chelmno and Treblinka; three crematoria burning Jews at Oswiecim (the Polish for Auschwitz), with two more under construction; 25,000 "legals" left in the Warsaw ghetto. Eliyahu Dobkin challenged the account of one of these women as exaggerated; her slap across both his cheeks shocked the agency's immigration director into reality.

The Jewish Agency Executive, still unable to grasp the Nazi plan for *total* destruction, decided to issue a public declaration on November 22, 1942. It spoke (erroneously) of a special "Vernichtungs Kommission," set up by one Feu of Warsaw after SS *Reichsführer* Heinrich Himmler's visit to Warsaw the previous spring, continuing its systematic slaughter of "tens of thousands" of Jews in Poland under a "drastic tempo." Children and the old were said to be particular targets, with hundreds of thousands of men capable of work sent to unknown destinations. The statement made no mention of poison gas operations; it gave figures totaling only some 115,000 deaths and said only of Warsaw and Lodz that these ghettos had witnessed a "frightening loss" in recent months. Nonetheless, the Jewish citizens of Palestine had finally received public assurance that the stories published throughout 1942 in the Yishuv's newspapers were to be believed.[56]

A report issued in London by the Polish government-in-exile two days later strengthened the Jewish Agency's pronouncement. Having suppressed earlier underground information regarding the mass deportations during the summer from the Warsaw ghetto, it now asserted that Himmler had ordered the death of one-half of the Jewish population of Poland by the end of the year. From July through September about 250,000 had been killed under this program; only about 4,000 were picked for "slave labor" on the battle front. The 130,000 ration cards issued by the Germans for September had fallen to only 40,000 for the succeeding month. A special Nazi battalion had shot the old and crippled; half of the remaining population, children and babies included, died in trains dispatched to camps in southeastern Poland. Starvation and suffocation from intense overcrowding and fumes of lime or chloride in the freight cars claimed many of the deported. Those so-called "settlers" who somehow survived the harrowing journey were then sent on to Treblinka, Belzec, and Sobibor, where they were "mass murdered." The *Reichsführer*'s order, the Polish statement emphasized, was "a first step toward complete liquidation."[57]

Simultaneously, Stephen Wise received a telegram from Under Secretary Welles on the morning of November 24, asking him to come to the State Department to look at certain documents. Boarding a train to Washington the same day in the company of his son, Wise entered Welles's office that afternoon. Explaining that he held materials forwarded by the American legation in Berne, Welles somberly stated: "I have reasons to believe that everything in these documents is correct." Keeping copies for the department, he handed the original affidavits, which supported Riegner's August telegram, to Wise, and added: "There is no exaggeration. These documents are evidently correct." Welles authorized the WJC president to make them public on condition that all newspapers receive the information at the same time and that the names appearing in the documents not be disclosed. Released from his earlier pledge, Wise and his son James hurriedly called a press conference for that evening.[58]

Through sources confirmed by the State Department, the WJC chairman began, he had just learned that half of the estimated four million Jews in Nazi-occupied Europe had been slain in an "extermination campaign." Hitler had ordered the murder of the entire number by the end of the year; the Warsaw ghetto had already been reduced from 500,000 to about 100,000. When Nazi leaders speak of killing "Jews in Poland," Wise continued, they refer to four-fifths of the Jewish population in Hitler-ruled Europe, since that many either are in Poland or are on route there under a Nazi "grouping plan." The Nazis have established a price of 50 reichsmarks for each corpse (mostly Jews), and are reclaiming bodies of slain civilians to be "processed into such war-vital commodities as soap, fats and fertilizer." Hitler "is even exhuming the dead for the value of the corpses," Wise emphasized. Injecting air bubbles into the veins of the victims was one of the "simplest and the cheapest methods" in this campaign, one physician able to kill more than 100 men in an hour.

Most of this information, he noted, came from various sources other than the State Department, but State had confirmed the documents as authentic. In an allusion to his October 20 meeting with Myron Taylor, Wise also quoted "a representative of President Roosevelt recently returned from Europe" as saying that the "worst you [Dr. Wise] have thought is true." Wise attributed Hitler's campaign to "a last desperate effort—one of his last mad acts before he is destroyed, or called to his judgment." He estimated that some half of the five million Jews in the territories occupied by the Nazis "had already been destroyed."[59]

The veil had been lifted at long last. How would the free world respond?

II

Wise's tragic news brought eight American Jewish organizations, responding to his cable, to the offices of the American Jewish Congress on November 25. Opening with an assurance that this special Joint Emergency Committee for European Jewish Affairs would be dissolved "as soon as its task was achieved," the chairman summarized his talk with Welles and the terrible documents concerned, and proposed to release the facts to the press. He also wished to secure a hearing before President Roosevelt (which Welles had promised to help arrange); cable a few hundred prominent non-Jews to comment on the situation; ask 500 newspapers by telegram to devote editorials to the problem; and set a day after Chanuka for Jewish prayer and mourning.

Breaking into tears, a representative from Agudas Israel suggested that a day of mourning be decreed during that very holiday, but Rabbi Aaron Kotler rose to object. Although the Jewish people possessed an entire *Mesechta* [tractate] *Ta'anis* on related subjects, such a proclamation "would mean that all is lost already." A day of fasting, prayer, and repentance was called for, the Torah sage concluded. Jacob Pat of the Jewish Labor Committee supplied additional information that afternoon as transmitted in a cable from Zygielbojm, and agreed to provide the press with the documents. Kubowitzki kept his silence, thinking the various proposals from a divided community too late. The group finally gave its consent to these various steps. Two reports (by Zivian and Sommer) thus became common knowledge, along with Wise's summary of the messages Riegner had sent since August. The WJC leader also admitted publicly that he was one of the group that had always believed such conditions could not be true until the documents submitted by the State Department proved anew that "nothing that has been said before was an exaggeration."[60]

Whitehall received a copy of the official Polish news about the Warsaw ghetto's liquidation from Silverman and Easterman on the morning of November 26. Eduard Beneš had informed the WJC's British section recently that his sources could not confirm the existence of a German plan for "wholesale extermination," but on the 25th Schwartzbart gave the WJC his government's statement about the more than one million

Jewish dead in Poland since World War II began. Leaning now on State's release of relevant documents to Wise, Silverman suggested to Law that a four-power declaration be issued warning that the perpetrators would receive due punishment and that the German people could not escape responsibility for the criminal acts of their government. The Allies should also broadcast to encourage Jews and those Gentiles who might be willing to protect them, the latter step perhaps serving an important weapon of general political warfare.

Privately doubtful that these proposals would do much good, but worried that the Foreign Office would be in an "appalling position if the stories should prove to have been true and he would have done nothing about them," Law promised the M.P. that he would enunciate the Foreign Office's view in Commons the next week. His subordinates in the meantime expressed their own preference for a vague denunciation of the "reported atrocities" and a warning of the Allied retribution that would follow the war.[61]

At the behest of its two Jewish members, the Polish National Council unanimously adopted a resolution of protest on November 27. Schwartzbart had already publicized the first Polish reports; Zygielbojm had just received a detailed letter from Bundist Leon Feiner in Poland about an unprecedented "mass, nightmarish mystery of death," warning that only immediate retaliation against German citizens in Allied countries could check this "war *sui generis*." The council's final statement avoided Feiner's request for reprisals, however, and made no demands on Poles to help rescue their Jewish countrymen.[62]

Jan Karski, who brought the Feiner report and other personal impressions to London, also gave Zygielbojm a special message. Having recently visited the Warsaw ghetto and the "selection" camp near Belzec in the uniform of an Estonian policeman, the underground messenger conveyed Feiner's own words to his old party comrade. Jewish representatives wished their leaders in the free world to lay siege to the important Anglo-American government offices and to accept no food or drink until some rescue action were undertaken. If necessary, these leaders should die a slow death and perhaps thus shake the world's conscience. After pacing up and down a small room in Stratton House for a few minutes, a startled Zygielbojm responded: "They would simply bring in two policemen and have me dragged away to an institution. . . ."[63]

Jewry in Palestine, responding spontaneously to the collective news, united in a paroxysm of grief. Thousands marched with black flags through the streets of Tel Aviv shouting "Save Our Brethren!" and "Death for the Germans!"; the entire Hebrew press appeared with black-bordered pages for a week. While some attacked the Yishuv's blindness to past reports of the impending catastrophe, most accused the Allied powers of "remaining unmoved by the hundreds of Jewish Lidices." The Jewish children should receive first priority in achieving a place of safety, insisted a consensus, and "the world must not remain silent." A meeting sponsored by the Revisionist New Zionist Organization inserted in the traditional "El Maleh Rachamim" memorial prayer the sentence, unprecedented in Jewish history, "because the whole Jewish people demands vengeance for the blood that was shed." Retaliatory action, neutral shelters, opening the gates of Palestine, ICRC aid, exchanges of Germans for Jews, a Jewish army, different diplomatic moves—all were suggested from various sides.

For the first time since the destruction of the Second Temple almost 2,000 years earlier, a great rabbinical assembly gathered in the Holy Land. From Jerusalem's oldest synagogue, Chief Rabbi Isaac HaLevi Herzog called upon the world's government and church powers to rescue Israel in its supreme agony. Robed in black, the more than 400 rabbis present rent their garments, recited prayers of supplication, and concluded with a march to the Western Wall. World Jewry was asked to set aside December 2 as a day of mourning and prayer.[64]

The WJC's British branch, in conjunction with Ignacy Schwartzbart, continued to widen the gap in the official wall of silence. The Polish National Council arranged a conference for Easterman and Barou on November 27 with Foreign Minister Eduard Raczynski, where the delegation suggested a formal memorandum summarizing the underground reports from Poland and a *demarche* seeking an Allied expression of protest. The congress wrote to all Christian churches and political organizations requesting that they express their indignation, and see to it that "the whole civilized world" exert its influence upon the occupied countries to resist the Nazi example. Beneš, Maisky, and other prominent diplomats were asked in interviews to support a collective declaration dealing specifically with the Jewish catastrophe and with immediate measures of rescue. A press conference sponsored by Silverman and Easterman on December 1 publicized the slaughter of a minimum of two million Jews, with Schwartzbart warning the West, in the recently received words of the Polish underground movement, to "believe the unbelievable!"[65]

Count Raczynski had not believed the original Bund cable about the annihilation of Polish Jewry. When Zygielbojm, speaking with "passion and despair," first conveyed its message to him a half-year earlier, the foreign minister doubted that the Nazis were carrying out the "total genocide" of a people. The information, which Raczynski then imparted to Prime Minister Sikorski and other officials of his government in May, had been confirmed a few days later by other sources, however. Still, as late as November 25 Raczynski had informed the anxious Representatives of Polish Jewry in Palestine only that the evacuation of all Jews from the Warsaw ghetto had not been confirmed. Zygielbojm's impressive pleas, prodding by Schwartzbart and the WJC, and particularly Karski's eyewitness report finally made their decisive mark.[66]

On December 1, the Polish ministry of information issued a special press bulletin that reported in full the destruction of the Warsaw ghetto. That same morning Raczynski drew Foreign Secretary Eden's attention in a private audience to the "wholesale destruction" of Jews in Poland. He also suggested that another conference of the occupied countries be held at St. James Palace, with HMG only required there in the capacity of an observer. This seemed "cold comfort" for the Jews, the British official replied, but the Polish diplomat felt that the occasion would cause them "some measure of satisfaction" and might be used to warn Laval against further deportations from France. Eden promised to give an official response within 48 hours.[67]

When December 2, 1942, dawned, Jews in 29 countries began a day of fasting, prayer, and mourning for their murdered families in Europe. Thousands of Jewish children in Palestine converged on the Western Wall while their parents crowded houses of prayer; aged Kabbalists gathered in their synagogue in Jerusalem's Old City and proclaimed anathemas on the Nazi hierarchy. Jews in Safed donned the yellow stars that marked their families in Europe for death, while a crowd of 100,000 in Tel Aviv, marching silently behind Torah scrolls, gathered at Habima Square to burn the swastika and an effigy of Hitler. About 500,000 Jewish workers in New York City observed a ten-minute work stoppage, joined by non-Jews who participated in shop meetings that condemned the massacre abroad, while rabbis carried the Torah in an East Broadway procession. Several radio stations in the metropolitan area observed two minutes of silence and then broadcast a memorial service over the Blue Network. The entire Jewish press in America appealed to the United Nations from black-bordered editions for effective rescue measures. Jewish businesses closed for the day in South America and Canada; synagogues were filled to overflowing. Newspaper editorials across the free world expressed sympathy to those singled out by the Third Reich for death.[68]

The Joint Emergency Committee in New York issued a proclamation to commemorate Jewry's "unspeakable grief and travail." Calling Hitler's satanic success "the greatest calamity in Jewish history" since the razing of the Second Temple, the leading Jewish organizations turned "once again to Him who has been the Guide and Guardian of Israel throughout all generations" for solace. By then the group had expected American Jews' mortal savior to agree to receive a small delegation at the White House, its purpose to obtain an official statement like the one

Roosevelt had made after the destruction of Lidice and its inhabitants. White House staffer David Niles was pressed by Wise to intervene for this end as well.[69] With still no reply in hand on this day of universal mourning, Stephen Wise penned a personal appeal to the "Boss" he worshipped.

"I do not wish to add an atom to the awful burden which you are bearing with magic and, as I believe, heaven-inspired strength at this time," the WJC president began. "But you do know that the most overwhelming disaster of Jewish history has befallen Jews in the form of the Hitler mass-massacres." Together with the heads of other Jewish organizations, he had kept the reports out of the press at Welles's request until the State Department confirmed that two million "civilian Jews" had been slain in Europe. The joint committee that he chaired wished to present Roosevelt with a memorandum on "these unspeakable horrors." "It would be gravely misunderstood," he closed, "if, despite your overwhelming preoccupation, you did not make it possible to receive our delegation and to utter what I am sure will be your heartening and consoling reply." Wise's *Congress Weekly* published some of Riegner's reports in full two days later, yet editorialized at the same time that "the spirit will triumph" against the dominance of force.[70]

British Jewry decided to mobilize its own forces on the afternoon of December 3. Selig Brodetsky, chairman of the Board of Deputies, insisted at an emergency meeting of major Jewish organizations that the Ministry of Information, the BBC, and the Department of Political Warfare had yet to raise the question before the public; the Foreign Office, the final arbiter, would just not be persuaded that the most authoritative sources were reliable. The different representatives offered their views about action, some cautiously arguing that a demonstration would be "out of keeping" with the public mood. Zygielbojm and Schwartzbart reported on their meeting with Jan Karski the previous day, in which the secret courier reiterated the substance of his previous talk with the Jewish Bundist. Easterman then relayed information, just received in a telephone call from Silverman, conveying Eden's private statement that Whitehall's doubts had now been overcome: it would support an Allied declaration dealing expressly with the Jewish crisis. The group then agreed to press for a United Nations declaration and to seek an appointment with the foreign secretary. Chief Rabbi Joseph H. Hertz issued a call for December 13 as a day of mourning and fasting by all Jews in the empire.[71]

The WJC's initiative and mounting pressure from various quarters brought about the significant reverse in the Foreign Office position. Frank Roberts of the Central Department, who thought that Raczynski's suggestion for an Allied conference would only result in vague resolutions, had stressed to his colleagues that "reliable evidence" did not exist for the atrocities reported. But Ivan Maisky told Eden that a three-power declaration was desirable and also "might give the unhappy Jews some comfort," a view in which the United States' John Winant concurred. Eden followed up this prompting by sending the two ambassadors a draft for their respective governments' views on the morning of December 8. ("Speed seems desirable," Denis Allen privately minuted, because Silverman had scheduled a question in Commons on the subject, and an aroused public wished Britain's response.)

Reports from Europe, HMG's proposed statement read, "leave no room for doubt that the German authorities are now carrying into effect Hitler's oft-repeated intention to exterminate the Jewish population in Europe." The three governments, it concluded, "condemn in the strongest possible terms this bestial policy," and "affirm their resolve to ensure that those responsible for these crimes shall not escape retribution, and to press on with the necessary practical measures to this end."[72]

At noon the same day, Wise, Henry Monsky of B'nai Brith, Adolf Held of the Jewish Labor Committee, Maurice Wertheim of the American Jewish Committee, and Israel Rosenberg of the Union of Orthodox Rabbis of the United States and Canada took seats in the Oval Office.[73]

"I am a sadist, a man of extreme sadist tendencies," Roosevelt began. He had appointed Herbert Lehman, New York's Jewish governor, to head the new Office of Foreign Relief and Rehabilitation Operations not only for his great administrative skills. The president hoped to stand behind a curtain in Germany after the war, and have the "sadistic satisfaction" of seeing some "Junkers" on their knees before Lehman, asking for bread. "And, by God, I'll urge him to give it to them." With the chief executive's permission, Rabbi Rosenberg then delivered the traditional Jewish blessing upon a country's head of state. Wise followed with a reading of the Joint Emergency Committee's declaration about the Holocaust, submitted the group's detailed 20-page memorandum on how almost two million Jews had been killed by the Nazis, and appealed to Roosevelt to do all in his power to bring this to the world's attention and "to make an effort to stop it."

"The government of the United States is very well acquainted with most of the facts you are now bringing to our attention," the president replied. Unfortunately, confirmation had come from representatives of the American government in Switzerland and other neutral countries. The problem was very difficult, he continued, because Hitler and his entourage "represent an example of a national psychopathic case." At the same time, the Allied cause ought not to make it appear that the entire German people were murderers or agreed with Hitler's actions. There must be elements in Germany, now completely subdued, who "at the proper time" would protest against the atrocities and the entire

Hitler regime. It was too early to make pronouncements in the fashion of President Wilson during the last world war, but he would certainly be glad to issue another statement such as they requested.

He then asked those present for suggestions and, only after a minute or two, plunged into a discussion of the problem of Jewish rights in North Africa. No reason existed for Jews and Frenchmen there to enjoy greater privileges than the area's 17 million Moslems. The United States supported equal rights for all, and thus "so vehemently" opposed attacks on Jews in Germany and Poland as an assault on American ideals of freedom and justice. As for the country's support of Vichy's Admiral Darlan in North Africa, a proverb recently heard from a Yugoslav priest was most apt: "When a river you reach and the devil you meet, with the devil do not quarrel until the bridge you cross."

Some hidden button must have been pushed, for at that moment the president's adjutant appeared. As the delegation rose, Roosevelt granted the group permission that its press release carry his statement to the July mass meeting in Madison Square Garden, but it had to be quoted exactly. "We shall do all in our power to be of service to your people in this tragic moment," he concluded. The four men, after shaking hands with the president, filed out of the room.

The delegation issued its release the same day. Quoting Roosevelt— "The mills of the gods grind slowly, but they grind exceedingly small"—it repeated his July and October assertions that the guilty would be held strictly accountable after the war. Departing, however, from the president's actual remarks, the release claimed that Roosevelt was "profoundly shocked" to hear that two million Jews had perished, and that the assurance had been extended that "the United Nations are prepared to take every possible step" to halt the massacres and "save those who may still be saved."[74]

"Most encouraging," the American Jewish Congress cabled to Easterman and Barou. Wrote Wise to Niles: "We ought to distribute cards throughout the country bearing just four letters TGFR [Thank God for Roosevelt], and as the Psalmist would have said, thank Him every day and every hour." Yet Roosevelt, who gave the Jewish spokesmen but six minutes to comment in the half-hour interview, had said nothing of the immediate action requested in the delegation's covering letter.[75] What if the remaining victims died by the time the mills of retribution ground to their fine end?

Demands for specific efforts mounted from various quarters. The Jewish National Council of Palestine urged the three major Allied statesmen to issue warnings, exchange Germans for Jews, rescue children, and approve a Jewish army to fight Hitler. Congressman Samuel Dickstein (Democrat from New York) appealed on the floor of the House for the

Vatican's intervention. Sixty-three senators and 182 congressmen, insisting that "the case for a Jewish homeland is overwhelmingly stronger and the need more urgent now than ever before," petitioned Roosevelt to support the restoration of the Jewish national home in Palestine.[76]

More diversified reactions were powerfully expressed in Great Britain. The day after reviewing the Nazi "Deliberate Plan for Extermination," the *London Times* published a letter from William Temple, the archbishop of Canterbury, that called for an Allied statement and the granting of asylum in Britain to any Jew able to escape the Nazi inferno. Such a declaration, the British WJC publicly emphasized, should contain an appeal that all Europeans protect Jews, especially children; that the neutral countries open their frontiers to escaping refugees; and that the United Nations stand as their guarantors. The Polish government, Count Raczynski informed Zygielbojm, sought to obtain Allied approval for reprisals against Nazi prisoners in Allied hands and the dropping over Germany of reports about the atrocities. On the same day that Schwartzbart issued Karski's report to the press, the *London Times* reported that the Nazi radio was broadcasting the date when each occupied country must be cleared of Jews; the august newspaper wondered if the Allied governments even now could do anything to check this diabolic murder plan. Jan Masaryk exhorted Czechs and Slovaks over the BBC airwaves to "do everything in their power to make easier the life of their Jewish fellow-citizens." Temple, also president of the British Council of Christians and Jews, simultaneously repeated his appeal to Eden and asked the foreign secretary to receive its delegation.[77]

The drumbeat of pressure intensified on December 9, 1942, when Raczynski addressed a diplomatic note to the Allied governments concerning Germany's clear efforts to destroy the Jews in his native country. Information received from underground sources in recent weeks, the memorandum began, indicated beyond doubt that "the German authorities aim with systematic deliberation at the total extermination of the Jewish population of Poland" and of many thousands of Jews "deported there from Western and Central Europe." Of the 3,130,000 Jews in Poland before the Nazi invasion, over one-third had perished. The Polish government confidently believed that the United Nations would condemn the barbarities, punish the criminals, and find means of "offering the hope that Germany might be effectively restrained from continuing to apply its methods of mass extermination."[78]

The note required a formal response. Writing on Eden's behalf, Roberts conveyed HMG's deep sympathy for the suffering now being inflicted upon "the unfortunate inhabitants of Poland." These atrocities strengthened Britain's resolution to achieve final victory, at which time all the guilty would be punished. The suggested joint declaration of the three

major Allies would condemn the German policy "so ruthlessly pursued."
No word was said of "Jews" or the immediate action requested in the
Polish *aide-mémoire*.[79]

Three days passed before the State Department accepted the Foreign
Office's draft for an Anglo-American declaration. Cautious regarding
rescue and anxious to avoid the "host of unguarded statements" made
by statesmen immediately after World War I, Secretary Hull inserted
"numerous" before "reports" and omitted the phrase "leave no room for
doubt." His designated specialist on Jewish affairs, however, objected to
the entire statement: while the proposed draft did not mention the "soap,
glue, oil and fertilizer factories," publication would support Wise's claim
of State verification. "The way will then be open for further pressure
from interested groups for action which might affect the war effort,"
Robert Reams observed to his superiors. Various memoranda from the
Polish and Czech governments-in-exile, Donald Lowrie of the YMCA,
and other Gentile organizations about the Nazi killings had indeed
cleared his desk throughout the past few months. Yet Reams now privately told various concerned quarters that these reports had not been
authenticated and that, he quickly added, the primary sources about the
alleged order for complete annihilation were Jewish. A reaffirmation of
the previously expressed Allied statements on war criminals would, in
his opinion, be "adequate."[80]

Whitehall bureaucrats expressed concern over the delay. Allen considered it "tiresome" in view of postponed parliamentary questions since
July, the Polish government's concern, and the forthcoming debate on
the question in Commons. Besides, the prime minister himself had dem-
onstrated a personal interest, having asked the Foreign Office for further
information after seeing Raczynski's note. Reams's objections to the
"extremely strong and definite" British draft, as expressed to a member
of the British embassy in Washington, included his feeling that its public
issue would aggravate the fears of world Jewry, augment "increased pressure from all sides" for the Allies to "do something more specific in
order to aid these people," and "might well strengthen German oppres-
sive measures." These reservations, HMG now concluded, appeared most
questionable.[81]

When Ambassador Halifax in Washington discussed the matter with
Welles on the morning of December 11, the American under secretary
expressed annoyance at his ally's anxieties. Certainly State wished to go
along with London regarding a statement, Welles insisted, although it
might have made some verbal suggestions. Hull's changes, together with
Reams's insistence that the words about deportations "irrespective of
age and sex" be excluded, since (he incorrectly asserted) that had not
been the case up to the present in France and might not be true else-

where, completed the American amendments. As the clock struck midnight, Hull wired Winant his approval subject to these revisions.[82]

The Russian government's response followed. The Soviets had never adopted a specifically humanitarian policy to save Jews *per se* during the war, and their official silence about Nazi brutalities in Poland prior to June, 1941, had made hundreds of thousands of unaware Jews an easy mark for the SS *Einsatzgruppen*. The German invasion, however, led Molotov to include the mass slaughter of Jews in his January, 1942, note about German atrocities against the Russian population, and to announce that his government was preparing a detailed registry of these crimes for punishment. Ambassador Maisky in London consistently supported the British WJC in its campaign for an Allied joint statement directed to Jewry's singular fate. In mid-October and again in early November Molotov applauded Roosevelt's conviction that the Nazi leadership should be brought to trial, but he added that these individuals should appear before a "special international tribunal" and be punished without delay. The draft declaration on the Final Solution would therefore be acceptable. Only one sentence, echoing Molotov's January note, was added on December 12 to that touching on mass executions: "The number of victims of these sanguinary punishments is taken to amount to many hundreds of thousands of quite innocent, men, women and children."[83]

The three major allies reached unanimity on December 14. By then the Poles had abandoned their proposal for another conference at St. James Palace. Still, they and the various Allied governments in London wished to participate as signatories: any absence, they argued, would be misunderstood by their home populations, since the great majority of the victims were their nationals, while German propaganda chief Joseph Goebbels would assert that it reflected differences on the issue within the Allied camp. A disturbed Welles thought it unnecessary that Charles DeGaulle's French National Committee be included at all, Halifax reported, and, as a last resort, wished the word "also" to separate the committee from the other signatories. Eden replied that since all concerned had given their consent to this customary diplomatic parlance, it would be impossible to clear the change before the agreed time of release.[84]

A meeting between Law and Christian representatives from the British Council of Christians and Jews the same day suggested the constraints then operating within Foreign Office counsels. William Temple echoed the delegation's interest in a firm United Nations declaration condemning the atrocities and promising refuge to any who might escape. Guarantees to neutral countries, his colleagues added, as well as a less rigid policy by British Home Secretary Herbert Morrison would markedly help. The group expressed an interest in a detailed, factual statement of

the massacres in order to convince skeptics of the problem's seriousness
and urgency.

In reply, Law announced that a declaration would be forthcoming.
While "the balance of probability . . . overwhelmingly" favored the "substantial truth" of the atrocity stories, the Foreign Office had "very little
clear evidence." If such statements were published with the reports at
hand, although "the broad picture" would be correct, the great likelihood
that many details could be in error presented the danger that "the whole
story would be discredited." The subsequent effect on our influence in
Europe would be "very bad." The danger also existed, he agreed with
one visitor, that the practical effect of a moral "harangue" to the Nazis
might goad them into further excesses. As for the observation that assurance of asylum would benefit escaping Jews and have a much more
"positive effect on public opinion at large," Law explained in confidence
that such a step might get us "involved in some kind of super-Balfour
Declaration which would dog our footsteps forever." He promised to
inquire regarding the neutrals most disposed to be friendly, but did not
hold out very high hopes.[85]

It only remained for Law to arrange that Silverman, the most appropriate choice, introduce the subject in the Mother of Parliaments. The
under secretary had shown the declaration to Easterman, who was visiting him during the morning of the 14th on behalf of Silverman. The
WJC's political secretary had wished to see the words "directly or indirectly" inserted concerning those responsible, as well as an appeal to
non-Jewish populations to protect Jews and a St. James Palace conference for the sake of wide publicity. Law replied to these requests in a
private talk with Silverman, followed by a letter to Easterman, arguing
that "tinkering" could hardly take place after Allied approval had been
obtained. The British authorities were also "pressed to state their attitude with the least possible delay," and a public conference would entail
further procrastination. Easterman's point about those responsible, which
Law appreciated, could be met by Silverman's addressing a supplementary question following Eden's announcement of the declaration.[86] The
statement would be issued on the morrow at noon British War Time,
and simultaneously in Washington and Moscow.

On December 17, 1942, Foreign Secretary Eden rose in the House of
Commons. Responding to Silverman's query as to whether he had any
statement to make regarding the German massacres of Jews, he respect-
fully informed the members that "reliable reports" had "recently" reached
HMG concerning "the barbarous and inhuman treatment to which Jews
are being subjected in German-occupied Europe." In particular, a note
from the Polish government, widely publicized in the press, had been
submitted to the United Nations. The British authorities had consequently consulted with their two major allies and the other democracies

concerned. All had agreed on the following declaration, which London, Moscow, and Washington were issuing at this hour:

> The attention of the Governments of Belgium, Czechoslovakia, Greece, Luxembourg, the Netherlands, Norway, Poland, the United States of America, the United Kingdom of Great Britain and Northern Ireland, the Union of Soviet Socialist Republics and Yugoslavia, and of the French National Committee has been drawn to numerous reports from Europe that the German authorities, not content with denying to persons of Jewish race in all the territories over which their barbarous rule has been extended the most elementary human rights, are now carrying into effect Hitler's oft repeated intention to exterminate the Jewish people in Europe. From all the occupied countries Jews are being transported, in conditions of appalling horror and brutality, to Eastern Europe. In Poland, which has been made the principal Nazi slaughterhouse, the ghettos established by the German invaders are being systematically emptied of all Jews except a few highly skilled workers required for war industries. None of those taken away are ever heard of again. The able-bodied are slowly worked to death in labour camps. The infirm are left to die of exposure and starvation or are deliberately massacred in mass executions. The number of victims of these bloody cruelties is reckoned in many hundreds of thousands of entirely innocent men, women and children.
>
> The above mentioned Governments and the French National Committee condemn in the strongest possible terms this bestial policy of cold-blooded extermination. They declare that such events can only strengthen the resolve of all freedom loving peoples to overthrow the barbarous Hitlerite tyranny. They reaffirm their solemn resolution to ensure that those responsible for these crimes shall not escape retribution, and to press on with the necessary practical measures to this end.

Eden's further remarks reflected the declaration's deliberate silence on possible Allied relief and rescue for European Jewry. To Silverman's two supplementary questions for clarification, the foreign secretary agreed that all associated with the crimes would be held responsible, but as for alleviating these horrors, "I fear that what we can do at this stage must inevitably be slight." After another M.P. also failed to obtain a commitment from Eden on aid via the neutrals, James de Rothschild movingly thanked the British government as one of its grateful subjects who, but for the grace of God, might have been included among the Nazis' victims. Eden pointed out that BBC broadcasts to Axis-held territory would publicize retribution for all the guilty and appreciation for those aiding the persecuted. Again, however, unspecified "immense geographical and other difficulties" existed regarding the grant of asylum to fortunate escapees.[87]

At the spontaneous suggestion of a non-Jewish Labor party member from London's East End, center of British Jewry, the House then stood for two minutes of frozen silence. "It had a far greater dramatic effect than I had expected," Eden later wrote in his diary, a scene the likes of which Lloyd George for one could not recall in all his years in Parliament. A short while later Viscount Simon read the declaration in the House of Lords. The same expressions of gratitude followed, mixed with concerned appeals, as the bishop of London expressed it, to "remove that sense of impotence now to bring help to those who suffer."[88]

The quintessential issue remained unresolved: would the "immense difficulties" darkly alluded to by Eden bow before what one member termed "the plain call of common humanity"? For the first time since the war's eruption, the democracies had admitted publicly that the Jews were undergoing systematic annihilation. After four precious months had passed between the receipt in London and Washington of Riegner's cable and the United Nations Declaration on Jewish Massacres, the cries of a people writhing in agony received official acknowledgment. Only positive action, however, could bring some succor. Unknown to the Allies, the "improved" crematoria ordered for Auschwitz-Birkenau, which would prove capable before long of polluting Europe's skies with the ashes of 500 human bodies per hour, were not yet in operation. But while these devices remained on the drawing boards of Erfurt's I. A. Topf and Sons, other machines of death continued remorselessly to take their toll. Well over two million Jews, according to a secret German report prepared at Himmler's request, had already perished, and time was running desperately short for the rest of the entire community on Axis-held soil.[89]

CONCLUSION

An inability to perceive that Hitler actually meant to kill every one of their European co-religionists explains the initial response of Jews in the free world to Riegner's cabled alert. Not only did the Nazi decision and its efficient execution lack historical precedent, but earlier news reports, sometimes contradicting one another, had spoken of mass murder—never a total plan. Thus at the Biltmore conference of May, 1942, Chaim Weizmann optimistically concluded that some 25 percent of the Jews in southern and eastern Europe might be "liquidated" during the war, but the two to four million homeless Jews thereafter could be absorbed in Palestine. Even the August telegram in question, aside from its factual inaccuracies, passed on the rumor with "all necessary reservation." A leading Bundist and former member of the Polish Sejm mocked Reigner's reports, during a closed meeting that October of Jewish notables in Geneva, as the exaggerations of a fertile imagination. The hesitations of Stephen Wise, Alfred

Silberschein, Chaim Barlas, the Board of Deputies, the Jewish Agency Executive, and the *Jewish Frontier* staff could be further augmented by the receipt of Allied approval, concomitantly given, to send food parcels to the Polish ghettos. The word of government officialdom that deportations meant forced labor at the German front also proved comforting, especially as these assurances might lighten a crushing sense of despair and helplessness in the face of the gravest responsibility. Under these conditions, solitary individuals like Pozner, Riegner, Lichtheim, Kühl, Zygielbojm, Schwartzbart, Frischer, Easterman, and Kubowitzki faced almost insurmountable challenges in transforming the shocking truth into a grasped reality.[90]

Once the unbelievable had been comprehended, Jewish communities experienced great difficulty in overcoming continued interorganizational rifts and differences about rescue tactics. Only the agreement that their consultation would be temporary obtained the cooperation of rival American Jewish groups; the long-established Joint Foreign Committee did not coordinate activity with the WJC's British section and Agudas Israel. The Yishuv's different political bodies also moved slowly to achieve a unity of purpose. The specter of rising domestic antisemitism and restrictionist sentiment in the United States and Great Britain played another role in convincing many to temper demands on behalf of a foreign minority. While completely beguiled by Roosevelt's personality and promises of help, an anguished Wise also keenly realized that many examples could be drawn from American history of failed ethnic politics, particularly in time of war. Lacking political leverage and uncertain about the frightful telegrams from Switzerland, the venerable leader had to pledge silence to Welles in order to maintain a conduit to his primary Geneva source and obtain confirmation from the only receptive ear at State. Thus did he become a tragic partner, rather than simply stereotyped "court Jew," in State Department and Foreign Office procrastination.[91]

Skepticism within the Anglo-American Alliance contributed to the gruesome end result. Ample proof to establish "at least a *prima facie* case" for the existence of a plan of total murder existed in State's files prior to August, 1942, yet the department suppressed Riegner's cable as unreliable and not involving "definite American interests." It would do so again the coming February. While passing on Riegner's message to Silverman, and thus to Wise, the Foreign Office's logical doubts about particular incidents, about the use of corpses for soap and fertilizer reminiscent of World War I propaganda, and about an overall Nazi plan to kill the remaining Jews "at one blow" delayed a much-called-for response. Available Polish government sources focused on Himmler's order to wipe out the Warsaw ghetto, Whitehall's expert on the matter observed in early December, not on a Hitler directive for complete destruction. "In our exchanges of information with the British Foreign Office," the

Polish foreign minister reminisced years later, "we had to be absolutely precise and most careful not to expose ourselves to the reproach of exaggeration. The number of Jews massacred in 1942 could only be surmised." Increased public pressure and Raczynski's note brought final acknowledgment, but Eden's presentation of the proposed declaration before the War Cabinet on December 14 suggested the limits of belief: "... while there was no direct confirmation of these reports so far as concerned the methods used, there were indications that large-scale massacres of Jews were taking place in Poland. It was known that Jews were being transferred to Poland from enemy-occupied countries, for example Norway; and it might well be that these transfers were being made with a view to wholesale extermination of Jews."[92] Given these reservations, mention of specific measures for rescue never found its way into the final draft.

Official action did not follow information about the Holocaust because the survival of European Jewry rated a low priority in the titanic Allied struggle against Hitler. Durbrow of the State Department's European Division decided early that any assistance would be "impossible"; Squire's report of September 28 took almost a month to reach Washington; Reams warned that a declaration would bring unwelcome agitation that might jeopardize the war effort. Law expressed anxiety about getting HMG enmeshed in "some super-Balfour Declaration"; Eden, who preferred the return of Jews to their former countries in Europe after the war rather than their settling in Palestine, hinted in Parliament at tremendous difficulties regarding the possibility of rescue. The same day that Wise and the Polish government released their reports, the Allies decreed that all engaging in the purchase of exit visas to ransom Jews would be considered guilty of trading with the enemy. Reprisals against Germans were ruled out then and subsequently as not the best way to achieve quick victory. Other rescue suggestions would also be turned down later on the same principle.[93] Premature publicity by Wise and Silverman, then, against State and Foreign Office wishes would have accomplished little but alienating the two governments even further.

In not according Hitler's prime enemy a distinct national entity, the Anglo-American Alliance could conveniently relegate the difficult "Jewish question" to the postwar period. To shift a congressional focus on Palestine as the logical Jewish haven, particularly given State's fears of Arab hostility, Secretary Hull called for a world in which Jews should be as free as others "to abide in peace and honor." The principle had to be kept that each Allied government spoke for all its nationals, the Foreign Office consistently argued in like vein. To "segregate" Jews as "a racial problem in Europe," Law wrote the Conservative party chairman, "would play into the hands of anti-Semitism." Moreover, Whitehall would be in for "serious complications" (including rescue, the thorny

Palestine issue, and future reparations) if Jews received separate status. Even Winston Churchill, strongly moved by the Nazi atrocities and impressed with Zionist claims, promised retribution only after the hour of liberation had struck in Europe.[94] By then the doom of an entire people on that continent would be sealed.

The individual in whom the Jews placed their greatest trust also failed to seize the hour. Franklin D. Roosevelt had information on the Holocaust long before Wise's press statement of November 24, 1942, but, as with the War Crimes Commission, he allowed the issue to come to a head before making a move of, in fact, no immediate consequence. The chief executive turned down Sikorski's private appeal for large-scale bombing in retaliation for German savagery, arguing that "the victims" could be "entirely safe from these recurring cruelties only when the military might of the Axis powers has been thoroughly crushed." He also proved unwilling to ask Congress about admitting thousands of Polish women and children, currently released from Soviet camps, fearing "anti-semitic agitation" upon the inclusion of many Jews. When Sam Rayburn pointed out that the president's private suggestion of loosening immigration restrictions would meet with "great opposition," Roosevelt quickly assured the Speaker of the House that he only wished to "make it clear that the responsibility was that of Congress." The administration's silence kept the American public ignorant and therefore unaroused; it also let Nazi propaganda chief Goebbels, writing in his diary on December 13, 1942, conclude: "at bottom, however, I believe both the English and the Americans are happy that we are exterminating the Jewish riff-raff." The occupant of 1600 Pennsylvania Avenue chose not to press State and Whitehall for a dramatic shift to unequivocal rescue action, and refused to consider any compromise on the Allies' grand strategy of "Unconditional Surrender." Such a decision was considerably easier than grappling with the vexing and urgent problem at hand.

Rather, FDR looked to the future. He openly pledged punishment for some Nazi leaders after V-E day, and considered himself a "sadist" in appointing Herbert Lehman to handle postwar relief for Germany. Roosevelt preferred to speak to Secretary Morgenthau of later Jewish settlement in Palestine, Ecuador, some virgin territory west of the Colombian Andes, and elsewhere on the globe.[95]

No direct acknowledgment of the Holocaust ever came from the Vatican. Well before Riegner's cable had reached the State Department, Harold Tittman, assistant to Myron Taylor, informally reminded the Holy See that its failure to protest against the Nazi atrocities publicly was "endangering its moral prestige and undermining faith both in the church and in the Holy Father himself." Various Allied representatives unsuccessfully pressed the pope to assert his moral position. Years later the official Vatican documentary record explained that first reports were "enigmatic" regarding the ultimate destination of the deportees and the Nazi plan. Yet an Italian priest who had been in Poland wrote to Pius XII on May 12, 1942, that the Germans had by then completed the massacre of Ukrainian Jewry, and "equally desired" to follow suit in Poland and in Germany "with a system of mass killings." Polish memoranda received in St. Peter's as early as July 12 plainly spoke of gas chambers and provided figures of mass executions in Vilna, Lwow, and a number of other cities; at the end of August SS Lt. Col. Kurt Gerstein gave the legal advisor of Berlin's Bishop Preysing (among many others) his personal eyewitness account about the gassing of Jews in Belzec; a Vatican source on November 23 provided further details to the State Department on the death of thousands in Poland by poison gas or machinegun fire. Pius XII's Christmas broadcast allusion (at last) to the mass deportations of European Jewry was, as British minister Francis Osborne pointed out to London, inferential, did not specify the victims, "and came at the end of a long dissertation on social problems." In forwarding the United Nations Declaration on Jewish Massacres, HMG's representative suggested that the pope endorse it publicly or at least encourage German Christians, particularly Catholics, "to do all in their power to restrain these excesses." The Vatican firmly stood its pious ground.[96]

The International Commitee of the Red Cross in Geneva also held to a strict neutrality. Swiss medical missions, having visited Germany's eastern front at the end of 1941 and the spring of 1942, knew of the atrocities committed there. The chief physician in the northern military hospital of Smolensk, for example, told a member on the first inspection team about gas chambers, crematoria, and the testing of such instruments of murder in Auschwitz. This conversation and personal observations were passed in March, 1942, to the Judge Advocat General of the Army, as well as to numerous audiences in Switzerland. The second group visited the Warsaw ghetto, where people had learned "that for them there were only blows, hunger, and early death." Although the Swiss general staff obtained a prohibition on all statements about the two visits, Riegner would find out 37 years later that the president of the Swiss Red Cross had joined the second mission at the last minute and subsequently passed his impressions to his colleagues on the ICRC. Carl Burckhardt therefore had this information, along with the two other reports on the Final Solution which he mentioned to Squire. Still, his uncharacteristically bold and vitally important step in corroborating Guggenheim's affidavit on November 7 did not preclude Burckhardt from feeling satisfaction, as Riegner heard at the time from two sympathetic women on the ICRC, when his committee voted shortly thereafter not to condemn the atrocities. Burckhardt's subsequent wariness represented yet another failure of the will and of the heart.[97]

"WHERE ARE THE DEMOCRATIC GOVERNMENTS?" cried black-bordered placards in Tel Aviv on December 2, 1942. The Jews in the West, like those under the Nazi yoke, were naive in thinking that the Allies would respond meaningfully to the great moral issue at stake if knowledge of their fate became available. Riegner, who had written to Goldmann at the close of October, 1941, in favor of a declaration by the London-based governments-in-exile nullifying anti-Jewish Axis laws, greeted the United Nations declaration with the great expectation that action might follow at last. Yet, "sitting in a hole" in Geneva or living elsewhere in the free world, had he and other Jewish representatives any choice but to trust the democracies? And these governments, however "embarrassed" over demands for rescue and however illogical their argument, given the present awareness of the Final Solution, that some concrete effort might provoke "greater" Nazi excesses, also knew this question to be one-sided. Silverman poignantly captured the same tragic situation that confronted Wise, writing to Easterman that if he published Riegner's message without Foreign Office approval, "they won't transmit any other messages and will be impervious to further approaches. That would not stop me if publicity, or any other action, at once would be of active practical utility. Unfortunately it won't. It is, after all, the protest of the lamb to the wolf."[98] As long as the United Nations limited their acknowledgment to pieties rather than the deeds requested by Jew and Gentile once the facts became known, the sacrificial lamb in Europe would be drawn without check to the altar.

The historic declaration of December, 1942, accomplished nothing because both Western governments refused to treat Jews as a distinct ally requiring emergency rescue. Indeed, it represented the only Allied pronouncement on the Holocaust throughout the war. In April, 1943, Zygielbojm responded in his own heroic way to Feiner's message; a suicide note, pleading with Churchill, Roosevelt, and the free world to intervene at the twelfth hour, went unacknowledged. Half a year later the two leaders joined with Stalin to issue a long statement against German barbarities—with Jewry conspicuously absent.[99]

That people would fall victim to the democracies' procrastination and unsurpassed callousness, as well as to the Nazis' prussic acid, first mentioned to London and Washington in Riegner's cable of August 8, 1942. Zyklon-B, the efficient solidification of hydrogen and cyanide in crystal form, passed through concealed ducts into gas chambers crammed with blameless and forgotten human beings. Exposed to the damp air hovering over hundreds of naked bodies, the pellets formed a gas. Within 15 minutes all the tightly pressed innocents in the simulated shower rooms suffocated to death.[100] And from Allied and Axis camps alike, thunderous silence.

The Bermuda Conference
and Its Aftermath

THE AWAKENING OF the conscience of the Allied nations to the attempted annihilation of the Jewish people by the Third Reich began on December 17, 1942. That Thursday morning British Foreign Secretary Anthony Eden announced in the House of Commons that 11 of the United Nations and the French National Committee condemned "in the strongest terms this bestial policy of cold-blooded extermination" and resolved to bring its perpetrators to justice. That same hour Moscow and Washington saw publication of the United Nations Declaration on Jewish Massacres.[1]

It had been four months since the British and U.S. governments had first received a report from the Geneva office of the WJC about the rumored Nazi plan to kill all of European Jewry. On December 1 the Polish government-in-exile's ministry of information chronicled the horrors in a report entitled "Extermination of the Polish Jewry." But at a time when, as one U.S. senator estimated, Europe's Jews were being slaughtered at a rate of five per minute, most newspapers buried in the back pages the stark reality of some two million Jews killed since the beginning of the war.[2]

Jewish leaders in America and England hailed the United Nations declaration. Some of those who had recently met with President Roosevelt to urge Allied intervention on behalf of European Jewry asserted that the statement would "solace and hearten the Jewish people throughout the world." The same day that the declaration was broadcast in 23 languages to all countries in Nazi-occupied Europe, Selig Brodetsky, president of the Board of Deputies of British Jews, wrote Eden that Jews would see it as "a further high example of the traditional British attitude in all that concerns humanity and civilization."[3]

At the same time most demanded immediate action rather than retribution after the war. "It is good but not good enough," declared the *New York Post.* The United Nations Information Office's detailed memorandum *Persecution of Jews,* issued on December 19, resulted in a spate of editorials in Great Britain calling for action. While the Nazi ministry of propaganda termed (for the benefit of neutral countries) the declaration "a bit of typical British-Jewish atrocity propaganda," Eleanor Rathbone (Independent M.P.) urged her government to lead the neutrals by relaxing immigration restrictions. Polish officials called for retaliation against the Nazis. Others insisted that the 1939 White Paper limiting Jewish immigration to Palestine to 75,000 by April, 1944, be lifted, and that the United Nations welcome all Jews escaping from Axis Europe.[4]

The pressure on Great Britain to implement the intentions of the joint Allied statement mounted. Armed with a first-hand report from Poland about the murders that began in the Warsaw ghetto in mid-July and the burning of Jewish corpses within an area of 50 kilometers in Belzec, Bundist representative Szmul Zygielbojm of the Polish National Council conveyed to Churchill and Roosevelt on December 19 an appeal from Jewish survivors in Poland. Four days later a delegation of Britain's Jews recommended to Eden that the International Red Cross and the Vatican be asked to cooperate and that Jewish escapees be admitted to every Allied or neutral territory, especially Palestine. They wanted leaflets denouncing the atrocities dropped over Germany and the Third Reich asked to allow Jews, particularly women and children, to leave. Harold Nicholson (Laborite M.P.) urged the British government to "revise its obstinate policy on refugees" and to approach the Palestine problem "with greater energy, imagination and unselfishness." The *New Statesman and Nation* insisted that the British government request Sweden and Turkey to save Jewish children and open its own doors as well. Parliamentary Under Secretary Richard Law heard suggestions from the Board of Deputies on December 30 that neutral governments be given guarantees that the refugees would be moved from their territories by the war's end and that short-term accommodation could be found in North Africa, Palestine, the Isle of Man, Eire, and the United States.[5]

The Foreign Office had hitherto taken the lead in responding to the awesome tidings. Unlike its Washington counterpart, it had forwarded the Riegner cable about the Nazi murder plan the previous August. Only in this fashion did Stephen Wise learn of it and press Welles for help. The British authorities had often urged the State Department to establish a joint war crimes commission, and their threat of a unilateral commission or similar organization forced the American government to concur two days before the intended deadline of October 7. Eden and Law, "genuinely horrified and moved" by reports from the WJC's Alexander Easterman and others, had pressed for and finally achieved the Allied declaration.[6]

The Foreign Office objected, however, to emphasizing the plight of the Jewish people, and had grave doubts about the possibilities for rescue. It wished to treat Jews as "nationals of existing countries," and not to grant the formation of an individual Allied force composed of Palestinian and other Jews or separate representation of Jewish concerns at international conferences. Arab unrest, in Whitehall's opinion, required that Zionist agitation for a Jewish state in Palestine be dampened. The foreign secretary, when introducing the UN declaration, spoke in general terms of "certain security formalities" and "immense geographical and other difficulties," cautioning that "what we can do at this stage must inevitably be slight." Five thousand Jews, 4,500 of them children, would be allowed to enter Palestine under the White Paper quota from Axis-controlled Bulgaria, but the military situation, Eden informed a Jewish delegation, made North Africa "unstable" as a haven. In addition, Portuguese colonies were not "readily available" for refugees entering Spain at about 50 a day; the Swiss sought a relaxation of the Allied war blockade to receive food provisions before taking in more Jewish refugees; restrictive immigration laws existed in all countries of the Western Hemisphere, including the United States. The year 1942 closed with Zygielbojm's December 19 appeal hanging and the Foreign Office in receipt of a telegram from Ambassador Halifax asking his government to seek U. S. cooperation over the so-called "refugee problem."[7]

For three weeks the British authorities mulled over Halifax's cable and the incessant public demand for results. On January 6, 1943, Zygielbojm received his answer to the appeal: a copy of Eden's December 17 speech in Parliament, with its concluding words of hesitation, and the assurance that HMG "was investigating all practical means" for rescue. On the same day Eden sought a statement from Myron Taylor, U.S. member on the Intergovernmental Committee on Refugees and Roosevelt's personal representative to the Vatican, against Zionist claims for Palestine as "extremist." Three days later Eden secured the War Cabinet's approval to have Halifax inform the State Department that Great Britain, "despite its substantial contribution" in receiving refugees, was prepared to discuss further joint possibilities with the United States in the matter. On January 11 the Cabinet agreed to Eden's memorandum that "no differentiation" should be made between Jews and other refugees in all rescue efforts. Awaiting a final draft of the British position, Halifax urged Assistant Secretary of State Adolf A. Berle, Jr., to remove the approximately 4,000 Jewish refugees from France and Spain to safer North Africa without delay. In the meantime, Hitler's New Year message predicting the annihilation of "international Jewry" approached realization. The world read news bulletins of large deportations from the capital of eastern Galicia, a deportation rate of Belgian Jewry exceeding 20,000 per month, and the advancing Red Army's discovery of towns in the Caucasus strewn with thousands of dead Jews.[8]

Dissatisfied with official British reticence, English advocates of immediate rescue lost little time in formulating programs. A meeting of members of Parliament and Jewish representatives on January 7 had debated
Eleanor Rathbone's memorandum "The Case for an Offer to Hitler."
Several doubted its advisability, especially if Britain were to take the
lead. Most of those present agreed on "a token gesture" to accept a
number of refugees, and then, with the establishment of a special Allied
council, to ask other United Nations to do likewise. The Joint Foreign
Committee, representing the Anglo-Jewish establishment, called for a
UN body to carry out all practical measures. As if divining an S.O.S.
dated January 13 from the underground Jewish National Committee of
Poland, begging for arms, the rescue of 10,000 children through a German exchange, and $500,000 for self-defense and aid, Zygielbojm pub-
licly called for reprisals against the Nazis as the only way to save the
remnant of Polish Jewry.[9] Rathbone, vice-chairman of the National
Committee for Rescue from Nazi Terror, pressed in Parliament for a
specific reaction from the Vatican. There was no time to lose, the Zionist
representative on the Polish National Council, Ignacy Schwartzbart,
warned the WJC in New York, since the official German creation of 55
"compulsory ghettos" in Poland marked "the final step to complete
extermination." Could united world action even now stay the hand of
the determined executioner?[10]

The British *aide-mémoire* on "Refugees from Nazi-Occupied Territory" arrived at the State Department on January 20, 1943. The problem
at hand, it began, should not be treated as solely a Jewish one. Transportation difficulties, rising antisemitism where "an excessive number of
Jews are introduced," and the Axis's "embarrassing" other countries by
flooding them with aliens, as Germany had done before the war, posed
alleged dangers. Still, the British government would not take "a merely
negative response to a growing international problem." England had
found accommodations for nearly 100,000 refugees. This figure included
Palestine, which received 18,000 legal immigrants and some 20,000 "illegals" between April, 1939, and September, 1942, and expected to take
4,500 Bulgarian Jews and up to 29,000 others by March 31, 1944, under
the White Paper. Would the American government issue additional visas
for entry into its borders, and assist in shipping refugees elsewhere, such
as North Africa and Santo Domingo? If the Anglo-American Alliance
could arrive at some understanding, approaches could then be made to
other governments to examine possibilities, perhaps through a closed
Allied conference.[11]

The Americans received a disingenuous document. Conclusive figures
for the number of civilian refugees in Great Britain and the East African
colonies, as one contemporary analysis made clear, had not been sup-

plied. Only 300 refugees (not the 3,000 cited) came to Jamaica, and Palestine had never admitted the 1,500 "illegals" deported from its waters in December, 1940, to Mauritius. Nor should the British statement have included prematurely 4,500 Bulgarian Jews slated for acceptance or the 29,000 to be allowed entry into Palestine. Indeed, since the latter figure was simply that allowed by the prewar White Paper, there was no reason to mention this number as further evidence of Britain's efforts on behalf of Nazi victims. And HMG ignored entirely the specific Nazi project to murder all of European Jewry—and therefore the immediate need to concentrate on their plight—by combining this group with questionable members of all other refugees in Europe.[12]

Whatever the *aide-mémoire's* limitations, the State Department dragged its feet. Foggy Bottom did consult its representative in North Africa regarding British concern about the Jewish refugees in Spain, reporting to Halifax on January 30 that evacuation to that area had been accepted in principle. But the department employed war censorship to quash receipt of further cables from the WJC's Geneva branch to New York headquarters, privately contending that such private messages might cause neutral countries "to curtail or abolish our official secret means of communication." A long message of January 21 from Riegner and Jewish Agency representative Richard Lichtheim, which arrived before the department's ban, reporting even greater atrocities in Poland and the fact that 70,000 survivors of the 136,000 Rumanian Jews deported to Transnistria in the Ukraine faced death by starvation, convinced the WJC that more aggressive measures were necessary to attain some concrete Allied rescue effort. Stephen Wise began preparations for a rally in New York on March 1 to "Stop Hitler Now!"[13]

Proponents of speedy rescue claimed that Palestine represented the most obvious solution to the problem. A month earlier 63 senators and 182 congressmen had signed an appeal for "millions of homeless Jews" to be allowed to "reconstruct their lives in Palestine" after the war. Lord Herbert Samuel, first high commissioner for Palestine, gave Eden his personal opinion that the country could provide for a population of three million and the entry of Jews should be encouraged forthwith. Upon receiving Riegner's cable of January 21 from the Foreign Office, the WJC's British section drafted a memorandum on rescue that emphasized the need for an international authority to consider all havens, especially Palestine. Its proximity to eastern Europe and the presence in the Promised Land of an organized Jewish community of nearly 600,000 able to care for Jewish refugees made it "the most readily available sanctuary." The Jewish Agency informed both governments at the same time that Palestine west of the Jordan River could maintain at least another three million inhabitants, exclusive of the southern Negev region. The agency asserted that the mass colonization necessary to "meet the needs of Jewish migration after the war" could take place only in a self-governing Jewish commonwealth in the ancient Jewish homeland.

The Foreign Office and the State Department did not accept this perspective, however. Both London and Washington, preoccupied with the effect on their war effort of Arab unrest about Zionists' expressed intentions, remained hostile. The White Paper, Colonial Secretary Oliver Stanley announced in Commons on February 3, should be strictly adhered to: "Winning the war is the most important thing of all."[14]

But what would be the moral worth of this triumph if it coincided with Hitler's victory against his primary enemy, the Jewish people? The Germans, "with complete disregard for the flood of protests" that followed the UN declaration, "are cold-bloodedly carrying on with the completion of the murderous task," Zygielbojm warned the world. On January 27 the Polish government-in-exile reported that some 58,000 of the 85,840 prisoners in Oswiecim (which the Nazis called Auschwitz) had perished. Three days later a group of 15 women and children from Sosnowiec, who arrived in Istanbul on their way to Palestine in a second Allied-German civilian exchange scheme, confirmed the rapid annihilation of Jewry in Poland. German postal authorities in Poland and the Baltic states, according to a Stockholm dispatch, had begun to use a special stamp in returning letters addressed to the victims: "Died in the course of liquidation of the Jewish problem." Of the 86,000 Jews in Yugoslavia before the war, 95 percent were now dead, stated that country's government-in-exile. For the first time Berlin radio informed the German people that mass executions of Jews had been carried out in occupied territories as a "precaution against Bolshevism." A coded message received from the Jews of Poland on February 10 and published by the Jewish Telegraphic Agency read, "Is the world really unable to save us?" "Hurry," read another a week later, "otherwise our complete extermination is unavoidable!"[15]

Harassed by an impatient public, the Foreign Office kept its counsel. The Jews in the United States should give HMG due credit for accepting 4,500 of their Bulgarian co-religionists, it informed the Washington embassy. "Hopes of a move en masse should be gently discouraged," however, owing to the "overwhelming" transit problem from Turkey. Admitting privately that this grant of 4,500 and the 29,000 left under the White Paper was "really only scratching the surface," a senior member of the Eastern Department insisted to the Board of Deputies' secretary that "America had a considerable leeway to make up." The State Department could especially help in North Africa and with the Latin American countries. As for the Polish government-in-exile's repeated request for reprisals, this would interfere with "the most effective" targets in the

Allied strategic bombing offensive. Machinery did not seem to exist for dealing with reported atrocities in Lithuania, confidentially added the Central Department's W. Denis Allen to a colleague, especially as "we cannot allow the Poles to regard Vilna as Polish." A newspaper exclusive, first published in the *New York Times* on February 13, that Rumania would allow the remaining 70,000 Jews in Transnistria to be transferred by ship to Palestine, met with the Foreign Office's swift response: no nation would accept any such offer. The gesture, if successful, might open up the prospect of "unloading at a given price all unwanted nationals on overseas countries." Allied victory, went this standard reply, should be the only answer.[16]

Whitehall could not, however, remain impervious to sharp parliamentary debates, thundering newspaper editorials, and the memoranda of Eleanor Rathbone and others, and after a month, with no American response to its *aide-mémoire*, it presented an ultimatum to the State Department. Richard Law informed the U.S. *chargé* in London on February 20 that HMG could not postpone beyond the next week some reply in Parliament to persistent queries about its activities to help the Jews of Europe. The U.S. government should join the British in convening a United Nations conference in London to examine the refugee question. The State Department should grant special visas to refugees, then invite other nations to follow suit. International guarantees, including repatriation, could be given the neutral powers that they would be aided in carrying this burden at the end of the war.[17]

By February 25 the Foreign Office's threat had again produced its desired effect, and the State Department submitted a formal reply to the British *aide-mémoire* of January 20. The U.S. government had dispensed large amounts of public and private money for refugees and called the 1938 Evian conference, precursor to the Intergovernmental Committee on Refugees. Visas numbering 547,775 had been issued in occupied Europe between 1939 and June 30, 1942 (228, 964 in the war years), with many more authorized between 1939 and 1942. State had authorized over 5,000 visas for admission to the United States from France, Spain, and Portugal, sought help for refugees from Switzerland and other neutrals, and aided refugees in Spain, including the transfer of a number to North Africa. No new restrictions, except for security checks, had been placed on the number of aliens allowed to enter this country since Pearl Harbor. Thousands of civilian enemy aliens and dangerous Axis nationals were being taken care of in American camps, thereby freeing supplies abroad for refugees in need.

As to the future, congressional immigration laws must continue to bind the government. The executive committee of the Intergovernmental Committee on Refugees was best qualified to continue solving the refugee problem, which should not be confined to "persons of any particular race or faith." An informal "preliminary exploration" by the Anglo-American Alliance in Ottawa might facilitate action by the Intergovernmental Committee.[18]

Now it was the Britishers' turn to be handed a crafty document. Why quote Myron Taylor's July, 1938, statement as the U.S. delegate at Evian against "dumping" German Jews on the "international market," which had hinted at economic retaliation against Germany, when the only way to rescue Jews in 1943 was to remove them from Axis Europe? In addition, only 21 percent of Poland's immigration quota to the United States had been filled between 1933 and 1938, despite an excess of applicants for American visas. In fact, almost 100,000 *fewer* people than the number of authorized visas mentioned in State's note were actually admitted during the years from 1933 to 1942, and only a little more than half of this total came from all of Europe. According to the U.S. government's immigration reports, only 71, 290 of the entire number of immigrants from Europe, and about 60,000 of those from Nazi-occupied countries between 1939 and 1942, were Jews. The American offer to take 5,000 French children had not materialized, and thus should not have been included in a survey of actual help for Nazi victims. Internment camps for Japanese from the West Coast and Germans and Italians from the Americas had no bearing on the problem in question, except for the fact that suspected enemy Axis agents had been admitted—unlike Jews in peril of their lives—outside of visa restrictions. The State Department's note followed the British example in overlooking the exceptional threat facing the Jewish people. Only the previous day Hitler had rebroadcast his determination to complete the Final Solution.[19]

Unaware of these diplomatic maneuvers, an aroused Jewish opinion pressed for action. The American Jewish Congress's March 1 "Stop Hitler Now!" rally in Madison Square Garden attracted 75,000 people. There they heard Chaim Weizmann bemoan the apathy of the Christian world, while warm messages of support from England's archbishop of Canterbury and Arthur Cardinal Hinsley called for "speedy deeds" to meet the "most appalling horror in recorded history." The following day Under Secretary Welles publicly declared that the meeting's 11 point program of rescue was receiving the most serious and sympathetic consideration from both Roosevelt and the State Department. The call to conscience included approaches to the German government and its satellites to permit Jewish emigration; refugee sanctuaries; greater entry of immigrants into the United States, Great Britain, and Latin America; opening the gates to the Jewish national homeland in Palestine; UN financial guarantees for feeding and rescue; an appropriate intergovernmental agency to implement the program; and the establishment of a tribunal that would ultimately bring the criminals to justice. Wise forwarded the proposals to Secretary of State Hull on March 5, along with a reminder that little had been done to implement the UN declaration just when the Germans were accelerating their program of systematic mass murder.[20]

The same day, however, the State Department published a summary of its February 25 note to Great Britain, thereby leading outsiders to believe that State had initiated the call for a conference. The unsuspecting British had no time to consult with the proposed host, the Canadian government. WJC headquarters in New York was shocked, since the move completely undercut their understanding of Welles's assurances of March 2 by emphasizing the limited possibilities of rescue. But Welles, in a harsh interview with the British *chargé* in Washington, insisted that the British government must not continue to give the impression that "it was the great outstanding champion of the Jewish people." Since Ottawa officialdom—consistently blocking the admission of refugees—opposed a conference on its own territory, Eden ultimately acceded to Hull's recommendation of isolated Bermuda as the site for the meeting. On March 23 the secretary triumphantly informed Roosevelt, who heretofore had maintained a guarded silence on the subject, that everything was ready.[21]

Recovering from their surprise, the British authorities staked out their position for the talks. In Parliament Eden applauded the Polish government-in-exile's support of repatriation as "the best way to solve the immediate and post-war problems." While the Foreign Office forwarded another cable to the WJC from Riegner, depicting continuing deportations from Berlin, Holland, and France, it dismissed his "pretty far-reaching proposals" (accepted by the World Council of Churches' secretariat in Geneva) to exchange Jews for Germans *en bloc*. The Foreign Office informed the Board of Deputies that transport difficulties "are really immense," and that many British women in Nazi Europe would have to be released before other exchanges with Germans for Jews could take place.[22]

The private comments Eden made in the United States at the end of February no doubt most sharply reflected his government's views. In an interview with Wise and the president of the American Jewish Committee, Joseph Proskauer, representing American Jewry's Joint Emergency Committee for European Jewish Affairs, Eden rejected as "fantastically impossible" their principal request that the United Nations ask Hitler publicly to release the Jews. Refugees in Spain and Portugal could not be sent to Palestine because "the Mediterranean is not clear." To the suggestion that England help additional Jews out of Bulgaria, the foreign secretary replied, "Turkey does not want any more of your people." The joint committee's second major proposal that the UN send food to occupied Europe for the Jews, the way the Allies had saved a starving Greece during the winter of 1941, seemed to make no impression upon the man who in 1938 resigned from the British cabinet rather than accede to Neville Chamberlain's appeasement of Hitler and Mussolini. Hewing to Britain's earlier stance on the Rumanian offer of 75,000 Jews from Transnistria's concentration camps, Eden more candidly warned Hull in the presence of Roosevelt that acceptance of the threatened Bulgarian Jews might well lead Hitler to make similar offers for Poland and Germany. Aside from the problem of ferreting out enemy agents, he went on to the unprotesting pair, "there simply are not enough ships and means of transportation in the world to handle them."[23] Rarely has a death sentence been more casually approved.

Of all the major government officials involved in these matters of rescue, Myron Taylor best sensed the immediate plight of the Jews. He had regularly forwarded Wise's requests that Pope Pius XII intervene on behalf of the Jewish people. Wise and Proskauer found Taylor very cordial and pleased with the joint committee's memorandum on rescue, saying that it followed the lines along which he had been thinking for some time. But he was unsuccessful in persuading Eden to hold a meeting of the Intergovernmental Committee without delay to take up the refugee question.[24]

Given his independent views, Taylor refused to head the American delegation to Bermuda. A leading member of FDR's Advisory Committee on Postwar Foreign Policy, he believed that private conversations with Eden and other British officials could attain as good a result as "a well advertised conference which must not fail." Taylor recognized that both governments, as he wrote the State Department, had to decide in concrete terms on temporary havens, cost, and guarantees regarding permanent refugee settlement. Assistant Secretary Berle, heading departmental discussions of postwar migration and settlement problems, should immediately initiate such action regardless of a conference that might "result in unexpected developments and commitments."[25]

Taylor's analysis, conveyed personally to Roosevelt on March 18, erred only in not grasping that both governments had already decided to exclude Jewish representatives from a conference that would be used not for meaningful rescue but for cosmetic effect. Bermuda's inaccessibility would keep away the public, with no interested organizations invited to attend the closed sessions. Europe's Jews were dying every day by the thousands, but both governments announced that the discussions would be "primarily exploratory" in nature.[26]

The State Department, where refugee matters were under the direction of Assistant Secretary Breckenridge Long, did all it could to ensure that the conference would yield minimal results. Maintaining a zealous control since Pearl Harbor over visas for aliens on the broadest grounds of "security," Long never altered his view that Jewish agitators were responsible for the unceasing pressure on State to effect a radical rescue policy. He was particularly anxious lest the conference's possible aid to Jews, together with public meetings, newspaper advertisements, Senate resolutions, and speeches by prominent Americans, be exploited by Joseph Goebbel's Nazi propaganda office as proof positive that Jews commandeered the country's military drive. Long shared with his subordinates a suspicion of British intentions. HMG's desire for a camp in North Africa would spark Moslem resentment, in Long's opinion, and he pressed for revival of the virtually defunct Intergovernmental Committee on Refugees as the sole end of the Bermuda proceedings.

While the British announced a delegation of first rank, their opposite numbers were decidedly inferior. From London came Richard Law, Home Office Under Secretary Osbert Peake, and Admiralty Financial Secretary G. H. Hall, with A. W. G. Randall of the Foreign Office's Refugee Department to serve as the trio's secretary. William Dodds, president of Princeton University, and Senator Scott Lucas of Illinois, on the other hand, had no background in refugee matters; Long counted on Chairman of the House Foreign Affairs Committee Sol Bloom of New York, more interested in personal recognition within executive and State Department circles than in championing Jewish causes, to serve as a sop to some Jews and to toe the given line. Three other advisers, who had previously indicated their support of Long's position, would go along to guarantee that all proceeded without a hitch.[27]

Both governments arrived at final positions before the conference began. On April 2 the British War Cabinet's Committee on the Reception and Accommodation of Refugees unanimously agreed that their government should not undertake any commitments beyond transporting the 5,000 refugees from Bulgaria to Palestine. Allied agreement with the Axis powers to accept Jews from central Europe was "out of the question"; the most important objective was the return of Jews in "large numbers" to "their own countries" after the war. The U.S. delegates received instructions on April 13 to make no commitments on shipping, funds, or new agencies for relief. The Americans could only grant monies to neutral governments aiding refugees. Nor could Palestine be considered as a temporary place of refuge, the State Department's Near Eastern Division hastened to add. Such resolution "would create serious risks of disaffection, perhaps accompanied by outbreaks in the Arab and Moslem world," and thereby interfere with combat operations. With these positions set, the American team joined their British allies in Hamilton on April 16, 1943.[28]

Four months had passed since the UN declaration. Little help had been forthcoming from the Anglo-American Alliance during that time, and now its representatives found themselves ensconced in quarters graciously put at their disposal by the Bermuda legislature to mark the island's first international conference. "Unless action is undertaken immediately," the Joint Emergency Committee for European Jewish Affairs warned Under Secretary Welles, "there may soon be no Jews left alive in Europe."[29] Those still surviving and all others interested in their rescue and relief would discover in time that they had no cause to place their last hopes either in the deliberations about to commence at—unconscious bitter irony—"The Horizons," or in their aftermath.

II

The statements made by some delegates shortly before the Bermuda conference began already signaled the defeatism of the two governments. "We will not fail in this crisis," Senator Lucas assured Americans, but he added that only Congress could determine their government's immigration policy. ("He is not too hopeful," the Foreign Office privately noted.) The few reporters in Bermuda were informed that shipping difficulties precluded immediate rescue. Law, heading the British group, insisted that only the triumph of the Allied armies would help the refugees. Professor Dodds, his opposite, added that "the problem is too great for solution" by the two governments at this first international meeting to discuss refugees since the *Wehrmacht* invaded Poland and began to fulfill Hitler's prophecy concerning the destruction of European Jewry in the event of global conflict.[30]

Although the conference had its genesis in the public's outcry to the UN Declaration on Jewish Massacres, the Jews had no staunch allies at Bermuda. The Americans, who could claim neither knowledge nor responsibility for the refugee problem, followed their instructions to the letter. They accepted the British agenda and arrived at a harmony of minds. Dodds and the State Department officials squelched Bloom's timidly expressed hope of negotiating with the Axis, and they agreed with the British that the Roosevelt-Churchill policy of unconditional surrender must remain inviolate. No exchange of prisoners or lifting of the Allied blockade to bring relief to European Jews would be permitted. The State Department's expert on shipping (and head of its Visa Division) even outdid the British in dismissing all possibilities of using Allied vessels for rescue, although the Americans did agree to share the cost of chartering two Rumanian ships to transport the offered 5,000 Bulgarian Jews to Palestine.[31]

Proposals for places of refuge died aborning. A British suggestion that Portuguese ships bring up to 15,000 refugees to Angola led Breckenridge Long's chief assistant on refugee matters, Robert Reams, to counter that neutral Portugal might not wish to help: Dodds recommended that the proposal be sent to the ineffective Intergovernmental Committee on Refugees. Mention of Santo Domingo, Madagascar, British Honduras, and Cyrenaica as refugee centers, to be referred to their respective governments for future discussion, all suffered a similar fate. British pressure for a center in North Africa met with the rejoinder that, aside from objections of the U.S. military, "American troops would not tolerate that any country occupied by them should put Jewish refugees in concentration camps"! The British found the Americans willing to accept the restrictive White Paper quotas, Dodds again clamping down on Bloom. As a quid pro quo, congressional immigration laws would also not be open to question. Nor would the conference discuss a Swedish offer—dependent upon assurances of Anglo-American aid—to admit 20,000 Jewish children from Axis-controlled countries.[32]

One of the American contingent tried but failed to stir his colleagues to undertake what he termed "an act of moral force, an act against reason ... that those who are now helpless and cannot help anyone will be saved from disaster." George Backer, former owner of the *New York Post* who now headed the American branch of the Organization for Rehabilitation Training (ORT), had been invited to wait outside the Horizons' conference doors as a concession to Jewish and newspaper pressure. When the U.S. delegates called in their entire staff for a frank discussion after the official talks had ended, Backer let loose. Far more must be done than merely transport the estimated 5,000 Jewish refugees then in Spain to a camp in North Africa and accept the White Paper, he urged. The Bermuda conference would be a failure unless negotiations were undertaken with the neutrals and the Vatican for removal of at least 125,000 Jews from eastern Europe. At least allow the Jews, who have lived in Europe for 1,900 years, to "have their seed saved," Backer pleaded. The Jewish Agency, whose memorandum Backer had forwarded to the American representatives, would take 94,000 immediately into Palestine, he added. Unspecified military and shipping difficulties served as the convenient foil to these arguments, however, and his poignant appeal went unheeded. On his return to the States, Backer confided his frustration to the Jewish Labor Committee. "The Jewish question met a deaf wall at Bermuda," he exclaimed. Had he known beforehand of such opposition to save European Jewry, Backer would not have made the trip.[33]

This "facade for inaction," in the later words of British chief delegate Richard Law, ended as inauspiciously as it had begun. A brief public statement, making no reference to Jews as such, assured the world that "a substantial number" of refugees would be aided through concrete recommendations. The proposals decided upon could not, however, be made public at this time. In fact, the conferees recommended only the "resurrection" (Law's word to his superiors) and expansion of the Inter-governmental Committee and its responsibilities, and the movement of 21,000 refugees, including the estimated 5,000 Jews, from Spain to North Africa. The Jewish organizations, in absentia, had called for negotiations with Germany via the neutrals to free Jews, shipment of food to Jews not permitted to leave Europe, and havens in the United States, Latin America, the neutral countries, and Palestine. Their memoranda were quickly dismissed, relegated to archives.[34]

The conference results satisfied the State Department entirely. Assistant Secretary Long, reflecting in early May on the March 1 Madison Square Garden rally, worried that the "hot headed masses" would "take the burden and the curse off Hitler." He could now rest content. Assistant Secretary Berle could also breathe more easily, having ruled out two weeks earlier, on military and moral grounds, a threat of raids against German towns and having dismissed Palestine as a place of refuge because of the inevitable Arab agitation to follow. (At that very moment he was secretly urging a joint Anglo-American statement on Palestine to postpone any answer for that vexing problem until after the war, thereby acceding to the White Paper.)[35] Even Under Secretary Welles, supporter of the Zionist cause and assurer of Wise and Proskauer that Bermuda would be a success if it rescued only 50,000 Jews, officially wrote Wise in June that "constant efforts" were being made to carry out the conference's recommendations, "including several mentioned by you." Only Myron Taylor again challenged his colleagues' smugness, refusing to organize a meeting of the moribund Intergovernmental Committee until the American and British governments first obligated themselves to ensure temporary and permanent havens for the Jews. "The Bermuda Conference was wholly ineffective, as I view it," he wrote Hull, Welles, and Long, "and we knew it would be."[36]

The British delegation also left Bermuda fully content. Its three members, in a confidential memorandum to the Foreign Office that Eden forwarded to the War Cabinet but specifically not to the dominions two months later, expressed pleasant surprise at the frank concord that had reigned. Unanimity had been achieved, and although the American representatives regularly put on the Intergovernmental Committee "difficult or disagreeable tasks which the United States government was clearly unwilling to carry out alone," the two groups had arrived at a mutually satisfactory position regarding that committee as well. The conference "achieved very little" regarding the immediate relief and rescue of refugees; how far it would succeed in "more modest aims will appear as time goes on."

But in one respect the discussions proved "thoroughly profitable." The note of "asperity, jealousy and suspicion" of His Majesty's Government in certain American official circles was dispelled, and it seemed that a foundation of understanding and cooperation on the refugee issue had been established in its stead. If so, the British government could "appeal confidently to American goodwill in all such refugee burdens in the future as we consider should not be placed exclusively on our own and British Colonial Governments." This welcome result should not be publicized, but "our ten agreeable days of discussion with the Americans in Bermuda will not have been wasted if we can succeed in keeping this one reality alive."[37]

Such optimism just when Goebbels published the Nazi order to annihilate the Jews "without mercy" could hardly be justified, and mounting voices denounced the Bermuda proceedings as a tragedy of unfathomable proportions. The Committee for a Jewish Army, led by an Irgun delegation from Palestine, blasted the conference on May 4 with a full-page advertisement in major American newspapers: "TO 5,000,000 JEWS IN THE NAZI DEATH TRAP BERMUDA WAS A CRUEL MOCKERY." Not long before, that same group had similarly attacked the failure of London and Washington to respond to Rumania's offer of the remaining Jews in Transnistria. Its Emergency Conference to Save the Jews of Europe subsequently urged the American government to create a specific agency without delay to rescue Jews, with international agencies aiding in their protection and emigration. Pointed criticism in Congress and especially Parliament also exposed the sterility of the conference. Eduard Beneš, president of the Czech government-in-exile, privately compared the Allied disregard for the fate of beleaguered Jewry to the betrayal of his country by the same governments five years earlier.[38] When food reached Greece through the Allied blockade, exchange of prisoners took place via the International Red Cross, Allied boats returned empty from theaters of war, and England's prime minister threatened to retaliate in kind if the Germans used poison gas on the Russian front, a mantle of "callous indifference" covered the major Allied powers.[39]

Manifest at the very moment when the Jews of the Warsaw ghetto took up arms to avenge their people murdered in the death camps, the apathy of the two governments represented at Bermuda appeared especially criminal. The final German assault against the remaining 60,000 inhabitants of the ghetto's more than 400,000 Jews began on the very day that the Bermuda conference opened, coincidentally the same evening of the Passover holiday commemorating Jewry's exodus from Egypt. Radio and newspaper bulletins conveyed to the world the ghetto's resistance, which would last longer than that of the entire Polish Army in September, 1939, but help never reached these defenders. "Aware that our last day is at hand," wrote 24-year-old commander Mordechai Anielewicz on April 26 in a final message to counterpart Yitschak

"Antek" Cukierman (later Zuckerman) on the "Aryan" side, "we demand from you to remember how we were betrayed." During the second week of May Cukierman and some associates cabled London: "While the epic heroism is nearing its end and remnants of Jewish centres in the provinces are being completely wiped out, the free world, the world of justice, remains silent and apathetic. It is unbelievable."[40]

In a last attempt to stir Roosevelt, Churchill, and the Allied peoples from passivity to action, Szmul Zygielbojm took his life. Despite the entreaty of Gentile PPS comrade Adam Ciolkosz that he work for postwar socialism in Poland or the United States, Zygielbojm no longer wished to live apart from his martyred people; the Bundist also just received word that the Allied high command had turned down his proposal to bomb Auschwitz and/or the Warsaw ghetto. A letter explaining the motives behind his suicide on May 12, 1943, included this singular *cri de coeur*: "Let my death be an energetic cry of protest against the indifference of the world which witnesses the extermination of the Jewish people without taking any steps to prevent it. In our day and age human life is of little value; having failed to achieve success in my life, I hope that my death may jolt the indifference of those who, perhaps even in this extreme moment, could save the Jews who are still alive in Poland."[41] Hitler would not wait patiently for their reply.

The originators of the Bermuda conference, who apparently had convened the sessions not so much to save the Jews from death as themselves from public censure, now felt pressed to give proof of their professed intentions. They were not prepared to accept the view of James G. McDonald, first League of Nations high commissioner for refugees who had resigned from that post in December, 1935, in protest against Allied inactivity to save Jews, that the Jewish refugees had "no other land to go" but their Promised Land of old. Roosevelt studiously avoided mentioning Palestine in messages at the time to Zionist organizations, and he gave that and the rescue of European Jewry low priority in winning the war. Even Churchill, unyielding advocate of a large Jewish state in Palestine, seconded the Foreign Office's position on British refugee efforts.[42] Both governments had decided well in advance of the Bermuda meeting not to press for large-scale havens. To where now could they turn? With an air of desperation these reluctant rescuers snatched at North Africa to meet their critics.

The first move in this direction at the highest level took place on May 7, with Secretary Hull's memorandum to FDR about the Bermuda proceedings. The secretary had declared his preference in November, 1942, just when Wise gave the world the detailed facts of Jewry's plight, for the return of refugees after the war to their homes "in a world in which Jews, like every other race, are free to abide in peace and honor." He now asked Roosevelt if he would agree to the conference's suggestion for a temporary camp in North Africa, to be followed by postwar repatriation. Hull would not, at the same time, support changing constrictive U.S. immigration laws or bringing in refugees as temporary visitors, thereby risking prolonged, bitter controversy in Congress and other forums.

On May 14 the president gave his approval to Hull's recommendations. As for moving refugees, costs should be shared with Great Britain, the American contribution to be taken out of relief funds assigned to former New York governor Herbert Lehman, director of the State Department's Office of Foreign Relief and Rehabilitation Operations (OFRRO). North Africa could be used as a "depot" for the 20,000 refugees presently in Spain, Roosevelt agreed, but not on a permanent basis without full approval of all authorities concerned: "I know, in fact, that there is plenty of room for them in North Africa, but I raise the question of sending large numbers of Jews there. That would be extremely unwise."[43]

The president's personal caution about the mass movement of Jews to North Africa reflected the concerns of the State and War departments. As early as June, 1942, State tried without avail to persuade FDR that a declaration regarding Palestine's future along the principle of self-determination enunciated in the Atlantic Charter would counter Axis broadcasts to the Middle East, which promised Arab independence and total elimination of the Jewish national home. Similar fears led the president's personal representative in North Africa, Robert Murphy, to join the State Department in successfully recommending that the 1870 Crémieux Decree, the law rescinded by Vichy that had granted French citizenship at birth for Algeria's Jews (excluding Moslems), not be restored by the Free French government. At the same time, the chief of the War Department's Military Intelligence Division (G-2) cautioned that pro-Zionist statements by eminent American officials would alienate the Moslem world and threaten the security of American troops in the Middle East. On the same grounds, in January, 1943, Allied headquarters in North Africa turned down a suggestion from the Committee for a Jewish Army that a Jewish legion be formed from native French and European refugee Jews located there.

Accordingly, the head of G-2 informed Breckenridge Long during the Bermuda talks that the War Department's strong objections to transporting Jewish refugees to North Africa "should preclude any further consideration of the matter." To shift attention from Palestine and North Africa as large havens for Jews, a confidential study on April 30 by G-2's Middle East section, embracing a totally pro-Arab position for Palestine, concluded that the Cameroons in central Africa should be the place of shelter for those European Jews who survived the war.[44]

Until Roosevelt's memorandum of May 14 to Secretary Hull, the

American government had limited its commitment to the estimated 5,000 Jewish refugees in Spain. Funds in the amount of $200,000 had been allotted for these and the other 15,000 refugees there, and the President's Advisory Committee on Political Refugees had recommended that 1,000 Jews go to Palestine and between 500 and 1,000 proceed to Jamaica. Replying to the British government's first expression of interest in a joint refugee program in North Africa, Hull had cautioned that military considerations were paramount. A second British request on March 24 met with Assistant Secretary Long's rebuff that only the French, then in political control of the area, could decide the issue. At most, the two governments, with a personal assist from Churchill, had protested in mid-April against the Spanish government's closing the Pyreneean frontier to Jews fleeing France.[45]

Roosevelt and Churchill discussed the matter in mid-May. The prime minister's interest in settling Jews in the former Italian colonies of Tripolitania and Cyrenaica, to serve as "satellites" of a future Jewish state, sparked the opposition of Roosevelt's foremost adviser on postwar settlement, Isaiah Bowman. Bowman's fears of a violent reaction in the Arab world found their way into a State Department memorandum that FDR handed Churchill while the latter visited Washington. During that same trip Eden cabled from London that he was "dismayed and depressed" at the strong objections of the U.S. joint chiefs to a small center somewhere in North Africa. The camp could get British pilots and other Allied prisoners out of France, he pointed out. The few Jewish refugees involved would not pose a problem of shipping, while the center might be located sufficiently remote from important Arab areas. A favorable decision would also halt "extremely serious" criticism in Parliament. "It is our last hope of carrying through a modest suggestion to which we attach great political and military importance," Eden implored. Churchill agreed to his foreign secretary's request that he take up the recommendation with the president at the White House and then left for England to work it out.[46]

Complete agreement between Roosevelt and Churchill for the refugee camp was obtained only in early July. Both Eden and his superior did not think the difficulties cited in Bowman's memorandum insurmountable so long as temporary havens were contemplated, although the British War Office opposed Cyrenaica because of probable Arab antagonism. For days the British embassy in Washington pressed the matter. At last, on June 18, following Under Secretary Welles's suggestion that Churchill send a personal message to FDR, Eden drafted a note that the "former naval person" forwarded at the end of the month: "Our immediate facilities for helping victims of Hitler's anti-Jewish drive are so limited at present that the opening of the small camp proposed for the purpose of

removing some of them to safety seems all the more incumbent on us."
Roosevelt finally gave his approval on July 9; "I am most grateful,"
Churchill replied a few days later.[47]

Still, the camp that was to receive an original estimate of 5,000–7,000
Jews was not even organized by the end of 1943. Having the American
and British governments' agreement to contribute $500,000 each, OFRRO
director Lehman instructed his chief of the North African mission in
Algiers that plans for setting up the camp "should be vigorously developed." The use of French military barracks occupied by the U.S. Army
at Camp Maréchal Lyautey, ten miles north of Casablanca near Fedhala, was approved by the State Department, General Eisenhower, and
the French authorities "in principle" on September 1. Moses Beckelman
formerly of the American Jewish Joint Distribution Committee, was
appointed as the project's director.

By the time the United Nations Relief and Rehabilitation Agency
(UNRRA) came into being in November under Lehman's directorship,
the French government, which had thought of imposing internment conditions on the center, finally agreed to turn over the facilities to the UN
relief body. It set down two conditions, however: the refugees must be
limited to 2,000 and eventually be removed by the Intergovernmental
Committee on Refugees. But UNRRA had as yet virtually no funds, and
while Lehman assured the State Department of his new organization's
willingness to take over the camp, the Foreign Economic Administration
was given temporary responsibility for the proposed site. Not one Jewish
refugee had been moved from Spain to the Moroccan location.[48]

A further complication arose during early 1944 in the difficult relations
between the newly formed U.S. War Refugee Board (WRB) and the
American ambassador to Spain, Carlton J. Hayes. The WRB sought to
remove promptly to Camp Lyautey as many "stateless and unprotected
refugees" as facilities permitted, and to have the Spanish government
encourage the entry of refugees into Spain. Such efforts, it suggested to
Hayes, would include easier border controls and the setting up of camps
on Spanish territory until the refugees were moved southward. The ambassador replied on February 28 that a total of some 1,300 (not the earlier
estimate of 5,000) refugees might be classified as stateless. They included
about 400 Spanish Sephardic Jews from Greece, who had been allowed
by the Germans to leave for Spain, and who would in the main apply for
admission to the Fedhala camp. Another 450 persons had also applied
for evacuation to Fedhala. The Spanish government, for diverse reasons,
opposed any further relaxation of its border controls, and to push for
this action, in Hayes's opinion, could seriously jeopardize the escape of
Allied soldiers from German-held territories to that country.[49]

The WRB's subsequent argument that its vigorous efforts, Allied victories, and the melting of snow in the mountainous region should stimulate the flow of refugees to Spain failed to convince the American ambassador. Hayes did press for better treatment of Jewish refugees in Spain's worst internment centers. At the request of WRB director John Pehle, he reluctantly urged the Spanish government to intercede with the Germans on behalf of a few hundred additional Sephardic Jews transferred from Athens to the Theresienstadt ghetto. But he remained at odds with the WRB; Eleanor Roosevelt's personal intercession with the president, which Pehle obtained, failed to secure Hayes's removal. Given his personal reading of Spanish nationalism and the country's strategic position vis-à-vis Germany during the war, the ambassador failed to accept the board's assignment of chief priority to rescue.[50]

Eventually, the bulk of these Sephardic Jews arrived at Camp Maréchal Lyautey. Beckelman, meanwhile, spent weeks in Spain early in 1944 helping the American and French governments screen the refugees, but the number, as Hayes had predicted, proved disappointingly small. UNRRA rejected about 25 percent of the applications from Jews, notwithstanding the ambassador's requests for a broad definition of "refugee," while Beckelman would not encourage refugees to leave for the camp because of UNRRA's uncertain "voluntary" status. The French continued to refuse refugees at the Fedhala center permits to work or to leave the camp area. Finally, Germany's tightening grip on France halted the stream of refugees to Spain. As this pressure on Spain decreased, the local authorities improved their treatment of the "stateless," and the urge to leave the country lessened. The first consignment reaching Casablanca on May 12 numbered only 38. By the end of June, 1944, nearly 600 more arrived from Madrid.[51]

In July UNRRA director Lehman gave his consent to the eventual liquidation of the camp. The bill authorizing an appropriation from the U.S. government to UNRRA had become law on March 28, but Lehman had trouble getting the center transferred from the Foreign Economic Administration to his agency's jurisdiction. Beckelman estimated that no more refugees would arrive from Spain, and he thought it impractical to continue the expense of operating a camp population of never more than 700. Relations with the local French authorities continued to be exceedingly difficult, and supplies from the army and the United States were virtually non-existent. Beckelman began to urge that the haven be closed, and Lehman overrode the WRB's objections and concurred in July. That same month, the center director finally secured the French provisional government's approval of the camp's transfer to UNRRA. The British continued to withhold their consent, however, and only when the camp reached the point of liquidation did the actual transfer take place—on October 5 retroactive to September 1, 1944.[52]

While the camp at Fedhala thus proved to be as limited a gesture as the conference that spawned it, the suggestion of complementary centers at Tripolitania and Cyrenaica came to naught. The British had been asked at Bermuda to consider Cyrenaica, and Roosevelt expressed to Churchill in July, 1943, his interest in the possibility of both areas as refugee havens. Assistant Secretary Long again made the proposal informally to the British minister in Washington six months later in an attempt to shift the public's focus away from Palestine. In March, 1944, the WRB indicated its readiness to share costs and transportation with the British as a "real opportunity" to rescue many Jews via Turkey and the Black Sea. Secretary Hull seconded the idea as "extremely important," adding that the two proposed camps could also take refugees from southern Italy. But the British minister for war refused to accede even to Tripolitania, writing Richard Law that Arab alarm and "Zionist propagandists" would create "an additional security problem for us at a time when we are already hard pressed to meeting existing commitments in Palestine and elsewhere in the Middle East."

The Foreign Office failed to convince its military authorities that acceptance of Tripolitania would be a "far less objectionable alternative" than opening Palestine to Jewish refugees beyond the White Paper quota. Moreover, while Roosevelt made it clear that there should be "no discouragement under any circumstances" of the escape of refugees to Italy from the Balkans, Robert Murphy, now the U.S. political adviser on the staff of the supreme Allied commander, Mediterranean theater, saw to it that help would not be tendered Marshal Tito's willing partisans in evacuating Jews then in Yugoslavia by Allied ships returning to Italy. The British government's approval in early June, 1944, for a camp in Tripolitania for 1,000-1,500 refugees never materialized; the Foreign Office "reluctantly" ruled out Cyrenaica because of "the political problems involved."[53]

The final saga of the 432 Sephardic Jews in the camp near Casablanca epitomized the classic fate of the "Wandering Jew," especially during the years of the Holocaust. Negotiations for their transfer to the Middle East had been complicated by the fact that the Egyptian government regularly refused to admit refugees lacking guarantees of repatriation. As an international agency UNRRA could supply no such assurance, and the Greek government seemed reluctant to allow the members of this group to return to their original homes. By early October they found themselves in the Greek colony at Nuseirat in the southwest of Palestine, a *fait accompli* that the British and Displaced Persons Division in Cairo had to accept uneasily. These officials correctly suspected that the majority would immediately leave the camp to join Jewish settlements nearby. Indeed, by January 15, 1945, 229 had done so. The remainder returned with the Nuseirat colony to Greece. The Greek government later protested strongly to UNRRA against what it viewed as an "unwarranted concealment" of these people, whose official return it would have refused. Athens even called (to no effect) for the removal of the UNRRA representative in charge of repatriation from the Middle East.

The Casablanca camp closed its doors on November 23, 1944. Despite the fact that 1,000 Jewish refugees in Spain still needed an outlet, the U.S. Army got the center back in February, 1945, to house prisoners of war.[54] The Bermuda conference attained its complete *dénouement.*

CONCLUSION

Thus did the British and American governments undertake a quest for "refuge"—not rescue—in the Bermuda conference and in its aftermath, the camp near Casablanca. Beset by public demands for forthright action, each hid behind questionable immigration figures on their admission of people desperately in need. Ships were found to bring more than 400,000 German prisoners of war to internment in the United States outside current visa regulations, but not for Jews facing death. Palestine's available doors also remained closed, except for the prewar White Paper quota. With the final decisions arrived at even before the conference opened, it is understandable that the two powers took leave of the proceedings fully satisfied. Disinterring the defunct Intergovernmental Committee on Refugees, Breckenridge Long's tactic to silence those truly interested in rescue, was a cynical ploy. In the greatest irony of all, the Bermuda conferees limited their attention to the small number of refugees who had in fact already found a precarious haven in neutral Spain. The Jews in Nazi transit and concentration camps, the subject of the December, 1942, U.N. declaration, were not on the diplomatic agenda. Indeed, the word "Jews" could not be found in the final communiqué from the conference. And the Fedhala camp, which Eden so aptly characterized as "a modest suggestion" primarily to still critics and save Allied soldiers, ultimately sheltered only a few hundred Jews who had the good fortune to cross General Franco's borders.

The paltry efforts of the conference and the consequent North Africa refugee center failed to either save the people expressly marked for destruction or enhance the Allied powers' moral prestige. Nor could it have been otherwise, when the Anglo-American Alliance refused to match Hitler's fanatic determination to murder all of European Jewry with an equally determined effort to rescue them. So long as the authorities most capable of action maintained, as Eden put it to Parliament a month after the empty show staged at Bermuda, that "the only real solution for this problem that can be found is a solution of final and complete Allied victory," the *Führer's* Final Solution for the "Jewish problem" could not be thwarted. Generosity, courage, and speed, which Eleanor Rathbone and others valiantly but vainly demanded, went wanting. These attributes could not be found in officials who feared, in Richard Law's frank phrase at Bermuda, that negotiations with Berlin might succeed and that "would be relieving Hitler of an obligation to take care of *these useless people.*"[55]

Rather than risk such embarrassment, it would be much less troublesome to call on the exigencies of war and not to admit that the fate of the Jews uniquely differed from that of other refugees. The Anglo-American notes calling for a primarily exploratory series of secret, isolated meetings, as well as all replies from State and the Foreign Office to their ever-growing number of detractors, must be viewed in this light. Definite possibilities for the rescue of Jews in Transnistria and Bulgaria; Sweden's offer for 20,000 Jews; reception centers in Palestine, Latin America, the United States, Cyrenaica, and Tripolitania; exchanges for prisoners of war; food parcels; funds for self-defense and relief; threats of reprisals; Allied guarantees to neutral countries—all scarcely received that serious consideration merited by the one people for whom delay meant death. The two governments found it far easier to sidestep the great challenge and to breathe the very spirit of defeatism and despair.[56]

This attitude seized the two leaders of the West as well.

Roosevelt failed to champion an active rescue program. When 400 Orthodox rabbis, organized by the Emergency Committee to Save the Jewish People of Europe, marched on Washington in October, 1943, to demand an Anglo-American governmental agency for rescue, FDR chose to dedicate a few bombers to the Free Yugoslav forces rather than receive the clergymen's delegation. Apart from fighting a global war, the president found himself confronted with restrictive immigration quotas, a possible recurrence of "Jew Deal" charges, a hostile Congress, and State Department apathy if not antisemitism. Assistant Secretary Long continued to trumpet the worth of the impotent Intergovernmental Committee, to brand rescue advocates as "emotionalists who are misled by Hitler," and to provide 1600 Pennsylvania Avenue with the same inflated number of refugees admitted to the United States that the American delegation had used at Bermuda. Not until December did critics succeed in unmasking the hollowness of the State Department's touted rescue record. Pressure from the public, members of Congress, and Treasury Secretary Morgenthau, all disgusted with the dilatory tactics of Long and others in the department, finally forced FDR to end State's obstructive monopoly on rescue and relief by creating the War Refugee Board in January, 1944, through executive order. He resorted to that instrument only once again—to admit 918 Jews and 64 other refugees to Fort Oswego, New York, where they were interned for the rest of the war.

The president spent much time on planning postwar settlement for Jews who would not live to see these memoranda when Hitler's *Götterdammerung* sounded.[57]

Churchill relegated the travail of European Jewry to secondary importance during the war. In private correspondence he emphasized "the great difficulties we are encountering and shall continue to encounter." Even if the Germans were to release all Jews under their stranglehold, "transport alone presents a problem which will be difficult of solution . . . but we shall do what we can." For him, these efforts included an understanding with the Foreign and Colonial offices to let the White Paper run its course, with no attempt made to create an agency parallel to the War Refugee Board across the ocean. He turned to the Foreign Office to answer in his place Harold Laski's cry of anguish on behalf of the Laborite's fellow Jews: "Can not even now something be done to give them a sign to relieve their agony?" He and Roosevelt omitted the Jewish people from the Moscow conference's formal statement in October, 1943, about those victim to Nazi atrocities. Neither leader, in the course of their secret correspondence with one another, raised the possibility of rescuing the particular targets of Hitler's obsessive hatred. In light of this response, Zygielbojm's suicide had been in vain. Like FDR, Churchill focused on the period after the war. His firm support for a large Jewish state in Palestine came too late, however, for those whose traditional homelessness such a commonwealth would have ended.[58]

The United Nations Declaration on Jewish Massacres, therefore, awakened the world's conscience but did not arouse the major Allies to translate that urgent moral call into action. That declaration remains the single international document dealing solely with Jewry's unparalleled plight in World War II. "Deeds commensurate with the gravity of the hour," called for in a last cable from the doomed fighters of the Warsaw ghetto uprising while the conference's delegates basked in the Bermuda sun, had not followed. The pleas and reasoned proposals of a concerned public could not move London and Washington to meaningful action. Chaim Weizmann's bitter observation, included in a memorandum to the conference which the Jewish Agency could not deliver in person, that "the world is divided into countries in which the Jews cannot live and countries which they must not enter"[59] had proved only too true during the Holocaust.

The Creation of
the U.S. War Refugee Board

ONE WEEK BEFORE Warsaw surrendered to Adolf Hitler's *Blitzkrieg* and the curtain fell on the first act of World War II, German Security Police Chief Reinhard Heydrich began to extend the Nazi persecution of Jewry beyond the borders of the Third Reich. Empowered by Hermann Goering the previous January to "solve the Jewish question," Heydrich ordered the mass resettlement and later concentration into ghettos of the two million Jews in German-occupied Poland as measures "leading to the fulfillment of the ultimate goal." Until final destinations would be approved, the Nazis turned the closed urban centers into death traps. Spotted typhus, tuberculosis, dysentery, and starvation ravaged the inhabitants. By September, 1942, 80,000 persons had died in the Warsaw ghetto alone. The Lodz Jewish community of originally 160,000 had a death-birth ratio of about 29:1 between 1940 and 1942; its Warsaw counterpart, 470,000 at its maximum, registered 45:1. In the end, one historian has estimated, one-fifth of Polish Jewry under the swastika perished behind these sealed walls.[1]

The American Jewish Joint Distribution Committee (JDC), formed in November, 1914, to bring relief to its fellow Jews in central and eastern Europe during World War I, kept warm a spark of life in this Jewish heartland. The "Joint" had spent some $2.6 million in Poland alone during 1933-38; in 1939 its expenditures reached $1.2 million. In 1940 and 1941, $859,400 and $972,000 respectively, reached the beleaguered Polish ghettos. By 1942, one in every nine Jews obtained meals at the JDC soup kitchens in Warsaw; the ratio stood at 1:3 in Lublin and 1:4 in the Radom and Warsaw districts. Medical aid helped 34 hospitals, and 30,000 children received daily care.[2]

Not one dollar of these funds entered Nazi-occupied Poland. Soon after the *Führer's* advent to power, the JDC decided not to provide aid that might benefit the German economy. All campaign monies raised were placed in U.S. banks, while zlotys arrived in Poland through the extension of a financial clearance arrangement that the Joint employed with its affiliated groups in the Third Reich: Berlin, Vienna, Prague, and Bratislava. This insistence on a relief policy "conforming in the closest degree" with U.S. State Department regulations had its drawbacks. The JDC, for example, refused to transmit funds from Geneva to Poland at the much higher black market rate or to send foodstuffs there from Bratislava against valuta or Swiss franc payments, contending that such moves would aid the German invader.[3]

Other Jewish organizations in the United States felt less constrained in the face of the crisis confronting their people abroad. The WJC, through its Geneva RELICO office directed by Alfred Silberschein with the aid of Gerhart Riegner, dispatched food parcels, visas, medicines, and clothing to Poland's interior (designated the "General-government") by a chain of paid messengers, a diplomatic consul's pouch, and a representative of the Catholic church. The Jewish Labor Committee and the Bund used Socialist contacts in London and even an employee of the Japanese embassy in Stockholm to forward sums to comrades in Warsaw; Agudas Israel employed ties to the Polish consulate in New York through which messages, monies, and parcels safely arrived in the ghettos.[4]

Few in the free world grasped in the first years of the war that Germany had consciously made starvation a weapon of annihilation, while public opinion believed that the blockade was the deadliest weapon in the British arsenal. "No form of relief can be devised," categorically asserted Prime Minister Churchill on August 20, 1940, in Commons, "which would not directly or indirectly assist the enemy's war effort." The British embassy in Washington reaffirmed Churchill's conviction on March 9, 1941, and in a letter to the Foreign Relations Committee a half-year later Secretary of State Hull opposed plans to feed occupied Europe on the assumption that "the responsibility and manifest duty to supply relief rests with the occupying authorities." To do otherwise, declared some prominent American Catholic laymen with the concurrence of the Unitarian Service Committee, "is contrary to the best interest of Christianity and America."[5]

The issue divided the Jewish organizations in the United States, and ultimately halted all sending of food packages from there to the Polish ghettos in the summer of 1941. The Joint Boycott Council, formed in the 1930s by the American Jewish Congress and the Jewish Labor Committee to boycott all trade with Nazi Germany, opened a drive in July, 1941, to "end the food package racket" and prevent the "feeding of Hitler's war machine." "Anything which will hinder the British war effort is contrary to the interests of the Jewish people," declared council president Joseph Tenenbaum, who stigmatized Agudas Israel as "a sickly weed transplanted from foreign soil to the liberal American environment." Pressure from the British embassy and the U.S. State Department having ended this activity by the WJC and the Federation of Polish Jews in America, WJC president Stephen Wise particularly anxious about "endangering everything by this wretched business," the council picketed the offices of Agudas Israel of America for disregarding official British requests to halt package service to relatives in Poland. Ultimately, the Aguda World executive in London under the direction of Harry Goodman announced on August 26 that it would henceforth be "guided entirely by the wishes of the British authorities in Washington." RELICO's Dr. Silberschein in Geneva, assisted by the WJC's Isaac Weissman in Lisbon, continued quietly to send food at the rate of 1,500 parcels per week. But this could hardly suffice when one-third of the Warsaw ghetto population could not even afford to pay the two-zloty tax on ration cards imposed by the *Judenrat* (Jewish Council), and living corpses collapsed and died every day in ghetto streets.[6]

The inability of Jewry in the free world to ease the Allied blockade was especially frustrating when the Anglo-American Alliance allowed food to reach Nazi-held Greece in 1942. While the Allied blockade and the U.S. Trading with the Enemy Act continued to hold back supplies to European Jewry, rapidly dwindling in number, 15,000 tons of wheat and 3,000 tons of other materials were sent to hold off starvation in Greece, with the help of the West and the International Committee of the Red Cross (ICRC). One ship even left from Haifa Bay. Jewry's singular agony, publicized in regular news dispatches, went unheeded, however.[7]

At this juncture the General Jewish Council in New York decided to consider sending a delegation to intercede with the State Department regarding relief supplies for Jews in Poland. On April 17, 1942, the Jewish Labor Committee, B'nai Brith, and the American Jewish Committee, in conjunction with the American Jewish Congress, drew up a draft memorandum. At the suggestion of the JDC's vice-chairman, Joseph Hyman, the group invited Christian and nonsectarian organizations to the deliberations. The issue, not confined to Jews, presented international, military, and diplomatic questions that had to be viewed "in relationship to the necessities of our country in prosecuting the war," Hyman argued. Delay thereby ensued. In the interim the State Department had insisted to the Representatives of Polish Jewry in Tel Aviv that "the successful prosecution of the war effort is of paramount importance even to suffering civilian populations," since only through an Allied victory would these people be "enabled to live again in a free society with an opportunity to lead normal lives." The American Jewish Congress's Maurice Perlzweig and the General Jewish Council's Isaiah Minkoff persisted nonetheless, and on November 13, 1942, the memorandum was ready.[8]

A promising breakthrough occurred simultaneously in London. Following a suggestion from Harry Goodman in mid-February, the Board of Deputies of British Jews had requested its government to permit food shipments to Poland's ghettos along the lines of the Greek relief example. On June 23, 1942, the British Ministry of Economic Warfare agreed to the board's sending one-pound packages of canned sardines, dried fruit, and like native products from neutral Portugal to specific individuals, with the Polish government-in-exile transferring funds for these shipments up to a maximum of $12,000 per month to its representative in Lisbon. Whitehall insisted on secrecy, as the British authorities were not prepared to sanction the project on any large scale or to encourage the sending of foreign exchange to Portugal. The Jewish Telegraphic Agency broke the story, however, on September 10, leading Hyman to insist to all queries that the JDC had to be "governed entirely" by American policy, which had not been ascertained.[9]

The WJC, in the meantime, had independently raised the question in Washington of relief to Jews in Poland. Reports published in early July, 1942, from the Bund and the Polish government-in-exile that at least 700,000 Jews had perished there stirred the WJC to press Washington again for aid without delay. On July 23 the WJC's Aryeh Tartakower and the president of the Central Representation of Polish Jews suggested to the U.S. Board of Economic Warfare that two tons of tea be sent to Poland for valuable exchange purposes via the International Red Cross (IRC) in Lisbon. James Waterman Wise, son of WJC president Stephen Wise, submitted a memorandum and legal brief to the Washington representative of the IRC asking that the ICRC in Geneva ship medicine and condensed milk to the ghettos, and that the Jews there be accorded the treatment demanded by international law under the 1929 Geneva Convention for all war prisoners.[10]

The Wises, father and son, together with WJC administrative committee head Nahum Goldmann, urged the Greek precedent on Assistant Secretary of State Dean Acheson. On October 5 they heard from Treasury Secretary Morgenthau that the State and Treasury departments had agreed "in principle" to follow the British example and to grant licenses of $12,000 monthly for the Belgian, Dutch, and Polish governments, two other organizations, and the WJC. Elated, the congress began reporting to its affiliated bodies that anti-typhus vaccine could be sent to the Warsaw ghetto, and it asked the Joint for financial support.[11]

Hearing this, the JDC promptly notified the other organizations of the General Jewish Council, which quickly sent a delegation to Washington. Minkoff and JDC representatives Hyman and Moses Leavitt assured Treasury Foreign Funds Control director John Pehle that the JDC, as the oldest and most substantial relief organization in the country, should be granted the license. In the meantime, the WJC and the Joint hurled verbal brickbats at each other with no hope for a mutual settlement.

Stephen Wise pointed out to Hyman that for several months the WJC had been discussing means with the American government of alleviating the tragic situation in eastern Europe; a united Jewish effort, to include the WJC's well-to-do South American affiliates, would be "welcomed" in Washington. Paul Baerwald, honorary chairman of the Joint, reviewed in turn the General Jewish Council's efforts with JDC support. He emphasized that his organization, which consistently focused on "humanitarian reconstruction and rehabilitation," considered the relief department of the WJC an integral part of the congress and therefore mainly concerned with "political objectives." The JDC received the Treasury license on December 11, 1942, just as the Allies first acknowledged that two million Jews had fallen victim to Germany's Final Solution.[12]

But the twelfth hour had already struck for Polish Jewry. The license was not even changed to allow packages to individuals; Portugal also made export of commodities very difficult. While Szmul Zygielbojm in London pleaded for "punitive measures against the Germans at once" as the only possible means of saving Polish Jewry, 7,000 of 12,000 packages of figs dispatched through the Board of Deputies between February and April, 1943, remained unaccounted for. In September JDC Lisbon representative Herbert Katzki reported that addresses for Warsaw and Crakow, along with Upper Silesia and the entire General-government except for Galicia, had to be eliminated on Nazi orders. "For the time being," the IRC's Washington delegate concluded in a letter to Agudas Israel two months later, the sending of supplies to Poland was "impossible."[13] Indeed, the large core of Polish Jewry had long since met death in the ghettos and labor camps or gone up in smoke in Treblinka, Chelmno, Belzec, Majdanek, Sobibor, and Auschwitz-Birkenau.

The WJC refused to forsake sending packages to Jewry in Poland. It first urged the ICRC to extend the use of its food parcel service from Switzerland to Jews in occupied Europe. In February and March, 1943, the congress pressed the Board of Economic Warfare to extend its new regulation of the previous November, allowing gift parcels to specified war prisoners and civilian internees, to Jews deported from Allied countries to eastern Europe and those in the ghettos. While the board, the State Department's Office of Foreign Relief and Rehabilitation Operations, and the ICRC delayed their replies, they all cautioned that American authorities would not approve of such schemes without firm German guarantees respecting such conditions. The full burden had again been shifted to the enemy's shoulders.[14]

But, unknown to the WJC, at that very moment career officers in the State Department had moved to withhold further information about the Holocaust from the Jewish community and even from certain authorities in the government. State officials had spent three months the previous year before confirming Gerhart Riegner's first report in August, 1942, about a rumored Nazi plan to kill all of European Jewry. On January 21, 1943, Minister Leland Harrison in Berne forwarded cable 482 for Wise to Under Secretary Welles, in which Riegner reported that 6,000 Jews were being killed daily in one Polish town, that Berlin Jews were facing their end, and that of 136,000 Jews deported to Rumanian-controlled Transnistria, 60,000 had died. Welles passed on the cable to Stephen Wise, and the American Jewish Congress readied for a Madison Square Garden mass demonstration calling for immediate Allied rescue. Yet on February 10 cable 354 arrived on Harrison's desk, referring to "YOUR CABLE 482, JANUARY 21," and suggesting that he *not* accept reports destined for "private persons" in the United States unless under "extraordinary circumstances." Welles apparently signed this routine-sounding dispatch without realizing the connection to cable 482, for on April 10, following Wise's request of March 31, he cabled Harrison to contact Riegner for "important information" about the fate of European Jewry that the WJC delegate wished to send to Wise.[15]

Welles's new order bewildered Harrison and especially mystified Riegner, who suddenly found his channel to Wise through Welles open once again. An embarrassed Paul Squire, the American consul in Geneva who with Harrison had done much to verify Riegner's August, 1942, report, could not tell the WJC man particulars about State's February 10 cable. To cover up the difficulty, he asked if Riegner could pay for sending off the requested information. "If necessary, I will," Riegner instantly replied. Harrison paraphrased Riegner's detailed two-page message of April 14 and mailed it to State four days later, along with his personal plea that the "helpful information" that Riegner's messages "may frequently contain" not be subject to the restriction imposed by cable 354.[16]

Riegner's telegram, forwarded on April 20, 1943, from the American legation at Berne, proposed a revolutionary change to WJC headquarters: funds from the United States could bring about the rescue—not just relief—of a substantial number of Jews within Nazi Europe. German authorities, he began, had approved ICRC collective shipments to the Theresienstadt ghetto near Prague, and might do likewise for Jewish labor camps in Upper Silesia. Much more significantly, "considerable amounts" of currency could bring about "wide rescue action" in Rumania, especially Transnistria, and France. An urgent appeal from Rumania's Jews for 100 million lei ($600,000), 60 million immediately to clothe and feed Transnistrian children and orphans who should be transferred to Palestine, could be met by guaranteeing that the funds would be deposited in Switzerland or the United States and paid *after* the war. Large sums, not to be transferred to French territory, would also aid in maintaining Jewish children underground in France and in transferring young people and certain "political friends" from that country to Spain and North Africa.[17]

The WJC central office in New York, seizing this new ray of hope, pressed the State Department to approve the financial arrangements hinted at in Riegner's telegram. His proposal seemed to bear directly on a February 12 news exclusive in the *New York Times* about the Rumanian government's offer to free the 70,000 Jews still alive in Transnistria—concerning which the Allies had done nothing. On April 23 Wise had written Welles to support a Treasury license for the WJC to send food packages to the Polish ghettos. A week later Wise and Nahum Goldmann asked the under secretary if he would recommend to Treasury that a license be issued to the WJC to deposit a substantial amount of money with the American legation in Switzerland for rescue work, as Riegner had outlined: "No military or economic objection from the point of view of the war effort could be made for the plan." Welles replied that he "saw the point," and asked for a memorandum on the subject.[18]

Welles then handed the matter over to State's economic adviser, Herbert Feis, who turned to Bernard Meltzer, acting chief of its Foreign Funds Control Division, for advice. On May 12 Meltzer saw Goldmann, who thought that by means of the scheme about 12,500 children could be transported from Rumania to Istanbul in two Rumanian boats and thence to Palestine with British visas, the Maquis rescuing political leaders and about 2,000 Jewish children from France to Spain or North Africa. Feis and Meltzer then worded a cable to Harrison that sought information, rather than "envisaging immediate action," about Riegner's proposal. These two Jews in Foggy Bottom, well aware of the negative attitude to the relief and rescue of European Jewry exhibited by Assistant Secretary Breckenridge Long from the beginning of the war through the recently concluded Bermuda conference, thereby kept the matter afloat.[19]

On June 14 Harrison cabled Riegner's confirmation that wealthy Rumanian Jews could provide the necessary funds to support the 70,000 remaining Jews in Transnistria, and would be reimbursed at black-market rates in American dollars or Swiss francs after the war through the American Jewish Congress's blocked account. Wilhelm Filderman, former president of the Jewish communities in Rumania, would disperse the WJC-backed funds via an underground relief agency manned by WJC members in that country; the WJC would try to evacuate immediately as many of these Jews as possible. As for France, at least 15,000-20,000 francs a month would be necessary. People in Switzerland having francs in France would release them to the underground through intermediaries trusted by the WJC in return for American dollars, converted into Swiss francs within Switzerland, at the prevailing black-market rate. Harrison, for his part, warned that these schemes in France could not be controlled, and that the transfer of enemy funds would be involved. At the same time he conveyed an ICRC report that the Rumanian government had taken a "helpful attitude toward [the] amicable settlement of Jews."[20]

Riegner's response only strengthened the division in State. While Feis and Meltzer favored action to implement the proposal, Long, his executive assistant, George Brandt, and his specialist on refugee matters, Robert Reams, particularly opposed this step. The trio emphasized that foreign exchange would thus be made available to the enemy, although Meltzer pointed out that the "economic warfare" aspects of the matter were questions for Treasury's decision. Long's Special Division finally made a slight concession: Meltzer could present Treasury with the economic warfare aspects alone at stake. Accordingly, on June 25 John Pehle received a copy of Riegner's cable.[21] This step, bringing Treasury for the first time officially into direct contact with the Final Solution, may have only suggested that Long and his subordinates intended further delay. Instead, to the amazement of both departments, it would ultimately swing the bolted doors of State's refugee policy wide open.

II

The State Department decision that Treasury had to be consulted on the WJC rescue proposal for Rumania and France delighted WJC headquarters. When first approached by the WJC to permit a license for food packages to the Polish ghettos, Treasury had unhesitatingly consented. In addition, in the WJC's view, bribery could bring results: New York headquarters had just received through the Polish diplomatic pouch an arresting letter from two Slovakian rabbis indicating that the deportations from Slovakia had temporarily ceased in this manner. "One of the highest Nazi officials," the long communication went on, would try to halt all the deportations and extermination of Europe's Jews, with the exception of Germany and the Protectorate, in exchange for an agreed amount of money to be deposited in Switzerland.[22] Now Riegner's letter suggested further possibilities.

But those American Jewish relief organizations that might raise the sums needed for significant rescue hesitated to accept the WJC's repeated urgings to take action. While the WJC could probably raise the ransom funds necessary to permit the evacuation of Transnistria's 70,000 Jews, the millions suggested for relief and larger rescue projects would be the responsibility of others. And they refused to apply to the U.S. government for permission to transfer money to Europe for rescue in Nazi-held territory, claiming that such deals, contravening the Trading with the

Enemy Act, were unpatriotic. At the end of May, for example, the JDC emphasized to State its interest in offering financial aid for "every possible measure of rescue and relief that will not conflict with military considerations" which the U.S. government "may devise and undertake." The Joint's representative in Switzerland, Saly Mayer, hesitated regarding the $2 million requested by the Slovakian Jewish "Working Group," partly on the assumption that the Allies would not permit him to make this transfer in the necessary Swiss francs. The WJC had no alternative, consequently, but to challenge the financial blockade on its own. Treasury seemed a far better address than State for this purpose.[23]

Indeed, these views proved to be well founded. James Wise and Goldmann met with Pehle and an associate in Treasury on July 1, 1943, to discuss the connection between Riegner's plan and "some indications" that for $170,000 certain government officials in Rumania would permit the evacuation of almost 70,000 Jews from their territory; Morgenthau was kept informed. Riegner and Harrison, in the meantime, prodded State for a reply, pointing out that an ICRC delegate could expedite the rescue project. At a State-Treasury departmental meeting on July 15 Pehle and the assistant general counsel, Josiah E. DuBois, Jr., insisted that various nationals of the German-occupied countries had agreed in previous cases to trade their own currency for dollars. By blocking the American relief funds in U.S. bank accounts, Treasury could ensure that the Germans would not get these dollars in later sales. Most of the foreign currency dealers, they observed, had consented to just such transfers. State officials continued to drag their feet, however. Feis and Meltzer could do no more than send a memorandum to Hull against the economic warfare argument raised by Long and company.[24]

Wise's intervention with Franklin D. Roosevelt on July 22, 1943, appeared to break the bottleneck. It had taken nearly two months to enter the Oval Office since Wise had first asked FDR for an "early appointment, because of the continued annihilation of our fellow Jews and the negative results of the Bermuda Conference." Roosevelt expressed his sympathy with the evacuation proposal, and said that he would take it up immediately with Morgenthau. Jubilant, Wise cabled his wife the good news before catching a return train to New York. The next day he expressed his "deep satisfaction" in a letter to the chief executive and urged approval of the proposal. A copy went to Morgenthau, along with Wise's expression of certainty that the secretary would be "deeply sympathetic ... to any undertaking which may save the lives of those otherwise doomed Jews."[25]

Wise's faith in Morgenthau was well placed. The dour Jew of German parentage had almost no knowledge of the traditions of his people, and always kept a low profile to avoid antisemitism and charges of divided loyalty. But Henrietta Klotz, his life-long secretary and watchdog over all Treasury appointments, fed Morgenthau Jewish culture regularly "with a teaspoon." This daughter of an Orthodox Jewish home also cultivated her boss's budding association with Zionists like Chaim Weizmann and Meyer Weisgal. German Jewry's worsening plight in 1938 had first led Morgenthau, and Roosevelt, to seek havens in South America and Africa for Jews and other refugees. But a vacation trip to the JDC's small DORSA refugee settlement in Santo Domingo, together with Weizmann's eloquence, convinced him by 1941 that only in Palestine could the harried Jews of Europe find security.[26]

Morgenthau's background and stolid temperament (Washington circles referred to "Henry the Morgue") had not prepared him for the Holocaust. When Wise, who had officiated at Morgenthau's wedding as the leader of the Reform Free Synagogue, told him in September, 1942, of Nazis converting Jewish bodies into fat for soap and pulling their teeth for gold, Morgenthau shielded his eyes in horror and implored: "Rabbi Wise, spare me!" That account and later press stories had a searing effect. He contacted the papal nuncio in Washington to have Pius XII intercede for Jewry's sake. A special Emergency Conference to Save the Jews of Europe received the secretary's message of "earnest hope" that those assembled would devise a specific plan to halt the "complete extermination" facing the Jewish people in Hitler's Europe: "Along with every other freedom loving American, I am deeply interested in seeing that every possible step is taken to stop this needless slaughter." The Riegner proposal signified just such a step. On July 31 the Treasury Department advised the American Jewish Congress that it was prepared to implement the evacuation proposal.[27]

Another week passed before State approved a cable about the license to Minister Harrison. As State preferred to make "no comments" on the Riegner proposal, however, only Treasury's approval made its way to the Berne mission on August 6. At the end of September the minister finally received word that he could definitely issue Riegner the license. Morgenthau even approved a memorandum, drafted by the department's general counsel, Randolph Paul, that Treasury could countenance other, similar projects "in view of the broad humanitarian considerations involved."[28]

By then, concerned members of the Treasury Department had had some indications of State's attitude toward assisting European Jewry. These included its objections to the immediate release of 1,500 Jewish refugees from camps in Algiers; its attempt, as reported by Drew Pearson in the *Washington Post,* to obtain a joint Anglo-American statement that would endorse the White Paper by barring any further discussion of Palestine until after the war; its hesitation to permit funds to be sent via Switzerland for the relief of Jewish refugees in Chunking; its stalling in the grant of JDC food packages to the "privileged ghetto" of Theresien-stadt. Foreign Funds Control director Pehle, who stepped in to approve the latter after receiving the JDC's plea in early September for a final ruling, now wished to ensure that State would do nothing further to hold up the Riegner plan.[29]

Suddenly, Minister Harrison mentioned two difficulties concerning Treasury's green light for the proposal. He required specific instructions from *State,* and the British commercial secretary also opposed the scheme so long as the Ministry of Economic Warfare (MEW) had not given its approval. Treasury, never told previously by State to get British ap-proval, only heard of Harrison's cable in mid-October through under-cover sources in the State Department. In response Pehle informed Long that U.S. funds had been transmitted in the past to other foreigners in need abroad, whereas British clearance was never necessary after Trea-sury had exercised its licensing authority in a *specific* case. Long finally gave a qualified approval, but Harrison, realizing State's dissociation from Treasury's enthusiastic support, checked with HMG's commercial secretary. The latter received word from his superiors—three weeks later—that the proper Washington authorities had to be consulted before MEW would finally agree.[30]

Morgenthau's circle in Treasury, stunned at State's dilatory tactics, urged Hull to have Ambassador John Winant officially press for MEW's withdrawal of its objections. Yet on December 6 Hull replied to Mor-genthau's letter by disclaiming responsibility for the three-and-a-half month delay! Treasury had never formulated a workable proposal for financing such a program, Hull countered, and it had never obtained British agreement.[31] The ball was back in Morgenthau's court.

Again, Morgenthau's "boys" provided a strong response. DuBois shared with the staff Meltzer's confidences about the division within State during the previous summer, including the significant news that the British embassy had in fact received information of the proposal at the time from Nahum Goldmann. Immediately contacted by Treasury, the British admitted this, but added that *State* had still not replied to a request for all the pertinent cables (at a time when State was holding up the whole program on the ground that *Treasury* had failed to clear it with the British). The staff decided to take full responsibility for issuing a license, and a ten-page memorandum by Paul, refuting Hull's conten-tions, arrived in Morgenthau's hands on December 17. A cable just received from Winant added fuel to the fire by hinting darkly that, according to MEW, which would have agreed to the license on purely financial grounds, "the Foreign Office are concerned with the difficulties of disposing of any considerable number of Jews should they be rescued from enemy occupied territory." Nothing should therefore be done, Whitehall declared, to implement the Riegner proposal, envisaging as it did the rescue of some 70,000 Jews.[32]

Recovering from this candid message, a very angry Morgenthau called for a two-page memorandum from Paul to present to the secretary of state and to the president, calling for immediate action on the Riegner proposal. Pehle, DuBois, and the others, however, urged that the time had definitely come for Roosevelt to establish an agency that would deal sympathetically with all rescue possibilities. Lend Lease counsel Oscar Cox of the Foreign Economic Administration (FEA), a Jew who had first proposed such a course to Morgenthau after the Bermuda conference had ended its secret deliberations, was especially persuasive in supporting this position during Treasury's "Jewish Evacuation" conference of December 19.

The secretary agreed but insisted that he confront "old man Hull" personally with the facts before turning to FDR in the last resort. He wished to tell Hull: "After all, if you were a member of the Cabinet in Germany today, you would be, most likely, in a prison camp, and your wife [a Jewess who had changed her maiden name from Wirtz to Whitney] would be God knows where." The time had come, as Paul's revised memorandum concluded, for State and Treasury "to cut the Gordian knot *now* by advising the British that we are going to take immediate action to facilitate the escape of Jews from Hitler and *then* discuss what can be done in the way of finding them a more permanent refuge.... Even if we took those people and treated them as prisoners of war it would be better than letting them die."[33]

An even more shocking revelation moved Morgenthau to face head on what Pehle called the "real issue." In early December DuBois asked Donald Hiss, a friend at State, if he could provide a copy of the mysterious cable 354 referred to in Harrison's dispatch of April 20, which Pehle had received in mid-July. DuBois obtained the signed copy and the previous telegram (482) to which it referred, Riegner's report of January 21, thereby giving Treasury the sudden realization that State wished to suppress vital information about the Holocaust.[34]

At a meeting with Hull on December 20, 1943, Morgenthau therefore read with amazement Hull's sharp reply to the Foreign Office, refusing to accept Whitehall's view about difficulties in the disposal of many rescued Jews. Long chimed in self-defensively that he had even ordered Harrison two days earlier to issue the license to Riegner. Hull's cable to Winant "took the wind completely" out of Treasury's sails, but Morgenthau and Paul jointly agreed on the spot to hand Morgenthau's memorandum to Hull. After a hasty reading of the document, the genuinely furious secretary of state conceded that the "people down the line" got "hold of these things and didn't understand them.... You just sort of have to rip things out if you want to get them done."[35]

Despite this victory, the Treasury officers wished to go beyond the license and obtain a governmental rescue commission, together with havens in neutral territories for Jews escaping death. Morgenthau had taken a great risk in pushing State: Hull might not have wished to be bothered with the issue, or anti-Roosevelt congressmen might still get a copy of the memorandum. Oscar Cox, armed with drafts for a press release and an executive order (first written by Milton Handler of his staff) to set up a "Committee on War Refugees" under Hull, Morgenthau, and the director of the FEA, reported that Edward Stettinius, Jr., Welles's newly appointed successor, had privately expressed sympathy for the Jewish refugee question.[36]

Long, moreover, had sent over cable 354 (a few hours after the Hull-Morgenthau conference) *without* the reference to cable 482. The only tangible clue to the message's true meaning would have been lost forever if DuBois had not ascertained the facts. Eventually an exact copy of 354 was obtained from State, along with that of Welles's first request for more information in October, 1942, and subsequently in April, 1943, concerning Riegner's August, 1942, report. The Treasury staff informed Morgenthau of these facts in a memorandum stamped "secret," charging that the efforts of Long and his "diabolical" associates to dam Riegner's vital information made them "accomplices of Hitler" and "war criminals in every sense of the term." Long's obstruction over the Riegner proposal for eight months until his abrupt approval on December 18 because of Treasury's unremitting pressure followed this pattern.[37]

A concerned American public, sparked particularly by the rigorous efforts of an Irgun Tsva'i Leumi delegation from Palestine, had also begun to question the State Department's response to the annihilation of Europe's Jews. That small band, headed by 33-year-old Hillel Kook (alias Peter Bergson), first captured national headlines and prestigious support with a dynamic, nonsectarian campaign to raise a 200,000-strong Jewish army of stateless and Palestinian Jew for the Allied cause. When Washington confirmed the dimensions of the Final Solution at the end of 1942, the young mavericks shifted their propaganda war to checking the massacre of their people in Europe. Shrill full-page advertisements by Pierre Van Paassen and Ben Hecht; the latter's "We Will Never Die" pageant, which played to overflow crowds across the country; cables to Churchill attacking the British White Paper; and blasts against the closed Bermuda conference as a "cruel mockery" of five million Jews caught in the "Nazi death trap"—all gradually succeeded in piercing the silence shrouding the Holocaust.[38]

The real danger—that with the advance of the Allied armies the Nazis would speed up their destruction of the Jews, as Joseph Goebbels currently threatened—drove Kook's entourage on to further activity. Convinced that governments would act only when public opinion compelled action, the sponsors of Van Paassen's "Proclamation on the Moral Rights of Stateless and Palestinian Jews," in cooperation with the Committee for a Jewish Army, decided to call an "Emergency Conference to Save the Jews of Europe." Meeting on July 20–25, 1943, at New York's Hotel Commodore, outstanding experts examined questions of international relations, military affairs, transportation, and relief, and restored the disaster to its rightful place as a specific Allied problem capable of definite solution. The conferees urged the U.S. government to create an official agency charged with rescuing this one people marked for death, the other United Nations free to participate if they so wished. The International Red Cross, neutral governments, and the Vatican, for their part, should oversee better treatment of Jews in the satellite governments, and press for their emigration from Axis-held territory. Ample food and shipping, particularly Allied vessels bringing troops to Europe and food to Greece which returned with empty holds, were available to help the persecuted. In four months 600,000 Jews from the satellite nations could be evacuated to Palestine, with an additional 150,000 brought to other temporary locations in neutral countries. Punitive raids and the promise of postwar reprisals would follow if Germany's satellites refused to let the Jews leave.[39]

The conference elicited wide coverage and pressured the nation's foremost political leaders to take a stand. Responding to a telegram from Max Lerner, Williams College professor, chief political writer for *PM*, and chairman of the emergency conference's resolutions committee, Roosevelt seconded Hull's assurance that the Intergovernmental Committee on Refugees and other Anglo-American efforts represented this government's "repeated endeavors" to rescue the Jews of Europe. Among other dignitaries, Morgenthau and Mrs. Roosevelt, who had expressed to Welles her feeling after the *Struma* tragedy that the White Paper policy "just seems to be cruelty beyond words," sent more personal messages of concern.[40]

Accompanied by American Labor party leader Dean Alfange and the sculptor Jo Davidson, Kook met with Hull and Long on August 12. The delegation suggested sending three three-man teams to investigate rescue possibilities, including temporary havens in Spain and Turkey, and to ask Palestine's high commissioner about temporary visas and the possibility of releasing the last 29,000 certificates under the White Paper. Similar camps at Jewish expense, they added, could be set up in Switzerland, Sweden, Portugal, and Morocco. The secretary retorted at the time that he viewed favorably the dispatch of such delegations, and would take their suggestion for camps into consideration.[41]

Still, finely expressed intentions did not result in concrete action. At the end of August the State Department announced the formation of a special U.S. commission to save European art, but the Emergency Committee's request for a specific agency to rescue Jews went unheeded. The Intergovernmental Committee on Refugees and the Bermuda conference championed by Roosevelt and Hull, by ignoring the unique Jewish tragedy, had proven distressingly inadequate to meet the crisis. State and Downing Street, as Lerner tellingly put it in a column addressed to the president, continued to "insist on giving the Jews in their death the civil national status that Hitler denies them in life." Van Paassen returned to the battle in September with a full-page "open letter" to Roosevelt and Churchill, appealing for the immediate establishment of a joint rescue agency so that humanity could say, in the language of the Bible, "our hands have not shed this blood." He received no reply. The mission of Congressman Will Rogers, Jr. (Democrat from California), sent by the Emergency Committee to London, also failed to achieve positive results in the way of rescue.[42]

Confronted by bureaucratic shuffle and silence, the "Bergson boys," as Kook's group increasingly became known, increased the public pressure on Washington. To coincide with the ten Days of Penitence preceding Yom Kippur, 400 Orthodox rabbis marched on the Capitol on October 6. After presenting a petition to Vice-President Henry Wallace on the steps of the Senate that called for rescue without further delay, the bearded, black-coated assembly heard one of their number chant Hebrew prayers at the Lincoln Memorial for Hitler's victims and (to the tune of "The Star-Spangled Banner") for the U.S. government. From there the patriarchal-looking group silently proceeded to the White House for an expected interview with Roosevelt, only to be told that the president was away on "other business."[43]

The foremost leaders of 6,000 churches in America proclaimed October 10 a Day of Intercession, requesting their followers to pray for "your Jewish brethren" in Europe and to aid the Emergency Committee. As "the last-ditch stand to prevent inaction from countenancing the slaughter of European Jewry," the committee then initiated a drive for ten million signatures to the president and Congress favoring the establishment of a separate intergovernmental rescue agency. It also staged the first rally honoring Sweden's heroic action to save Danish Jewry, at which 6,000 heard former Office of Price Administration director Leon Henderson castigate the Allies' "moral cowardice" and challenge Roosevelt and Churchill to right their countries' dismal rescue record. When the Moscow conference's Declaration on Atrocities still pointedly excluded the Nazis' prime target, Hecht penned an advertisement entitled "My Uncle Abraham Reports," an elegy that concluded bitterly with small hope of hearing anything worthwhile about Jews from Roosevelt's 1600 Pennsylvania Avenue study.[44]

The unparalleled tragedy of Jewry abroad and the success of the Emergency Committee's enlightenment campaign inspired the Bergsonites to try their last card—resolutions in both the House and Senate to move the administration. Congressmen Will Rogers, Jr., and Joseph Baldwin (Republican from New York) and Senator Guy Gillette (Republican from Iowa) introduced identical resolutions on November 9, 1943, urging Roosevelt to create a rescue commission "designed to save the surviving Jewish people of Europe from extinction at the hands of Nazi Germany." For Breckenridge Long, the demand appeared "an unwarranted duplication of effort" of the Intergovernmental Committee he had disinterred during the Bermuda conference. Only after protracted delays and Treasury Department intervention had he recently agreed to Kook's request that Ira Hirschmann, vice-president of Bloomingdale's, be sent to investigate rescue possibilities from the vantage point of Istanbul. Seeking to blunt the attack on State's handling of the Jewish refugee question, Long released the Bermuda final report the following day. Its lack of substance, however, merely strengthened the resolve of his opposition.[45]

While the Senate Foreign Relations Committee took the resolution under its wing, Sol Bloom, chairman of the House counterpart, decided to hold hearings in the matter. The elderly Jewish congressman from New York, having been pilloried by the Bergson boys for serving at the Bermuda fiasco as a stalking horse for State's position, now saw the chance to rehabilitate his image. Witnesses Dean Alfange, Congressman Baldwin, William Ziff, Kook, Frances Gunther, and New York Mayor Fiorello LaGuardia, however, unsparingly accused the American government and the Allies of sabotaging all effective rescue of European Jewry, and thereby encouraging the Nazis to continue their annihilation campaign with unremitting fury.

The mounting pressure of cables demanding action, speared by the Emergency Committee's advertisement "HOW WELL ARE YOU SLEEPING?," convinced Bloom to have Long himself testify in State's defense. For four hours in executive session on November 26, the star witness described the department's rescue steps and dwelt on his revival of the Intergovernmental Committee at Bermuda. His confidential assertions that the allied body had the authority to negotiate with the Axis through neutral governments and that 580,000 refugees had been admitted since 1933 to these shores contributed to a very favorable reception; even Rogers, co-sponsor of the rescue commission proposal, hailed his "fine and brilliant exposition."

The appearance of Rabbi Wise before Bloom's committee six days later further weakened the resolution's chances of success. The American Zionist spokesman had opposed the Irgun group's independent methods from the start as unrepresentative of the American Jewish community at large. A few months earlier Wise had persuaded the U.S. delegate to the Intergovernmental Committee not to attend the Emergency Conference to Save the Jews of Europe. He had also rejected a suggestion from Samuel Rosenman, Roosevelt's chief speech writer and adviser, that Kook be invited with the most prestigious Jewish organization leadership to a conference for unity; he and Rosenman (both of the Reform persuasion) had advised FDR in October not to receive the Orthodox rabbis. The executive board of the established Emergency Committee for Zionist Affairs worried about Rosenman's periodic warnings that the tactics of the Bergson clique alienated the "sympathetic" president, and no Jewish leader venerated the occupant of the White House more than Stephen Wise.

Speaking as a co-chairman of the recently established American Jewish Conference, Wise lost no time in throwing a damper on the resolution. He first smeared those "rashly written and rashly published advertisements" (of Kook's group) that always asked for help and funds not accounted for, and casually dismissed the Emergency Committee as representing "no one but a handful, a very small number of Jews and a number of Christians." The Zionist official then called the resolution "inadequate" for its lack of a specific program, especially for not mentioning open entry into Palestine, the Jewish national home promised in Britain's 1917 Balfour Declaration. In their own counsels Kook, chief lieutenant Samuel Merlin, and their associates were sure that the governmental commission they championed would quickly realize that country's central value. But in assigning rescue first priority, the Irgunists and their congressional supporters had purposely avoided this knotty political issue for fear it might jeopardize the resolution. For Wise and other leading Zionists, however, rescue and Palestine were inseparable in the redemption of their beleaguered people. Having carried the banner of a Jewish state in Palestine for many lonely years, and having now captured most of the country's major Jewish organizations for that cause at the American Jewish Conference, they were not prepared to tolerate any compromise on principle. Public attacks followed against the Emergency Committee as one of many "fronts" designed to undermine the recognized national Jewish agencies.[46]

Despite these setbacks, the mounting pressure initiated by the Emergency Committee blew the cover off State's case. Convinced that Long's "extensive report" obviated the need for a separate rescue commission running counter to the policy fixed at Bermuda, Bloom asked for and received Long's approval to make the assistant secretary's testimony public. The vacuity of the Bermuda conference now became common knowledge, especially after the Jewish Telegraphic Agency printed a statement it had obtained from the director of the Intergovernmental Committee on Refugees that it had no authority whatsoever to negotiate with the Axis. State's duplicity also appeared blatant when Jewish groups calculated the number of all refugees actually admitted to the United States at no more than a third of the figure given by Long, who had erred in the number of visas issued. "If men of the temperament and philosophy of Long continue in control of immigration admission," reacted New York Congressman Emanuel Celler, "we might as well take down that plaque from the Statue of Liberty and black out the 'lamp beside the golden door.'" Just before the Christmas recess the House Foreign Relations Committee shelved the resolution, as Long had wished, but Gillette and the Senate committee stood firm. Utah's Elbert Thomas moved swiftly the day that Roosevelt-inspired, hostile chairman Tom Connally was ill. Gillette's resolution, which drew the unprecedented co-sponsorship of 12 colleagues from both parties, was adopted unanimously on December 20, 1943. What would Congress do, observers asked, when it reconvened in three weeks?[47]

These latest revelations cemented Morgenthau's irrevocable decision to take Treasury's indictment of State directly to the White House. Randolph Paul would have three weeks in which to prepare a memorandum of the case for a scheduled appointment with Roosevelt on January 16, 1944. The secretary's gambit would be an explanation of the delay between Wise's July meeting with FDR over the Riegner proposal and the issuance of the license to the WJC on Christmas eve.[48]

While Paul and his colleagues, particularly DuBois, revised the memorandum, some of the staff heard from the WJC about State's "willful attempts" to prevent rescue ever since Riegner's first cable regarding the Final Solution had reached it. The WJC's Irving Miller, who had waited anxiously outside the gates of the White House while Wise met with Roosevelt on July 22, frankly explained to Paul, Pehle, and DuBois about the "run-around" that the WJC received from State, and about the way in which the department had torpedoed the Bermuda conference even before it convened. Pehle also discovered that Treasury's approval four months earlier for a JDC license to rescue abandoned Jewish children in France had also been stymied by the department. He issued the license forthwith, and exchanged $100,000 worth of Swiss francs for Saly Mayer's work, on his own.[49]

Meeting with Morgenthau on January 12, Hull agreed with his Cabinet colleague's assertion that the U.S. government's record in rescuing the Jews was "most shocking." Yet State's aging chief showed no knowledge of Eden's view, cabled by Winant five days earlier, that possible "transportation and accommodation problems" that might be "embarrassing" to both governments could well ensue from the adoption of Riegner's scheme. An ashen-faced Long sought unsuccessfully to hold back the record of his suggestion to the British minister in Washington that HMG make havens available for Jewish refugees in Cyrenaica and Tripolitania, the former Italian colonies in North Africa, and so divert mounting public pressure away from the most logical refuge, the Jewish Yishuv in Palestine. Only days earlier the British had turned down the JDC's month-old request to set aside sufficient Palestine certificates *within* the White Paper quota to assure the evacuation from Switzerland of 5,000 French Jewish children after the war, although this step alone would persuade the Swiss authorities to admit these children facing the gravest danger of deportation and death. The moment "the heat was off," Treasury privately concluded, nothing helpful would be forthcoming from State.[50]

The final brief for the president, written by DuBois, Pehle, and Paul—three Protestants—flayed the State Department's failure to use the available governmental machinery to help rescue European Jewry. Included in the *Report to the Secretary on the Acquiescence of This Government in the Murder of the Jews* was a most recent revelation about the WJC's inability to obtain Anglo-American funds for aiding European Jewry through ICRC auspices. Goldmann had suggested to Long in September that the two governments contribute $8 million to the ICRC for medicines and concentrated foods for Jews in central Europe. Long replied then that State had no money, the president possessed limited special funds, and the WJC would have to obtain a congressional appropriation. He agreed, however, to recommend the measure if approved by the Intergovernmental Committee in London, a move that effectively stifled Goldmann's proposal from the start. The JDC, informed by Goldmann of Long's interest, had immediately offered State to make an initial grant of $100,000 to the ICRC while a decision on the larger proposal was pending. While the Intergovernmental Committee produced no quick response, the Treasury staff reported to Morgenthau on January 14 that the president's special fund contained $70 million and that State officials could get whatever sum they wished "with a snap of their fingers."[51] Long had apparently not made the crucial gesture.

A startling piece of evidence just uncovered about the attitude of the American Joint Chiefs of Staff toward rescue also found its place in the explosive charge. On October 12, 1943, Goldmann had cabled Hull about information from the WJC's British section that 4,000 Jewish refugees and Yugoslavs recently in internment camps in Ugo had been freed by Tito's partisans and removed to the Adriatic island of Rab. In view of the possible recapture of that island by the Germans, the WJC asked that the U.S. military authorities be requested to move the refugees quickly to a safer area, such as southern Italy, Sicily, or North Africa. Hull referred the matter via Winant to the Intergovernmental Committee in London, whose principal heads recommended on November 2 that State ask the military's advice and also consider sending funds to the refugees so they could effect their own escape. Winant, who contacted the American military in London, finally heard on December 15 that the joint chiefs had turned down the request on operational grounds. But the august body also used the occasion to declare that "to take such action might create a precedent which would lead to other demands and an influx of additional refugees for the care of which the military authorities would be unable to provide facilities and supplies." This position, Morgenthau observed, like that taken by State and the Foreign Office, fundamentally "was no different from Hitler's attitude." The Nazis recaptured Rab.[52]

Morgenthau had doubts about how Roosevelt would react to the memorandum, as well as to the executive order redrafted by the Treasury youngsters, Handler, and Office of War Mobilization counsel Ben Cohen, but he was determined to force the issue to a head. The president's closest Cabinet associate had generally succumbed in the past to FDR's infectious charm, and he cautioned his circle that Roosevelt might say "I'll take this off your hands, I don't want you to get involved," or "You have to take this off my hands." Yet Morgenthau, moved to the core ever since Wise had given him a wrenching picture of the Jewish martyrdom on Europe's blood-soaked soil, would no longer settle for such replies. Although he preferred Treasury's case to be settled on its merits, he was prepared, if necessary, to capitalize on the "boiling pot on the Hill" regarding Gillette's bipartisan resolution and to let the memorandum invoke the danger of a "nasty scandal" in an election year should public suspicions of State antisemitism be confirmed.[53]

And, as a last resort, the secretary was ready to carry out the threat of his own resignation. Confidante Henrietta Klotz reminded Morgenthau, as he cast about for a way to shake Roosevelt to take decisive action, that he had threatened the president several times to retire to his Dutchess County farm. Her superior took the suggestion in complete earnest.[54]

Morgenthau, Pehle, and Paul confronted Roosevelt in the White House on January 16, 1944, as he quickly read the secretary's *Personal Report to the President*. The secretary had condensed the original draft and had altered its title, but he had left the original sting intact. Its eight single-spaced typed pages began with a direct attack on the State Department for completely failing to "take any effective action to prevent the extermination of the Jews in German-controlled Europe." The indictment focused on the delays over Riegner's evacuation proposal and on the fate of his cables about the Holocaust at the hands of men "who are indifferent, callous and perhaps even hostile." The delegation then provided additional examples of repeated inaction and opportunities lost under Long and his staff, and Pehle explained why a determined governmental effort to save European Jewry would not harm the economic blockade.[55]

The overwhelming weight of the argument and Morgenthau's rock-like stance, along with the mounting pressure for a presidential rescue commission from Congress and the public after Long's House committee testimony became common knowledge, combined to produce the desired effect. Roosevelt responded with enthusiasm to the executive order, proposed that Hull and Secretary of War Henry Stimson join Morgenthau as the War Refugee Board's nominal heads, and urged a greatly relieved Secretary of the Treasury to discuss the proposal with Under Secretary Stettinius. Six days later the president announced the formation of the War Refugee Board by Executive Order 9417, John Pehle to be its acting director. FDR assigned the new agency $1 million from his emergency funds, but private rescue agencies would have to cover all expenses thereafter.[56]

With strong support from Stettinius, who (in a forthright memorandum to Hull) questioned as final the joint chiefs' position about rescue operations, a discernible shift from past State Department practice occurred. Back in September he had received FDR's encouragement for a three-man rescue commission, but Hull and Long had killed the idea by convincing the sincere but uninformed under secretary that it would "cut across" the Intergovernmental Committee and "upset" the Bermuda conference's conclusions. Now Stettinius assigned Long, who persuaded Hull to keep the "hot potato" entirely out of State, to drop all refugee questions and handle congressional relations. Treasury's draft of an unequivocal cable from State on January 25 to all its diplomatic missions abroad—at a record cost of $10,000—to facilitate by all possible means the War Refugee Board's future work for the rescue and relief of "the victims of enemy oppression" also went forward under Stettinius's guiding hand.[57]

The telegram, Pehle aptly concluded, effectively changed "the whole government policy." Eight hundred fifty thousand letters of support, clear indication that the Bergson boys had been very effective, flooded the White House. Gillette removed his resolution from the Senate floor, noting that Roosevelt's abrupt action "attained the goal we were seeking." Unaware of Morgenthau's personal involvement, newspapers credited the Emergency Committee's "industrious spadework" solely with the outcome.[58] A promising beginning, critics agreed. But the lateness of the hour and Adolf Hitler's ruthless determination to complete the murder of all the Jews in Europe made the odds of success more than questionable.

CONCLUSION

Four years had elapsed between the Nazi conquest of Poland and Roosevelt's creation of the War Refugee Board. The State Department's inaction and "gross procrastination," as Morgenthau then characterized it,[59] had been clearly reflected in the case of food relief to the ghettos, cable 354, and Riegner's rescue proposal. Especially striking was State's opposition to the WJC evacuation plan, given Roosevelt's initial encouragement and the support of the department's own economic specialists and the Treasury Department's Foreign Funds Control Division. Only Treasury's increasing pressure finally brought about the department's retreat in these matters.

The Foreign Office's record suffered even more by comparison. While it approved a limited license for food to Poland and Theresienstadt before State did, Whitehall expressed reluctance on political grounds even to accept its *own* Ministry of Economic Warfare's approval of the preliminary financial arrangements for Riegner's scheme. Morgenthau appropriately termed its views "a Satanic combination of British chill and diplomatic double-talk; cold and correct, and adding up to a sentence of death." The persistent worry about "disposing" of any "considerable number of Jews" from Nazi-occupied Europe also explains the vexation of a prominent Foreign Office official on suddenly hearing of the War Refugee Board's creation: "It is fundamentally all part of a Zionist drive and is liable to make much trouble for us in Palestine and with our relations with America over Palestine." In like vein, the British would register a protest in March, 1944, against the board's new licensing policy to private organizations; HMG did not set up a parallel refugee agency during the remainder of the war.[60]

Both governments appeared uneasy with the possibility of truly aiding the Jewish people in their blackest hour. According to the Allied rationale, supplies to the ghettos would "almost certainly" be diverted for the Germans' personal use or granted the Jews just to free the Third Reich from its "responsiblity" to feed them. Either way, the argument could not lose and the Jews died. Actual rescue, on the other hand, raised "technical difficulties" which might be "embarrassing" to both governments. Anthony Eden's choice of words in January, 1944, simply echoed his earlier fear, expressed to Hull and Roosevelt in March, 1943, that acceptance of Bulgaria's 60,000–70,000 Jews might cause Hitler to make similar offers in Poland and Germany just when shipping and accommodation could not "handle" the Jews. State's European Division had turned down a related offer for Rumanian Jewry in November, 1941, on similar grounds. Both governments jointly took this position at the Bermuda conference, Robert Reams of Long's staff later informing Stettinius that "in the event of our admission of inability to take care of these people, the onus for their continued persecution would have been largely transferred from the German Government to the United Nations." Officialdom had no intention of conceding, as Will Rogers, Jr., emphasized at the Emergency Conference in July, 1943, that the problem had to be "taken out of the dossiers of the diplomats and placed in the hearts of humanity."[61]

Morgenthau and the Treasury circle reacted differently, understanding the moral issue involved and the possibility of helping the Jews without sacrificing the major war effort. Realizing, with Cox and Stettinius, that the annihilation of the Jews by the Nazis challenged the basic principles of humanity and civilization for which the Allies had taken up arms, they argued that bringing the Jews relief and rescue would both thwart the Axis and further a fundamental objective of the United Nations in view of Germany's announced policy to destroy this one people. A proud American, Morgenthau deeply believed in the concept of the United States as a refuge for the persecuted the world over; as a Jew, the Holocaust shocked him profoundly. Guided by a concerned staff, he displayed courage and statesmanship in first approving Riegner's evacuation project, then challenging State, and finally confronting Roosevelt himself.[62]

Had the definite possibilities which existed been taken up without delay by the Anglo-American Alliance, as Treasury championed, countless thousands of Jews would have survived the Third Reich's *Götterdammerung*. Food and medical supplies could have provided immediate sustenance throughout Europe, while dollars and Swiss francs would have been used for false documents, South American passports, bribes, and large ransom efforts. Some in the Nazi hierarchy did allow wealthy Jews to buy their way to safety. Taking note of this fact when defending State's "reluctance" to allow blocked accounts in Switzerland, which "apparently could not be used by the Nazi leaders" during the war, Cordell Hull later unwittingly admitted the probability of rescue: "... the State Department did not have the large sums of money and the personnel needed to carry out a plan of reaching and bribing the German officials in charge of the extermination program."[63] Treasury revealed, however, that the attitude of State and the Foreign Office precluded attempting such plans in the first place.

Some Jewish efforts had shown what successes even limited funds could achieve in underground activities. JDC funds via Saly Mayer enabled the Oeuvre de Secours aux Enfants (OSE) to shelter thousands of children in Christian homes throughout 1942, until the U.S. government cut diplomatic relations with Vichy in November and the Trading with the Enemy Act closed off legal payments to southern France. Three Palestinian Jewish emissaries in Istanbul, assigned to work exclusively to save their people in Europe, reported to American Jewish organizations in May and July, 1943, how "with money one can save lives." They wrote that bribery had postponed the expulsion of the entire surviving Slovakian Jewish community three times, and that Jews could be smuggled out of Poland, Slovakia, and Hungary, a view Alfred Silberschein confirmed in a November letter to WJC headquarters. But by the time the War Refugee Board managed to take its first concrete steps to alter the financial blockade, the German armies occupied Hungary and speedily carried out the last act of the Final Solution with a ruthlessness unsurpassed heretofore. Even then the board favored drawn-out negotiations over Gestapo offers at the end of 1944, rather than allowing the payment of inconsequential sums for the swift release of Jews in Nazi hands.[64]

Organized Jewry in the United States failed at times to measure up to the unparalleled catastrophe. The inability to grasp that the Third Reich employed starvation as a weapon to destroy European Jewry, coupled with sincere but misguided doubts about challenging the Allied blockade against Germany, ended its food parcel projects in August, 1941.[65] The more established JDC executive insisted on complying with all American regulations and refused throughout the war to contemplate some *modus vivendi* with the WJC, while Jews abroad underwent mass annihilation.[66] Patriotic considerations not to confront the financial blockade, together with fears of dual loyalty charges, overrode the desperate need to raise and transmit substantial funds for ransom and similar activities. A traditional philosophy of relief in accordance with governmental law, rather than obligatory large-scale rescue measures, fundamentally could not cope with the crisis at hand.

Even those organizations that challenged the economic warfare argument did not always comprehend the dimensions of Nazi policy. One major Agudas Israel leader, for example, continued to focus as late as March, 1943, on sending the (already doomed) ghettos food to save the Jews and thereby "disrupt" the Nazi propaganda line in occupied countries: "One Jew less—one bread more!" In mid-July he still pressed the Joint Emergency Committee for European Jewish Affairs to dispatch food by boat for the "still several million Jews in Poland."[67] WJC headquarters in New York, although maintaining constant pressure on various departments in Washington and elsewhere to save Jewry, also erred occasionally in evaluating the crisis. Thus, in a memorandum to the Bermuda conference it expressed the conviction that starvation represented the major cause of Jewish death at German hands. The second factor, it declared, was the high death rate Jews suffered while being transported from Poland to labor camps on the Nazi-Soviet front.[68]

In the final analysis, however, the JDC correctly concluded that the ultimate solution to helping European Jewry lay "in the hands of governments from whom permission must be secured." Rather than grapple with the "technical difficulties" involved in relief and rescue, the State Department and Foreign Office, the Board of Economic Warfare and MEW, the ICRC, the joint chiefs, and the Intergovernmental Committee on Refugees all passed their responsibilities onto the enemy. Roosevelt did nothing until pressed by Wise in July, 1943, and, far more important, by Morgenthau and political considerations in January, 1944, even though he had received an eyewitness report on July 28, 1943, from Jan Karski of the Polish underground about the gassing of Jews at Belzec.[69]

"I don't know how we can blame the Germans for killing them when we are doing this," observed Randolph Paul in December, 1943. "The law," he concluded, "calls them *para-dilecto,* of equal guilt." At a time when the two closest Allies received accurate information on the full scope of the Jewish tragedy, the *New York Post*'s Samuel Grafton raised the issue most succinctly in a column that found its way into Morgenthau's personal diaries: "Either we consider the Jews part of Europe, and therefore we retaliate against their murderers as against the murderers of Europeans, or we must consider them a special case, and therefore devise a special means of rescue. There are no other alternatives, in logic or in honor; only these two."[70] The powers of the free West refused to pick up the challenge.

Confronted by the Holocaust, the American and British governments discriminated in their unwillingness to save European Jewry. State Department wires regularly sent reports from Switzerland to private American and British firms giving the status of their property holdings in Europe, but cable 354 argued that further cables from Riegner about the Final Solution should be suppressed because such "private messages" might endanger official secret communications.[71] The telegram approved of this service in "extraordinary circumstances," but State did not regard the mass murder of millions of Jews as such.

A massive food relief program to Greece could be carried out, but not to the ghettos of Poland and only slight quantities to Theresienstadt and elsewhere. (The Jewish organizations, particularly the JDC, immediately covered the substantial cost of these relief services when tardy governmental approval provided an opportunity to do so.) While both Washington and London allowed a Zurich firm to purchase substantial amounts of material in German-held territory—even manufacturing radio transmitters for the Nazi war effort—funds for aiding European Jewry in its bleakest hour became suspect. Whitehall quickly transferred £3,000 sterling to Guernsey to feed English children in the Channel Islands occupied by the Germans without even asking for U.S. approval, but it turned a deaf ear to similar relief for Jewish children in Rumania,

France, and all over Axis Europe facing certain death. British imperial policy kept the people most in need from their national homeland in Palestine, tantalizingly close to the charnel house of Europe. State did finally challenge this rationale concerning the Riegner proposal, but it acceded to the more basic White Paper at the Bermuda conference and zealously guarded entry into the United States.[72]

Hidden behind the special classification "stateless refugees," the Jews could not hope to exercise any meaningful leverage in the international arena. Assistant Secretary Acheson attempted to explain away the fundamental differences between the Greek and Jewish ghetto situations in terms of a German perspective, but actually, as Nahum Goldmann observed at the end of 1944, the Jews could not duplicate the Greek "bargaining point" with the Allies of ships, a geographic base, and other factors. The most expensive cable Gerhart Riegner ever sent in his life, 700 francs for the April, 1943, telegram about evacuation possibilities, was really his cheapest, the WJC official mused after the event: it eventually made possible the breaking of the financial blockade and the subsequent sending of large funds abroad by American Jewish organizations for relief and rescue.[73] But had State and the Foreign Office felt compelled, as they did for other groups of civilian refugees and prisoners of war, to lift such restrictions once they comprehended Nazi designs, the annihilation of the Jews might have been considerably checked well before Riegner's first rescue proposal crossed their desks.

By the mutual consignment of the two Western Allies, the unique tragedy of the Jewish people was either lost among "suffering civilian populations" of different nationalities, or dismissed as a separate circumstance that could only achieve redress after victory in a new "free society." Other peoples already possessing the benefits of statehood fared far better than the Jews, although operating as governments-in-exile.[74] Even the title of the War Refugee Board, like the camouflaged vocabulary Germans specifically employed in their attempt to kill all of Jewry, followed the example of the Evian and Bermuda conferences, the Intergovernmental Committee on Refugees, and the British War Cabinet's Committee on the Reception and Accommodation of Refugees to disguise its real objective. The WJC and the Bergson boys, under such circumstances, could do no more in the war years than besiege Washington regularly and hope that some understanding would result in action.

"Only a fervent will to accomplish, backed by persistent and untiring efforts, can succeed where time is so precious," read Morgenthau's January, 1944, memorandum to Roosevelt. That fervent will and compassion were missing in the councils of the Western powers. The Jews could not wait for the Allied victory. Adolf Hitler would not let them wait. His grim executioners, working day and night, reaped a bloody harvest.

Rescue from the Balkans

"RUMANIA PROPOSES TRANSFER OF JEWS" ran the headline on page five of the *New York Times,* February 13, 1943. Adolf Hitler's ally, according to C. L. Sulzberger's dispatch from London, had communicated to the Allies a plan for the departure of 70,000 of the 185,000 Jews originally deported to Transnistria in the southern Ukraine. Those chosen would be taxed 20,000 lei each to board Rumanian ships, displaying the Vatican insignia to ensure safe passage. Palestine was intimated as the "most convenient" end destination.

Some circles raised doubts about the plan, the foreign correspondent pointed out. Enemy agents might easily mix with the emigrés; successful transfer would risk stirring up the "latent discord" surrounding Arab and Jew in Palestine, with ensuing repercussions throughout the Moslem world; "numerous great difficulties" existed regarding any mass shipment of refugees at this juncture in World War II. Observers in London viewed the striking offer as evidence of the Rumanian government's effort to disengage itself from the losing Axis coalition, and thus lessen the postwar Allied retribution to be exacted against those enemies who "were responsible for inflicting suffering on the innocent." An announcement by Jewish affairs commissar Radu Lecca the previous August that 185,000 Jews had been "settled" in Transnistria contradicted earlier pronouncements by Premier Ion Antonescu about the area's becoming "a model Rumanian home," Sulzberger observed, since Marshal Antonescu did not consider Jews to be Rumanian citizens. The democracies, in any event, had apparently made no decision as yet regarding the proposal.[1]

The journalist's exclusive did not disclose that during October, 1941, Antonescu had ordered the concentration of Jews between the Dniester and Bug rivers in occupied Russia for the purpose of their "liquidation." Coming to power in September, 1940, the marshal had survived an attempt by anti-Jewish Iron Guard "legionnaires" to overthrow his government four months later. His success provided scant comfort for Rumanian Jewry, however, which lost hundreds on that occasion to green-shirted Guardists incited by Viorel (later Valerian) Trifa; among the victims were Bucharest Jews literally butchered in a horrible parody of the Kosher ritual. Far worse was the massacre of some 8,000 Jews by government soldiers at Iasi (Jassy) toward the end of June, 1941.

Not long thereafter Rumanian army units drove Jews from the former Russian territory of northern Bukovina and Bessarabia across the Dniester into the arms of Nazi mobile killing force *Einsatzgruppe* D. When the German military protested that "eliminating" these Jews should be accomplished in a more "systematic and slow manner," the Rumanian premier ordered the establishment of deportation quotas. With starvation and mass shootings commonplace throughout the Transnistrian concentration camps, about two-thirds of all those Jews forcibly evacuated there were dead by May, 1942.[2]

The American minister to Rumania had wired home substantive accounts of these atrocities, together with information on opportunities for rescue, but the State Department merely filed his cables away. Throughout 1941 Francis M. Gunther relayed reports on the "incredible horror of the bloodthirsty vengeance wrecked on the Jews," including his conclusion that the "modern captivity" known as Transnistria "would seem deliberately calculated to serve a program of virtual extermination." When the Turkish minister in Bucharest had requested American support that November for a novel plan to transport some 300,000 Rumanian Jews across Turkey to Syria or Palestine for temporary settlement, Minister Gunther had sought State's instructions. Cavendish Cannon of the Division of European Affairs quickly squelched the rescue idea. Shipping and the Arab question, as well as doubts over the "temporary goal" mentioned, posed immediate problems. Endorsement, moveover, would likely bring about new pressure for an asylum in the Western Hemisphere, relieve the Rumanian government from responsibility in an overall settlement of the Jewish question, and encourage similar offers in Hungary and elsewhere where Jews had suffered "intense persecution." "So far as I know," Cannon reminded his superiors, "we are not ready to tackle the whole Jewish problem." The brief accomplished its end, for the suggestion never caught a favoring wind.[3]

His Majesty's Government in London, for its part, definitely did not wish to come to grips with the awesome plight of Europe's Jews. Determined to adhere to the May, 1939, White Paper throughout the war, the Mandatory power for Palestine regularly pressed the Balkan and other countries of Europe to halt what it termed "illegal" Jewish immigration to the Promised Land. Refugees who nevertheless took the route to Palestine aboard vessels so unseaworthy they were referred to as "floating coffins" were turned away from their destination. This occurred first in December, 1940, to a large group exiled to Mauritius, while the drowning at that same moment of over 200 Bulgarian Jews aboard the *Salvador* drew an appreciative comment from the head of the Foreign Office's Refugee Section: "There could have been no more opportune disaster from the point of view of stopping this traffic." Palestine High Commissioner Harold MacMichael reluctantly accepted the 792 passengers on the *Darien II,* mainly survivors of the Iron Guard pogroms and the *Salvador* disaster, who reached Haifa Bay from Constanza in March, 1941. These fortunate few had to remain, however, in the Atlit camp for 17 months more. Irrespective of increasing German efforts to seal off escape channels from Axis-held Europe, the Colonial Office continued to dole out the precious entry permits to Palestine with a penurious hand.[4]

The Jewish Agency for Palestine barely shook this official resolve. Only after difficult negotiation did its executive witness the arrival of 5,851 refugees holding certificates from enemy territories via Marseilles and Trieste. Yet this effort ended with the closing of the Mediterranean in June, 1940, once Italy entered the war on Hitler's side. Chaim Barlas, heading the agency's Palestine office in Geneva, reached Istanbul two months later and succeeded in rescuing thousands of mainly Polish Jews caught in Lithuania and Rumania with valid Palestine certificates in hand. In early 1941, responding to his continuous requests, the Turkish government announced that it would grant to all such refugees transit visas legal for two weeks from time of receipt. Barlas lost little time in submitting the required names to HMG's passport control officer in Turkey and thus saved another 1,200 refugees from Lithuania who traveled via Moscow and Odessa to Istanbul. But his supply of names and detailed supporting information had to be approved successively by the high commissioner's office in Palestine, the relevant authorities in London and Geneva (the Swiss acting on behalf of HMG as the protecting power abroad), and the various departments of the government in Ankara. Only then were the lists finally dispatched to the Turkish consulates at Bucharest, Budapest, and Sofia. The process, which took half a year on the average, was complicated by the Turks' insistence that only 50 Jews per week could pass through their borders on the way to Palestine.[5]

Seven hundred sixty-nine Jews who witnessed the deportation to Transnistria could not wait for British approval, and they crammed into the *Struma* for passage to Palestine on December 12, 1941. The voyage of the 56-foot-long cattle boat, organized under the courageous Revisionist Zionist leader Eugen Meissner, miraculously made it to Istanbul after three days and weighed anchor to await engine repairs offshore. The Turkish authorities would not let the Jews land without onward papers to Palestine, which the British, in turn, refused to grant.[6] MacMichael and Colonial Secretary Walter Moyne warned that a positive decision would have "a deplorable effect" throughout the Balkans by encouraging further attempts, and they urged the *Struma*'s return to the Bosporus. Never had a Nazi agent infiltrated into Palestine via these ships, the Jewish Agency countered; the JDC expressed its willingness to guarantee the passengers' absorption in Palestine. Three days prior to the Turkish deadline for transferring the boat outside her territorial waters, High Commissioner MacMichael agreed to accept every child between the ages of 11 and 16. The Turks refused to let even these travel overland to the Syrian border, however. All on board, who had been trapped there for two months, could do no more than paint a large sign visible on shore: "SAVE US!"

In the evening of February 23, 1942, a Turkish tug cut the *Struma* loose five miles out of the harbor with the thought that it should, somehow, return to Rumania. The next morning an explosion tore the rickety vessel apart. David Stoliar alone survived. He and a woman who had earlier been granted permission to disembark to deliver a baby (stillborn) would eventually be admitted to Palestine—as an exception on humanitarian grounds.[7]

The *Struma* disaster brought about a subtle change in HMG's immigration policy concerning the Holy Land. Moyne's successor, Robert Cranborne, admitted to Chaim Weizmann that he had been "greatly shocked" at the turn of events, and did not know why a number of the associates of the pro-Nazi former mufti of Jerusalem, Haj Amin el-Husseini, were freed concomitantly from imprisonment abroad to reenter Palestine. Spirited opposition to British policy by Josiah Wedgwood, M.P., and Lord Davies in Parliament, together with official protests from Jewish organizations, congressmen, and the American press, further made their mark. While Foreign Secretary Anthony Eden thought it "more merciful in the end to turn these ships back" rather than deport to Eritrea illegals reaching the Holy Land, Viscount Cranborne proposed to the Cabinet the announcement that all unauthorized immigrants who made Palestine on their own would be admitted after a security check but deducted from the regular White Paper quotas. His colleagues refused at first to thus encourage the traffic, but finally agreed to his proposal that the measure be carried out without publicity.[8]

Cranborne informed the Jewish Agency of this modification on May 22, but insisted that HMG would continue to deny facilities for such immigration to Palestine. Those reaching Turkey, he noted, would therefore *not* be eligible for entry certificates. When historian Lewis Namier pointed out that Jews in Rumania, who could not obtain Palestine visas, should be eligible for certificates if they reached neutral territory just as were those arriving in England, the colonial secretary demurred: "If people were to come here in shiploads helped by the Nazis, it would be a

matter for grave suspicion." Three small boatloads of Jews from Rumania who made it to Palestine waters were admitted as a result, but the
few arriving in Turkey usually ended up in Cyprus. The agency protested against the anti-Jewish discrimination, to no avail.[9]

By the end of 1942 the Jewish Agency official with the best appreciation of rescue opportunities through Turkey, then "window to the Balkans," could report little success. A scheme for the emigration of 270
Rumanian and Hungarian Jewish children up to 16 years of age, discussed between the agency and HMG in February, received final approval only in April, Swiss confirmation by June, and the protection of the
ICRC in September. The British and Turks turned down Barlas's suggestion that they increase the figure to 400 so that the 270 total would be
assured; none arrived by the New Year. Another plan to cover 400
Rumanian children who had received Palestine certificates prior to the
war fell through when HMG refused to guarantee their quick passage
through Turkey. Having failed in various efforts to charter a boat for
this purpose, Barlas vainly turned to the Swedish minister in Ankara for
a vessel that occasionally carried food supplies to Greece. During 1942,
3,743 Jews entered Palestine, the lowest figure for the entire war.[10]

Concurrently, the German organization in Bucharest sought to carry
out the Final Solution against the Jews of Old Rumania (the Regat).
Ever since the Wannsee conference of January 20, 1942, designed to
implement fully the Third Reich leadership's decision to annihilate European Jewry, had marked 342,000 Jews in Rumania (including Bessarabia)
for death, the Nazi hierarchy had been pressing Bucharest for the intended victims. A Jewish council supervised by Lecca, supplanting the
federation of Jewish community organizations under the strong presidency of lawyer Wilhelm Filderman, had already been established with
this end in mind. In June Adolf Eichmann spoke of preparations for a
general deportation transport to Auschwitz, and a month later his representative in Bucharest reported that Mihai Antonescu, the premier's
second-in-command, agreed to a series of transports beginning in September. A technical conference under Eichmann's direction, held that
month at the Reich Security Main Office (RSHA) in Berlin, decided to
run German-supplied "special trains" for 2,000 Jews every two days to
the murder center at Belzec, Poland. Antonescu assured Nazi Foreign
Minister Joachim von Ribbentrop during a visit to Hitler's headquarters
that Rumania stood ready to satisfy Germany's wishes.[11]

By then, however, Marshal Antonescu entertained second thoughts. He
had personally approved the deportation of Rumanian Jews then living
in the Reich and the expulsions to Transnistria. Those of Old Rumania
were deemed indispensable to the country's economy, however, a fact
that Filderman raised most effectively in numerous memoranda to the

premier, his former classmate. Protests by Filderman, Chief Rabbi Alexander Safran, and Zionist leader M. Benvenisti made their impact on various government officials, the Vatican, and the leaders of the two largest opposition parties. One month after the German foreign office's department for Jewish affairs, *Abteilung Deutschland,* snubbed Lecca during his August visit to Berlin, the premier decided to cancel the deportation order. Following heavy losses among the 27 Rumanian divisions on the Russian front, he put out peace feelers via the neutral powers and the Vatican's emissary in Bucharest. Antonescu's plan for emigration of Jews, in his mind a possible link to the Allies, logically followed.[12]

On November 30, 1942, Jewish Agency representatives in Istanbul reported that the Rumanian government would allow 70,000 Jews from Transnistria, at 200,000 lei apiece, to exit for Palestine or anywhere else. Speaking in Lecca's name, a Mr. Gur indicated that the head of the Jewish Council, Christian convert Nandor Ghingold, would be permitted to discuss transport arrangements with the agency and the JDC in Switzerland or Lisbon. Four days earlier Zionist leader Wilhelm Fisher in Bucharest had telephoned Barlas's associate Joseph Goldin to indicate that Gur spoke for him and Samuel Enzer, head of the agency's local Palestine Office. Goldin, who saw to it that the memorandum arrived in Jerusalem via the uncensored Polish diplomatic pouch, heard a confirming story one week later from a Dutchman who served as director-in-chief of Phillips radio in the Balkans.

Lecca himself made the offer official in a talk to Filderman, Benvenisti, and other Jewish leaders on December 3. The underground Zionist movement quickly sent the information from Bucharest via courier to the agency office in Geneva, while the Jewish leadership asked Lecca to improve the health of the Transnistrian deportees prior to their emigration by returning them to Rumania proper without delay. (Lecca, at the same time, secretly informed the German authorities, who vetoed the proposal.)[13]

The sudden news caught the Jewish Agency Executive unprepared to move decisively. The Yishuv in Palestine had not given full credence to earlier reports about the Nazis' systematic murder of Jews across the map of occupied Europe. Cables since the summer to that effect from Barlas's subordinate Chaim Pozner (later Pazner) in Geneva continued to go unanswered. Since the war began, no concerted rescue effort had been mounted from Turkey by the different Zionist political organizations; only Zvi Yechieli of the Mossad, the agency's body for underground immigration, and the Histadrut's Venya Pomeraniec (later Ze'ev Hadari) of HaKibbutz HaMeuchad were there by the year's end to resume *Aliya Bet* beyond Barlas's official purview. The arrival in mid-November of 78 survivors from Hitler's hell, in a first exchange agreement with the Germans, shattered many illusions, but a sense of impotence generally took hold in turn.[14]

Fatalism permeated the Agency Executive's discussion of the Transnistrian offer on December 23, 1942. Treasurer Eliezer Kaplan noted the refusal of the Anglo-American Alliance to permit funds into enemy territory, and others agreed that the agency could only inform HMG in London and ask for the plan's quick implementation. Doubts conveyed by Benvenisti and Fisher found a receptive audience, with those present insisting on the presence of Fisher, not Ghingold, for official negotiations. Although Barlas vouched at the meeting for the reliability of the neutral informant and the fact that the British in Ankara had already been notified, he was asked to check further in Istanbul.[15]

The Foreign Office indeed obtained the information from its ambassador at the end of the month, soon after Colonial Secretary Oliver Stanley received Cabinet approval to let 4,500 Jewish children from Bulgaria, accompanied by 500 adults, enter Palestine. Having turned down the agency's request in early November to accept all Jews released by the willing Bulgarian authorities, High Commissioner MacMichael now acceded to the agency's supplication that at least the children be saved. The vast Rumanian project presented a far more "frightful prospect" to Whitehall's Refugee Department, but it did not wish to risk another *Struma* incident and incur the wrath of "wild Jewish opinion," particularly in the United States. Still, comfort was taken in the private observation that Rumanian shipping could hardly handle 70,000 Jews. Just to be sure, Whitehall would try to see that the JDC did not "pull a fast one" in paying the required funds to an enemy power; if a mass migration did indeed commence, the Cabinet would reconsider its decision.[16]

Hearing nothing of these deliberations, the Palestinian representatives in Istanbul pressed their superiors for more aggressive action to save the Jews of the Balkans. Menachem Bader, who arrived after British procrastination in early January, 1943, on behalf of HaKibbutz HaArtsi and HaShomer HaTsa'ir, dramatically described the massacre of European Jewry in a memorandum to Papal Nuncio Angelo Roncalli (the future Pope John XXIII) and asked for his intervention with the local authorities. The Rumanian offer should be taken seriously, Bader and Yechieli reported home, while Shaul Meyerov (later Avigur), director of the Mossad since mid-1938, urged that boats be purchased for this purpose.

British-Turkish sluggishness in granting visas, especially evident in the slow transit of 270 children from Hungary and Rumania, and the unanswerable accusation of "where were you?" leveled by the first arrivals, heightened the frustration of the young emissaries. Letters brought by paid couriers from the valley of slaughter, carrying frantic appeals in

Hebrew code of "mercy fast" and "we live in neighborhoods of death," gave them no respite.[17]

Stanley's announcement in the House of Commons on February 3, 1943, about the Bulgarian negotiation and Sulzberger's story in the *New York Times* ten days later on the Transnistrian proposal did not aid the cause of rescue. HMG quickly sought to discourage any "hopes of a move en masse" to the Promised Land, and persisted in not considering it "practicable" to give the Turkish government a general assurance that all unauthorized Jewish immigrants reaching its shores would be admitted to Palestine. Members of an Irgun delegation under Hillel Kook (alias Peter Bergson) assured the American public in a full-page newspaper advertisement campaign that Transnistria's Jews could be saved at $50 each, only to be attacked by Stephen Wise and other Zionist officials as giving weight to unconfirmed rumor. But internal Jewish quarrels were of small moment once Whitehall, with the State Department's private approval, dismissed the scheme as—if serious—a piece of blackmail. In addition, the Turks stuck to their limited transit regulations, noting that only two trains ran weekly on the Taurus Express by which the children in question could travel from Istanbul to Aleppo.

In the meantime the German foreign office's *Abteilung Deutschland* and Eichmann did everything in their power to pressure both Balkan allies to halt all emigration. Prodded by ex-Mufti Haj Amin el-Husseini of Jerusalem, the Nazis refused safe conducts from Rumania for ships with ICRC markings, and ultimately ruined an Anglo-American *demarche* to charter the Rumanian liners *Bessarabia* and *Transylvania* for the Bulgarian evacuation. Only trickles got through.[18]

To the Yishuv delegation in Istanbul, HMG represented the major stumbling block. Thanks to Barlas's untiring efforts, the Turkish government expressed its willingness in mid-February to simplify the transit of immigrants in groups of 50, but no change was forthcoming. Eliezer Kaplan, who arrived at the end of the month to review the situation, concluded that British policy lay behind Ankara's lethargy. In March he heard the British ambassador agree to have a special representative appointed to handle the Jewish emigration to Palestine, help bring 2,000 Jews from Alexandretta, and aid in the purchase of neutral boats for travel from the Balkans to that port. Lack of adequate railroad equipment did not permit the Turks to fulfill the agency treasurer's request that five train carriages be relegated per week for the transfer of Jewish children; at most, they agreed to enlarge the group quota to 75 every ten days. Transport by sea, he concluded, was imperative. Only diplomatic demands on London might bring about the necessary breakthrough.[19]

Jewish Agency headquarters, a block away from the British Museum in Bloomsbury, were not lax in applying just such pressure, but its officials had met with regular delay and evasion. As early as January 19, 1943, Joseph Linton requested that those allotted immigration certificates be given the necessary papers in Balkan capitals directly by Swiss consuls without rechecking, as in the past, with Geneva, Istanbul, and Palestine. When political department director Moshe Shertok (later Sharett) again raised the issue on February 5, Colonial and Foreign Office representatives expressed no definite objections. In the following weeks Barlas cabled that without HMG's official green light, the Turks would not help; that exit permits for 5,000 Jewish orphans from Transnistria could be obtained, according to Filderman; and that masses of Jews were being deported from Thrace and Macedonia to Poland. Yet by the end of March, as Namier reminded the Colonial Office, the necessary order to dispense with the "unnecessary formalities" and so save precious time had not been given.[20]

The White Paper lay at the heart of the matter, and Washington chose not to challenge its closest war ally on this issue. Despite public pressure on both sides of the Atlantic to bring Europe's Jews to Palestine via the Balkans and Turkey, Cranborne announced in the House of Lords on March 23 that HMG's shipping and food resources to maintain "vast quantities of refugees" were "greatly stretched." Foreign Secretary Eden repeated the point when American Secretary of State Hull pressed him four days later for help to Bulgaria's threatened 60,000-70,000 Jews, adding that acceptance might well serve as a dangerous precedent. Hull echoed this position in a talk with Stephen Wise and American Jewish Committee president Joseph Proskauer the same day. No new commitments in excess of the 5,000 Jews from Bulgaria would be undertaken, the two governments agreed during the Bermuda conference in April.[21]

Not privy to these deliberations, the Palestinians in Istanbul anguished over lost opportunities to save their people through cracks in Germany's mighty Fortress Europe. Money and letters had gotten through to comrades who warned in Hebrew code that since "ami" (my nation) is soon to "marry Mrs. Harigavitch" (be murdered), "darkia" (passports), "chiluf" (exchange for German civilians), or "hatsalaski" (rescue) would have to hurry if the Yishuv wished to "extend a mazal tov" (save them). Definite possibilities for exit from Slovakia, Hungary, Italy, Croatia, and the Balkans existed, the Palestinians pointed out, but Palestinian and especially far more substantial American Jewry did not grasp and thus respond to this immediate reality.[22]

HMG, in particular, squandered valuable months. Its experts in Istanbul had approved three ships for the voyage between Bulgaria and Turkey, yet London did not follow up with an application to the Turkish authorities. Many thousands of Bulgarian Jews were already transported down the Danube River toward Slovakia, reported the Budapest underground "Va'ada" rescue circle to Istanbul, and from there by train "to the city of murder" in Poland. Marshal Antonescu assured the ICRC of his continued interest in facilitating emigration, this one month after Gerhart Riegner in Geneva first transmitted to New York information about rescuing the survivors in Transnistria with the cooperation of the ICRC and Jewish leaders like Filderman, Fisher, and Benvenisti. The Anglo-American Alliance continued to drag its feet, even as the former mufti urged Hungary's foreign minister not to permit Jewish emigration to Palestine—but only somewhere marked by "active control" such as Poland— and the Germans moved decisively to seal all paths to freedom.[23]

London agreed to depart from the strict letter of the White Paper in July, 1943, but this concession was to have limited effect. In a memorandum to the War Cabinet, Stanley recommended that all Jews reaching Turkey would be eligible for admittance to Palestine. The colonial secretary doubted that the number who managed to escape would make this "a serious problem," but he assured disturbed associates that the prewar restrictive quotas would remain in force to ensure stability. The Cabinet approved the proposal on July 2, agreeing also to continue Jewish emigration to Palestine beyond the original White Paper deadline of April 1, 1944, until the 75,000 maximum figure was attained. The decision, intended primarily to quiet mounting attacks in the public sector against HMG's rescue effort, was passed on to British embassies and to the Jewish Agency in confidence. The refugees had to arrive "under their own steam," Stanley informed an agency delegation on July 12, and no publicity could be given the matter. If the possibility of organized migration from the Balkans were improved, Palestine's chief secretary emphasized to Shertok, the new arrangement would be "subject to immediate reconsideration." Unknown to the agency at the time, the Turks received no word at all.[24]

A plan to rescue a first group of 1,000 Bulgarian Jews brought Britain's actual intentions to the surface. Danny (Ze'ev) Shind, *Aliya Bet* pioneer who joined the Pomeraniec-Bader Histadrut team as the Mossad's chief delegate at the end of February, had made contact with an elderly Bulgarian merchant seeking to recoup his fortune through the shipping business. Shind and Teddy Kollek, then representing the agency in work with British intelligence, reluctantly allowed Jordan Spassof to purchase a ship under his name for two trips from Bulgaria or, if impossible, Rumania to the Turkish port of Mersin. An old cargo vessel named the *Maritza* was purchased by the Mossad at great cost to carry some 250 passengers each voyage. His ties with the foreign ministry and army fortified by liberal bribes, Spassof received a letter dated June 19, 1943, from the Bulgarian minister of public affairs and health that authorized the departure until the end of August of 1,000 Jews not of military age. The agency's Palestine Office director in Sofia was not, however, convinced by Shind's confirmation and a list of 1,300 names that Barlas supplied from Istanbul. Should the dangerous sea voyage be undertaken, he wondered, just when it appeared that Bulgarian Jewry no longer faced death? Resolved to expedite matters, Barlas turned to the British ambassador in early July.[25]

Although the agency's request appeared certain of fulfillment, HMG again torpedoed the possibility of rescue. Spassof's permit, lists of available Turkish boats (aside from the recently purchased *Milka* in Spassof's possession), and the promise of cooperation from ICRC delegate Gilbert Simond in Ankara all augured well for success, Barlas thought. His British hosts insisted, however, that they had to cable home for instructions, notwithstanding Barlas's reminder of their agreement with Kaplan in March and of the need for immediate action. HMG, Barlas discovered a week later, decided to verify Spassof's letter through the Swiss legation in Sofia. The unprecedented move infuriated the Jewish representatives. It clearly spelled doom for the project, for the Bulgarian government would hardly authenticate a letter of permission that had been obtained through unofficial channels and against German wishes. As the Jewish representatives had foreseen, the Bulgarian foreign ministry denied the entire story. The agency refused to give up. Shertok traveled to Istanbul to investigate, and he concluded that the negotiations should be pursued seriously. The local British authorities agreed to recognize the June 19 permit and to find an additional vessel, but their decision had scant value. The terminal date for Spassof's permit had passed by then, and the Bulgarians revoked the license.[26]

In the face of such intransigence, only attaining a possible *modus vivendi* between the agency and the JDC nourished some hope among the rescue advocates in Istanbul. Leery of weakening the effectiveness of its independent relief activities worldwide, the JDC had vetoed financing *Aliya Bet* while providing consistent support, at Barlas's request, to those aboard the *Salvador, Europa, Viitoriul,* and the *Struma* who reached Turkey's shores in this fashion. Transports having British sanction, such as the 270 children scheme and the offer for 5,000 Bulgarian Jews, received JDC help through funds deposited in Barlas's bank account. But, to the consternation of impatient agency representatives in Istanbul and Bratislava seeking large-scale rescue through the "Europa Plan," the JDC refused to challenge the Allied blockade on money to Axis-held territory. Further, its directors rejected the proposal of a formal joint committee with the agency in relation to Palestine matters, and dissolved such an effort in Teheran on the same grounds. The prospect, then, of the JDC helping the agency's Balkan rescue work seemed most unlikely.[27]

Joseph Schwartz's arrival on the scene signaled the beginnings of a decisive reversal in JDC circles. Scion of an Orthodox rabbinical family from the Ukraine, the American-born scholar of Hebrew and Middle Eastern affairs had pursued his studies at Yeshiva College and the University of Cairo before turning in 1939 to JDC work in western Europe. Subsequently appointed director of JDC European headquarters in Lisbon, Schwartz wired to the New York central office his support for Barlas's efforts on behalf of Balkan Jewry throughout 1943. During a visit to Palestine that summer he came to a significant agreement with agency representatives Kaplan and Eliyahu Dobkin and Mossad chief Meyerov. The JDC would cover £35,000 sterling for the 1,000 Jews permitted in the Spassof charter, those transit costs that Jewish refugees to Palestine could not afford, and a guarantee of £20,000–25,000 per month (the dollar equivalent placed in American banks) to free local currency for rescue activity in enemy countries.

When Schwartz reached Turkey in August to finalize the technical aspects involved, Barlas sought to obtain his complete trust by opening all records for inspection. The dynamic, dedicated work of the Yishuv's representatives made a strong impression on the tall Jew in the uniform of an American Army colonel, and at the end of the month a complete understanding between the two forces had been reached. Schwartz pledged $70 per passenger for travel and maintenance from Istanbul to Palestine as the JDC's contribution. Before leaving, the aggressive JDC emissary also initiated talks, in conjunction with Barlas and others, for the shipment of 250 tons of food to Transnistrian Jewry through ICRC channels.[28]

Yet it all seemed too late, for by then the Palestinians' earlier illusions about the fate of their people in Europe had been rudely, totally shattered. The different representatives, now including Revisionist Zionist Joseph Klarman and Agudas Israel's Jacob Griffel, first came fully prepared to send thousands of letters and parcels from Istanbul to old addresses in Poland. The absence of receipts, including from what they considered at the time to be the "work camp" of Auschwitz-Birkenau, initially led to speculation that the oppressed Jews in such camps either could not cover related mail costs or wished to remain anonymous under the Nazi occupation. The horrible truth could not be denied for long, however, with the delivery in early August of a letter to the Pomeraniec-Bader-Shind trio from Bendzin sealing more than just faint hopes.

HeChalutz's Frumka Plotnicka and four other Zionist pioneer workers acknowledged the dispatch from Istanbul of 50,000 German marks for rescue. The group then poignantly reported the "systematic destruction" of Polish Jewry; the gassing centers at Chelmno, Treblinka, and Auschwitz; the Warsaw ghetto revolt; the *Judenrein* policy executed in western Europe, Lithuania, and the Ukraine. "We expect these are our very last days," they wrote in great haste on July 17 before the courier's scheduled departure. "Our hope to reach Palestine will unfortunately never be realized."[29]

Pomeraniec, who knew the signees personally and had focused his efforts on such correspondence these past months, broke down. Plotnicka had refused the personal offer of a safe journey to Istanbul, the Gentile courier reported, choosing instead to share the lot of her comrades and that of all European Jewry. A message from Slovakia soon thereafter, confirming the letter's grim prophecy, plunged the Yishuv's representatives into a painful crisis of spirit. Had they the moral right to live in freedom without doing everything possible to penetrate the barriers of Hitler's Europe? Just then a story came through about some Jews who, before their death, entered a synagogue and cursed world Jewry for standing silent from afar. Pomeraniec returned to Palestine in September to secure more funds for rescue and to plead that emissaries be dispatched forthwith to contact those still surviving in occupied Europe. By then the agency had finally received British approval to send Jewish commandos to Axis territory, and at a discussion on the subject that he attended in the home of Hagana leader Eliyahu Golomb, the participants chose the dangerous mission's first member, Yehuda Achishar for the Jews of Rumania.[30]

Not one to wait for an outcome to such developments, Shind picked up the threads of rescue in his individual fashion. The Spassof affair and the rift it created within Bulgarian Zionist groups convinced the young redhead that more independent control and direct influence over endangered Jewish communities abroad had to be centered in his hands. Samuel Enzer, head of the agency's Palestine Office in Rumania, had failed after valiant attempts that spring to obtain ships for emigration; the ICRC refused another Jew's separate offer to supply a boat bearing relief supplies for Greece on the condition that each return trip bring 50 Rumanian Jews to Istanbul. With exit from Bulgaria at least temporarily closed, Shind decided to renew the Mossad's contact in Bucharest with the one non-Jew possessing *Aliya Bet* experience and good ties in the relevant Rumanian loci of power. He turned to a suave Greek named Yanaki Pandelis, who enjoyed illicit business deals provided that their reward matched the ensuing danger.[31]

Shind and Ehud Ueberall (later Avriel), who arrived in August to replace Teddy Kollek, fully realized Pandelis's unscrupulous nature, but they had no stronger reed on which to lean. The Greek's earlier cramming the *Struma* in order to gain higher profits, as well as fears that he might yet seek revenge over his imagined loss regarding the *Darien II*, caused the Mossad considerable worry. It counted on the local Zionist youth organizations, guided by the rare teamwork among Revisionists Meissner, Lipa Chaimovic, and Shmuel Ariel (with whom Klarman had daily telephone contact), Enzer, and his associate David Nussbaum, to check the extortionist tendencies of the so-called "fat one." That September Pandelis used Mossad funds to buy "ORAT," a dying travel bureau, and set up his shop undercover. The motley group of conspirators, informed by Shind's coded telephone calls that the *Maritza* and *Milka* were at their disposal, began work under the very noses of the Nazi occupation forces.[32]

Deteriorating German-Rumanian relations seemed most propitious for the realization of these efforts. Antonescu had already blamed Hitler, at a private conference in mid-April, for the loss of 18 Rumanian divisions at Stalingrad; the loss of an additional eight that summer to the rapidly advancing Red Army convinced the premier that new secret peace feelers had to be made to the West. Alexandre Cretianu expressly flew to Istanbul with these orders, while others pursued the course in different neutral countries. On November 15 Antonescu denied the *Führer's* request for additional Rumanian soldiers and control over the Transnistrian railroad system. Two days later, in search of a culprit—without fully realizing his own guilt—for the murder by Rumanian forces of over 120,000 Jews who had been deported to Transnistria, Antonescu ordered that the Germans cease the "terrible murders" and that the survivors be evacuated to Bukovina.[33]

The Jewish organizations in Rumania exploited this *dénouement* in masterly fashion. Even after the Germans engineered his deportation to Moghilov in May, 1943, Filderman sent a memorandum requesting the government to return all the Jews in Transnistria to the Regat. Antonescu approved this step for some categories on July 8. Returning soon thereafter to Bucharest, the brave Jewish leader continued the struggle, and helped ensure that all refugees from Poland would remain on Rumanian soil. Benvenisti and Fischer continued to obtain help on behalf of those deported from Czernowitz and Transylvania through former Prime Minister Iuliu Maniu and ICRC's Charles Kolb. The Zionist youth movements passed on information to HeChalutz representative Nathan Schwalb in Geneva, who in turn forwarded JDC money through the ICRC to appropriate circles in Transnistria. Similar contacts brought valuable Chilean passports via Alfred Silberschein in Geneva for the underground movement ("tiyul" in the Hebrew code) of Jews from Poland to Slovakia, Hungary, and Rumania. Thus, too, did Gerhart Riegner in Geneva transmit reliable information after April to the ICRC and the U.S. State Department about rescue opportunities with the use of blocked funds from American sources.[34]

Washington and London hardly facilitated the rescue effort. The State Department dragged its feet on Riegner's proposal, on the suggestion of the World Jewish Congress's Nahum Goldmann that $8 million be con-

tributed by the Anglo-American Alliance for Jews abroad through the
ICRC, and on increasing calls for a separate government agency dedicated to meaningful action to save Europe's remaining Jews. In September the Foreign Office, which already received a report that all deportations to Transnistria had ceased, confidentially transmitted to State news
of its July reversal; it still persisted, however, in keeping the vital information from the Turkish government for fear that it might open the way
to a "flood of refugees" and thus prejudice the future Palestine settlement.
Similarly, the approval by the U.S. Treasury Department of Riegner's
plan drew Whitehall's objection in mid-December over the "difficulties
of disposing of any considerable number of Jews should they be rescued
from enemy occupied territory." Under the circumstances the ICRC,
which had received Antonescu's approval to transfer 150 orphans weekly
to Palestine, could claim with some logic that the lack of Allied funds
and shipping necessitated its "very limited" assistance. The two governments made no direct approach to Antonescu on behalf of Rumanian
Jewry, although Alexander Easterman of the WJC's London office made
such a request in early November and both capitals received peace proposals from the Antonescus and Cretianu that winter.[35]

The Palestinians in Istanbul had ample reason for bitterness. Seized
by the monumental tragedy, Bader tried desperately to encourage European comrades facing death and to shake the Yishuv's leadership with
their letters, filled with "much blood that will scream and boil and froth
for thousands of years because it was spilled in vain." Barlas secured the
Turkish grant of individual visas at a rate of nine families per week in
Bucharest, Budapest, and Sofia, but the continued difficulties regarding
transport and Palestine certificate authorization made even this slight
concession of minor importance. Further, Benvenisti and some others
(as had occurred previously in Bulgaria) objected strenuously to travel
aboard the Mossad ships without suitable documents in the face of possible German retaliation. Kolb and Simond considered such boats too
risky for the extension of ICRC protection, prudence their superiors
seconded in view of the *Struma* disaster. As a result of the confluence of
these factors, a mere 526 Jews passed through Turkey in all of 1943 from
Bulgaria, Hungary, and Rumania. Four hundred thirty more escaped the
Nazis in small boats from Greece to Izmir and thence to Palestine.[36]

The year 1944 brought but dim prospects for significant change. The
British-Turkish bottleneck and German designs, dissension within Rumanian Jewish circles vis-à-vis *Aliya Bet,* news that the first two Jewish commandos from Palestine had been captured soon after landing, continued
delays in obtaining additional vessels, and a split between Barlas and
Shind over operational techniques—all served as dire omens.[37] According
to reports from Enzer in Bucharest, the Rumanian government was

prepared to release Jews in Transnistria for cash and to allow the *Milka* and *Maritza* to sail. Transit of 150 Rumanian Jewish children and their adult escorts by rail to Turkey had also been authorized by the Bulgarians on the proviso that the British obtained the necessary transit visas from Ankara. Yet, other than the American government's tardy grant of a $100,000 license for the JDC to carry out Joe Schwartz's plan concerning supplies from Istanbul to the Transnistrian deportees, the Allies and neutral powers moved languidly. The arrest on January 26, 1944, of the underground Zionist leadership in Rumania, following German disclosure of their rescue activities and communications with Jewish organizations abroad, brought these myriad difficulties to an unnerving climax.[38] Who among the Palestinians, faced with these conditions, would be foolhardy enough to raise his glass high to the New Year?

II

At this crucial juncture a 43-year old vice-president of Bloomingdale's in New York City resolved to expedite the rescue of Balkan Jews to their Promised Land. Early an advocate of boycotting Hitler's Germany, Ira A. Hirschmann had personally guaranteed the U.S. immigration affidavits of some 200 Viennese Jews after bearing witness to what he later called the "aimlessness and lethargy" of the 1938 Evian conference. Back home, he became increasingly agitated over newspaper accounts of the Jewish catastrophe and the apparently ineffectual Intergovernmental Committee on Refugees and the Bermuda conference. The aggressive calls for determined governmental action, particularly in Turkey, by Mrs. John Gunther and others on the Emergency Committee to Save the Jewish People of Europe impressed the Jewish business executive. Accompanied by its head, Hillel Kook (Bergson), he visited Assistant Secretary of State Breckenridge Long in September, 1943, and requested air priority for a personal investigatory mission to Ankara.[39] Long contended that the government's lengthy record of relief activity on behalf of the oppressed was continuing "to the best of the Department's ability in the present situation in Europe." He also disputed Kook's contention that an official agency should be delegated to focus on the plight of Jews under Nazi control, but eventually agreed to telegraph the ambassador.[40]

Laurence Steinhardt's career reflected the current perils of an American Jewish diplomat. His dispatches about security risks, while serving as the country's ambassador to the Soviet Union, had provided Long valuable ammunition in 1940 for State's campaign against accepting prominent refugees on the special American visa list. When transferred to Turkey two years later, Steinhardt moved to limit the number of American Jews assigned to diplomatic service there; the Turks' excessive "varlik" tax on minorities' property and the ensuing imprisonment of defaulters for hard labor was protested only as regards U.S. citizens. Yet the past Zionist Organization of America member also had a long talk with the Turkish foreign minister, which contributed strongly to the removal of the official stipulation that each group of 75 refugees had to depart from Turkey before another could be admitted. He obtained Ankara's intervention with Berlin for the fate of 10,000 Jews of Turkish origin in France and backed Barlas consistently. Steinhardt informed a group of New York Agudas Israel leaders in confidence that he had also personally helped Jewish children across the Bulgarian frontier, and concluded that "no laws existed for me when people had to be saved."[41]

With some reservations, Steinhardt cabled Secretary Hull his agreement in principle. Hirschmann, whom he had once met, might join the several representatives of Jewish organizations already in Turkey who sought to achieve his identical objective. Yet the harsh Bulgarian decrees promulgated by Interior Minister P. Grabovski, the ambassador cautioned Hull, did not allow for Jewish transit to Turkey. With this apparently single means of transportation from the Balkans closed, he harbored little hope for the possibility of rescue.[42]

Four months later Hirschmann left the States as a special attaché to Steinhardt on behalf of the U.S. War Refuge Board (WRB). First intending to travel to London as a private citizen and try to open the doors of Palestine, he obtained a pledge of financial support from Joseph Proskauer and some other prominent American Jewish leaders and a six-week leave from Bloomingdale's. The few officials in Washington, like Oscar Cox, who pressed for a separate government rescue agency tapped him for service, however, as soon as President Roosevelt ordered the establishment of an agency dedicated to "the immediate rescue from the Nazis of as many as possible of the persecuted minorities of Europe, racial, religious or political, and all civilian victims of enemy savagery." Acting director John Pehle briefed Hirschmann on the opportunities for concrete action, including a request to try to break up the concentration camps in Transnistria, and promised the board's full support. As an extra precaution, Isador Lubin provided a code word for direct contact to his "boss" in the White House should the British create difficulties concerning the fundamental visa issue. On January 30, 1944, the zealous Hirschmann boarded a C-54 in Miami for the long haul to the Bosporus.[43]

Within a month after the WRB representative's arrival, the transit bottleneck via Turkey had been broken. Red tape and indifference on the part of British and Turkish officials, he soon discovered, explained the pigeonholing of some 1,200 visas that had been approved since September. In addition, with London still not informing Ankara by official letter that all Jews reaching the country would be allowed to proceed for

Palestine within 24 hours, the Turks refused to honor their earlier promises to receive groups of 75 per week. Bolstered by Pehle's efforts in Washington and Steinhardt's local contacts, Hirschmann saw the required
documents emerge from the British embassy labyrinth. As a result, the
Turks agreed to move Jewish refugee children by rail at the rate of 140,
with an escort of 10 adults, every ten days across Anatolia to Aleppo; the
arrangement would be exclusive of their previous commitment of nine
families weekly from the Balkans. This and a consolidation of the inefficient visa system brought quick results. Within ten days 90 Jews arrived
from Bulgaria and 74 from Greece, to move on to Palestine.[44]

HMG's anxiety over Palestine, as Hirschmann and Pehle suspected,
determined its Balkan rescue policy. Notwithstanding representations by
Shertok and others that the parceling out of White Paper certificates
should be speeded up in light of the Holocaust, the Foreign and Colonial offices privately decided that filling the outstanding balance of 27,535
places should be stretched out to "about the end of 1945." A sudden
deluge of Jewish immigrants would add to Hagana strength, according
to War Office calculations, forcing the immobilization of many British
divisions during the expected second front against Germany. The agency's requests for Jewish parachutists to save some of Balkan Jewry from
destruction, as well as its own relief team to liberated areas, understandably encountered strong opposition in these quarters. MacMichael even
opined that the granting of quotas after the White Paper's final deadline
was "a grave mistake." His argument failed to carry, but Stanley assured
the nervous high commissioner that the agency's attempt to force the
White Paper pace would be "firmly resisted and a crisis avoided." Accordingly, while the Foreign Office sent the Turkish government informal word at last on March 17 of the Cabinet's July, 1943, ruling, the
Palestine authorities were to be informed regularly of all visa and arrival
details so "they can watch and regulate the flow."[45]

Hardly at one with such convictions, the energetic Hirschmann did
everything in his power to charter well-built passenger ships with appropriate safe conducts to ply the waters between the Black Sea ports and
Istanbul. A plan, suggested in January by Murray Gurfein of the U.S.
Office of Strategic Services in Turkey, that ships be obtained from the
Anglo-American shipping pool had been deemed "impolitic" by Gurfein's intelligence superiors in view of the Palestine issue. Pehle did
obtain assurances to the Turkish government that the *Vatan* would be
replaced if lost, but Barlas' negotiation fell through when Hirschmann
concluded that the small, old cargo vessel would not do. When the
Swedes stalled on releasing the *Bardaland,* Steinhardt secured Turkish
approval for charter of the 4,000-ton liner *Tari.* Through Pehle's intervention, the field director of the U.S. War Shipping Administration in

the Middle East even came to negotiate its price. Hirschmann looked forward to bringing 1,500 Jewish children from Transnistria in early April, particularly once the ICRC's Simond claimed to have German Ambassador Franz von Papen's promise that Berlin would grant safe passage for a direct voyage from Constanza to Haifa.[46]

With his unique authorization to negotiate with the enemy, Hirschmann moved to obtain Antonescu's release of Transnistria's surviving 48,000 Jews to Old Rumania. On March 7 the State Department requested Steinhardt and the American minister in Berne to communicate to the Balkan governments that, "fully responsible for the actions of persecution committed on their territories," they should "desist immediately" and allow refugees to depart to any neutral countries prepared to receive them. With Steinhardt's full agreement, Hirschmann personally conveyed the unequivocal message to Cretianu on March 13, 1944, in the privacy of Simond's home.

The Rumanian minister's expressed fear of the advancing Russians sparked Hirschmann to make a remarkable offer, one he rightly termed later "a shot in the dark," on his own initiative. American visas would be awarded the four members of the ambassador's family in exchange for freeing the Jews still alive in Transnistria, 5,000 children to leave Constanza for Palestine, and for ending all persecution against minorities. Apparently realizing what would transpire if the Russian armies provoked the Germans to take over control of Transnistria, Cretianu agreed to send an urgent cable to Bucharest recommending in the strongest terms that these Jews be transferred to the interior of Rumania proper. On March 16 Cretianu informed Hirschmann that the removal had begun and that Antonescu pledged exit permits to all those who wished to leave for Palestine. Four days later Kolb cabled Simond that the transfer from Transnistria was complete.[47]

Emigration out of Rumania was an entirely different matter, however, and only the Mossad's tireless spadework over the previous year and a half made this a reality. Without HMG's knowledge, it informed Bucharest about Britain's unofficial policy of permitting illegals in Palestine; preparations for departure aboard the *Milka, Maritza,* and *Bellacita* continued, despite ICRC unwillingness to grant them safe conduct. ORAT, even given Pandelis's handsome profits (some going to Lecca), filled the vacuum created after the Zionist leadership's arrest in January, 1944, by supplying false documents, smuggling refugees across Rumania's borders to safety, and arranging government-sanctioned transport lists. An important helping hand came from parachutist Achishar, who directed HeChalutz emigration plans from a hospital bed while under guard. Energetic appeals by Filderman, the Zionist author and well-connected industrialist, A. L. Zissu, and others to the government, the diplomatic corps, and the ICRC gradually secured the release of those officials arrested. The Zionist underground, too, continued to function, and had obtained the return of all Jewish orphans under 15 years from Transnistria at the end of February. Hirschmann's *demarche* coincided with these activities, some Rumanian efforts to join the Allied camp, and, especially significant, the Red Army's offensive.[48]

On March 28, 1944, the telephone rang in the livingroom of Shind's and Ueberall's apartment in Istanbul, around the corner from the German embassy. The *Milka* had just left Constanza, they heard. Some 250 survivors from Czernowitz, the capital of Bukovina, were aboard.

The Mossad agents immediately informed Barlas, who left to activate diplomatic channels in Ankara. The Jewish ambassador without diplomatic credentials got nowhere with his regular contact at the foreign office, while HMG's chief representative was told that landing the unauthorized refugees would encourage mass arrivals of other Jews—not in Turkey's interest. Foreign Minister Numan Menemenciogalu first informed Steinhardt that the *Milka* would not be allowed to enter the port: its passengers lacked Turkish visas and Palestine entry certificates, and he contemplated taking the "most severe action" against those in Istanbul organizing this traffic. After a second talk, which lasted for over an hour and a half, the foreign minister finally agreed as a special courtesy to his American friend to allow the refugees to land and proceed on a special train to the Syrian frontier. Indefatigable Jewish businessman Simon Brod arranged all technical details with the Turkish police and the sympathetic British intelligence official who had confidentially informed the Palestinians seven months earlier about HMG's July, 1943, decision.

The sight of 239 survivors boarding four cars on the Orient Express marked "Reserved for Passengers to Palestine" deeply stirred Meyerov and his cohorts. Shind composed a letter to Mossad headquarters in Tel Aviv, expressing both joy over the departure and disgust at those "well wishers" who had abandoned the remnant of the Jewish people in its darkest hour. He emphasized: "Let the *Milka*," which proved that the Mossad's work had not been in vain, "bear witness to the sin of neglect on the part of the enlightened world."[49]

"We only hope that we have time to save greater and greater numbers," Shind concluded, and rescue they did. With indispensable financial aid from the JDC, over 1,200 Jews from the Balkans passed through Turkey during the next two months aboard the ORAT-directed vessels without the full assurance of safe conduct. Adolf Eichmann sought the German foreign office's intervention on April 4, 1944, against the migration of Jewish orphans to Palestine, but the Russian capture of Czernowitz carried more weight with the Rumanians. The *Maritza* delivered 244 Jews to Istanbul on April 8, followed by another 272 aboard the

Milka and 153 on the *Bellacita*. The *Maritza* brought 318 more on May 23. The passengers on its second voyage, including Hungarian and Polish refugees who had been smuggled into Bucharest by the Rumanian Zionist youth organizations, also provided the Yishuv and the Allied governments with the first eyewitness accounts of Eichmann's preparations for the "mass extermination" of Hungarian Jewry.[50]

The Mossad's determined effort proved fundamental, for the hopes Hirschmann placed on the *Tari* as the harbinger of what he publicly heralded as a future "bridge of ships" came to naught. The Turks' abrupt discontinuance of chromite shipments to Germany, after numerous Allied requests, ended von Papen's promise of safe conduct. The British in Ankara, who at last informed their hosts officially of the July, 1943, decisions and had a ship ready to sail for Rumania provided the safe conducts were obtained, blamed Hirschmann (as did the Jewish Agency) for telling a news conference, on returning in April to New York, that the *Tari* would make for Haifa in "the largest single evacuation of the war" as soon as German safe conduct had been obtained. On that occasion Hirschmann also proclaimed that the WRB, with Steinhardt's help, had saved thousands of Jews. The urge for publicity, despite knowledge that the Nazis sought to encourage Arab aspirations, was further aggravated by Steinhardt's eagerness to concretize the voyage. His convincing the foreign minister to approach the Germans officially in this regard, notwithstanding the two countries' steadily deteriorating relationship, courted further disaster. Last-minute efforts by Steinhardt in Ankara and Hirschmann in Washington to realize the scheme via safer Bulgaria ended in complete failure.[51]

The Palestinians' hard-won successes hardly dispelled their sense of fundamental powerlessness, as the arrival of Joel Brand in mid-May with Eichmann's "blood for money" offer made agonizingly clear. While they tried everything to aid the Hungarian Jew, the Turkish government prepared to expel Brand and companion Bandi Grosz to Budapest and certain death, and even refused Moshe Shertok a visa to interview Brand. British local intelligence, suspecting both Nazi intentions and the Jewish Agency of exaggerating the Holocaust's dimensions in order to elicit concessions regarding Palestine, did not cooperate. "Open" cables (purposely meant for the eyes of interested German agents) arrived from Pomeraniec, then reporting to the Jewish Agency Executive in Jerusalem; these noted diplomatic activity but nothing concrete. In desperation, Bader and Brand wrote a bogus agreement dated May 29, and dispatched it by secret courier to Eichmann in Budapest. Ultimately, after Bader had at last convinced him to return home, Brand got HMG's permission to set off on June 5 with Ueberall for Aleppo to see Shertok. The British spirited him away from the railroad station to house arrest in Cairo, however, and never returned the Jewish messenger to Turkey and Hungary as promised. Bader's willingness to negotiate with the Germans—at their request—in Budapest, notwithstanding Hirschmann's fear and the possibility of a trap, met with a firm refusal on HMG's part a month later, as well.[52]

Differences within the large Yishuv representation created other problems. Those overseeing *Aliya Bet* thought the indefatigable Barlas too possessive in his duties, and worried over his dependence on Hirschmann and Steinhardt. The separate triumvirate of Griffel, Klarman, and former Czech businessman Ludwig Kastner, seeking to increase the percentage of agency certificates assigned to Aguda and Revisionist members in the Balkans, cabled the Orthodox Va'ad HaHatsala in New York for $200,000 to enlarge the Mossad's activities.[53]

Confronted with the telegram's contents by Steinhardt, an astonished Barlas agreed with the American ambassador that these appeals were "not necessary." Such independent moves, in Barlas's opinion, would also endanger the private agreement made between Steinhardt and Turkey's foreign minister to allow this unsanctioned movement to Palestine. He therefore immediately wired Nahum Goldmann in New York that no funds should be sent from the United States unless requested by Steinhardt, Barlas, the JDC, or the War Refugee Board; the board, in turn, advised the Orthodox Jewish rescue organization to try to reach an agreement with JDC and agency representatives in Istanbul. Distrustful of the JDC headquarters' legalistic approach, the reliance of Barlas and Steinhardt on the Turkish authorities, and Steinhardt's past attitude toward Jewish refugees while serving in Moscow, the Va'ad HaHatsala concluded that Barlas was guilty of the unpardonable act of informing on fellow Jews.[54]

A split in the Rumanian Jewish community proved of far greater danger to the Mossad's continued work. Pandelis's exorbitant charges, going well beyond costs covered by the JDC–Jewish Agency agreements, infuriated many Zionist youths and refugees who could not afford the, going rate. A. L. Zissu, assuming both the Benvenisti and Enzer posts, went so far as to ask the Rumanian government on April 1 to close ORAT's doors. His step had the full support of ICRC representative Kolb, then deeply involved in emigration preparations for the *Tari* and similar vessels, and long furious with Pandelis's "traffic in slaves." The loss of ORAT's charter, just when Pandelis's liaison man in Istanbul helped Shind sign contracts (despite limited funds) for the Turkish boats *Kasbek, Bulbul, Morina, Mekfure,* and *Salahattin,* brought all departures to a sharp halt.[55]

Equally damaging, the uncompromising Zissu refused to cooperate with the non-Zionist Filderman and his central committee in drawing up the departure lists. Zissu did much, with Kolb's help, to have the Antonescu government protect Jewish refugees crossing the border from Hungary's northern provinces during the deportations to Auschwitz-Birkenau; Filderman addressed a special appeal to the ambassadors of the United States, Soviet Union, and England in Istanbul on their behalf, and maintained close ties with the WJC's Riegner in Geneva to help finance rescue. But despite Filderman's repeated urgings that fair consideration be given non-Zionists for prospective entry into Palestine, as mandated by the agency's own constitution and Barlas's written instructions, Zissu opposed relinquishing full control.[56]

The Rumanian authorities refused to countenance what Mihai Antonescu designated these "detestable agitations," and on July 19, 1944, there came into being an interministry committee under Vice-Premier Antonescu's direction to oversee departures and an emigration office with his friend Zissu at its head. Zissu initially refused to give in regarding the committee's makeup and the recruitment of passengers, and insisted that Pandelis's boats not leave Rumanian ports until they paid full damages to the government and the Jewish community. To ensure the government's interest in facilitating the exit of some 10,000 Jews per week under Rumanian Red Cross protection, Filderman and other Jews involved in the negotiations stayed their ground. Children, young pioneer "*chalutzim*," and refugees from Hungary and Poland facing the greatest danger would receive first priority without regard to party affiliation, and would leave immediately.[57]

Hirschmann returned to Istanbul at this moment, carrying WRB orders to keep the Eichmann-Brand negotiations afloat and to revive the flow of Balkan immigration. The hesitant HMG minister resident, Middle East, Walter Moyne, permitted him to interview Brand only after being shown a letter from Roosevelt (obtained by Pehle via Lubin), expressing full support for the WRB and its envoy's mission "in the interests of humanity." Hirschmann then began to straighten out the "organizational chaos" that had developed in Istanbul since his first tour of duty. Aware that the growing presence of zealous representatives from various Jewish groups had disturbed Steinhardt's other duties and angered the Turkish foreign office, he quickly streamlined activities with the assistance of board associate Herbert Katzki. The JDC would pay 80 percent of actual rescue costs, retroactive to and replacing Schwartz's first flat-rate commitment of August, 1943, in addition to all charges from Istanbul onward to Palestine. A working committee of Hirschmann-Katzki, Barlas, Shind, David Schweitzer of HIAS-ICA, and the JDC's Reuben Resnick began to eliminate much overlapping and confusion.[58]

Coordination came not a moment too soon. Shind received information at the end of June about the Rumanian government's new emigration agency and its permitting ORAT to proceed with the departure of some 3,000 Jews. Tension mounted with von Papen's sudden departure and a blackout over Istanbul, when word arrived on July 7 that the *Kasbek* was en route. The 140-ton wooden ship with motor propulsion, expected to accommodate 450 people, arrived two days later carrying 759 tired survivors from Poland, Rumania, and Hungary. Necessary transit documentation was secured, and the entire group, including 214 emaciated orphans from Transnistria, boarded a special Turkish train for the three-day ride to the Syrian border. The *Morina, Bulbul,* and *Mefkure* did not follow as expected, however, Hirschmann discovering from renewed contact with Cretianu that Zissu's tactics were creating complications. Kaplan of the Jewish Agency responded in a sharp letter to the obdurate Zionist, insisting that his sectarian quarrels with Filderman and Agudas Israel representatives should not jeopardize the one duty of "emigration at any cost." Hirschmann reiterated the theme in similar fashion, also throwing the board's support behind Griffel's efforts to engage additional ships and so break the Rumanian deadlock.[59]

The board emissary also essayed his direct diplomacy with the Bulgarian authorities. No results paralleling the Cretianu *demarche* had resulted from Hirschmann's talk with Ambassador Nicholai Balabanoff the previous spring, but current reports that the new Bagryanov government was moving away from Nazi control to the Soviet camp suggested a more favorable atmosphere. Through Floyd Black, former president of the American College in Sofia and son-in-law of a Bulgarian general, he sent off a memorandum on July 22 requesting the new prime minister to emulate Rumania's assistance to Jewish refugees. Two days later the seasoned Balabanoff informed him in Simond's home that Bulgaria would take "gradual steps" to ameliorate the condition of the Jews, as well as to facilitate their departure eastward. Exploiting Balabanoff's transparent wish to secure some American good will, Hirschmann took a gamble and asked that he commit this position in writing to Simond.

When the unprecedented letter arrived on Balabanoff's personal stationery the following afternoon, an excited Hirschmann decided to test the Bulgarian's sincerity. A communication dated August 1, written to Black but aimed for Sofia, insisted that the Bulgarians abrogate Gabrovski's two nefarious anti-Jewish laws, reconstitute the prewar privileges of its 45,000 Jewish citizens, and publicly permit the exit without delay of all Jews wishing to leave for Palestine. Balabanoff met the American envoy at his request four days later. While expressing sympathy, he seemed to be playing for time. Possessing knowledge about the secret discussion of peace terms then going on between the Bulgarians and Moscow, Black worried that the Bagryanov government might fall any day.[60]

By now Hirschmann had come to realize that the Palestinian "boys," as he termed them, had correctly focused on *Aliya Bet*. First leaving the United States as a non-Zionist, the WRB representative became converted during a brief visit to Palestine by the pioneering, constructive spirit of the Yishuv and the determination of leaders like David Ben Gurion and Henrietta Szold to receive the remnants of a decimated European Jewry. His work in Turkey further provided Hirschmann the candid realization that because Palestine represented, as he told the press, the "only beckoning open door to hundreds of thousands" of human beings seeking a refuge from certain death at Hitler's hands, that country was their inevitable haven. And only the Mossad's small boats, without German and ICRC safe conduct, had ultimately brought Jews to their ancestral homeland. No longer could the WRB envoy maintain the luxury of distance from the youngsters' clandestine activities on the rationale that "a subway cannot work above water—nor a ship below." Following a meeting with the entire group at which Bader spoke with special force, Hirschmann pledged the intrepid Histadrat representatives his full support. When thereafter hearing from Shind about further delay, he immediately asked Simond to inform Bucharest via Kolb that all expenses for ORAT's four ships had been covered.[61] The clandestine meeting of minds received its most dramatic test that summer.

Late on August 3, 1944, one day after Turkey joined the Allied camp, the *Mefkure, Morina,* and *Bulbul* finally sailed from Constanza for Istanbul. Shind understood from a telephone call the same Thursday that ORAT and Zissu's emigration office had foiled German obstructionist intentions. He, Meyerov, and Ueberall, joined by Bader and Pomeraniec, kept the long vigil over an American navy map, while Moshe Averbuch (later Agami) sat alone reading the Psalms for divine guidance. The lead vessel *Morina* arrived two days later, bringing 308 passengers, with the *Bulbul* sighted fighting a gale in the Black Sea. No word came of the *Mefkure,* however, and the Palestinians' anxiety grew.[62]

Late Sunday evening an agitated Katzki called his superior at the American embassy: a German warship had torpedoed the *Mefkure* some 40 miles from Istanbul, with a loss of almost 300 Jewish lives, including 96 children. The *Bulbul,* Hirschmann subsequently discovered from garbled reports, had anchored in the safety of Igneada Bay and was about to steam for Istanbul. Rather than have the boat chance its journey's last leg through mine-filled, stormy waters, Hirschmann got Ankara—in exchange for a handsome contribution in JDC secret funds to the Turkish Red Crescent—to deliver a message that those aboard should be landed forthwith. A supply convoy of ox carts, with one of the "boys" in attendance, made its way through the desolate Asiatic mountains to the stranded party of 395. Once the refugees reached Istanbul, Simon Brod took over until they left from the little railroad station, the "Hatikva" on their lips.[63]

The tragedy of the 140-ton motor schooner shook the Palestinians, but they unanimously decided to press on. Risks had to be taken, Mossad chief Meyerov concluded, recalling his part in the 1940 *Patria* disaster. Hirschmann, backed by Pehle and the JDC, promised additional support for future illegal transports. As for the *Mefkure,* a private review by Barlas, Meyerov, and Resnick concluded that the Turkish captain had abandoned the overcrowded ship without helping his passengers. The three-man board could not establish the attacking vessels' identity, although some of the five *Mefkure* survivors stated that these were German. Among the five, who stayed afloat for four hours until picked up by the *Bulbul,* were a newly married couple. Vera Fulop, 18 years old and in advanced pregnancy, gave birth to a healthy baby precisely one month later.[64]

Hirschmann, for his part, thought that the entire rescue program would "suffer lamentably" as a result of the *Mefkure's* fate, and therefore decided it soundest policy to press the Bulgarians for revocation of the anti-Jewish laws. Hearing of Bagryanov's plans not to include the Jewish problem in an emergency session of parliament, aimed to legitimize its country's withdrawal from the Axis, he reinforced the position that continuance of the Nuremberg-type laws would be interpreted unfavorably in Washington's eyes. The Bulgarian prime minister did convoke such a session on August 17, where he referred to Bulgaria's need and ability to "liquidate" the Jewish issue without causing new, unnecessary suffering. The State Department took Hirschmann to task for his promise to Balabanoff of U.S. assistance for the rehabilitation of Bulgarian Jewry, insisting that the WRB had no authority to discuss any possible postwar commitments. Nothing came of this rap on the knuckles, and at the month's end the parliament in Sofia voted to revoke its anti-Jewish legislation and to restore full rights and property to all.[65]

The *Mefkure* catastrophe bore a different lesson for the Griffel-Klarman-Kastner team. More acceptable transports, such as the purchase of a Swedish liner at a half-million dollars for 5,000 Rumanian passengers to Palestine, were better than the Mossad's small vessels. The more seaworthy boat would actually be cheaper in the long run than the present method, they wired the Va'ad HaHatsala on August 12. The scheme would also balance Zissu's discriminatory award of Palestine certificates, information corroborated by Chassidic leaders who had reached Bucharest and Palestine with Va'ad HaHatsala support.[66]

A delegation led by Rabbi Aaron Kotler immediately pressed JDC headquarters to contribute most of the requested funds, emphasizing that Steinhardt had spoken highly of Griffel during his previous stay in

New York. Since the War Refugee Board's advice and approval were indispensable in this instance, the JDC advised the group to contact Pehle's office. The following day Rabbi Kotler telephoned, informing Henrietta Buchman of JDC's accounts department that they had spoken to Steinhardt and received a favorable reaction. In a second call he advised that a new cable from Griffel complained about Barlas's insistence on limiting the small boat sailings to one a month, with Zionists alone being booked for departure. The JDC would be guided by the board's recommendation, Buchman insisted in reply, a point she repeated when Steinhardt telephoned the next afternoon. Quite annoyed, the ambassador noted that, in truth, he thought the suggestion entirely impracticable. If, he had told the Va'ad HaHatsala representatives, they could prove the plan workable, consideration would then be given to supplying the necessary funds.[67]

Eri Jabotinsky of the Emergency Committee to Save the Jewish People of Europe, who had reached Istanbul in May with Pehle's help, shared the Griffel group's approach. A pioneer in arranging large illegal Revisionist transports to Palestine until his arrest by the British in February, 1940, he first contemplated acquiring the swift Rumanian liners *Transylvania* and *Bessarabia* for $4 million each. When the Turks made these inoperative, at Allied request to avoid German capture, he proposed the purchase of the 500-ton Turkish boat *Toros* to rescue 1,000 Jews from Budapest by transporting them down the Danube to Istanbul. This unorthodox plan would also break the shipping monopoly of the Jewish Agency, which had excoriated the Bergsonites in the United States and their new Hebrew Committee for National Liberation. Hirschmann, who judged Jabotinsky an opportunist and an obstructionist, questioned the Danube route as gravely dangerous. Jabotinsky was prepared to proceed nonetheless, and he wired the Emergency Committee that the JDC's Joseph Schwartz was uninterested in the $100,000 project.[68]

With Schwartz denying the story, JDC secretary Moses Leavitt asked Pehle for clarification. The board director stood by Hirschmann's position, especially since developments in the Balkans at the end of August cast doubt on the immediate feasibility of this or similar schemes. A decision by the Joint Chiefs of Staff, opposed to granting American safe conduct to the voyage in view of extensive Allied mining operations on that international waterway, ended the matter.[69]

The time had come to bid adieu to Turkey and rescue duties, Hirschmann decided. Suggestions to implement a Jewish Agency plan to rescue 8,000 of Budapest's endangered Jews by moving them via rail to Rumania and thence by boat to Istanbul for the Holy Land, as well as transports from Bucharest and Sofia aboard the *Smyrnie* and *Alba Julia,* were overtaken by Russian conquests in southeastern Europe. (The commander in chief of British Mediterranean operations, for his part, judged the Rumanian government's donation of the latter vessel for this purpose "undesirable.") German evacuation of the Aegean islands also obviated the board's belated interest in a rescue base to save Greek Jews reaching Izmir by sea. The Soviet expulsion of an Anglo-American military team to Bulgaria ended Hirschmann's own plan to enter the Balkans on a mission of mercy. In a final collaboration with Steinhardt, he therefore advised Pehle in mid-September that Katzki could take over relief operations that were sure to follow.[70]

After touching farewells with the young Palestinians and Floyd Black, Hirschmann made a last request of the Russians to have their advancing armies take the Balkan Jews under their protection. Cretianu and Balabanoff, he learned from First Secretary Mikhailov on that occasion, had been judged friends of the Allies and so retained in office by the Soviet occupation authorities. The special attaché cabled this news to Pehle as completely justifying the board's mandate to deal directly with the wartime enemy. As Hirschmann took his leave, Jewish organizations extended their gratitude for his "magnificent efforts," and urged the continuation of the board's historic endeavor.[71]

Responding to the lightning change of events in the Balkans, the members of the Palestine Rescue Committee in Istanbul went their separate ways. Pomeraniec entered the first liberated country of eastern Europe as a correspondent of the Jewish Telegraphic Agency, where he helped revive prewar Jewish organizations and broadcast on Friday evenings in Hebrew over Sofia Radio. Klarman and Averbuch traveled as reporters to Bucharest, where they joined some of the Jewish parachutists from Palestine in bringing the Zionist message to their decimated, weary people. The Revisionist representative even secured a statement from the new foreign affairs minister that favored emigration to Palestine for Jews not subject to the military draft, an "irresponsible" move which Steinhardt thought ran counter to board policy favoring full reinstatement of Jews as Bulgarian citizens.[72]

Barlas, considered far more respectable, received British permission to resume agency activity in Rumania. Calculating those rescued via Istanbul between January and September, 1944, at 1,101 by land and 3,268 by sea (aboard the "illegal" Mossad boats), he left for Palestine in eager anticipation of continued work throughout the Balkans. But the JDC seconded Hirschmann's estimate that with the restoration of rights to Bulgarian and Rumania Jewry, no need existed any longer for their evacuation to Palestine. Accordingly, it terminated the $3 million appropriation earmarked for Mossad voyages, informing the agency that henceforth each case would have to be judged on its own merits.[73]

The British, always apprehensive of a Jewish exodus to Palestine, moved to stem any mass movement from the Balkans. This anxiety had determined London's earlier frenetic search for refugee centers in Tripolitania and Sicily when Hungary offered to release its Jews, as well as Minister Resident Moyne's warning not to jeopardize HMG's security commitments with "unlimited numbers" beyond the White Paper. The Foreign Office therefore sought to "stiffen" the State Department with the need to delay congressional resolutions favoring a Jewish state, especially in light of rising Irgun and Stern attacks against the British forces in the Holy Land. In like vein, despite Shertok's appeal for a reconsideration of the White Paper with particular regard to Rumania and Bulgaria, the Colonial Office on October 5, 1944, withdrew its July, 1943, pledge "in view of the changed situation in the Balkans." The new rate of entry to Palestine would be 1,500 immigrants per month, reallocated to cover the remaining 10,300 certificates.[74]

The Jewish reality in eastern Europe challenged these calculations of officialdom head on. Of 270,000 survivors in Rumania, 150,000 lacked food and shelter; the new under secretary of state for interior was the very general who three years earlier had been responsible for the Iasi massacre. Almost half of the 40,000 surviving Bulgarian Jews faced similar desperate circumstances; typhus, malaria, and diphtheria were rampant in both countries. The substantial supply of emergency JDC funds did not meet the crisis, while concrete relief from international organizations like UNRRA would not be expected for months.[75]

And so the Jewish refugees made for their ancient homeland. A group of 160 Rumanians and Poles, including 119 children under a specially arranged scheme, reached Istanbul directly by rail on October 25; the Mossad's *Salahattin* finally arrived four days later with 547 persons, including 25 just liberated from the Bor labor mines of Yugoslavia. The same week 50 crossed the Bulgarian-Turkish border at Svilingrad without difficulty, followed by 80 on rail. In mid-November, 172, including a group of 43 Polish refugees, arrived from Bulgaria and Rumania. The Bulgarian station master at Stara Zagora stopped 600 Hungarian Jews from Rumania, wanting to check with the Soviet occupying power first. Another 300 failed to get that far at Russe, and were turned around. On December 7, 925, including 370 Transnistrian orphans, made it aboard the Mossad's *Toros*. Parties of 37, 46, and 36 came the next week aboard Sofia rail. The Turkish and British authorities, following past arrangements, sent all these to Palestine.[76]

Panic seized HMG's officials. On November 4, three days after he had succeeded MacMichael, John Gort urged London to inform the Turks that the previous automatic entry of illegals into the Promised Land was hereby revoked. The Colonial Office hesitated, but it could not deny escalating activity by Jewish militants in Palestine, or its minister's report that several "tens of thousands" had registered in Bucharest for emigration. Whitehall officials spoke, in response, of the need to return Jews to their former homes. Lord Gort soon repeated his worry over the likely admittance of "undesirables," and asked for an end even to the new 1,500 monthly quota, while Minister Le Rougetel in Bucharest applauded Russian insistence on proper entrance visas as reducing the potential "flood" to Palestine.[77]

David Ben Gurion's week-long visit to Bulgaria in early December understandably gave the British much cause for concern. The Jewish Agency Executive chairman held court at Pomeraniec's apartment in Ueberall's company, and monopolized page one of the local press. He urged the prime minister, interior minister, and head of the Farmer's party to support the Jewish need for emigration and a state in Palestine. Ben Gurion's call for an independent Jewish commonwealth capable of accommodating four million Jews drew an enthusiastic response from a crowd of 7,000 Jews, over one-third of Sofia's Jewish population. The apathetic stares of barefooted children, during his visit the following morning to the impoverished Jewish quarter of Yüc Bunar, particularly stirred the Zionist leader. He resolved to accord 5,000 of these youngsters first priority to the Promised Land and to buy 10,000 pairs of shoes in Palestine for dispatch to the survivors. These included the remaining 300 Jews of Macedonia, who surfaced from hiding in the mountains and now lived in remote Skopie. They all had to be saved at once, Ben Gurion told colleagues on his return to Jerusalem, or they would be lost forever.[78]

Reacting to this pressure, London informed the Turkish government on December 18 that the 1943 guarantee for illegals had come to an end. Although admitting to its own minister that a haven other than Palestine had not been secured, it instructed him to justify the reversal on the grounds that the Balkan situation had improved, and that "satisfactory departure controls" had not yet proven possible. If Ankara did not maintain the refugees temporarily with *ad hoc* arrangements, the Foreign Office pointedly advised, they should be returned to Rumania and Bulgaria overland—not in the same small craft aboard which they had reached Istanbul. When controls became satisfactory, it added, the guarantee would be reinstituted. That never came to pass.[79]

With the British decision, Katzki thought the WRB's work in Istanbul finished. Not including a third exchange the previous July of 283 from Bergen-Belsen and Vittel for German nationals, 6,527 Jewish refugees had passed through to Palestine during the last year, he informed Pehle. Rumania and Bulgaria claimed the lion's share, including approximately 1,000 orphans repatriated from Transnistria. The group at Stara Zagora finally came through in January, thanks to Steinhardt's vigorous intervention with the British ambassador in Ankara, but HMG's new decree made future passages of note unlikely. Five million dollars in British gold sovereigns, which had arrived unsolicited in March, 1944, for rescue activities, would be returned in full by diplomatic pouch to the American legation in Cairo. The order to close down the office came back from Washington on February 3, 1945.[80]

The British showed their claws one last time, engineering Eri Jabotinsky's arrest when he attempted to challenge the White Paper. Notwithstanding information from the board that HMG's October, 1944, decision limited Balkan emigration to 3,500 over the next six months, Jabotinsky had found a freighter capable of carrying 1,500 Jews from Constanza directly to Haifa. The Turks were prepared to back the trip just as soon as the American ambassador closed the *Tari* transaction, a stipulation the indignant Steinhardt feared might convince the Turks to charge the board $150,000 for lapsed negotiations. In early December Jabotinsky received approval to proceed with the *Tari*'s charter from Hillel Kook, who hoped that success might lead to future trips. A month later, however, the Turkish minister of communication turned down the scheme.[81]

A shocked Jabotinsky attributed this reversal to British intervention; Katzki thought it consistent with HMG's December 18 note to the Turkish foreign office. Considering his mission unproductive, Jabotinsky proposed to return to New York. The State Department, always wary about the Kook-led activists, refused him a visa. Before an appeal could be made, however, the Turks extradited Jabotinsky to Palestine in February at the formal request of the British. HMG charged him with being involved in Moyne's assassination by Sternists the past November, a fabrication which Jabotinsky's supporters blasted in the New York press and the House of Representatives as an act, in Ben Hecht's phrase, of "international intimidation." He was released from prison a few days later.[82]

The Jewish Agency, even with White House support for two ships to carry 1,000 certificate holders from the Balkan countries to Palestine, enjoyed no better fortune. Did the Allies, able to transport 20,000 Moslem pilgrims from Egypt to Mecca and 40,000 Yugoslav refugees from Italy to Egypt during the war, "owe nothing to the Jewish people?" executive member Bernard Joseph asked War Refugee Board headquarters at the end of 1944. The agency turned in the last resort to Isador Lubin, whose code word to Hirschmann had uncovered "lost" Palestine visas for one Mossad vessel thanks to a quick telephone call from Roosevelt to Churchill. The Zionist sympathizer got his friend Maurice Boukstein in touch with the War Shipping Administration's deputy director, who indicated that approval from "the proper sources" might indeed enable two Liberty ships to accomplish the task. The transport of 3,500 Jewish children, scattered in Christian homes and monasteries, from France and Belgium to Palestine was also deemed a possibility.[83]

Those sources went into action. A White House request bestirred the State Department, which uncovered important information in mid-April, 1945: Palestine certificates were not being issued by British passport control in Bucharest; the Soviets were not issuing any exit permits; the *Smyrnie* was being held in a Black Sea port for the purpose of making such trips. When Boukstein conveyed news just received from Eliezer Kaplan that a Jewish Agency representative had given HMG's passport officer in the Rumanian capital the list of persons for certificate distribution and that the *Smyrnie* was actually not available, the department's George Warren made State's fears clear.

The British might compel a shipload of legal immigrants arriving in Haifa to transfer to Philippeville in French North Africa as it had recently done for Jewish concentration camp inmates reaching Switzerland, should the monthly White Paper quotas be exceeded by that time, Warren stated. Roosevelt and State knew that the immigrants wished to go to Palestine, and the American government was "quite displeased" about the British maneuver. If the British cooperated, he added, the two Liberty vessels could travel to Constanza within a month. The necessary word never reached the War Shipping Administration.[84]

V-E day came, bringing HMG the additional victory that its prewar White Paper remained intact. Moyne's successor, Edward Grigg, warned Eden that partition of Palestine, then being deliberated by a special Cabinet committee, would "very likely bring into existence a Jewish Nazi State [*sic!*] of a bitterly dissatisfied and therefore aggressive character." To Ben Gurion's mid-March appeal for a Jewish state there—in some way linked to the British commonwealth, capable of taking in one million refugees over some years—High Commissioner Gort replied that he foresaw "grave difficulties attending such grandiose schemes." In long, top-secret dispatches back home, Gort echoed Grigg's fears, and insisted on a maximum 2,000-monthly quota until the peace conference.[85]

Their colleagues in London agreed. The refugees had to be forced into what Shertok called the "10,000 straitjacket," although the thousands of Holocaust survivors clamoring for entry into their national homeland made this small number of remaining certificates look ludicrously anachronistic. Receiving reports about the frequent killing of Jews as they emerged from hiding in Poland and Hungary, the Agency Executive found its inability to provide even a few entry certificates a strain "humanly unbearable."[86] The two sides were on a direct collision course.

CONCLUSION

The mark of Cain branded not only the German brow during the Holocaust, particularly in the case of Balkan Jewry. The fanatical designs of

Abteilung Deutschland, Adolf Eichmann, and ex-Mufti Haj Amin el-Husseini notwithstanding, unique opportunities existed for rescuing a people targeted for murder in Rumania and Bulgaria. Even Ion Antonescu, after bringing about the death by his soldiers of over 120,000 Jews in Transnistria, offered a door to safety for the survivors. Authorities in Sofia presented definite exit possibilities as well. Those powers most capable of meaningful counteraction, however, responded slowly to the challenge.

Moral callousness especially pervaded the British camp. Wanting to maintain the White Paper, HMG consistently sought to check any mass movement of Jewish survivors, which it feared might bring, in Walter Moyne's caustic phrase, a "flood of gatecrashers" to the Promised Land.[87] Difficulties raised concerning alleged enemy agents, Arab hostility, Palestine's resources, and Allied shipping conveniently masked the fundamental wish to secure Palestine in the interest of imperial strategy. A cumbersome certificate process, reactions to the Transnistria and Spassof proposals, revocation of the July, 1943, decision favoring "illegals" (passed to quiet public agitation but long kept from the Turks) as soon as Balkan mass emigration became probable, suspicion of the War Refugee Board, and the arrest of Jabotinsky—all reflected Britain's stance. The Jewish national home in Palestine, as a result, was denied its logical purpose to the war's end.

The Turkish government's record was hardly better. Aside from Ankara's indifference to the 769 human beings aboard the *Struma,* its languid visa procedure assisted the White Paper's implementation. Humanitarian considerations meant little in a country where only "baksheesh" brought results, and an onerous capital levy discriminated against Jews and Christians possessing Turkish citizenship. The Jewish communities of Istanbul and Izmir could have absorbed some 5,000 Jews without difficulty, yet even temporary havens for Jewish refugees, which the American government offered to help finance, were outlawed: the public, the foreign minister informed Steinhardt, would resent "Bulgarians [*sic*] eating white bread while Turks starve."[88] Ankara did expand use of an antiquated railway system at the American ambassador's request, but the limited service hardly sufficed to meet the dire emergency.

Until 1944 Washington was equally unconcerned about the fate of Balkan Jewry. Minister Gunther's report about a plan to transport 300,000 Jews in November, 1941, to Syria or Palestine received short shrift in the State Department, which opposed Riegner's plan to save the remnants of Transnistria's concentration camps and formally acceded to the White Paper at the Bermuda conference in April, 1943. One year later a State delegation discussing postwar plans in London repeated this official assurance. With justification could a surprised Rumanian ambassador query Ira Hirschmann about his government's abrupt change of heart: "If this means so much to you in the United States, why did you not come sooner? You could have saved more lives."[89]

The resolve shown by the U.S. War Refugee Board indicated, as Max Lerner characterized it in *PM*, that compassion could replace indifference and that a democracy might be strong in acting for the cause of freedom. Hirschmann's determination, his bold initiatives strengthened by Pehle in Washington and Steinhardt in Ankara, brought dramatic change. Even the skeptical British implicitly perceived this shift of purpose: "The S.D. [State Department] was friendly but futile; the W.R.B. is offensive but effective." The board also established the important precedent that one free nation could, in the midst of global war, not only destroy people but save them.[90]

Ultimate rescue lay in the hands of the representatives from Palestine who converged on Istanbul after 1942. As initial doubts gave way to a keen understanding of the Holocaust, the bold youngsters discarded legal convention to sustain with some measure of help fellow Jews facing annihilation. Food, money, false papers, word of the Yishuv, letters linking one threatened community in occupied Europe to another, and finally "illegal" boats all raised abandoned European Jews from the very depths to the lower rungs of Hitler's hell. Difficulties beyond their control made dealing with uncertain couriers (some Gestapo agents) and businessmen like Pandelis, as well as a tragedy such as the *Mefkure,* risks that had to be assumed. The Yishuv group, after all, lacked power in the councils of the free world. Theirs was therefore a mission "wretched and dismal," as Menachem Bader concluded in a final account of the more than £1 million sterling expended for rescue: "these were only a drop in a sea frenzied with blood and tears, in which millions of our brothers sank and drowned." Miraculously, the Palestinians brought a few thousand souls to the Jewish homeland and safety.[91]

Their grasp of Jewry's unprecedented plight eluded not only the Anglo-American Alliance but others as well. The Palestinian and American Jewish communities—when aware of the tragedy's dimensions—often lapsed into a fatalistic sense of impotence, although Kaplan and Schwartz, for example, changed their views after visits to Istanbul. Even some in Rumania and Bulgaria hesitated when the Mossad offered transports to freedom. The imperative to save fellow Jews from impending death weakened Zionist party loyalties among those in Turkey, but a few leaders like Zissu remained true to particularist politics. Hirschmann spent much time vainly seeking safe conducts for large ships; Kolb and Simond provided valuable support, but would not take Mossad vessels under International Red Cross protection. When the Nazis met defeat in the Balkans, Hirschmann and the JDC began to stress prewar Jewish rights rather than necessary evacuation.

A relatively limited percentage of Jews perished in southeastern Europe primarily because the Rumanian and Bulgarian leadership realized that the Germans were headed for defeat. National, not humanitarian, considerations motivated overtures to the West, especially given the rapid advance of the Red Army. Courageous Jewish leaders in Rumania played effectively on this anxiety, and stirred religious and political opposition figures to support their cause. Paradoxically, Antonescu believed along with other wartime antisemites in the canard of universal Jewish power.[92] The Rumanian premier sought to employ his "Jewish question" to gain a separate peace with the capitalist democracies, who in fact accorded the Jews a very low priority during the years that witnessed their quintessential tragedy.

Jewish powerlessness, a bi-millenial disability that made the Holocaust possible, had to undergo a radical transformation if Auschwitz-Birkenau were not to be repeated. In April, 1945, Anthony Eden and Herbert Emerson, chairman of the Intergovernmental Committee on Refugees, might call for a halt to "the centrifugal movement from Europe" and an end to discriminatory racial laws as a basis for solving the Jewish problem. Roosevelt expressed a similar attitude in more specific terms two months earlier, telling the staunchly anti-Zionist Muslim monarch of Saudi Arabia, Abdul Aziz Ibn Saud: "The Germans appear to have killed three million Polish Jews, by which count there should be space in Poland for the resettlement of many homeless Jews." The survivors had small reason, however, to trod any longer on earth that served as the shroud for their families, to breathe the air that still reeked with the stench of burnt flesh from the crematoria. In Rumania, for example, 100,000 registered by that January for emigration to Palestine.[93]

Spontaneously, they and many others made for the one land which had seen their birth as a people and which beckoned now as the end to their anguished wanderings in exile. Thus was fulfilled Shertok's prophecy, set down in a 1943 letter from Turkey to the remnant on *Tisha B'Av,* that they would one day appear as "the bearers of the solution" in Jewry's postwar struggle for independence.[94] The veterans of the Mossad, supported by the JDC understanding first obtained with the Jewish Agency in Istanbul, would be there to ease the return home.

Auschwitz-Birkenau and
the Martyrdom of Hungarian Jewry

MICHOEL DOV WEISSMANDEL, hiding out "in a cave near Lwow" on May 16, 1944, sat down to dispatch a long cry *de profundis* to the central office of HeChalutz in Geneva. "Yesterday they started deporting from Hungary the Jews east of the Tisza River (Transylvania, Carpatho-Russia, and the district of Kosice)—a first phase in the deportation of all Hungarian Jewry—and this first phase reaches 320,000 people, the Lord should guard and save them." Every day, the 42-year-old ultra-Orthodox rabbi went on in his biblical Hebrew style, 12,000 persons are scheduled to be shipped, 75-80 to a railroad freight car, via Kosice-Presov-Orlova-Musina to Auschwitz-Birkenau in Upper Silesia. Upon arrival, some 95 percent immediately will perish by Zyklon vapors in Birkenau's gas chambers and then be cremated. The testimony of two Jews who had recently escaped from that camp and an attached diagram of its physical layout, corroborated by a non-Jewish fugitive, indicated that facilities there had been expanded months earlier in order to put the Jews of Hungary to death.

With "six times a million Jews" slaughtered until now and tens of thousands murdered daily, Weissmandel begged the Pioneer Zionist youth movement and its colleagues to take immediate action. Widespread publicity, warnings to the German and Hungarian nations by the Allied powers, and vigorous protests from the pope and the International Red Cross should follow. More important, the death vaults in Auschwitz had to be bombed from the air, and all roads and bridges from eastern Hungary to Poland must be regularly destroyed. Aside from this, substantial funds had to be transmitted for bribes, false documents, concealed bunkers, food, and the hiding of Jewish children with Gentiles. "Our brothers, sons of Israel, are you insane?" Perhaps you, like the victims, have been beguiled by the shrewd murderers, despite our previous reports. The despairing advocate ended, "May God open your eyes and give you the privilege and the ability in the final hour to rescue the surviving remnant. . . ."[1]

The son-in-law of Neutra's chief rabbi, David Ungar, could not have much reason for hope. The Bratislava Jewish underground, led by Weissmandel and his distant relative, the Zionist (Mrs.) Gisi Fleischmann, had helped end transports from Slovakia to Poland two years earlier with the payment of $50,000 to SS deportation chief Dieter Wisliceny. These funds were obtained through Weissmandel's local associate Binyamin Shlomo Stern and Philip (Fülöp) von Freudiger of the Budapest Orthodox community, not the major Jewish organizations abroad. Saly Mayer, representing the American Jewish Joint Distribution Committee (JDC) in Switzerland, pointed out that American government regulations outlawed such transfers as assisting the enemy. "Onkel Saly" also expressed some doubts about the actual need, and asked the Slovak "working group" for detailed budgets. Mayer's HeChalutz counterpart, Nathan Schwalb, initially replied in favor of armed sacrifice to gain Allied postwar support for Zionist goals. Hungary's elder leadership rejected any "illegal" transaction whatsoever. When Weissmandel subsequently obtained a proposal through Wisliceny's superiors, Adolf Eichmann and ultimately *Reichsführer* SS Heinrich Himmler, that all deportations to Poland from western Europe and the Balkans be halted in exchange for $2 to $3 million in foreign currency and further negotiation with JDC representatives, Jewish groups in the free world gave the matter limited credence. (In any event, they lacked a method of transmitting this large sum in the face of the Allies' financial blockade.) Some funds eventually arrived from Mayer and emissaries of the Palestinian Yishuv in Istanbul, but these hardly met the Nazis' figure. In early September, 1943, Wisliceny halted the discussions, telling the Bratislava group that its self-styled "Europa Plan" might be taken up by Berlin at some later date.[2]

The dire peril confronting Hungary's 800,000 Jews after the German occupation on March 19, 1944, had galvanized Weissmandel and his colleagues to a valiant but seemingly vain effort. Four days after the invasion Wisliceny, now attached to Eichmann's "Special Operations Group" in Budapest, paid a quick trip to the Bratislava rescue organization: they could "reap the fruits of a new Europa Plan," but the 320,000 Jews of Hungary's provinces were doomed. Weissmandel quickly had letters of introduction drafted for the SS official to Freudiger and two others, but he simultaneously told Freudiger in a secret message to warn Jews in the northeastern zones that entry into ghettos meant death. The German-Slovak decision in April to ship the latter the following month via Kosice-Presov to Auschwitz was also relayed to Freudiger and to Switzerland. But the submissive Jewish Council under Samu (Samuel) Stern, bewildered by Eichmann's deceptive combination of threats and assurances, refused to believe the worst. Speed and secrecy, techniques honed to perfection from Eichmann's total European experience and aided by zealous antisemites in the Hungarian ministry of the interior further paralyzed the Nazi-designated *Judenrat*. Its official protests—after brutal ghettoization had already taken place—were met with disclaimers, and the timetable of the Nazi hierarchy continued, unchecked, on schedule.[3]

Even as Eichmann and Auschwitz commandant Rudolf Hoess made final preparations to "stomach" their expected arrivals, the Bratislava committee spread the truth beyond the country's borders. The miraculous arrival of Walter Rosenberg (later called Rudolf Vrba) and Alfred Wetzler at the Jewish underground in Slovakia on April 25, 15 days after their escape from Auschwitz-Birkenau, shattered all illusions. In separate statements the two young Slovak Jews, aided by eyewitness information supplied Wetzler by Jewish *Sonderkommando* Filip Müller, described the process of annihilation and the ghastly end of a "cautiously" estimated 1,765,000 Jews in Birkenau's four crematoria during the last two years. The "selections," the gassing of unsuspecting victims with cans marked "Zyklon—For Use against Vermin," and the cremating by the *Sonderkommando* of bodies to ash for fertilizer were all meticulously recounted. The fugitives' information and their warning of mounting preparations to receive the last major Jewish community of Europe corroborated fragmentary reports and official transport listings then in the Slovak group's possession. A 26-page summary statement, accompanied by an architect's professional sketches of both main camps and a request that Allied planes quickly destroy the killing apparatus and approaching railroads, went out by secret couriers to HeChalutz's Schwalb in Geneva, the Vatican via its nuncio in Bratislava, Rudolf (Reszö) Kastner of the Zionists in Budapest, and the delegates of the Palestinian Jewish community in Istanbul. Using these "Auschwitz protocols" for the substance of his May 16 letter to Schwalb, Weissmandel also dispatched a coded cable to Isaac Sternbuch in Switzerland, urging that Great Britain's Royal Air Force bomb Kosice and Presov and the single-track line between the two cities.[4] The Slovak Jewish underground could do nothing more.

In Budapest the illegal Zionist Assistance and Rescue Committee, the "Va'ada," stepped in to fill the vacuum for aggressive Jewish leadership. This group, headed since its formation in January, 1943, by Otto Komoly, his deputy Kastner, and Joel Brand in charge of smuggling Polish Jews into Hungary, had long established contact with the Weissmandel-Fleischmann organization. Knowing of the Europa Plan discussions, Kastner and Brand convinced Wisliceny that he should negotiate with them directly for the original $2 million figure in return for no ghettoization or deportations, as well as departure for 600 possessing emigration certificates to Palestine. By the third week of April the two young representatives had managed to pay Wisliceny a $200,000 down payment and informed Saly Mayer by courier of the pressing need.[5] With no quick results in sight, Wisliceny's superior continued the course of rapid ghettoization while taking over his place in the bargaining.

"Blood for money, money for blood," Eichmann abruptly offered Brand on April 25, 1944. Over three subsequent talks the SS official directing Germany's Final Solution suggested the freeing of one million Jews for goods such as 10,000 trucks, 800 tons of coffee, two million bars of soap, and 200 tons each of cocoa, sugar, and tea. If agreement were reached in principle, a token number of Jews would be let out of Hungary, but Brand had to complete the task soon. Jews released could not exit for Palestine because of the adamant objections of the ex-mufti of Jerusalem; they had to head for Spain and the West. The trucks must be winterized, for they would be "required exclusively for the Eastern front." The last crudely put hint from Himmler (without Foreign Secretary Joachim von Ribbentrop's knowledge) to the Allies, the occasional presence during the talks of SS representative Edmund Vessenmayer and the SD's Otto Clages, and the handing over to Brand of captured material sent the Va'ada from Schwalb and Mayer in Switzerland were all meant to convince him of the mission's seriousness.[6]

Some in the Va'ada like Kastner doubted Brand's talents for the job, especially after hearing that a shady smuggler and turncoat espionage agent named Andor "Bandi" Grosz was to accompany him, but they were confronted with a *fait accompli*. A cable was sent off seeking a visa in Brand's name from the Jewish Agency in Istanbul, his personal choice for contact abroad. Kastner's sudden arrest on May 10 and the first deportations five days later, of which Eichmann had warned Brand at their last meeting, certainly darkened the horizon. A week later Brand and Grosz left by train to Vienna, whence they took a German plane on May 19 for the short flight to Istanbul.[7]

Totally unaware of these developments, the disoriented Jews in the northern ghettos were boarding the cattle cars to Auschwitz-Birkenau on the average of 12,000 a day. The *Judenrat*'s indecisiveness, complemented by Kastner's own doubts and his decision not to disclose the Rosenberg-Wetzler report in early May lest the Va'ada's broader negotiations be halted and greater damage to the country's Jewish community ensue, contributed to a widespread paralysis.[8] But Hungarian Jewry, like its co-religionists across Hitler's Europe, had been rejecting reliable information about the Final Solution since 1942. Reports from thousands of Slovak and Polish refugees dispersed throughout the country, Western broadcasts in the Hungarian language, and eyewitness accounts of thousands who served in the east as Hungarian soldiers or as Jewish forced laborers all had told of systematic slaughter. Members of Zionist youth movements, operating from a *Judenrat* office, did reach the provinces in

April, 1944, with warnings of imminent disaster, but to no avail. The individual managing this *Judenrat* department sent forged papers and money to enable at least some to get to the capital, but good news about the Red Army's advance and the psychological inability to forsake orthodox values overnight led to meager results. Even Transylvanian Jewry, advised by a few of its own leaders to attempt a crossing over the nearby border to Rumania, refused to absorb reality. Isolated politically, highly vulnerable to native antisemitism, having no easy resource to weapons or young fighting men (most already in the Hungarian forced work battalions), and stunned by the lightning execution of Eichmann's plans, these trapped human beings, devoid of hope, passively went to meet their fate.[9]

The Anglo-American Alliance possessed some reliable knowledge of the impending catastrophe. On April 5 the Office of Strategic Services in Washington received two reports about the Nazis' apparent plans to make this "the most efficient pogrom of them all." The following day a Jewish Agency representative warned British intelligence in Cairo of a Nazi radio broadcast that the Germans proposed "eliminating a million Jews in Hungary." Gerhart Riegner, the World Jewish Congress's representative in Geneva, learned from a trustworthy German source at the same time that the Nazis planned to kill Hungary's 800,000 Jews within six months. He gave this information to the U.S. War Refugee Board's newly appointed delegate in Switzerland, Roswell McClelland, who immediately passed it on to his superiors in Washington. The British authorities received this news at the end of the month. On May 19 the anti-Nazi Hungarian minister in Berne notified his British counterpart that half a million Jews were to be deported to Poland, and asked that the BBC warn the Hungarian people without delay not to assist in the deportations. Yet nothing happened for several precious weeks.[10]

The Jewish Agency also stood powerless while the Mandatory power for Palestine first responded to Joel Brand's startling information with uncertainty and delay. Although David Ben Gurion and Moshe Shertok in Jerusalem pressed HMG on May 26 for spirited action on the presumption that the planned deportations "have been deferred pending negotiations," the antiseptically named War Cabinet Committee on the Reception and Accommodation of Refugees remained skeptical. Furthermore, discussion within that committee reflected the worry that consent "might lead to an offer to unload an even greater number of Jews on to our hands," particularly regarding Palestine. Eden warned Churchill on June 1 that Middle Eastern oil and strategic communications necessitated the establishment of a state there that would satisfy the Arabs of the area. Accordingly, Shertok could not obtain a visa to interview Brand in Turkey.

The Jewish messenger from Hungary, having received word sent by

Weissmandel to the Yishuv band in Istanbul that the death transports to Auschwitz had begun, as well as some hint that Grosz had actually been ordered by the Germans to send out peace feelers to the Western Allies, realized that only by returning soon with some concrete response could he possibly check the mass slaughter. Brand voluntarily left for the Syrian border on June 5 to see agency political director Shertok and plead that the British and Americans offer the SS not trucks but money. (Shertok traveled there after being told by Palestine's chief secretary that Brand would not be allowed back in Turkey if he set foot on Palestinian soil.) The British whisked Brand off to Cairo the moment he reached Aleppo, however, and then reneged on their earlier promise to let him quickly return home. "This is wartime," High Commissioner MacMichael told a protesting Shertok.[11]

On June 5, the eve of the Normandy invasion, HMG also warned Washington that while some "Jews in position of extreme distress and danger" (undefined) could be received in Spain and Portugal, acceptance of the "blackmail" proposal "is equivalent to asking the Allies to suspend essential military operations." A week later Whitehall received Cabinet approval to turn down a suggestion from Chief Rabbi Joseph Hertz and the Jewish Agency that all Jews in enemy territory be declared "British protected persons"; this priority, it argued, "would overlook the fact that German brutality has been directed very extensively, above all in Poland, against non-Jews."[12]

The Americans, informed immediately by their ambassador in Ankara, adopted a more positive attitude. Director John Pehle of the WRB, the rescue organization considered by Foreign Office personnel to be an irresponsible body aimed at bringing Franklin D. Roosevelt Jewish votes, obtained the president's agreement that "we should keep the negotiations open if possible" to gain time and thus perhaps spare "the lives of many intended victims." This approach resembled the Jewish Agency Executive's position, Nahum Goldmann in Washington adding that ransom and IRC help might be offered; Shertok, after finally seeing Brand, insisted that a meeting with "accredited German representatives" had to take place in neutral Lisbon or Madrid and so "defer the killings." Ira Hirschmann was dispatched to contact Brand and report back to the board, while a message for the Soviets on June 9 informed Moscow of U.S. wishes. Ten days later London received the State Department's reply to its June 5 note: subject to the "necessities of military operations," it "should be made clear to the Germans by actions as well as words" that both governments will find "temporary havens of refuge for all Jews and similar persons in imminent danger of death whom the Germans are willing to release."[13]

Information then reaching Freudiger from Weissmandel, however, was about to blast prevalent fears and hopes that further negotiations over the Brand proposal would check the deportations. Taking over the talks with Eichmann and Clages separately in Budapest after Brand's departure, Kastner and colleague Andreas Biss respectively had managed to raise the original 600 exit figure to almost 1,700 persons and to obtain a promise for 18,000 to be placed in Austria's Strasshof concentration camp until Brand returned. (Indeed, Kastner's wire to Istanbul on June 17 that Brand come back at once or "everything will be lost" strengthened Shertok's hope that this be done to "prevent precipitation of calamity.") Yet this quiet diplomacy had no effect on the vast destruction currently taking place, Vessenmayer delightedly reassuring the head of the Nazi press on June 8 that "no marked public reaction" had yet occurred in the West to the deportations. At that very moment a courier from Bratislava delivered the Auschwitz protocols with a significant supplement to Freudiger.[14]

Appended to the original Rosenberg-Wetzler account was the testimony of two more Jews, Arnost Rosen and Czeslaw Mordowicz, who had fled Auschwitz on May 27 and succeeded in bringing the Slovak Jewish underground word of the Hungarian transports themselves and their appalling fate. The leader of Budapest's Orthodox community passed the text to his associates in the *Judenrat*. Shocked into absolute certainty at last, they began spreading the report in government and church circles. Freudiger also showed the report to Miklós (Moshe) Krausz, the Jewish Agency official in charge of emigration to Palestine.[15]

Strongly at odds with Kastner on personal and political grounds, Krausz had sometime earlier concluded that pressure from the neutral powers rather than negotiations with the SS might save his people. After obtaining refuge in the Swiss legation through the support of Charles Lutz, chief of the division for foreign interests, Krausz had discussed with his Gentile friend the possibility of issuing protective papers, and had asked Sweden's envoy if a special delegate of that country's Red Cross could be sent to help Budapest's Jews. Receipt of the full eyewitness report on Auschwitz, together with the ominous Nazi order for complete ghettoization in Budapest within a week of June 16, required far more drastic measures. Krausz had received no word from his superior, Chaim Barlas in Istanbul, since a notice three months earlier of the 600 available Palestine certificates. Accordingly, he entered Lutz's office and placed the briefest telephone call on June 19 to his Jewish Agency Geneva counterpart: "I have an important message and can't get through. You must do everything!"[16]

Chaim Pozner, on the other end of the wire, moved so successfully that he had Krausz's information in hand within a week. A Rumanian courier, sent by diplomat Georges Mantello with Pozner's calling card, left the same afternoon for Budapest. He returned to Berne early on June 23, carrying a letter Krausz had written immediately following his talk with Pozner, the original Auschwitz protocols, and an account of the deportation of 335,000 Jews from the Hungarian provinces between May 15 and June 7, 1944, and an additional 100,000 transported since. Pozner obtained the entire package that same morning and read Krausz's bitter conclusion: "the whole Jewish race in Hungary is condemned to death." "No escape" existed, although the granting of Palestinian citizenship to certificate holders would save a few thousand, and passports of neutral states might be issued. At that very minute some 350,000 Jews were being concentrated in Budapest and environs, settled in chessboard fashion in the city proper so they would not escape Allied bombardment. His letter and the reports, Krausz ended, should receive widespread publication. Attached was the (Weissmandel) appeal that the railroad lines to Auschwitz be bombed.[17]

Unknown to all but a few, the last request had actually been relayed to Switzerland and to Washington well beforehand. Weissmandel's coded cable of May 15, sent to his friend Hugo Donenbaum for Isaac Sternbuch, ultimately reached the representative of the American Orthodox Jewish rescue committee Va'ad HaHatsala late Friday afternoon on the 19th. In view of the extreme emergency, Sternbuch violated the Sabbath by immediately traveling from Montreux to Berne, where he woke up the British military attaché at midnight and pressed for the bombing of the Kosice-Presov route to Auschwitz. After repeating this information and plea to the American military attaché, who wired Washington, Sternbuch sent off similar cables in secret code via Julius Kühl of the Polish legation to the offices of Agudas Israel in New York and London so that they would take necessary steps. A similar telegram a few days later, warning that 15,000 Jews were being deported daily to Auschwitz, he passed on to the sympathetic American attaché in Berne. Sternbuch and his dynamic wife Recha did the same with other Weissmandel wires arriving at a frantic pace thereafter. The WRB received his coded cable of June 2 to the Union of Orthodox Rabbis in New York that "airmail" be urgently sent to Munkacs, Kosice, and Presov, "as this is the one means of rescue."[18]

That same day Isaac Gruenbaum, chairman of the Jewish Agency's rescue committee, made a related request of the American consul in Jerusalem while relaying information he had just received via Istanbul (from Weissmandel). Among other suggestions to check the ongoing transports, he asked on his own initiative that American planes bomb the death camps in Poland. Lowell Pinkerton refused to transmit the proposal through regular diplomatic channels to Washington, arguing strongly that bombing would cause the death of many Jews and might lead Nazi propaganda to claim that Americans, too, were helping in the destruction of the chosen victims. Jews in such centers were condemned to die in any event, Gruenbaum insisted. Some might escape in the confusion resulting from the air attacks; German SS guards would die; and perhaps the raids would disturb the tempo of mass slaughter and prevent the future construction of similar killing installations. The agency representative failed to win over his listener, but did receive Pinkerton's promise to forward the idea of bombing the railway lines between Auschwitz and eastern Hungary. The WRB got this information as well.[19]

Neither Sternbuch nor Gruenbaum received a reply.

Back in Geneva, the shocking news about Auschwitz and Hungarian Jewry received broad dissemination. Pozner immediately informed the various Jewish rescue organizations there, obtained from the usually fractious group a front for united action, and cabled Barlas the news for transmission to Jerusalem and London urging "necessary speedy action," as well as a reply about "Haftzazis [bombing in Hebrew code] proposals in this matter." Mantello initiated a press campaign that achieved impressive coverage through the efforts of Walter Garrett of the British news agency Exchange Telegraph; Gerhart Riegner of the WJC undertook a joint approach to the IRC with the help of Czechoslovak Minister Jaromir Kopecky. Kopecky, in receipt of the Auschwitz protocols from the Czech resistance, had wired London earlier in an attempt to stop the scheduled murder reported therein of the second contingent from Theresienstadt for June 20. With Riegner translating the document from German into English, Kopecky then cabled to the Czech government-in-exile the suggestion that the camps be bombed. Kopecky's figures on the Hungarian deportations, challenging previous ones supplied by Sternbuch, pushed WRB representative Roswell McClelland to obtain additional information.[20]

On June 24, 1944, McClelland integrated the Krausz dispatch with information received from Sternbuch, Kopecky, and a Swiss official just returned from Budapest. He wired board director John Pehle their consensus that vital sections of five stretches of railroad, especially bridges along the Csap-Kosice-Presov route, be bombed "as the only possible means of slowing down or stopping future deportations"; at least 1,500,000 Jews had been gassed in Birkenau since mid-1942. Two days later the British minister wired London a summary of the Krausz letter and the Auschwitz report, prepared by Richard Lichtheim in Geneva for Chaim Weizmann and Shertok. Aside from widespread publicity and warnings to the Hungarian government, "reprisals against Germans in Allied hands" and the bombing of railway lines, death camp installations, and all government buildings in Budapest should quickly follow, Lichtheim advised.[21]

Pehle relayed McClelland's telegram to Assistant Secretary of War John J. McCloy on June 29, along with a covering letter that emphasized bombing the deportation railroad lines, unaware that War's Operations Division had just rejected a proposal to strike the Kosice-Presov link. That idea, recommended on June 18 by Agudas Israel president Jacob Rosenheim after receiving word from Sternbuch, Pehle had forwarded to the War Department on June 21. Basing itself on a departmental decision of the previous February that "speedy defeat of the Axis" would most effectively bring relief to "victims of enemy persecution," the Operations Division asserted on June 26 that Rosenheim's request "could be executed only by diversion of considerable air support essential to the success of our forces now engaged in decisive operations." McCloy, also asked by the White House to investigate the proposal without a strong priority designation, reiterated this position in responding on July 4 about McClelland's wire. The assistant secretary, whose department thought this "certainly not a major affair" considering the Overlord invasion campaign, added to Pehle that the suggested operation "would in any case be of such doubtful efficacy that it would not amount to a practical project."[22]

Receipt of the Lichtheim cable in Whitehall early on June 27 produced more dramatic results. Winston Churchill picked it out of the sea of war dispatches, and scrawled a note to Foreign Secretary Eden: "What can be done? What can be said?" Weizmann and Shertok sought an immediate interview with Eden, but he fobbed off "these two Jews," as he put it, to Undersecretary Richard Law. At that meeting on June 30 Shertok again requested that Brand be returned to Hungary, with the Allies informing the Germans through the Swiss protecting power of their willingness to discuss the rescue of European Jewry in general. The WRB should meet Gestapo representatives, provided that the deportations "would stop in the meanwhile." A wireless warning to Hungarian railway workers not to transport Jews to death camps and the plea to bomb those installations completed the agency's demands. The following day a more responsive Foreign Office cabled its ambassador in Washington that HMG might agree to send Brand home and to negotiate with American support via the Swiss for transferring to safety "a stated number of Jews in conditions of particular distress," especially children. In principle, Eden personally supported the bombing proposal; broadcasts to workers on Hungary's railroads quickly followed.[23]

On July 6, as the deportations from the Hungarian provinces had almost come to an end and the American magazine *PM* published an exclusive summary of the Auschwitz report, Eden consented at last to receive Weizmann and Shertok. By then the foreign secretary had obtained a summary of the Auschwitz protocols from Stockholm and Geneva, although he doubted, as he put it to the War Cabinet, "if there was any effective action we could take." Beginning with his grasp of Krausz's June 19 message, Weizmann observed that "the stage of temporizing in the hope of prolonging the victims' lives is over." With messages in this vein already received from the Agency Executive in Jerusalem, the Yishuv's Va'ad Leumi, and the Jewish rescue organizations in Switzerland, he went on to stress the continuation of the negotiations. Brand should be allowed to return in the company of Menachem Bader, a member of the Palestinian Histadrut representation in Istanbul whom the Nazis had invited for talks at Kastner's suggestion. They would carry the message that a meeting of Germans with a WRB and a British representative would take place, ransom to be paid if necessary, and a declaration issued that all Jews released would be received by the Allies.

Interjecting at this point, Eden declared that the Foreign Office did intend to press for the entry of 20,000 Jewish children into Switzerland, a similar proposal for Sweden, and the admission into Palestine of those possessing proper certificates. Weizmann finished by reading the "urgent suggestions" in the agency's accompanying *aide-mémoire*: there must be a public declaration that the Swiss, in particular, issue protective documents in Budapest; a second warning had to be sent to the Hungarian population, with Russian premier Joseph Stalin approached to join; the railway line from Budapest to Birkenau and the death camps must be bombed. That same day Eden sent a report of the talk to Churchill, expressing approval of the warning and bombing suggestions but also his dislike of anything such as Bader's trip, "which might be interpreted as negotiation with the enemy."[24]

The prime minister replied in decisive fashion. "You and I are in entire agreement," he minuted to Eden on July 7. "Get anything out of the Air Force you can and invoke me if necessary. Certainly appeal to Stalin. On no account have the slightest negotiations direct or indirect with the Huns." Four days later Churchill endorsed his last point. The persecution of Hungarian Jewry and their deportation to Auschwitz, he wrote his foreign secretary, "is probably the greatest and most horrible crime ever committed in the whole history of the world," carried out "by scientific machinery, by nominally civilized men in the name of a great State and one of the leading races of Europe." Precisely for that reason, all involved and found guilty had to be put to death. The Allies should declare the policy in public, with "no negotiations of any kind on this subject."[25]

Churchill's response put a finish to the Brand mission, the last nail of its coffin driven in on July 19. Skeptical throughout concerning the proposal and fearing that the Jewish Agency wished to employ it to break the 1939 White Paper, Whitehall now dropped the original idea of negotiating with the Swiss. The willing Bader, a Palestinian (and therefore British) subject, was refused permission to leave. The Americans, who had heard from Soviet Deputy Foreign Minister Andrei Vyshinsky on June 20 that his government did not consider it "expedient or permissible" to carry on any such talks, went further on July 7. Overriding British objections, Washington relayed to Moscow all details it had lacked a month earlier, including Brand's informal conversations indicating that the Germans had promised not to use the 10,000 trucks in question on the western front. Secretary of State Hull emphasized that eventually an offer might be received "which can be considered seriously," but his new information clearly ruled out any Russian approval. If this were not enough, the Foreign Office heard a week later from HMG Middle East intelligence's interrogation of Grosz that high Gestapo officials were using the mission to seek peace feelers with the West, "which might embarrass us with the USSR." Extremely nervous at these implications, London cabled the reasons for its change of policy to the State Department on July 18, and a day later leaked news of the Brand-Grosz trip to the press. While the aghast Palestinians in Istanbul saw this move as a "clear manifestation" of HMG's antisemitism, the *New York Herald Tribune* and the BBC termed the Nazi proposal a "monstrous" offer.[26] The Allied front, all triumphantly declared, would stand firm.

Ironically, on that same July 19, 1944, the press reported a halt to the deportation of Hungary's Jews.

World protest at the end of June had played a major part in this dramatic reversal. Pope Pius XII had received dispatches about German activity from Nuncio Angelo Rotta in Budapest, as well as the American government's request a month earlier to "express himself" by threat of excommunication and other means; he finally wrote to Regent Miklós Horthy on June 25 to help those "persecuted because of their nationality or race." The following day, pressed by the WRB, which supported a plea from the WJC's Leon Kubowitzki on May 31 for a strong diplomatic note to the Hungarians, Roosevelt threatened reprisals and bombing of Hungarian towns if the deportations did not cease. Secretary Hull repeated this theme via the Swiss 24 hours later. The Swiss government, alerted by Consul Lutz and others, intervened, as did Madrid and Ankara. King Gustav V, receiving eyewitness accounts from his Budapest representatives and formal requests to step in from Sweden's chief rabbi and the Jewish community of Budapest, wrote the regent on June 30 "in the name of humanity" and that of the "reputation of Hungary among the nations of the world" to save Jews from death. The Riegner-Kopecky *demarche* resulted in a similar letter from Max Huber, president of the ICRC in Geneva. Information passed on by the *Judenrat* in Budapest and the unprecedented publicity resulting from Mantello's immediate effort also played their role. Horthy alluded to all this in a talk with German Ambassador Vessenmayer on the evening of July 4.[27]

More significant, Vessenmayer concluded in a report to Berlin after talking with Prime Minister Döme Sztójay on July 4, was the interception and deciphering by Hungarian counter-intelligence in Switzerland of Krausz's dispatch as relayed to the American and British governments by their men in Switzerland. (German authorities had intercepted the message to the Foreign Office.) Their description of the fate of the deportees, the suggested bombing of Budapest and the Hungarian railways, together with another teletype message (sent by Kastner) naming 70 Hungarian and German culprits, could not be denied by the Nazis. Nor could the Allied bombing of Budapest, publicly demanded of Roosevelt in May by *Jewish Forum*'s editor to demonstrate unequivocally that "the United Nations are concerned for the lives of Jews," on July 2. Horthy and other antisemites in his entourage might easily have viewed these developments as further proof of their conviction that Jews controlled London and Washington.[28]

Horthy could not overlook the strategic position of the Allied offensive. While the West had launched the invasion of France, Soviet troops were quickly approaching the Carpathian region. In addition, as Sztójay pointed out to Vessenmayer, Rumania and Slovakia had allowed Jews from Hungary to enter their own borders.[29]

Perhaps most important was the 76-year-old leader's fear of an internal *coup d'état*. Eichmann, in collaboration with Political Secretary László Endre, had carefully arranged for a one-day "sweep" of Budapest's Jews on July 7. Gendarmerie Secretary László Baky and 600 Hungarian policemen under his jurisdiction from the provinces were to seize the capital and topple the regent simultaneously. The latter got wind of the plan, partly through word to his son from Ernö (Ernest) Petö of the *Judenrat*. He ordered the deportations stopped on July 7, and crushed the rebellion. On the 12th the neutral ministers were informed that all anti-Jewish measures were to be suspended, and two days later Horthy succeeded in checking Eichmann's zealous attempt to ship 1,200 Jews from the Kistarcsa camp to Auschwitz after being notified of this through Freudiger. Eichmann did get these and 1,500 other Jews at Savar deported aboard an express train to Auschwitz on the 19th, but with that "victory" the supreme architect of destruction had to be content for the time being.[30]

The curtain was about to rise on the second act in a unique tragedy. On July 19, the same day that Reich Deputy Press Chief Sunderman denied the reported atrocities and the ICRC communicated to the world Horthy's decision to stop the deportations, the ICRC made a major announcement: the Hungarian government had authorized the relief organization "to cooperate in the removal of all Jewish children under 10 years of age who are granted a visa by some acceptor country ... emigration to Palestine has been permitted to every Jew who is in possession of the necessary visa." In the space of 55 days 437,402 Jews had been deported to Auschwitz-Birkenau, some 90 percent to a quick death. Their suitcases at the railroad siding, according to a Polish underground report broadcast by the BBC on July 17, had left a mute pile 300 meters long, 5 meters high, and 200 meters wide.[31] The West had done nothing to check this massacre. Now it would have to respond publicly to the "Horthy offer." Still not fully resolved were some issues raised by Weizmann and Shertok with Eden on July 6, particularly the bombing proposals. Perhaps the eclipse of the Brand-Grosz project, moreover, did not rule out unofficial negotiations? In the wings, Budapest's 300,000 Jews anxiously awaited their fate.

II

The reported halt to the deportations strengthened the doubts of those British officials skeptical about the entire bombing scheme. Armed with Churchill's approval of July 7, Eden had immediately informed Air Secretary Archibald Sinclair of this fact, and requested that he examine the feasibility of the Jewish Agency's request. On the 15th Sinclair ruled out the strike against railways as beyond the distance of British bases. For the same reason, he noted, HMG's Bomber Command lacked the capacity to fly against Auschwitz-Birkenau during a nighttime raid. The Americans might do so by daylight, but the "costly and dangerous" operation might be ineffective and would not afford the victims great opportunities of escape. The air secretary agreed to present the matter to Washington, although he was "very doubtful" that its estimate of the situation would be otherwise. Eden was not at all satisfied with this "characteristically unhelpful letter," but the head of his Refugee Department thought that the technical difficulties and Horthy's announcement suggested reserve.[32]

When in early August the Air Ministry pressed Whitehall for photographic information about Birkenau, the Foreign Office suggested to the Jewish Agency in London that it might wish to drop the bombing request, given the end of transports out of Hungary. Political secretary Joseph Linton rushed to demur, pointing out that the death factories could be used in the future. Upon hearing that the lack of topographical data was causing the delay, he immediately obtained information from the Polish government-in-exile on Auschwitz and Treblinka, and sent it to the Foreign Office. Linton's reports were *withheld*, however, from both the Air Ministry and the foreign secretary, Eden only given a memorandum that the apparent improvement in the Hungarian situation and the "very great technical difficulties involved" called for a negative decision by HMG. The deception received official status on September 1. A letter from Under Secretary Law to Weizmann employed the second reason alone; Law's note to Sinclair, on the other hand, accorded it inferior significance.[33]

Across the Atlantic, rescue advocates offered sundry plans to the War Refugee Board. By July 1 John Pehle had received a suggestion from WRB assistant Benjamin Akzin that Auschwitz-Birkenau be bombed, as well as Kubowitzki's alternative proposal that Soviet paratroopers and members of the Polish underground destroy the installations. The WJC's British branch, influenced by members Ignacy Schwartzbart of the Polish National Council and Ernest Frischer of the Czech government-in-exile (who also proposed the razing of Budapest), backed the Kopecky-Riegner request for air sorties against the camps. Kubowitzki, however, feared for the resulting victims, and worried that the Germans would thereby be given a "welcome pretext" to deny that they had committed the killings. Receipt on July 6 of the summarized Auschwitz protocols from both McClelland and the Czech authorities in London led Pehle to review the matter again.[34]

The impracticability of air operations continued to dominate the response of U.S. officialdom. Pehle considered the suggestion regarding paratroopers a nonmilitary matter and an inefficient operation that would also involve the sacrifice of American troops. "The apparently deep-rooted anti-Semitism" in Polish circles, on the other hand, raised strong doubts that their weak underground forces would attack the death centers "in good faith" without the assertion of strong political pressure and support. The WRB director decided, therefore, not to refer these proposals to the War Department. Getting no response, Kubowitzki appealed directly to McCloy on August 9 with Frischer's proposal that the death camps and railroad junctions be bombed. Five days later the assistant secretary repeated the substance of his July 4 letter to Pehle, adding that "such an effort, even if practicable, might provoke even more vindictive action by the Germans."[35]

There remained the Horthy offer, which had its genesis in the Hungarian government's June 27 request of the Germans that "approximately 7,000 persons" and 1,000 Jewish children under ten years of age be permitted to depart for Palestine. Consul Lutz, working in tandem with Krausz from the newly established Department of Emigration of the Swiss legation's Representation of Foreign Interests, reported to both governments that his bureau had immigration certificates to Palestine for 8,700 families, a total of about 40,000 persons. At the suggestion of Foreign Secretary von Ribbentrop, Hitler actually approved this official "resettlement" to Sweden, Switzerland, and the United States in exchange for a free hand from the Hungarians concerning the Jews of Budapest. To finalize matters, a collective passport for a first group of 2,200 Jews, having Rumanian permission for transit to Constanza and thence to Haifa, was discussed on July 17 by Lutz and Krausz with the German and Hungarian authorities.[36]

Eichmann lost no time in registering a personal protest against the Krausz-Lutz scheme. The 38-year-old SS official insisted that he understood Himmler strongly disapproved of such "biologically valuable material, including very many old Zionists whose migration to Palestine is extremely undesirable," being allowed to proceed in that particular direction. Secretly, he wished to resume the deportation of Jews from the Hungarian capital so suddenly and rapidly that they would be on their way to Auschwitz "before the necessary formalities could be arranged." In the face of Horthy's firm stance against further deportations, Eichmann at least managed to have the *Führer* revoke the 2,200 exit permits to Palestine.[37]

Unaware of Eichmann's machinations, senior officials in London panicked over the distinct possibility of a mass Jewish exodus from Budapest to the Promised Land. A flurry of cables suggesting emigration assistance to Palestine from the Swedish and Swiss governments, along with Shertok's urging that as many Hungarian Jews as possible be brought to that most obvious center of refuge, led the Colonial Office to warn Whitehall that Palestine only had "limited room" and "we may be on the verge of a flood of refugees." The Foreign Office agreed: possible havens should be far from Palestine, preferably in the Western Hemisphere. Pehle and his associates, strong supporters of a plan currently being advanced by the Emergency Committee to Save the Jewish People of Europe for temporary refugee shelters in Palestine, would have none of this. When the State Department, at WRB urging, informed London on July 31 of its wish to announce in a week's time that it would have the ICRC arrange havens "for all who are permitted to leave Hungary and who reach neutral or UN territory," the Foreign Office requested a postponement until the War Cabinet discussed the matter.[38]

At the Cabinet Committee on Refugees' meeting of August 4, Colonial Secretary Oliver Stanley cautioned that the 40,000 figure might turn out to be considerably larger. The proposals conveyed by Brand had spoken, after all, of close to a million Jews; the British empire, concluded the committee, lacked the capacity for further accommodation. Five days later the War Cabinet ruled against making an indefinite commitment, particularly in view of a wire from High Commissioner MacMichael that the Holy Land could take but a maximum of 4,000 immigrants from Hungary within the remaining 11,000 White Paper

unallocated quota. The State Department, on the other hand, strengthened by the presence in London at that moment of Treasury Secretary
Morgenthau and WRB general counsel DuBois, pressed Eden and his
staff to drop HMG's proposed reply of qualified cooperation. Eliminating the word "all" before "Jews," London finally muted its fears about
upsetting the White Paper and bowed to the pressure. At midnight
August 17, 1944, the two Allies announced their acceptance of Horthy's
offer. A precious month had passed by.[39]

The same anxiety of "risking civil war in Palestine owing to an inroad
of Jews from Hungary into the Levant," as Eden put it in a memorandum to Churchill, caused a little delay in HMG's granting bogus Palestine certificates to some of the Jews still around Budapest. Krausz's June
19 suggestion that Palestinian passports be granted to certificate holders
had immediately been passed on to Shertok via Pozner. The latter,
working with his Jewish Agency colleague M. Kahany, drew up a broad
formula stating that these documents "virtually gave citizenship" to their
holders. Having these ideas in tow, Moshe Shertok asked the Colonial
Office in early July to issue "some fictitious device" by which the imper-
iled Jews would "be regarded for present purposes as Palestinian citizens." The agency, Shertok quickly added, would give a written assurance that the special document constituted no permanent guarantee.
MacMichael expressed grave misgivings about "so demonstrable an act
of bad faith," while a Whitehall official thought that the Germans "would
put the screw on even harder." But on July 28 Stanley agreed that the
Swiss should be authorized to issue certificates in Budapest for 5,000
Jews, which would allow the holder to enter Palestine "as an immigrant
. . . at any time at which he/she may reach that country." After two years
Palestinian citizenship would follow.[40]

The Jews of Budapest needed far more help than diplomatic evasion
as a counterforce to the relentless Eichmann, and they received it from
Sweden in mid-July. Just as the first Hungarian deportations began,
Sweden's chief rabbi, Marcus Ehrenpreis, had discovered an eminent
non-Jew who might organize rescue activities in Budapest. Koloman
Lauer, a Hungarian Jewish refugee in charge of a substantial export firm
operating from Stockholm, suggested to the Reform clergyman that his
business associate, Raoul Wallenberg, undertake the mission.[41]

The 31-year-old unassuming bachelor, coming from a long line of
Swedish diplomats and bankers, had first become sensitized to the plight
of European Jewry when he met German refugees in 1936 during a six-
month stint at the Holland Bank in Haifa. Furthermore, he spoke German well, and had received a broad education in the United States and
on trips as Lauer's representative in central Europe. Ehrenpreis, then in
his mid-seventies, entertained doubts about Wallenberg's age and the

suggestion that the Swede resort to bribes for rescue. After two weeks he passed on the information to the Swedish Foreign Ministry, which at the same time also received a request from the U.S. ambassador and from Ivor C. Olsen, WRB delegate and financial attaché in the American Embassy, that it send someone to the Hungarian capital. When Lauer met with Olsen, whose office was adjacent to his own, the choice was concluded. Carrying full diplomatic accreditation as third secretary of the Swedish legation at Budapest, the promise of a first installment of $100,000 from JDC funds via the WRB, and a list of helpful contacts and Jews to be given rescue priority, Wallenberg prepared for an August departure. But ministry reports about Jewry's agony, particularly the Rosenberg-Wetzler eyewitness testimony on Auschwitz-Birkenau which the legation had dispatched on June 24, convinced him to leave immediately for his rendezvous with destiny.[42]

Arriving in Budapest on July 9, Wallenberg quickly set to work with unparalleled zeal. His Section C, devoted to "humanitarian aims," went far beyond the 700 provisional passports and certificates issued by Minister Carl Danielsson via Swedish Red Cross delegate Valdemar Langlet to Jews with relatives or commercial ties in Sweden. Using his academic training gained a decade earlier at the University of Michigan, Wallenberg designed an elaborate-looking protective passport that ultimately covered some 5,000 people. A widespread relief organization employing 400 Jews further helped lift the overriding apathy he had found on his arrival. High-ranking government officials were bribed or promised Swedish diplomatic support after the Nazi collapse.[43]

This single-minded devotion infected others. The ICRC's Robert Schirmer followed in the distribution of supplies and, upon obtaining Horthy's grant of protective extra-territoriality, the marking of Red Cross seals on houses where Jews were concentrated. Lutz took in close to 3,000 Jews at the Swiss Department of Emigration, located at 29 Vadasz St. in the combined "glass house" of magnate Arthur Weisz and the empty headquarters of the Hungarian Football Association, and ultimately issued protective papers for an additional 30,000 in Swiss-marked dwellings. The Spanish and Portugese embassies sheltered other Jews and, with Langlet, issued thousands of protective documents. Monsignor Rotta gave out thousands of Palestine immigration certificates forwarded by the apostolic delegate to Turkey, the future Pope John XXIII, who had been approached by Palestine Chief Rabbi Isaac Herzog, the Jewish Agency's Chaim Barlas, and the WRB's Ira Hirschmann; Rotta also issued "safe conduct" passes over his own signature. Together the neutral government representatives formed Section A of the IRC, headed by Zionist leader Otto Komoly, whose children's shelters ultimately housed 8,000 Jewish children.[44]

To alleviate the precarious situation further, Jewish circles in Budapest pressed to pick up the thread of the defunct Brand negotiations. A transport arranged by Kastner of 1,684 Jews had left for the Spanish frontier on June 30, all necessary documents secured by Barlas and Jewish Agency immigration head Eliyahu Dobkin, after 5 million Swiss francs were promised to *Obersturmführer* Kurt A. Becher. (This SS cavalry officer, serving as a personal emissary of Himmler in Hungary, had already negotiated the transfer of valuable property to the SS as the price of flight to Portugal for the Manfred Weiss family and Baron von Oppenheim.) Local resources, including the delivery of three suitcases filled with diamonds, gold, and platinum to Becher, covered 3 million of the total payment, with the remainder to come from a Swiss credit to purchase tractors there and sheepskins in Slovakia. As part of this deal, Freudiger and Orthodox Jewish businessman Gyula Link asked Sternbuch to open a credit for 40 tractors and so assure the safety of 1,200 religious Jews, a good portion of whom were on what Kastner called his "Noah's Ark" to Spain. Eichmann personally shifted the Kastner train to Bergen-Belsen on July 8, however, placing its fate, that of the 18,000 in Strasshof, and that of 600 Jews protected by Kastner at a camp on Budapest's Columbus St. in grave straits.[45]

JDC intervention appeared crucial at this point. Kastner urged Schwalb in Geneva that the Freudiger-Link negotiation be supported fully, but the JDC's Mayer refused Sternbuch's individual request for 500,00 Swiss francs to this end: Nazi guarantees had not been obtained and Mayer wished, above all, to focus on all Jews in need ("Klal"). Fortunately, Biss's memorandum for Himmler via Clages and funds from Agudas Israel's Jacob Rosenheim to cover a Swiss credit for ten tractors arrived in time to keep these three groups temporarily from the gas chambers of Birkenau. While Eichmann fretted, Kastner obtained Himmler's agreement through Becher to let Joseph Schwartz, the JDC's European director, proceed with the original discussions. Following the July 20, 1944, attempt by some German generals on Hitler's life, Berlin ordered that Kastner join Schwartz at the Spanish-French border for the talks.[46] Would Washington agree?

Unlike the British, the director of the WRB still wished to keep the door to negotiations open. Grosz's interrogation, the German willingness to talk with Menachem Bader in Berlin, and a report from Ivor Olsen in Stockholm on June 28 that three Nazis had offered to release at least 2,000 Latvian Jews in exchange for medicine, nonstrategic materials, and apparently Western "good will" all suggested the enemy's seriousness in continuing where Brand's project had left off. Schwartz, an American, could not negotiate and thus create Soviet suspicions, Pehle and Under Secretary of State Edward Stettinius, Jr., decided on

July 27—but someone not of Allied nationality could. Hearing this, the Germans agreed instead to meet Saly Mayer, a citizen of neutral Switzerland, at the Austro-Swiss border. As proof of good faith and on Kastner's insistence, they also consented unconditionally to release a convoy of 500 Jews from the 1,684 at Bergen-Belsen to Switzerland and not to deport the remainder involved in the Va'ada's broader scheme.

Knowing of the various details from Mayer, Schwalb, and Sternbuch, McClelland (in Mayer's code, "Chanuka") recommended to Pehle on August 11 that the JDC man be given the green light. The Swiss would have to approve this effort, designed to "gain as much time as possible without, if possible, making any commitments," he added. While awaiting board approval, Mayer followed McClelland's advice and informed Budapest that the 500 would have to arrive in Switzerland prior to any meeting. Kastner had cabled a hesitant Mayer that only the Freudiger-Link tractor plan could obtain the release of the 40,000 broached by Lutz and Krausz, and he urged that at least "Alpayim Alafim Salys" (2 million Swiss francs in Hebrew code) be made available. McClelland had his own doubts, however, thinking that "at this juncture it is impossible to embark upon a program of buying Jews out of Nazi hands," especially in exchange for goods that might prolong the war.[47]

The 62-year-old Mayer entered the talks with three Nazis and Kastner on August 21, 1944, bound by the impossibility of offering money or goods and authorized to speak only as a private Swiss citizen. The JDC's European office had privately insisted that he first clear everything with headquarters in New York; the head of the Swiss alien police, Heinrich Rothmund, informed Mayer that ransom could not be involved; the ICRC, for its part, claimed that it "could on no account associate with people who would use illegal means for salvaging goods." The Swiss even refused to let Becher, his assistant Max Grueson, and Eichmann associate Hermann Krumey cross the border, and Mayer had to talk with them pacing back and forth on the bridge between St. Margarethen and Hoechst, Austria. In a first private meeting Kastner warned Mayer that failure would see a different Nazi group, currently urging the deportation of Jews, succeed in its goal of "100% destruction." Becher then suggested that American freighters deliver 10,000 trucks for postwar use, returning home with 2,500 Jews per trip. Sticking to his previous instructions, the very proper Jew insisted to the four ("Arba," in his code) that he would never undertake "immoral" slave trade. Further discussion as to money and other materials needed by the Germans was necessary, he advised, and until then "no annihilation" should take place.[48]

The first encounter satisfied both sides. The first group of 318 Jews—Eichmann cut this from the original 500, and purposely excluded Kastner's entire family and Joel Brand's mother and three sisters—arrived from Bergen-Belsen that afternoon. The War Refugee Board, whose reply seconding McClelland's position arrived the next day, urged Mayer to continue his stalling efforts without any payment of ransom. While the JDC delegate sought an immediate $2 million credit from his superiors, Becher cabled Himmler that, with "300 pieces" just "rolled across" into Switzerland, the Jewish side had begun to view the negotiations seriously. Becher's telegram came just in time for Budapest Jewry, since Eichmann had obtained Horthy's consent to carry out a "limited deportation" from the capital on August 25. (Actually, 66 trains were ready for a sweep of Budapest's remaining Jews.) The fall of Rumania to the Red Army during the night of August 23 abruptly made the regent rescind the order, however, causing the furious head of the "Special Operations Group" to have Wisliceny flown to Berlin in an appeal for Himmler's help. Becher's report and Germany's particular need for her Hungarian ally at that very moment led to the *Reichsführer*'s wire at 3 A.M. on August 25 that the deportations were to be discontinued. Eichmann's commando team was finally dissolved a month later, Himmler awarding him an Iron Cross, second class, in compensation.[49]

Throughout September, 1944, Mayer continued, in McClelland's apt phrase at the time, "playing off the killing group against [the] undecided group pushing goods for nothing." Shifting the negotiations from trucks to money in a talk with Grueson and Becher representative Wilhelm Billitz, he declared a willingness to deposit 5 million Swiss francs locally, provided Swiss consent were obtained, in the name of his organization for discussion involving *all* Jews under German control. When Grueson demanded a final reply within 24 hours and negotiations with someone who had "full political powers," the Swiss Jew asked for a detailed list of what goods in Switzerland the Germans would buy with the money given them. The slaughter of Jews (including the last deportations then beginning in Slovakia on Himmler's order, after Jewish youth participated in the national uprising of August 28) would have to be halted, he added. Mayer's unauthorized mention of specific funds, prodded by Kastner's warning that "Nazis are not retailers—all or nothing" and an urgent memorandum from Biss that "a few small advances" be made to save the talks, was not revealed to McClelland. An ambiguous cable to Budapest from Mayer on September 26, confirming his promise about the 20 million Swiss francs, delighted Clages and Becher, who promised to inform Himmler immediately. As a result, Kastner was allowed to leave two days later with Billitz and SS equipment specialist Herbert Kettlitz for yet another meeting on the bridge at St. Margarethen.

As the clock ominously struck "11:59!" with a furious Mayer still lacking any word from his superiors, the JDC representative reiterated his position to the Nazi contingent. He would not resort to blackmail. Two million dollars had been promised for the purchase in installments of Swiss goods; as long as the talks continued, the Jews of Slovakia and Budapest must be protected and the remainder of the transport at Bergen-Belsen released. Billitz wired Becher of these facts without delay, also expressing doubts to his chief that Mayer could actually make the transaction involved. "The whole affair is becoming very restrained," McClelland informed Pehle, particularly with Kastner's report that Eichmann and Wisliceny had just been transferred back to Budapest.[50]

Unaware of these confidential meetings, the WJC's Kubowitzki renewed his pressure on Washington to destroy Auschwitz-Birkenau and other death camps by use of operational ground forces. "It is difficult to imagine any vindictive action by the Germans which could still deteriorate the present desperate plight of the Jewish population in occupied Europe," he wrote McCloy on August 30. Echoing a letter from Ignacy Schwartzbart to the Polish prime minister, Kubowitzki asked for the use of Polish, Soviet, and even Anglo-American troops to destroy these installations. The Mediterranean commander in charge has been fully informed of the situation, the assistant secretary replied a few days later, and perhaps "an alteration in the tactical situation" might allow him to take some such effective steps "to check these ghastly excesses of the Nazis." McCloy confirmed this point at the end of the month, and promised to contact British commander Henry M. Wilson again.[51]

Concurrently, the Va'ad HaHatsala once again put forth its plea for bombing the railroad junctions between Budapest and Upper Silesia. On August 28 Sternbuch had cabled Weissmandel's warning that this offensive could check continuing deportations, 12,000 Jews having been shipped to Auschwitz two days earlier. Receiving this wire at night, Rabbi Abraham Kalmanowitz immediately called the WRB's Benjamin Akzin with a plea that he deliver this message directly to Pehle in the morning. In transmitting the report over the head of his immediate superior, Akzin pointed out that the board had been created precisely to overcome past inertia and insufficient government interest in rescuing European Jewry. Pehle had spoken to the president the previous April in support of the "free port" idea, not a matter of life and death. The identical course should be followed now, Akzin urged. Surely Roosevelt, aware of the United Nations' present air superiority, would at once "cut through the inertia-motivated" objections of the War Department when acquainted with the facts and give the order. But the board director had recently echoed War Department policy in refusing to second requests from Jewish organizations to destroy Auschwitz by bombing or parachutist commando action, to use American airplanes to fly children out of Hungary, or to permit payment of ransom in light of the 318 Jews just released from Bergen-Belsen. Akzin's memorandum remained in Pehle's files.[52]

"For such consideration as it may be worth," the board director did transmit to McCloy a telegram of September 29 from the WRB's James Mann in London regarding the bombing of Auschwitz-Birkenau and other death centers. Earlier that month, upon hearing that "the Germans are increasing their extermination activities," the Polish government-in-exile and the WJC's British section had asked Mann to convey to his superiors the need for precision air strikes against the gas chambers and SS barracks. By then the State Department had in hand an ICRC report that the Germans intended to deport the Jews still alive in Hungary, as well as McClelland's information, emanating from the Bratislava Jewish underground, about the imminent deportation of all Jews left in Slovakia. McCloy, however, followed his executive assistant's advice not to take action on Mann's cable in view of the matter's full review in the past. Quite independently, the War Department's Operations Division had the message radioed to the commander in chief of the U.S. Strategic Air Forces in Europe, Lt. General Carl Spaatz, on October 4 for his consideration. The next day Spaatz's deputy commander summarized that body's findings and offered his conclusion: the "unfortunate Poles herded in these concentration camps" would not have "their status improved" thereby, while the Germans "would be provided with a fine alibi for any wholesale massacre that they might perpetrate."[53]

Similar requests in London met with Whitehall's traditional attitude. On September 18 the newly appointed head of the Refugee Department discovered to his surprise that the Jewish Agency's donation of topographical material on Auschwitz and Treblinka had not been forwarded to the air secretary, despite the latter's assertion that lack of such information precluded a strike operation. "We are therefore *technically guilty* of allowing the Air Ministry to get away with it without having given them (tho' we had it) the information they asked for as a prerequisite," concluded Paul Mason. Two days later the agency's Linton submitted a cable just received from Gruenbaum in Jerusalem (again from Weissmandel via Istanbul). Reports about daily transports being prepared for 10,000-12,000 Jews to Auschwitz via Zelina and Pruska and one that 15,000 had just been sent to Germany, Gruenbaum pleaded, necessitated UN warnings to the Hungarian authorities, the bombing of the railway line to Auschwitz, and the bombing of that death factory itself. While attaching a note on the four railway routes from Budapest to Poland, Linton called for a reconsideration of the bombing request on his understanding that the fuel depots in the area had already been targets of Allied air strikes on two occasions. The Foreign Office rejected the appeal, however, on the ground that a halt had been called in the Hungarian deportations since July, and it still kept the plans of Auschwitz from the Air Ministry.[54]

On October 12 A. G. Brotman of the Board of Deputies of British Jews asked whether HMG had considered a joint bombing attempt with the Soviets. In reply, Mason pointed out the risk of Germany claiming that the Allies had done their best to murder the Jews. In fact, a week earlier the Colonial Office had set entry of Jews into Palestine at a maximum of 1,500 per month, in line with another Eden memorandum that oil and other British interests in the Middle East militated against a Jewish state there. HMG never pursued Brotman's proposal either.[55]

Secret negotiation and official decisions in Washington and London could not meet the immediate crisis facing the remnant of Hungarian Jewry. On October 14, 1944, with the Red Army marching on Budapest, Horthy announced over the airwaves that his country was deserting the Axis. The *Wilhelmstrasse* had long been notified of a Hungarian mission to Moscow seeking an armistice. Bolstered by the 24th Panzer Division with 40 Tiger tanks, the Nazis moved quickly now, spiriting the regent's son away to Mauthausen and then offering Horthy a 24-hour ultimatum. The old man collapsed, and the Germans appointed Ferenc Szálasi of the Arrow Cross party (Nyilas) to head the new puppet government. Eichmann, whom Himmler called "the master," arrived on October 17 in the capital.[56] The final act was on hand.

III

Within a week, the long-dreaded nightmare became reality. Members of the Hungarian Arrow Cross looted and killed hundreds of Jews in the open streets. The new interior minister, Gabor Vajna, agreed to Nazi requests that 50,000 Jewish men and women be marched to the Reich, with four labor camps to be set up for all capable of work. Any others were to be segregated in one ghetto. (Confidentially, the German foreign office heard from Vessenmayer, Eichmann planned to deport another 50,000 later on.) Vajna publicly announced on October 18 that he did not consider baptized Jews and those holding protective passports free from the new government's determination to "solve the Jewish question." Two days later doors marked with the yellow star for Jews were assaulted by the Hungarian police. All males from 16 to 60 fit for labor were rounded up, followed by women between 16 and 40, and sent to work on fortification lines. By October 26 they numbered 35,000.[57]

The neutral embassies swiftly rose to the challenge. Hearing from Krausz and the Swiss legation that the German authorities had agreed to the departure of "about 8,000 Jews" by November 15, Pozner and Kahany got the Swiss Political Department to cable its assurance that the number would be admitted into Switzerland. The American and British ministers privately agreed to supply guarantees for final destination, and soon repeated this pledge for 4,500 Jews holding Swedish documents. In Budapest Wallenberg made contact with the wife of Foreign Minister Gabor Kemenyi and obtained the rescinding of Vajna's order. The ICRC, pressed by Riegner and his superiors in New York, strengthened the hand of its representatives in the beleaguered city and protested vigorously to the Szálasi government.[58]

This could not divert Eichmann from starting the 120-mile march to Strasshof, Austria. On November 2, as the Soviet spearhead reached the city's suburbs, some 15,000 remaining members of the Jewish labor battalions were shifted west of the Danube. Six days later, joining about 25,000 Budapest Jews of all ages, they set out on the perilous journey. Without food and driven ruthlessly by Hungarian gendarmes in the freezing weather, thousands died of bullets and hand grenades, disease and starvation. Children born in barracks across the border died within an hour or so, the victims of lice.[59]

Throwing personal safety to the winds, Wallenberg carried out his own rescue operation. In an official Swedish truck he followed after the death marches, pulling out people by the use of protective documents and distributing food, shoes, and warm clothing to others. A volunteer worker for the Red Cross, armed with "safe-conduct" certificates from Angelo Rotta, did the same with the aid of nuns roaming through the endless lines. Issuing its own documents, the ICRC also filmed the horrors for the papal nuncio. The neutral emissaries protested to Szálasi, who then informed the Germans that women should only be removed by transport vehicles. While a furious Eichmann wangled a few trains from Vienna to finish the job, Wallenberg's contacts provided the Swedish attaché with lists of the deportees, and false papers were prepared in their names for the Hungarian police. Usually Wallenberg appeared at the assembly centers to get the release of those arrested, and on one night even drove to catch a train and free "his" charges just before the sealed carriages reached Germany's border.[60]

When the city's remaining 100,000 Jews were ordered into a small central ghetto in Pest, the one-man army of mercy and other neutral government authorities moved to avert this step to ultimate murder. Aside from affording protection to those already housed in Swedish, Swiss, and Red Cross buildings, they established an "international ghetto" for some additional 15,000. Wallenberg began by transferring his office there from Buda on the right side of the Danube, and obtained 32 apartment buildings near the Margit Bridge for new "Swedish houses." The neutral embassies save for the Turks followed his example, and continued issuing false papers. Foods and medicines were regularly supplied via Olsen and the ICRC with funds from Saly Mayer of St. Gallen.[61]

On another front, General Dwight D. Eisenhower, commander of the

Allied Expeditionary Forces in Europe, issued a stern warning to the German people on November 7 that they take no part in the program of mass murder and terror. Throughout September the WRB's Pehle had been receiving reports from various organizations that the Nazi forces, in retreat before the Red Army, might kill the thousands of prisoners left in centers like Auschwitz. These sources also ventured the suggestion that Roosevelt and military authorities warn the Germans against taking such action. Thinking that a nonpolitical gesture by one presumably involved in the future occupation of Germany might have some effect, the board's director suggested to McCloy on September 28 that SHAEF's overall head issue a statement referring to the plight of people "without regard to their nationality and whether they are Jewish or otherwise." Roosevelt gave his approval to this draft in mid-October, just when an initially reluctant War Department heard that SHAEF's Political Warfare Division preferred to substitute "religious faith" for "Jewish," and so avoid giving the Nazis a "powerful propaganda line." While the Washington bureaucracy smoothed over the discrepancy, McClelland weighed in with a lengthy request that all the Allies and major organized churches issue a concerted, powerful warning on behalf of political prisoners and those the Germans considered "stateless" (primarily Jews). SHAEF's change in wording was accepted on October 30, and the State Department requested Moscow to join with a comparable declaration "in view of the urgency of the situation." The Soviets did not reply.[62]

The day following Eisenhower's warning, Pehle urged McCloy to bomb the Auschwitz gas chambers and industrial plant. Pehle's sudden reversal came after receiving the complete Auschwitz protocols from Geneva on November 1. In a covering letter dated October 12, McClelland had referred to his summary of their contents three months earlier, and provided various reasons why he believed them authentic. Shocked out of his earlier hesitation, his WRB superior forwarded the materials to McCloy and strongly recommended that the War Department give serious consideration to precision air raids. The arguments he advanced had long been advocated by different Jewish organizations: the Germans could not reconstruct elaborate murder installations at Birkenau for some time; the Krupp, Siemens, and Buna factories, as well as the SS living quarters, would also be destroyed; the morale of the Auschwitz-Birkenau underground (discussed in the protocols) would be visibly strengthened; and possibilities existed that some of the prisoners could escape. A precedent existed: Pehle enclosed a recent *New York Times* clipping about a British air attack that had freed almost 100 members of the French resistance in an Amiens prison, killing the guards in the process. Simultaneously, the director cabled Mann in London to obtain precise information and maps from Polish and Jewish sources for just such air strikes.[63]

The War Department's Operations Division was unmoved. McCloy replied to Pehle on November 18: air power would be diverted from industrial targets vital for Germany's weakening war potential. Heavy bombers could alone strike the area, but these would have to fly an approximate 2,000-mile round trip unescorted over enemy territory. "The positive solution to this problem is the earliest possible victory over Germany," McCloy emphasized. He returned the report on Auschwitz for Pehle's records.[64]

Facing this decision, the board director made the complete Auschwitz protocols public "in the firm conviction that they should be read and understood by all Americans." Pehle provided a week's delay on the release date in order to allow reporters to prepare their stories, when suddenly the director of the Office of War Information phoned him and asked that the news bulletin be recalled. The public would regard the report in the same vein as the atrocity stories circulated during World War I, Elmer Davis argued, and would consequently be inclined to question the government's credibility on other information released concerning the war effort. Pehle disagreed with this reasoning but complied with a request that he attend a meeting of Davis's staff. To a man, they stressed that the feature should be killed. Although he respected Davis as an intelligent journalist and a recognized liberal, Pehle stood his ground lest skeptical reporters be led to think that the accounts were untrue. His associates backed this position, and the full eyewitness accounts of Auschwitz-Birkenau saw publication soon thereafter.[65]

The gruesome facts received broad and sympathetic coverage, but this *dénouement,* far too late for its authors' original intention, actually came after Hitler's second in command had decided to end the mass-murder process. As early as the evening of September 30, soon after Himmler heard a report about Mayer's wire to Kastner and Grueson, Clages had informed Biss that the *Reichsführer* SS would issue an oral order to halt the "actions" in the death camps. The following month this was done, although two more convoys were gassed on arrival in Auschwitz. Anglo-American warnings on October 10–11 that "those guilty of murderous acts would be brought to justice"; Becher's persuasions regarding the Mayer-Kastner talks and a *demarche* to Himmler by the Sternbuch group; Himmler's continued attempts to seek a separate peace with the West, particularly as the Soviets advanced on the eastern front; the need for an alibi after the war—all these factors played a part in this decision. Rudolf Hoess, who had taken command of Auschwitz in May specifically to oversee the killing of Hungarian Jewry, received Himmler's order a half-year later to stop the gassings. The murderous equipment of crematoria I and II was dismantled and sent to Gross Rosen and Mauthausen, and buildings were demolished. The first transport of evacuees went off to Bergen-Belsen, Sachsenhausen, and other concentration camps, with the personal effects of the victims sent from the Auschwitz warehouses (so richly stocked they were nicknamed "Canada") to Germany.[66]

Himmler finally got his long-sought wish when Becher met on November 5, 1944, with an American who appeared to possess political authority: Roswell McClelland. At the end of October the American WRB attaché had obtained entry visas into Switzerland for Becher, Billitz, Kastner, and German purchasing agent Kettlitz. The latter had no idea what he wanted to buy, Mayer soon realized, although Becher declared unequivocally for the first time that Himmler himself was directing the German overtures. Fully aware of the urgency of the situation, Mayer produced McClelland in a private meeting with Becher at a Zurich hotel. Mayer dominated a good portion of the hour-long talk, beginning with his translation from a Dorothy Thompson article that favored Allied encouragement of all democratic tendencies in Germany after the Third Reich's defeat. Following his prior arrangement with Mayer, McClelland repeated this theme. The tactful JDC representative then appealed to the cavalry officer as a gentleman, not of the "killing group," who could use an alibi. He presented a memorandum urging that the murder of all civilians be "entirely halted," that permission be given the ICRC to intervene in the camps, and that orphaned children be transferred to Switzerland, a condition to which the Swiss government had given assent. To show that the negotiation was serious, Mayer then produced an October 29 cable from Secretary Hull indicating that the JDC had "authorized" a credit of 20 million Swiss francs for Mayer's disposal, subject to U.S. government approval.[67]

McClelland subsequently reported to Washington Mayer's apparent success. Becher would submit a number of stipulations to Himmler, "Deviller" in the JDC representative's notes, on or about November 10. These included a halt to the killing of all civilian internees, particularly over 100,000 Jewish aged, invalids, and children still in Budapest, and the release of all individual Jews specified through the JDC, such as Fleischmann, Weissmandel and others in Bratislava. All Jews holding documents promising exit to neutral and Allied countries, including some 8,000 at Bergen-Belsen, should be allowed to leave, and information was to be supplied about the welfare and whereabouts of any other groups of Jews requested henceforth.[68]

The expected transfer of funds did not arrive quickly, as Mayer and Becher had both hoped, but a ruse kept the delicate talks going. While putting off Kettlitz with the demand for a detailed list of goods to be purchased, Mayer frantically urged the JDC to respond to the pressure of what he privately termed "Chicago! Al Capone" and forward the money. Hearing more favorable promises from the Sternbuch group, Kettlitz cabled this fact to Budapest on November 18, along with his conclusion that the Mayer funds would not be forthcoming. Becher, who at their previous meeting told Kastner of the intrigues against his position with Himmler and even against the *Reichsführer* himself, was about to report to Berlin on the progress of the negotiations. Faced with disaster, Biss and Kastner (perhaps with Becher's knowledge) got Billitz to telephone an optimistic evaluation to Himmler's headquarters, which reached Becher after his arrival there. His status reinforced, the cavalry officer pressed his chief to renew in writing his instructions to cease the annihilation at Auschwitz and to halt Eichmann's forced marches if he wished the negotiations to continue. The intercession of *Wehrmacht* General Juttner and Commandant Hoess, who had even reacted in indignant fashion when witness to the brutal expulsions, strengthened Becher's case. In Berlin Himmler called a disobedient Eichmann on the carpet in Becher's presence, and ordered him to stop them immediately. In return, Eichmann received a Cross of War Merits, First Class With Swords.[69]

The State Department, in fact, forbade the use of any funds for ransom. Under the erroneous impression that "transportation difficulties" and a "disorganized" Szálasi regime precluded a "concerted anti-Jewish pogrom" in Budapest, McClelland advised the board of November 16 *not* to transfer the funds Mayer had requested. The talks should be discontinued, "with all due credit to SM for a magnificent and difficult piece of work," he cabled. Acting Secretary Stettinius echoed his agreement about the money in a cable a few days later, while expressing nonetheless the WRB's confidence "that you will take into consideration the fact that because of recent military developments each day that can be gained is of increasing importance." As an additional blow, Mayer heard at the month's end that the JDC's Schwartz, while coming to Switzerland, could not participate in the discussions.[70]

Aided by Kastner, Mayer still kept up the bluff. Eichmann was delighted at Kettlitz's negative cables to Becher, who also began to realize that "an old Jew was leading him by the nose." He sent an assistant, *Haupsturmführer* SS Krell, to accompany Kastner and Billitz to the Swiss frontier. Hearing privately from a desperate Mayer the actual truth on December 1, Kastner boldly convinced Krell and Kettlitz to cable Becher without delay that an initial 5 million Swiss francs were in fact available, and that Eichmann's holding up the other part of the test convoy at Bergen-Belsen hampered further progress. Mayer, now recovering more self-assurance, proposed to Krell that the funds be used by the ICRC to feed and clothe all Jews under Nazi rule. Thinking that the money was forthcoming, Becher obtained Himmler's approval to release the remaining 1,368 Jews from Kastner's original convoy. They reached Switzerland in the early hours of December 7.[71]

Not taken in by the Mayer-Kastner negotiations, Eichmann did everything in his power to finish off the remnant of Budapest Jewry. On December 3 his Bureau of Jewish Affairs instigated the Hungarian police to attack the Columbus Street camp. The gendarmerie overcame some armed resistance and dispatched two trains carrying all men and women capable of work to Bergen-Belsen. The camp's children, the sick, and the aged he moved, following Biss's intervention, into the central ghetto. But two days after the regular long-range Soviet bombardment of Budapest began, Eichmann sealed off the ghetto as a preparatory measure to final deportation. Arrow Cross and Gestapo patrols raided protected houses, threw people into prison, and tortured them for ransom or sent them to work on fortifications. The Arrow Cross ultimately shot 10,000-15,000 Jews, who were left in the streets or dumped into the icy waters of the Danube.[72]

Wallenberg proved indefatigable in restoring some humanity to this world of bloody chaos. He acquired stores of vitally needed supplies for two hospitals and soup kitchens. Attempts were made on Wallenberg's life after Eichmann personally threatened the "Jewish dog" who, in a dinner conversation, advised the Nazi official to give up with the war lost. The young attaché persevered, resorting to a bicycle after his official car was "stolen." He removed his protected people from jails and once ordered an armed Hungarian patrol out of the Swedish quarter, fully meriting John Pehle's concurrent praise for the "splendid cooperation, vigor and ingenuity" he brought to their common humanitarian endeavor. Informed that the Hungarian government intended to drop leaflets by airplane in which "workers, Jews and suppressed" were encouraged to rise and fight the enemy, Wallenberg frustrated the provocation scheme by appealing directly to Szálasi himself. Aryan-looking Jews, members of Zionist pioneer movements, were also dressed in SS uniforms and sent to protect "safe" houses.[73]

These Zionist youth, led by Rafi Friedl (later Benshalom) of HaShomer HaTsa'ir, never put faith in negotiating with the enemy. Survivors from Poland and Slovakia had reached Budapest before the coup of October 15 thanks to such as HaNoar HaTsiyoni's Siegfried Roth, while a few thousand were smuggled out of Rumania and back into Slovakia in a movement ("tiyul" and "retiyul") organized by Moshe "Pil" Alpan and Menachem Klein. With the aid of an SS officer, the youngsters freed several dozen prisoners from the Kistarcsa camp just prior to their deportation. Operating from the "glass house" headquarters of the Swiss Department of Emigration, they took charge of the IRC children's shelters. Aided by the talents of artist Shraga Weil, the indomitable band also forged thousands of papers and rubber stamps (including that of Eichmann himself). Wallenberg and Lutz, aided much that winter by his wife, did not repudiate "their" signatures when confronted with some of these forgeries.[74] On one occasion, a plan devised by Palestinian Hagana emissaries resorted to Jews in labor service uniform and a few bribed Hungarian gendarmes in order to free leading resistance fighters like Zvi and Nashka Goldfarb from a Buda jail. "So near the fire," recalled one of the participants, "we became immune to fear."[75]

In besieged Budapest, Becher still had not received final confirmation about the promised 20 million Swiss francs. When Krell returned to inform him of the mission's poor results, the Nazi colonel cabled Geneva that the full amount should be paid forthwith. At that point, hearing from Joseph Schwartz that New York headquarters did not even have sufficent funds to buy the requested war materials, Mayer suggested that the francs be transferred for Red Cross supplies to Jews still alive in occupied Europe. The JDC's European director agreed, and McClelland now recommended the undertaking in a cable of December 13 to Washington. The attaché's superiors expressed their doubts six days later. Could such material be obtained in shortage-ridden Switzerland and reach the oppressed? Even if so, the major Allies would have to consent to the novel scheme.[76]

Such delay notwithstanding, a desperate plan to destroy the entire Pest ghetto was actually averted at the twelfth hour. On learning from a reliable Arrow Cross publisher via the former *Judenrat* chairman that "ultras" in Szálasi's cabinet wished to massacre every Jewish witness before the Russian entry into the capital, Biss promised Becher the 15 million Swiss francs outstanding and, as an advance, gave an order for 30 trucks to a Slovak dealer named Alois Steger. He and the Va'ada's Otto Komoly then obtained Kastner's cabled approval, and Becher got Himmler's intervention to have the senior officer in the German Budapest garrison warn the ultras' leader not to go through with the plan "for reasons relating to German's economic interest." On his own, Wallenberg warned the commander of all German forces in the city that he would be held personally responsible. Several Hungarian police officials, bribed by the promise of the morally driven Swede to help them diplomatically after the war, repeated the threat. The intended pogrom was called off.[77]

At 3 P.M. on Christmas eve, 1944, as the Red Army encircled Budapest, Eichmann and his commando staff took a hurried leave forever. Making an effort to snatch the last of his prey, he had set up a chain of Jews to carry shells from an ammunition depot to the besieged German positions some eight kilometers away. He also prevailed on Interior Minister Vajna to remove all Jewish children into the ghetto for an obvious grim end, and just before leaving tried unsuccessfully to abduct the members of the Va'ada. Hansi Brand, wife of Joel Brand who on her own printed thousands of forged certificates to save Jews in Budapest, escaped the dragnet by feigning another identity in response to a Gestapo telephone call. The Arrow Cross would soon exact its revenge, executing Komoly and associate Szulem Offenbach, Arthur Weisz, and Simcha Hunwald of HaShomer HaTsa'ir.[78]

The fighting raged on for several weeks. Even before it subsided, the Jewish community sought to honor their noblest friend. Attempting to secure food for his protected houses, Raoul Wallenberg denied colleague Per Anger's insistent request to join him in moving to the Swedish embassy on the safer Buda side. On January 10, 1945, he moved to an IRC building nearer to the front in an effort to obtain Soviet protection for the Jewish survivors. A Russian patrol entered the premises three days later and took Wallenberg to their headquarters. He reappeared briefly on the 17th at his former office, 6 Tatra Street, and told associates that he was being taken to meet the USSR commander, Marshal Malinovsky, at Debrecen. "Whether as a guest or as a prisoner, I do not know," were the Swede's parting words. The next day the Russians took over Pest, including its ghetto of 100,000 Jews. Units of the 1st Perekop Division, commanded by Jewish Colonel Gregory Davidovich Yelizavetsky, liberated Auschwitz on January 26. Buda west of the Danube fell on February 13, with all of the country firmly in the victors' grasp two months later.[79] The tragedy of Hungarian Jewry had come to its close.

CONCLUSION

According to World Jewish Congress calculations, 596,260 Hungarian Jews were deported during the German occupation, with 21,747 others killed. Of the total, 116,500 lived to witness liberation by the Allied armies. Taking into account the 139,000 Jews left in the entire country (124,000 in Budapest itself), the number of survivors reached 225,000. The Jewish community, as a consequence, lost 68.4 percent of its members to the Nazis' Final Solution.[80]

The failure to check this systematic slaughter, even in the last year of World War II, is the paradigm *par excellence* of Jewry's personal experience during the epoch since known as the Holocaust. Isolated politically within and without, susceptible to native antisemitism, and stunned by Nazi speed and deception, Hungary's Jews denied clear evidence of the Third Reich's design. In the bitterest of ironies, Himmler actually believed that the Jewish people could advance a separate peace with the Anglo-American Alliance or, in Horthy's estimate, have Budapest bombed to stop the deportations. Infected by such thought, Joel Brand's assumption of the Jewish Agency's dominating influence was rudely shattered when he reached the West. His subsequent criticisms of its leadership, just like those leveled by Kastner and Biss against Mayer and

Brand, Sternbuch's attacks on Mayer and Kastner, Weissmandel's bitter recriminations against free world Jewry in general, and the Grunwald-Kastner trial in Israel leading to Kastner's murder in 1957, reflected a failure to grasp the fundamental powerlessness of a people abandoned to its fate. Another illusion that served to mask the horrible reality was Shertok's faith that Brand's return to Budapest would halt the expulsions. Witness, too, Gruenbaum's asking Istanbul in June, 1944, if "150,000" had indeed been moved eastward, and if food packages could be dispatched there. After the war, he had but one question for Kastner: why did resistance not take place?[81]

The leaders of the West, who alone could have checked the demonic reality that was Auschwitz-Birkenau and the tragedy of Hungarian Jewry—the Holocaust in microcosm—misjudged its dimensions and denied that the Jews were an entity meriting distinct consideration. Antisemitism played some role here, such as the observation of Whitehall's Southern Department director that "a disproportionate amount of the time of this office is wasted in dealing with these wailing Jews," or Eden's notation "Must I?" regarding the need to receive Weizmann and Shertok for an interview about the transports to Auschwitz. In addition, officials in London and Washington regularly expressed doubt about the extent of the killings, British authorities continuing to be taken in as late as October, 1944, by the Nazi deception regarding "Waldsee."[82] More significant was the masking of Jewry's singular agony: the Foreign Office's argument that awarding protective status to all endangered Jews would overlook very extensive Third Reich brutality "above all in Poland, against non-Jews"; the reference by Pope Pius XII, who never excommunicated Catholic murderers in Germany and Hungary, to "those persecuted because of their nationality or race"; Spaatz's deputy commander commenting about "unfortunate Poles herded in camps"; the Eisenhower warning concerning individuals then suffering because of "religious faith." Hitler's "mass extermination of the Jews was only one of a number of military measures" employed by the Nazis to execute their operations in a "most economic manner," averred John McCloy in December, 1944, when opposing the projected Allied prosecution of German prewar atrocities as if these were traditional war crimes.[83]

The abdication of moral responsibility to defenseless human beings reflected itself in other ways as well. Numerous delays occurred in responding to information about Nazi intentions, the Brand mission, and the Horthy offer. British anxieties never dissipated about "flooding" Palestine with "unmanageable numbers of Jews" and about the paramount need to secure Middle Eastern oil and strategic communications. The Americans kept the door to negotiations further open, but did not alter their immigration quotas either, vetoed ransom, and finally allowed

Mayer the requested funds in January, 1945, on condition that McClelland co-sign for any decision as to their use.[84] Both governments piously declared at the same time that any specific reprisals would provide the Germans with a "fine alibi" and/or lead to "more vindictive" (undefined) action. Rather than carefully deliberate over effective rescue, the consensus had been reached early on that a speedy Axis defeat would most effectively bring relief to the victims. This perspective even influenced a sympathetic Pehle to wait four months before pressing for the bombing of Auschwitz-Birkenau.

The bombing issue most poignantly mirrors Allied callousness toward rescue during the Holocaust. A message reaching Geneva in early September, 1943, from the Bratislava Jewish underground reported that Auschwitz was one of four known "annihilation camps"; a half-year later Kubowitzki had to ask his WJC colleague in Lisbon whether a report received from Poland to that effect was "absolutely reliable." There "has been a shuttle between Westerbork [in Holland] and Auschwitz for months," the usually *au courant* Kubowitzki pointed out, and it "seemed nearly impossible that Westerbork inmates should not have been informed of this matter."[85] Had the Allies permitted open, swift lines of communication, the vital (per the Latin root for pertinence to life) information could have been utilized to maximum effect without such loss of time. Again, more than a month passed before Weissmandel's flood of requests to bomb Auschwitz-Birkenau and its approaching railway lines finally broke through the dam of a silent Western bureaucracy. Even then civil servants stymied the strong approval of Churchill and Eden, following receipt of the Auschwitz protocols, and held back topographical data from the British Air Ministry. Only once did the U.S. War Department correspond with the competent European forces over the bombing proposal; Spaatz's staff did not accord it much careful consideration. The "many sided and far-reaching moral effect," which Shertok considered to be the bombing's main purpose, never received examination in either circle.[86]

Had the wish to destroy the gas chambers existed, the early data on file could have contributed decisively to their total demolition. Already on May 8, 1944, the commander of the Allied air forces in Italy indicated that the U.S. 15th Air Force based on Foggia had the capacity to attack simultaneously the Blechhammer oil-refining complex 47 miles from Auschwitz and the war industries at Auschwitz and Odertal. The first mission on June 2 of "Operation Frantic," which allowed American bombers to extend their range by flying between Britain or Italy and Poltava in the Soviet Union, considerably impaired the Hungarian marshalling yards at Debrecen—on a deportation route to Auschwitz. A second shuttle, flying back to Italy from Russia on June 26 to strike the synthetic oil plant at Drohobycz, crossed directly over one of the five deportation lines—and trains—to Auschwitz and came within 30 miles of two others. That same day an American reconnaisance mission, seeking information on the I. G. Farben complex (Buna, or Auschwitz III) in Monowitz, flew over and by chance photographed Birkenau (Auschwitz II) nearby.[87] On June 29 McCloy received McClelland's cable listing the five rail lines to the camp and transmitting the request to bomb it. Yet London and Washington did not correlate the relevant information, even though both obtained a summary of the Auschwitz report, including an accurate diagram of the centers, during the first week of July.

Industrial plants near Auschwitz and even the camp itself came under constant Allied air attack between July and November, 1944. Bombers of the 15th Air Force flew across the three other deportation railroad tracks on July 7. Between that date and November 20, Blechhammer and other targets close to Auschwitz were struck on ten occasions by hundreds of planes carrying tons of bombs. Heavy bombers raided the oil refineries there and at Trzebinia, only 13 miles northeast of Auschwitz, on August 7. Two days after Joseph Linton brought the Foreign Office a map detailing Auschwitz on August 18, 127 Flying Fortresses, escorted by 100 Mustang fighters, dropped 1,336 500-pound high-explosive bombs over I. G. Farben factories less than five miles east of the gas chambers. American bombers, again taking pictures of the Monowitz industrial area near Auschwitz on August 25, also photographed Birkenau. A second raid against Monowitz took place on September 13, the same day Gruenbaum cabled that Auschwitz-Birkenau and railway lines approaching it should be destroyed. A few 500-pound high-explosive bombs, "captured" on camera, actually landed in Auschwitz II by accident and killed a number of SS guards, prisoners, and civilian workers. Two more raids against the I. G. Farben plant on December 18 and 26 brought the sorties to an end.[88]

This extensive campaign refutes McCloy's assertion that a strike against Auschwitz-Birkenau would have necessitated the "diverting of airpower" from "decisive operations elsewhere," yet the Allies never bombed the facilities or even designated them a target. The four gassing crematoria, standing in two pairs and topped by four tall chimneys, could have easily been pinpointed from the air by referring to the Auschwitz protocols, the American aerial photographs, and maps then on file with the Polish government-in-exile in London. Notwithstanding the "serious technical difficulties" raised by the Air Ministry and the War Department's judgment that the proposed raids would have been of "doubtful efficacy," flak resistance and 19 German fighters were ineffective against the very successful strike on Auschwitz during the morning of August 20. The less accurate September 13 raid, drawing no German planes but receiving intense ground fire that downed 3 of 96 Liberators, did considerable damage to the I. G. Farben factories. The final raid of 1944 on December 26 struck the SS hospital in Birkenau, no more than 1,500 meters from the death vaults themselves.[89]

While major deportations from Hungary ended in July, the SS overseers of Auschwitz-Birkenau continued to fulfill their task with grisly precision. The Jews of Rhodes, the final mass transport from Paris, passengers on the last deportation from Holland (carrying Anne Frank, among others), more than 60,000 survivors of the Lodz ghetto, over 20,000 (particularly children) from the Theresienstadt ghetto, the remainder of the Slovakian community, and thousands of others were deported and gassed there. Weissmandel reported (via Sternbuch) these deportations during August, but his error in attributing them to the fate of Hungarian Jewry, which Kastner refuted, led McClelland to dismiss the exhortations as the "customary 'Notgeschrei' of the Holy Men." The scale of this slaughter was immense, 24,000 bodies burned in the crematoria and open pits nearby during one 24-hour period in August. Heavy bombers flying at their normal altitude of 20,000–26,000 feet could not have missed this pitch-black sickly smoke in the Polish air. And even if precise bombing had been tried and failed, one saturation bombing, as well as a few Mitchell bombers flying at lower heights or some Lightning dive-bombers refueling at the island of Vis, could have accomplished the destruction.[90]

Had the order to do so been given soon after Sternbuch first relayed Weissmandel's cables to the Anglo-American military attachés in Berne, hundreds of thousands of innocent lives would have been saved. (The Allied command apparently suffered no qualms when its planes were raining death concurrently upon thousands of guiltless slave laborers in German plants, although the British War Cabinet did express concern to Roosevelt over the loss of French lives inflicted by the bombing that preceded the Normandy invasion.) Birkenau internees would have died, but the mass killing, as many inmates realized at the time, would have been stopped.[91]

The West accorded a far higher priority to the Warsaw uprising during August and September, 1944. As Soviet forces crossed the Vistula and neared Warsaw, the Polish Home Army under General Bor-Komorowski decided to rise against the Nazis. When Russian air activity suddenly ceased, the British responded to the pleas of the Polish government-in-exile by flying in arms and supplies on 22 missions from southern Italy between August 8 and September 22. Of 181 bombers sent during the hazardous night flights, again passing within a few miles of Auschwitz, 31 did not return; the effort "achieved practically nothing." Churchill cabled Stalin on August 5 and 12 to send machineguns and ammunition, and on the 20th Roosevelt joined in a request of the Russian leader for arms or permission to let Allied planes refuel behind the Soviet lines. Five days later Churchill wished this last point repeated, but, given Stalin's obdurate refusal to help, Roosevelt "did not consider it would prove advantageous to the long-range general war prospect" to join in the desperate appeal. The British War Cabinet wired Moscow in a final effort on September 4 for "whatever help may be in their power," particularly landing facilities for American aircraft. One hundred seven Flying Fortresses of the Air Force Eighth Bomber Group, operating the last of the "Frantic" missions to Poltava, did drop 1,294 containers of arms and supplies over the Polish capital on September 18. The president, the War Department, and the U.S. Air Force all realized by then that "the Partisan fight was a losing one," and that much valuable airpower would be lost to the primary oil campaign against Germany. Still, what Churchill later called "the martyrdom of Warsaw," a non-military objective, did engender a humanitarian response.[92]

The Soviets refused to consider the Jewish problem at all. Immediately after the Third Reich take-over of Hungary, the WJC's Alexander Easterman in London had pressed for their intervention. They did not, however, judge it "expedient or permissible" to carry on any talk along the lines of Brand's mission, while the State Department's request for a warning to the Germans against persecuting people for their "religious faith" went unanswered. Suspicious of Wallenberg's funding by the American government, his contacts with Hungarian police and the Nazis, and his plan for the rebuilding of Hungary after the war, could Moscow believe that the young man from an eminent capitalist family had come to Budapest expressly to save Jewish lives?[93]

In Soviet custody, Wallenberg vanished without a trace. On January 16, 1945, the Swedish government received an official statement that "measures have been taken by the Soviet military authorities to protect Mr. Raoul Wallenberg and his belongings." Deputy Foreign Minister Andrei Vyshinsky, in reply to Swedish inquiries, declared on August 18, 1947, that Wallenberg "was not known in the Soviet Union" and was assumed to have died during the fighting in Budapest. After several war prisoners from Axis countries, freed by the Soviet Union, reported that Wallenberg was in a forced labor camp, the circumspect Swedish Foreign Ministry again sent a formal inquiry. Deputy Foreign Minister Andrei Gromyko announced on February 6, 1958, that Wallenberg had died in Moscow's Lubyanka prison on July 16, 1947, of a heart attack. Still, some 15 reports came in subsequently that he was alive, the last in 1978 from Jan Kaplan, a Russian Jew who claimed that he met a Swede in the hospital of the Butyrka jail with 30 years' prisoner experience. After conveying this information during a telephone conversation from

Moscow with his daughter in Tel Aviv, Kaplan was rearrested by the Soviet police and has since disappeared. The next year, following the death of Wallenberg's mother and stepfather, a tree was planted in his name in Jerusalem on the Avenue of the Righteous of the Nations at Israel's Holocaust memorial, Yad Vashem.[94]

A few "Righteous of the Nations" did respond to the summons of history. Against the Germans' stalking death and in the face of the complicity—by their silence—of the Allies, such individuals as Wallenberg, Lutz, Rotta, Schirmer, Kopecky, and McClelland expressed in their actions the values for which the West waged war. In the deeply engrained pseudo-religion of the Third Reich, Jews were transformed into ashes or numbers; if the latter, these goods could be traded for trucks and other merchandise, as in the offer via Brand and Becher's expression to Himmler that 318 "pieces rolled across" the Swiss border. Washington and London did not share this dehumanized attitude, but they considered German oil supplies and Middle East petroleum a greater priority than saving human flesh and blood by bombing the instruments of mass murder and engaging in fundamental rescue activity. A few non-Jews, with a profound feeling for their fellow man, rejected such a perspective. In a world gone mad, they proved to be an oasis of sanity and decency.

Dismissed in Allied circles because they lacked international consequence, the Jews of Hungary and other European countries were the quintessential figures of tragedy. The West "kept faith" only with its political allies, including French resistance fighters and the partisans of the Warsaw uprising. Chaim Weizmann understood this full well when he appealed on June 19, 1944, to South African premier Jan Smuts and to Winston Churchill for the establishment of a Jewish commonwealth in undivided Palestine before the war had ended: "The parlous position of the Jews is due to the fact that they have no country which they can call their own.[95] Indeed, given the Nazis' zeal and the Jewish people's lacking the essential ingredient of state sovereignty, it is a wonder that Weissmandel, Fleischmann, Kastner, Komoly, Biss, Krausz, the Zionist youth of Budapest, Mayer, Sternbuch, and Pozner—tenacious figures who stayed at their posts and seized the hour—saved the many that they did. Adolf Eichmann, after all, had done everything humanly possible to claim the entire Chosen People of the Bible for his own.

Most remarkably, a group of Jews in Auschwitz-Birkenau, as forlorn as their people across occupied Europe, staged the camp's only revolt on October 7, 1944. While the Poles and other groups in the underground Camp Military Council made an uprising contingent on outside support and on clear evidence that the SS intended to gas the "Aryan" prisoners, the Jews and the Russians went ahead with their own practical preparations. Explosives, smuggled by Jews from one of the Krupp slave-labor plants, were turned by Soviet prisoners into grenades and bombs. The Jewish *Sonderkommando* of Birkenau, aware that their ranks were gassed every two to three months, and finally broken at the fate of Hungarian Jewry, continually pressed the council to take action. One scheduled operation miscarried, although David Szmulewski, one of the Birkenau underground who had directed Rosenberg's activities prior to his April escape, managed to secure three photographs of the Hungarian mass murder "action." (The pictures, which reached Crakow on September 4, had been taken through the endeavor of several Jewish groups in a last attempt to convince the West to bomb Germany's largest death factory.) At the end of September, after a quarter of the *Sonderkommando* 800-man squad had been gassed, the Polish resistance leaders discovered that outside help could not be expected. While deciding to give up the plan of revolt, the council, commanded by future Polish Premier Jozef Cyrankiewicz, continued to tell the Jews to wait for a general attack. Hearing through underground sources of their imminent death, the *Sonderkommando* of crematoria III and IV acted on their own. Crematorium III was blown up with oil barrels, grenades, and bombs; the uprising then spread to crematorium I.[96]

The *Sonderkommando* revolt ended quickly. Three SS men were killed (with 12 injured), and about 250 Jews died in the fighting. Twenty-seven escaped into German Silesia and survived the war in a local concentration camp. The majority of those captured who had fled the camp were shot the same day. The *Sonderkommando* of crematorium II, who had not participated, were killed after the final gassing in Birkenau's chambers on October 28. For weeks the Gestapo tortured four Jewish girls involved in getting the explosives, but even those tactics obtained no information. The last message to her comrades from Roza Robota, who had passed the powder to the *Sonderkommando,* concluded with "Chazak V'Ematz"—be strong and brave. The two who somehow survived their oppressors' brutality were hanged, one dying with the cry "Revenge!" on her lips, before the assembled women prisoners in Auschwitz I on January 6, 1945.[97]

Ultimately, the *Sonderkommando* provided a post-Holocaust world with the noblest prescription for its survival. Auschwitz, mankind's subsequent synonym for absolute evil, occurred because "it was far away, in the back of beyond." Not merely 50 miles west of Crakow on the River Sola in Poland, as Rudolf Hoess wrote in the opening line of his autobiographical memoir,[98] but also in the minds of those who alone could have wiped out that scourge from the face of the globe. Yet most of the *Sonderkommando* refused to yield to Western civilization in abandoning their sense of moral dignity. In choosing death on their own terms, they avenged the murder of fellow Jews and heroically asserted the values of life's highest purpose. Before embarking on this final end, some even buried fragmentary testimonies of "the tragic universe in which we lived" among the very ashes of Birkenau's dead. The diaries, discovered in that 750 by 1,800 meter area after the war, of Leib Langfus, Zalman Gradowski, and Zalman Lewenthal illuminate most powerfully the reasons why Jews failed to fall victim entirely to the Nazi plan for a total brutalization of personality prior to murder: the Warsaw ghetto survivors who attacked a group of SS guards in the undressing rooms; the old Polish rabbi who danced to the gas chambers in his eagerness to die for *Kiddush HaShem* (santification of the Divine Name); the two Hungarians from the provinces who produced a bottle of brandy before one of the *Sonderkommando,* insisted that he live to revenge their blood, and therefore join them in drinking "l'chayim!" (to life); some 4,000 of the Czech family camp who sang their country's national anthem and the Zionist one of hope, "Hatikva," as they waited in crematoria I and II. These and others inspired the *Sonderkommando* to resist the Germans by telling "future generations" of what had taken place on the earth's most accursed spot, and, forsaken within and without, then taking up arms in a revolt that defied all reason.[99]

The last deeds of such chroniclers bear particular witness that the deadliest nihilism ever to envelop mankind's landscape did have a counterforce. As they realized, some gesture must be forthcoming against a world—killers and indifferent spectators—that could gas 2,000 people in less than half an hour at the cost of one-half cent per body, until Hoess ordered that Hungarian Jewish children be thrown alive into Birkenau's burning pits to economize on Zyklon-B insecticide.[100] In the never-ending struggle between the forces of good and evil, the blood of the murdered brother cries out still. For humanity's sake, the voice of Abel and his messengers, the few survivors, must be heard and heeded before it fades from consciousness forever.

The World Jewish Congress
Confronts the International
Red Cross

IN OCTOBER, 1944, Gerhart Riegner became obsessed with one fear: the survivors of the Third Reich's concentration camps might be liquidated in a Nazi *Götterdämmerung* during the last phase of World War II. The man who had alerted the skeptical Allied powers in August, 1942, to an unconfirmed rumor that Adolf Hitler's order for the annihilation of European Jewry would be implemented that autumn knew now that close to five million Jews were already victims of the *Führer's* master plan. In April, 1944, Riegner had cabled his superiors in New York the report that came to him from a Basel source with contacts in the German defense ministry that Berlin had made special provision for the murder of Hungary's 800,000 Jews within six months. Eleven weeks later the Berne representative of the U.S. War Refugee Board, Roswell McClelland, confirmed that at least 335,000 members of the last major Jewish community in Europe had already been deported to Poland, many to the Auschwitz-Birkenau "extermination camp," and sent to their deaths.[1] Efforts by the United States and Swedish governments, the pope, the WJC, and other sources had subsequently helped obtain Hungarian Regent Miklós Horthy's promise to stop further deportations. While the American and British governments procrastinated in rescue action, however, the Gestapo regained the upper hand. Horthy was deposed in mid-October; Adolf Eichmann, fanatical architect of destruction, and the Hungarian Arrow Cross began forced marches of 40,000 Jews to Austria and the concentration of the remainder into a ghetto within range of Russian artillery not many miles from Budapest.[2]

Complete realization of the Final Solution appeared within sight. The Anglo-American Alliance had been unresponsive to the fate of the Jews of Europe during the war years. In August it turned down requests from various Jewish organizations, made since June, to destroy Birkenau and railroad lines leading to the Auschwitz gas chambers. London and

Washington could hardly be counted on now to intervene.[3] To whom, then, could Riegner, tormented by his *idée fixe,* turn for help in this eleventh hour?

The International Red Cross would seem to have been the most logical choice. The fundamental idea expressed by the founder of the Red Cross, Henri Dunant, in his booklet *Un souvenir de Solferino* (1862), was "to care for the sick and wounded in time of war." Subsequently, the worldwide Red Cross broadened its objective to "act as a benevolent intermediary between Governments, peoples and nationalities for the purpose of itself carrying out or making it possible for others to carry out the humanitarian task of relieving sufferings arising out of war, sickness or disaster." Thanks to the IRC's headquarters in Geneva, the International Committee of the Red Cross (ICRC), thousands of missing soldiers were traced, letters and parcels sent to prisoners of war, and camps of war prisoners and interned civilians inspected during World War I. The ICRC also made regular visits for the evacuation of civilians from occupied districts and for the repatriation or internment in neutral territory of the more severely wounded in that conflict.

In the years after World War I the IRC continued its humanitarian tradition. It sent two medical missions to the Ukraine from 1921 to 1923 and visited political prisoners in Hungary, Poznan, Lithuania, and Ireland. The Geneva Convention of July, 1929, which provided guarantees for members of the armed forces, also recommended a study of methods to protect civilian internees. IRC resolutions to this effect, strongly expressed in the 1934 Tokyo Project, failed to receive international ratification before the outbreak of World War II, but nearly all the governments concerned observed them in practice. Indeed, the German foreign office was among the first to give such assurances to the ICRC, and ultimately some 160,000 civilians enjoyed the same legal status and safeguards as prisoners of war under the convention of 1929.[4] With its internationally recognized standing and contact with virtually all governments, the IRC stood in a unique position to relieve the tragic plight of European Jewry.

Knowing that the Jewish population in the war zone would "suffer most heavily from the ills that war creates," in view of Germany's well-known attitude toward Jews, the WJC's Geneva office immediately decided in September, 1939, to place its services at the disposal of the ICRC. To avoid difficulties with Germany in and outside of Switzerland, Riegner and former Polish parliament delegate Alfred Silberschein substituted a new title for the congress's letterhead: RELICO (Committee for Relief of the War Stricken Population). RELICO induced the Red Cross to intervene in many cases with the belligerent powers on behalf of Jews, provided it with staff to handle correspondence in Yiddish and

Hebrew, and worked together with the ICRC in searching for 10,000 missing persons. After long negotiations in November and December, 1939, with the ICRC and the American Red Cross, RELICO received permission to send collective consignments of food, clothing, linens, and medicines to the largest Jewish communities in Nazi-occupied Poland. The first substantial shipment of medications, 15 boxes worth about $12,000 from Swiss-Jewish doctors, reached the head of the Jewish Council in Warsaw through the German and Polish Red Crosses and the ICRC. Jewish war prisoners in Yugoslavia and Greece received RELICO packages with ICRC assistance. In addition, vital information on Nazi activities found its way to Riegner via IRC headquarters, at times from the German Red Cross.[5]

Yet such aid paled in comparison with the IRC's acceptance of the Third Reich's technical distinction between international safeguards to be accorded all "civilian internees" and the lack of such protection for Jews, who were classified as "detailed civilians." Except for visits paid during July and October, 1941, to nine internment camps for Jews in Nazi-occupied France, the ICRC did not visit similar centers anywhere else in occupied Europe, nor did it inspect the Polish ghettos and the death camps.[6] The congress's New York headquarters stopped sending funds and packages to Poland when Britain sharply condemned this activity in April, 1941, as thwarting the Allied blockade; concurrently, the Allies and the ICRC saw to it that 15,000 tons of wheat and 3,000 tons of other supplies arrived in Nazi-held Greece to stave off famine during the early winter of 1941-42.[7] The WJC's central office pleaded with the ICRC throughout 1942-43 to bring pressure enabling the doomed Jews in Polish ghettos and elsewhere to be recognized as civilian prisoners of war. Had not Germany publicly declared that its measures against Jewry were necessitated by the fear that "the Jews are a power waging war on Germany" and, for reasons of security, should therefore be "eliminated"? The appeal went unheeded.[8]

The IRC insisted that it could not challenge the Nazi onslaught against European Jewry. First, the German authorities considered their treatment of these people an internal matter. Second, the protection of even "civilian internees" had not yet received legal sanction in a separate convention. Norman Davis, chairman of the American Red Cross, added that "it would seem an exceedingly doubtful procedure to jeopardize the smooth operation" of activities protecting all prisoners of war in an attempt to broaden the treaty of 1929. Nor could the IRC threaten the Third Reich that it would not assist German prisoners of war or civilian internees if Jews continued to suffer privation and death: "Our first duty is to the individuals regardless of their nationalities, creed or race."[9] Accordingly, the IRC could not discriminate against Germany, but "detained civilians" remained a class apart, as the Nazis themselves desired.

Matters did not improve greatly in the first half of 1944. Prodded by a magazine article's attack on the IRC's "unfulfilled testament" and a subsequent speech on the floor of Congress by Congressman Emanuel Celler of New York, Secretary of State Cordell Hull noted the need for international protection of "certain categories of civilians" under German control. The possibility of such legal action in the future, however, did not stop the death camp chimneys from belching forth their acrid smoke. The ICRC only began sending individual packages on its own in early 1944 to civilian internees and Jews in Theresienstadt.[10] A suggestion from the congress's vice-president, Nahum Goldmann, to Assistant Secretary of State Breckenridge Long in September, 1943, that the American and British governments supply the IRC with $8 million for relief work seemed to be making headway. Long informed the House Foreign Affairs Committee in November that the American government had agreed in principle to underwrite $4 million for this purpose. Yet nine months elapsed before the War Refugee Board informed the House that the ICRC had been assured the necessary funds would be made available. In another instance the ICRC hesitated to give food parcels to 1,200 Jews interned in camps in Croatia, arguing that its packages, earmarked for the officially recognized "civilian internees," might be confiscated and the entire service threatened. More than three months passed before the blockade authorities finally allowed a three-month trial shipment to begin from Switzerland in August, 1944.[11]

Also behind the IRC's position lay the conviction—which the WJC failed to alter—that the central office in Geneva, composed of a few private individuals, lacked the power of authority to influence Germany. A. Leon Kubowitzki, head of the congress's department of European Jewish affairs and a Belgian refugee from Hitler, found this attitude a "disgrace." With the number of both Nazi victims of the war and Nazi prisoners so great, surely the IRC was now in a position to bring pressure to bear upon Berlin. But Marc Peter, the IRC representative in Washington, D.C., replied in a frank conversation: "We are but a Committee of goodwill. . . . What can we do with a great power which is determined to justify its policy?" An ICRC delegation in London echoed these sentiments to Goldmann and other congress representatives: everything depended on "the goodwill of the German authorities, which cannot be assumed to exist in this particular case." The WJC faced "a blank wall of stubbornness and bad will," Kubowitzki had to conclude in April, 1944. Two months later, in a memorandum on the necessity of making Red Cross food parcels available for Jews in Nazi internment and labor camps, he warned: "It should be remembered that the Jews . . . who are undernourished are being killed off when they have no strength left."[12]

The people having "the greatest moral claim" upon the urgent assistance of the IRC could find precious little salvation from the symbol of world humanitarianism, yet the WJC, with no alternative, continued to pound on a closed door. Goldmann and Kubowitzki cabled Riegner about their attempt to have the IRC issue a public statement recognizing Jews as civilian internees under the convention of 1929. When notified of the precarious Hungarian situation in early October, 1944, Kubowitzki urged Riegner to arrange the immediate dispatch of a special governmental or Red Cross mission there. Such a task force should be authorized to issue so-called protection documents and to concentrate holders of those papers in a building under Swiss aegis, following the example of the Swedish legation's special department led by Raoul Wallenberg in Budapest. A week later, the same day that Eichmann re-entered the Hungarian capital to finish accelerating the Final Solution, Kubowitzki informed his colleagues in New York of "definite reports" and instructions that "the inmates of the extermination camps would be wiped out and all the buildings razed." His only hope was "the will of our people to survive on their ingenuity, on the human solidarity of their Gentile neighbors, and on the incredible heroism of our youth in Europe."[13]

Gerhart Riegner knew better than most of the ICRC's attitude, especially through an early, cordial relationship with its vice-president, Carl Burckhardt. As a young attaché in Vienna during the 1920s, Burckhardt was fascinated by and had drawn close to that city's Jewish intellectuals, in particular Hugo von Hoffmansthal, librettist for most of Richard Strauss's operas. Yet this *Weltmensch* and connoisseur of the arts, with his aristocratic pedigree, also soothed the ruffled feelings of Nazi representatives Constantin von Neurath and Joseph Goebbels in 1933 at the request of his government, when the League of Nations diplomatic circle cut them off socially and the Swiss feared retaliatory measures. Later, when Burckhardt's *Richelieu* had attracted Hitler's interest, the Swiss diplomat again found himself chosen to keep the peace as League of Nations high commissioner for Danzig. Given the existing balance of forces between Germany and Poland, Danzig represented an untenable post unless one cooperated with the Third Reich. It was in this context that Riegner, a close student of Burckhardt's at the Institut des Hautes Etudes Internationales in Geneva, and Nahum Goldmann had first jousted with Burckhardt throughout 1937-1939 on behalf of Danzig's 6,000 Jews and the broader issue of the constitutionality of German racial laws according to the League of Nations mandate.[14]

Burckhardt's attitude toward the plight of European Jewry was ambiguous in the first years of the Holocaust. In November, 1942, he confirmed Riegner's reports about the Nazi plan of annihilation on the basis of two of his own local German sources for the U.S. minister in

Berne. This vital collaboration from such a respected source, first conveyed to Paul Guggenheim, the congress's legal expert and a colleague of Burckhardt's at the Institut, helped convince the American authorities of the reality of Hitler's *Endlösung.* "This was a very courageous act," Riegner emphasized years later, as the IRC heretofore had adopted a neutral position vis-à-vis Germany. Still, Burckhardt thought, as he told Riegner soon thereafter, that if the ICRC were to speak out against the destruction of European Jewry, its other activities would be hampered. He was therefore satisfied that a resolution protesting this systematic mass murder, a step recommended by two women on the ICRC, failed to receive the necessary majority vote. Riegner, who discovered this at the time, could take little comfort from Burckhardt's position.[15]

Riegner knew, too, that Burckhardt's superior, ICRC president Max Huber, held a strictly legalistic attitude throughout these trying years regarding the fate of Jewry. The aging Huber, formerly president of the International Court of Justice at the Hague, consistently opposed the WJC's argument that the endangered Jewish people be protected under the 1929 convention. At the end of June, 1944, the congress's Geneva representatives stressed to the ICRC that the Red Cross had a responsibility to intervene on behalf of Hungarian Jewry, especially when Horthy seemed prepared to cast off his allegiance to Germany. Guggenheim finally persuaded Huber to write a personal letter to Horthy on July 6. Twelve days later Horthy promised in reply that no more Jews would be "transported forcibly out of Hungary." Yet Huber's action represented, as Riegner later characterized it, "an appeal, not a protest." The ICRC could not undertake the latter, he informed Guggenheim and Riegner on October 2, almost two months after they had forwarded the congress's memorandum calling for a public statement from that organization.[16]

Some straws in the wind, however, indicated to Riegner that the congress's interventions were at last beginning to produce a positive change in IRC circles. In spite of the "very prudent terms" of Huber's letter of October 2, the ICRC addressed a note on the same day to the *Wilhelmstrasse* demanding the guarantees of the Tokyo Project of 1934 for all people designated *"Schutzhäftlinge"* of foreign nationality. The term, according to Burckhardt's report to Riegner on the 24th, covered not only foreign workers and political detainees, but also all foreign Jews who were deprived of their liberty of movement in Germany and German-occupied territories. This move, which the congress had urged since 1942, had not simply been repelled by the Nazis; the ICRC was informed that an unofficial reply would be shortly forthcoming.[17]

Aggressive and courageous action by ICRC representatives, however, could also achieve results, as the congress had urged all along. Two ICRC delegates, first Friedrich Born and then Robert Schirmer, had stood up to the Arrow Cross since August, and succeeded in their bluff that protection of Jews through special passes and Red Cross markings on houses was included in the IRC convention. Their daring exploits had saved thousands of Jews so far in Budapest. A full report on these activities from Schirmer to Riegner in early November further convinced the WJC official that such energetic, determined action taken by the ICRC much earlier would have impeded the Nazi annihilation of Jewry. It might possibly now.[18]

Riegner could not let the opportune moment slip by. He replied with Guggenheim on the 23rd to Huber's letter of October 2, 1944, that "total war" called for the "imperative" interpretation of conventional law and the Tokyo Project in the broadest manner. Riegner had no patience to wait for the German response to Huber's October 2 note, however. Burckhardt himself was a politician astute enough to realize that the obvious shifting winds of war in favor of the Allied cause allowed for greater IRC maneuverability. Yet, curiously, this Swiss student of history did not grasp the fact that extraordinary measures alone could deal with the unique tragedy of the Jewish people. In November, 1942, Riegner had privately pleaded with Burckhardt to either protest publicly or quietly seek German permission to send delegates to inspect the Jewish camps and ghettos, to no avail. Now, at the height of the Hungarian crisis, Burckhardt called Riegner to his office and asked if the ICRC should bow to requests to distribute many more protection passes than was its wont. "Give as many as you can," the 32-year-old refugee from Hitler's Berlin replied. "This is not Switzerland. This is a country governed by gangsters. These are not normal times. The more people you give a chance, the better." Although the ICRC vice-president eventually followed Riegner's advice, his limited perception of the situation forced the WJC representative to cast around for other sources of pressure that might shake the legalistic neutrality of IRC headquarters to its foundations.[19]

Well before the Hungarian forced marches of October, 1944, Riegner had approached various Red Cross delegates and other governmental representatives in Geneva in efforts to obtain a united front for rescue and relief. These concerns, after all, affected every country, but help was only forthcoming in individual cases. Silberschein and Riegner sent food, false papers, and money through some South American diplomats, the Poles (with limited confidence), the Yugoslavs, and the Czechs. The congress could not get the ear of the big powers, as Riegner agonizingly discovered even when the value of his confidential sources often proved superior to those of the Allies. The Swiss government, eager to maintain its neutrality, limited the entry of Jewish refugees to its borders after 1939. In addition, diplomatic relations in Geneva circles were shrouded in uncertainty, particularly regarding the status of Free French leader Charles de Gaulle and the question of recognizing Italy after her surrender to the Allies. With no official international status, as Riegner put it years later, the congress was ultimately "gornischt" (nothing) in the diplomatic arena.[20] In whom, then, could Riegner have confidence?

One individual and the nation he represented in Geneva had proven their understanding and sympathy for the Jewish cause: Dr. Jaromir Kopecky, permanent delegate of the Czechoslovakian government-in-exile to the League of Nations and delegate of the Czech Red Cross. He had helped supply the congress with parcels of farina, rice, and milk powder for Theresienstadt, forged documents, and money for the congress's activities in Europe. Kopecky gave Riegner the first detailed report on Auschwitz-Birkenau, received through the Czech underground from two Jewish escapees. Another copy with additional documents about the Hungarian situation, destined for Chaim Pozner of the Jewish Agency's Palestine emigration office in Geneva, had arrived a few days later into the hands of a Jew named Georges Mantello serving in El Salvador's consulate. While Pozner immediately passed the report on to his superiors in Istanbul, Jerusalem, and London, Mantello, on his own, handed the material to the local press. The strict Swiss censorship permitted information on the camps and the deportations to see print for the first time; the WJC representative, more interested in alerting the world and wishing to avoid difficulties with the Swiss government, advised Kopecky to cable immediately to the Czech embassy in London. The report had actually reached London from Sweden a little earlier; the BBC now broadcast Riegner's (erroneous) deduction that the Auschwitz "six-month quarantine" for the Czech Jews really meant two or three days until death. President Eduard Beneš and Foreign Minister Jan Masaryk of the Czech government-in-exile maintained personal friendships with Goldmann and WJC representatives in London Alexander Easterman and Noah Barou, while the Jewish Czech counselor Ernest Frischer, also a member of the WJC executive, regularly cabled the New York office important details of the Holocaust and of the need to bomb the railways leading to the death centers.[21]

Kopecky received the desperate Riegner one fine October morning in his office, "Listen." his friend began. "We all have the same problem and there isn't any coordination at all. Terrible things will happen in the camps in Germany to the Jews, the Czechs, all the other nationalities. Let us try at least to do something together." It was "absolutely amazing" that the initiative had to come from Riegner, the WJC representative noted in retrospect. Yet since the congress lacked international standing, only through Kopecky could a meeting be called to discuss possibilities for rescue in the last months of the war. Some Nazi officials, Riegner knew from the Hungarian Zionist Reszö Kastner, had been negotiating since mid-August with the American Jewish Joint Distribution Committee's representative in Switzerland, Saly Mayer, possibly to save themselves before the inevitable German defeat. Since the pendulum could still swing from the extremity of a Nazi bloodbath against all camp internees to saving the survivors en masse, surely a final, united effort was in order. Perhaps a group of interested parties would agree to approach their individual governments requesting that the ICRC intervene in Berlin with the highest German authorities to stop the killings, permit inspection of the camps, and quickly allow for supplies to the inmates before imminent starvation and disease?[22]

Riegner's appeals made a profound impression on Kopecky, and he at last agreed to call a meeting of various government delegates to consider the matter. A letter drafted by Riegner (and also addressed to him, since Kopecky wished the congress executive to state the case before those assembled) went out on November 14 from Kopecky's office. In cold prose Riegner masked his deepest feelings. Employing his and Guggenheim's characterization in their October 25 letter to Huber of "total war" which Germany was waging against occupied Europe and particularly Jewry, the invitation went on to state the WJC's basic position: the 1929 Geneva Convention and the 1934 Tokyo Project called for protection of *all* civilian internees and deportees from occupied countries. The "favorable evolution" of the war now constituted a "particularly propitious" time to obtain from the Third Reich application of these judicial guarantees. A "collective *demarche*" by all countries occupied in part or wholly should urge neutral governments and the ICRC to obtain such safeguards from Berlin. Riegner and Kopecky drew up a list of sympathetic invitees, based on their previous contacts, and called the meeting for November 17 at 3 P.M., at the Czech legation in Geneva.[23]

Who would make their way to the second floor of 24 Ave. de Champel? Could a consensus be obtained for immediate, joint action? Would the Nazi murder mills continue to grind away to their inexorable end before the Allied governments and the IRC moved? Riegner had no reason to assume that a last-minute warning to the German people by Allied supreme commander Dwight D. Eisenhower on November 7, not to "molest or otherwise harm or presecute" the inhabitants of the forced labor and concentration camps in their midst ("Jews" had been deliberately omitted), would have any tangible effect.[24] The sands were rapidly running out. The fate of the remnant of European Jewry still in *Festung Europa* hung in the balance.

II

The confidential session of November 17, 1944, confirmed the correctness of Riegner's and the WJC's analysis, and set the stage for united action calling for firm IRC intervention with Germany. The initiator of the conference, arriving late from a sudden, urgent trip to Berne, found ten representatives awaiting him. Aside from Jaromir Kopecky, four Red Cross delegates from Rumania, Yugoslavia, Poland, and the Netherlands, together with representatives from the governments of France, Greece, Italy, Norway, and Belgium, were seated around the table. After summarizing the contents of his letter of invitation, Kopecky opened with a warning that the Nazis might employ "hot-headed" methods as the war wound to its finish. The time seemed most opportune for the ICRC to seek protection from Germany for all civilian internees, he noted, to the agreement of the Yugoslav delegate. A joint effort on behalf of political prisoners would offer greater possibilities, however, whereas the question of civilian populations was "more delicate," interjected Norway's representative. His Rumanian counterpart insisted that greater difficulties existed for his own country than others.

Sensing that the meeting might degenerate into a discussion of individual concerns, Riegner took the floor and emphasized that all situations and categories of persons should be encompassed in a *demarche* to the neutral powers and the ICRC. The still unanswered note of October 2, which IRC headquarters had sent to the *Wilhelmstrasse* after the WJC had urged protection of all civilians and particularly Jews, would be strengthened by your governments' action, he argued. Indeed, rejoined the French delegate, but only the Allied capture of large numbers of German soldiers could achieve success in this respect. Concrete proposals are needed, Kopecky insisted, for without them, there is no point in calling in the American and British governments. Exchange of reports? Unanimously agreed. Reprisals? Imprudent, all assented. That would not conform to the principles of morality by which the Allies were fighting, added the representative from Norway. Should we not choose among reprisals, merchandise, and bribes? asked Italy's consul general. Drawing the meeting to a close, Kopecky promised to provide a report to all present. This and other information could lead to further discussion and plans.

Riegner tried to steer the group back to his original intention, but Norway's delegate countered that humanitarian and juridical arguments did not impress the Germans: threats alone would. The deportations were up to Himmler and the Gestapo, as well as the concentration camp directors, noted others. All present had agreed on the need and value of a united front.[25] Riegner and Kopecky had achieved their first breakthrough. They now had to suggest the next step.

Encouraged by this initial exchange of views, Riegner and Kopecky next decided to recommend a concrete plan of action. On December 7 a letter over Kopecky's signature made its way to all who had attended the conference. Aside from enclosing a record of those deliberations, Kopecky proposed that each delegate ask his government to consider a collective step via the ICRC, the Vatican, and/or the Swiss government and the neutral powers. German safeguards should be asked for all civilians, including Jewish deportees, analagous to the 1929 prisoner of war convention, and protection of civilian internees as recommended in the Tokyo Project. These guarantees would include communication with a neutral organization, treatment "compatible with human dignity" regarding lodging, food, and hygiene, the right to be visited by a neutral representative and to receive all necessary supplies for their welfare from a neutral source. Until then, the letter concluded, Kopecky looked forward to sharing information in such matters, which would serve as a basis for convening a second meeting of those interested.[26]

While Riegner and Kopecky could only wait for official replies to this proposal, the WJC continued its pressure on the IRC. Congress president Stephen Wise received word from the Swiss government that its legation in Budapest, working in tandem with the ICRC representative there, had expressed its willingness to grant interrupted transit to 12,000 Hungarian Jews. The congress's London office found the IRC prepared to ask the Anglo-American Alliance to extend financial grants originally designated for help in concentration camps to people now rescued and in urgent need. But Kubowitzki's co-worker, Aryeh Tartakower, who had failed to obtain IRC support for Polish Jewry during 1941-42, lacked confidence in that organization's cooperation. In addition, even if the United States and England granted the necessary funds, months might pass before concrete relief work would be accomplished.[27] To try and break the bottleneck, Kubowitzki decided to go to Europe and press for immediate action.

Kubowitzki's London talks in January, 1945, were exercises in frustration. The sympathetic War Refugee Board representative there, James Mann, could only promise to pass on WJC suggestions for the bombing of death camps, the extension by neutrals of the Hungarian protection papers scheme for Jews, the immediate delivery of food parcels via the ICRC to Jewish camps, and for an IRC public declaration recognizing Jews as civil prisoners of war with full care and visitation rights. United Nations Relief and Rehabilitation Administration (UNRRA) officials presented a picture of uncertainty regarding their mission after the war. Herbert Emerson, director of the Intergovernmental Committee on Refugees, shocked Kubowitzki with a categorical denial that the $8 million fund noted by Assistant Secretary Long in November, 1943, had ever existed! As for the safety of Jews and others endangered by Germany, Emerson believed it impractical to ask the Allied authorities to take any special measures for the safety of one element of the population during a time of military crisis. The ICRC's London representative, Kubowitzki also learned, knew nothing about Huber's correspondence with Guggenheim and Riegner; nor did he, while favoring energetic action along the lines pursued by Schirmer in Hungary, share the congress's opinion about the IRC's strength and authority. This attitude depressed Kubowitzki just when the WJC's British section received startling news of a Nazi order to liquidate the camp occupants before imminent Allied capture. Kubowitzki and an associate could only cable the ICRC, urging that one of its top executives travel immediately to Berlin and convince the Third Reich leadership to halt further killings.[28]

Kubowitzki was especially exasperated that all his attempts to call a similar conference in London of those governments represented at the November 17 Geneva meeting had failed. Aside from interest expressed by the National Committee for Rescue from Nazi Terror, a nonsectarian organization sparked by MP Eleanor Rathbone which had done much to alert England to the horrors of the Holocaust, no further encouragement could be found. The acting Czech foreign minister informed Kubowitzki that, upon receiving Kopecky's report, he had brought the matter to the Vatican's attention; no answer had yet been received. Czechoslovakia maintained no diplomatic relations with the neutral powers, and could not call a meeting in view of the delicate Polish-Russian situation. The Czech government-in-exile had immediately intervened in London and Moscow in the matter of bombing Auschwitz-Birkenau, as Kopecky and Riegner had urged the past June when forwarding eye-witness accounts of that death camp, again without success.[29]

Still, the congress's pressure began to have telling effect on IRC headquarters that same month. American Secretary of State Edward Stettinius, Jr., who had halted all ransom negotiations to save Jews in November, 1944, between Nazi representatives and Saly Mayer, now modified his position. On January 8 he requested War Refugee Board delegate McClelland to approach the Swiss government and the ICRC to declare all surviving Jews under their protection, get permission to visit the camps, and obtain figures and lists of interned persons. A second cable sped to McClelland on January 17, urging that the 300,000 food parcels given by the board to the ICRC also be sent to Jews in Nazi hands. This action would make Berlin aware of the neutral governments' interest in the Jews. Five days later the ICRC cabled the WJC, which was confidentially shown Stettinius's cables by the board in Washington, that it had asked the Nazi government to allow its delegates to visit all concentration camps, distribute supplies, and obtain lists of inmates.[30] The German response had not yet been received, but these requests were precisely what Riegner's and Kopecky's plans had called for in November (which McClelland reported on earlier to Washington). Some governments evidently had replied positively to that *demarche* and had made their influence felt in Geneva.

Yet the WJC could not rest content with this achievement. It discovered that the IRC's American representative continued to insist that sending delegates to death camps containing Jews would be "discreditable as well as dangerous to the cause itself"; to undertake such negotiations again would only irritate Berlin and jeopardize IRC work. The committee had to focus on the distribution of supplies to prisoners of war, Marc Peter argued, and blockade and war operations made even this increasingly difficult. Privately, a War Refugee Board administrator in Washington advised congress visitors to increase their pressure on the ICRC and the Intergovernmental Committee on Refugees, since both organizations "could do much more in this particular case than is actually being done at the present moment." Riegner, too, cabled that amelioration of the plight of Jews under the swastika could be secured if the Soviets would give assurance or make concessions regarding their German prisoners. Lack of sufficient means of transport, he added, was also hampering IRC relief activities on behalf of these Jews.[31] On February 2, 1945, the congress therefore again appealed to the ICRC to take extraordinary steps to protect the lives of the surviving Jews. While awaiting a reply, the WJC learned that the American Red Cross only envisioned a relief scheme for Poland of some $50,000 and was concentrating its activities on Greece and Yugoslavia, despite the desperate plight of Jewish survivors in liberated Rumania, Bulgaria, and Hungary.[32]

Under such frustrating circumstances, Kubowitzki decided to join Riegner in Geneva at the end of February to confront the newly elected president of the ICRC directly. Professor Burckhardt, who had succeeded Huber in this post a month earlier, reiterated his belief in an interview on February 20 that to accede to repeated requests by the congress for a public statement on the status of the Jewish deportees would only endanger Red Cross activities. At the same time he had been asked to see *Reichsführer* Himmler and had decided to do so. It would be a "terribly unpleasant interview"; the SS chief was a "frightful man" to whom Burckhardt had nothing to offer, for Himmler "knew that he was lost." Yet Germany needed IRC assistance without delay to avoid the most terrible chaos, argued Kubowitzki. The Reich's leadership was very divided, Burckhardt replied: while Hitler wished "to take along with him in his downfall the war prisoners, the hostages and all the civilian internees," others were "afraid of such a monstrous crime." Thanking Burckhardt for his decision, Kubowitzki explained that the congress had constantly insisted on an IRC statement because the Jewish people and public opinion in general could not understand the continued silence of the Red Cross in the face of the annihilation policy.

This was "an exceptional opportunity for the Red Cross" which should be exploited to the fullest, he emphasized.[33]

So Riegner's estimate of the situation had been correct all along. His own German sources, together with the knowledge that Himmler had recently sanctioned the transport of 1,210 Jews from Theresienstadt to Switzerland through the good offices of the Va'ad HaHatsala and its intermediary, the former Swiss president Jean-Marie Musy, had hinted at the split between Hitler and Himmler. Riegner also knew something about the successful efforts of the congress's Hilel Storch to intervene with a few German officials and, especially Himmler's physiotherapist, the Finn Felix Kersten, on behalf of the Jewish camp inmates. Burckhardt, unaware that the initiative had come from Riegner, now indicated that Allied pressure for IRC aid to Jews had influenced him greatly. The time had come, in Riegner's view, to finalize the *demarche*.[34]

To ensure that Burckhardt would proceed to Germany at once, Riegner and Kubowitzki persuaded Kopecky to call a second meeting of the November 17 group for February 26, 1945. A "grandiose plan" should take place in the very next days, Kubowitzki urged, to the agreement of all present. One or two of the earlier attendees did not come, but a most significant addition was Roswell McClelland of the WRB. McClelland, who had helped issue Riegner's bulletins regarding the Hungarian situation in mid-1944 through the Quakers, and who knew from Riegner of Huber's October 2 note to the Germans, had expressed some doubts to his board superiors regarding Kopecky's involvement in the November meeting. But events since January convinced him that SS officials were willing to cooperate with the ICRC, and he wired the board to place trucks at the Red Cross's disposal and to speed parcels from board stocks at Göteborg to the camp inmates. The chief ICRC delegate from Berlin had also indicated to McClelland only days before that such measures could save thousands of Jews being evacuated from concentration camps and regrouped in two areas between Munich and Hamburg-Lübeck.

At this meeting McClelland indicated that he would ask his government to support united appeals to the ICRC and the Swiss Confederation. After lengthy discussion all agreed to hand deliver an identical letter (drafted by Riegner) to Burckhardt between 9 and 10 A.M. the next day. This memorandum urged the president of the ICRC to make "a supreme effort" on behalf of the Jews in his talks with the Reich authorities, and to dispatch a Red Cross delegation without delay to negotiate the liberation of *all* civilian internees.[35]

The congress continued to press the *demarche* until Burckhardt left for Germany. On March 3 Kubowitzki obtained from the president of the Swiss Confederation the information that his government had decided to intercede with Berlin. If Himmler agreed to let the *Schutzhäftlinge* leave, Switzerland would allow them entry, as it had permitted two transports of Jews the past December and February. That very afternoon Burckhardt indicated to Kubowitzki that Germany had agreed to repatriate civilian internees—including Jews—of certain nationalities. The Red Cross would try to bring people back to Switzerland on empty supply trucks and on a boat from the Swedish Red Cross. "What can we give you of more value than the burden of our hopes?" asked Kubowitzki, as he took his leave and signed the ICRC's Golden Book at Burckhardt's request.[36]

Still not satisfied—had not Burckhardt's reply to the group's February 27 memorandum spoken of resistance in Germany to saving Jewish lives at the last hour?—Riegner and Kopecky convened two more meetings at the Czech legation. On March 5 they succeeded in having those present agree to impress upon the reluctant Anglo-American Alliance indirectly the need for trucks and ships for civilian relief and repatriation, as well as for prisoners of war. A week later the group agreed to challenge the American and British governments' decision to limit supplies to prisoners of war. Centralized relief and rescue action with UNRRA and the ICRC would be undertaken immediately upon Burckhardt's return.[37]

Burckhardt's visit to Germany achieved precisely what Riegner, Kopecky, and those who had joined in the united effort since November had intended. The first news of his success came to the WJC on March 15, when its British section reported (incorrectly) that the Nazis had allowed Burckhardt to fill his empty supply trucks with 1,210 Jews from Theresienstadt ghetto. Germans, now needing the camps themselves, were willing to include Jews among specific nationalities for release. The War Refugee Board heard more reliable information from McClelland a week later, and Burckhardt reported in detail at IRC headquarters on the 26th to those whose concerted action had finally led to his trip.[38]

Himmler had given full power to his second-in-command, Ernst Kaltenbrunner, to negotiate with the ICRC president on March 12-13, 1945. Ten years earlier Nazi intelligence chief Reinhard Heydrich, later author of the first plan in 1939 to ghettoize all of European Jewry, had refused Burckhardt permission to bring relief to the concentration camps. Heydrich's successor had altered that policy dramatically in 1945. Encouraged by Kaltenbrunner's agreeing to speed delivery of food parcels to prisoners of war and to have Red Cross observers live in such camps until the end of the war, Burckhardt asked for and obtained the same benefits for civilian internees. "In fact," Kaltenbrunner added, "you may even send permanent observers to the Israelite camps."[39]

Three centers of distribution would be set up at Lübeck, Ravensbrück, and Bayreuth, Burckhardt informed his rapt audience on March

26, because trucks from Switzerland could reach them within a range of 300 kilometers. Camps would be organized by nationality, with evacuation taking place for women, the aged, and children. Answering Riegner's question regarding nonrepatriables (he assumed that Jews would make up large numbers in this category), Burckhardt responded that the ICRC contemplated separate camps with full privileges for such people. As he left the meeting Burckhardt took the initiator of the entire *demarche* aside and indicated that German SS officials had assured him that the ICRC would have "very large possibilities in caring for Jewish detainees." It was "an enormous step forward," concluded Riegner in his report to WJC headquarters that day.[40]

Unknown to Riegner at the time, Burckhardt's success reflected Himmler's general wish to curry Allied favor just when the Russians and American armies converged on the Rhine. The plan of the WJC's Hilel Storch to rescue Jews and send supplies from Sweden for Jewish camp inmates in Germany had been brought by the indefatigable Kersten to Himmler for approval. After a week of stormy argument Himmler signed a document on March 12 promising to hand the camps over intact to the Allies, thereby in effect countermanding Hitler's orders. Acting on an impulse, Kersten also persuaded the SS chief to receive Storch for further negotiations. Storch's substitute, Norbert Masur, met Himmler secretly on April 21, some hours after Hitler's birthday party, and got the *Reichsführer's* promise that 1,000 Jewish women would be released from the Ravensbrück camp along with a number of French women and 50 Norwegian Jews. A few hours later, Count Folke Bernadotte, vice president of the Swedish Red Cross who had been in touch with Storch and WJC London representative Lev Zelmanovits, obtained Himmler's additional word that a Red Cross bus convoy would be allowed to take not only 1,000, but as many as it could manage. Ultimately, the total came to 4,500. Two nights later, Himmler admitted to Bernadotte that "Germany is defeated." The next day, despite his irritation at Allied publicity over atrocities at Buchenwald and Bergen-Belsen, Himmler signed a letter confirming his promise to hand over all camps and their inmates to the approaching Allied armies.[41]

Riegner still had one more battle to face with the IRC: the segregation of Polish-Jewish prisoners of war by Germany in these final days of war. A cable from the WJC's Aryeh Tartakower had informed Riegner on the morning of March 13 that reports indicated such segregation was taking place just before German evacuation of the concentration camps. Since recently liberated French and Yugoslav prisoners had given Riegner similar reports at the time, he immediately asked for and received an appointment on the same day from the ICRC's vice-president, Jacques Chenevière. Just prior to the meeting the WJC executive obtained additional confirmation from inmates of three camps recently freed by the Red Army.[42]

A last-minute catastrophe seemed in the making. Riegner presented a hastily drawn-up memorandum to Chenevière and ICRC legal advisor Beck, insisting that IRC headquarters intervene at once with the German authorities. This segregation, unlike the question of civilian internees and "detainees" which had now been successfully resolved by the WJC, clearly violated the 1929 convention. Could not the ICRC immediately cable instructions that its Berlin delegation strive for this order's nullification, with general orders to all ICRC representatives in Germany to hinder any similar moves elsewhere? Again, Riegner was consumed by his *idée* fixe. Perhaps such separation of Jewish from non-Jewish military prisoners was not a violation, suggested a doubting Beck that afternoon, but similar to the way in which Allies separated Nazi and non-Nazi prisoners? Hardly, retorted a shocked Riegner: "After the extermination of almost the totality of the Jews of Europe, separation can only be a preparatory measure to extermination in the camps!" Holding a lengthy cable just received from the WJC's New York office along the same lines, Chenevière ended the spirited encounter by promising to investigate further.[43]

As in the past, the IRC's response to this particular question indicated that it completely failed to grasp the unique fate of Jewry in the Final Solution. Four years earlier Burckhardt had assured Riegner that the IRC admitted no discrimination whatsoever between war prisoners, "notwithstanding their origin or creed." He did see to the safety of Jewish Palestinian war prisoners, including Yitschak Ben Aharon (future chief executive of the labor Histadrut organization). Now the ICRC president returned to his organization's long-held rigid interpretation of the law. In a letter on March 23 he asserted that although segregation *had* actually taken place, this did not in the opinion of the ICRC delegates in Germany affect the treatment of the Jewish prisoners of war. The ICRC, he concluded, had asked its representatives on the spot to find out the reasons for this segregation.[44]

Such action, however, was a "flagrant violation" of the 1929 convention, responded Guggenheim and Riegner on March 29. With "consternation" they noted that Burckhardt's letter accepted the Nazi position (just as the ICRC had until the previous January regarded Jews as "detained internees"). Article 4 of the convention stipulated "explicitly, completely and with no equivocation" against this discriminatory action on lines of religious and ethnic action. Especially in view of the record of annihilation by Germany of virtually all Jewish civilians during the war, this segregation of prisoners could only be interpreted in similar fashion. It qualified as the "gravest violation" of war prisoners' rights, one which the two WJC representatives were immediately prepared to discuss further at Burckhardt's wish.[45]

The president of the ICRC remained immovable. In reply a week later he argued that the Geneva convention did not apply with "sufficient juridical" strength so long as the segregated Jewish war prisoners received the same treatment as others, while a French Jewish officer had informed the ICRC in Berlin that the segregation in question only applied to living quarters. These Jews could still move freely about, and they received the same treatment as their Gentile "companions in captivity." ICRC representatives in Germany would continue to monitor the situation when visiting these camps.[46]

Highly displeased with this rejoinder, Riegner and Guggenheim prodded the ICRC further in a meeting with Burckhardt on April 11, 1945. After repeating the WJC view that this separation in itself constituted differential and illegal treatment according to international convention, an exasperated Guggenheim added that eventual mass destruction must be the logical objective of the German action before the Allies liberated the camps. This did contradict the principle of the absence of segregation among civilian prisoners (except for nationality), Burckhardt admitted, but the ICRC's Berlin delegate had just assured Geneva headquarters that the Nazi differentiation of Polish-Jewish soldiers was "steadily regressing."

What about the basic principle? Riegner shot back. Even if the Jews received similar treatment, this represented an unacceptable "moral discrimination." The ICRC president retreated slightly: other sections of the Geneva Convention strongly indicated segregation to be inadmissible. At any rate, separation was opposed to the "spirit" of the convention, and ICRC delegates had since been instructed to oppose its execution. "Radical measures" might be taken by the Germans at any moment, the WJC spokesmen emphasized. "I understand your inquietude," Burckhardt replied, in confirming Riegner's reports that Hitler would gain the upper hand over Himmler by insisting on "the total extermination" of the Jews. The legal aspects of the entire question, he concluded, should be taken up with Professor Huber and other legal consultants of the ICRC.[47]

Gaining no real satisfaction from the ICRC, Riegner had Kopecky call a final meeting of the November group to discuss this segregation of Jewish military prisoners. After a quick review of the congress's confrontation with Burckhardt over the issue, Riegner reminded those present that something disastrous could happen at the last hour. In view of Burckhardt's attitude and most recent information, a second collective action would not be necessary. At the same time, all should have their governments individually request the ICRC to maintain a guarded watch on the matter. Such separation is "absolutely inadmissible," seconded Kopecky. The meeting agreed to follow up the question on an individual basis.[48]

The end of World War II, fortunately for the captured Jewish soldiers, ended the issue. The ICRC's vacillating policy might have led to further disaster, as Hitler raged in his Berlin bunker and expelled Himmler from the Nazi party and all his state offices for compromising the *Führer*'s war to destroy the Jewish people. In effect, the Jews, as Aryeh Tartakower wrote in retrospect, "were asked to wait until the Germans would start killing the Jews."[49]

For Riegner and the WJC, the IRC could and should have done far more in bringing relief and rescue to European Jewry during the years of the Holocaust. In some instances it had proven helpful, but not in the most crucial moments of need. The IRC had failed to grasp that the plight of the Jews—*sui generis*—deserved special attention. Faced with the unparalleled plan of one nation to annihilate an entire people, IRC headquarters remained wedded to the organization's pre-1939 legalistic standards. It had accomplished much prior to the Nazi *Blitzkrieg* against Poland, but the experiences of World War I were hardly a sufficient preparation for what would occur during World War II. Energetic action on the part of such ICRC officials as Schirmer in Hungary indicated one alternative. The united *demarche* on behalf of civilian internees and Jews, which Riegner had to initiate and oversee to its successful completion, constituted another. The congress, however, commanding no international status, lacked the authority throughout this period of catastrophe to gain wide support for its position. In the end, all Riegner could do in the final moment of the war on behalf of the segregated Jewish military prisoners was to address a communication to the ICRC's legal expert, Max Huber, reserving the right to be consulted on the revision of the 1929 convention.[50] Whether or not the IRC and the world community would learn from the Holocaust remained to be seen.

CONCLUSION

Not long after the end of World War II, the IRC began to publicize what it considered to be its achievements on behalf of the Jewish population of Europe during that global conflict. Its vice-chairman devoted an article in the committee's monthly organ to the ICRC's relief work for "Israelites," an essay that subsequently appeared in pamphlet form. In reply to various attacks, another ICRC pamphlet justified its position on the basis of the same arguments given the WJC during the war years: with no existing international convention for civilians, the belligerents could make the claim that many had to be arrested for "security reasons—in itself valid ... and none could say it nay." This argument notwithstanding, the ICRC had continued to ask the Third Reich to relent, visited Theresienstadt, sent collective supplies in the summer of 1944 at "a risk," and transferred the funds of the Joint Distribution Committee and other Jewish organizations to Hungary, Rumania, and Slovakia. Burckhardt's mission in 1945 to Germany (the WJC's efforts went unnoticed) represented a "daring step" that had achieved substantial results. "To engage in controversy about the Jewish question would have interfered" with all the IRC's other tasks. Nevertheless, it had saved several thousands in Hungary from mass deportation and brought relief to thousands of Jews in Rumania. "Lastly, in one way and another, individually or in groups, several thousands more of these unhappy people were saved from the fate which awaited them."[51]

The onset of the Cold War, however, brought into question the IRC's authority to speak for the cause of international humanitarianism. In early March, 1947, the Soviet Union insisted that the League of Red Cross Societies be designated the official world humanitarian organization, and the Swedish Red Cross seemed to veer to its side. With the Russian government not even having representation in Switzerland, the IRC's executive body realized that nothing could be accomplished if Washington and Moscow clashed on the issue. To check the Soviet move, it called a special conference of various world humanitarian organizations to obtain a vote of thanks for its past work and to define its relationship to these 15 societies.[52]

Honorary president Max Huber, leading the ICRC delegation, confessed that certain provisions of the previous international conventions for "the dignity of the human personality" would have to be "adapted" to the present needs "in the light of the experiences of the last war." The agenda, however, was limited to a discussion of the religious and cultural needs of military prisoners, who alone had been covered in past conventions, and centered on technical problems. In the discussion that ensued, general agreement prevailed on eventual changes in the respective articles.[53] The IRC plan in this political struggle appeared to be heading for success, when the representative of the lone Jewish group present upset the carefully ordered applecart.

Riegner now had a unique opportunity to challenge the IRC's record during the Holocaust and its posture of self-congratulation. After obtaining an amendment that the cremation of war prisoners would not be allowed as a rule, he voiced his true feelings and those of the WJC about the IRC's failings in the World War II years. Adequate provisions should be incorporated into the conventions to prevent future segregation of war prisoners, as had occurred with Jews at the close of the last war. Only the quick advance of the Allied troops prevented German execution of these Jews, he reminded his listeners. The ICRC did not intervene, despite continued congress protests. Seeing no unanimity on this question, Riegner asked that the minutes record his calling attention to this important matter. The IRC should give it special consideration; he reserved the right for the WJC to submit "a more satisfactory formula."

Outraged that during these deliberations, meshed in international politics, the basic revision of the 1929 convention and what had happened to the most obvious victims of World War II had not been discussed, Riegner then, without warning, turned to the question of civilian internees. In a lengthy statement the individual most responsible for the united action of November, 1944–March, 1945, reviewed the entire story of the WJC's confrontation with the IRC. How could a vote of confidence be given in the light of this history, unless the Geneva convention were at least extended to the civilian population? Having "dropped a bombshell," he later recalled, the invited guest in the IRC house "wanted to disappear." Following some tense moments, those assembled decided that the issue should be discussed after they finished their deliberations on technical matters. Riegner thus received the opportunity to submit his proposals the following day.[54]

March 4, 1947, saw Riegner rise as the spokesman for the Jewry of Europe that was no more, and for all other civilian victims of World War II. He recalled for the conference that millions of civilians had been victims of arbitrary measures of internment, deportations, and mass murder because of the complete lack of any legal protection for them in the conventions. On behalf of the WJC executive board, he proposed that IRC protection be extended to *any* persecuted minority in time of peace or war. This should be mandatory for any circumstance, and such persecutees entitled to the same rights as war prisoners. Visits by the ICRC, supplies, medicines, exchange of mail, and all other assistance must be given them, and no country should be permitted to benefit by the conventions unless it pledged to observe these principles. Riegner urged speedy adoption by governments and particularly by the IRC, which, strongly criticized in recent years for not making sufficient efforts to protect the concentration camp inmates, should take the lead in this regard.

During the debate that followed, Riegner found limited support for his position. Although various Catholic and Protestant organizations expressed full sympathy with his argument, most did not commit themselves. Huber, who had previously defended the ICRC's action in a published apologia in which "Jews" were hidden under "persecutees," repeated the IRC's standard defense and left it to the Human Rights Commission of the United Nations to deal with the problem. Finally, a consensus appeared to accept a resolution offered by the World Council of Churches supporting the ICRC on the ground that only a neutral agency in a neutral country could protect military prisoners and civilian internees in wartime. Under the circumstances, Riegner could not stand publicly in opposition. He therefore asked for the floor, proposed that the vote of confidence omit "and civilian internees"—and sat down. A chill settled over the chamber.

Another hour's discussion failed to resolve the matter. Huber indicated that he had spent many "sleepless nights" wondering if the ICRC had done the correct thing in following its legal position consistently. Yet a "gentlemen's agreement" between the belligerents had protected many civilians, he added, and the Allies had not ratified the Tokyo Project at the time the war broke out. Jews were not covered by these "agreements," Riegner tilted: "You have your public opinion, and I have mine. If I speak of 'civilian internees', Jews do not think of 50 thousand or more foreigners saved, but of Auschwitz, Buchenwald, and Birkenau." The heated debate continued back and forth, with Riegner diplomatically adding that this was not the place to make the historic evaluation. To end the argument, a delegate then proposed to substitute *persons assimilées* for *civilians internées* in the resolution of confidence. Realizing the mood that afternoon, Riegner replied: "No one will understand that phrase anyhow, and I cannot have anything to do with it." The problem of civilian internees, as a result, had been postponed once again.[55]

Riegner's presentation and the changing historical climate eventually had their impact, however. The WJC opened up a full-scale publicity campaign pointing out the IRC's rigidity during the war, while it also took up resolutions to amend the Geneva Convention with the various governments concerned. In April, 1947, a conference of government experts met in Geneva to study the international guarantees for the protection of war victims. The delegates, divided as to whether or not the IRC should be the competent body to protect civilians, left that question open. The third commission, however, went beyond the IRC proposal that the stipulations of the 1929 convention be applied by analogy to civilian internees, declaring that a special statute was required: "The general rules of humanity and the law of nations are applicable to the treatment of Civilian War Internees as a body." Accordingly, these people merited visits, hygienic living conditions, food, and medical attention to maintain health and prevent loss of weight, relief and information bureaus, elected representative bodies, and adequate clothing. They should remain in possession of all personal effects and articles, and not be moved more than 15 kilometers per day and at a rate proportionate to their strength under conditions at least equal to those applicable to the forces of the detaining power.[56] Some lessons from the Holocaust had been learned after all, and guilty consciences tried at least to improve possibilities for the future.

Two years later the IRC's reversal of policy received international sanction. The IRC drew up the complete texts of the 1947 governmental findings and presented them to its seventeenth international conference at Stockholm in August, 1948. Professor Huber, clearly impressed by Riegner's argument at the March, 1947, conference, reverted to the very phrase Riegner and Guggenheim had used in their last confrontation with him as World War II ended: "War as it becomes more and more total, annuls the differences which formerly existed between armies and civilian populations in regard to exposure to injury and danger." Those present adopted principles that closely resembled the directives of a memorandum from the WJC's legal division; Riegner, Storch, and Zelmanovits represented the congress at this historic gathering. Almost every country in the world, in turn, approved the IRC recommendations in the Geneva Conventions of August 12, 1949. The adoption of guarantees for civilian internees, as the ICRC noted for the national Red Cross Societies in a brief analysis of these conventions, "is essentially new. In the evolution of protective international legislation, it is of the greatest import."[57]

The confrontation between the World Jewish Congress and the International Red Cross had ended. Ten years had passed since Hitler had invaded Poland and unleashed what would become the first stage of the Final Solution. Riegner, Guggenheim, Kubowitzki, and their colleagues would not take comfort in their triumph. It had come too late for six million of their fellow Jews, who heard not the bells that pealed out victory and freedom. For these martyred dead, just like the WJC, commanded no audience in the international corridors of power during the years of the Holocaust.[58]

The only other course left open to the congress during World War II would have been to assail the ICRC publicly, but, judging from the continued inability of even the American government to move that august relief organization, such an effort would have been fruitless. In March, 1944, as soon as the determined Nazis entered Hungary to complete their annihilation of European Jewry, the War Refugee Board urged the ICRC to send "effective representation" to that country to protect the Jews; the ICRC denied the request as inconsistent with the agency's "conventional competence." A month later the WRB cabled a stronger appeal to Geneva to ask Germany and all her satellite governments to give Jews full treatment or at least food packages as accorded to civilian internees under the 1929 Geneva Convention, only to be told that such moves would go far beyond the limits of the IRC's "traditional capacity" and lay it open to the objection that it was intruding upon internal affairs of state. The ICRC indicated in July that its activities would not be jeopardized for the sake of an attempt to distribute relief generally to "unassimilated persons who are confined in camps." On the same grounds, the IRC's central office did not press Berlin for authorization to examine Jewish camps under Nazi control, or accept a board request in September that an official visit by the ICRC to the Theresienstadt ghetto could halt deportations and check "well known tendencies in certain circles in Germany to exterminate [the] maximum number of Jews before [the] end of war [which] may make [a] sudden deterioration of [the] position of Jews in Theresienstadt and elsewhere likely." Only beginning in January, 1945, did the State Department challenge the IRC outright, and this took place in conjunction with the Kopecky-Riegner *demarche* and the inevitable collapse of the Third Reich.[59]

The ICRC's stubborn legalism correctly convinced the congress that any public attack on this unswerving position, in Riegner's words years later, "would not have helped at all" during the war. Contemporary awareness of the War Refugee Board's lack of success, amply reflected in the WJC's files, gave the congress further reason for despair and for the decision to keep its own confrontation with the IRC since 1939 hidden from the public eye. At least behind-the-scenes diplomacy—the *demarche* instigated by Reigner—had wrested a sizable number of Jews from Hitler's grasp. And, as Kubowitzki put it at the height of the Hungarian crisis, every Jew who survived in occupied Europe was "a kind of itinerant miracle."[60]

The World Jewish Congress had failed to shatter the "persistent silence" of the International Red Cross during the years of the Holocaust.[61] Yet it could look forward to continuing its fight for the equality of Jewish rights the world over with the knowledge that the congress had accomplished much despite overwhelming odds. In truth, the failure was not its own.

The Sternbuchs, Storch, and the *Reichsführer* SS

IN THE LAST WEEK of October, 1944, the Va'ad HaHatsala received a startling telegram from its chief representative in Switzerland. Through channels of the War Refugee Board, 42-year-old Isaac Sternbuch informed the rescue organization of America's Orthodox Jewish community that those Jews removed from the Vittel internment camp the past spring had, according to French underground information, been deported in two groups about the middle and end of May. Ask the government of Paraguay via the Spanish embassy in Berlin to "ascertain present location," he implored the New York–based agency. "At our request," Sternbuch ended the cable, "Federal Councilor Musy has announced his readiness to visit Berlin and try and rescue them."[1]

The Va'ad, headquartered at 132 Nassau Street in the offices of its parent body, the Union of Orthodox Rabbis of the United States and Canada, had its genesis five years earlier. Responding to an appeal from Vilna's Rabbi Chaim Ozer Grodzinski for financial aid to more than 20 Talmudic academies that had fled Poland for "the Jerusalem of Lithuania," the union quickly formed the Emergency Committee for War-Torn Yeshivoth in mid-November, 1939. Under the driving chairmanship of American Agudas Israel head Rabbi Eliezer Silver, his effort strengthened by the arrival in early 1940 of Mir Yeshiva president Rabbi Abraham Kalmanowitz, the Va'ad HaHatsala (as the Emergency Committee became known) raised over $128,000 by that fall.[2]

Efforts continued in 1941. The longer established and far more substantial American Jewish Joint Distribution Committee (JDC) objected to what it viewed as the Va'ad's disruptive, particularistic campaign, as well as the new group's supply of funds to Lithuania without a Treasury Department license after Soviet annexation of the Baltic republic. Certain, however, that the rescue of these Torah centers demanded unique priority for the future of world Jewry, the independent Va'ad persisted. Collections by Young Israel pioneer Irving Bunim and others, even held occasionally on the Sabbath in view of sudden life-and-death emergencies, bore fruit. The $135,000 spent by the Va'ad HaHatsala during 1941, when added to even larger sums given by the JDC, brought some 500 Yeshiva people to the safety of Vladivostok, Kobe, and Shanghai and 125 to the Western Hemisphere before the year's end.[3]

Invaluable help came from the Agudas Israel Youth Council, then centered in its Williamsburg branch at 616 Bedford Avenue, under the energetic leadership of Michael G. Tress. Having come under the influence of Yeshiva Torah VaDa'as dean Shrage Feivel Mendlowitz and Rabbi Elchanan Wasserman of Baranowitz during the latter's 1938 visit to the United States, the textile house executive resolved to dedicate his entire energies to beleaguered co-religionists in Europe. The council's refugee and immigration division opened a refugee home in May, 1939, and during the next two years took care of more than 150 such families in need. Thousands of kosher food parcels were sent through Agudas's Yugoslavia branch to various occupied German territories until external pressures halted the program in mid-1941. Volunteer committees secured vital affidavits of support that went off to different American consulates overseas for thousands of prospective immigrants. Tress and Agudas's Meir Schenkolewski also helped obtain a few hundred special visas from the State Department for Orthodox leaders abroad, thus enabling World Aguda president Jacob Rosenheim and such rabbinic authorities as Aaron Kotler of Kletsk and Reuven Grosovsky of Kamenetz to reach New York before the Japanese attack on Pearl Harbor.[4]

The United States' entry into World War II boded ominously for the Va'ad's continued work. Rosenheim's private appeal that the President's Advisory Committee on Political Refugees (PACPR) ask Roosevelt to grant several thousand emergency visas without consular formalities for Jews facing deportation from the Reich to Poland, these individuals to be examined by a security board on Ellis Island, enjoyed no chance of realization. Assistant Secretary of State Long had already secured the complete defeat of PACPR chairman James McDonald and his colleagues with the ending of the emergency visa program in July. When Rosenheim, accompanied by Polish-born Isaac Lewin and a rabbi recently arrived from France, beseeched Long to overcome the department's fear of security risks by at least opening camps in islands along Florida's coastline to those confronting death, his tears met with a friendly but firm refusal.[5] American war censorship cut off all contact with Nazi-held Europe soon after, just as Germany's Final Solution for the so-called "Jewish problem" moved into high gear.

Fortunately, at that very juncture a crack in Hitler's Fortress Europe opened for the Va'ad in Switzerland. Germany's *Anschluss* with Austria in March, 1938, had stirred St. Gallen's Recha Sternbuch, the 33-year-old daughter of chief rabbi of Antwerp Mordecai Rottenberg, to inaugurate an individual rescue campaign. Bribing Swiss frontier guards, she illegally brought several hundred Jews from Dachau and other concentration camps across the border by means of fictitious visas with the help of St. Gallen police chief Paul Grüninger before her arrest in 1939. The spirited woman, released from prison despite her refusal to disclose the names of confederates whatever the penalty, was exonerated after a two-year-long law suit. Understandably, when she and her husband, Isaac, a dress manufacturer, received an urgent cable in 1941 to help the Mir Yeshiva students stranded in the Far East, they moved quickly to dispatch funds and create the Hilfsverein für jüdische Flüchtlinge im Shanghai (HIJEFS). This independent effort, with headquarters in Montreux once the Sternbuchs moved there, came to Rabbi Kalmanowitz's attention, and activity with the Va'ad ensued.[6]

Daring innovation marked HIJEFS's first efforts. Eli Sternbuch, Isaac's brother, established contact with Paraguay consul Rodolfe Hügli, who agreed to issue 1,000 protective passports for Jews in Poland, Belgium, and Holland at a mere 100 Swiss francs apiece. Other South American countries followed for a cost of $200–$400. With the aid of RELICO's Alfred Silberschein in Geneva, thousands of temporary affidavits at little or no cost were also obtained from the Honduras consulate and Georges (Mandel) Mantello, a Hungarian-born Jew employed as first secretary with El Salvador's counterpart. The Polish diplomatic code, thanks to envoy Aleksander Ladós and his subordinate, the Jewish refugee Julius Kühl, in Berne, ensured HIJEFS's dedicated small band a secret line of communication to Agudas's Isaac Lewin through the consulate general of Poland in New York City. Thus did the first eyewitness news about the mass deportations from Warsaw arrive at Rosenheim's office in early September, 1942.[7]

Throughout the following year the Va'ad HaHatsala engaged on various fronts to extend its program of salvation. While Tress approached Treasury Secretary Morgenthau for a license to forward sums for food parcels abroad, Kalmanowitz maintained ties to his Mir Yeshiva community in Shanghai via neutral countries, despite FBI warnings of impending arrest. Lewin transmitted sums to Rabbi Eliyahu Botchko, the Sternbuchs' brother-in-law and head of the Novogrudok Yeshiva Etz Chaim in Montreux, and to Agudist leader Chaim Eiss for the rescue of individual families and Chassidic rabbis. (Contacted by Eiss one summer day, Kühl used a courier from Papal Nuncio Philippe Bernardini to rush a passport to the Belzer Rebbe, thereby enabling the Polish Jewish leader to leave Budapest for Palestine.) The Union of Orthodox Rabbis intervened on behalf of a reported offer to release 70,000 Rumanian Jews, successfully pressed for a joint congressional resolution excoriating Germany's systematic slaughter of European Jewry, and obtained the Polish government's willingness to include 500 Yeshiva students for evacuation to Mexico.[8] Rosenheim applauded James McDonald's attack on Great Britain's "scarcely conceivable" 1939 White Paper regarding Palestine, and asked the PACPR chairman if his group might explore the possibility of a mass Jewish settlement on the high plateau of Portuguese Angola. Aguda director Harry Goodman in London secured 100 immigration visas from the Irish government, and saw the apostolic delegate concerning the fate of Italy's Jews. Following cables from Va'ad representatives Jacob Griffel and Ludwig Kastner in Istanbul about the desperate plight of the remaining 80,000 Jews in Transnistria's concentration camps, Rosenheim intervened with U.S. ambassador to Turkey Laurence Steinhardt and requested the JDC to send 250 tons of food to Rumania via the International Red Cross.[9]

As Allied callousness to the fate of Europe's Jews became increasingly manifest, the Va'ad adopted a more radical stance. Rabbis who in mid-1942 had refused to support public demonstrations and demand an Allied reprisal policy to counter European Jewry's destruction now had to confront the stark reality of the Holocaust. How, further, would they contend with the ineffectual Bermuda conference on refugees, which Secretary of State Hull applauded in a letter to the Union of Orthodox Rabbis—two months after a delegation had requested concrete results? At the instigation of the Emergency Committee to Save the Jewish People of Europe, 400 of its members marched on the nation's capitol and the White House, urging that Jews evading death be admitted to the United Nations, neutral countries, and Palestine. The union's presidium also lobbied for congressional passage of resolutions masterminded by the Emergency Committee to create a separate government agency bent on rescue.[10]

Fund-raising activity logically shifted in emphasis as well. Letters from Satmarer Rebbe Joel Teitelbaum, Neutraer Rov David Ungar, and his son-in-law, Rabbi Michoel Dov Weissmandel, appealing for funds to smuggle Polish, Rumanian, and Hungarian Jews to safer Slovakia, convinced the Va'ad that Isaac Sternbuch's call for an immediate campaign to this end warranted priority action. At its annual convention in early January, 1944, the Orthodox body resolved to drop its earlier focus on eastern Europe's Torah community in favor of helping all endangered Jews. HIJEFS, which had been remitted a total of $47,000 during all of 1943, consequently obtained $100,000 within a month via the newly created U.S. War Refugee Board.[11]

At last Recha and Isaac Sternbuch's circle could lay claim to some tangible means, but just then the news arrived in New York that the Germans had confiscated all South American and Latin American passports from Jews in the camp at Vittel, a spa in southern France. (The majority of these documents originated with HIJEFS, but a good number had been purchased from a Gestapo-run operation in Warsaw's Hotel Polski.) The Swiss authorities' negative attitude particularly disturbed the Sternbuchs, for Recha's parents and two sisters-in-law, as well as other relatives and the family of colleague Saul Weingort, had been brought to that internment center some months earlier. Rosenheim, Tress, and Shabse Frankel, Agudas Israel of America director whose family was also imprisoned there, immediately contacted the State Department and Apostolic Delegate Amleto Cicognani in Washington; these authorities, in turn, obtained the assurance of Paraguay and some other governments that they would continue to recognize both the validity of the papers and similar protective certificates for internees in Bergen-Belsen, Libenau, Tittmoning, and Compiègne.[12]

Yet remarks of the camp's officials, conveyed to the Va'ad in both IRC-sponsored letters and coded messages from internees in Vittel, made it clear that only swift exchange with Germans in Allied hands would save the Jewish inmates. Accordingly, the Va'ad sought and obtained the WRB's intervention with the State Department on February 21, then again in mid-March, that the U.S. minister in Berne approach Berlin via the recalcitrant Swiss federal government on their behalf. Since all attempts to contact the largest group in Bergen-Belsen had failed to date, Rosenheim also requested the understanding board director, John Pehle, on March 23 to exert the strongest pressure on the Third Reich's leadership to permit IRC supervision of the camp prisoners.[13]

One week later Isaac Sternbuch relayed to Kalmanowitz through WRB channels the *cri de coeur* of 238 Jews in Vittel: "Isolated for deportation" on March 20, only the announcement of a protecting power about imminent exchange might save them. Accompanied by Frankel and Baruch Korff of the Emergency Committee, Kalmanowitz brought the grim tidings to Morgenthau on April 6. The Treasury Secretary, instrumental in creating the board in January, 1944, at the expense of Foggy Bottom, heard that for six weeks State had held up the WRB's request concerning the protective documents on the ground that these were either forged or issued by the Gestapo. Korff noted the interest of New York's Senator James Mead and House Majority Leader John McCormack in the matter, but Kalmanowitz's dramatic intercession proved decisive with the usually stolid Morgenthau. The sight of "this grand old rabbi, with a wonderful beard like the Catholics wear in the Near East," breaking down into hysterical weeping and a faint unnerved the Reform Jew. Following four hours of constant work that afternoon, a jubilant Morgenthau got the strong cable in dispute released from State to Minister Leland Harrison in Berne the next morning.[14]

The danger had scarcely passed, however, Further SOS telegrams re-

ceived from Sternbuch on the eve of Passover, including a report that the
Vittel group had already been moved, induced Rabbis Kotler and Korff
to travel again to Washington on the night of the second Passover Seder.
The zealous 28-year-old Korff, who broke the story of State's procrastination to columnist Drew Pearson, impressed an angry but honest Cordell Hull to override his subordinates. Cables were quickly sent off to the
various U.S. legations in South America and the unsympathetic American ambassador to Spain, Carlton J. Hayes, backing the validity of the
foreign documents and declaring the Polish Jews to be "exchange material" for Germans in South America. Vatican representatives Bernardini
in Berne and Cicognani in Washington also supported the respective requests of Sternbuch and Kalmanowitz, but they got nowhere with the
Western Hemisphere countries concerned when also raising the question
of eventual immigration as a result of the possible exchange.[15]

On April 26, 1944, Lewin heard from Sternbuch that all internees in
Vittel had been deported, for the time being, to Drancy. Two escapees
who provided this information added that the protecting states, Spain and
Switzerland, had not yet informed the Germans about recognizing the papers in question. If an intervention by both neutrals did not occur within
24 hours, the HIJEFS chairman warned, "all these people are doomed."[16]

The quickening tempo in the last stage of the Nazis' Final Solution gave
HIJEFS and the Va'ad, which received no definite word about the Vittel
Jews during the next four months, scant cause for hope. Neither rescue
center could move the Allies, as Weissmandel had implored, to bomb the
railroad junctions through which Hungarian Jewry was deported in packed
cattlecars to Auschwitz-Birkenau. WRB representative Roswell McClelland
in Berne refused to give in to what he privately termed "pressure from the
Holy Men" that 40 tractors be sent to Hungary as ransom for the exit of
1,200 rabbis and prominent Jews. Those refugees from Bergen-Belsen and
Vittel who arrived on July 10 in Palestine, saved through the third civilian
exchange conducted by London and Berlin during the war, indicated that
the Vittel deportees were sent to Poland, "presumably to Oswieszien [sic]
... well known as a slaughtering camp." The Va'ad joined Palestine Chief
Rabbi Herzog's appeal to Pope Pius XII that he excommunicate all Christians participating in the murder of European Jewry, and all the American
Orthodox organizations pressed the three Allied warlords to rescue the
remnant in Hungary quickly—both to no avail.[17] The Va'ad's attempt to
procure 5,000 protective passports from the Dominican Republic for
$72,000, enjoying the strong backing of the WRB but not the State De-
partment's Adolf Berle, did not materialize. A warning from New York that
German evacuation of 7,000 Jews in Kovno to the east Prussian border
suggested "extermination will ensue" elicited a despairing reply on August
29 from Va'ad representative Shlomo Wolbe in Stockholm: his repeated
endeavors to communicate with Lithuania had all failed.[18]

Two days later Sternbuch finally cabled concrete information to Lewin about the Vittel group. German and Jewish sources indicated that all but 20 were deported to Auschwitz. If the U.S. government threatened Berlin with reprisals or ceased to give information about German prisoners of war in Allied hands, HIJEFS's chairman suggested, perhaps they could yet be rescued.[19]

The Va'ad's financial assets, while accomplishing much, could hardly meet the demands of the rapidly unfolding catastrophe. Between July and September, 1944, $300,000 in Swiss francs was credited to HIJEFS's account in St. Gallen. Money sent to Weissmandel with Bernardini's help for bribing the Tiso regime in Slovakia allowed some 1,800 Jewish refugees to enter that Catholic country from Hungary, the greater part in labor camps. The American minister to Morocco helped Renee Reichman in Tangiers send thousands of food packages to Jews in Theresienstadt, Birkenau, and Oranienberg in the name of the Spanish Red Cross; this Orthodox woman from Hungary also played a role in securing the Spanish government's promise to extend diplomatic protection over 1,200 Jews still alive in Budapest. With Soviet permission, Va'ad executive secretary Jacob Karlinsky sent off thousands of 12-pound food packages to Jewish refugees in Siberia and Samarkand. Griffel helped the Bobover and Wysnitz Chassidic dynasties, among others, while Sternbuch relayed funds to Angelo Donati for the sake of Jews in Italy and France. The amounts received for the vast rescue imperative were "ridiculous," however, a frantic Weissmandel exhorted HIJEFS's Hugo Donenbaum and Sternbuch by way of paid Gentile couriers. Expecting at least $1 million for the audacious program of the Bratislava Rescue Committee, on which he worked closely with JDC representative Gisi Fleischmann, he called on "heaven and earth as witnesses" that the Gaon of Tschechoiw and many others could have been saved had more funds been made available.[20]

The Va'ad HaHatsala's strained relations with the Joint Distribution Committee, dating from the former's activities for Polish Yeshiva groups and exacerbated by the advent of its broader campaign since January, 1944, precluded financial subvention from that essential quarter. The Sternbuchs never forgave "Joint" representative Saly Mayer for a letter, written in his former capacity as chairman of the Federation of Swiss Jewish Communities, supporting Swiss policy against the influx of east European refugees after the *Anschluss*. Recha's arrest ensued, HIJEFS's executive was convinced, consistent with Mayer's reluctance during 1939 to help Revisionist-Zionist Reuven Hecht direct the "illegal" migration of European Jews to Palestine through Switzerland and Marseilles.[21] Mayer's hesitation over Weissmandel's plea at the end of 1942 for a $2–3 million "Europa Plan" to check the Holocaust, followed by the JDC delegate's unwillingness to endorse a 700,000 Swiss franc line of credit for the 40-tractor proposition in mid-1944, infuriated the Orthodox organization. HIJEFS hoped for more understanding in Mayer's superiors, but JDC headquarters in New York continued to belittle the Va'ad's experience and methods in a "ferocious" propaganda war that World Jewish Congress administrative secretary A. Leon Kubowitzki privately villified as "jeopardizing the little rescue work that is actually being done." Griffel's urgent request for $200,000 to hire a large ship for the rescue of Jews from the Balkans died aborning, as did Weissmandel's $1 million appeal at a time when the Slovak rabbi reported that an additional 12,000 Jews had been deported on August 26 past his country to Auschwitz.[22]

In desperation, HIJEFS sought out other Jewish groups in Switzerland to finance the tractor ransom proposal. Mihaly Banyai's Committee for Jews in Hungary, which included Rabbi Zvi Taubes, Zurich businessman Josef Mandel, and his brother, Georges Mantello, had already established contacts with Swiss businessmen known for their good standing in Nazi circles. Two of these introduced Curt Trümpy, intermediary between the Messerschmidt works in Switzerland and a Swiss named Bührle. In mid-July Trümpy attempted to negotiate on the committee's behalf with SS leaders in Vienna for the exit of 20,000 Hungarian Jews to Rumania. The Germans were actually prepared to negotiate "on a commercial basis," a surprised emissary reported back to the committee just when Recha Sternbuch and Donenbaum received McClelland's firm negative concerning the tractor exchange. After Mrs. Sternbuch turned to Mantello for a loan of 600,000 Swiss francs to obtain the tractors, the Mandel-Mantello brothers agreed to extend half that amount in a blocked account on certain conditions, with 200,000 each provided by the Sternbuchs and a circle around Chief Rabbi of Zurich T. Loewenstein.[23]

Saly Mayer, about to embark on separate talks with Nazi representatives from Hungary led by *Obersturmbannführer* Kurt Becher, wondered if Bührle's added influence was strong enough to consummate the desired deal for the first 1,200 Jews in question. Mantello retorted that a trip to rescue these unfortunates could be undertaken by Trümpy, who contacted Mayer in early August. Mayer then gave the young Swiss a memorandum for the Nazis, demanding that Becher or someone else get instructions from *Reichsführer* SS Heinrich Himmler regarding actual Third Reich policy. At a meeting in Germany on August 12, according to Trümpy's later account, the Nazis announced that they would release part of a Hungarian transport held in Bergen-Belsen if additional ransom were paid. His first talk with Becher et al. at the end of the month did convince Mayer that "Himmler knows and approves"—318 Jews from that convoy also arrived in Switzerland on August 21—but his doubts regarding Trümpy lingered. At last he secretly provided HIJEFS, against the advice of McClelland and the WRB, with a first payment of 260,000 Swiss francs ($59,000) to cover some of the tractors. Sternbuch thought the delay "deplorable," certain that his organization's own credit deposit two months earlier had saved the contingent of 318. HIJEFS immediately supplied Trümpy with 100,000 Swiss francs to secure the release of the Orthodox individuals still held in the transport in Bergen-Belsen, particularly Joel Teitelbaum of Satmar, and waited on edge for the outcome.[24]

Impending disaster for their people yet alive on Axis European soil gave the Va'ad HaHatsala and its centers abroad no rest. Nothing transpired on Reuven Hecht's plan, transmitted directly to the White House by American consul in Zurich Sam Woods, for a mass emigration to Palestine in response to the Hungarian government's rescue offer. American authorities continued to turn down Va'ad-HIJEFS ransom and bombing proposals just when governments-in-exile reported from London about the German deportation in sealed freight cars of Holland's last 3,000 Jews and the remainder of the Slovakian Jewish community (destined for Auschwitz-Birkenau). Liberated Lublin and vicinity uncovered only ten children among 1,000 Jewish survivors in Majdanek, while the 20 remaining Jews who greeted the first American tanks reaching Vittel on September 12 still lacked precise information about the fate of the earlier two transports. Agudas's Harry Goodman obtained 500 Irish and 400 Mexican visas for Hungarian Jewry, an impressive but fundamentally limited achievement. In the wake of Polish information, received on September 25, 1944, that the Nazis had ordered the immediate murder of 45,000 "civilian prisoners" in Auschwitz, Kalmanowitz got Cicognani to bestir the pope and asked American Jewish Committee president Joseph Proskauer and the WRB to support a government declaration threatening stern punishment against all such atrocities. Sternbuch's warning on October 5 that the Germans intended in the last moment to "exterminate all internees in concentration camps," Himmler reportedly having worked out these plans with camp officers, secured State Department intervention via the Swiss and a strong statement from Secretary Hull five days later.[25]

On October 14, 1944, Rosenheim, Tress, Kalmanowitz, and Schenkolewski, after waiting the entire Sabbath day at the White House, presented the desperate case of European Jewry's remnant before Eleanor Roosevelt. Her husband would "do his utmost" to save the camp inmates, the First Lady assured Agudas's delegation. At the same time, FDR thought that recognizing these Jews as prisoners of war, reprisals to follow by Americans against German prisoners if the Jews came to harm, would lead to a "chain of violence without end" on both sides.

She would plead with the president to approve a warning, currently under discussion, by SHAEF commander Dwight D. Eisenhower that the officers of these camps would be held responsible for any crimes against the internees. Rosenheim's proposals that Franklin Roosevelt appeal directly to "the last spark of honor and humaneness in the hearts of the German people," that Eleanor do the same to "German motherhood," and that some leading Americans of German origin launch a similar last-minute plea elicited her great interest, if guarded optimism.[26]

Fully alive to the catastrophe, and particularly concerned about the Vittel deportees' fate, the Sternbuchs made contact that same moment with Jean-Marie Musy. The 75-year-old former federal councilor and president of the Swiss Confederation, Recha learned from her Catholic friend Louise Bolomey, had successfully intervened in Paris during the summer with Gestapo head General Hoberg for the liberation from Drancy of a Jewish couple, and had recently undertaken a similar effort for the son of a Lausanne widow named Thorel. Publicly acknowledged Catholic leader of various fascist movements in Switzerland, this avid anti-communist lawyer seeking to refurbish his image at the war's end appeared a godsend to the HIJEFS executive board. At Recha's urging, the well-connected widow Bolomey finally convinced Musy to meet Mrs. Sternbuch.[27]

In mid-October Recha and Isaac, claiming to act on behalf of the Union of Orthodox Rabbis of the United States and Canada, pleaded with the pronounced Germanophile to intercede in Berlin personally on behalf of Jews in Nazi camps and particularly Recha's immediate family in Vittel. An agreement was signed between Recha and Musy on October 18: one million Swiss francs (copies supplied in checks on HIJEFS's bank account for half that amount) would be paid to the latter for the rescue of 216 "Israelites," deported from Drancy in two groups between around April 18 and mid-May to "an unknown site in Germany or in a German-occupied region."[28]

Although without a reply from Himmler to his previous letter for an appointment to discuss the young Thorel, Musy had made up his mind to depart for Berlin. Soon thereafter the German legation informed Musy that if he wished to see the *Reichsführer* SS, he should come to the Nazi capital. With 60,000 Swiss francs from the Sternbuchs for a car and other expenses, an additional million and perhaps more to be paid (Isaac wired the Va'ad HaHatsala) "only when designated persons shall cross Swiss frontier," Musy and son Benôit left on October 29 for his rendezvous with Adolf Hitler's second-in-command.[29]

A German official conducted the pair from the Constanz border station, and on All Saint's Day Musy met *Brigadeführer* SS Walter Schellenberg in Berlin for the first time. The head of the Reich Security Main

Office (RSHA) division for foreign intelligence had already concluded in the late summer of 1942 that only a separate peace with the West could save the Third Reich from total disaster. Assisted by Felix Kersten and *Obergruppenführer* SS Karl Wolff, Himmler's masseur and command staff director respectively, the calculating 32-year-old lawyer attempted through various channels during the next two years to reach the leaders of the Anglo-American Alliance with the *Reichsführer's* vacillating approval. Only the previous month Himmler had allowed Schellenberg to contact Swedish banker Jakob Wallenberg by means of anti-Nazi conspirator Carl Goerdler, without result. Schellenberg's concern had not heretofore encompassed the Final Solution—he had even drafted the agreement between the *Wehrmacht* and the SS *Einsatzgruppen*—but Musy's mission might well benefit his own diplomatic ends. The *Altbundesrat* appreciated the *Bridgadeführer's* "modest, very calm" demeanor, and they came to fundamental agreement during the journey to Breslau, where they secretly boarded Himmler's special train heading for Vienna.[30]

At 4 P.M. on November 3, 1944, Musy entered Himmler's car for their scheduled private interview. The two had met at anti-communist meetings prior to the war, Musy even an honored guest at previous Nuremberg party rallies. The 44-year-old *Reichsführer* now listened attentively to the appeal that he free Thorel, several other designated individuals, and all the Jews confined in concentration camps. The latter action would both solve the "Jewish problem" for the Third Reich and create favorable worldwide publicity, Musy argued. The American government, according to a document submitted by the Sternbuchs, was prepared to assume all costs for Jewish refugees unable to settle in Europe or Palestine.

At the end of two hours an agreement in principle had been reached. The 600,000 Jews estimated by Himmler and Schellenberg to be under German control could be released to Switzerland in transit without Hitler's authorization. Himmler did not challenge Musy's claim that Germany would not win the war; indeed, he had already halted deportations from Budapest to Auschwitz-Birkenau and ordered an end to "final extermination" of the Jews. The *Reichsführer* insisted on goods, especially trucks and tractors, in compensation, precisely as his agents secretly conveyed on different occasions to the West through Joel Brand, Philip von Freudiger, Becher, and Trümpy. Musy countered by pointing to severe Allied controls on such war materiel; when Himmler refused to consider medicines, the elderly Swiss suggested that it would probably be easier to secure large sums, a possibility mentioned to him by Sternbuch. The commander of the SS Order of the Death's Head still preferred payment in goods, but ultimately concluded that a compromise might be effected on the ground of foreign exchange. No contact could be established with the Vittel group, but Schellenberg would see to the freeing of Thorel and certain others, and keep in close contact with the former federal councilor.[31]

After numerous discussions Musy and the Sternbuchs agreed on a line of strategy. While Mrs. Bolomey went to Paris to discuss the question of obtaining goods, all agreed that the pressing hour demanded a cash proposition. For 20 million Swiss francs ($5 million), 300,000 Jews could be evacuated to neutral countries, the sum perhaps deposited in a Swiss bank on a monthly basis of one million Swiss francs for each 15,000 persons reaching safety. Musy informed Himmler by letter on November 18 that the American authorities had sanctioned the appropriation, with 20 million francs already allocated! While the Union of Orthodox Rabbis was awaiting the *Reichsführer*'s list of required goods, the *Altbundesrat* personally sought large quantities of pharmaceutical products. He was prepared to travel immediately to see Himmler, Musy concluded his communication, and entertained the "best hope" for the entire operation's success. HIJEFS's chairman, for his part, urged the union in Polish code to cable acceptance of the scheme through the American embassy, an immediate decision "exclusively addressed to us for utilizing perhaps this only chance for rescue of a great number of Jews." Simultaneously, another secret wire to Lewin emphasized that one million Swiss francs be placed at Sternbuch's disposal without delay for releasing the initial 15,000 Jews.[32]

Tress quickly received WRB director Pehle's approval to have McClelland give Sternbuch the Va'ad HaHatsala's reply: "We completely agree with your rescue work and are ready to obligate ourselves for large sums of money." The British Foreign Office, worried that unclear messages about the matter smacked "closely of Nazi blackmail" reminiscent of the "notorious" Brand proposals, refused to pass on a report to New York from Agudas's Goodman. With more information at his own disposal, McClelland entertained similar fears. Sternbuch, who thought a 20 million Swiss franc figure concurrently under discussion between Mayer and an agent of Himmler emissary Becher related to the Musy *demarche,* asked the board representative to support the total request. Not having placed great stock in Sternbuch's rescue programs since assuming his diplomatic post eight months earlier, McClelland cautioned Pehle on December 9 about the "vagueness and unreliability of this 'whole' scheme." With Musy, known as the "Swiss Quisling," involved, the board could not actively participate in any event, he noted. That did not preclude Sternbuch's receiving the Va'ad's first remission of $100,000 in Swiss francs a few days later, one week after the remainder of the Hungarian transport from Bergen-Belsen, including the Satmarer Rebbe, arrived in Switzerland.[33]

HIJEFS actually had no intention of negotiating with Himmler over huge sums of money or war materiel. The former tack might well spur German extortionists to additional deportations or, if failure ensued, a savage bloodletting, while the American authorities would be unlikely to grant Swiss firms on the "black list" authority to send goods into the Third Reich. A direct political line, however, exploiting Himmler's illusion that he could secure more favorable Allied treatment for his country by means of the Musy-Sternbuch connection, seemed promising with the Nazi defeat plainly in sight. Unable to find in Saly Mayer an ally for these calculations, HIJEFS had to wait until the remaining $150,000 arrived after the New Year from its New York headquarters to cover 15,000 Jews. Musy immediately wrote to the *Reichsführer* SS for a second interview, and received Himmler's favorable reply a few days later.[34]

As soon as Musy sat down in a hotel room at Wildbad-Schwarzwald on January 15, 1945, Himmler questioned the importance of the Union of Orthodox Rabbis. "Sally Meier," after all, had brought about the Becher-McClelland meeting two months ago. A shocked Musy retorted that, according to Sternbuch, HIJEFS alone could negotiate on political grounds, since the JDC dealt exclusively in philanthropic concerns. "Who is it that the American government is really in contact with. Is it a Rabbi-Jew or is it the Jioint? [*sic*]," Himmler wondered. He was prepared to continue the discussion provided Musy explore the nature of Mayer's mission and this most fundamental question of all.

Agreeing, the old gentleman presented a list of non-Jewish Swiss and French nationals and Recha Sternbuch's relatives, to be freed forthwith, and then explained that compensation in goods for the release of the remaining Jews would be impossible. In response, the *Reichsführer* summarized his previously stated position: ever since talks had begun on improving the fate of the Jews, whose earlier "high death rate" resulted from their engagement in "hard labor" projects, they were assigned to "armament factories" and other "normal work." The Third Reich did not wish Jews under any circumstances living in its territory, and merely sought guarantees that those freed through Switzerland would never be transferred to Palestine, since "we know that the Arabs hate them in the same measure as we." Tractors, trucks, and machine tools were desired, not the proffered medical supplies or even foreign exchange; the American press had to "comment favorably" on the transaction. An enthusiastic Schellenberg, the only other individual present that Monday evening, received an order to ensure the liberation of those on Musy's list. "All the Jews" in the concentration camps would be evacuated to Switzerland without delay.[35]

Musy crossed the border two days later, while Schellenberg returned his car to son Benôit, then waiting in Berlin to pick up Recha's two brothers and some others whom Himmler had pledged. Sternbuch informed McClelland about the talks and cabled a summary to the union, which quickly wired back via the Polish consulate pouch confirmation of its political *bona fides*. Musy returned to Germany on January 21 to concretize evacuation plans with Schellenberg, who received a copy of the union's declaration from the German legation in Berne by special courier. Further discussions produced a comprehensive agreement: 1,200 Jews would arrive by train in Switzerland every two weeks; after delivery of the first convoy, 5 million Swiss francs were to be deposited with a Swiss bank in an account under Musy's name. Such funds, paid to the IRC in return for food and medicines needed by the German population, would be acceptable in lieu of goods. While Frank Göring, a close subordinate of Schellenberg's, set out to locate those on Musy's list and implement the general scheme, Musy returned home on February 1 to ensure a smooth reception of the impending arrivals.[36]

At this point, Roswell McClelland's positive intercession in Berne proved timely. A supplementary report from Musy, mentioning a "blackmailing scheme" by Hermann Goering and other leading Nazis to have foreign personalities like Marshal Petain and Belgian King Leopold suffer the final fate of those retiring into a "German reduit" unless Reich chiefs received equal right of exile in Switzerland, raised serious misgivings in the American Quaker's mind. Nor could he ignore the "most unclear purpose," which Sternbuch also conceded to McClelland in private, behind the token Swiss franc deposit to Musy. Yet the WRB representative also knew that Becher's actual "*mandat*" from Himmler, according to Mayer's own estimate, seemed quite uncertain; that Schellenberg's longtime contact man with the chief of Swiss army intelligence deprecated the Mayer-Becher negotiations; and that on February 5 Becher agent *Hauptsturmführer* Krell received orders from Berlin to halt his talks because the Musy effort would yield "astonishing results" within a few days. Accordingly, while advising Sternbuch to stall on payment until the first convoy might arrive, McClelland told Swiss police chief Heinrich Rothmund that he thought the U.S. government would agree to transfer such groups to Allied soil, just as it had guaranteed the transfer of refugees from Hungary the previous summer.[37]

Dispatching the first transport of Jews from the German side was fraught with great difficulty, however. Forced marches of those prisoners "in condition to leave" from concentration camps to Germany's interior, begun in mid-January at Himmler's order, were claiming thousands of lives each day. RSHA director Ernst Kaltenbrunner and Gestapo chief Heinrich Müller, in keeping with this demonic side of the vacillating *Reichsführer's* personality, actively obstructed Frank Göring's efforts to implement the Himmler-Musy agreement. When Göring, using Schellenberg's personal conduit to the Reich transportation ministry, finally cleared one train to depart from Theresienstadt, he found that only 1,600 had answered the German call on February 3 for half of the remaining 12,000 internees to leave for Switzerland. "We are being sent to Osweicz, not to Schweiz," the vast majority feared, recalling that 1,689 of their number had on October 30, 1944, joined close to 90,000 previously deported to Auschwitz (Oswiecim in Polish) for "resettlement."[38]

Finally, on February 5, 1945, 1,210 anxious Jews (including 58 children) boarded the comfortable third-class carriages at 5 P.M. While the Theresienstadt transport made its perilous way over Eger, Nuremberg, and Augsberg, the predominantly elderly group received more than ample food and vitamins such as they had not seen for years. "In the name of *Reichsleiter* Himmler you are now free," declared Major Göring to the ecstatic passengers as their train crossed the border at Kreuzlingen just before noon two days later. Upon receiving signed postcards of their safe arrival, Schellenberg's deputy returned home to prepare a succeeding convoy of 1,800.[39]

Three hours later HIJEFS's Reuven Hecht briefed Swiss Confederation president Eduard von Steiger on the Musy mission. U.S. Consul General Woods, first to bring Hecht and Sternbuch together after developing a close professional and personal relationship with Hecht, had managed on short notice to secure the important interview. Firm advocate in the fateful year 1942 that Switzerland could admit no more refugees because "the lifeboat is full," the reserved von Steiger now told his visitor that all Jews arriving at the frontier would be granted asylum. (Benôit's return with Recha Sternbuch's brothers and two others—her parents and all those deported from Vittel "could not be located"— strengthened HIJEFS's case considerably.) After the two drew up an official communiqué regarding the transport, an elated Hecht set off to win the support of the local press.[40]

While Swiss newspapers echoed von Steiger's public praise of Musy, said to be acting on behalf of the "Executive European Council" of the union and World Agudas Israel, and the promise of bi-weekly transports, Sternbuch openly cabled New York and London of the wondrous outcome. At the same time he warned the union in Polish diplomatic code that it should not hesitate to dispatch the remaining 4 million Swiss francs for Musy's account in the Swiss national bank and to forward favorable press clippings. "It is possible that the release of the Jews may be the forerunner of proposals of much greater importance to the Germans," McClelland wired the WRB, particularly as Musy also achieved the concomitant liberation of some 540 French citizens and nine Swiss nationals. When Sternbuch arranged for a paper credit of the necessary francs to save time, McClelland suggested to Washington that a Treasury license for the Va'ad HaHatsala to remit its $1 million equivalent might be issued in their joint names, as had been done a month earlier for $5 million sent Mayer by the JDC.[41]

Musy's insistence to Recha Sternbuch, however, that he would not return to Berlin before receiving definite reports in the American press about the Nazi "change of heart" reinforced McClelland's suspicions. HIJEFS's chairman strongly denied rumors that the admission of every refugee cost 1,000 Swiss francs and the entry of major Nazis, and he implored the WRB's delegate to back this humanitarian endeavor. Finally, in possession of the 4 million franc paper credit and added interest expressed by the Dutch and French governments, HIJEFS convinced Musy to leave on February 19 to expedite the release of additional transports.[42]

The Va'ad HaHatsala made every effort to meet Sternbuch's insistent pleas, but circumspect authorities in Washington held up a license until the month's end. Upon raising $63,000 in a blitz campaign, a delegation including Kalmanowitz, Bunim, and Frankel approached JDC headquarters for help. Worried about U.S. trading with the enemy regulations and, in Rosenheim's view, beset by fear of "the anti-Semitism complex," its executive finally agreed under "inescapable pressure" to lend the remaining $937,000 with the proviso that government approval had to be given. The State Department, notwithstanding London's reluctance to take the negotiations seriously, was willing to grant permission if the funds to Musy could be blocked somehow in Switzerland. Newly appointed WRB director William O'Dwyer allowed Bunim to send Sternbuch a photographic montage of positive accounts from the nation's press on the Theresienstadt train, but he preferred to recommend to the Treasury Department McClelland's suggestion concerning any financial remittance.[43]

Talk that the staunchly anti-Roosevelt *Chicago Tribune* was about to run a story concerning Morgenthau's "dealing with Himmler" to free only Jews made the Jewish Secretary of the Treasury especially apprehensive. He insisted that the Va'ad immediately halt its clandestine use of the Polish diplomatic channel and that the three Cabinet officers overseeing the War Refugee Board arrive at a consensus on the matter. On February 28 Secretary of War Henry Stimson, Acting Secretary of State Joseph Grew, and Morgenthau agreed to a $1 million deposit in the name of Sternbuch-McClelland, no funds to be used for ransom or without prior board authorization.[44]

This limited success appeared to have come too late, for on March 3 the *Altbundesrat* telephoned HIJEFS secretary Herman Landau with a brief message as soon as he came back to Switzerland: "If no more trains leave Germany, you have to thank Saly Mayer." The same day

Musy explained to the Sternbuchs that, according to information received from Schellenberg and Göring, Mayer's negotiations with Becher to keep the Jews alive in Germany proper were "sabotaging" his separate efforts. Some negative press reports regarding the latter, including a story that 200 members of the SS would gain asylum in America thereby, had been passed on by Becher to Kaltenbrunner. Sternbuch immediately cabled the Va'ad via Kühl at the Polish legation to intercede with the JDC. He then secured a confidential letter from McClelland, stating that Washington had formally assured the Swiss government of its willingness to cover all expenses involved in the prompt evacuation "to Allied territories overseas" of those Jews freed with the former federal councilor's help.[45]

Musy wished an additional statement from Sternbuch, showering praise on the Third Reich without mention of him or HIJEFS. In the end, after consulting McClelland and von Steiger, HIJEFS decided to publish a declaration under its own name on March 16: the Germans, contrary to various rumors, had claimed "no indemnification" for their assurances regarding the liberation of Jews via Musy, whose activities "are exclusively charitable." With these two documents and a copy from Reuven Hecht of the Sternbuch-McClelland bank account in Basel's Fides Truehand, Musy sallied forth with his son once again to the tottering Reich.[46]

Thinking that only Washington could help realize the Musy plan and so check a possible Nazi slaughter of Europe's surviving Jews in the final hours of the war, a Va'ad HaHatsala delegation made one last attempt to ease the bottleneck with an afternoon visit to Morgenthau on March 13, 1945. After Baruch Korff noted the problems involved in the restrictions placed on the $937,000 license, the obtaining of trucks carrying relief supplies from Switzerland to Germany, and the evacuation of Jews to safety, the Treasury Secretary took the floor. Speaking frankly as a government official with deep sympathy for their work, he went on to emphasize that, given the government's primary concern with winning the war, the remittance in question required attendant safeguards. The Jews in America, he added, could harm themselves greatly and spark dangerous antisemitic publicity if it were ever revealed that any of their co-religionists were negotiating directly with Himmler for such rescue.

These last words stung Rabbi Kotler. Incensed, he pointed a finger at Morgenthau and exclaimed to Irving Bunim in Yiddish: "Sogt ihm efshar hut er moira far sein shtelle. Ein Yiddisches leben ist mehr wert wie die ganze shtelle seine!" Bunim tried to lighten the impact when the puzzled Treasury director asked for a translation, but, at Kotler's insistence, he explained verbatim: "The Rabbi said, 'Tell him perhaps he is afraid to jeopardize his high office. One Jewish life is more valuable than that entire position of his!'" At least save invaluable time, Bunim recommended, by permitting Sternbuch to use the original one million Swiss franc license for legitimate expenditures under McClelland's authorization. "Tell the Rabbi, I am a Jew, and I am willing not only to give up my office, but my life to save my people," Morgenthau responded. He would clear an affirmative cable on Bunim's request with the State and War Department secretaries. As to the other issues raised, the board was exploring every possibility. The group, including Rabbi Kalmanowitz, took their leave after presenting a written memorandum of the points raised in the interview.[47]

Hardly had the Va'ad HaHatsala time to savor this small victory when Berlin warned over DNB radio three days later that all Jews, including prisoners of war, would be killed. A shocked Kalmanowitz appealed to Cicognani for Vatican intervention, while the Va'ad presidium cabled Roosevelt to prevent this last-minute slaughter. Bunim drafted an accompanying memorandum for the chief executive, which concluded, in language similar to that used in the declaration to Morgenthau, by referring to "a very sad drop of the curtain" on 2,000 years of murdering the Jewish people. Fearing that "if Roosevelt will see that it was done for two thousand years, he will say, let it be another year," Kotler struck the paragraph.[48]

As the hour inexorably neared midnight, HIJEFS could offer no solace. Musy and son crossed the frontier on the afternoon of March 24 empty-handed, and reported to the Sternbuchs, Hecht, and Bolomey that their efforts to extricate additional convoys had been unsuccessful. In desperation, Sternbuch wrote to the ICRC in Geneva that the 5 million Swiss francs were now at its disposal, specifically for freeing Jews from Germany. Even as Hecht shifted to this new arena of activity, Sternbuch received a WRB message from Kotler and Kalmanowitz on March 26: internees, starving in all camps, should receive more food parcels and be evacuated in ICRC trucks returning empty to Switzerland. "Worried about DNB report," they concluded. "Every effort should be made to stop exterminations and to rescue, every minute counts."[49]

HIJEFS's chairman certainly agreed with this grim estimate, but his last major card to save the remnant of the Jewish people on the blood-soaked soil of Europe had been thrown. Factors beyond his group's control spelled an end to the "Musy action." He would again press the *Altbundesrat* to continue negotiating for at least one additional convoy, but the prospects for achievement appeared nigh impossible. In the depths of despair, Sternbuch cabled the Va'ad HaHatsala a terse message the same day: "No further transport arrived."[50] How could the surviving Jews be rescued now?

II

Unknown to Sternbuch, the answer appeared to come in a letter dated
March 24, 1945, from Felix Kersten to WJC representative Hilel (Gilel)
Storch in Stockholm. Having just conducted secret talks at Storch's urgent request with Heinrich Himmler on the fate of the last Jews in German hands, the *Reichsführer*'s masseur reported most dramatic success.
Food parcels sent by Storch for some time now to specific persons in the
concentration camps would be distributed to other Jews if the addresses
were not to be found; the possibility of placing these survivors in specially arranged camps, gradually to come under Red Cross control, had
"met a great understanding." Himmler had issued a written order "saying that cruelties and the killing of Jews are forbidden," and he intended
to issue new instructions to camp commandants at a meeting that same
day regarding "a more humane treatment of the Jews." A new investigation would look into the matter of releasing certain groups to Switzerland or Sweden, while Kersten still hoped for word on Storch's list of
individual prisoners to be evacuated. Any publicity in the world press,
however, would halt these improvements forthwith. Finally, at Kersten's
suggestion, the *Reichsführer* SS was prepared to "negotiate with you
personally" about these questions. Willing to sacrifice himself completely,
as he had already done for numerous "unfortunates," Kersten now
awaited Storch's response.[51]

The 43-year-old businessman from Latvia had special reason to celebrate this wondrous *dénouement*. Arriving in Sweden before the Russian occupation of Riga, Storch's excellent financial connections with
the Soviet Union, Latvia, and Sweden had proven decisive in bringing
his wife and child to safety. But attempts to rescue other relatives, holding Palestine certificates, from subsequent German occupation in the
Baltic area failed. In addition, the local Jewish community organization,
Mosaika Forzamlingen, and Chief Rabbi Marcus Ehrenpreis showed
themselves extremely reluctant to press for visas from a government
whose official neutrality inclined toward Hitler's interest. German troops
and war supplies openly passed through Swedish territory, and a stringent residence permit policy granted a total of only 4,000 Jewish refugees (including 900 from nearby Norway) entry by the end of 1942. Such
developments gave Storch, also serving as representative of the Jewish
Agency's rescue committee, understandable anxiety at a time when the
first published Nazi regulations regarding Jewish fortunes in the *Ostland*
appeared most ominous for his people in Latvia and Lithuania.[52]

In the Va'ad HaHatsala's local representatives he found a more kin-
dred element. Hans Lehmann, an import-export businessman formerly
of Leipzig, had begun rescue work with the transfer to Stockholm of

Hamburg's only remaining synagogue after *Kristallnacht*. Classes in Congregation Adath Jeshurun were conducted by Rabbi Shlomo Wolbe, originally a German Reform Jew who had studied at the Mir Yeshiva in Byelorussia after first coming under the influence of Eliyahu Botchko in Montreux, and who was brought from Riga to tutor the Lehmann children. The two became a conduit for the Va'ad's efforts on behalf of the Polish *yeshivot,* joined in April, 1940, by Abraham I. Jacobson, the Tiberias-born outspoken rabbi of Trondheim who was visiting Sweden when the Nazis invaded Norway. Through Wolbe's intercession, the 2,386 end-visas for Curaçao issued by honorary Dutch Consul A. M. de Jong at only $1.00 apiece between January and April, 1941, enabled a large group to depart Lithuania for Vladivostok on its way to Japan. Lehmann's contacts with South American diplomats and Jacobson's personal ties to Consul Borrera of Ecuador also resulted in the transfer of diplomatic passports to some 2,000 Dutch and other Jews in Germany's *Festung Europa* during 1943.[53]

The initial Swedish response in April, 1943, to the possibility of admitting 20,000 Jewish children immediately from territories under Third Reich control boosted Storch's spirits, but the Anglo-American Alliance's "inert and indifferent bureaucracy" stifled any hope for its realization. Advanced by the Jewish Agency's S. Adler-Rudel, the proposal had required London and Washington to pay a daily upkeep of $1.00 per child, permit additional foodstuffs through Göteborg for this project despite the Allied blockade, and agree to evacuate the youngsters after the war. The matter went unmentioned at the Bermuda conference on refugees. The British Foreign Office subsequently refused to commit His Majesty's Government to eventual removal—the "only bait" Swedish Foreign Ministry Chief Secretary Eric Boheman felt would attract the Nazi authorities, not wishing to acquiesce in Germany's *Judenrein* policy for Europe.

After a silence of three months the State Department indicated to London its interest in the plan, but stressed that no final decision had been reached as to procedural method. By then, Sweden's annulment of iron ore shipments and German transit rights, the result of Stalingrad and other Allied victories, made a successful *demarche* most improbable. Upon additional prodding by Whitehall and the Intergovernmental Committee on Refugees, Washington finally advised London on October 11 that it would give consideration to the proposal if Stockholm were prepared to take up the matter now with the *Wilhelmstrasse.* This "word game" ended soon thereafter when the sympathetic Social Welfare Minister Gustav Moeller indicated his government's unwillingness to approach the Germans, citing as its reason the Quisling regime's refusal to allow Norwegian children exit for Sweden.[54]

Stockholm's forthright rescue that same month of almost 95 percent of Danish Jewry signaled its official shift toward humanitarian values. Information about impending mass deportations had drawn a protest to Berlin from Foreign Minister Ernest C. Günther on September 29, 1943, some hours before Danish Minister Hendrik de Kauffman asked WJC president Stephen Wise in New York to help secure Sweden's apparent readiness to receive these desperate human beings. Wise and colleague Nahum Goldmann, in touch with Storch, raised the matter with Assistant Secretary Long on October 1; State cabled appropriate encouragement. The next day, at the instigation of the Danish underground and some prominent Swedes, the Danish Jewish refugee and internationally acclaimed physicist Niels Bohr asked 85-year-old Swedish monarch Gustav V to publicize Günther's note. That evening Swedish radio broadcast the news of the government's intervention with Germany and its willingness to harbor all of Denmark's Jews.[55]

While this official announcement propelled the hitherto quiescent Danish Jews and their Christian neighbors to organize a "little Dunkirk," some activist Jews on the Swedish side had already taken steps in this direction. At the instigation of Adler-Rudel, who received Moeller's promise in March to view favorably the admission of any Jews escaping from Denmark, the *Julius* was purchased to convey Zionist pioneer youth and other Jews to these safe shores. A young Orthodox Jewish businessman, Fritz Hollander, and fellow Zionist partner Norbert Masur went on to establish contact with the Danish underground movement in Stockholm; the attorney Ivor Philipson oversaw technical aspects for the transport system with substantial funds from the Jewish community, deposited only after the government's encouraging position became public. To expedite the opening of Sweden's frontiers, Storch asked the American minister to intercede with Gösta Engzell, chief of the Swedish foreign office's legal department, who in turn obtained an affirmative response from Tage Erlander, then police minister. Over 7,000 Jews were ultimately ferried to safety that fall.[56]

Sweden's changed attitude stood the test when Hungarian Jewry faced its turn on the Nazi timetable of mechanized death. In mid-April, 1944, Masur suggested to Ehrenpreis that they search for a prominent Swedish Gentile to initiate a rescue program with the country's embassies in Bucharest and Budapest to bring Jews from these two capitals to Turkey. Some influential politicians convinced Storch and his few associates that government intervention could not be obtained at that moment, however, while the national Council of Bishops turned down Ehrenpreis's appeal that it openly denounce the persecutions in Hungary. A month later Raoul Wallenberg's Jewish business partner suggested his name to Ehrenpreis and WRB delegate Ivor Olsen. The intervention of Sven Salen, a well-known shipping man, eased Wallenberg's appointment to the Swedish legation in Budapest as secretary for humanitarian concerns.[57]

Storch contributed to Stockholm's resolve. Even before Wallenberg's departure, he worked tirelessly at getting hundreds of names, forwarded by the WJC's Argentine section, of individuals having different ties to Sweden included in protective documents which that legation had issued after the Germans occupied Hungary. At the end of June Storch received a cable from the Jewish Agency's Isaac Gruenbaum in Jerusalem, urging that that Swedish monarch be asked to use his personal influence on the Hungarian government to stop the current deportations to "death camps Poland for annihilation." While he immediately contacted the foreign office's Engzell and Prime Minister Per-Albin Hansson, Ehrenpreis wrote to the king's chamber on June 29, 1944, and pleaded for Gustav's intercession. The monarch, whose government had recently received a similar letter from the Jewish community in Budapest and eyewitness information about Auschwitz-Birkenau, cabled Hungarian Regent Miklós Horthy the following day "in the name of humanity to take measures to save those who still remain to be rescued of this unfortunate people." One week later Wallenberg set out for what would be an unparalleled mission of mercy.[58]

Simultaneously, War Refugee Board representative Olsen reported home about an offer by Nazi official Peter Kleist and two other individuals named Klaus and Boening to release at least 2,000 Latvian Jews against a cash payment. Although $2 million, then 2 million Swedish kroner, were mentioned, the group stated that perhaps no money at all would be required. The important consideration, they emphasized, was that the Swedish foreign office had to express strong appreciation of the proposal and a willingness to receive these refugees gladly, as well as to promise that the arrivals would not spread anti-Nazi propaganda. During Olsen's one meeting with Boening on July 3, Kleist's personal business representative suggested that in exchange for evacuating the Jews from the Baltic countries, the Swedish Red Cross would offer nonstrategic medical supplies for Germany's bombed-out civilians. Boening, officially German cultural attaché, added that Kleist had resigned over severe disputes with Nazi foreign minister Joachim von Ribbentrop as his special representative for civilian administration in Poland and the Baltic area, but maintained close ties with important individuals in the hierarchy of the National Socialist regime.[59]

The three governments directly involved reacted gingerly. Washington instructed Olsen to seek Swedish Red Cross examination of concrete terms without permitting reference in any future negotiations to the American government or its interest. Taking seriously what he characterized as Hitler's "general policy" of killing all Jews, Swedish official

Boheman believed that Kleist's activities were "directly inspired" by Himmler, known to be strongly opposed to the violently anti-Swedish attitude taken by Hitler and von Ribbentrop and interested in currying favor with the West before Germany's inevitable defeat. London concurred, particularly in light of proposals, which Britain's Cairo intelligence center concluded had emanated from the *Reichsführer* himself, secretly carried a month earlier by Joel Brand to the West. Swedish intelligence, on the other hand, also reported to the Americans' Office of Strategic Services counterpart that Klaus had arranged for Kleist to spend some time at the Soviet legation during his most recent trip to Stockholm. It did not know that, following the Nazi debacle at Stalingrad, von Ribbentrop had asked Kleist at Hitler's order to maintain his contact with Klaus and seek out Soviet intentions.[60]

Olsen continued discussion of the dubious proposition, hoping to secure better treatment of Jews and other civilian internees. He arranged with Folke Bernadotte, vice-president of the Swedish Red Cross, to handle all negotiations with Kleist and Boening regarding the evacuation to Sweden of some 4,500 Jews holding South American visas in Bergen-Belsen and other camps. Storch was intimately involved in these negotiations, having asked Klaus earlier for Kleist's intervention on behalf of his relatives in Latvia and eastern Germany. Nothing came of this appeal, which reached Kaltenbrunner, but Kleist reported that an order had been issued to halt the shooting of Jews moved to east Prussia during the German evacuation of the Baltic countries. In fact, the Jews in the Siauliai (Shavli) and Kaunas (Kovno) ghettos were transported to concentration camps in Germany proper that July.[61]

At a meeting with Kleist and Klaus on September 20, 1944, in Stockholm, Storch raised the possibility of payment for the release of the 4,500 Jews. Kleist, who approved of concentrating the Jews in Germany in order to pressure the Allies not to bomb the Reich, preferred a political solution: peace with the West in return for the preservation of the surviving Jews. A meeting in Storch's apartment between Adler-Rudel and Boening suggested the freeing of a certain number of Jews at a cost of $250,000, to be spent by the Swedish Red Cross on medical equipment for Germany. In October Storch heard from Kleist, currently negotiating with the Swedish foreign office and Bernadotte over the freeing of 100,000 Estonians in Osel, that money could not extricate Jews under the Nazi jackboot. Berlin, he claimed, was then debating the possibility of using Jewish camp inmates as hostages, and he would try to satisfy Stockholm's interest in a release of some sort. All these discussions came to naught, however.[62]

Other rescue operations bore modest fruit. Olsen's direct efforts brought a total of about 1,200 people to Sweden that fall from Estonia,

Latvia, and Lithuania in hazardous circumstances, but Jews were not to be found amongst them. For Storch, who had transmitted to the American embassy a detailed eyewitness report in early 1943 from a Latvian Jew, Leonidas Sebba, of the *Einsatzgruppen* mass executions in the Baltic region, the outcome was particularly bitter. Following the report of one Jew whom Storch had saved that a Latvian committee's story about 800 Jews hidden in the Dundaga forest was a blatant hoax, he refused to authorize a receipt for JDC payments to Olsen, thereby earning the board representative's disfavor. In the end, the Riga-born businessman could do little more than inform the World Jewish Congress's central office in New York about the massacre of 4,000 Jews in Kovno and 11,000 in Dvinsk during the *Wehrmacht*'s retreat westward.[63]

Storch's dogged campaign to send food parcels to Jews in the concentration camps proved more successful. Despite strong protests from his WJC associates in New York and Geneva, the Anglo-American Alliance and the ICRC had refused to help the segregated Jews in this fashion. Only in the fall did a first trial shipment of 15,000 three-kilogram parcels leave Göteborg for specific camps, not individuals. After limitless perseverance and just when ICRC parcels from Switzerland drew to a halt, Storch obtained a Swedish license in October to send 20,000 three-kilogram food packages to individuals in Bergen-Belsen, Theresienstadt, Ravensbrück, and other camps filled with Jews where food conditions were reported as desperate. Since use of the WJC's name would jeopardize the project, he got the Swedish YMCA to oversee implementation and to request confirmation by letter or card from recipients to its representatives in Germany. Stockholm's lord mayor and president of the corporative federation, Carl Anderson, provided Storch credit, while Koloman Lauer helped obtain Jewish names from the concentration camps. In order to save time, personal guarantees for the first 10,000 parcels were provided by Storch, his colleagues Akim Spivak and Leon Lapidus, and Marcus Kaplan.[64]

The latter arrangement was necessary because internal Jewish disputes threatened to vitiate the program. Differences soon arose with the autocratic Ehrenpreis, whom he had persuaded in October to chair the newly formed Swedish section of the WJC. Storch therefore resigned from its executive and continued the parcel scheme as part of the WJC's relief and rehabilitation department. The JDC's Laura Margolis, Ehrenpreis, and the Mosaika board of directors refused to cooperate, however, without receiving license control. Early in 1945 Storch even managed to send the vital packages by railway trucks directly to Bergen-Belsen, receipt confirmed by 136 inmates to Switzerland in a last exchange for German civilians living on Allied soil. Lev Zelmanovits, secretary general of the WJC's London branch who had obtained Bernadotte's promise in

November to support its broad rescue program with the Swedish government, finally adjudicated the conflict during a trip to Stockholm in the company of associate Ben Rubenstein.[65]

Yet what ultimate value had these food packages when the WJC heard repeated reports that the concentration camps and their inhabitants were to be blown up, upon Hitler's order, just prior to the Allies' anticipated arrival? In connection with his "complicated conversations," Storch heard the foreign ministry further confirm on February 2, 1945, that Sweden would accept all the Jews incarcerated in Bergen-Belsen and some in Theresienstadt, and even be prepared to offer transport from Germany. Bernadotte, he also cabled Zelmanovits, had just left for "SUPPORTING COVERSATIONS WITH HEAD NEGOTIATOR WITH WHOM HAVE BEEN NEGOTIATING SINCE SUMMER 1944." In point of fact, Günther, Boheman, and Swedish Red Cross president Prince Carl had ordered Bernadotte to *limit* his talks with key Nazi officials (especially Himmler) to the specific release of Norwegians and Danes in German camps. The SS chief's release of seven Swedish employees in Warsaw, 50 ill Norwegian students, and the 1,210 Jews via Musy convinced the Swedish officials to grant a formal request for this mission from N. Ditleff, head of the Norwegian organization in Sweden for aiding prisoners of war. Count Bernadotte succeeded to a large extent, obtaining Himmler's permission to have the Scandinavians assembled in a special camp at Neuengamme near Hamburg.[66]

Unaware of this outcome, Storch sought a direct link to the one man who could halt execution of the *Führer*'s satanic directive—Heinrich Himmler. Every previous effort to rescue Jews from the camps, with a few minor exceptions, had met with failure. The situation had, moreover, deteriorated considerably since issue of Hitler's command. Storch's well-placed friend, Riga-born Ottokar von Knierim of the Dresdener Bank branch in Stockholm, proposed the answer: 47-year-old Felix Kersten, personal doctor to the *Reichsführer* SS.[67]

No better choice could have been made. The Estonian-born manual therapy specialist then living in Holland, while curing Himmler's intestinal spasms during professional visits to Germany in 1941, had gotten his patient's consent to postpone carrying out Hitler's proposal that the Ukraine be colonized with three million "irresponsible" Dutchmen. Minister T. M. Kivimäki of the Finnish legation in Berlin and former Dutch Minister Baron von Nagell used this Finnish subject, whose intervention also prevented the deportation of Finland's Jews to Poland in mid-1942, to rescue Norwegian and Dutch prisoners. His treatment of and talks with Schellenberg in August, 1942, led to the SS *Brigadeführer*'s separate talks with Carl Langbehn, Jakob Wallenberg, and Abraham Hewitt, claiming to represent Roosevelt, in Stockholm the following year.[68]

Soon after Kersten had moved to Stockholm in October, 1943, Foreign Minister Günther, welcoming his efforts to free seven officials of the Swedish Match Co. arrested for espionage, broached the prospect of the masseur's intervening with Himmler to release all Scandinavian prisoners to Sweden. Ultimately, on December 8, 1944 (confirmed in writing two weeks later), Himmler promised Kersten the confidential release of all Danes and Norwegians, with the use of Swedish buses. As a personal Christmas gift, the SS chief pledged as well the lives of 1,000 Dutch women, 1,500 French women, 500 Polish women, and 400 Belgians in a future rescue to Sweden. Kersten unsuccessfully sought the release of 20,000 Jews from Theresienstadt at the request of a former Swiss patient, but received a promise that between 2,000–3,000 could go.[69]

At the end of February, 1945, the man Himmler called the "magic Buddha" was about to return to the Berlin lion's den. His close ally Schellenberg, interested in using Bernadotte to bring about a German surrender to the West at a time when Himmler fell ill owing to the collapsing war front and bitter rivalries within Hitler's entourage, telephoned Stockholm for Kersten's urgent service. Wishing Kersten to ensure the realization of Bernadotte's mission, to free other select individuals, and to avert war in Scandinavia after the collapse of the German front, Günther eagerly approved.[70]

Not surprisingly, therefore, when an agitated Storch pressed him on February 25 in von Knierim's company to ask Himmler to nullify Hitler's concentration camp order, Kersten gave his consent. The next day the two decided to use the Finn's intervention for a major rescue effort. Storch submitted a two-page memorandum on March 2, which began with a request to dispatch food and medicine to Jews in Germany, who should be placed in camps under Swedish Red Cross care and control. This was necessary because the Anglo-American authorities refused to send Storch's additional shipments without such distribution. (The recent 2,700 arrivals in Switzerland confirmed receipt of the first parcels.) Liberating the approximately 3,000 Jews having South American passports in Bergen-Belsen and certain other named Jews should be a first priority. Stockholm agreed to this plan of evacuation, he pointed out, envisaged by Storch and Kersten at a figure of 5,000–10,000. The World Jewish Congress representative expressed his thanks for Kersten's past humanitarian achievements, and concluded with the hope for similar success in this "very desperate situation."[71]

While awaiting Kersten's report, the indefatigable Storch tried one final avenue to rescue his people in its twelfth hour. From Bernadotte's reply to his note of February 23, which had forwarded a letter by Zelmanovits, he gathered that Stockholm would not, for the present, have the Red Cross representative handle the Jewish crisis. He was therefore most receptive when Fritz Hesse approached him on March 1 at Kleist's recommendation.

He had come from the Nazi ministry of foreign affairs with an offer to end "any further Jewish slaughter in Germany," Hesse emphasized. Could Storch help forward a letter to Stephen Wise, asking him to inform Roosevelt of the matter? He also wished the American president to know how the Russians were horribly mistreating the Germans, such as in the Soviet capture of east Prussia, and to intervene on behalf of "humanizing" the war; von Ribbentrop was prepared to evacuate the Jews in France on condition that Allied bombing cease. A communication to Wise would be superfluous, the Jew retorted: he could quickly arrange a meeting between Hesse and one of Roosevelt's personal agents in Stockholm, Ivor Olsen. The WRB delegate himself knew that the foreign ministry's Engzell was "rather optimistic" that this approach, when tied to the talks Storch had conducted with Kersten and Klaus, would bring out at least a few thousand Jews to Sweden. He agreed to meet Hesse on the understanding that their *tête-à-tête* would be a personal, unofficial exchange of views on humanitarian problems.[72]

Hesse presented himself to Olsen on the afternoon of March 8, 1945, as a German public relations official and intermediary to the British government in 1939 who later "pressed vigorously" within high Nazi circles against the persecution of different minority groups. Certain key officials in the German high command, worried over the heavy tolls exacted by Allied bombing against German civilians, were most receptive to a broad agreement that would "humanize the war." To Olsen's expressed doubts that Himmler, von Ribbentrop, Goebbels, and others of their rank had serious inclinations in this direction, Hesse responded that they were indeed receptive to any suggestions, at least for now. In exchange for a quickly instituted agreement to protect civilian populations, he was delegated to say that "every Jew in Germany" would be permitted to leave as soon as technical details could be worked out. The British and Americans, the conservative Junker went on, had very little time left to realize their "fatal mistake" in setting Russia up as "the ruler of Europe" after the war.

No German entertained the faintest thought of agreeing to the Allies' dictum of unconditional surrender, Hesse insisted, nor were the Jews advanced for bargaining purposes in the Third Reich's "more or less hopeless" situation. Perhaps, at the same time, millions of innocent noncombatants could be saved. The National Socialist government, he declared, had "definitely abandoned any idea of mistreating" the Jews further; their condition would be the same as that of any other civilian population now in Germany. Olsen asked for concrete proposals and promised to contact Washington without delay. Further discussions, he had no doubt, could lead to progress.[73]

Having received the *Führer*'s skeptical nod to forge a direct link to the British or, optimally, Roosevelt in this fashion, a despondent, neglected von Ribbentrop found Hesse's conclusions about the possibility of discussion with the Americans especially interesting. Yet Hitler, perhaps impressed with Jakob Wallenberg's fleeting remark to Hesse about the better prospects of negotiating with Stalin, first proposed on March 13 that the envoy return to begin talks through Aleksandra Kollontai of the Soviet embassy. The next day, after an injection from charlatan Dr. Theodor Morrel and some Wagner music had fortified his conviction to show no "sign of weakness" for the present, the isolated *Führer* forbade "any further discussion with foreigners." Von Ribbentrop confided in his personal emissary that both he and Himmler, at daggers drawn, had independently decided nonetheless to challenge Hilter and deal with the West. Conflicting accounts of the initial mission, which splashed across the world press's front pages through Hesse's indiscretion in Stockholm, ended any possibility of his future service to the powerless foreign minister, however.[74]

The *Reichsführer* SS was indeed defying Hitler at that very moment, granting concessions in the privacy of Kersten's residence at Gut Hartzwalde beyond Storch's and Günther's wildest expectations. Although first insisting that he would obey "to the last detail" the *Führer*'s direct order to have Germany's "enemies and the criminals in concentration camps" share in the nation's downfall, the man Hitler had always thought of as "faithful Heinrich" then contemplated freeing all the Jews on condition that enemy bombings would cease for at least a fortnight. The Allies would never consent, Kersten replied, countering with the suggestion that if he truly wished to help suffering human beings, Himmler should immediately send 20,000 Jews to Switzerland or Sweden. Having borne the brunt of Hitler's fury on reading some negative Swiss accounts about the Musy transport, Himmler emphasized that his chief had strongly outlawed any such releases in the future.

After difficult negotiations in which Himmler adjutant Rudolf Brandt strengthened Kersten's arm, the *Reichsführer* affixed his name at 2 P.M., March 12, 1945, to an unprecedented document. Himmler attested that the camps would be surrendered in an orderly manner to the Allies, further killing of Jews should cease, and prisoners, not to be evacuated, might receive food parcels. His physician impulsively countersigned: "In the name of humanity, Felix Kersten."[75]

Ever under Hitler's hypnotic influence and in constant fear of especially Joseph Goebbels and omnipresent head of the party chancery

Martin Bormann, Himmler still agreed to have several thousand prisoners, including 5,000–6,000 Jews, transported to Sweden. Kersten's original thought to have Himmler see Storch brought a prompt refusal at first: "I can never receive a Jew. If the *Führer* were to hear of it, he would have me shot on the spot." But again reversing himself, the SS leader pledged his life and honor to Storch's safety for a secret appointment at Hartzwalde in the company of Brandt and Schellenberg. On March 21, just before Kersten's departure, Brandt wrote the masseur that the *Reichsführer* was looking into his individual wishes "in a well-disposed manner."[76]

Himmler confirmed this in an extraordinary letter the same day. Thanking Kersten for his visit and his consistent humanitarian attitude, the SS chief pointed to the some 2,700 Jews who had arrived in Switzerland as a continuation of his colleagues' prewar interest in the emigration of Jews from Germany. Effective measures had been taken in Bergen-Belsen to check the great outbreak of typhus, "very often" found in "people from the East." He would "decide generously," as in the past, on Kersten's wishes. "Heartfelt greetings" to your honored wife, children, and especially to you, concluded Himmler the day after Hitler withdrew his command of Army Group Vistula.[77]

Kersten's report, coupled with requests received from the World Jewish Congress, persuaded Stockholm to have Bernadotte also seek the rescue of non-Scandinavians (including Jews) in his future talks. Learning from Hesse in early March that clothing and blankets to bombed-out German civilians might obtain the large release of Jews, Storch in tandem with Zelmanovits urged the foreign ministry and Swedish Red Cross to move Jews to special camps and from there, in Swedish buses, to safety. Sweden would spare no effort or expense in fetching those Himmler had pledged in December, Günther told Kersten on his return. The foreign secretary, although skeptical of the eventuality, also thought it a great step if Himmler and Storch should meet. Receiving Kersten's report, which also mentioned Brandt's assurance that the 5,000 figure could be doubled in oral negotiations with Himmler, a delighted Storch agreed to see the *Reichsführer* SS in Kersten's company and pressed the Swedish foreign office to admit 10,000 Jews.[78]

The British provided no encouragement for the scheme. Certain that Kersten was "a Nazi and a thoroughly bad man," Minister Victor Mallet turned down Storch's request that he tell Stockholm to accept all Jewish refugees. He forwarded to Whitehall copies of the Kersten correspondence (intended for the WJC's London office), as well as Storch's information that Engzell had reported the Swedish government's desire to give "all positive assistance" to the maximum rescue of Jews. Foreign Secretary Anthony Eden was anxious not to be "dragged into" the

Himmler-based proposal, particularly after *Pravda* had questioned the admission into Sweden of many Nazis holding Finnish passports and once Stalin sharply criticized General Wolff's negotiations with American intelligence in Switzerland; he preferred saying nothing to the Swedes. A year earlier Churchill had protested to the Russian premier about a false allegation in *Pravda* that von Ribbentrop had secretly talked with British agents in Cairo, and categorically opposed any negotiations over the Brand proposal. Now the British prime minister registered a succinct reply to Eden's note: "I agree. No truck with Himmler."[79]

The U.S. minister, perhaps on Olsen's advice, also did not transmit to Stephen Wise a cable from Storch on March 27. Stockholm, Storch reported, had decided to admit 10,000 Jews with the aid of convoys, and considered (as did Bernadotte) his journey to Himmler important. Four days later the Swedish foreign office on its own forwarded to the WJC president a brief telegram from Storch about the impending trip and Stockholm's interest, despite the "very difficult" transport question, in giving all possible help that "number of Jews to be rescued will not be curtailed."[80]

A nervous and depressed Himmler greeted Bernadotte on April 2, 1945. Still hoping for a separate peace with the West and worried that Kaltenbrunner might renege on his promises to ICRC president Carl Burckhardt, Schellenberg had pressed his superior throughout March to have Bernadotte convey to SHAEF commander Eisenhower the *Reichsführer*'s personal capitulation offer. Himmler hesitated once again, insisting that he maintain the SS oath of absolute loyalty to Hitler. For this reason had he forbade Wolff to continue his negotiations over surrendering the German forces in Italy to the West. When Hitler ordered the Waffen SS division members in Hungary stripped of their armbands as a mark of dishonor, Himmler remained steadfast in his first fealties.[81]

The war, although lost, must go on, the *Reichsführer* SS now told Bernadotte. He owed everything to Hitler, and would therefore not take the proper course that Bernadotte advanced—unconditional surrender. He agreed, at the same time, to the gradual release of some Scandinavians. The next day Himmler complained to the Swede that he would have liked to evacuate the Jews from Germany, as he did in the case of the Musy transport. Unfortunately, the *Führer* had issued strict orders against any repetition after receiving reports of this action in the Swiss press. Schellenberg did not give up, however, telling Count Bernadotte during the latter's trip to Berlin that he would try and convince his superior to accept the Red Cross official's terms for a special flight to see Eisenhower: Himmler should declare himself Hitler's successor, dissolve the National Socialist party, and release all Scandinavian prisoners.[82]

Musy had by then returned to Berlin, where he urged Himmler to offer a four-day truce proposal to the Allies for the evacuation of all the camp inmates. Schellenberg favored the humanitarian gesture, thinking that it might lead to a "general compromise" with the West, and received invaluable backing from SS head office and prisoner-of-war chief *Obergruppenführer* Gottlob Berger. Himmler indicated agreement with this suggestion as well, but, lacking courage to present it to Hitler, asked Schellenberg to raise the subject with Kaltenbrunner. "Have you gone off your head?" the RSHA chief reacted on April 3. Transcripts of an "Atlantiksender" broadcast originating from one of Charles de Gaulle's centers in Spain and current reports in the Swiss press that Himmler had negotiated with Musy to "save his skin" and that of 250 Nazi leaders, brought to the *Führer*'s attention by Kaltenbrunner, resulted in the *Führer*'s command that all the detainees be marched to a "reduit" in the Bavarian Alpine region to join the Nazis' last stand. Upon hearing from Göring that only some 10,000 of 18,000 scheduled to leave Buchenwald, for example, would probably survive the 300-kilometer ordeal, Musy wondered if it would not be more humane to shoot these inmates. He wanted a personal audience to discuss the question with the *Führer,* whom he had never met, but was told: "If Hitler so ventured, he would have you shot."[83]

As a last resort, the former Swiss Confederation president asked Himmler to risk his life and order that all camps not be evacuated. On April 7 the indefatigable Schellenberg informed Musy that Himmler, who had earlier agreed to Kersten's appeal on this score, had consented. The surviving Jews in Bergen-Belsen and Ravensbrück would stay put. Himmler also halted evacuation from Buchenwald, where on April 4 all prisoners had been readied for the march. In return, stipulated the *Reichsführer,* the Western armies had to agree that the SS guards and administrative personnel of the 15 main camps would be accorded prisoner-of-war treatment. Musy immediately took the hazardous drive back to Kreuzlingen, where, in the company of Sternbuch and Donenbaum, he heard McClelland indicate that there was little likelihood the SS guards would be summarily shot if they laid down their arms. Musy cabled Schellenberg on April 10 that Washington had reacted favorably, and then made preparations to return to Germany.[84]

For HIJEFS's executive, working determinedly with ICRC help since mid-March to bring food to the camps and rescue at least some Jews, Musy's account only augmented a pervading sense of anxiety. At Hecht's urging, Marcel LeClerc of the division of special assistance secretly obtained ten trucks (with funds from Saly Mayer) for a plan to bring back 600 Jews on Musy's list from Bergen-Belsen and Theresienstadt. The ICRC's Hans Meier was simultaneously intervening in Berlin with Kaltenbrunner under his organization's name for the release of Jews, as

Burckhardt had originally been promised by the RSHA director on March 12. The Germans refused any entry into Bergen-Belsen, however, and the ICRC did not know if its insufficient relief parcels had been distributed there. Four trucks with HIJEFS supplies eventually reached Theresienstadt in early April, but the camp commandant did not permit the ICRC delegates to give out the packages or depart with Jews. On the night of April 10 the first ICRC truck convoy to reach Switzerland from Germany, carrying 299 French women—only seven Jews—out of Ravensbrück, reported that the Nazis were "simply working detainees to death." Hecht and Donenbaum quickly set about getting more trucks off for Theresienstadt, while Musy and Recha Sternbuch crossed the border at Bregenz to follow up the liberation of the camps and perhaps yet locate her parents.[85]

The forced evacuations were, in fact, proceeding apace despite Himmler's pledge, as Benôit Musy discovered when he returned to Buchenwald on April 10 to locate some of those Jews promised his father by the *Reichsführer* SS. He at once drove to Berlin, where he bitterly reproached Schellenberg. The shocked *Brigadeführer* telephoned Himmler's headquarters, to be assured by Brandt that everything would be done to halt the evacuations; Himmler personally called back a few hours later to confirm this. The same day, following a conference of office chiefs, the Gestapo's Müller explained that he had started the expulsion operation three days ago on Kaltenbrunner's orders. The latter admitted on the spot that he had given this instruction following Hitler's personal command to evacuate "all the important internees" to the south. In a mocking dialect the RSHA head then remarked to Schellenberg: "Tell your old gentleman [Musy Sr.] that there are still enough left in the camps. With that you too can be satisfied."[86]

Trusting on Himmler to override Kaltenbrunner's directive, Schellenberg authorized Göring to drive with Benôit Musy to Theresienstadt. There they were told on the evening of April 15 that the Berger-Rothenberg families had been deported to Auschwitz in early 1945, and that "persons ostensibly not in the camp were to be considered as having been sent to Auschwitz." They returned to Berlin, where Schellenberg advised them to cut through the Russian lines and make for Ravensbrück at the earliest opportunity.[87]

Kersten meanwhile was standing by in Stockholm, awaiting Himmler's formal invitation to Storch. On April 3 the WJC representative had received Kersten's confirmation that Himmler would henceforth end the "present horrors" and surrender the camps intact to the Allies. An impatient Storch thanked Kersten the same day for this assurance, but warned of news just received that at least part of Bergen-Belsen was being evacuated. Kersten immediately called his secretary at Hartzwalde, who then heard from Brandt about Himmler's orders to safeguard the camps and that a "good reception" was assured for their impending visit. Yet on April 7 both Kleist and Klaus informed Storch that Kaltenbrunner had ordered the bombing of Bergen-Belsen for 6 A.M. the next morning. Losing little time, Storch got Kersten to telephone Brandt directly under special number 145 from Kersten's apartment.[88]

Three days later the Swedish Red Cross vice-president returned to Stockholm bearing a personal letter from Brandt to Kersten. Himmler's adjutant stated therein that the search for individual prisoners was being pursued, that Bergen-Belsen had been assigned a more humanitarian commandant, and that the International Red Cross had received permission to visit Theresienstadt. Bernadotte, who had transported 40,000 kosher food parcels that Storch received from McClelland's stocks in Switzerland through the intercession there of WJC colleague Gerhart Riegner, simultaneously confirmed to the WJC man that Brandt had informed him about Himmler's frustration of the Kaltenbrunner directive. Finally, on Thursday, April 12, Kersten's secretary called to say that the *Reichsführer* SS would talk with them in three days. Unable to reach Storch by telephone, the physiotherapist dispatched a hastily written note urging that he be prepared for an early Sunday flight at the latest.[89]

While no final word had yet come from Himmler, Storch and the small circle considering the trip raised doubts as to its value. In giving his consent, Storch had initially intended to gain time for the threatened Jews. Assurances now from Kersten regarding Himmler's orderly surrender of the camps and Bernadotte's ongoing activity suggested that the journey would not gain much. This conclusion was mutually arrived at during a conference which he attended in Engzell's office with associates Masur and Hollander. The great danger personally facing Storch, who had lost 18 members of his and his wife's families to the Nazis, presented a second consideration of much weight. Ehrenpreis and Storch colleagues Lapidus and Spivak concluded that the stateless ex-Latvian should not depart without a temporary Swedish passport, which Engzell and some other highly placed officials were prepared to consider. Günther refused, perhaps influenced by the fears of Mallet and Olsen that the zealous Storch had either exaggerated his actual authority with the Allies, or that the Nazis were employing him as a "stalking horse" for their own goals.[90]

Unknown to those in Stockholm, Himmler's postponement reflected his continued self-torturing indecision during the final weeks of the war. He listened with great interest to a medical specialist, brought by Schellenberg, describe Hitler's marked deteriorating physical condition, yet on April 13 informed his close subordinate that he could not bring himself to overthrow the *Führer*. When Schellenberg reminded him on that occasion of the promises to Musy and the necessity for him to see

Storch, he countered: "How am I going to do that with Kaltenbrunner about? I shall be completely at his mercy!" Furthermore, widespread Allied publicity about the horrors in liberated Buchenwald and Bergen-Belsen irritated Himmler greatly, especially as he had personally ordered their peaceful surrender to the Western armies. When his "little Wolff" was confronted by the sinister Kaltenbrunner on April 16 with an intelligence report concerning secret talks about the surrender of the *Wehrmacht* in Italy, Himmler dared not accompany the two adversaries to Hitler's bunker. Finally, he accepted Schellenberg's suggestion to invite Kersten and Storch for the 19th, during a period when Kaltenbrunner was known to be traveling to Austria.[91]

Storch would not be Kersten's companion, however. Engzell issued a protective document to Storch on April 16, which declared that he was about to depart for Berlin "to negotiate the release of certain internees" in "collaboration" with the Swedish foreign office. Yet a securer Swedish passport was still denied the World Jewish Congress representative.[92] In addition, Bernadotte had just confirmed by letter to Storch that Himmler pledged not to evacuate the Jewish camps, particularly Theresienstadt, Bergen-Belsen, and Buchenwald, and that all 423 of the Danish Jews in Theresienstadt were expected to reach Sweden (listed as "Danes") the next day; the WJC official in turn asked Bernadotte to focus on convoys from Ravensbrück, not included in Himmler's promise to Kersten because that camp was in the Red Army's sphere of operations. Still, the visiting Kleist told Storch on the 18th that Kaltenbrunner was sabotaging the Himmler-Kersten camp agreement. According to Storch's future account, Bernadotte erred in telling Kleist that same day of Himmler's invitation: the WJC representative feared that the acerbic von Ribbentrop–Himmler relationship would cause the *Wilhelmstrasse* envoy to inform von Ribbentrop of Storch's trip the minute Storch departed with Kersten. Perhaps, too, Himmler would make any release contingent on an Allied bombing halt, as Hesse had hinted earlier regarding a German *demarche* via Wise to Roosevelt. Deciding that he could not travel under these varied circumstances, Storch persuaded his friend Engzell to have Masur, a native of northern Germany who had taken Swedish citizenship after settling in Stockholm in 1921, to go in his stead.[93]

On the morning of April 19, two hours before the scheduled flight, Storch asked Masur to undertake the hazardous mission. Masur had previously volunteered his services if for any reason Storch could not depart and, with Hollander, had kept the principal legations informed of the latest talks. Doubting that a trip at this late date could still be of any value in view of Germany's highly critical position, he telephoned Engzell. Upon receipt of an encouraging reply, however, as well as a list of

Jewish and non-Jewish prisoners for possible liberation, he set off with
scant knowledge of the lengthy Storch-Kersten negotiations. At 2 o'clock
that afternoon a swastika-marked aircraft, loaded to capacity with Red
Cross packages, embarked with only these two passengers (Masur traveling incognito) for the four-hour trip via occupied Copenhagen to Berlin's Tempelhof airport.[94]

"Heil Hitler," a group of SS greeted the pair. "Good evening," Masur
coolly replied, with a doff of his hat. Holding on to Schellenberg's safe
conduct pass, they entered an SS staff car for the drive to Kersten's
estate. Having conferred the same afternoon in Berlin at Schellenberg's
request with the German minister of finance, whose views resembled
those of the opportunistic *Brigadeführer,* Himmler dispatched his trusted
subordinate to prepare the ground for his appointment at Hartzwalde.
The *Reichsführer* SS decided that he had better appear at the party in
honor of Hitler's fifty-sixth birthday, to be celebrated the next day in the
great bunker 50 feet under the courtyard of the Reich Chancellery,
before confronting the Jew on equal terms.[95]

In the preliminary talks Schellenberg expressed his complete sympathy
with their desires. While an anxious Masur tried to sleep through the
continuous crump of Allied bombs, Kersten emphasized the Swedish government's interests and the great importance that Himmler show his
"goodwill" to Masur with the release of as many Jews as possible. After
Friday breakfast Masur insisted to Schellenberg that he had come as a
private individual and needed to leave Berlin by Monday at the latest.
Schellenberg promised to support all their proposals. That afternoon
Bernadotte called him from the Swedish legation in Berlin and asked for
a conference with Himmler before returning home early the next morning. Schellenberg arranged for the count to await Himmler at the
Hohenlychen hospital, and then picked up his chief and Brandt at Wus-
trow for the 45-minute drive back to Hartzwalde. On hearing the auto
arrive at 2:30 A.M., Kersten stepped outside to speak with Himmler.[96]

At Kersten's personal request, the indecisive *Reichsführer* agreed to
do all in his power to avert possible war in Scandinavia. Would Kersten
fly from Sweden as his ambassador to begin negotiations with Eisenhower for an armistice, Himmler suddenly asked, so that a single front
with the West against Russia might be undertaken? Kersten suggested
that he discuss the subject with Bernadotte, then urged his patient to be
magnanimous to Masur so that history would not make a one-sided
judgment of the German people. In an ill-chosen phrase the SS chief
replied: "I want to bury the hatchet between us and the Jews."[97]

Entering the candle-illuminated library, the electric lights switched off
because of an air-raid alarm, the elegantly uniformed *Reichsführer*

greeted Masur that April 21, 1945, with "Good morning" and said he was glad the guest had come. After Kersten had served some Swedish tea and coffee, Himmler launched into a lengthy, fantastic apologia.

Not one of the countries that professed friendship to the Jews had agreed after the Nazis came to power to accept the Himmler offer of Germany's "alien element," he argued. The proletarianized Jewish masses of eastern Europe aided the partisans during the war and fired on SS troops from their ghettos. To check epidemics of contagious diseases like typhus, which these Jews carried, their innumerable corpses had to be destroyed in specially constructed crematoria. If the Jewish people suffered from the ferocity of war, the Germans did too, particularly against the implacable Russian foe. All those in the "educational camps" of the Third Reich worked hard and received just treatment.

Masur's occasional protestations bringing no disclaimer, Kersten intervened with a request to discuss how many human beings could still be saved. At least the Jews still in Germany should be assured of their lives if "a bridge between our two peoples" were to be built in the future, Masur appealed. To this end, he asked the *Reichsführer* for the freeing of those Jews in camps near Sweden or Switzerland and the good treatment of the remainder until the Allied forces arrived.

Himmler responded by attacking the Anglo-American "atrocity propaganda" about Bergen-Belsen and Buchenwald and the press campaign against him for releasing the Musy transport. Such continued releases, Masur suggested, would make a good impression in the world press, gain the favor of the Swedish and Allied governments, and have importance for the judgment of history. After the *Reichsführer* defended Theresienstadt as an ideal city run by Jews, the talk shifted to releases from Ravensbrück, which Himmler had promised Kersten previously. Masur pressed the subject, fearing that the Jews there might yet be slaughtered by the Nazi leadership in the course of its death agonies. When Himmler hesitated to commit himself, Kersten asked for a review of the Swedish foreign ministry lists for special consideration. While Masur went with Schellenberg into an adjoining room to decide on other points to be discussed, Kersten urged Himmler, with Brandt's approval, to stand by their March 12 understanding. "Then I'll fix the figure at a thousand. But there will be more," Himmler replied, agreeing also to liberate those specified by Stockholm.

Himmler kept his word to Kersten. On Masur's return, he pledged that 1,000 Jewish women in Ravensbrück could be freed on Swedish Red Cross convoys, provided that they be designated as "Poles" to circumvent Hitler's expressed prohibition regarding Jews. Fifty Norwegian Jews, 100 French women, 50 Dutch Jews, 50 Dutch women, and some

Swedes would also be liberated. The *Reichsführer* fully intended to adhere to his March agreement with Kersten (a memorandum to this effect was given Kersten by Brandt), demanding nothing in return. He then veered back to justification: Hitler alone resisted the Bolshevik menace, and his fall would bring chaos to Europe; the National Socialist state had reduced crime and given work to all.[98]

As the conference broke up at 5 A.M., Himmler and Kersten walked outside for a private talk. The Finn obtained Himmler's confirmation not to have the Hague, Clingendael, and the Dam blown up. "The finest elements of the German people perish with the National Socialists," the *Reichsführer* emphasized in presenting his valedictory view of Germany's tragedy, and whatever followed did not matter. On this nihilistic note, Himmler bade the man who had been his physician for the past six and a half years a tearful farewell and departed with Schellenberg for the Bernadotte appointment.[99]

Carrying Brandt's clearance letter on their drive to gutted Berlin, Kersten and Masur witnessed the "Master Race" in frenzied retreat and a forced evacuation of camp inmates from Oranienburg. At the Gestapo building Göring promised to divert the Swedish Red Cross bus column, then on its way to Denmark carrying Scandinavians from Neuengamme, to Ravensbrück. With Russian shells showering down on the capital, the pair flew to Copenhagen that afternoon aboard a Condor troop transport. At 9 P.M. they reached home soil.[100]

Their mission over, each reported to Günther. Summarizing the negotiations resulting in this bizarre interview, Kersten stressed that Himmler had finally agreed to keep his earlier promises. Masur warned that as many Jews as possible should be evacuated: "it was not inconceivable" that Himmler or other Nazi leaders might yet order the murder of all Jews before the guns were silenced. A skeptical Storch expressed this same anxiety to Kersten, who asked him in turn to ensure that the Swedish Red Cross formally receive the released Jews as "Polish" prisoners. "In a moment of confusion" Himmler's orders might be frustrated, Kersten admitted to Storch, but Brandt and Schellenberg would do their best to prevent such a possibility. Thanks to their interview, Bernadotte secured from Himmler on April 21 the release of all females in Ravensbrück. Soon thereafter, approximately 7,000 women of different nationalities (half of them Jewish) reached Lübeck, and from there a haven in Denmark and Sweden.[101]

Himmler did not relinquish his hope of joining the Western powers as "a sworn enemy of Bolshevism." Three days after Bernadotte refused to take a message to Eisenhower on his behalf, by which time Hitler had independently resolved to depart the failed Third Reich with suicide in his bunker, the *Reichsführer* drafted a letter of surrender to the West that the Red Cross official agreed to deliver to Günther. Churchill and Roosevelt's successor Harry S Truman saw the move as a last effort to split the Big Three and, after immediately informing Stalin, replied that simultaneous surrender alone would be acceptable. Eden's private disclosure at the San Francisco conference of his proposal leaked out to a Reuters correspondent, who had the exclusive printed in the early hours of April 28. Hitler turned livid on hearing of the betrayal that evening, screamed that "a traitor must never succeed me as *Führer*," and ordered Field Marshal Ritter von Greim to arrest Himmler at all costs. He had Fagelin, Eva Braun's brother and the *Reichsführer*'s contact at headquarters, shot on the barest suspicion of disloyalty; in the *Führer*'s last will and testament Himmler was expelled from the Nazi party and all offices of state. On April 30, 1945, Adolf Hitler, whose demonic hatred of one people dragged the world into a bloody conflict and ultimately destroyed European Jewry, killed himself. The following morning Goebbels sent Admiral Dönitz an explicit signal that Hitler had died, and indicated that the naval commander would head a new cabinet in which Himmler's name was conspicuously absent.[102]

To the last, thousands of Jewish lives hung perilously in the balance, as Sternbuch, Storch, and their colleagues feared, during this onrush of the Nazis' all-consuming Wagnerian *Götterdämmerung*. About 28,000 prisoners, mostly Jews, were evacuated by the SS in death marches on the eve of Buchenwald's liberation to camps in southern Germany. Two of these open freight car transports set off on April 7 with 6,000 half-starved souls; some 170 reached Flossenbürg alive; one survived a ghost train that was abandoned ten miles west of Dachau. Three thousand inmates on one train from Rehnsdorf, a branch of Buchenwald, lost their lives to an Allied bombing attack and machinegun executions by their Nazi guards. With American troops closing in, thousands of men were mowed down by machinegun fire on Natzweiler's *Appellplatz,* the rest hurriedly packed off to Dachau. Mass graves and little more than living skeletons greeted Nordhausen's liberators on April 13. About 7,000 "exchange Jews" were driven out of Bergen-Belsen, where 13,000 more prisoners died within a few days *after* British troops arrived to find 10,000 unburied bodies between April 6 and 11. Air raids, spotted typhus, shootings, and exhaustion took many victims until two of the three convoys were rescued by the Americans near Magdeburg and by the Russians close to Torgau. Of the third shipment, 1,712 reached Theresienstadt on April 21.[103]

The Nazis' original declared goal to make Europe *Judenrein,* frantically implemented even in the last hours of World War II, spelled near doom for the inmates of Dachau and Theresienstadt. Two transports and 137 VIPs left Dachau in the first stage of execution of Himmler's April 14 order that no prisoners from Germany's first concentration camp (1933) fall into Allied hands. A truckload of poison was dispatched from Munich laboratories on April 29, possibly to be mixed with the inmates' lunch. When American troops freed the camp that day, they discovered to their horror a trainload of 2,206 men, 83 women, and 21 children—all dead—and about four days' accumulation of corpses stacked behind the crematorium in a room measuring 40 feet by 20. In Theresienstadt, the "model" ghetto that fooled two ICRC delegations, the doors to newly constructed gas chambers were returned three times because they did not fit. The camp population, swelled in its last three weeks by 12,000 inmates from the rest of the Reich in the worst stages of malnutrition and disease, were saved from this danger when Red Cross official Paul Dunant returned in early May. His few colleagues were no protection against a German regiment, however, which fired off its excess ammunition on retreating from Prague. Only with the Red Army's arrival on May 8 could the ecstasy of freedom fill the air.[104]

Preparations for "Operation Cloud A-1; Fire-Cloud," a directive ascribed to Kaltenbrunner for the blowing up of these two concentration camps and Mauthausen, together with their inmates, reached their nearest success in the latter. Kurt Becher may have secured Commandant Franz Ziereis's tacit consent on April 27 to halt the slaughter ordered by the RSHA chief of the remaining 60,000 in Mauthausen and environs, but four days later Swiss ICRC delegate Louis Haeflinger heard from *Obersturmführer* SS Guido Reimer about the Nazis' true intentions: 24½ tons of dynamite had been placed in a subterranean aircraft-construction hangar in Gusen to destroy the prisoners and the neighboring residents, "who knew too much," during the evening of May 5. On the morning of the scheduled operation Haeflinger and Reimer departed in an Opel to seek out American spearhead columns reported to be in the area. The U.S. commanding officer, joined by three tanks and three armored cars, received orders to return immediately with them. The audacious bluff secured the camp's liberation.[105]

Less than 48 hours later Eisenhower received Alfred Jodl's signature on Dönitz's behalf of the *Wehrmacht*'s unconditional surrender, Wilhelm Keitl repeating this in Soviet headquarters at Karlshorst on May 9. Himmler, finally realizing that he was lost, shaved off his moustache and fled Flensburg for the Elbe River. Brandt and a few of the remaining faithful accompanied the man now sporting a black eye patch and bearing papers in the name of Heinrich Hitzinger; Schellenberg had already departed for Denmark to seek a peaceful resolution of the German occupation of the Scandinavian countries. The British caught up with this small group on May 23 near Luneburg. As a doctor routinely examined him the same evening, the *Reichsführer* SS bit on a hidden phial of cyanide. Death came almost instantly. Two days later his body was buried close by in an unmarked grave.[106]

CONCLUSION

In a savage world that claimed six million of their people, some Jews understood that morality transcended man-made law. While established organizations like the JDC and the Swiss and Swedish Jewish communities hesitated to challenge current government policy, Recha and Isaac Sternbuch and Hilel Storch stopped at nothing in their heroic, near hopeless struggle to rescue European Jews during World War II. Kalmanowitz, Kotler, Tress, Bunim, Lewin, and their associates merited WRB director Pehle's postwar encomium: "for imagination and constructive ideas, for courageous programs, for ingenuity and singleness of purpose," the Va'ad HaHatsala "need bow to none." Across the Atlantic, HIJEFS's executive and the WJC's representative in Stockholm, using bribes, fictitious protective documents, smuggling of "stateless" refugees, relief parcels, and constant diplomatic intervention, served as distinguished exemplars of this fitting appraisal. And when the unparalleled slaughter of an abandoned people also required secret dealings with the likes of Musy, Kleist, and Hesse, these intrepid souls resorted to the insight of an old Yiddish maxim: "When one needs a thief, you take him off the gallows."[107]

Paradoxically, the foremost missionary of the Nordic gospel for whom Adolf Hitler's word was law, the high priest at the altar of the New Order who methodically, ruthlessly executed the Final Solution, was nevertheless also open to their respective intercessions. The leader of the Nazi elite guard, whose SS carried on their belts the motto "My Honor is My Loyalty," devoutly believed in his *Führer*'s manichean view of an uncompromising, universal struggle between the "Aryan" Germanic race and world Jewry. According to a sympathetically received memorandum from Heinrich Himmler to Hitler in May, 1940, the non-Jewish populations of eastern Europe were to be denationalized by means of selective murder and their reduction to a mass of toiling Helots. Germany had to witness, however, the complete removal of the Jews, as Hitler insisted in his earliest extant political statement, September 16, 1919. When, therefore, the Third Reich's expulsion efforts during 1933–41 failed to receive Allied encouragement, a program aimed at the total annihilation of European Jewry followed. Still, the *Reichsführer* SS never doubted the Nazi ideology's central postulate that "international Jewry" dominated the world of Germany's opponents. Accordingly, releasing Jews to the West in exchange for saving the Third Reich by a separate peace against Moscow seemed to promise the perfect approach, which he and most trusted subordinates Schellenberg and Brandt confidentially pursued with Musy, Kersten, and Bernadotte. At a time when other diehard murderers like Kaltenbrunner, Müller, and Eichmann avidly implemented the *Führer*'s designs against Jewry, Himmler risked his own life in the most remarkable meeting of the war, driving 80 kilometers to the Masur conference some hours after Hitler's birthday party in order to realize this incredible illusion.[108]

The leaders of the West, far more conscious of Jewry's scant international weight during the Holocaust, had no intention of even responding to the ethical imperative of saving innocent lives. Consistent procrastination over papers for those in Vittel and elsewhere, over the Adler-Rudel scheme to save 20,000 Jewish children, and over licenses to deposit funds abroad doomed thousands of men, women, and children. Reprisals, bombings, and fundamentally inconsequential ransom payments were all forbidden, the British particularly anxious not to support the Musy and Kersten *demarches*. SHAEF ignored the SS death marches, begun in mid-January 1945, completely. The American Joint Chiefs of Staff even refused the Va'ad HaHatsala's plea of March 16, 1945, for a warning against the Nazis' last-minute threat to kill all surviving Jews, arguing that "our position on this subject has been clearly indicated, and that any further statement along these lines might weaken the affect [*sic*] of previous statements"; an Allied warning, issued one month later under increasing public pressure, failed to mention "Jews." Prisoners of war, enjoying a much securer status than Jewish camp internees, got first priority regarding freedom transports and food packages from restrictive Switzerland. Even neutral Sweden, whose rescue record markedly surpassed that of any other government, chose to liberate only Scandinavians until Kersten's success and WJC prodding tilted the scales at the war's end in the Jews' favor.[109]

Given this scale of priorities, the Jewish tragedy during those years infinitely overshadows the bitter recriminations over rescue that were traded after the war. Saly Mayer did frustrate HIJEFS at the time, but the Sternbuchs' charge that his supply of press accounts to Becher ended further convoys beyond the Theresienstadt train must be measured against Musy's wish for publicity; against Schellenberg's Nuremberg testimony about the Free French broadcast that especially infuriated Hitler; and against the possibility (which McClelland noted at the time) that an empty-handed Becher, frustrated by Mayer's shrewd dilatory tactics, may have informed Kaltenbrunner on his own in order to discredit Musy's status as a negotiator and to maintain his own prestige. Storch and Kersten made the major overtures to Himmler, yet Masur's courageous trip, as Kersten wrote Günther a few days later, and Bernadotte's talks brought their entire activity full circle. Thanks to the humanitarianism of such as Philippe Bernardini, Felix Kersten, a few ICRC representatives, and Gösta Engzell—the only delegate at the 1938 Evian conference on German and Austrian "political refugees" who urged his colleagues to deal with "the problem of European Jewish emigration as a whole"—additional lives were saved. But these amounted to no more, borrowing a survivor's later phrase, "than a tear in the sea."[110]

"A nation of Jobs" became easy prey for the murderous Third Reich, no one desiring European Jewry in their "utter powerlessness," wrote Yitschak Katzenelson three months after arriving in Vittel. On April 18, 1944, he and remaining son Zvi were deported on the first of two transports to Drancy and eleven days later sent to history's greatest slaughterhouse at Auschwitz; left behind was an awesome 15-canto elegy in Yiddish, "The Song of the Murdered Jewish People." Joseph Goebbels had no quarrel with the poet's final agonized cry. For all of his delusions (shared by many in the fool's paradise that was Hitler's bunker) in the last weeks before emulating Hitler's suicide, the Nazi minister for propaganda and enlightenment most pointedly captured the stark truth on March 13, 1945: "No one can say with certainty which nations will be on the losing side and which on the winning at the end of the war; but there can be no doubt that the Jews will be the losers."[111]

Four days after Himmler took his own life, Zalman Grinberg echoed this reality in addressing the first organized activity of the Jewish survivors, a concert in St. Ottilien. Hitler "won the war against the Jews of Europe," declared the Kovno physician whom American troops had rescued from the two convoys sent out of Dachau on the evening of April 26, 1945. During the past month the 33-year-old Orthodox Jew and Zionist had been able to take over the former Nazi military hospital at St. Ottilien for his fellow Jews (this time accorded the anonymous designation by the Allies as "displaced persons"). This celebration of mutual liberation, Grinberg now reminded his listeners, was also a day of mourning: "We unlearned to laugh, we cannot cry any more; we do not understand our freedom: this probably because we are still among our dead comrades!" The more than 400 assembled silently rose that Friday afternoon to commemorate their people's martyrs, and a cantor intoned the traditional prayer for the dead, "El Maleh Rachamim."

The famed Kovno ghetto orchestra, most of whose members had survived the transports to Germany in mid-1944, began to play. Henye Durmashkin brought the audience to tears with a rendition of "I Long for Home" from the Vilna ghetto. A medley of ghetto Yiddish folksongs and Hebrew melodies from Palestine gradually transformed the mood to one of exhilaration. The concert ended with all present singing the Zionist anthem of hope, "Hatikva."[112] The *Sh'eirit HaPleita*, the name by which the "saved remnant" were to become known, determined to live.

Epilogue

"Believe the Unbelievable!"

ONE RESPECT IN WHICH the blackest of tragedies which we call the Holocaust defies historical analogy is that the victims have been taken to task for their own destruction. The dehumanizing process of any totalitarian regime, Bruno Bettelheim and Hannah Arendt contend, affects persecutors and victims alike. Thus the collaboration of the Jewish councils, a disintegration of personality in the ghettos and concentration camps, and the mindless resignation of a folk that went to its doom "like sheep to the slaughter." Raul Hilberg's pioneering analysis of the Nazi bureaucracy amply refutes Arendt's thesis that Adolf Eichmann and numerous others below him in the Nazi command structure took no initiative in making Europe *Judenfrei*. Yet even his massive volume postulates that the one group marked for complete annihilation during World War II was "caught in the strait jacket" of a four-millennia-old history that "always" reacted to force with "alleviation and compliance," and that the Jews consequently "plunged themselves physically and psychologically into catastrophe." Jewish experience, Edward Alexander has most recently argued, contributed to the fate of the Jews, for it harbors a "deep-seated unwillingness, ultimately, to credit the existence of evil."[1]

Such observations often are factually unreliable, are produced by the dubious gift of hindsight, and suffer from a failure of imagination. Their authors, fortunate not to possess an intimate awareness of what David Rousset termed *l'univers concentrationnaire,*[2] hazard oversimplified formulations where precise study is especially required. The circumstances that faced each *Judenrat* and community before and after actually comprehending the Nazi design of total murder, as well as the alternatives for rescue then present in and outside Germany's Fortress Europe, are crucial issues that call for examination. These specific questions should also be placed within the context of Jewish traditional values and of the war itself.

Any effort that seeks, while avoiding what Yehuda Bauer properly designates "mystification," to understand how the legions of the swastika attained their ultimate *raison d'être* must commence with the riddle of human perception, particularly as it operates in time of acute danger. Clinical analysis of behavior in *extremis* indicates that people facing an uncertain threat tend to deny its imminence. Human beings seek to reduce constant tension and actively avoid situations and information that would be likely to increase a feeling of unrelieved stress. The inability to make decisions follows as well, particularly since reaching judgment does not guarantee the reduction of "dissonance."[3] Disbelief and defense mechanisms that dull reaction prevail, especially where cues pointing to calamity are ambiguous and when a disaster-stricken population is uncertain about the means available for escape. And when people are finally devoid of hope, like French Huguenots in the St. Bartholemew's Day Massacre, Turkish prisoners drowned at Napoleon's order, and individuals confronting a hangman's noose or a terrorist's bullet, passivity is also commonplace.[4]

The behavior of non-Jews caught in the Nazi vise illustrates the same psychological responses. Occupied Europe, after all, provided both the administrative apparatus that made possible the invader's continued occupation and the labor force for Third Reich armament factories and large-scale industrial projects. There were no rebellions among the more than seven million foreign workers exploited in Germany itself, where few *Wehrmacht* members of military age could be found. The civilians wiped out in Lidice, Rome's Fosse Ardeatine caves, Oradour-sur-Glâne, and Bande did not resist their killers. Uprisings in major cities only began in Polish Warsaw and Paris during the summer of 1944—one year after the Warsaw ghetto revolt. "Poland is not yet lost as long as we live" resounds the first line of the Polish national anthem, yet her Gentile citizens and intelligentsia went without opposition to graves dug by their own hands. Millions of Soviet prisoners of war, notwithstanding much military experience and their slogan "We shall strike the enemy in his own territory," acted in similar fashion whether on the soil of Holy Mother Russia or in Auschwitz. So, too, did the British 2nd Battalion's Norfolk Regiment at Paradis, more than 70 American soldiers near Malmédy, and countless prisoners of war subject to the "Bullet Decree" in Mauthausen.[5]

Viewed in this context, what could have been expected of European Jewry under Hitler's heel?

Irrespective of various uncritical generalizations about their hereditary sensibilities, the march of history from the rise of Adolf Hitler in 1933 until the outbreak of world war six years later fully revealed the Jews as the outcasts of Western civilization. Buffeted by mounting antisemitism wherever they lived, Abraham's seed found possible havens firmly closed.

Nations outdid one another at the 1938 Evian conference in professing all good will while refusing entry to a people in its time of greatest need. The serene tenor of life went on for others, outwardly unruffled and complacent, but Jews everywhere could not escape the ominous implications of the Nuremberg laws, *Kristallnacht,* and Hitler's Reichstag declaration in January, 1939, concerning "the destruction of the Jewish race in Europe" in the event of global conflict. On the eve of September 1, 1939, Poland initiated a ruthless program to force out of her borders the largest concentration of Jews on the continent, while His Majesty's Government in England aimed to bar the most obvious available shelter, the Jewish national home in Palestine.[6]

Soon after the huge, finely tuned German war machine lunged eastward, the entire Nazi state apparatus began working with speed and in silence to resolve what it officially designated the "Jewish question." The head of the Security Police, Reinhard Heydrich, issued a "strictly secret" order on September 21 to all *Einsatzgruppen* chiefs that Jews be gathered into the larger cities as "the first prerequisite for the final aim." *Judenraete,* yellow star markings, expulsions from the Reich-Protektorat to the General-government, and ghettoization followed in the search for the so-called "Final Solution." The first mass killings—the last alternative in securing a *Judenrein* Europe, carried out by SS *Einsatzgruppen* immediately after the invasion of the Soviet territories in June, 1941— caught the Jews there completely unaware. Limited Jewish groups in Poland, isolated in sealed-off ghettos with no radio or telephone communication to a usually hostile outside world, grasped their true predicament only by the summer of 1942. During the past year and a half, for example, the Bund had sent "Aryan-looking" Jacob Celemenski from town to town, dispensing funds but also organizing delegations for a scheduled national conference in Warsaw. HeChalutz and other Zionist movements across Europe focused on retraining their youth for a better economic future.

The essential German ministries hitherto uninvolved in the program for total annihilation met covertly on January 20, 1942, in Berlin's Grossen Wannsee suburb to expedite it; not until December 17 did the Allies formally acknowledge the Reich's design. By August, 1943, an estimated four million Jews in eastern and western Europe were no more. *Reichsführer* SS Heinrich Himmler felt supremely confident that October in gloating before some district leaders that they were creating "an unwritten and never-to-be written page of glory" in Germany's history. The mass slaughter never stopped. Hungary, which had the last major Jewish community in Europe, lost more than 400,000 from her provinces between May and July, 1944. A year later the total number of dead reached six million.[7]

Deception, the most fiendish ingredient in accomplishing the Nazi murder plan, took an especially great toll. Heydrich's concentration order stated that Jews "have most decidedly participated in sniper attacks and plundering action," a pretext that later was amended to include the need to separate the natural disease carriers from clean "Aryans" and to provide the former with a kind of cultural-social autonomy. Before embarking on a full-blown catastrophe, the Nazis introduced the ghetto, yellow star, death from hunger and typhus, and the random bullet as part of a general effort to break the spirit. All these had been encountered by the Jews for generations, however. A Warsaw publication in 1940, for example, could therefore quite reasonably look to past Jewish heroism and suffering for some comfort in the present crisis. Amidst the shock involved in the constant shifting of walled-in boundaries, the brutal caprice of an ever-present armed guard, planted rumors, and abrupt "selections" for "labor" units, the enemy always offered the minutest ray of hope. A plethora of differently stamped exemption cards for work, assurances that only "foreigners" (followed by the sick and old) would be sent to special "Jewish territories," and improved living conditions after mass deportations all blinded the designated victims. The noble Jewish tradition of collective responsibility was perverted by the German moloch so as to hamper further any thoughts of resistance. Many a *Judenrat* member and young partisan alike struggled, as a result, with the agonizing possibility of heavy reprisals against the community for their actions in a world of permanent terror.[8] "Special treatment," "registration," "transport eastward," "hospital," "resettlement," and hundreds of other phrases also served to conceal the raw reality of diabolic intentions.[9]

The fine art of deceit continued to its fiery completion. "In transit to Bialystok" read the sign over a dummy train station, equipped with a ticket office and a hand-painted clock whose hands pointed to 3:00 for the next departure, as Jews alighted from jammed railroad cars before being driven brutally to Treblinka's gas chambers. A massive Star of David topped a building, called the "*Judenstaat*" by the executioners, which housed ten vaults restricted to one people alone. "Work Makes One Free" (*Arbeit Macht Frei*) greeted all eyes over the main entrance to Auschwitz, where many arrivals printed names and birthdates in bold letters on their suitcases, expecting to get these back. Postcards stamped "Waldsee," each reading, "I am well. I work and am in good health," had to be written on occasion to relatives back home. The strains of fine music, performed by an all-inmate orchestra, accompanied millions on their last walk past a landscaped garden leading to underground chambers. Zyklon-B gas was then delivered to simulated shower rooms in vans with Red Cross markings, and the condemned met their death with cakes of soap in hand.[10]

Under these circumstances, the first Jews who finally realized what

ultimately awaited European Jewry as a whole met with a staunch refusal to believe among their own people. Jewish leaders dismissed the
first news of Chelmno and other mass slaughter camps from Yehoshua
Aronson at the end of 1941 as atrocity propaganda; the head of the
Jewish councils in Upper East Silesia (Moses Merin) added that steady
jobs in German army workshops alone could save the Jews, while an
eminent Orthodox rabbi found traditional consolation in Psalm 23, verse
4: "Yea, though I walk through the valley of the shadow of death, I will
fear no evil, for Thou art with me." At about the same time, after
receiving testimony from some survivors of the first Ponary massacre,
listening to anti-Nazi *Wehrmacht* officer Anton Schmidt, and recalling
the grim prophecies of Hitler's *Mein Kampf,* Abba Kovner concluded
that the Jews of Europe faced total destruction; on January 1, 1942, he
drew up the first call for armed resistance. The United Partisans' Organization (FPO) in Vilna lost its leader, Yitschak Wittenberg, in a confrontation with that ghetto's remaining populace and the *Judenrat* chief six
months later, however; a revolt in "the Jerusalem of Lithuania" never
took place.[11]

FPO emissaries and a Chelmno survivor reaching the Warsaw ghetto
in early 1942 were not believed, while Jewish notables and party chiefs
meeting there that April resolved to wait and not let young "provocateurs" bring on harsh German retaliation. Told about Auschwitz-
Birkenau in September by a messenger from Sosnowiec, the Vienna
Judenrat responded: "*Unmöglich!*" A realistic appraisal only set in subsequent to the first mass deportations. One year later, after a handful of
weapons were obtained against the greatest of odds, militant rebellion
remarkably broke out across Poland.[12]

Even then, Jewish communities yet unscathed refused to give credence
to reports of complete destruction. The majority in Rumania, Bulgaria,
and Denmark discounted reliable information in 1943 that they faced
mortal danger. Receiving a letter that same year from Palestinian Jewish
representatives in Istanbul about the vast slaughter in Poland, a leader
of the Hungarian Zionist movement dismissed the news as mere propaganda, notwithstanding eyewitness accounts from Polish and Slovakian
Jewish refugees who had been living in Hungary since 1942. The Budapest *Judenrat,* quickly assured by Eichmann and others they had no
need to worry, did not believe an April, 1944, message from Bratislava's
Michoel Dov Weissmandel that Europe's last major Jewish center faced
deportation. Members of Zionist youth movements, operating from a
Judenrat office, reached the Hungarian provinces with warnings of
imminent disaster—to no avail. Transylvania Jewry, advised by a few of
its own leaders to attempt a crossing over the nearby border to Rumania,
also refused to assume the worst. Isolated politically and highly vul-

nerable to native antisemitism,[13] the disoriented Jews of Hungary boarded the cattle cars to Auschwitz denying the certainty of their journey's end.[14]

More decisive than the human response to disaster and German cunning in a hostile environment was European Jewry's natural inability to comprehend the irrationality of the Holocaust. Not that the victims refused to "credit the fact" that they had enemies capable of murder: history had provided them with an overabundance of persecutors. Could most go any further, however, than that heroine of *The Shop on Main Street* who cried out, in a final stab at recognition: "Pogrom!"? The closest parallel would have been the Turkish annihilation of Armenians during World War I, yet not all Armenians were then targeted for death, and, in any case, that act of genocide had receded from the memory of most Europeans by 1939. Moreover, as Emmanuel Ringelblum noted in his Warsaw diary after grasping Hitler's fanatical plan for the Jews, "History *does not* repeat itself. Especially now, now that we stand at the crossroads, witnessing the death pangs of an old world and the birth pangs of a new."[15] Now birth itself constituted the most heinous crime in the Third Reich canon, expiated only by death.

Lacking a complete analogy to draw upon, the Jews could view the enemy's emphasis on survival by work as entirely logical. After all, asked such different *Judenrat* leaders as Adam Czerniakow, Ephraim Barash, Jacob Gens, and Mordecai Chaim Rumkowski, would the Third Reich's military machine sacrifice thousands of valuable laborers, much less divert precious rolling stock for death transports, during the war? Indeed, the labor ghettos enjoyed the longest duration; it is moot whether the halt of the Russian advance during the summer of 1944 prevented the survival of thousands of Jews in Lodz, Kovno, and elsewhere.[16]

Incredulity also stemmed from a deeply rooted belief of many in the culture and conscience of the West. Assimilated Jews failed to fathom that the Germany of Kant and Goethe could be capable of humanly unimaginable barbarism. Communist party members were betrayed by the "comrades" with whom they had built up cities like Minsk or by the Soviet partisans in the forests of Byelorussia. Those especially who had taken part in the steady development over the past two centuries toward equality for all, thereby contributing to new Jewish welfare institutions, schools, synagogues, newspapers, movements, and communities across the European landscape, maintained their trust in liberty and humanism. Finally, the Jews clung to the noble but naive faith that if only the Allies knew, the death factories would cease their grisly operation. Alexander Donat spoke for them all, in writing after the war: "We fell victim to our faith in mankind, our belief that humanity had set limits to the degradation and persecution of one's fellow man." The abrupt shattering of this conviction for Czerniakow, the realization that all his liberal and reasonable defenses were illusions and that the Nazis planned to ship every one of "his" charges to Treblinka, led the idealistic head of the Warsaw *Judenrat* to take cyanide rather than sign the second deportation order in July, 1942. The transports rolled inexorably ahead.[17]

As for the West, which alone could have checked the tempo of Germany's Final Solution, its political leaders were also slow to grasp the singular nature of the Jewish catastrophe. Reports constantly reached London and Washington of Jewish suffering, but these were scattered and "atrocity" conjured up propaganda stories from earlier wars. Even after realizing that the Third Reich had made starvation a weapon of annihilation, public opinion agreed with Winston Churchill's publicly expressed conviction that "no form of relief can be devised which would not directly or indirectly assist the enemy's war effort." A research paper in January, 1942, for Great Britain's Royal Institute for International Affairs surveyed the future possibilities of European Jewish assimilation, "considerable economic stratification," and a "relative decline" in German areas; it offered no word, moreover, regarding the war's possible effects on east European Jewry. Government officials continued their policy of the previous decade to dampen news coverage about Jewry's plight and so avoid the charge of antisemites at home and abroad that the Allies were fighting a "Jewish war." Rumors conveyed through Jewish sources in Switzerland during the summer of 1942 of a Nazi plan to murder all surviving Jews "at one blow" and to use the corpses for soap and fertilizer, recalling British intelligence's admitted fabrication about a German "cadaver conversion plant" during World War I, were thus suspect. Deportation to Poland, both governments taken in by Axis propaganda, meant forced labor at the Nazi war front. This information suited prior expectations, much like American experts erred some months earlier regarding a Japanese attack in the mid-Pacific. Only confirmation from such groups as the Polish government-in-exile and the International Red Cross, as well as mounting publicity from Jewish and other organizations, after more than two million had already perished, led the Allies to declare in December that the perpetrators of this "bestial policy" would not escape retribution.[18]

Still, disbelief continued to the war's end. The chairman of the British Joint Intelligence Committee, upon receiving reports in July, 1943, of the use of gas chambers to murder the victims, asserted: "The Poles, and to a far greater extent the Jews, tend to exaggerate German atrocities in order to stoke us up." On July 11, 1944, Jewish Agency spokesman Moshe Shertok felt the need to point out, among other reasons for the bombing of the death installations, that such an act would "go far towards dissipating the incredulity which still persists in Allied quarters with regard to the report of mass extermination perpetrated by the Nazis." Indeed, that very day even the well-informed Churchill expressed his sudden shock at the massacre of Hungarian Jewry, particularly since, as he wrote his foreign secretary, "probably the greatest and most horrible crime ever committed in the whole history of the world" was being carried out "by scientific machinery, by nominally civilized men in the name of a great State and one of the leading races of Europe." The BBC refused to use an eyewitness account by its own correspondent in August, 1944, of *liberated* Majdanek, thinking the detailed story "a Russian propaganda stunt." As late as that December the American under secretary of war asked the World Jewish Congress's administrative secretary: "Tell me, do you really believe that those terrible things happened?" "One notable tendency in Jewish reports on this problem," noted an official of the Foreign Office's Refugee Department to his colleagues the following month, "is to exaggerate the numbers of deportations and deaths." It is not surprising that isolated Jewish survivors in Rumania, Belgium, and Greece refused to acknowledge the utter depravity of the Holocaust after their rescue.[19]

Official opinion, even when convinced of the facts, remained skeptical that publicity would have the desired effect. Repeated warnings, various quarters argued, tended to "debase the currency," might result in "increased maltreatment" to the victims, and aid Joseph Goebbels's propaganda that Jews abroad ran the Allied war. But in addition, as the *Reichskommisar* for the *Ostland* had observed to his superior in June, 1943, those hearing and reading the facts would not be prepared to give them credence. The Office of War Information did follow a policy of restraint, even attempting to hold up publication in November, 1944, of a report on Auschwitz-Birkenau by four Jewish escapees and one Polish officer on the ground that the American public would regard its contents as similar to World War I atrocity tales; as a result, the government's reliability on other information released concerning the war effort would be open to doubt. A Roper poll taken one month later indeed revealed that the great majority of Americans could not believe that millions of Jews had perished in the Nazi onslaught. The British and American people, concluded an official with SHAEF's Plans and War Division in early 1945, were still as a whole not willing to entertain the awful truth. His opposite number in the British Political and Intelligence Division agreed, adding that individuals who would be likely to respond to cruelty to a child or an animal in peacetime "will, after years of being told about brutalities, become anesthetized even to a Lublin."[20] War, after all, entails suffering, while the Holocaust beggared the imagination.

Even those who viewed the annihilation process first-hand found it difficult to internalize it as reality. Three Jews, officially visiting Belzec to examine rumors about the first big "action" from Crakow in March, 1942, witnessed that "very hectic work was taking place." Eichmann completely took in an International Red Cross delegation, on an inspection of Theresienstadt in June, 1944, with a specially built Potemkin-type village; the report of a second visit several months *after* the liberation of Auschwitz, where most of the camp's Jews had perished, accepted at face value the SS *Obersturmbannführer's* explanation that the Third Reich wished the camp to serve "as a practical experiment, on a small scale, for the future Jewish State to which a certain strip of land should be allotted after the war." Six Jehovah's Witnesses who lived by the side of the gas chambers and crematoria in Birkenau doubted their own eyes; on their return to Holland *during* the war, they, like others before them, were not believed. "How could it be possible for them to burn people, children, and for the world to keep silent?" agonized a young Elie Wiesel after being confronted with Auschwitz. "No, none of this could be true. It was a nightmare...."[21]

This psychological hindrance also affected Palestinian Jewry. As early as October, 1939, a meeting in Jerusalem of *chalutz* organizations projected the destruction of Poland's Jews as the first victims of "an awesome holocaust [*shoa ayuma*] which has engulfed the world." Yet a sustained study about the plight of European Jewry, published in Tel Aviv in September, 1941, failed to speak of systematic annihilation. One year later, three months after a Bund cable to London gave the first (underestimated) news about the slaughter of 700,000 Jews in Poland, an eminent Polish refugee wrote that "millions" were awaiting salvation. Jewish Agency officials continued to question Geneva reports of mass killings across Europe until survivors from Poland reached the Promised Land in mid-November, 1942, just when confirmation came from New York and London. Still, Palestinian emissaries to the Yishuv's rescue committee in Istanbul during the spring and summer of 1943 fully intended to send thousands of letters and parcels to old addresses in Poland. Isaac Gruenbaum, chairman of the rescue committee, asked Istanbul in June, 1944, if 150,000 Hungarian Jews had indeed been moved eastward, and if food packages could be dispatched there; after the war he had but one question of Hungarian Zionist Reszö Kastner: why did resistance not take place? The Zionist leadership never wavered to the war's end in publicly supporting the May, 1942, Biltmore program (all of Palestine as a Jewish state), although the millions for whom it was intended had obviously perished.[22]

American Jewish organizations were not immune either. Publications hesitated at first to print news of the death centers, and some persisted in writing of continued Jewish life in Poland. The Joint Distribution Committee refused to accept the argument that drastic measures, even if contravening government policy, should be taken. One Agudas Israel executive, opposed to this position, still pleaded for an Allied mercy ship laden with food and drugs to save "millions" in Poland—this on the eve of the Warsaw ghetto uprising. A memorandum to the Bermuda conference on refugees concurrently submitted by the World Jewish Congress, whose centers in New York and abroad also attempted a more radical program of rescue, unconsciously accepted German propaganda in asserting that transports to build fortifications at the Russian front took the heaviest Jewish toll. Most other groups, as epitomized by the umbrella-type American Jewish Conference of August, 1943, focused on the postwar relief and reconstruction of European Jewry. As in Palestine, life went on, despair giving way to resignation.[23]

Allied callousness toward the Jewish people reflected a different elementary failure of perception. Having at first misjudged the dimensions of the Holocaust, London and Washington continued to deny Jewry the sense of communal distinction that had accounted for its mysterious survival these past 4,000 years. Heir to the Enlightenment's emphasis on personal freedom and the good inherent in all human beings, the West concluded that according the one people lacking national sovereignty special consideration as an independent entity would mean the vindication of Hitler's philosophy of *das Volk*. Not by accident did Secretary of State Cordell Hull take the occasion of the Balfour Declaration's twenty-fifth anniversary to declare that the postwar world should ensure Jews the full rights of citizens everywhere, a view eagerly applauded by a British government in retreat from its previous pledge of 1917 to establish a Jewish national home in Palestine. Paradoxically, this meant, in point of fact, that the unique fate of Jewry was either concealed under "Poles," "Belgians," etc., or refused sympathy because Jews were classified as "enemy aliens" when found in countries loyal to the Axis.[24] In either instance Hitler—who thought otherwise—secured his primary objective.

Thus it never occurred to the Anglo-American Alliance that European Jewry, like other peoples opposed to the Third Reich, should be assigned any role in the general war strategy. Greeks would obtain relief to avert famine, Poles and Czechs arms for resistance, but not Jews. French youngsters in very impressive numbers could be spirited to safety across the Pyrenees, but not a marked people to Spain and Turkey. Tens of thousands of Yugoslavs and Greeks received a cordial welcome in Middle East refugee camps, yet HMG continued the draconian 1939 White Paper throughout the hostilities for those most needing their national and accessible homeland. Worried lest the Third Reich's leadership "embarrass" the Allies by "flooding" them with unwanted Jews, the two major Western powers sought a joint declaration on Palestine to quash public agitation over that haven in the war years, and mutually consented not to alter their respective limited immigration quotas. (Enemy prisoners fared far better: boats were found to ferry some 430,000 to camps in the United States during the world conflict.) Not a word of the infamous SS death marches appeared in SHAEF directives or in the Western press. The Intergovernmental Committee on Refugees, the British Cabinet Committee on the Reception and Accommodation of Refugees, the Bermuda conference on refugees, and the War Refugee Board all omitted mention in their titles of the one group for which each had been principally created; rarely did Allied statements refer to the persecution of the Jews. For most of World War II, these officially designated nonpersons did not fare better with self-professed guardians of humanitarianism and morality like the International Red Cross and the Vatican, or with the neutral governments. Moscow ignored the entire matter.[25]

Only one Jewish battalion and a tiny parachute unit from the Yishuv saw action, and these grudging concessions from 10 Downing Street and 1600 Pennsylvania Avenue were not granted until toward the end of the war. Nineteen RAF de Havilland Mosquito bombers escorted by Spitfires successfully attacked an Amiens prison in "Operation Jericho" on February 18, 1944, to free nearly 100 members of the French resistance, but the crematoria and the railroad lines leading to them never became prime targets. Reprisals on German cities expressly for atrocities against Jews, the dispatch of funds for underground rescue, and delaying negotiations over the Eichmann "goods for blood" offer were all ruled out by the West. Responses to specific evacuation proposals concerning Jews in Transnistria, France, Rumania, Bulgaria, and Hungary were not commensurate with the urgent need. Szmul Zygielbojm's suicide, meant to move Churchill, Franklin Roosevelt, and the free world to action in mid-1943, went unheeded. FDR fled from 400 Orthodox rabbis who marched on Washington that October; the British prime minister avoided World Zionist Organization president Chaim Weizmann. Instead, to defeat the enemy and have the Jews return to their European "homes" after the war served as the fixed philosophy for the duration.[26] Alas, that policy proved bankrupt for a powerless people.

A few courageous souls attempted to shatter the Allied conspiracy of silence, as well as the prevailing illusion that nothing could be done. Near insuperable difficulties, analyzed in the preceding chapters, confronted various Jews and Gentiles who responded to the cry of conscience. The Babylonian Talmud prescribes their reward: "Whosoever saves a single Jew, Scripture ascribes it to him as though he had saved an entire world." Yet these individuals' valiant race against calculated mass-production death wrested only limited successes. Killers and indifferent bystanders, by depersonalizing the Jews of Europe, marked these innocents for doom. Hitler, Himmler, Eichmann, Antonescu, Horthy, and others of such ilk believed with apocalyptic certainty that a demonic international Jewry controlled Germany's opponents; the West, in whose councils the stateless Jews commanded no political leverage, consigned the Third Reich's primary victim to one category: expendable.[27] Behind the mask called twentieth-century civilization, as a consequence, countless more worlds were destroyed.

THEREAFTER

Buchenwald, liberated by Combat Team A of the U.S. Army's 6th Armored Division on April 11, 1945, at last allowed mankind to peer into the abyss that had ultimately claimed these six million human beings. Stark horror gripped the parliamentary and congressional missions, soon visiting the camp at the invitation of SHAEF commander Dwight D. Eisenhower, which testified about "the organized crime against civilization and humanity" and "the lowest point of degradation to which humanity has yet descended." Edward R. Murrow's terse live radio broadcast—"There were two rows of bodies stacked up like cordwood. They were thin and very white"—and a film of bulldozers pushing heaps of dead naked bodies like refuse into a pit shocked people everywhere. The holder of the Keys of St. Peter, who had moved so cautiously to save the Jews, tried to distinguish between a minority of war criminals and a docile, deluded majority of the Germany nation (at least 50 percent Catholic), reported Great Britain's delegate to the Holy See. Eisenhower's son later recalled that it was "impossible actually to believe that what one was seeing was real," just as the distances between galaxies escape full appreciation. Some Polish Jews in Buchenwald even wrote to relatives, long since victims of the Final Solution, asking to look after their affairs and obtain from Gentile neighbors the keys to prewar dwellings.[28]

A barrage of graphic, first-hand accounts from across the blood-soaked soil of Europe could not be denied for long, however. Richard Crossman, then deputy director of SHAEF's Psychological Warfare Division, expressed the sudden transformation of attitudes: "Though we had heard and reported many stories of Nazi massacres of Jews and Slavs, we had never believed in the possibility of 'genocide.' . . . Now we were to realize that our propaganda had fallen far behind the truth." Few had shared Edgar Snow's publicly articulated vision in October, 1944, grasped after his inspecting Majdanek, of the diabolic system which "for the first time made a totalitarian industry out of the reduction of the human being from an upright ambulatory animal to a kilogram of gray ashes." So intense was the trauma that war correspondent Murrow, on reaching Dachau in early May, 1945, began a memorable broadcast with the words, "I pray you will believe me."[29]

The human mind slowly awakened to the reality of the Holocaust after V-E day. The Nuremberg, *Einsatzkommando,* and Eichmann trials, among others, revealed beyond doubt that the Oxford English Dictionary's illustration, printed in the year of Hitler's ascension to power, that "Louis VII once made a holocaust of thirteen hundred persons in a church" would no longer suffice. Man now could not help but "believe the unbelievable!," as the Polish underground frantically cabled London during the summer of 1942.[30] The same liberals who reassuringly thought that Adolf Hitler could be placated in the 1930s now had to grapple with the existence of evil incarnate, as well as their own fundamental inaction at a time when men, women, and children pleaded for the sacred breath of life. This catastrophe is, therefore, far more than the sum of its victims.

A methodical German fervor to destroy not matched by an Allied will to save carried out the inconceivable. In January, 1944, Arthur Koestler warned about the current disbelief in the Nazi *Endlösung*: "A dog run over by a car upsets our emotional balance and digestion; three million Jews killed in Poland cause but a moderate uneasiness. . . . We are unable to embrace the total process with our awareness; we can only focus on little lumps of reality." He should have added that indifference to deeds of barbarism also stemmed from Western civilization's gradual loss of the sense of solidarity.[31] A slow decay of conscience took place in the world before and while the storm clouds of war rolled across Europe. Without that loss of a sense of certain decencies, the Jews, many of whom resisted Nazi attempts at dehumanization and miraculously adhered to their basic values *de profundis,*[32] would not have gone abandoned into the night. Christianity and Western humanism avoided the moral imperative to try to save an innocent people, including 1,500,000 children who perished, and through their silence became accomplice to mass murder. The kingdom of barbed wire and ashes, as a consequence, enjoyed an unbridled reign.

Mankind has forgotten too soon. "Something terrible had fallen like a meteorite into history," as Abba Kovner expressed it years later, when the Holocaust showed the whole world that the blood of a people could be shed with impunity. The seeker after an etiology for modern-day genocides in Tibet, Bangladesh, Biafra, Paraguay, Burundi, parts of southeast Asia, as well as the most recent grave threat to Jewish existence in Israel during October, 1973, should scrutinize Babi Yar, Sobibor, and the diaries of the *Sonderkommando*. The post-Auschwitz recognition of what Emil Fackenheim has denominated "radical evil" must, in turn, be a guide to radical humanist action. Only thus can the victims be snatched from oblivion and complacency give way to personal commitment. Once and for all, the calamitous fallacy that what happens in one part of the globe is not another's affair must be shed, lest one day a brother's keeper be again found wanting in the face of extremity. The madness of an escalating arms race that currently casts a lengthening shadow of omnicide—the transformation of our planet into a universal nuclear crematorium—mandates that active compassion which flows from mutual need replace the crime of indifference.[33]

The cancer of bestiality is the concern of us all, and the infinite preciousness of life requires daily affirmation. *The Plague,* one of the first artistic renditions of the years of France's occupation under the Nazi jackboot, sounded this quintessential lesson of the Holocaust unequivocally in June, 1947. Albert Camus's allegory contains a passage that might well serve as the epitaph for European Jewry's fate during World War II:[34]

> Sometimes at midnight, in the great silence of the sleep-bound town, the doctor turned on his radio before going to bed for the few hours' sleep he allowed himself. And from the ends of the earth, across thousands of miles of land and sea, kindly well-meaning speakers tried to voice their fellow-feeling, and indeed did so, but at the same time proved the utter incapacity of every man truly to share in suffering that he cannot see. "Oran! Oran!" In vain the call rang across oceans, in vain Rieux listened hopefully: always the tide of eloquence began to flow, bringing home still more the unbridgeable gulf that lay between Grand and the speaker. "Oran, we're with you!" they called emotionally. But not, the doctor told himself, to love or to die together—"and that's the only way. They're too remote."

Therein, as well, lies the key to our own *human* survival.

Notes

Abbreviations Used in the Notes

AJC	American Jewish Committee Archives, New York
BD	Board of Deputies of British Jews Archives, London
BGA	David Ben Gurion Archives, Sde Boker, Israel
CAB	Cabinet Papers
CO	Colonial Office Papers
CZA	Central Zionist Archives, Jerusalem
FDRL	Franklin D. Roosevelt Library, Hyde Park, N.Y.
FO	Foreign Office Papers
FRUS	*Foreign Relations of the United States*
HA	Hadassah Archives, New York
Hag. MSS	Hagana Archives, Tel Aviv
IMT	*Trial of the Major War Criminals before the International Military Tribunal*, 42 vols. (Nuremberg, 1947–49)
JAEJ	Jewish Agency Executive Jerusalem
JAEL	Jewish Agency Executive London
JDC	American Jewish Joint Distribution Committee Archives, New York
JOMER	*Jewish Observer and Middle East Review*
JTA	*Jewish Telegraphic Agency Daily News Bulletin*
LC	Library of Congress, Washington, D.C.
MA	Moreshet Archives, Givat Chaviva, Israel
MD	Henry Morgenthau, Jr., diaries, FDRL
MPD	Henry Morgenthau, Jr., presidential diaries, FDRL
NA	National Archives, Washington, D.C.
PREM	Premier MSS
PRO	Public Record Office, Kew, England
SD	Records of the State Department, NA
SM	Saly Mayer MSS
Tress MSS	Michael Tress MSS, Agudath Israel of America Archives, New York
UJA	United Jewish Appeal Archives, New York
VH	Va'ad HaHatsala MSS, Yeshiva University, New York
WA	Chaim Weizmann Archives, Rechovot, Israel
WJC	World Jewish Congress Archives, New York
WJCL	World Jewish Congress, British section, Archives, Institute of Jewish Affairs, London

WO   War Office Papers
WRB   War Refugee Board MSS, FDRL
YV   Yad Vashem Archives, Jerusalem
ZA   Zionist Archives and Library, New York

Preface

1. Elie Wiesel, *One Generation After* (New York, 1970), pp. 46–47. Even George Steiner's metaphor of "hell on earth" is inadequate. See the observations of Lawrence Langer and Emil Fackenheim in Alvin H. Rosenfeld and Irving Greenberg, eds., *Confronting the Holocaust* (Bloomington, Ind., 1978), pp. 46, 106.

2. Raul Hilberg, *The Destruction of the European Jews* (New York, 1973 ed.); Philip Friedman, *Roads to Extinction: Essays on the Holocaust,* ed. Ada J. Friedman (New York and Philadelphia, 1980); Lucy S. Dawidowicz, *The War against the Jews, 1933–1945* (New York, 1975). For previous studies on different aspects of the bystanders' conduct, see the bibliography.

Chapter 1—The Struggle for an Allied Jewish Fighting Force

1. Weizmann to Chamberlain, Aug. 29, 1939, WA. The League of Nations mandate for Palestine, assigned by the major Allies to Great Britain in 1920, recognized the Jewish Agency as representing the Jewish people on all matters concerning the Jewish homeland there.

2. Yehuda Bauer, *From Diplomacy to Resistance: A History of Jewish Palestine, 1939–1945* (Philadelphia, 1970), p. 212.

3. Ibid., pp. 47–48; Ben Gurion in *JOMER,* Aug. 30, pp. 10-12, and Oct. 25, 1963, pp. 16–18; Goldman to Brandeis, Sept. 5, 1939, 53, Robert Szold MSS, ZA.

4. Chamberlain to Weizmann, Sept. 2, 1939, WA.

5. Ben Gurion in *JOMER,* Nov. 1, 1963, pp. 20–23. Ben Gurion quickly realized that only the reality of increased power, particularly expressed in immigration and Jewish armament in Palestine, might sway the British in the Yishuv's favor. Ben Gurion diary, Sept. 22, 1939, BGA.

6. Moshe Sharett, *Yoman Medini,* 4 (Tel Aviv, 1974): 331–38, 343; Bauer, *Diplomacy,* pp. 81–82; Bernard Joseph, "Memo on Palestine," Jan., 1941, Jewish Agency confidential 1939 files, ZA.

7. Ben Gurion in *JOMER,* Dec. 20, 1963, p. 18; Jacob Lifschitz, *Sefer HaBrigada HaYehudit* (Tel Aviv, 1947), p. 20; Shertok report, Oct. 9, 1939, American Jewish Conference files, HA; Sharett, *Yoman Medini,* 4:436–38; Yitschak Lamdan, ed., *Sefer HaHitnadvut* (Jerusalem, 1949), pp. 39, 41–42.

8. Weizmann-Halifax talk, Sept. 18, and Weizmann-Churchill talk, Sept. 19, 1939, WA; memo, Sept. 26, 1939, JAEL, WA; JAEJ, Oct. 22, 1939, CZA. For more on Wingate's stance, see Christopher Sykes, *Orde Wingate, a Biography* (Cleveland, 1959), pp. 206-9, 219–20; Weizmann notes, Oct. 24, 1939, WA.

9. Sharett, *Yoman Medini,* 4: 364, 368; *The Autobiography of Nahum Goldmann: Sixty Years of Jewish Life* (New York, 1969), pp. 187-88; Goldmann to

Wise, Oct. 4, 1939, American Jewish Congress 1939 file, Louis Lipsky MSS, New York.

10. ZOA-Hadassah meeting, Sept. 9, 1939, Rose Jacobs MSS, HA; ZOA conferences with Hull and Lothian, Sept. 11, 1939, 112, R. Szold MSS.

11. MacMichael to MacDonald, in reply to Sept. 2, 1939, FO 371/23239, PRO; MacMichael-Ben Gurion-Shertok talk, Sept. 26, 1939, CO 733/406/75872/12, PRO.

12. Shertok-MacDonald talk, Oct. 11, 1939, 112, R. Szold MSS; Sharett, *Yoman Medini,* 4: 417-18; meeting Oct. 19, 1939, CAB 65, PRO; Gabriel Cohen, *Churchill U'Sheailat Eretz Yisrael, 1939-1942* (Jerusalem, 1976), pp. 27-28.

13. Ben Gurion in *JOMER,* Nov. 8, 1963, pp. 16-19; Barker memo, Nov. 2, 1939, in Luke to Baggallay, Nov. 13, 1939, FO 371/23251, PRO; MacDonald-Shertok talk, Oct. 20, 1939, American Jewish Conference file, HA; Weizmann-Ironside interviews, Oct. 30 and Nov. 14, 1939, WA. The sentences were lowered to 16 months' imprisonment. Bauer, *Diplomacy,* p. 101.

14. Ben Gurion in *JOMER,* Nov. 15, 1963, pp. 19-20; Bauer, *Diplomacy,* pp. 85-86; Weizmann-Shertok-MacLeod talk, Nov. 16, 1939, WA; Sharett, *Yoman Medini,* 4: 500, 523; Weizmann to Ironside, Dec. 1, 1939, WA.

15. Ben Gurion in *JOMER,* Nov. 15, p. 22 and Nov. 22, 1963, pp. 15-17; Weizmann-Wavell talk, Dec. 8, 1939, WA; Halifax-Weizmann talk, Dec. 18, 1939, FO 371/22983, PRO; Halifax to Weizmann, Dec. 19, 1939, WA; Sharett, *Yoman Medini,* 4: 535-36; meeting, Dec. 1, 1939, 216A/16, WJC; Lamdan, *Sefer HaHitnadvut,* pp. 39-40, 53-96. Leading American Zionists also had decided to oppose a Jewish legion, irrespective of their country's neutrality laws, out of fear of contributing to "tremendous agitation" then current against Jews as "war mongers." Schultz to Goldmann, Nov. 6, 1939, 214A, WJC.

16. Cohen, *Churchill,* pp. 29, 56-61; GOC-in-Chief, ME, to WO, Feb. 2, 1940, FO 800/13, PRO; *New Judea,* Mar.-Apr., pp. 86-118; protests of Mar. and Apr., 1940, L 22/91, CZA; Yehuda Slutsky, *Sefer Toldot HaHagana,* vol. 3: *MiMa'arach LeMilchama* (Tel Aviv, 1972), pp. 125-32.

17. Winston S. Churchill, *The Second World War: Their Finest Hour* (New York, 1977 ed.), pp. 541, 141, 149; Lloyd to Churchill, May 22 and June 27, 1940, FO 371/24566, PRO; Ben Gurion in *JOMER,* Dec. 13, 1963, pp. 15-17; Bauer, *Diplomacy,* pp. 106, 87-89; visit to Lothian, June 20, 1940, Isidor Breslau MSS, Washington, D.C.; Montor to Kaplan, June 25, 1940, Eliezer Kaplan MSS, ZA; JAEL, Aug. 9, 1940, CZA. At the same time Churchill killed the Colonial and Foreign offices' support of a secret offer from Iraqi Foreign Minister Nuri Said to have HMG begin implementing the White Paper's constitutional clause in exchange for Iraqi support for the Allied cause, with a public declaration for full implementation after the war. Cohen, *Churchill,* pp. 63-73.

18. JAEL, Sept. 9 and 18, Oct. 16, 1940, Z4/302/24, CZA; Leonard Mosley, *Gideon Goes to War* (New York, 1955), pp. 89-92; N. A. Rose, ed., *Baffy: The Diaries of Blanche Dugdale, 1936-1947* (London, 1973), pp. 174-78; Lloyd to Weizmann, Oct. 17, 1940, WA; Thompson to Churchill, Jan. 23, 1941, and Churchill's note, PREM 4, 52/5/II, PRO; JAEJ, Feb. 16, 1941, CZA.

19. Haining to Shuckburgh, Aug. 22, 1940, and to Moyne, Feb. 8, 1941, WO

32/8502, PRO; MacMichael to Lloyd, Nov. 12, 1940, FO 371/24565, PRO; Ben Gurion in *JOMER,* Dec. 20, 1963, p. 19.

20. Wavell to WO, Feb. 26, and Churchill to Moyne, Mar. 1 and 4, 1941, PREM 5, 51/9/II, PRO; Ch. 2; Moyne to Weizmann, Mar. 4, and Weizmann to Moyne, Mar. 6, 1941, WA; Amitzur Ilan, "HaMinimax VeOrmat HaHistoria," in Yosef Gorni and Gedalia Yogev, eds., *Medina'i Beltot Mashber, Darko Shel Chaim Weizmann BaTenua HaTsiyonit, 1900–1948* (Tel Aviv, 1977), p. 153, n. 22. The British discriminated against the 1,600 "Palestinians" in their subsequent retreat from Greece to Crete in May, and these Jews fell into German hands. Bauer, *Diplomacy,* p. 126.

21. Bauer, *Diplomacy,* pp. 153–62; Robert Stephens, *Nasser: A Political Biography* (New York, 1971), ch. 2; Moyne to Weizmann, Aug. 28, 1941, WA; Lyttleton to Eden, Aug. 9, 1941, S 25/1555, CZA; Weizmann to Churchill, Sept. 10, 1941, WA; Margusson to Moyne, Sept. 22, 1941, WO 32/9502, PRO; Moyne memo, Sept. 30, 1941, PREM 4, 52/5, I–II, PRO. At this time, Moyne favored east Prussia and Madagascar as places for large-scale Jewish settlement after the war. Moyne–Ben Gurion talk, Aug., 1941, BGA; Weizmann to Moyne, Oct. 20, 1941, S 25/7569, CZA.

22. Moyne to Weizmann, Oct. 15, 1941, WA; minutes of delegation's talk, Oct. 17, 1941, WO 32/9502, PRO; *Palcor,* Nov. 10, 1941; *JTA,* Nov. 26, 1941; ex-Mufti diary entry, Nov. 26, 1941, Virginia Gildersleeve MSS, Special Collections, Columbia University, New York; London *Jewish Chronicle,* Nov. 14, 1941.

23. Ben Gurion in *JOMER,* Feb. 21, 1964, pp. 20–21; meeting, Mar. 11, 1941, Minutes, BGA; ECZA minutes, May-June, 1941, ZA; Ben Gurion memo, "Outlines of Zionist Policy," Oct. 17, 1941, WA.

24. Jabotinsky to Chamberlain, Sept. 4, 1939, FO 371/23250, PRO; Jabotinsky-MacDonald talk, Sept. 6, 1939, FO 371/23242, PRO; Vladimir Jabotinsky, *The Jewish War Front* (London, 1940; later reprinted as *The War and the Jews,* New York, 1942); FO 371/24566, PRO; Jabotinsky to Czech foreign minister, Aug. 1, 1940, Box 2, NZO U.S. files, Metsudat Ze'ev, Tel Aviv. The Zionists turned down Jabotinsky's plan to meet the crisis facing their people with the formation of a World Jewish Committee. Meeting, May 28, 1940, ECZA files, ZA.

25. Interviews with the author: Hillel Kook, June 22, 1972, and Samuel Merlin, Mar. 27, 1972; Bergson to Silver, Apr. 10, and to Wise, May 7, 1941, Hebrew Committee of National Liberation MSS, Metsudat Ze'ev; Monty N. Penkower, "In Dramatic Dissent: The Bergson Boys," *American Jewish History* 70 (Mar., 1981):282–85; Yitshaq Ben-Ami, *Years of Wrath, Days of Glory* (New York, 1982), pp. 213–24, 241–44.

26. Pierre Van Paassen, "World Destiny Pivots on Palestine," *New Palestine,* Dec. 12, 1941, pp. 9–10; Kook interview; Bergson to Halpern, Apr. 9, 1942, Box 26-40, Committee for a Jewish Army MSS, Metsudat Ze'ev; Greenberg to Brodetsky, Nov. 30, 1942, Selig Brodetsky MSS, AJ 3/165, Mocatta Library, London; Committee for a Jewish Army MSS, Metsudat Ze'ev.

27. Diary, Nov. 28, 1941, BGA; Ben Gurion to Locker, Jan. 4, 1942, S 25/41, CZA; Ben Gurion in *JOMER,* Apr. 3, pp. 16–18, Apr. 10, p. 18, and Apr. 24, 1964, pp. 17–19; *Extraordinary Zionist Conference New York, 1942, Stenographic Protocol,* ZA. For the deepening split between Weizmann and Ben Gur-

ion on this and other issues see Yosef Gorni, *Shutfut U'Ma'avak* (Tel Aviv, 1976), chs. 4-5. The rift actually began when Ben Gurion refused to accept the offer of a Jewish division because its 3,000 Palestinian Jews would have to leave for service anywhere at HMG's order. Diary, Sept. 11, 1940, BGA; JAEL, Sept. 18, 1940, Z4/302/24, and JAEJ, Feb. 16, 1941, both CZA.

28. Bauer, *Diplomacy,* chs. 3-5; Slutsky, *Sefer Toldot HaHagana,* 3:chs. 20-21. MacMichael also released 58 "illegals" from detention to produce hundreds of cannon in Persia for the British Army. When their services ended two years later, however, the high commissioner refused to admit them to Palestine; 30 had to return to Czechoslovakia, where they joined the Skoda works. Lifshitz, *Sefer HaBrigada,* pp. 34-36.

29. Ben Gurion to Casey, Apr. 15, 1942, Z5/1361, CZA; Shertok to Auchinleck, Apr. 17, 1942, Jewish Agency files, 16/3, ZA; Weizmann to Winant, Apr. 25, 1942, Box 30, John Winant MSS, FDRL; S 25/6005, CZA; Bauer, *Diplomacy,* pp. 219, 183-84.

30. Weizmann to Welles, July 2, 1942, and to Roosevelt, same date, and BJS note attached, Z5/1444, CZA; July 3, 4, and 7, 1942, vol. 5, MPD; July 7, 1942, vol. 547, MD; Weizmann-Roosevelt talk, July 7, 1942, Z5/1378, CZA; Frankfurter to Roosevelt, July 6, 1942, PPF 140, FDRL; Weizmann to Locker, July 15, 1942, WA.

31. Churchill to Cranborne, July 5, and Cranborne to Churchill, July 6, 1942, PREM 5, 51/9/II, PRO; Churchill message in *JTA,* July 23, 1942. Although the War Department was critical regarding a memorial service for Wingate, the prime minister spoke "warmly" in Cabinet of the "great loss" sustained by HMG at his death and entirely supported Wingate's proposal. Leopold Amery diaries, Apr. 3, 1943, London.

32. Cranborne to Grigg, July 15, 1942, WO 32/10258, PRO; parliamentary debate on Aug. 6, 1942, quoted in *New Judea,* Aug.-Sept., 1942, pp. 163-71; Secretaries' memo, Aug. 1, 1942, WP 42 (332), CAB 66, PRO; Lamdan, *Sefer HaHitnadvut,* pp. 97-131; Bauer, *Diplomacy,* pp. 220-21.

33. Bauer, *Diplomacy,* p. 191; Locker to Henderson, Nov. 11, 1942, Jewish Agency files, 16/3, ZA; Shertok to Pinkerton, Nov. 23, 1942, Correspondence, BGA; JAEJ, Dec. 13, 1942, CZA; Ben Gurion in *JOMER,* May 22, 1964, pp. 17, 19; Shertok-Gater et al., talk, Dec. 30, 1942, S 25/7566, CZA.

34. Murray to Hull, Aug. 5, 1942, 867N.01/1812 and 4/5, RG 59, SD; Halifax to Welles, Oct. 29, 1942, 867N.01/10-2942, SD; British embassy's Jewish army memo, n.d., Box 3045, Morris Lazaron MSS, American Jewish Archives, Cincinnati, Ohio; Pope to LaGuardia, Nov. 7, 1942, Box 2674, Fiorello LaGuardia MSS, New York City Archives, New York; Halifax to FO, Oct. 6, 1942, FO 371/31379, PRO; *New Judea,* Dec., 1942, p. 48.

35. Ch. 3; Shertok statement, Dec. 21, 1942, Box 1, Labor ZOA papers, YIVO Archives, New York; I. Beer, *Let the Truth Be Told,* 1 (Mar. 1, 1947), Box 16, Labor ZOA, YIVO Archives; ZOA Admin. Committee minutes, Feb. 21, 1943, ZA; British Ministry of War Information report, Mar. 11, 1943, Box 39, RG 28, United Nations Archives, New York; William Stevenson, *A Man Called Intrepid: The Secret War* (New York, 1976), pp. 377-78, 385-91; I. S. O. Playfair, *The Mediterranean and the Middle East,* vol. 2 (London, 1956); Joseph

B. Schechtman, *The Mufti and the Fuehrer* (New York, 1965), chs. 3 and 4. On Feb. 21, 1943, Shertok brought American Zionists the latest figures from Palestine; as against 21,000 Jews, about 8,000 Arabs had been recruited, while the proportion in the Palestinian population was then one Jew to two Arabs. The 8,000-Arab total included Arabs from Transjordan and Syria, with about half of this figure evaluated as "came and went." ZOA Admin. Committee minutes, ZA.

36. Wedgwood and Moyne clash in Commons, June 9, 1942, quoted in *New Judea,* May-June, 1942, pp. 122–27. The joint idea of the Jewish Agency and the Va'ad Leumi, in response to the Allied acknowledgment of the Holocaust, for a Jewish army consisting of stateless Jews to serve outside Palestine came to naught. Memo, Dec. 7, 1942, Correspondence, BGA. For an exhaustive analysis of the subject under discussion up to this point, focusing on events in Palestine and London, see Yoav Gelber, *Toldot HaHitnadvut,* vol. 1: *HaHitnadvut U'Mekoma BaMediniyut HaTziyonit VeHaYishuvit, 1939–1942* (Jerusalem, 1979).

37. Shertok report, Feb. 23, 1943, Jewish Agency files, ZA; Ben Gurion in *JOMER,* Jan. 6, 1954, p. 19; Joseph to GOC, ME, Mar. 5, 1943, Correspondence, BGA; Bauer, *Diplomacy,* pp. 267–68; Lamdan, *Sefer HaHitnadvut,* pp. 50–51; Va'ad HaPoel minutes, May 5–7, 1943, Histadrut Archives, Tel Aviv; JAEJ, June 13, 1943, CZA.

38. Monty N. Penkower, "The 1943 Joint Anglo-American Statement on Palestine," *Herzl Yearbook* 8 (1978):212–21; Middle East conference memo, May 19, 1943, FO 371/34975, PRO.

39. Casey, Attlee, Cripps, and Lyttleton memos, all in CAB 66, PRO; Ettel memo, Mar. 24, 1943, and addendum, reprinted in *Nation Associates* memo, June, 1948, Box 14, Clark Clifford MSS, Harry S. Truman Library, Independence, Mo.; chiefs of staff memo, July 25, 1943, quoted in Nov. 4, 1943, meeting, CAB 95/14, PRO.

40. Penkower, "1943 Joint Statement," pp. 221–33. Amery first broached the idea of a generous partition of Palestine for the Jews in a much earlier memo to Churchill. Amery to Churchill, Oct. 4, 1941, PREM 4, 52/5, PRO.

41. Ben Gurion in *JOMER,* Jan. 10, 1964, pp. 18–19; Golda Meir, *My Life* (New York, 1975), pp. 184–89; Jewish Agency to Linton, Aug. 12, 1943, S 25/1670, CZA; Shertok to Goldmann, Aug. 30, 1943, S 25/73, CZA; Slutsky, *Sefer Toldot HaHagana,* 3:176–80; *New York Times,* Oct. 7 and 8, 1943.

42. Jessie Lurie, "Guns in Palestine," *Nation,* Jan. 22, 1944, pp. 92–94; Slutsky, *Sefer Toldot HaHagana,* 3:181–87; Shertok-MacMichael talk, Nov. 17, 1943, Jewish Agency 1939 files, ZA; Jewish Agency to Weizmann, Nov. 19, 1943, S 25/1670, CZA; JAEL minutes, Nov. 26, Dec. 3, 1943, Z4/302/28, CZA.

43. Slutsky, *Sefer Toldot HaHagana,* 3:730–32, 774–76; Yoav Gelber, *Toldot HaHitnadvut,* vol. 2: *HaMa'avak LeTsava Ivri* (Jerusalem, 1981), ch. 3. The last-named concessions proved short-lived, however. Lamdan, *Sefer HaHitnadvut,* pp. 136–42.

44. *Political Report of the London Office of the Executive of the Jewish Agency, Submitted to the Twenty-second Zionist Congress at Basle, Dec. 1946* (London, 1946), pp. 37–38; Shertok to Locker, Sept. 13, 1943, Z5/1217, CZA; Slutsky, *Sefer Toldot HaHagana,* 3:664; JAEL, Oct., 1943, meetings, Z4/302/27, CZA; Churchill-Weizmann talk, Oct. 25, 1943, WA.

45. Bauer, *Diplomacy*, pp. 348, 311–23; chiefs of staff memo, Jan. 22, 1944, CAB 95/14, PRO; Goldmann to Shertok, Apr. 4, 1944, Z5/778, CZA; Joseph to Weizmann, Mar. 31, 1944, S 25/560, CZA.

46. Lifschitz, *Sefer HaBrigada*, p. 42; Weizmann to Grigg, Mar. 28, 1944, Correspondence, BGA; Shertok report, May 8, 1944, JAEJ, CZA; Grigg to Weizmann, June 21, 1944, WA; commanders-in-chief memo, May 2, 1944, CO 733/461/75872/II, PRO; Grigg memo, June 26, 1944, CAB 66, PRO.

47. Weizmann to Churchill, July 4, and Grigg to Weizmann, July 7, 1944, WA; Abba Eban, "Tragedy and Triumph, 1939–1949," in Meyer Weisgal and Joel Carmichael, eds., *Chaim Weizmann: A Biography by Several Hands* (London, 1962), pp. 272–73; Ch. 7; Lamdan, *Sefer HaHitnadvut*, p. 146.

48. Ch. 7; Churchill to Eden, June 29, 1944, PREM 4, 52/5/II, PRO; discussion, July 3, 1944 (86/44/1), CAB 66, PRO; Winston S. Churchill, *The Second World War: Triumph and Tragedy* (New York, 1962 ed.), pp. 590–91n.

49. British fears of Zionist political aims limited the entire program's potential ever since the idea of Jewish parachutists had been raised by the Jewish Agency in early 1943. Again, Churchill's sympathies went counter to those British authorities ultimately responsible for the decision, and the large-scale program failed to materialize. Bauer, *Diplomacy*, pp. 274–86; Zerubavel Gilad, ed., *Magen-BeSeter* (Jerusalem, 1952), pp. 193–97, 211–617; Slutsky, *Sefer Toldot HaHagana*, 3:ch. 32. For a related *dénouement* regarding the bombing of Auschwitz-Birkenau, see Ch. 7.

50. Churchill to Weizmann, Aug. 5, 1944, and Weizmann to Churchill, same date, WA; Grigg to Churchill, Aug. 6, 1944, PREM 5, 51/9, PRO; Grigg to Weizmann, Aug. 17, 1944, WA; Shertok to Ben Gurion, Aug. 24, 1944, Correspondence, BGA; meeting, Aug. 27, 1944, S 25/5092, CZA; agency-WO conference, Sept. 18, 1944, Hag. MSS; Lamdan, *Sefer HaHitnadvut*, p. 147; Bauer, *Diplomacy*, p. 349.

51. Shertok to Weizmann, Aug. 17, and Weizmann to Churchill, Aug. 5, 1944, WA; Churchill to Roosevelt, Aug. 23, and Roosevelt to Churchill, Aug. 28, 1944, PREM 4, 51/9/I, PRO; decision, Sept. 4, 1944 (116/44/6), CAB 65, PRO. At one point Weizmann even suggested that the brigade banner include the Union Jack in the upper left corner of the Jewish flag, "because it is our conviction that the future of the Jewish Nation is bound up with the British Empire." As the War Office objected, Shertok's original design for the Jewish flag alone prevailed. Weizmann to Churchill, Sept. 21, 1944, and addendum, PREM 4, 51/9/I, PRO.

52. *Political Report ... Basle*, p. 39; Great Britain, *Parliamentary Debates* (Commons), vol. 403, col. 474, Sept. 28, 1944.

53. Gelber, *Toldot HaHitnadvut*, 2:422–23, 431–32, 436–48; Weizmann to Churchill, Sept. 20, 1944, WA; Ben Gurion remarks, Sept. 24, 1944, Va'ada HaMerakezet, Histadrut Archives; Ben Gurion to Churchill, Oct. 1, 1944, S 25/7569, CZA; Lamdan, *Sefer HaHitnadvut*, pp. 148–49; *JTA*, Oct. 1, 1944.

54. Shertok to Silver, in AZEC exec. committee minutes, Oct. 12, 1944, ZA. The debate regarding the possibility of a Jewish force to serve outside Palestine's borders began immediately within the Yishuv and its leadership. JAEJ, Sept. 24, 1939, CZA; Bauer, *Diplomacy*, pp. 94–96, 174–78, 211–18; Gelber, *Toldot HaHitnadvut*, vol. 1.

55. Ch. 4; Penkower, "Bergson Boys," pp. 297–309; Halifax to FO, Aug. 24, Sept. 11, 1944, FO 371/40145, PRO; CO memo, Sept. 8, 1944, CO 733/461/75872, 14A, PRO; Pierre Van Paassen, *The Forgotten Ally* (New York, 1943). HMG's spokesman in Parliament, in ridiculing Strabolgi's continued insistence on a large Jewish army, could intimate publicly for the first time that a Jewish brigade might be in the offing. Strabolgi and Croft statements in Commons, July 4, 1944, quoted in *New Judea,* June–July, 1944, pp. 157–58.

56. Hoskins report, Apr. 20, 1943, Box 5, PSF confidential files, State Department, FDRL; Laski's remarks in JAEL meeting, Oct. 13, 1943, WA; Churchill to Bridges, Oct. 1, 1944, PREM 4, 52/5, PRO; Churchill, *Second World War,* 6:453; Great Britain, *Parliamentary Debates* (Commons), vol. 410, col. 1509, May 2, 1945.

57. Slutsky, *Sefer Toldot HaHagana,* 3:668–69, 797, and ch. 39; Lamdan, *Sefer HaHitnadvut,* pp. 950, 675–794; Lifschitz, *Sefer HaBrigada.*

58. Churchill to Ismay, Jan. 25, 1944, PREM 4, 51/11, PRO; Slutsky, *Sefer Toldot HaHagana,* 3:729; Eban, "Tragedy and Triumph," pp. 274–75, 277–79. According to the British official record, the total strength of the brigade at war's end stood at 4,021, of whom 3,170 were serving in Europe. The casualties: 33 killed, 157 wounded, and four missing in action. Great Britain, *Parliamentary Debates* (Commons), vol. 439, col. 1125, July 1, 1947.

59. Baxter to Halifax, Mar. 9, 1943, FO 371/35032, PRO; Ben Gurion in *New Palestine,* Oct. 27, 1939, p. 5; JAEJ, Oct. 22, 1944, CZA. These assumptions also colored British Ministry of Information statements about Palestine and Zionism. Weizmann to Bracken, Mar. 22, 1944, S 25/7569, CZA. For a classic example of this unbridgeable divide, see Ben Gurion—MacMichael talk, diary, Apr. 3, 1944, BGA.

60. Ben Gurion in *JOMER,* Jan. 10, 1964, p. 21; MacMichael to colonial secretary, in reply to Sept. 2, 1939, FO 371/23239, PRO; I. S. O. Playfair, *The Mediterranean and the Middle East,* 1 (London, 1954):17, 93.

61. Ben Gurion in *New Judea,* Aug., 1940, pp. 172–74; Ben Gurion in *Palestine and Middle East* 17 (July, 1944):123–24; Grigg comments in Commons, Aug. 21, 1940, quoted in *New Judea,* Aug., 1940, p. 175. And see Moyne–Ben Gurion–Weizmann talk, Oct. 23, 1941, quoted in Lamdan, *Sefer HaHitnadvut,* p. 47.

62. Facsimile in H. R. Trevor-Roper, *The Last Days of Hitler* (New York, 1947), p. 180. For Shertok's perception of this reality, see his incisive speech to the Jewish Brigade on the occasion of its disbandment. Lamdan, *Sefer HaHitnadvut,* pp. 950–57. It is estimated that, apart from the contribution of the Yishuv, some one and a quarter million Jews served in the Allied armies during World War II. Lifschitz, *Sefer HaBrigada,* p. 58n.

Chapter 2—The *Patria* and the *Atlantic*

1. *Palcor,* Nov. 22, 1940; Slutsky, *Sefer Toldot HaHagana,* 3:152–53.

2. Shertok diary, Nov. 10 and 17, 1940, S 25/10582, CZA; JAEJ, Nov. 18 and 21, 1940, CZA; Szold to Bertha, Nov. 21, 1940, file 1, Henrietta Szold MSS, HA. The 1939 White Paper limited Jewish immigration to Palestine to 75,000 until Apr. 1, 1944, thereafter only with Arab consent.

3. Ch. 1; Lloyd to MacMichael, Nov. 17, 1940, FO 371/25242, PRO; Weizmann to Lourie, Nov. 18, 1940, file 32a, Robert Szold MSS, ZA; Rose, *Baffy,* p. 178.

4. Monty N. Penkower, "Ben Gurion, Silver, and the 1941 UPA National Conference for Palestine: A Turning Point in American Zionist History," *American Jewish History* 69 (Sept., 1979):66-71; JAEJ, Feb. 16, 1941, CZA.

5. Lloyd to MacMichael, Nov. 9, 1940, FO 371/24565, PRO; Nov. 1, 1940, WP 40 (431), CAB 66, PRO; Lloyd to Churchill, Nov. 21, Martin to Seal, Nov. 21, and Martin to Eastwood, Nov. 22, 1940, all in PREM 4, 51/11, PRO; Churchill, *Second World War,* 2:592; MacMichael to Lloyd, Nov. 24, 1940, FO 371/25242, PRO.

6. *Sefer HaMa'apilim,* ed. Moshe Basok (Jerusalem, 1947), pp. 246, 250-60; Joseph report, Nov. 26, 1940, S 25/2631, CZA; Gershon A. Steiner, *Patria* (Tel Aviv, 1964), p. 204.

7. David Nemeri oral testimony, Hag. MSS; Munya Mardor, *Strictly Illegal* (London, 1964), pp. 74-75; Szold to Bertha, Nov. 28, 1940, file 1, H. Szold MSS, HA.

8. Avigur interview with Jordan S. Penkower, Nov. 17, 1977 (notes in the author's possession); Avigur to Mardor, Jan. 13, 1950, Hag. MSS. The claim that Katznelson knew of the sabotage plan is but conjecture. Anita Shapira, *Berl,* 2 (Tel Aviv, 1980):601. Avigur's later recollection (Dalya Ofer, "HaAliya-HaBilti Chukit LeEretz Yisrael BeTekufat Milchemet HaOlam HaShniya 1939-1942," Ph.D. dissertation, Hebrew University 1981, pp. 60-61) that he consulted with Katznelson and not Shertok does not square with the facts (see nn. 37 and 57 below).

9. Kahn to JDC, Mar. 15, 1938, Austria Genl., JDC; Herbert Rosenkranz, "The Anschluss and the Tragedy of Austrian Jewry, 1938-1945," in Josef Fraenkel, ed., *The Jews of Austria: Essays on Their Life, History and Destruction* (London, 1967), pp. 482-85; *JTA,* Mar. 16 and 17, 1938.

10. Testimony of Moritz Fleishman, Eichmann trial, Apr. 26, 1961, session 16 (copy at ZA); Israel Cohen report, May 1, 1938, Box 24/29, Zionist Organization files, ZA. For the Evian conference, see A. J. Sherman, *Island Refuge: Britain and Refugees from the Third Reich, 1933-1939* (London, 1973), ch. 5.

11. Rosenkranz, "Anschluss," pp. 486-90; Lauterbach report, Apr. 29, and Cohen report, May 1, 1938, Box 24, Zionist Organization files, ZA.

12. Martin Gilbert, *Exile and Return: The Struggle for a Jewish Homeland* (Philadelphia, 1978), pp. 196-97, 202; Shertok to chief secretary, May 8, 1938, Box 15/3, Jewish Agency files, ZA; Ehud Avriel, *Open the Gates!* (New York, 1975), p. 15.

13. Yehuda Braginski, *Am Choter El Chof* (HaKibbutz HaMeuchad, 1965), pp. 19-35, 43-44, 67, 77, 104, 106-7; Shertok testimony, Dec. 8, 1936, in Palestine Royal Commission, *Minutes of Evidence Heard at Public Sessions* (London, 1937), p. 99.

14. Chayim Lazar, *Af Al Pi, Sefer Aliya Bet* (Tel Aviv, 1957); Wolfgang von Weisl, "Illegale Transporte," in Fraenkel, *Jews of Austria,* pp. 165-72. The Austrian crisis and danger in eastern Europe led the NZO executive after the abortive Evian conference to shorten the time to one to three years. Jabotinsky memo, Oct. 15, 1938, 840.48 Refugees/848, RG 59, SD. For Perl's other activi-

ties in this connection, see William R. Perl, *The Four-Front War: From the Holocaust to the Promised Land* (New York, 1979).

15. Katz to JDC, June 10, and Jaretski diary, June 20, 1938, Austria Genl., JDC; Rosenkranz, "Anschluss," p. 487.

16. Rosenkranz, "Anschluss," pp. 491, 496–98; Gilbert, *Exile and Return*, pp. 203, 207; Ruth Aliav (Kluger) and Peggy Mann, *The Last Escape* (New York, 1973), p. 506; Kultusgemeinde report, Jan. 14, 1939, Austria Genl., JDC.

17. *Documents on German Foreign Policy, 1918–1945*, ser. D, 5 (Washington, D.C., 1950):904–5, 926–36; Benno Cohen testimony, Eichmann trial, Apr. 21, 1961, session 15, ZA; Rosenkranz, "Anschluss," p. 502.

18. Braginski, *Am Choter*, pp. 157–59; Avriel, *Open*, pp. 48–77; K. I. Ball-Kaduri, "HaAliya HaBilti-Chukit MeiGermania HaNatsit L'Eretz Yisrael," *Yalkut Moreshet* 8 (Mar., 1968):134–35; Ueberall to Storfer, Dec. 1, 1939, SM-31, JDC; Ofer, "HaAliya-HaBilti Chukit," pp. 226–247.

19. Gilbert, *Exile and Return*, pp. 236–39, 223; Braginski, *Am Choter*, p. 130; Michael Bar-Zohar, *Ben Gurion*, 1 (Tel Aviv, 1975):399–400; Avigur interview with the author, July 15, 1976.

20. *New Judea*, Sept., 1939, pp. 330–32, 336, 340.

21. Ibid., pp. 340–41. The full address can be found in *The 21st Zionist Congress* (Geneva, 1939) (in Hebrew), pp. 112–56, ZA; Aliav and Mann, *Last Escape*, pp. 220–47.

22. *New Judea*, Sept., 1939, pp. 346–47; Shapira, *Berl*, 2:580–82.

23. Aliav and Mann, *Last Escape;* Malka Ben-Shachar, *Masa Tiger Hill* (Tel Aviv, 1980); Gilbert, *Exile and Return*, pp. 242–45; Weizmann-MacDonald talk, Sept. 29, 1939, WA; Apr. 27, 1940, CO 733/426/75872/16, PRO; MacDonald-Shertok talk, Oct. 24, Nov. 24 and 29, 1939, all in file 112, R. Szold MSS, ZA.

24. Gilbert, *Exile and Return*, p. 245; memo, Jan. 17, 1940, 840.48 Refugees/2358, SD; the Marquess of Dufferin and Alva, Feb. 13, 1940, cited in *New Judea*, Feb., 1940, p. 59; Elchanan Oren, *Hityashvut BeShnat Ma'avak, Istrategya Yishuvit BeTerem Medina, 1936–1947* (Jerusalem, 1978), pp. 96–108. The Colonial Office took the lead in trying to check unauthorized immigration, even at the expense of international law. Leni Yahil, "Mivchar Teudot Britiyot Al HaAliya HaBilti-Ligalit LeEretz Yisrael (1939–1940)," *Yad Vashem Studies* 10 (1974):184–86.

25. Hilberg, *Destruction*, p. 138; national board minutes, Feb. 29, Oct. 8 and 17, 1940, HA. For the Kladovo-Darien affair as reflective of official Zionist ambivalence regarding *Aliya Bet*, see Ofer, "HaAliya-HaBilti Chukit," pp. 74–144. For Freier's difficulties with the Zionist establishment, see Recha Freier, *Let the Children Come* (London, 1961).

26. Penkower, "Bergson Boys," pp. 282–83; Millstein and Ussoshkin to JDC, Dec. 14 and 30, 1939, Czech Genl. Refugees, JDC; Spicer to Hecht, Jan. 20, 1941, Reuven Hecht MSS, Haifa; Lazar, *Af Al Pi*, pp. 402–35; Eri Jabotinsky, *Avi, Ze'ev Jabotinsky* (Tel Aviv, 1980), pp. 168–208; Ben-Ami, *Years of Wrath*, pp. 253–67.

27. Rosenkranz, "Anschluss," pp. 507–8, 510; diary, Nov. 30, 1939, BGA; *New York Times* and *JTA*, Feb. 29, 1940.

28. Rosenkranz, "Anschluss," p. 509; Frank testimony, Apr. 2, 1958, 01/227, YV; Beth-Or (Lichtheim) memo, Mar. 30, and Lichtheim to Caplan, Mar. 31,

1940, Jewish Agency confidential files 1939, ZA; Bernstein to Kaufman, Dec. 3, 1940, file 57, R. Szold MSS, ZA.

29. Yehuda Bauer, *My Brother's Keeper: A History of the American Jewish Joint Distribution Committee, 1929-1939* (Philadelphia, 1974), pp. 286-89; Bauer, *American Jewry and the Holocaust: The American Jewish Joint Distribution Committee, 1939-1945* (Detroit, 1981), pp. 147-51; SM-31, JDC.

30. Erich Steiner, "Zwei Jahrzeite nach der 'Patria,'" *Jedioth Chadashoth,* Oct. 25, 1960, Hag. MSS; Neuman to JDC Paris, Apr. 1, 1940, Czech Genl., JDC; SM-31, JDC; Loewenherz to JDC, May 20, and Storfer to Troper, July 10, 1940, Austria Genl., Emigration, JDC.

31. Rosenkranz, "Anschluss," pp. 508, 510; Troper to JDC, Dec. 11, 1939, Austria Genl., JDC; Ofer, "HaAliya-HaBilti Chukit," pp. 241-44; Frank-Wendel to Burg, June 11, 1940, SM supplement-56, JDC; Blum-Jakobson to Troper, July 11, and Schwartz to JDC, Oct. 25, 1940, Czech Genl., JDC. Otto Hirsch, *Reichsvereinigung* executive director who completed the transaction that made the transport possible, had participated in early 1939 in a conference of Jewish, Catholic, and Protestant representatives in Germany, where his colleague Dr. Julius Seligsohn predicted that "in the future an abrupt end will be put to the Jewish question." The minutes of that meeting ominously record that "Mr. Eichmann, who first handled the Jewish problem in Vienna and later on in Prague, is now in Berlin." Namier to Harvey, Nov. 2, 1939, FO 371/24085, PRO.

32. Ofer, "HaAliya-HaBilti Chukit," pp. 265-81; Popper to Rosenfeld, May 12, 1941, FO 371/29163, PRO; Jakobson-Blum report to JDC, Aug. 9, 1940, Czech Genl., JDC; *Milos* committee to Va'adat HaEzra, Oct. 4, 1940, Hag. MSS; 03/3290, YV.

33. *Sefer HaMa'apilim,* pp. 236-37; Aaron Zwergbaum, "Parshat Mauritius," *Yad Vashem Studies* 4 (1960):194-95; Jakobson-Blum report, Sept. 24, 1940, Czech Genl., JDC. For the *Pentcho,* see Boris Lawrence, "Sipur Shel HaOniya Pencho, 1940-42," *Yalkut Moreshet* 20 (Dec., 1975):35-50, and S 5/2664, CZA.

34. *Milos* committee, Oct. 4, 1940, Hag. MSS; Ofer, "HaAliya-HaBilti Chukit," p. 271; Steiner, "Zwei Jahrzeite"; *Sefer HaMa'apilim,* p. 236. Fully informed by British intelligence of these developments, HMG in London asked the high commissioners of Mauritius and Trinidad if they could absorb a few thousand Jewish illegal refugees, "probably" to include some enemy agents. Yahil, "Mivchar Teudot," pp. 188-89.

35. Bracha Habas, *Gate Breakers* (New York, 1963), p. 129; Joseph, "Memo on Palestine," Jan. 1941, Jewish Agency confidential 1939 files, ZA; *Sefer HaMa'apilim,* pp. 237-39; O-33/976, YV. A baby girl who had been born in Haifa port on Nov. 19 was returned with her mother by the British authorities to the *Patria.* Both survived. "Remember the Patria," *Jerusalem Post,* Nov. 27, 1970.

36. *Milos* committee, Oct. 4, 1940, Hag. MSS; Steiner, *Patria,* pp. 165-85; Leavitt to Herman, Nov. 23, 1940, MRD 1, 2/1, UJA.

37. Avigur interview with J. S. Penkower; Slutsky, *Sefer Toldot HaHagana,* 3:152-53; A. Zisling testimony and Sharett to Bloch, Mar. 28, 1962, Hag. MSS. Coincidentally, Shertok and Meyerov were brothers-in-law.

38. Mardor, *Strictly Illegal,* ch. 8; David Nemeri testimony, Hag. MSS.

39. Zwergbaum, "Parshat," pp. 195-201; *Sefer HaMa'apilim,* pp. 240-41; 03/2615, YV.

40. Joseph, "Memo," ZA; *HaOlam,* Dec. 5, 1940, p. 139.

41. Shertok-MacMichael talk, Nov. 27, 1940, S 25/2569, CZA; *New York Times,* Nov. 27, 1940.

42. *New York Times,* Nov. 27, 1940; JAEJ, Nov. 28, 1940, CZA. After the report became public years later, Sharett confirmed to Avigur that he had recorded it immediately after meeting with the high commissioner. Avigur to Slutsky, Dec. 2, 1958, 426, Hag. MSS.

43. Penkower, "Ben Gurion, Silver," pp. 71-72.

44. Ibid.; Ben Gurion remarks, JAEJ, Feb. 16, 1941, CZA.

45. Nov. 26 and 28, 1940, JAEL, Z4/302/24, CZA; Weizmann-Halifax talk, Nov. 27, 1940, FO 371/25242, PRO; Rose, *Baffy,* p. 179; Chaim Weizmann, *Trial and Error* (New York, 1949), p. 403.

46. Meeting, Nov. 27, 1940, CAB 65/10; Wavell to Eden, Nov. 30, 1940, PREM 4, 52/5; Churchill to colonial secretary, Mar. 1, 1941, PREM 5, 51/9/II; meeting Dec. 2, 1940, CAB 65/10; Churchill to Wavell, Dec. 2, and Wavell to Churchill, Dec. 3, 1940, PREM 4, 51/2, all in PRO. For Wavell's frustrating the formation of an Allied Jewish fighting force not long thereafter, see Ch. 1. A British military report confirmed Churchill's estimate, noting later that the effect on the Arabs of the *Patria* passengers' admission had been "remarkably small." Gilbert, *Exile and Return,* p. 250.

47. Nemeri testimony, Hag. MSS. Other factors were the British removal of some watertight bulkheads (in order to cram in more illegals), the passengers' seeking shelter below from fear of an air attack, and Wendel's decision to place more material on top of the explosive. S. Wilenski testimony, Hag. MSS; Sharett to Bloch, Mar. 28, 1962, Hag. MSS.

48. "Yizkor" proclamation, Nov. 28, 1940, Hag. MSS; Mardor, *Strictly Illegal,* pp. 77-78.

49. *Sefer HaMa'apilim,* pp. 274-78; reports of Dec. 13 and 14, 1940, S 25/2631, CZA; Bernard Wasserstein, *Britain and the Jews of Europe, 1939-1945* (Oxford, 1979), pp. 74-75; Zwergbaum, "Parshat," pp. 202-3. The oral testimonies of passengers aboard the *Patria* and the *Atlantic,* many of which later appeared in *Sefer HaMa'apilim,* were first published as a pamphlet entitled *Bivrit Ha'apala,* Apr. 23, 1941, Hag. MSS.

50. Zwergbaum, "Parshat," pp. 204-5; Yitschak Noy testimony, Hag. MSS; Wasserstein, *Britain,* pp. 75-76; 03/2376, YV. For lists of the deportees and the *Patria* victims, see memo, Mar. 26, 1941, S 25/2631, CZA.

51. Mapai executive meetings, Dec. 12, 15, and 25, 1940, Hag. MSS; Shapira, *Berl,* 2:601-3. For the first analysis of these deliberations, see S. B. Beit-Tsvi, *HaTsiyonut HaPost-Ugandit BeMashber HaShoa* (Tel Aviv, 1977), pp. 302-3.

52. Mapai executive meeting, and Golomb remarks, Dec. 25, 1940, Hag. MSS; Avigur to Mardor, Jan. 3, 1950, Hag. MSS; Avigur interview with J. S. Penkower. The Jewish Agency's official report to the 1946 Zionist congress gives the total of 257 dead. In Aug. 1953, a salvage operation on the *Patria* brought up additional remains of the victims. Lazar, *Af Al Pi,* p. 459.

53. Mapai executive meetings, Dec. 12, and 15, 1940, Hag. MSS; Kaplan re-

marks, JAEJ, Mar. 2, 1941, CZA; Rosenbloom to author, Mar. 1, 1978; Beit-Tsvi, *HaTsiyonut,* pp. 311-13.

54. Shertok-MacMichael talk, Nov. 27, 1940, S 25/2569, CZA; JAEJ, Dec. 15, 1940, CZA; Shertok to Weizmann, Dec. 17, 1940, S 25 (A15), CZA. My thanks to Jordan S. Penkower and Gedalia Yogev for uncovering this letter on my behalf.

55. Shertok to Weizmann, Dec. 17, 1940, S 25/1716, CZA. The original Hebrew handwritten drafts of this letter, showing that Shertok assigned it a special importance, are in S 25/10682, CZA; the English version is in Hag. MSS. According to Avigur, Shertok's messenger was probably Lt. Col. Tony Simmonds, who had served with Orde Wingate in Palestine and subsequently, as head of MI 19's Cairo branch, brought a few dozen Greek Jews to safety on caiques. Avigur-J. S. Penkower interview.

56. Shertok to Weizmann, Dec. 17, 1940, S 25 (A15), CZA; Rose, *Baffy,* p. 179. Also see Shertok's view of Weizmann, quoted in Ofer, "HaAliya-HaBilti Chukit," p. 56. Students of Zionist history have overlooked this communication, which may be a decisive key in understanding Sharett's decision to stand by Ben Gurion when Weizmann lost the WZO presidency at the Zionist congress in Dec., 1946, in Basle.

57. Sharett to Mardor, Apr. 29, 1957, and to Bloch, Mar. 28, 1962, Hag. MSS. Also see Sharett quoted in Beit-Tsvi, *HaTsiyonut,* pp. 309-10.

58. Avigur to Mardor, Jan. 3, 1950, Hag. MSS; *Sefer HaMa'apilim,* pp. 197, 282-85. Significantly, Avigur (Meyerov) participated in the defense of Tel Chai, and directed both the settlement of Chanita and *Aliya Bet* activity. Shaul Avigur, *Im Dor HaHagana,* 1 (Tel Aviv, 1970):87-125, and 2 (Tel Aviv, 1977):57-99.

59. Berl Katznelson, *Kitvei Berl Katznelson,* 5 (Tel Aviv, 1947):11-26; Eliyahu Golomb, *Chevyon Oz,* 2 (Tel Aviv, 1955):113-15. While the NZO supported the declaration, Ben Gurion's firm opposition ended acceptance of the manifesto and the WZO-NZO alliance. David Niv, *Ma'archot HaIrgun HaTsva'i HaLeumi,* 3 (Tel Aviv, 1967):60-66. Shapira, who discusses an earlier Katznelson-Ben Gurion-Jabotinsky negotiation (*Berl,* 2:585-92), makes no reference to this manifesto.

60. JAEJ, Mar. 2, 1941, CZA; national board meeting, Nov. 26, 1940, HA. Upon his return to Palestine, Ben Gurion privately asserted that he would not have prevented the *Patria* sabotage plan. Meeting, Mar. 11, 1941, BGA.

61. Penkower, "Ben Gurion, Silver," pp. 72-74; Zalman Shazar, *Tsiyon VaTsedek,* 2 (Tel Aviv, 1971):471. The authoritative biographies by Bar-Zohar and Shapira, which properly underscore Katznelson's singular influence on Ben Gurion, both miss this development completely.

62. Penkower, "Ben Gurion, Silver," pp. 74-75. Brandeis privately urged leading Jewish businessmen, then attending the conference, to have their communities aid the Yishuv fully. Meeting, Jan. 26, 1941, Minutes, BGA.

63. Abba Hillel Silver, "The Cause of Zionism Must Not Be Minimized," *New Palestine,* Jan. 31, 1941, pp. 7-8, 25-27; Wise to Goldmann, Dec. 5, 1940, Box 110, Stephen Wise MSS, American Jewish Historical Society, Waltham, Mass.

64. Penkower, "Ben Gurion, Silver," p. 76; Joseph interview with the author, June 21, 1972.

65. Niv, *Ma'archot,* 3:68; Natan Yelin-Mor, *Lochamei Cheirut Yisrael* (Jerusalem, 1975), pp. 55–70; Gerold Frank, *The Deed* (New York, 1963). Avigur received formal confirmation of the Irgun's plan years later. A.B. testimony, May 9, 1957, Hag. MSS.

66. Gilbert, *Exile and Return,* p. 251; Zwergbaum, "Parshat," pp. 208–44; Kohn to Linton, June 29, 1942, Box 16/3, Jewish Agency files, ZA; S 5/711, CZA; Slutsky, *Sefer Toldot HaHagana,* 3:158.

67. Namier-Moyne talk, Mar. 21, 1941, S 25/9802, CZA; Shertok-Gater talks, Feb. 24, Mar. 30, 1944, CO 733/462/75872, 26C, PRO; Pehle memo to Hull, Mar. 29, 1944, 840.48 Refugees/5461, SD; Stanley announcement, Feb. 21, 1945, quoted in *New Judea,* Feb.-Mar., 1945, p. 86; Zwergbaum, "Parshat," pp. 206, 246–47. For the creation of the War Refugee Board, see Ch. 5.

68. Yahil, "Mivchar Teudot," 191; Gilbert, *Exile and Return,* pp. 250–51, 259–62; Va'ad HaPoel minutes, Mar. 19, 1942, Histadrut Archives, Tel Aviv; correspondence, Feb., 1942, PREM 4, 51/1, PRO. For more on Moyne's anti-Zionist views at the time, see Ch. 1.

69. Strabolgi, House of Lords, Feb. 7, 1945, quoted in *New Judea,* Feb.-Mar., 1945, pp. 85–86; Yehuda Slutsky, "The Palestine Jewish Community and Its Assistance to European Jewry in the Holocaust Years," in *Jewish Resistance during the Holocaust* (Jerusalem, 1971), p. 417; Ch. 6.

70. Wedgwood, House of Lords, Feb. 26, 1942, quoted in *New Judea,* Mar., 1942, p. 85; Bauer, *American Jewry,* pp. 54–55, 160; Leni Yahil, "Madagascar Chazon Ta'atuim Shel Pitaron HaShe'ela HaYehudit," *Yalkut Moreshet* 19 (June, 1975): 159–74; Hilberg, *Destruction,* pp. 260–61. By this time the *Führer* also had received an unequivocal pledge of allegiance from the former mufti of Jerusalem in exchange for Nazi support of Arab independence in Palestine. Husseini to Hitler, Jan. 20, 1941, *Documents on German Foreign Policy, 1918–1945,* ser. D, 9 (Washington, D.C., 1960):1151–55. For the German Army's view of "Jewish Bolsheviks," see Jürgen Förster, "The Wehrmacht and the War of Extermination against the Soviet Union," *Yad Vashem Studies* 14 (1981):7–34.

71. *Extraordinary Zionist Conference New York, 1942, Stenographic Protocol,* ZA; Bauer, *Diplomacy,* pp. 242–50. The emphasis on diplomacy, however more militant, failed to appreciate the value of *Aliya Bet* as a political weapon against HMG. Ofer, "HaAliya-HaBilti Chukit," pp. 66–72, 390–405.

72. Cranborne, House of Lords, Feb. 7, 1945, and Stanley, Commons, Feb. 21, 1945, quoted in *New Judea,* Feb.-Mar., 1945, pp. 85, 87; Ch. 6.

Chapter 3—"The Final Solution" Unveiled

1. Edgar Salin, "Über Artur Sommer, den Menschen und List-Forscher," *Mitteilungen der List Gessellschaft* (Basle) 6, nos. 4/5 (Nov. 30, 1967):85–86; Chaim Pazner interview with the author, July 14, 1978.

2. Walter Laqueur, *The Terrible Secret: Suppression of the Truth about Hitler's "Final Solution"* (Boston, 1980), pp. 67–73, 138–40; copy of the full Molotov statement, WJCL; *Life,* Feb. 23, 1942, pp. 26–27; Yoav Gelber, "HaItonut HaIvrit BeEretz Yisrael Al Hashmadat Yehudei Eiropa," in *Dapim LeCheker*

HaShoa VeHaMered, ser. 2a (Tel Aviv, 1969), pp. 32–34; *New York Times,* Apr. 5, 1942; Alex Grobman, "What Did They Know? The American Jewish Press and the Holocaust," *American Jewish History* 68 (Mar., 1979):327–52.

3. Yehuda Bauer, "When Did They Know?" *Midstream* 14 (Apr., 1968):51–56; Sikorski broadcast, FO 371/31097, PRO; London *Jewish Chronicle, London Times,* and *JTA,* June, July, 1942; Gelber, "Haltonut"; Laqueur, *Terrible Secret,* pp. 103–12.

4. Perlzweig to Easterman, July 23, 1942, 177a/86, WJC; Laqueur, *Terrible Secret,* pp. 65–76, 83–96; *JTA,* July 27, 1942. A most recent official account indicates that the British also knew almost immediately something of the mass executions in occupied Russia, the Nazis' first implementation of the Final Solution. F. H. Hinsley et al., *British Intelligence in the Second World War: Its Influence on Strategy and Operations,* 2 (London, 1981):671.

5. Salin, "Artur Sommer," pp. 81–90. For the first appreciation of this message, see Shlomo Derech's introduction to the Hebrew edition of Arthur Morse's *While 6 Million Died* (*VeHaOlam Shatak, Et Nispu Shisha Milyonim,* Tel Aviv, 1972), pp. v–vii.

6. Pazner interview. Pozner-Salin correspondence for 1941 can be found in Pazner MSS, P12/46, YV. After the war a letter of introduction by Farrell (July 27, 1945) certified that during the years 1940–45 Pozner "rendered useful service to the Allies by putting at my disposal information concerning the enemy, which was passed to the competent authorities. Dr POZNER gave his services gratuitously and spared no effort to loyally assist the cause of the Allies." P12/46, YV.

7. Pazner interview; Pazner to the author, Dec. 12, 1979.

8. Pazner interview with the author, June 20, 1979 (hereafter Pazner interview-2); Pozner to Neustadt, July 9, and to Barlas, Aug. 29, 1942, P12/46, YV. For other surviving Pozner letters about Salin's information, which reached individuals in Palestine then involved in rescue work, see Pozner to Neustadt, Aug. 28, Dec. 2, 1942, and Pozner to Pomeraniec, Feb. 9, 1943, all in P12/46, YV. Also see Salin to Pazner, Apr. 22, 1969, P12/46, YV.

9. Pazner interview-2; Stoll to author, Nov. 6, 1979; Salin, "Artur Sommer," p. 86, does not refer to his connection with the Jewish Agency official, but he acknowledged this privately when informing Pazner, upon the article's publication, for the first time of Sommer's name. Salin to Pazner, Apr. 22, 1969, and Dec. 20, 1972, P12/46, YV. Sagalowitz recalled Pazner's name in this regard during an interview with Professor Yehuda Bauer. Bauer to Pazner, Sept. 6, 1971, P12/46, YV.

10. Riegner still maintains silence on the industrialist's identity, and Walter Laqueur's recent investigations, based on Sagalowitz's memoir (P13/62, YV), have only determined that Sagalowitz introduced that mysterious German to Riegner in Feb., 1945. Aside from uncovering the identities of Schulte and his Swiss contact Koppelman, I have discovered that WJC administrative secretary A. Leon Kubowitzki (later Kubovy) also met them via Sagalowitz when visiting Riegner in Feb., 1945. On that occasion Koppelman informed Kubowitzki that a nephew of one of his female acquaintances had seen the draft of this order signed by Nazi chieftains Himmler and Bormann on Hitler's table, and that it had later received the *Führer*'s signature. Schulte confirmed that "an extermina-

tion order seems to have existed." My correspondence with the relevant German archives has also disclosed that Schulte (mentioned to Laqueur as the general manager of a Breslau mining :ompany who defected after apparently bringing important information to the West) was born on Jan. 4, 1891, in Duesseldorf. Although Nazi war production chief Albert Speer could not recall Schulte's name years later, Schulte became in fact a manager of the board of directors of some German companies, and was appointed "Wehrwirtschaftsfuehrer" on Sept. 1, 1941. A copy of his plan for Germany's economic rehabilitation after World War II is in the Sagalowitz papers. Walter Laqueur, "The Mysterious Messenger and the Final Solution," *Commentary* 69 (Mar., 1980):54–64; Laqueur, *Terrible Secret,* pp. 78, 100n; Riegner conversation, Kubowitzki diary, Feb. 16, 1945, in Miryam Kubovy, *Ultimate Rescue Efforts, 1944* vol. 3 (n.d.), YV; Kubowitzki memo of talk with Schulte and Koppelman, Feb. 24, 1945, WJCL; Speer to the author, Aug. 28, 1981; Simon to the author, Apr. 22, 1981; P13/117, Benjamin Sagalowitz MSS, YV.

11. Riegner interviews with the author, Apr. 22, 1977, and Nov. 9, 1979; Riegner in *Jewish Affairs* 1 (Oct.-Nov., 1947):10–12; memo, Feb. 24, 1945, WJCL; Kubowitzki diary, Feb. 16, 1945, in Kubovy, *Ultimate Rescue Efforts,* vol. 3. The first expanded account, based on Riegner's reminiscences, of an anonymous German industrialist as the sole source of information was Arthur Morse's *While 6 Million Died: A Chronicle of American Apathy* (New York, 1967), ch. 1. Riegner subsequently identified Sagalowitz as the intermediary in *Das Neue Israel* (Zurich) 5 (Nov., 1968), but steadfastly maintains that by Aug. 1, 1942, Sagalowitz had only heard from the industrialist. In accepting this position, Laqueur relegates the Salin-Sommer connection to an appendix and neglects Pozner's contribution entirely (*Terrible Secret,* pp. 213–14). Derech, who presented Pazner's version, concluded that no such German source existed, and that Sagalowitz had mistaken the economist Sommer with the unnamed industrialist given in Morse's account. (Natan Eck repeated this assumption in *Shoat Ha'Am Ha Yehudi BeEiropa* (HaKibbutz HaMeuchad, 1975), p. 314.) It appears, however, that two separate reports arrived almost simultaneously in Sagalowitz's hands. Also see the Pazner cable quoted in n. 22 below; the conjecture of Salin in his letter to Pazner, Jan. 23, 1973, P12/46, YV; and Bauer to Pazner, Sept. 6, 1971, P12/46, YV.

12. Riegner to Silverman with memo attached, Mar. 19, 1942, 264, WJC; Riegner to Tartakower, Apr. 29, 1942, 184a/54, WJC; Riegner interview, Apr. 22, 1977.

13. Riegner interview, Apr. 22, 1977; Pazner interview-2.

14. Riegner interview, Nov. 9, 1979. Morse, *While 6 Million Died,* p. 13, adds that Riegner and Guggenheim meant three and a half to four million exclusive of the Jews in the Soviet Union.

15. Riegner interview, Nov. 9, 1979; see nn. 16 and 18 below for transmission to London and Washington; Elting memo, Aug. 8, 1942, 862.4016/2234, RG 59, SD. Sagalowitz must have transmitted the substance of the report to the Swiss Jewish federation, since its central committee repeated the rumor in a confidential meeting with head of the police Heinrich Rothmund one week after he had ordered the border closed to Jews escaping from France. Its members failed to

get the order rescinded, however, Rothmund thinking then that the entry of 10,000 refugees would be intolerable. Alfred A. Häsler, *The Lifeboat Is Full* (New York, 1969), pp. 126–29; McClelland-Bauer interview, July 13, 1967, Institute for Contemporary Jewry, Hebrew University, Jerusalem.

16. Riegner statement in *Jewish Affairs* 1 (Oct.-Nov., 1947):9; Durbrow memo, Aug. 11, 1942, 862.4016/2235, SD. State Department policy up to this point can be studied in Henry Feingold, *The Politics of Rescue: The Roosevelt Administration and the Holocaust, 1938–1945* (New Brunswick, N.J., 1970); David S. Wyman, *Paper Walls: America and the Refugee Crisis, 1938–1941* (Boston, 1968); Saul S. Friedman, *No Haven for the Oppressed: United States Policy Toward Jewish Refugees, 1938–1945* (Detroit, 1973).

17. Durbrow memo, Aug. 11, 1942, 862.4016/2235, SD; Baerwald to Welles, Aug. 11, 1942, State Dept., JDC; Welles to Harrison, Aug. 17, 1942, 862.4016/2233, SD; Riegner statement in *Jewish Affairs* 1 (Oct.-Nov., 1947):9; Michael R. Marrus and Robert O. Paxton, *Vichy France and the Jews* (New York, 1981), ch. 6.

18. Baxter minute, May 29, 1942, FO 371/32698, PRO; John R. Fox, "The Jewish Factor in British War Crimes Policy in 1942," *English Historical Review* 92 (Jan., 1977):91–93; Walker minute, Aug. 15, 1942, FO 371/30917, PRO; Silverman statement in *Jewish Affairs* 1 (Oct.-Nov., 1947):2. For a good analysis of the overall British position, see Wasserstein, *Britain*.

19. S. Levenberg interview with the author, Aug. 2, 1979; Alexander Easterman interview with Andrea P. Rosen, Oct. 25, 1977 (notes in the author's possession); Easterman interview with the author, July 31, 1979.

20. Schwartzbart statement, Box 1, Israel Cohen MSS, YIVO Archives, New York; diary, June 25–30, 1942, M2/767, Schwartzbart MSS, YV; *The Ghetto Speaks,* Aug. 5, 1942, and Szmul Zygielbojm and Josiah Wedgwood, *Stop Them Now!* (London, 1942), Bund Archives, New York; Allen memo, Sept. 7, 1942, FO 371/31097, PRO; Laqueur, *Terrible Secret,* pp. 108, 110, 128–31. A summary of the WJC press conference, highlighted in the *London Daily Telegraph,* saw print in the middle pages of the *New York Times.* Laqueur, *Terrible Secret,* pp. 74–75.

21. Photostat of Silverman cable to Wise, Aug. 24, 1942, *Jewish Affairs* 1 (Oct.-Nov., 1947); Silverman to Easterman, Aug. 28, 1942, WJCL.

22. Memo quoted in Beit-Tsvi, *HaTsiyonut,* pp. 78–79; Julius Kühl interview with the author, Feb. 17, 1982; Kühl to Mayer, July 12, 1942, Julius Kühl MSS, Miami Beach; Schwalb to Mayer, Aug. 19, 1942, SM-25, also SM-64, JDC; Pozner to Barlas, Aug. 29, 1942, S 26/1428, CZA, and P12/46 (from Barlas MSS, Jerusalem). The "one month" in Pozner's cable, which I have emphasized here, confirms that Pozner immediately wired Barlas upon receiving Salin's news from Sommer about the Final Solution.

23. Morse, *While 6 Million Died,* pp. 15–16; Donald A. Lowrie, *The Hunted Children* (New York, 1963), chs. 20–21.

24. Riegner interview, Apr. 22, 1977.

25. Silverman to Wise, Aug. 28, 1942, 740.0011 EW 1939/553, SD; Western Union cable, New York stamp 2:28 A.M., Aug. 29, 1942, 206A, WJC; Israel Miller interview with the author, May 14, 1978.

26. Wertheim, Wise, Monsky and Held to Hull, Aug. 27, 1942, Genl. France deportations, JDC; Perlzweig telephone conversation with the author, May 3, 1981; Tartakower to the author, Aug. 3, 1981; Tartakower interview with the author, June 25, 1982; Laqueur, *Terrible Secret,* p. 161; Tartakower to Riegner, Sept. 3, 1942 (quoted in Beit-Tsvi, *Ha Tsiyonut,* p. 87), and BK (Kahn) memo, Sept. 1, 1942, Poland Genl., JDC.

27. Wise to Welles, Sept. 2, 1942, 840.48 Refugees/3080, SD. It is suggestive of Wise's constricted position that he wrote, rather than telephoned, Welles.

28. Atherton to Welles, Sept. 3, 1942, 840.48 Refugees/3080, SD (with notation that Welles contacted Wise on the 3rd, and also thus marked on Wise's letter to Welles, attached); Wise to Goldmann, Sept. 4, 1942, Box 109, Stephen Wise MSS, American Jewish Historical Society, Waltham, Mass.; Stephen Wise, *Challenging Years: The Autobiography of Stephen Wise* (New York, 1949), p. 275. Laqueur, *Terrible Secret,* p. 224, errs on this chronology.

29. Isaac Lewin, *Churban Eiropa* (New York, 1948), p. 134; Laqueur, *Terrible Secret,* p. 115; Rosenheim to Roosevelt, Sept. 3, 1942, 740.00116 EW 1939/570, SD; Halifax to FO, Sept. 4, 1942, FO 371/31097, PRO; Shuster to Waldman, Sept. 8, 1942, Poland 1942, AJC. For Sternbuch, see Chs. 7 and 9.

30. Rosenblum to M. Wertheim, Sept. 8 and 9, 1942, Poland 1942, AJC; D. Wertheim "strictly confidential" memo to Poalei Zion members, Sept. 9, 1942, 264, WJC; Lewin interview with the author, Oct. 5, 1979; Shabse Frankel interview with the author, Dec. 28, 1981.

31. Wise to Frankfurter, Sept. 4, 16, 1942, Box 109, Wise MSS; McDonald secretary to Frankfurter, Sept. 4, 1942, PAC files, James McDonald MSS, Columbia University, New York; Laqueur, *Terrible Secret,* p. 95; Wise to Korn, Sept. 9, 1942, Box 113, Wise MSS.

32. Wise to Frankfurter, Sept. 16, 1942, Box 109, Wise MSS; Ch. 5, n. 11; *JTA,* Sept. 9, 1942; Riegner to Wise, Sept. 24, 1942, WJCL. Feingold, *Politics,* pp. 170, 333, n. 10, states that the *JTA* broke the Riegner story on Oct. 9, "so that the press was able to give wide circulation to the first reports of the Final Solution in operation." The *JTA* has no such release for that date. An editorial entitled "Nazis' Extermination" in the London *Jewish Chronicle,* Sept. 25, 1942, echoing the *Christian Science Monitor,* stated that "everything points to a planned deliberate increase" in Hitler's proclaimed principle to exterminate the Jews. Laqueur points to that newspaper's report of Oct. 2, 1942, "Nazis' Master Plan for Jews," as "the Riegner report without attribution" (*Terrible Secret,* p. 118). Yet the printed account only spoke of a "new and comprehensive" design to drive every Jew out of western Europe, probably to put them in a gigantic reservation in the former Polish-Russian zone, where they would be treated as "prisoners and hostages" according to the "situation that may arise out of war developments." In any event, no extended publicity came until the end of November ff., after Wise released the story (see pp. 79ff., below).

33. Goldmann interviews with the author, Mar. 14, 1974, and Nov. 7, 1976; Goldmann remarks, Nov. 29, 1944, 81/1, WJC. My conclusion here disagrees with the judgment expressed in Friedman, *No Haven,* pp. 143, 151, and with Bauer's conclusion in *Holocaust,* p. 23, that silence was "a logical step," since Wise "had not acted upon the much more detailed and unequivocal Bund cable."

Wise called the Madison Square Garden July rally in direct response to that telegram, and sought to have food packages sent to the Polish ghettos. It is true that others in the WJC executive felt more militant steps were in order (see pp. 76-77, 324n68 below). Laqueur, *Terrible Secret*, pp. 161n, 194, accepts Bauer's position on this and subsequent activities, but the WJC did seek the relief and rescue of its co-religionists abroad throughout the war. See Chs. 4-9.

34. Fox, "Jewish Factor," p. 93; WJC, British section, *Outline of Activities, 1936-1946* (London, 1948), pp. 11-12; Easterman interview with Rosen, Oct. 25, 1977.

35. Elizabeth Eppler, "The Rescue Work of the World Jewish Congress," in *Rescue Attempts during the Holocaust,* Yisrael Gutman and Efraim Zuroff eds. (Jerusalem, 1977), pp. 59-60; Roberts memo, Feb. 24, 1942, FO 371/30914, PRO; Roberts memo (with Eden notations), Sept. 3, 1942, FO 371/30885, PRO; Allen minute, Aug. 28, 1942, FO 371/31098, PRO; Roberts minute, Sept. 2, and Eden to Bobbety, Sept. 8, 1942, FO 371/31097, PRO; Fox, "Jewish Factor," pp. 93-94.

36. Lichtheim to Gruenbaum, Aug. 27, 1942, L22/103, CZA; Lichtheim to Jewish Agency London, Aug. 30, 1942, C 11/7/2/6, BD; Lichtheim to Jerusalem, L 22/149, CZA; Wise to Halifax, Sept. 24, 1942, 16/3, Jewish Agency files, ZA; Lourie to Lichtheim, Sept. 25, 1942, L22/149, CZA. For earlier detailed reports by a pessimistic Lichtheim, see L 22/95 and 149, CZA.

37. *FRUS, 1942,* 3:775-77; Taylor memo of conference, Sept. 25, 1942, Box 5, Myron Taylor MSS, FDRL; Pierre Blet et al., *Actes et documents du Saint-Siege relatifs à la Second Guerre Mondiale,* 8 (Vatican, 1974):665, 669, 679.

38. Squire to Riegner, Oct. 8, 1942, WJCL; Squire to State, Sept. 28, 1942, 862.4016/2242, SD; for Domb's letters of Sept. 4 and 12, 1942, to E (Eli) Sternbuch, see 184a/58, WJC, and also see Ch. 9, n. 13. Riegner sent off a summary as well to Silverman-Easterman, Oct. 3, 1942, WJCL. Hillel Seidman of Warsaw also dispatched a coded message to Chaim Eiss of Zurich that 10 percent of Warsaw's original 450,000 Jews had survived. Eiss, who worked on rescue with the Sternbuch family, replied that he understood the hint from Amos 5:3. Hillel Seidman, *Yoman Ghetto Varsha* (New York, 1957), pp. 75-76.

39. Lichtheim to Linton, Aug. 27, 1942, C 11/7/2/6, BD; Riegner to Wise, Sept. 24, 1942, WJCL; Häsler, *Lifeboat* (quoting Mann), p. 185; Fox, "Jewish Factor," p. 95. Also see Lichtheim to Jewish Agency, Sept. 15, 1942, C 11/7/2/6/, BD.

40. Lichtheim to Lourie (of Jewish Agency, New York), Sept. 29, 1942, 264, WJC; Welles to Harrison, Oct. 5, 1942, 740.00116 EW 1939/600, SD. For the constraints then operating on the WJC in New York, see Perlzweig to Easterman, Oct. 1, 1942, 177a/86, WJC.

41. Riegner interview with the author, Apr. 22, 1977; Lichtheim to Lourie, Oct. 5, 1942, U-134, WJC; Riegner to Silverman-Easterman, Oct. 3, 1942, WJCL; *Manchester Guardian,* Oct. 30, 1942; Riegner memo to WJC, Oct. 8, 1942, 266, WJC; Riegner conversation, Kubowitzki diary, Feb. 16, 1945, in Kubovy, *Ultimate Rescue Efforts,* vol. 3; memo, Feb. 24, 1945, WJCL; *Congress Weekly,* Dec. 3, 1942, p. 5; Lichtheim to Lauterbach, Oct. 20, 1942, L 22/149, CZA. Schulte's information about Backe's rationale coincided, in fact, with

Martin Bormann's concurrent explanation to Nazi administrators that "the elimination of millions of Jews living in the European economic area is an imperative rule in the struggle to secure the existence of the German people. It is in the nature of things that these somewhat difficult problems can only be solved with ruthless severity...." Marlis G. Steinert, *Hitler's War and the Germans,* trans. Thomas E. J. De Witt (Athens, Ohio, 1977), pp. 141–42. For the *Führer's* actual order, see n. 90 below.

42. Harrison to Hull, Aug. 11, 1942, 862.4016/2234, SD; Harrison to Hull, Oct. 6, 1942, 740.00116 EW 1939/601, SD; Lichtheim-Riegner memos of Oct. 22, 1942: "Aide-Mémoire Concerning the Persecution of the Jews of Europe," 184a/54a, WJC; "Note Regarding the German Policy of Deliberate Annihilation of European Jewry"; "Documents"; "Note Regarding Hitler's Instruction Concerning the Annihilation of the Jews of Europe," all WJCL.

43. Riegner interviews, Apr. 22, 1977, and Nov. 9, 1979. This account differs from Morse's version in *While 6 Million Died,* p. 21. For the WJC's ongoing confrontation with the International Red Cross, see Ch. 8.

44. Morse, *While 6 Million Died,* pp. 21–23. For the Guggenheim and Zivian affidavits, see 184a/56, WJC. For the British response, see n. 92 below.

45. Beit-Tsvi, *HaTsiyonut,* pp. 80–84; Pozner to Neustadt, Dec. 12, 1942, P12/46, YV; Natan Eck comment about Silberschein's skepticism that September, in *Peulot Hatsala BeKushta 1940-1945* (Jerusalem, 1969), p. 41; Ch. 8 n. 5, for RELICO. The Yishuv leaders cabled New York two weeks later. Ben Zvi et al. to American Jewish Congress, Nov. 10, 1942, 204a, WJC.

46. Harold Ickes diaries, Oct. 5, 1942, LC; Ickes to Wise, Oct. 7, and Wise to Goldmann, Oct. 9, 1942, Box 1001, Wise MSS; Goldmann report in Oct. 6, 1942, minutes, 264, WJC; Ch. 5.

47. Fox, "Jewish Factor," p. 96; Goldmann in Oct. 6, 1942, minutes, 264, WJC; *JTA,* Oct. 6 and 15–17, 1942; London *Jewish Chronicle,* Oct. 2 and 16, 1942. Roosevelt in fact moved at the last minute only because the Foreign Office, seeking a war crimes commission since August, threatened to act independently. *FRUS, 1942,* 1:48–59.

48. Taylor memo for Roosevelt and Hull, Oct. 20, 1942, Box 11, Taylor MSS. I have been unable to locate these two memos to Roosevelt in either the Taylor or the voluminous Roosevelt files, but the WJC's British section had submitted a memo on the Final Solution to Taylor dated Oct. 7 (740.00116 EW 1939/634, SD). He acknowledged it by asserting that prior Allied statements sufficed, and that one of the war's main objectives was to ensure that "all the peoples of the world" would not be subject to mass persecution in the future. Taylor to Easterman, Nov. 2, 1942, WJCL.

49. Goodman to secretary of Joint Foreign Committee, Sept. 23, 1942, C 11/13/16/1, BD; Easterman to Perlzweig, Oct. 8, Nov. 1, 1942, U-134, WJC; board's talk with Law, Oct. 1, 1942, C 11/7/3a/2, BD, and FO 371/30885, PRO; *JTA,* Oct. 28, Nov. 1, 1942; Beit-Tsvi, *HaTsiyonut,* p. 71.

50. Churchill to Temple, Oct. 29, 1942, and attachments, PREM 4, 51/7, PRO; Churchill note, B 5/2/6, BD.

51. Riegner interview, Oct. 19, 1977; Morse, *While 6 Million Died,* p. 24; Bauer, *Holocaust,* p. 23; Tzipora Hager Halivni, "The Birkenau Revolt: Poles Prevent a Timely Insurrection," *Jewish Social Studies* 41 (Spring, 1979):145–46,

n. 11. In a private meeting with Riegner soon thereafter, Burckhardt insisted that the IRC could do nothing substantial to aid European Jewry. Conference, Nov. 17, 1942, L 22/3, CZA. A pessimistic Lichtheim agreed with the Red Cross official; Riegner did not. Lichtheim to Josef, Nov. 30, 1942, L 22/103, CZA; Ch. 8.

52. Hayim Greenberg, "The Plan of Destruction," *Jewish Frontier,* Nov., 1942, p. 8.

53. Kubowitzki to Wise et al., Aug. 21, 1942, 268/90, WJC; Beer memos, Sept. 2, 1942, 264, and Sept. 3, 1942, 268/90, WJC; Kubowitzki to Cantor, Aug. 6, 1942, 264, WJC; Aryeh L. Kubovy, "Criminal State vs. Moral Society," *Yad Vashem Bulletin* 13 (Oct., 1963):6; Marie Syrkin letter in *Midstream* 12 (May, 1968):62-63. Visiting Riegner in Feb., 1945, Kubowitzki criticized him for accepting Guggenheim's objection to mentioning reprisals in his Aug., 1942, cable. Riegner interview with the author, Nov. 9, 1979.

54. Syrkin in *Midstream,* pp. 62-63; Poalei Zion minutes, Sept. 16, 1942, 264, WJC. With most of the information for this issue deriving from the World Jewish Congress and its affiliates, it seems evident that Wise by then also approved this step, notwithstanding his pledge of silence to Welles. "If Wise was so worried about publicity," wrote the *Jewish Frontier*'s Marie Syrkin years later, "we would have heard from him or some one close to him after the Sept. '42 issue." Syrkin to the author, Jan. 19, 1980.

55. "Jews under the Axis, 1939-1942," *Jewish Frontier,* Nov., 1942; Poulos to Greenberg, Dec. 6, 1942, *Jewish Frontier*'s files, New York; *New York Post,* Dec. 2, 1942. For Greenberg's scathing attack soon thereafter on the American Jewish leadership, see "Bankrupt," *Yiddishe Kemfer,* Feb. 12, 1943, reprinted in *Midstream* 10 (Mar., 1964):5-10.

56. Beit-Tsvi, *HaTsiyonut,* pp. 84, 69; Silberschein for Schwartzbart via Easterman, Oct. 8, 1942, M-2/241, YV; reports in S 26/1159 I and II, CZA; Shapira, *Berl,* 2:666-67; Shertok to Linton, Nov. 20, 1942, S 25/1681, CZA; Nov. 22, 1942, JAEJ minutes, CZA; all Palestinian Hebrew newspapers, Nov. 23, 1942; Va'ad HaPoel minutes, Nov. 25-26, 1942, Histadrut Archives, Tel Aviv. The *New York Times* on Nov. 25, 1942, carried a brief mention in the middle of the paper, including information from its Jerusalem correspondent about "great crematoriums" at "Oswiencim" near Crakow, and noted that Polish Christian workers in Jerusalem had confirmed the news about the gas chambers on the former Russian frontiers, "in which *thousands* of Jews have been put to death" (my italics).

57. Yisrael Gutman, "The Attitude of the Poles to the Mass Deportations of Jews from the Warsaw Ghetto in the Summer of 1942," in *Rescue Attempts,* pp. 399-422; Laqueur, *Terrible Secret,* pp. 112, 114-17. For Himmler's order of July 19, 1942, regarding the Government-general, see NO-5574, Nuremberg documents, Columbia University Law Library, New York.

58. Gottschalk to Waldman, Nov. 27, 1942, Nazism 1942-43 files, AJC; minutes, Nov. 30, 1942, Emergency Joint Committee 1942-43 files, AJC. Wise later declared (*Challenging Years,* p. 276) that Welles had vouched for the truth of the documents, but his recollection at the meeting of Jewish leaders on Nov. 30 was more qualified. Not surprisingly, State would not confirm that Welles had fully done so. Editorial, *Christian Century,* Dec. 9, 1942.

59. *New York Times* and *New York Herald Tribune,* Nov. 25, 1942; *PM,* Nov. 25, 1942.

60. Gottschalk to Waldman, Nov. 27, Dec. 30, 1942, Nazism 1942–43 files, AJC; Kubowitzki diary, Nov. 25, 1942, in Kubovy, *Ultimate Rescue Efforts,* vol. 1; *JTA,* Nov. 27, 1942; American Jewish Congress release, Nov. 26, 1942, 206a, WJC. See also Laqueur, *Terrible Secret,* p. 193n. The temporary nature of the committee resulted from the fact that Wise, president of the American Jewish Congress, had earlier broken with the General Jewish Council, now consisting of the American Jewish Committee, B'nai Brith, and the Jewish Labor Committee.

61. WJC, *Outline of Activities,* p. 13; Polish government's statement to Easterman, n.d., and Law-Easterman-Silverman talk, Nov. 26, 1942, FO 371/30923, PRO; Fox, "Jewish Factor," pp. 99–100.

62. Schwartzbart statement, Nov. 25, 1942, 264, WJC; Feiner to Zygielbojm, Aug. 31, 1942, quoted in Wladyslaw Bartoszewski and Zofia Lewin, eds., *Righteous among Nations: How Poles Helped the Jews, 1939–1945* (London, 1969), pp. 719–28; Polish National Council resolution, Nov. 27, 1942, quoted in ibid., pp. 767–68. For earlier criticism by Jewish representatives about the council, see Tartakower to Goldmann et al., May 21, 1942, U-134, WJC, and Schwartzbart report, June 23, 1942, WJCL. Also see Tsvi Avital, "Yachaso Shel HaShilton HaPolani BaGola El Ha'Sh'eila HaYehudit," *Yalkut Moreshet* 16 (Apr., 1973):133–46; A. Reiss, "Perakim MiPeulot HaEzra VeHaHatsala," in *Dapim LeCheker HaShoa VeHaMered,* ser. 2a (HaKibbutz HaMeuchad, 1952), pp. 19–36.

63. Jan Karski, *Story of a Secret State* (Boston, 1944), pp. 320–52; *Zygielbojm Buch,* ed. S. J. Hertz (New York, 1947), pp. 34–40; Laqueur, *Terrible Secret,* pp. 232–35.

64. *JTA,* Nov. 27 and 29, Dec. 1, 1942; Gelber, "HaItonut HaIvrit," pp. 50–53; Pinkerton to State, Nov. 30, 1942, 740.00116 EW 1939/673, SD.

65. Schwartzbart report, n.d. (but written on Dec. 13, 1942), 264, WJC; Easterman-Barou to chairman, Nov. 27, and to Wise et al., Dec. 3, 1942, WJCL; British section statement, Dec. 1, 1942, 6/40, Ernest Bevin MSS, Churchill College, Cambridge University.

66. Raczynski to the author, Aug. 15, 1978; Gutman, "Attitude," pp. 407–8; Edward Raczynski, *In Allied London* (London, 1962), pp. 125–27. I have also profited much from an interview conducted in Aug., 1978 (tape in author's possession), by Rabbi and Mrs. M. S. Penkower with PPS leader Adam Ciolkosz, a Socialist member of the Polish National Council who enjoyed a close ideological friendship with Zygielbojm, and from relevant contemporary pamphlets graciously sent me by Mr. Ciolkosz. Also see Adam Ciolkosz, "In London mit Artur Zygielbojm," *Unzer Zeit,* May, 1965, pp. 23–24; Ch. 4, n. 41.

67. "Extermination of the Polish Jewry," *Polish Fortnightly Review,* Dec. 1, 1942, WJCL; Henderson minute, Dec. 1, 1942, FO 371/30923, PRO.

68. *JTA,* Dec. 3, 1942. For his part, Kubowitzki thought that Wise and the Jewish leadership in the United States were "not hysterical enough" in responding to the massacre of their people abroad. Kubowitzki diary, Dec. 3, 1942, and Kubowitzki to Wise, Dec. 4, 1942, in Kubovy, *Ulimate Rescue Efforts,* vol. 1. Greenberg wanted a half-million Jews to demonstrate in front of the White House for three days, demanding rescue. Va'ad HaPoel minutes, Dec. 31, 1942,

Histadrut Archives. See also Gov. Council, Dec. 3 and 10, 1942, American Jewish Congress Archives, N.Y.

69. Dec. 3–4, 1942, in Kubovy, *Ultimate Rescue Efforts,* vol. 1; minutes, Nov. 30, 1942, Emergency Joint Committee 1942–43 files, AJC; Wise to Niles, Dec. 2, 1942, Box 181, Wise MSS.

70. Wise to Roosevelt, Dec. 2, 1942, OF-76C, FDRL; *Congress Weekly,* Dec. 4, 1942.

71. Memo of meeting, Dec. 3, 1942, C 11/7/2/6, BD; *JTA,* Dec. 5, 1942.

72. Fox, "Jewish Factor," pp. 100–101; Allen minutes, Dec. 2 and 4, 1942, FO 371/30923, PRO; *FRUS, 1942,* 1:67–68. For Winant's earlier views regarding the tragedy of European Jewry, see AGB (Brotman) memo, July 6, 1942, E 3/508, BD.

73. The following is based on Held's detailed report of the visit, Dec. 8, 1942, pt. 3, sec. 1, no. 15, Jewish Labor Committee Archives, N.Y. Wertheim, overlooked by Held, later reported that FDR's views had "completely" identified with those of the delegation. Annual meeting, Jan. 31, 1943, transcript, AJC.

74. *JTA,* Dec. 9, 1942.

75. Ibid.; Perlzweig-Miller to Easterman, Dec. 9, 1942, 178A, WJC; Wise to Niles, Dec. 9, 1942, Box 181, Wise MSS. A copy of the detailed memo and letter dated Dec. 8, is in Nazism 1942–43, AJC. Wise publicized his own thoughts on rescue in *Opinion,* Dec. 23, 1942.

76. *JTA,* Dec. 3, 6, and 7, 1942; *FRUS, 1942,* 4:549–50.

77. *London Times,* Dec. 4, 5, and 7, 1942; memo, Dec. 4, and Masaryk broadcast, Dec. 8, 1942, WJCL.

78. Raczynski note, Dec. 9, 1942, FO 371/30924, PRO.

79. Roberts to Raczynski, Dec. 10, 1942, FO 371/30924, PRO.

80. Heller to Neumann, Nov. 6, 1942, misc. H. file, Emanuel Neumann MSS, New York; Morse, *While 6 Million Died,* pp. 31–34; Reams to Hickerson-Atherton, Dec. 10, 1942, 740.00116 EW 1939/694, SD.

81. Allen minute, Dec. 11, and Roberts minute, Dec. 14, 1942, FO 371/30924, PRO; Reams to Hickerson-Atherton, Dec. 10, 1942, 740.00116 EW 1939/694, SD.

82. Halifax to FO, Dec. 11, 1942, FO 371/30924, PRO; *FRUS, 1942,* 1:68; Laqueur, *Terrible Secret,* pp. 227–28. For Reams's later obstruction, see Chs. 4–5.

83. Dov Levin, "The Attitude of the Soviet Union to the Rescue of the Jews," in *Rescue Attempts,* pp. 225–36; Molotov to Kerr, Nov. 3, 1942, FO 371/30925, PRO; *FRUS, 1942,* 1:69.

84. Dominions Office to various dominions, Dec. 12, and Halifax to FO, Dec. 16, 1942, FO 371/30924, PRO; *FRUS, 1942,* 1:69–71.

85. Memo of meeting, Dec. 16, 1942, WJCL, and FO 371/32682, PRO. Law privately agreed with their criticism of the home secretary's stringent immigration policy. Ibid.

86. Law memo, Dec. 14, and minute of Dec. 15, 1942, FO 371/30925, PRO; Easterman to Law, Dec. 14, 1942; Law to Silverman and to Easterman, both Dec. 16, 1942, all WJCL.

87. Great Britain, *Parliamentary Debates* (Commons), 5th ser., vol. 385, cols. 2082–87, Dec. 17, 1942.

88. Barou-Easterman to Wise-Perlzweig, Dec. 17, 1942, 178a, WJC; Earl of Avon, *The Eden Memoirs: The Reckoning* (London, 1965), p. 358; Great Britain, *Parliamentary Debates* (Lords), 5th ser., vol. 125, cols. 607–12, Dec. 17, 1942.

89. Bishop of London in Great Britain, *Parliamentary Debates* (Lords), 5th ser., vol. 125, cols. 607–12, Dec. 17, 1942; Morse, *While 6 Million Died,* p. 46; Korherr report (first presented at the postwar Nuremberg trials), given in appendices of Serge Klarsfeld, ed., *The Holocaust and the Neo-Nazi Mythomania* (New York, 1978), pp. 163–211.

90. *Extraordinary Zionist Conference N.Y. 1942,* pp. 20–40, ZA; Laqueur, *Terrible Secret,* p. 77; Riegner interview, Nov. 9, 1979; Ch. 5, n. 12. For the most comprehensive analysis of a *Führer* directive regarding European Jewry's total destruction, see Martin Broszat, "Hitler and the Genesis of the 'Final Solution': An Assessment of David Irving's Theses," *Yad Vashen Studies* 13 (1979):73–125.

91. Easterman to Perlzweig, Jan. 15, 1943, U–134, WJC; Chava Vagman-Eshkoli, "Emdat HaManhigut HaYehudit BeEretz Yisrael LeHatsalat Yehudei Eiropa, 1942–1944" (M.A. thesis, Bar-Ilan University, 1977); OWI report, Oct. 27, 1942, Box 1528, Jewish Welfare Board Archives, New York; B 5/2/5/1–3, BD; Justine Polier interview with the author, May 17, 1976. For the sharpest criticism cᶠ Wise, see Friedman, *No Haven,* pp. 143, 151, who also quotes Elie Wiesel, "Telling the Tale," *Dimensions in American Judaism* 2 (Spring, 1968):11. Yet one month after the UN declaration, fewer than half of the American people believed that the Nazis were deliberately killing the Jews. Charles H. Stember et al., *Jews in the Mind of America* (New York, 1966), pp. 141, 155, n. 11.

92. Friedman, *No Haven,* pp. 135–36; Ch. 4; Savery to Roberts, Dec. 3, 1942, FO 371/31097, PRO; Savery to Roberts, Dec. 8, 1942, FO 371/30924, PRO; Raczynski to author, Aug. 15, 1978; Eden to War Cabinet, Dec. 14, 1942, CAB 65/28, PRO. Upon finally receiving a copy of Guggenheim's affidavit from the WJC's Maurice Perlzweig, the FO's Eastern Department observed that it would have added a rider to the effect that it "took no responsibility for the document's contents." Dec. 30, 1942, FO 371/34361, PRO.

93. *New York Times,* Nov. 25, 1942; Eden minute, Nov. 28, 1942, FO 371/31380, PRO; Raczynski to author, Aug. 14, 1978; Chs. 4–9.

94. *FRUS, 1942,* 4:548; Law to Jowitt, Nov. 14, 1942, FO 371/30885, PRO; Law to Dugdale, Dec. 7, 1942, FO 371/32682, PRO; *JTA,* Sept. 9, 1942.

95. Roosevelt to Sikorski, July 3, 1942, Box 65, PSF Poland, FDRL; Halifax to FO, Sept. 9, 1942, FO 371/32632, PRO; Henry Wallace diary, vol. 10, p. 1995, Nov. 26, 1942, Special Collections, Columbia University, New York; Feingold, *Politics,* pp. 305, 169; Roosevelt-Morgenthau conversation, Dec. 5, 1942, vol. 5, pp. 1200–1201, MPD. In the United States Kubowitzki realized early on the limitations of the chief executive in this matter. Kubowitzki to Wise et al., Aug. 21, 1942, 268/90, WJC. For Roosevelt's timidity during this period on other issues, see James MacGregor Burns's incisive *Roosevelt: The Soldier of Freedom, 1940–1945* (New York, 1970) and Robert Dalek's more comprehensive *Franklin D. Roosevelt and American Foreign Policy, 1932–1945* (New York, 1979).

96. *FRUS, 1943,* 3:772–78; Blet, *Actes et documents,* 8:53, 534, 670, 758; Polish report to the Vatican (and FO), July 12, 1942, FO 371/31098, PRO; Saul Friedländer, *Counterfeit Nazi: The Ambiguity of Good* (London, 1969), ch. 6; *Wiener Library Bulletin* 9 (May-Aug., 1955):22; Morse, *While 6 Million Died,* p. 24; Wasserstein, *Britian,* pp. 175–76; Harrison to State, Dec. 26, 1942, Office of the Chief, Box 42, RG 226, NA; Gitta Sereny, *Into That Darkness: From Mercy Killing to Mass Murder* (London, 1974), pp. 328–33. The Vatican did protest British bombing of nonmilitary objectives in Genoa and Milan. Harrison memo, Nov. 20, 1942, Bern, folder 4, RG 226, NA.

97. Häsler, *Lifeboat,* pp. 76–80, 187; Riegner interview, Nov. 9, 1979; Laqueur, *Terrible Secret,* pp. 62–64. For continuing ICRC practice in this vein, see Ch. 8. The Swedish government, too, although hearing from Gerstein at the end of Aug., 1942, about the gassing of Jews in Belzec, kept this to itself until after the war. Laqueur, *Terrible Secret,* pp. 48–50.

98. *JTA,* Dec. 4, 1942; Riegner interview, Nov. 9, 1979; Silverman to Easterman, Dec. 17 (should be 16), 1942, WJCL. In Nov. 1941, Lichtheim hoped for a statement from Roosevelt protesting the murder of European Jewry, just to show that "moral values still exist." Lichtheim to JAEL, Nov. 10, 1941, 16/3, Jewish Agency files, ZA.

99. *FRUS, 1943,* 1:768–69; Ch. 4 and the other chapters of this volume for Allied callousness after acknowledging the dimensions of the Holocaust.

100. Gerald Reitlinger, *The Final Solution: The Attempt to Exterminate the Jews of Europe, 1939–1945* (New York, 1961 ed.), pp. 145–52. For the UN declaration's legal influence *after* the war regarding the issue of "crimes against humaity," see Fox, "Jewish Factor," pp. 105–6.

Chapter 4—The Bermuda Conference and Its Aftermath

1. Great Britain, *Parliamentary Debates,* (Commons), vol. 385, cols. 2082–87, Dec. 17, 1942; Easterman to Perlzweig, Jan. 15, 1943, U 142/13, WJC.

2. Ch. 3; "Extermination of the Polish Jewry: What Happened in the Warsaw Ghetto," *Polish Fortnightly Review,* Dec. 1, 1942, WJCL; Edwin Johnson, extract of remarks, Dec. 16, 1942, U.S. Congress, Senate, *Congressional Record,* 78th Cong., 1st sess., 1943, 89, pt. 9:A125.

3. *JTA,* Dec. 20, 1942; Brodetsky to Eden, Dec. 18, 1942, C 14/16, BD.

4. *JTA,* Dec. 21, 1942; Rathbone to Linton, Dec. 14, 1942, Z4/14758, CZA; *New Judea,* Dec. 1942, pp. 39–42.

5. *The Ghetto Speaks,* Mar. 1, 1943, pp. 1–5, Bund Archives, New York; Zygielbojm to Churchill, Dec. 19, 1942, PREM 4, 51/6, PRO; memo of visit of British Jewish deputation to Eden, Dec. 23, 1942, C 10/2/8-1, BD; *JTA,* Dec. 27, 1942; memo of Law meeting, Dec. 30, 1942, C 10/2/8-2, BD.

6. Morse, *While 6 Million Died,* pp. 14, 26–28; Alexander Easterman interview with Andrea P. Rosen, Oct. 25, 1977 (copy in the author's possession).

7. Eppler, "Rescue Work," pp. 56–60; *New Judea,* Dec. 1942, p. 37; colonial secretary's memo, Dec. 14, 1942, CAB 65, 168/42/9, PRO; Eden's remarks to British Jewish deputation, Dec. 23, 1942, C 10/2/8-1, BD; FO memo, Jan. 1942, CAB 95/15, PRO.

8. FO to Zygielbojm, Jan. 6, 1943, PREM 4, 51/6, PRO; Halifax to Taylor,

Jan. 6, 1943, 867N.01/1837, RG 59, SD; Eden draft, Jan. 9, 1943, WP 43 (13), CAB 66, PRO; discussion, Jan. 11, 1943, CAB 65, 6/43/4, PRO; Halifax-Berle talk, Jan. 14, 1943, 840.48 Refugees/3557, SD; *JTA,* Jan. 3, 8, 14, and 18, 1943. The Intergovernmental Committee on Refugees, set up after the 1938 Evian conference, did little to save Jews and other refugees during the war.

9. Memo on meeting, Jan. 7, 1943, C 10/2/8/-2, BD; Joint Foreign Committee memo, Jan. 11, 1943, file 100, David Mowshowitz MSS, YIVO Archives, New York; Warsaw ghetto cable, Jan. 13, 1943, printed in *Zygielbojm Magazine,* Bund Archives, New York; *JTA,* Jan. 12, 1943.

10. Great Britain, *Parliamentary Debates* (Commons), vol. 386, cols. 184–86, Jan. 20, 1943; Schwartzbart to WJC New York, Jan. 19, 1943, 204A, WJC. The Joint Foreign Committee was composed of leading members from the Board of Deputies and the Anglo-Jewish Association.

11. *FRUS, 1943,* 1:134–37.

12. Ilya Dijour, "The Preparations for the Bermuda Conference," *YIVO-Bleter* 21 (1943):5–19.

13. *FRUS, 1943,* 1:250–58; Hull to Murphy, Jan. 16, 1943, 840.48 Refugees /3559 CF, SD; Morse, *While 6 Million Died,* pp. 42–43; Riegner and Lichtheim to WJC, Jan. 19, 1943, 206A, WJC. The Foreign Office also forwarded this cable to the WJC in London. Norton to FO, Jan. 25, 1943, FO 371/34361, PRO.

14. *FRUS, 1942,* 4:549–50; Samuel statement in memo of visit of British Jewish deputation to Eden, Dec. 23, 1942, C 10/2/8-1, BD; WJC British section draft of memo, Jan. 28, 1943, C 10/2/8-2, BD; Jewish Agency memo, Jan. 25, 1943, Z 5/1444, CZA; *FRUS, 1943,* vol. 4, for State Department opposition to Zionism; Stanley statement, Feb. 3, 1943, Great Britain, *Parliamentary Debates* (Commons), vol. 386, cols 863–67.

15. *JTA,* Jan. 2, 10, and 27, Feb. 1, 10, 17, and 18, 1943; Morse, *While 6 Million Died,* p. 45; memo, Jan. 30, 1943, S 26/1159 II, CZA. Such reports led the Polish government-in-exile, via Zygielbojm, to approach the Foreign Office informally on behalf of *all* Jews for the first time, Its proposals were, as in the past, quickly dismissed. Memo, Feb. 25, 1943, and Allen minute, FO 371/34362, PRO.

16. FO to Washington embassy, Feb. 3 and 26, 1943, FO 371/34967, PRO; Brotman-Roberts talk, Feb. 9, 1943, file 100, Mowshowitz MSS, YIVO Archives; FO memo, Feb. 17, 1943, FO 371/34550, PRO; Allen minute, Feb. 20, 1943, FO 371/34362, PRO; *New York Times,* Feb. 13, 1943. The Foreign Office's last response was prompted by Chaim Weizmann's urgent letter to Halifax, begging HMG to carry out this "humanitarian act." Weizmann to Halifax, Feb. 16, 1943, Weizmann file, ZA, and Ch. 6.

17. Rathbone memo, Feb. 12, and 24, 1943, C 10/2/8-2, BD; *JTA,* Feb., 1943; *FRUS, 1943,* 1:138–40; War Cabinet discussion, Feb. 22, 1943, 33/43/4, CAB 65, PRO; Palestine Elected Assembly statement, Feb. 22, 1943, FO 371/36661, PRO; Brotman to Law, Feb. 23 and 25, 1943, C 11/64-1, BD.

18. *FRUS, 1943,* 1:140–44.

19. Dijour, "Preparations"; Feingold, *Politics,* pp. 261, 264; *JTA,* Feb. 24, 1943.

20. "The 'Stop Hitler Now' Demonstration," *Congress Weekly,* Mar. 5, 1943; Dec. 31, 1943, vol. 688-II, MD; Wise to Hull, Mar. 5, 1943, 740.0016 EW

1939/815, SD. Wise also sent a copy to the president. "Memorandum of the Resolutions," PPF 5029, FDRL.

21. *FRUS, 1943,* 1:144–47; Dec. 31, 1943, vol. 688–II, MD; Irving Abella and Harold Troper, *None Is Too Many* (Toronto, 1982), pp. 130–39 and *passim.* According to the British minister, however, Welles admitted in effect that publication of the American note was "a calculated political action" designed to cast the United States in the "beau role." Halifax to FO, Mar. 6, 1943, FO 371/36655, PRO.

22. Eden statement, Mar. 3, 1943, Great Britain, *Parliamentary Debates* (Commons), vol. 387, col. 318; Norton to FO, Mar. 11, 1943, FO 371/34362, PRO; WJC-World Churches statement, Mar. 18, 1943, L22/92, CZA; Roberts to Brotman, Mar. 16, 1943, C 11/6/4–1, BD; Great Britain, *Parliamentary Debates* (Lords), vol. 126, cols. 811–21, 845–60, Feb. 23, 1943. Riegner's fresh information was not publicized on the BBC, the minister of information asserting that "it would be an insult to our Jewish fellow citizens to broadcast these lies." Bracken to Locker-Lampson, Mar. 12, 1943, FO 371/34362, PRO.

23. Joint Emergency Committee on European Jewish Affairs minutes, Mar. 29, 1943, Manson files, Abba Hillel Silver MSS, the Temple, Cleveland, Ohio; office committee minutes, American Emergency Committee for Zionist Affairs, Mar. 30, 1943, ZA; President's Advisory Committee on Political Refugees minutes, Mar. 30, 1943, PAC files, James McDonald MSS, Columbia University, New York; *FRUS, 1943,* 3:38.

24. Taylor to Cicognani, Feb. 26, 1943, Myron Taylor MSS, FDRL; Joint Emergency Committee memo submitted to Taylor, Mar. 22, 1943, Joint Emergency Committee files, AJC; meeting, Apr. 10, 1943, Joint Emergency Committee files, AJC. After the war Taylor opposed a Zionist solution for Palestine in favor of the broad dispersal of Jewish refugees. Taylor to Truman, May 15, 1946, and July 30, 1947, Box 8, Myron Taylor MSS, FDRL.

25. Hull to Roosevelt, Mar. 23, 1943, OF 3186, FDRL; Taylor memo, Mar. 17, and Taylor to Welles, Mar. 18, 1943, Taylor MSS, FDRL. Nahum Goldmann, vice-president of the World Jewish Congress, also told a Foreign Office representative during Eden's visit that no conference was necessary. In Goldmann's view the Allies should make the offer of food (for those not freed by the Nazis) and refuge, and leave it up to the Germans to accept or refuse. Strang memo, Mar. 24, 1943, FO 371/36658, PRO.

26. Refugees file, Isaiah Bowman MSS, Johns Hopkins University, Baltimore, Md.; Feingold, *Politics,* pp. 192–94; Wise to Welles, Apr. 14, 1943, Joint Emergency Committee files, AJC; Walker minute, Apr. 11, 1943, FO 371/36659, PRO.

27. Feingold, *Politics,* pp. 137–48, 159–66, 194–200, 231–37, 243; *The War Diary of Breckenridge Long,* ed. Fred L. Israel (Lincoln, Nebr., 1966), pp. 307, 309; FO to Washington embassy, Apr. 6, 1943, FO 371/36657, PRO; Halifax to FO, Apr. 7, 1943, FO 371/36658, PRO.

28. Cabinet Committee on Refugees meeting, Mar. 31, 1943, and decisions, Apr. 2, 1943, FO 371/36657, PRO; Morse, *While 6 Million Died,* p. 48; Alling to Reams, Apr. 14, 1943, Box 17, WRB.

29. *FRUS, 1943,* 1:148; Wise et al. to Welles, Apr. 14, 1943, Joint Emergency Committee files, AJC.

30. *JTA,* Apr. 13, 1943; FO memo, Apr. 16, 1943, FO 371/36659, PRO; Morse, *While 6 Million Died,* p. 49.

31. The American notes of the conference discussions can be found in Box 203, Breckenridge Long MSS, LC. The British record is in FO 371/36725, PRO. Also see the astute analysis in Feingold, *Politics,* pp. 197–204. I remain unconvinced by the defense of Dodds in Friedman, *No Haven,* p. 173. See also Ch. 6.

32. See n. 30 above; Ch. 9, n. 54.

33. Minutes of two meetings, Apr. 25, 1943, Box 203, Long MSS, LC; Halifax to FO, Apr. 15, 1943, FO 371/36659, PRO; Weizmann to Law, Apr. 15, 1943, WA; office committee minutes, May 6, 1943, Jewish Labor Committee Archives, New York. A Foreign Office member dismissed the Jewish Agency memo in this fashion: "It is naively assumed the United Nations could provide transport for all these people. That alone makes the memorandum fantastically out of relation to reality. This memorandum is obviously political ... Jewish dominance of Palestine by greatly increased immigration." Minute, Apr. 17, 1943, FO 371/36701, PRO. For the earlier dramatic shift in Backer's appreciation of Jewish sovereignty in Palestine, see Ben Gurion diary, Jan. 7, 1942, BGA.

34. Law quoted in Morse, *While 6 Million Died,* p. 57; *FRUS, 1943,* 1:173–74; Law to FO, Apr. 27, 1943, FO 371/36659, PRO. For copies of these memoranda, see n. 31 above. My analysis of these proposals and the response of the two major powers to them differs from the conclusions drawn by Beit-Tsvi, *HaTsiyonut,* pp. 321–26.

35. Feingold, *Politics,* p. 207; Berle memo to Hull and Long, Apr. 20, 1943, Box 202, Long MSS, LC; Penkower, "1943 Joint Statement," pp. 212–18.

36. Welles quoted by Proskauer in Apr. 10, 1943, meeting, Joint Emergency Committee files, AJC; Welles to Wise, June 24, 1943, 264, WJC; Taylor to Hull-Welles-Long, Apr. 30, 1943, cited in memo on Bermuda conference, Feb. 22, 1943, Box 3, WRB; Taylor to Emerson, May 25, 1943, Taylor MSS, FDRL.

37. Law, Peake, and Hall memo to FO, June 28, 1943, FO 371/36725, PRO. Assistant Secretary Berle's public insistence, immediately after the Bermuda conference ended, that "nothing can be done to save these helpless unfortunates" until the defeat of Germany, was to the FO a "valuable indication" that U.S. government circles "realized the difficulty in the rescue problem." Walker note on Berle speech in Boston, May 2, 1943, FO 371/36661, PRO.

38. *JTA,* May 7, 1943; *New York Times,* May 4, 1943; author's interviews with Hillel Kook, June 22, 1972, and Samuel Merlin, Mar. 27, 1972; Penkower, "Bergson Boys," pp. 281–90; *Congressional Record,* 89, pt. 10:A2154, A2389–90, A2566; Great Britain, *Parliamentary Debates* (Commons), vol. 389, cols. 1119–1204, May 19, 1943; Ch. 5; Weizmann-Beneš talk, May 18, 1943, Z5/1377, CZA.

39. Potter to E. Roosevelt, July 15, 1943, Emergency Committee to Save the Jewish People of Europe files, Metsudat Ze'ev, Tel Aviv; Goldmann to Gruenbaum, Apr. 5, 1943, Z6/18/15, CZA; Smertenko to Villard, May 27, 1943, file 3570, Oscar G. Villard MSS, Houghton Library, Harvard University. Boston, Mass.

40. Morse, *While 6 Million Died,* p. 52; *JTA,* Apr. 22, 1943; Reuben Ainsztein, *Resistance in Nazi-Occupied Europe* (London, 1974), p. 644; cable, May 11, 1943, in Schwartzbart to *London Times* editor, May 24, 1943, M2/243, Schwartzbart MSS, YV; Yisrael Gutman, *Yehudei Varsha 1939–1943, Ghetto, Machteret, Mered* (Tel Aviv, 1977), pp. 377–410. Allied complicity in these linked tragedies

led Jewish Agency rescue advocate S. Adler-Rudel to question if even 100,000 of his people in Europe would survive the war. "Warsaw and Bermuda," address, June 11, 1943, S. Adler-Rudel MSS, Leo Baeck Institute, New York. For an early evaluation by a Yishuv leader of the revolt's legacy for Jews, see Zerubavel remarks, May 5-7, 1943, Va'ad HaPoel minutes, Histadrut Archives, Tel Aviv.

41. *Zygielbojm Buch*, pp. 362-63; Adam Ciolkosz, "Paminci Bohaterow Ghetta Warszawskiego," *Robotnik Polski* (New York), May 18, 1958, pp. 1-5, and see Ch. 3, n. 66; Laqueur, *Terrible Secret*, p. 96n; Zygielbojm to Raczkiewicz and Sikorski, May 11, 1943, 0-55, YV. For the Foreign Office's hesitation about publishing the suicide note, see Roberts to Mark, May 22, 1943, FO 371/34362, PRO.

42. James G. McDonald, "The Time for Discussion Is Past," *New Palestine* 33 (Mar. 19, 1943):5-7; Welles to Early, Mar. 4, 1943, 840.48 Refugees/3721, SD; Roosevelt to Flynn, Apr. 9, 1943, OF 700, FDRL; Churchill quoted in *Palcor*, Apr. 8, 1943.

43. *FRUS, 1943*, 1:176-79. The Intergovernmental Committee's director had first suggested the North Africa camp for refugees in Nov., 1942, only to be informed by Taylor that the idea was "impractical." *FRUS, 1942*, 1:477-78, 481.

44. Penkower, "1943 Joint Statement," pp. 224-25; Robert Murphy, *Diplomat among Warriors* (New York, 1965 ed.), pp. 183-84; McIntyre to Roosevelt, Dec. 21, 1942, Box 69, PSF, FDRL; memo of Long-Strong talk, Apr. 22, 1943, Box 203, Long MSS, LC. Murphy was influenced by his (Jewish) adviser, Paul Warburg. Warburg to Murphy, Feb. 13, 1943, FO 600/67, PRO

45. *FRUS, 1943*, 1:258, 278, 137, 142, 282, 290-91; Long-Campbell talk, Mar. 24, 1943, Box 202, Long MSS, LC. The British dragged their feet on Palestine's admitting the 1,000 refugees. McDonald to Welles, Feb. 5, 1943, 840.48 Refugees/3593, SD.

46. Penkower, "1943 Joint Statement," p. 218; *FRUS, Conferences at Washington and Quebec, 1943*, pp. 342-46. The support of Generals Giraud and Eisenhower and the British chiefs of staff notwithstanding, the joint chiefs raised alleged difficulties of shipping and possible Arab unrest, as well as "an added and unwarranted administrative responsibility" on the supreme military commander in North Africa. *FRUS, 1943*, 1:295-97.

47. Churchill to Stanley and Eden, June 8, and Eden to Churchill, June 15 and 18, 1943, PREM 4, 51/4, PRO; *FRUS, 1943*, 1:307-25.

48. *FRUS, 1943*, 1:334-35, 339-40, 345, 359, 367; Ackerman memo, n.d., Box 39, WRB; "Report on Middle East Camps," UNRRA MSS, ME 1, pp. 28-29, Box 2755, United Nations Archives, New York.

49. *FRUS, 1944*, 1:992-94, 996-99. These Jews, who had lived in Salonika for several centuries, had continued to claim citizenship in the country from which their ancestors had been expelled in 1492. The Spanish government, with urging by Hayes, continued to recognize this claim, "albeit grudgingly." During the German invasion of Greece the Spanish consul prevented deportation of these Jews to Poland by giving them visas and arranging their transport to Spain on the promise of the American and British embassies that they would be moved elsewhere as soon as possible. "Report on Middle East Camps," pp. 31-32; John P. Wilson, "Carlton J. Hayes, Spain, and the Refugee Crisis, 1942-1945," *American Jewish Historical Quarterly* 62 (Dec., 1972):105-6. For the Nazi annihila-

tion of Salonika's Jewish community, see Schwartz to JDC, Mar. 25, 1944, Box 39, WRB.

50. *FRUS, 1944,* 1:1013–15, 1935–36; Joseph P. Lash, *Eleanor: The Years Alone* (New York, 1972), p. 109; Wilson, "Carlton Hayes," pp. 107–10. The WRB moved after obtaining a WJC report about the sympathy of Franco's brother for the Spanish Jews in Greece, and upon receipt from the WJC of a Jewish Agency cable warning of their deportation to Theresienstadt. Board to Madrid, May 27, and Goldmann to Pehle, May 11, 1944, Box 47, WRB. For the Spanish government's poor record on behalf of Jewish refugees, particularly given scant Allied pressure as regards the rescue of Jews, see Chayim Avni, *Sefarad Ve Ha Yehudim Be Yemai HaShoa Ve Ha Emantsipatsya* (HaKibbutz HaMeuchad, 1974). But also see Nathaniel Weyl, "Israel and Francisco Franco," *Midstream* 28 (Feb., 1982):11–16. For the fate of 288 Sephardic Jews who ultimately arrived in Bergen-Belsen, see Trobe to Mayer, Mar. 30, 1945, SM Supplement-4, JDC.

51. Wilson, "Carlton Hayes," p. 107; "Report on Middle East Camps," pp. 30–31; Beckelman to Anderson, Feb. 12, and 30, 1944; Friedman memo, Feb. 24, 1944; Beckelman's talk with French authorities, Mar. 25, 1944; Ackerman report, Apr. 20, 1944, all in Box 39, WRB; Intergovernmental Committee annual report, Apr. 1943, ERO files, Box 40,631, UNRRA MSS, UN Archives.

52. "Report on Middle East Camps," pp. 30–31; Board to London, July 21, 1944, Box 110; State Dept. to Winant, Aug. 15, and Board to Mann. Nov. 20, 1944, Box 39, all in WRB. The head of the Civil Affairs Office's refugee section foresaw these difficulties early, and urged (unsuccessfully) that only the admission of all endangered refugees by the United Nations would afford the "basic solution." Johnson to Fryer, Feb. 18, 1944, Box 30, WRB.

53. *FRUS, 1943,* 1:323–24; *1944,* 1:1007–1008, 1018–19, 1053–54, 1058–59, 1070–71; Law to Grigg, Apr. 3, and Grigg to Law, Apr. 4, 1944, FO 371/42728, PRO; Randall memo, Apr. 13, and Law to Grigg, Apr. 22, 1944, FO 371/42729, PRO; Vucinich memo, Apr. 20, and Vucinich to Green, May 29, 1944, Box 1, R and A, Meditn. Theater Corresp., RG 226, NA; Pehle to Stettinius, June 16, 1944, Box 70, WRB.

54. "Report on Middle East Camps," pp. 32–33; Perez Leshem, "Rescue Efforts in the Iberian Peninsula," *Leo Baeck Institute Yearbook* 14 (1969):255; Blickenstaff to Campbell, Jan. 8, 1945, Box 39, WRB.

55. Great Britain, *Parliamentary Debates* (Commons), vol. 389, cols. 1197 and 1133, May 19, 1943; Law quoted (my emphasis) in Feingold, *Politics,* p. 199.

56. For a similar lack of priority assigned by the Anglo-American Alliance to a WJC proposal in 1943 to send funds from the United States for underground rescue in Rumania and France, see Ch. 5.

57. William D. Hassett, *Off the Record with FDR 1942–1945* (New Brunswick, N.J., 1958), pp. 209–10; Chs. 5–6; Feingold, *Politics,* pp. 301–3; Pehle to Morgenthau, July 25, 1944, vol. 758, MD; Sharon Lowenstein, "A New Deal for Refugees: The Promise and Reality of Oswego," *American Jewish History* 71 (Mar., 1982):325–41.

58. Churchill quoted in Eppler, "Rescue Work," p. 59; Laski to Churchill, July 6, 1943, and Churchill note, attached, PREM 4, 51/8, PRO; *FRUS, 1943,*

1:768-69; Roosevelt-Churchill wartime correspondence, FDRL; Penkower, "1943 Joint Statement."

59. Morse, *While 6 Million Died,* p. 53; Weizmann (Jewish Agency) memo to Bermuda conference, Apr. 14, 1943, Box 59, Elbert Thomas MSS, FDRL.

Chapter 5—The Creation of the U.S. War Refugee Board

1. Hilberg, *Destruction,* pp. 128, 140, 143-44, 168-69, 173-74; Mordecai Lenski, "Problems of Disease in the Warsaw Ghetto," *Yad Vashem Studies* 3 (1959):283-93.

2. Memo, Feb. 8, 1940; Buchman to Rosen, Aug. 5, 1942; Kahn 1941-44 report, all in Poland Genl., JDC.

3. Kahn 1941-44 report, Poland Genl., JDC; Troper to JDC, Dec. 22, 1939, and Lisbon to JDC, Dec. 20, 1940, both in Poland Genl., JDC; Bienenstock report, Jan. 1942, 212/20, WJC.

4. Gerhart Riegner interview with the author, Nov. 7, 1977; Alf Schwartzbaum, "Peulot Ezra MiSchveits BaShanim 1940-1945," *Masua* 2 (1974): 139-40; Isaac Lewin interview with the author, Oct. 5, 1979; Kazimierz Iranek-Osmecki, *He Who Saves One Life* (New York, 1971), pp. 228-29.

5. A. Leon Kubowitzki, "Survey of the Rescue Activities of the World Jewish Congress, 1940-44" (mimeo), pp. 9-10, file 153, WJC. President Roosevelt's earlier appeal that limited quanities of milk and vitamin concentrates be sent to Vichy France under strict American Red Cross supervison failed to move the British. Roosevelt to Churchill, Dec. 30, 1940, Box 51, Norman Davis MSS, LC. Also see Renchard to Davis, July 18, 1940, Box 54, Davis MSS.

6. Kubowitzki, "Survey"; Wise to Perlzweig, May 9, 1941, in Kubovy, *Ultimate Rescue Efforts,* vol. 1, YV; *JTA,* July 10 and 30, Aug. 5, 15, and 27, 1941; *Independent Jewish Service,* Aug. 8, 1941; *Divrei Yemei Va'ad Hatsala* (New York, 1957), pp. 11-20; Beit-Tsvi, *HaTsiyonut,* pp. 251-52; *Unity in Dispersion: A History of the World Jewish Congress* (New York, 1948), p. 175; Yitschak Weisman, "My Experience with the Joint" (n.d.), 228, WJC.

7. *Inter Arma Caritas: The Work of the International Red Cross during the Second World War* (Geneva, 1947), pp. 79-80; *JTA,* Jan. 1 and 8, Feb. 1 and 23, Mar. 15, 17, and 24, 1942. A representation of Polish Jewish refugees in Palestine was the first to raise (unsuccessfully) the Greek example, in a plea of Mar. 30, 1942, to the London-based Polish government-in-exile. Reiss, "Perakim," p. 23.

8. Hyman to Baerwald et al., Apr. 1, 1942; Minkoff to Hyman, Apr. 17, 1942; Hyman to Buchman, May 1, 1942; Pinkerton to representatives of Polish Jewry, June 22, 1942; Perlzweig to Minkoff, Sept. 1, 1942; Leavitt to Lehman, Nov. 13, 1942, all in Poland Genl., JDC; Perlzweig to Easterman, June 30, 1942, U-142/14, WJC.

9. *JTA,* Feb. 18, 1942; Rosenheim to JDC, Sept. 10, 1942; Hyman to Waldman, Sept. 23, 1942; Hyman to Waldman, Sept. 14, 1942, all in Poland Genl., JDC.

10. Ch. 3; Tartakower to Wise et al., July 24, 1942, 267/46, WJC; J. Wise memo to Peter, n.d., 212/20, WJC.

11. J. Wise memo, Oct. 14, and meeting of Oct. 6, 1942, 264, WJC; Susman to Hyman, Nov. 9, 1942, Poland Genl., JDC.

12. Hyman memo, Nov. 17, 1942; Minkoff to Pehle, Nov. 17, 1942; Wise to Hyman, Nov. 18, 1942; Baerwald to Wise, Nov. 27, 1942; Baerwald to Wise (not sent), Dec. 1, 1942; Hyman to Minkoff, Dec. 15, 1942, all in Poland Genl., JDC.

13. Zygielbojm report, Jan. 4, 1943; Katzki to Brotman, July 2, 1943; Katzki to New York, Aug. 19, 21, 1943; Peter to Rosenheim, Nov. 11, 1943, all in Poland Genl., JDC. For further contemporary reports on the unreliability of the Crakow *Judische Unterstutzung Stelle,* see two accounts sent to Leavitt, Mar. 17, 1944, Poland Genl., JDC, and Iranek-Osmecki, *One Life,* pp. 229–35. A more positive evaluation, including the JDC's contribution after 1942, can be found in Bauer, *American Jewry,* pp. 84–92, 332–34.

14. Tartakower to Kubowitzki, Feb. 9, 1943, 265, WJC; Tartakower to Wise et al., Feb. 19, 1943, U-134, WJC; Wise and Goldmann to board, Feb. 25, and Tartakower to Peter, Mar. 4, 1943, 265, WJC; Ch. 8.

15. Morse, *While 6 Million Died,* ch. 1, and pp. 42–43.

16. Ibid., p. 65; Riegner interview with the author, Apr. 22, 1977; Riegner to Wise, Apr. 14, 1943, Riegner Archives, Geneva. Harrison privately had Riegner informed that while he transmitted his message to State, he was "endeavoring to arrive at such an understanding" with the department and with Rabbi Wise, and that "I shall be glad to render him all assistance which I may deem appropriate under the instructions which the Department of State has issued to me." Squire to Riegner, Apr. 27, 1943, Riegner Archives.

17. Morse, *While 6 Million Died,* p. 65, erred in writing that the cable mentioned rescue of French children in the "concentration camps of the South." Riegner's original message to Wise (see n. 16) spoke of rescuing French children "who are being lodged at non-Jews or hidden." Harrison's paraphrase to State altered this to "being lodged at Suez (camp?) or hidden." The minister's error became Morse's 30 years later.

18. Ch. 6; Wise to Welles, Apr. 14, 1943, Emergency Jt. Committee on European Jews, 1942–43 files, AJC; Wise to Welles, Apr. 23, 1943, 264, WJC; Wise-Goldmann-Welles talk, Apr. 30, 1943, State Dept. files, ZA.

19. Meltzer-Goldmann talk, May 12, 1943, 840.48 Refugees/3827, RG 59, SD; DuBois memo, Dec. 9, 1943, vol. 688-I, MD; State to Harrison, May 25, 1943, 862.4016/2269, SD; Ch. 4.

20. Harrison to State, June 14, 1943, 862.4016/2274, SD.

21. DuBois memo, Dec. 9, 1943, vol. 688-I, MD: Harrison to State, June 14, 1943 (with notation that cable was given to Pehle on June 25, 1943), 862.4016/2274, SD. Welles would soon transmit a message to Wise from Riegner and the Jewish Agency's Geneva representative, giving the figure of "about four million victims." Welles to Wise, Aug. 6, 1943, Box 66, Stephen Wise MSS, American Jewish Historical Society, Waltham, Mass. Yet an official Allied statement currently listed Jewish victims at 1,702,500. *New York Times,* Aug. 27, 1943. For Reams's earlier obstruction, see Ch. 3, n. 80.

22. Tartakower to Wise et al., Apr. 12, 1943, 266, WJC. The letter, dated Dec. 8, 1942, conveyed the "Europa Plan" of Rabbi Weissmandel and the Slovakian Jewish "working group." For the plan, see Ch. 7, n. 2.

23. Nahum Goldmann interview with the author, Mar. 14, 1974; Baerwald to Welles, May 28, 1943, Paul Baerwald MSS, Columbia University, New York; Ch. 7, n. 2.

24. Pehle and O'Connell memo to Morgenthau, July 1, 1943, vol. 646, MD; Morse, *While 6 Million Died,* p. 67; Paul memo to Morgenthau, Aug. 12, and DuBois memo, Dec. 9, 1943, vol. 688–I, MD.

25. Wise to Roosevelt, Apr. 28, 1943, PPF 3292, FDRL; Wise, *Challenging Years,* pp. 277–78; Wise to Roosevelt, July 23, 1943, 862.4016/2286, SD; Wise to Morgenthau, July 23, 1943, vol. 652, MD. Wise also used the interview to check on rumors about an impending official statement on Palestine. See Penkower, "1943 Joint Statement," pp. 222–23. Wise's later autobiographical recollection that Roosevelt called Morgenthau on the spot is suspect, as there is no mention of this either in Wise's letter the following day to the president or to the secretary. Similarly, notwithstanding Wise's memoirs, Riegner's plan mentioned nothing about smuggling Jews from Poland to Hungary. Goldmann's subsequent reminiscence (in *Holocaust and Rebirth: A Symposium* (Jerusalem, 1974), p. 96), confirmed in a letter of Nov. 22, 1978, to the author, that Eleanor Roosevelt was asked to intervene with FDR is not included in Wise's version or in any of the available archives. But it is possible, given her sympathy in 1939 for a bill to bring Jewish refugee children in to the United States and her strong opposition to Breckenridge Long's firm restrictive visa policy. Morse, *While 6 Million Died,* pp. 207–8, 238, 246, 31–32.

26. Henrietta Klotz interview with the author, Mar. 14, 1977; Morgenthau memo, Nov. 16, 1938, vol. 151; Nov. 21, 1938, vol. 152, both MD; Isaiah Berlin interview with the author, July 1, 1976.

27. Klotz interview; Ch. 3; Morgenthau to Cicognani, May 19, 1943, vol. 635, MD; *The Answer,* Aug., 1943, p. 4; Morgenthau memo to Roosevelt, Aug. 11, 1943, vol. 688–I, MD. In contrast to Morgenthau's personal message, Hull's statement, endorsed by Roosevelt, merely spoke of American support for the work of the (dormant) Intergovernmental Committee on Refugees, and emphasized that "no measure is practicable unless it is consistent with the destruction of Nazi tyranny." *The Answer,* Aug., 1943, p. 24.

28. DuBois memo, Dec. 9, 1943, vol. 688–I, MD; State to Harrison, Aug. 6, 1943, 862.4016/2269, SD; Paul memo to Morgenthau, Dec. 17, 1943, vol. 688–II, MD; Paul memo with Morgenthau's signature of approval, Aug. 26, 1943, vol. 688–I, MD; Morse, *While 6 Million Died,* p. 71.

29. Paul memo to Morgenthau, Aug. 12, 1943 and Morgenthau-Lehman telephone conversations, Sept. 15 and 20, 1943, vol. 688–I, MD; Penkower, "1943 Joint Statement," pp. 228–30; Pehle to Leavitt, Sept. 14, 1943, Genl. Czech, Terezin, JDC.

30. Harrison to State, Oct. 6, and Paul memo to Morgenthau, Nov. 2, 1943, vol. 688–I, MD; Pehle-Long talk, with Reams and Long memos, Oct. 26, 1943, attached, 862.4016/2292, SD.

31. "Jewish evacuation" meetings, Nov. 23 and 24, 1943; Morgenthau to Hull, Nov. 24, 1943; Hull to Morgenthau, Dec. 6, 1943, all in vol. 688–I, MD.

32. DuBois memo, Dec. 9, 1943, vol. 688–I, MD; "Jewish evacuation" meeting, Dec. 13, 1943; Paul memo to Morgenthau, Dec. 17, 1943; Winant to State

(and Morgenthau), Dec. 15, 1943, all in vol. 688-II, MD. Nor did State favor Treasury's attempt to have the Free French committee dispose of the fines levied on the Jews of Tunisia, and to make restitution for that community's past losses under the Vichy government. Paul-White memo to Morgenthau, Dec. 3, 1943, vol. 688-I, MD.

33. "Jewish evacuation" meetings, Dec. 12, and 20, and Paul "revision," Dec. 17, 1943, vol. 688-II, MD.

34. DuBois memo, Dec. 18, and "Jewish evacuation" meeting, Dec. 20, 1943, vol. 688-II, MD.

35. Morse, *While 6 Million Died,* p. 75; State to Winant, Dec. 18, and "Jewish evacuation" meetings, Dec. 20, 1943, vol. 688-II, MD.

36. Ibid. The drafts can be found in that volume on pp. 192-94. Milton Handler interview with the author, May 26, 1976.

37. "Jewish evacuation" morning meeting, Dec. 20 and 21, and "Secret" memo for "Secretary Morgenthau's Information Only," Dec. 23, 1943, all in vol. 688-II, MD. DuBois, *The Devil's Chemists* (Boston, 1952), p. 187, and Morse, *While 6 Million Died,* p. 77, erred in claiming that the exact text of cable 354 came into Treasury's hands only after the Hull-Morgenthau meeting of Dec. 20. DuBois's memo of Dec. 18 (see n. 34) quoted the full text of 354 and 482, and Morgenthau wrote "confidential" on that report.

38. Ch. 1; Penkower, "Bergson Boys," pp. 281-90.

39. Penkower, "Bergson Boys," p. 290; author's interviews with Hillel Kook, June 22, 1972, and Samuel Merlin, Mar. 27, 1972.

40. Penkower, "Bergson Boys," pp. 290-91; Max Lerner interview with the author, May 7, 1979; Justine Polier interview, Sept. 14, 1977, Eleanor Roosevelt Oral History Project, FDRL. For the *Struma,* see Ch. 6. For a British official's appreciation of the emergency conference's import, see Guest to FO, July 27, 1943, FO 371/36665, PRO.

41. Penkower, "Bergson Boys," p. 291.

42. Ibid.

43. Ibid., p. 292; S. Margoshes in *Jewish Day,* Oct. 10, 1943; S. Grodzensky in *Der Yiddishe Kempfer,* Oct. 15, 1943; "Zivyon," *Jewish Daily Forward,* Oct. 16, 1943. The president fled to dedicate four Liberator bombers at Bolling Field to the Free Yugoslavia forces. Hassett, *Off the Record,* pp. 209-10.

44. Penkower, "Bergson Boys," p. 292.

45. Penkower, "Bergson Boys," pp. 292-93; Ch. 6, n. 39.

46. Penkower, "Bergson Boys," pp. 293-95. To the challenge that they had no authorization to speak in the name of an established constituency, the Bergson boys relied on what Samuel Merlin termed "the mandate of conscience." *The Answer,* July 12, 1944, p. 20. For Merlin's early call for a UN agency to "Save the Jewish People of Europe," see *The Answer,* June 5, 1943, pp. 13-14.

47. Penkower, "Bergson Boys," pp. 295-96; Emanuel Celler interview with author, June 14, 1975; Celler quoted in *Report,* Jan. 13, 1944, vol. 693, MD; Kook, in Laurence Jarvik, director, "Who Shall Live and Who Shall Die?" (documentary film, 1981). For a congressman's defense of the Bloom-Long moves, see Wadsworth to Ehrhorn, Dec. 12, 1943, Box 25, James Wadsworth MSS, LC.

48. "Jewish evacuation" meetings, Dec. 28 and 31, 1943, vol. 688-II, MD.

49. Irving Miller interview with the author, May 14, 1978; "Jewish evacuation" meeting, Dec. 31, 1943, vol. 688-II, MD; Paul memo to Morgenthau, Jan. 3, and "Jewish evacuation" meeting, Jan. 4, 1944, vol. 690, MD. The JDC license focused on relief, unlike the WJC's for evacuation; this led to a further skirmish between Treasury and State. Jan. 6 and 7, 1944, vol. 691, MD.

50. "Jewish evacuation" meeting and Pehle memo, Jan. 12, 1944, vol. 693, MD; Leavitt memo, Jan. 7, 1944, and Eden to Winant, same date, vol. 692, MD; Long-Campbell talk, Jan. 11, 1944, 840.48 Refugees/5017A, SD. The British had also refused in mid-1943 to accept an exchange of 5,000 Jewish children under the Third Reich's control for interned Germans in Allied hands on the grounds that the children were not nationals of the British empire. Hilberg, *Destruction*, p. 721.

51. "Report to the Secretary on the Acquiescence of This Government in the Murder of the Jews," Jan. 13, 1944, vol. 693, MD; Long-Goldmann talk, Sept. 16, 1943, Box 202, Breckenridge Long MSS, LC; Hyman to Long, Oct. 6, 1943, 840.48 Refugees/4556, SD; "Jewish evacuation" meeting, Jan. 15, 1944, vol. 694, MD. The WJC's British section had first proposed that the UN provide the ICRC with £5 million immediately to relieve the "acutest suffering" of the Jews in Europe. Rubenstein-Barou-Easterman to Miller, Sept. 1943, 184A, WJC. Goldmann wished to expedite matters by involving only the two major Western Allies. He still failed.

52. "Report to the Secretary," Jan. 13, 1944, vol. 693, MD; Winant to State, Nov. 4, 1943, vol. 689, MD; "Jewish evacuation" meeting, Jan. 13, 1944, vol. 693, MD. Also see Daniel Carpi, "The Diplomatic Negotiations over the Transfer of Jewish Children from Croatia to Turkey and Palestine in 1943," *Yad Vashem Studies*, 12 (1977):109–21. Tito's partisans ultimately freed most of these Jews, of whom those fit for battle formed a Jewish battalion in his 7th and 8th Divisions. Popovich to Saxon, April ?, 1944, Box 1, R and A Meditn. Theater Corresp., RG 226, NA.

53. "Jewish evacuation" meeting, Jan. 15, 1944, vol. 694, MD.

54. Klotz interview.

55. "Personal Report to the President," pp. 111–18, vol. 694, MD.

56. Morse, *While 6 Million Died*, pp. 78–81; Feingold, *Politics*, pp. 241–47.

57. Reams to Stettinius, Oct. 8, 1943, Box 202, Long MSS; Stettinius to Hull, Nov. 17, 1943, 840.48 Refugees/4796, SD; *War Diary of Breckenridge Long*, p. 377; "Jewish evacuation" meeting, Jan. 25, 1944, vol. 696, MD.

58. "Jewish evacuation" meeting, Jan. 26, 1944, vol. 696, MD; Penkower, "Bergson Boys," pp. 296–97. When Morgenthau congratulated Hull on this "magnificent cable," at the first meeting of the board's nominal heads, the secretary of state immediately replied: "What you mean is you are congratulating yourself." Secretary of War Henry Stimson added: "That is better than throwing brickbats at each other anyway." "Jewish evacuation" meeting, Jan. 26, 1944, vol. 696, MD. Stimson attributed FDR's creation of the board to Morgenthau's initiative. Jan. 26, 1944, vol. 46, Stimson diaries, Sterling Library, Yale University, New Haven, Conn. My evaluation of the Bergson group, here and elsewhere in this volume, differs from that in Lucy S. Dawidowicz, "American Jews

and the Holocaust," *New York Times Magazine,* Apr. 18, 1982, pp. 46ff., and Marie Syrkin, "What American Jews Did during the Holocaust," *Midstream* 28 (Oct., 1982):10–12.

59. "Personal Report to the President," Jan. 13, 1944, vol. 694, MD.

60. Henry Morgenthau, Jr., "The Refugee Run-Around," *Collier's,* Nov. 1, 1947; Hankey minute, Feb. 4, 1944, FO 371/42727, PRO; *Aide-Mémoire* to State Department, Mar. 24, 1944, 840.48 Refugees/5977, SD. For an example of current British sensitivity regarding immigration to Palestine and War Refugee Board views on that subject, see Gallman to Hull, Mar. 11, 1944, vol. 709, MD. For hesitancy over a license, proposed by Ignacy Schwartzbart, for sending underground funds to Poland, see MEW to Randall, Jan. 26, 1944, FO 371/42775, PRO.

61. Chs. 4, 6; Reams to Stettinius, Oct. 8, 1943, Box 202, Long MSS; Penkower, "Bergson Boys," p. 309.

62. Paul memo to Morgenthau, Aug. 26, 1943, vol. 688–I, MD; Klotz interview. The "Jewish evacuation" meetings (the title deriving from Treasury's response to Riegner's proposal) in the Morgenthau diaries indicate that the Treasury staff exercised a strong influence on the Secretary's ultimate position. And to his personal secretary, who first inculcated in him an appreciation of the Jewish heritage and who participated in all these sessions, Morgenthau wrote just before leaving government service: "The Jewish people in this country have been kind enough to say that I helped in saving the lives of some of [the] Jews abroad. Whatever credit I deserve in this matter I want you to know that I want to share it equally with you. In the realm of Jewish affairs you were particularly understanding and helpful." Morgenthau to Klotz, Aug. 5, 1945. Henrietta Klotz MSS, private collection, New York City.

63. Hilberg, *Destruction,* p. 370; Ch. 6; Cordell Hull, *Memoirs,* 2 (New York, 1948):1539. Even Heydrich admitted the possibilities of rescue, telling those assembled at the Wannsee conference (Jan. 20, 1942) that "certain difficulties" existed, especially in Hungary and Rumania: "To this day, for example, a Jew in Rumania can for money obtain appropriate documents officially confirming him to be of some foreign citizenship." Lucy S. Dawidowicz, ed., *A Holocaust Reader* (New York, 1976), p. 77. At the same time, the Allies outlawed individual ransom payments by their nationals as contravening the economic blockade. *New York Times,* Nov. 25, 1942.

64. Bauer, *American Jewry,* ch. 10; Pomeraniec to Mereminski et al., May 30, 1943, 266, WJC; Pomeraniec, Bader, and Shind to Mereminski, July 25, 1943, Z6/17/9, CZA; Silberschein to Tartakower, Sept. 22, 1943, 206A, WJC.

65. In emphasizing these shortcomings, I take issue with the argument that Zionist philosophy expressly led to the halt in the food package scheme. For this position, see Beit-Tsvi, *HaTisyonut,* pp. 252–54, and Moshe Shonfeld, *The Holocaust Victims Accuse* (New York, 1977), pp. 45–49.

66. The JDC and the WJC would dissipate their potential combined strengths in a bitter battle over the rescue of Jews from France to Spain and Portugal, as well as in Switzerland and Sweden, during the war. For the first instance, see Bauer, *American Jewry,* pp. 213–16, and Yitschak Veisman *Mul Aitanei HaResha* (Tel Aviv, 1968); for the latter, see Ch. 9. The same held true in the JDC's relationship with the Orthodox Va'ad HaHatsala. See Ch. 9.

67. WJC's relief committee meeting, Mar. 24, 1943, 216A/33, WJC; Joint Emergency Committee, July 15, 1943, Emerg. Joint Comm. on European Jews 1942–43 files, AJC.

68. Beit-Tsvi, *HaTsiyonut,* pp. 324–26. This German propaganda had been conveyed to Stephen Wise by Washington government circles in Sept., 1942. Ch. 3. Again, I cannot agree with Beit-Tsvi (ibid.) that this mistaken evaluation stemmed from a Zionist ideology. Moreover, the congress, just as the Joint Emergency Committee, did call in its memo to the Bermuda conference for a separate government agency for rescue, negotiations with the Axis via neutral powers, and neutral and Allied havens to save European Jewry. The fundamental problem was that the Anglo-American Alliance decided, well before the WJC's memo had been presented, not to move in a positive way on any of these issues. Ch. 4.

69. Hyman to Rosenberg-Silver, Oct. 6, 1943, Va'ad HaHatsala MSS, Yeshiva University, New York; Jan Ciechanowski, *Defeat in Victory* (Garden City, N.Y., 1947), pp. 182ff.; Ch. 3, n. 63. FDR offered ringing phrases but no concrete help at the talk's end. Jan Karski address, Oct. 28, 1981, International Liberators' Conference 1981 of the U.S. Holocaust Memorial Council (notes in the author's possession).

70. Paul comment in "Jewish evacuation" meeting, Dec. 17, 1943, vol. 688–II, MD; Grafton in *New York Post,* July 22, 1943, vol. 688–I, MD. Again Beit-Tsvi, *HaTsiyonut,* pp. 331–33, assumes that the Zionist views of Wise and the WJC prevented rescue action after Wise had asked FDR to intervene on the Riegner proposal. Yehuda Bauer, although not sharing this political perspective, also faults Wise and the WJC (*The Holocaust in Historical Perspective* (Seattle, 1978), pp. 23, 25, repeated verbatim in *American Jewry,* pp. 191–92). My research in the WJC Archives and other depositories indicates beyond doubt that the congress, headed by Wise, vainly tried throughout the war to move the Allies to save European Jewry. Chs. 3–4, 6–9.

71. DuBois, *Devil's Chemists,* p. 188.

72. Paul memo to Morgenthau, Dec. 17, 1943, vol. 688–II, MD; Paul memo, Nov. 2, 1943, vol. 688–I, MD; also see Ch. 4, 6. For a record of the JDC's relief to Jews in Theresienstadt, see Reich to Speiser, Jan. 1, 1945, Genl. Czech, Terezin, JDC, and for the $100,000 which the Foreign Funds Control Division and the board permitted the JDC to use via the ICRC, see Schwartz letter, Dec. 23, 1944, Rumania Genl., JDC.

73. J. Wise memo, Oct. 14, 1942, 264, WJC; War Emergency Conference, Nov. 29, 1944, 81/1, WJC; Riegner interview with the author, Apr. 22, 1977. The Greek ambassador also informed Goldmann that after the Greek navy had lost almost two-thirds of its shipping and personnel in the early days of the war, his government had agreed to throw itself fully into the war only if Canadian wheat arrived in Greece. War Emergency Conference, Nov. 29, 1944, 81/1, WJC. Secretary Hull asserted the difference to the American *chargé* in London: "It must be clearly kept in mind that [the] Greek relief program is exceptional and is considered as completely separate from the food package program" involving Portugal, which the U.S. government approved on a $12,000-month basis. Hull to Bucknell, Dec. 7, 1943, 840.48 Refugees/4762, SD.

74. The same lack of political leverage explains why Jewish resistance move-

ments in occupied Europe remained singularly isolated and had, in Goldmann's later words, "no rational hope to be rescued." Goldmann, "Influence of the Holocaust," p. 89. Also see the incisive remarks in this regard by Henri Michel, "Jewish Resistance and the European Resistance Movement," in *Jewish Resistance during the Holocaust* (Jerusalem, 1972), pp. 365-75.

Chapter 6—Rescue from the Balkans

1. *New York Times*, Feb. 13, 1943. For the American government's surprise about the story, see Welles to Atherton, Feb. 15, 1943, 840.48 Refugees/3603 RG 59, SD.

2. Hilberg, *Destruction*, pp. 488-91; *FRUS, 1941*, 2: 860-65; Curzio Malaparte, *Kaputt* (New York, 1946), ch. 6; Howard Blum, *Wanted! The Search for Nazis in America* (New York, 1977), pp. 107-17; WJC report, Jan. 27, 1942, pt. 3/10, Jewish Labor Committee Archives, New York; *Jewish Frontier*, Nov., 1942, pp. 30-32.

3. *FRUS, 1941*, 2:870-76.

4. Wasserstein, *Britain*, pp. 52-55, 76, 78-79; Ch. 2. MacMichael's fears also led to his suggestion, which the colonial secretary accepted, that *Darien II* "illegals" be removed from Palestine in case of British withdrawal before a Nazi attack. MacMichael to colonial secretary, May 23, 1941, FO 371/29234, PRO.

5. Chaim Barlas, *Hatsala Be Yemei Shoa* (Tel Aviv, 1975), pp. 18-25, 230-35; Lichtheim to Linton, Oct. 18, 1939, L 22/91, CZA; Barlas to Silberschein, Nov. 19, 1940, M 20/35, A. Silberschein MSS, YV; Barlas to Troper, June 15, 1941, and attachments, Turkey Genl. Refugees, JDC; Chaim Barlas, "Mivtsa Aliyat Lita," in *Dapim Le Cheker HaShoa Ve HaMered*, ser. 2a (HaKibbutz HaMeuchad, 1969), pp. 246-55; *Reports of the Executives Submitted to the 22nd Zionist Congress at Basle, December 1946* (Jerusalem, 1946), pp. 164-66; Shertok-MacMichael talk, Dec. 2, 1941, S 25/23, CZA.

6. Sharett, *Yoman Medini*, 5:286-95. Following MacMichael's urgent request to have the *Struma* barred from passage through the Dardanelles, Whitehall had first requested Turkish authorities to intervene in this vein. MacMichael to CO, Oct. 9, 1941, and FO to Angora, Oct. 11, 1941, FO 371/29163, PRO.

7. Wasserstein, *Britain*, pp. 143-56; Ofer, "HaAliya-HaBilti Chukit," pp. 338-83; report, Feb. 27, 1942, L 15/222, CZA.

8. Cranborne-Weizmann talk, Feb. 25, 1942, WA; Wedgwood and Davies quoted in *New Judea*, Mar., 1942, p. 85; American Jewish organizations' memo to Welles, Mar. 19, 1942, WA; S 25/10082, CZA; Wasserstein, *Britain*, pp. 157-61.

9. Cranborne-Locker et al. talk, May 22, 1942, S 25/9802, CZA; Cranborne to Locker, May 22, 1942, 16/3, Jewish Agency files, ZA; Locker to Cranborne, May 27, 1942, S 25/9802, CZA; Ofer, "HaAliya-HaBilti Chukit," pp. 361-64, 384-89.

10. Dalya Ofer, "Peulot Ezra VeHatsala Shel 'HaMishlachat HaEretz-Yisre'eilit' BeKushta 1943" (M.A. thesis, Hebrew University, 1972), pp. 121-23, 129 (copy at YIVO Library, New York); L 15/190, CZA; Barlas memo, Sept. 20, 1942, 16/3, Jewish Agency files, ZA; *Reports of the Executives*, p. 154. Also see Shertok to chief secretary, Nov. 2, 1942, Correspondence, BGA.

11. Christopher Browning, *The Final Solution and the German Foreign Office* (New York, 1978), pp. 125–26; Teodor Lavi, *Yahadut Rumania BaMa'avak Al Hatsalata* (Tel Aviv, 1965), p. 111n; Teodor Lavi in Teodor Lavi et al., eds., *Pinkas HaKehilot,Rumania,* 1 (Jerusalem, 1969):175. For the Wannsee conference, see Hilberg, *Destruction,* pp. 263–66.

12. Hilberg, *Destruction,* pp. 498–502; Browning, *Final Solution,* p. 127; Lavi, *Yahadut Rumania,* pp. 41–42, 110, 73–74; Lavi, *Pinkas Rumania,* pp. 176–77, 179.

13. Ofer, "Peulot," pp. 100–101, Lavi, *Pinkas Rumania,* p. 179; "A Scheme for the Roumanian Jews," n.d., WJCL; S. Avni, "Al Tochnit Transnistria," *Yalkut Moreshet* 30 (Nov. 1980):201–2.

14. Pozner to Barlas, Aug. 28, and to Neustadt, Dec. 12, 1942, P12/46, Chaim Pazner MSS, YV; Pomeraniec to Silberschein, Nov. 29, 1942, M20/36, YV; Ch. 3. An observation soon thereafter (cited by Bauer, *American Jewry,* p. 194) regarding the "news that came from Geneva did not convince" therefore refers to information transmitted simultaneously that summer by Pozner and the WJC's Gerhart Riegner.

15. Vagman-Eshkoli, "Emdat," pp. 82–85. The Rumanian Zionists had legitimate doubts, given both Lecca's dubious stance and past Nazi opposition to any emigration projects.

16. MacMichael to CO, Nov. 9, and Stanley to MacMichael, Dec. 8, 1942, FO 371/32698, PRO; FO 371/32668, PRO; Wasserstein, *Britain,* pp. 79–80. The Yishuv was prepared to take at least 50,000 Jewish children immediately. Ben Gurion to Berl (Locker), Dec. 8, 1942, Correspondence, BGA. For Stanley's firm reservation against large-scale immigration from Rumania, see Jan. 7, 1943, War Cabinet Committee on the Reception and Accommodation of Refugees, CAB 95/15, PRO.

17. Pomeraniec to Silberschein et al., Dec. 23, 1942, M20/36, YV; Menachem Bader, *Shlichuyot Atsuvot* (Merchavia, 1954), pp. 51–53; Bauer, *Holocaust,* pp. 158–59; Vagman-Eshkoli, "Emdat," p. 86; Ofer, "Peulot," p. 123; Pomeraniec to all, Feb. 15, 1943, D.1.711/4, MA; Bader to Heini et al., Mar. 9, 1943, D.1.730.1, MA; Venya Pomeraniec, "Kushta, Merkaz LePeulot Ezra VaHatsala," in Zerubavel Gilad, ed., *Magen BeSeter* (Jerusalem, 1952), p. 199. Letters forwarded in 1943 to Palestine are in S 26/1428, CZA.

18. Great Britain, *Parliamentary Debates* (Commons), vol. 386, cols. 863–67, Feb. 3, 1943, FO to Washington, Feb. 3, 1943, FO 371/34967, PRO; FO to Ankara, Feb. 16, 1943; FO 371/36700, PRO; WJC release, Feb. 20, 1943, 236/9, WJC; FO to Washington, Feb. 26, 1943, FO 371/34967, PRO; Barlas, *Hatsala,* pp. 190–91; Browning, *Final Solution,* pp. 170–73; el-Husseini to von Ribbentrop, May 13, 1943, M-94/45 (8), YV; Frederick Chary, *The Bulgarian Jews and the Final Solution, 1940–1944* (Pittsburgh, 1972), pp. 131–32, 137; Wasserstein, *Britain,* p. 181. According to an Eichmann associate, the ex-mufti's intervention with Himmler in Nov., 1942, also halted a Nazi scheme to exchange 10,000 Jewish children from Theresienstadt for imprisoned Germans in Palestine. "As far as I know," the SS official added, "these children were subsequently killed." Dieter Wisliceny interrogation, July 16, 1946, UNRRA Czech., Box 60,032, UN Archives, New York.

19. Ofer, "Peulot," p. 132; Vagman-Eshkoli, "Emdat," pp. 70–76; Barlas to

colleagues, Feb. 19, 1943, Genl. Turkey, Refugees, JDC; Steinhardt to Hull, Feb. 20, 1942, vol. 702, MD.

20. Linton to Boyd, Jan. 19, and Walker minute, Feb. 9, 1943, FO 371/36699, PRO; Barlas to Bursan, Mar. 1, 1943, SM-54, JDC; Namier to Gater, Mar. 5, 1943, FO 371/36677, PRO; Namier to Randall, Mar. 19, 1943, FO 371/36711, PRO; Goldmann to Taylor, Mar. 24, 1943, Z5/1161, CZA; Namier to Boyd, Mar. 25, 1943, FO 371/36677, PRO.

21. *Great Britain, Parliamentary Debates* (Lords), vol. 126, cols. 851–52, Mar. 23, 1943: Hayter to FO, Mar. 27, 1943, FO 371/36677, PRO; Ch. 4.

22. Bader to Va'ad HaPoel, Mar. 29, 1943, D.1.699A, MA; Pomeraniec to Pozner, Mar. 14, 1943, P12/40, Pazner MSS, YV; Istanbul letter (excerpt), Apr. 30, 1943, 265, WJC; Pomeraniec-Bader-Shind to Mereminski, July 25, 1943, Z6/17/9, CZA; Venya et al. to Silberschein et al., Aug. 12, 1943, M20/36, YV. For some of the group's reports in 1943 on the Jewish situation across Europe, see L 15/201, CZA.

23. Ofer, "Peulot," pp. 73–76; Pomeraniec-Bader to Silberschein et al., Apr. 27, 1943, M20/36, YV; Barlas, *Hatsala,* p. 244; Antonescu to IRC, May 24, 1943, P-6/52, YV; Husseini (in Rome) to Hungarian foreign minister, July 28, 1943, Correspondence, BGA; Lichtheim to agency, May 28, 1943, FO 371/34362, PRO. For the Yishuv's capacity to absorb these refugees, see Jewish Agency to Linton, Apr. 15, 1943, C 2/2/5/1, BD.

24. Wasserstein, *Britain,* pp. 162, 339; Stanley memo, WP 43/277, CAB 65, PRO; McPherson to Shertok, July 16, 1943, Correspondence, BGA; Ofer, "Peulot," p. 36.

25. Ofer, "Peulot," pp. 149–53; Pomeraniec-Bader-Shind to Mereminski, July 25, 1943, Z 6/17/9, CZA; Avriel, *Open,* p. 137.

26. Ofer, "Peulot," pp. 154–55; Venya et al. to Dobkin, July 3, 1943, S 26/1158, CZA; Shertok to Weizmann, July 12, 1943, Correspondence, BGA; Hayter to Goldmann, July 30, 1943, 16/3, Jewish Agency files, ZA; Shertok report, JAEJ, Aug. 22, 1943, CZA. For a similar contemporary impact on Jews in Slovakia, see Yosef Kornianski, *Bishlichut Chalutzim* (Haifa, 1979), pp. 139–40.

27. Chs. 2, 5; Leavitt to Hayes, Apr. 15, 1943, Bulgaria Genl., JDC; Magnes to Baerwald, May 14, 1943, Genl. Turkey, Refugees, JDC; Leavitt note, July 9, 1943, Genl. Jewish Agency, JDC.

28. Ofer, "Peulot," pp. 53–54; Mayer-Schwartz talk, Mar. 13, 1942, SM-7, JDC; Schwartz to Leavitt, June 5, 1943, Bulgaria Genl., JDC; Resnick report, Aug. 28, 1944, Emerg. Turkey, JDC. For Schwartz's seminal influence on JDC activity in Europe during the war, see Bauer, *American Jewry.*

29. Joseph Klarman interview with the author, Jan. 14, 1982; Ofer, "Peulot," p. 43; Szner comment in *Peulot Hatsala BeKushta, 1940–1945* (Jerusalem, 1969), p. 45; Fredka Mazia, *Rai'im BaSa'ar* (Jerusalem, 1964), p. 185; Venya et al. to Jewish Agency et al., Aug. 3, 1943, S 26/1240, CZA. Also see Zerubavel [Gilad], ed., *Chantche VeFrumka, Michtavim VeDivrei Zikaron* (Tel Aviv, 1945).

30. Mazia, *Rai'im BaSa'ar,* p. 185; Ch. 7, n. 85; Avriel, *Open,* p. 156; Pomeraniec in *Magen BeSeter,* pp. 201–2; Hadari comment in *Peulot Hatsala BeKushta,* p. 8; Ze'ev (Venya) Hadari interview with the author, Jan. 18, 1982.

For additional sums that were soon collected in Palestine, see minutes, Sept. 23, 1943, BGA.

31. Ofer, "Peulot," pp. 156-57; Avriel, *Open*, p. 131; Perl, *Four-Front War*, p. 359.

32. Ofer, "Peulot," p. 158; Braginski, *Am Choter El Chof*, pp. 260, 284; Perl, *Four-Front War*, pp. 360-61; Klarman interview; Avriel, *Open*, pp. 139-40.

33. Lavi, *Pinkas Rumania*, pp. 179, 189; Hilberg, *Destruction*, p. 505. The most thorough study gives a total of 138,957 Jews killed there by the Rumanians, with a total of 215,757 Rumanian and Russian Jews murdered in Transnistria by Antonescu's regime and the *Einsatzgruppen*. Julius S. Fisher, *Transnistria: The Forgotten Cemetery* (New York, 1969), pp. 134-37.

34. Lavi, *Yahadut Rumania*, pp. 47, 174, 72, 84; Silberschein to Tartakower, Sept. 22, 1943, 206A, WJC; Ch. 5; Wise to Taylor, Nov. 29, 1943, 840.48 Refugees/4908, SD. Also see copies of correspondence to Istanbul from Hungary at the end of 1943 in Kornianski, *Bishlichut Chalutzim*, pp. 231-41. For one example of Kolb's efforts, see ICRC Geneva to ICRC London, Jan. 20, 1944, WJCL.

35. Ch. 5; Norton to FO, Sept. 14, 1943, FO 371/36705, PRO; Campbell to Hull, Sept. 9, 1943, 840.48 Refugees/4529 CF, SD; Helm to Jerusalem, Nov. 4, 1943, FO 371/36684, PRO; ICRC Geneva to Wash. office, Oct. 12, 1943, 265, WJC; *Report of the International Committee of the Red Cross on Its Activities during the Second World War (September 1, 1939-June 30, 1947)*, 1 (Geneva, 1948):654; Easterman-Hall talk, Nov. 11, 1943, WJCL; *FRUS, 1941*, 1:391-95; Füllemann to ICRC London, Feb. 1, 1944, WJCL.

36. Bader to Zvi et al., Sept. 25, 1943, D.1.735.1-2, MA (trans. in Bauer, *Holocaust*, p. 25); Bader to Mazkirut, Oct. 1, 1943, D.1.705-3, MA; Bader to Zvi et al., Oct. 23, 1943, D.1.735.3, MA; Venya et al. to Silberschein et al., Nov. 13, 1943, M 20/36, YV; *Report of the ICRC*, 1:655; Schwarzenberg to Kahany, May 12, 1944, L 15/395, CZA; Ofer, "Peulot," pp. 164-66. I have relied on Barlas's numbers for 1943 as given in the Resnick report, July 1-15, 1944, Emerg. Turkey, JDC. Of these "illegals," 252 ended up in Cyprus. Ibid.

37. Ofer, "Peulot," pp. 164-67; Pomeraniec in *Magen BeSeter*, pp. 202-3; *New York Times*, Jan. 5, 1944. The first photographs of Jewish corpses in Transnistria, along with one of a Treblinka death chamber, reached the Jewish Agency at this time. Lichtheim to Linton, Jan. 20, 1944, L 22/77, CZA.

38. Enzer memo, Jan. 18, 1944, FO 371/42723, PRO; Hugessen to FO, Dec. 30, 1943, FO 371/36684, PRO; Hugessen to FO, Jan. 30, 1944, FO 371/47241, PRO; *JTA*, Jan. 20, 1944; Lavi, *Yahadut Rumania*, pp. 135-37. For the Zionist youth movement in the country at the time, see Y. Artsi, "BeRumania BeYemei HaShoa," *Masua* 1 (1973):140-50, and S. Avni, *Ge'alani MiYad Tsar* (Tel Aviv, 1978), ch. 2.

39. Ira A. Hirschmann, *Caution to the Winds* (New York, 1962), pp. 48-49, 101-5, 130; Kook interview with the author, June 22, 1972. For the Emergency Committee, see Chs. 4-5.

40. Bergson-Hirschmann-Long talk, Sept. 1, 1943, Box 202, Breckenridge Long MSS, LC.

41. Feingold, *Politics*, p. 145; Barry Rubin, "Ambassador Laurence A. Stein-

hardt: The Perils of a Jewish Diplomat, 1940–1945," *American Jewish History* 70 (Mar., 1981):332–43; Yitschak Ben Zvi diary, Aug., 1943, 1/6/14/11, Yitschak Ben Zvi Archives, Jerusalem (courtesy of Shimon Rubinstein); Steinhardt to Hull, Feb. 20, 1944, vol. 702, MD; *FRUS, 1941,* 1:986–87; Isaac Lewin, *No'chen Churban* (New York, 1950), pp. 200–202; Goldmann-Steinhardt talk, Oct. 4, 1943, 264, WJC; Chaim Barlas, "Pegishot BeKushta," *Masua* 4 (1976):125–33.

42. Steinhardt to Hull, Sept. 7, 1943, Box 70, WRB.

43. Hirschmann, *Caution,* pp. 132–34; Hirschmann memo, Oct. 13, 1943, Box 1, Ira A. Hirschmann MSS, FDRL; Ira A. Hirschmann, *Lifeline to a Promised Land* (New York, 1946), pp. 18–19, 46; JAEJ minutes Mar. 5, 1944, CZA. For the board's early understanding of Turkey's importance to the cause of rescue, see Friedman memo, Jan. 25, 1944, Box 39, WRB.

44. Hirschmann, *Lifeline,* pp. 40–45; Steinhardt to Pehle, Feb. 26, 1944, Box 39, WRB; Hirschmann to Pehle, Mar. 4, and to Pehle, Mar. 6, 1944, vol. 709, MD; Payman handwritten memo, Mar. 4, 1944, Box 1, Hirschmann MSS.

45. "Draft," c. Feb., 1944, FO 371/42722, PRO; Gater-Shertok talk, Feb. 24, 1944, CO 733/462/75872/26C, PRO; FO 371/42722, PRO; FO 921/152, PRO; MacMichael to Stanley, Mar. 18, 1944, FO 371/42723, PRO; FO to Angora, Mar. 17, 1944, CO 733/454/75113-I, PRO.

46. Gurfein interview with the author, June 7, 1979; Hirschmann to Pehle, Feb. 18, Mar. 15, 1944, Box 39, WRB; Barlas-Steinhardt talk, Mar. 1, 1944, C 11/12/136, BD; Hirschmann, *Lifeline,* pp. 59–70; Steinhardt to Barlas, Apr. 3, 1944, BGA. Palestine Chief Rabbi Isaac HaLevi Herzog had also failed in his effort regarding the *Vatan.* His report of activities for rescue while in Istanbul is given in Herzog memo, *Av* 1944, S 25/1251, CZA.

47. Hirschmann, *Caution,* pp. 152–60; Friedman to Pehle, Apr. 15, 1944, Box 42, WRB; *FRUS, 1941,* 1:1045–46. At the personal instigation of State Department Assistant Secretary Adolf A. Berle, Jr., who had worked with Hirschmann on LaGuardia's New York mayoralty campaign, Roosevelt secretly approved the four visas to Cretianu. Hirschmann address, Mar. 5, 1981, CUNY-Eisner Institute for Holocaust Studies (notes in the author's possession).

48. Ofer, "Peulot," pp. 161, 165; Lavi, *Pinkas Rumania,* pp. 187–88, 190; *Magen BeSeter,* pp. 237, 255; Donovan to Roosevelt, Mar. 27, 1944, Box 6, PSF OSS, FDRL. For the children rescued from Transnistria, see Efraim Dekel, *Seridei Cherev,* 1 (Tel Aviv, 1963):282–302.

49. Avriel, *Open,* pp. 140–45; Hugessen to FO, Apr. 1, 1944, FO 371/42723, PRO; Steinhardt to State, Mar. 28 and 29, 1944, 840.48 Refugees/5465 and 5467 CF, SD; Steinhardt to Hull, Mar. 30, 1944, vol. 716, MD.

50. Avriel, *Open,* p. 145; Lavi, *Pinkas Rumania,* p. 193; Resnick report, July 1–15, 1944, Emerg. Turkey, JDC; HeChalutz report, May 23, 1944, Box 52, WRB; Ch. 7; Pinkerton to Hull, May 25, 1944, vol. 735, MD; L 15/117-II, CZA. The cable about Hungarian Jewry was sent by the agency to the World Jewish Congress in New York, which immediately published it. Memo, June 6, 1944, 178A, WJC.

51. *New York Times,* Apr. 11, 1944; Linton to under secretary, Apr. 14, 1944, Correspondence, BGA; Steinhardt to Hull, May 2, 1944, vol. 726, MD; Wasser-

stein, *Britain,* pp. 327-28; Rubin, "Ambassador Steinhardt," p. 344; Avigur remarks, Apr. 19, 1944, Va'ada HaMerakezet minutes, Va'ad HaPoel, Histadrut Archives, Tel Aviv. The agency even felt it necessary to announce that its efforts alone had brought Jews to Istanbul. Shertok to Goldmann, June 2, 1944, Z5/778, CZA.

52. Ch. 7; Bader, *Shlichuyot,* pp. 100-106, 110-13; Avriel, *Open,* pp. 177-188; Hadari interview; Shalom Rosenfeld, *Tik P'lili 124: Mishpat Gruenwald-Kastner* (Tel Aviv, 1955), pp. 53-54; Bader to Pomeraniec, May 27, 1944, D.1.719, MA; diary, July 8, 1944, Box 1, Hirschmann MSS; Bader to Ben Gurion, July 8, 1944, BGA; Magnes diary, same date, BGA. At Griffel's entreaty, Klarman had tried to convince Brand against completing the journey from Ankara to Aleppo. He did not think the Jewish Agency a conscious accomplice to Brand's arrest, however, and refused to testify to that effect for the defense at the 1954 Gruenwald-Kastner trial. Klarman interview.

53. Ofer, "Peulot," p. 166; Bader to Shertok, Mar. 18, 1944, D.1.745, MA; Klarman et al. to Va'ad HaHatsala, May 5, 1944, Rumania Genl., JDC; Klarman interview with the author, Jan. 14, 1982.

54. Barlas-Steinhardt talk, May 11, 1944, S 44/679, CZA; Kubowitzki memo, June 9, 1944, 76A, WJC. For the Va'ad HaHatsala, see Ch. 9.

55. Ofer, "Peulot," pp. 160-61; Kolb to Simond, Apr. 29, May 5 and 31, 1944, all in FO 371/42807, PRO; Avriel, *Open,* pp. 145-47; M[enachem] to Chaverim, May 19, 1944, Correspondence, BGA.

56. Filderman to Barlas, May 10, 1944, Box 40, WRB; Marton to Brothers, Aug. 19, 1944, Box 36, WRB; Mozes Weinberger-Carmilly, "The Tragedy of Transylvanian Jewry," *Yad Vashem Bulletin* 15 (Aug., 1964):23; L 15/255 and 180, CZA; Riegner to McClelland, May 16, 1944, Box 62, WRB; Filderman to Mayer, June 16, 1944, SM-55, JDC; Aryeh Morgenstern, "Va'ad HaHatsala HaMcuchad SheLeYad HaSochnut HaYehudit U'Peulotav BaShanim 1943-1945," *Yalkut Moreshet* 13 (June, 1971):74-75; memo, Oct. 22, 1944, S 26/1428, CZA; S 26/1235, CZA.

57. Kolb to Simond, May 31, 1944, FO 371/42807, PRO; Lavi, *Pinkas Rumania,* pp. 193-94; notes of meetings, June 18, 20, and 21, and Filderman to Barlas, July 7, 1944, all in Rumania Genl., JDC; P 6/91, YV.

58. Hirschmann, *Lifeline,* pp. 107-27; Roosevelt to Hirschmann, June 8, 1944, Box 194, PSF WRB, FDRL; Hirschmann to Pehle, Aug. 19, 1944, with reports, Turkey Emerg., JDC; Schweitzer to Bernstein, July 20, 1944, folder 3, HIAS-HICEM 1, ser. 18, YIVO Archives, New York; Kaplan report, July 28, 1944, S 26/1238A, CZA. For Steinhardt's continuing efforts, see Steinhardt to Resnick, June 15, 1944, Rumania Genl., JDC.

59. Hugessen to FO, June 26, 1944, FO 371/42726, PRO; Bader, *Shlichuyot,* pp. 109-10; Hirschmann to Pehle, Aug. 19, 1944, Turkey Emerg., JDC; Hirschmann-Cretianu talk, July 5, 1944; Kaplan to Zissu, July 17, 1944; Shind to Zissu, July 17 and 28, 1944, all in Box 37, WRB; Hirschmann to Zissu, July 21, 1944, Turkey Genl., JDC; Schweitzer to Asofsky, Aug. 8, 1944, folder 13/19, HIAS-HICEM 1, ser. 18, YIVO Archives. For some eyewitness accounts from *Kasbek* survivors, see *Voice of the Unconquered,* 2 (Sept., 1944):3.

60. Hirschmann memo, Apr. 6, 1944, Box 72, WRB; Hirschmann-Black talk,

July 21, and Hirschmann to Pehle, Aug. 19, 1944, Turkey Emerg., JDC; Hirschmann, *Lifeline,* pp. 150–62. For previous OSS efforts to detach Bulgaria from the Axis, see two memos to Donoⱱ n, Mar. 23, 1944, Box 6, PSF OSS, FDRL.

61. Hirschmann, *Caution,* pp. 137–39, 151; *New York Times,* May 17, 1944; diary, Mar. 10, 1944, Box 1, Hirschmann MSS; Avriel, *Open,* p. 169; Hirschmann to Simond, July 19, 1944, Box 37, WRB.

62. Avriel, *Open,* pp. 169–70; Hirschmann to Pehle, Aug. 15, 1944, vol. 764, MD.

63. Barlas to Gruenbaum, Aug. 5, 1944, Correspondence, BGA; Hirschmann, *Lifeline,* pp. 92–96.

64. Avigur interview with the author, July 15, 1976; Ch. 2; "Moladeti" (Pomeraniec) to JAEJ, Aug. 12, 1944, S 26/1428, CZA; JDC admin. committee, Aug. 8 1944, SM-13, JDC; report, Sept. 9, 1944, 264, WJC; Avriel, *Open,* pp. 171–73. Ya'akov Cruz, "HaLaila Bo Tub'ah 'Mefkure,'" *Yediot Acharonot,* Aug. 10, 1979, cites a German author's claim that the vessel involved was of Russian origin.

65. Hirschmann to Magnes, Aug. 7, 1944, Box 41, WRB; Hirschmann to Simond, Aug. 8, 1944, Box 3, Hirschmann MSS; Hirschmann, *Lifeline,* pp. 162–64; Pehle to Hirschmann, Aug. 18, 1944, Box 72, WRB.

66. Griffel et al. to Va'ad HaHatsᵃlᵃ, Aug. 5 and 12, and Sternbuch to Va'ad HaHatsala, Aug. 12, 1944, 265, WJC; July and Aug., 1944, protocols of testimony from *Kasbek* passengers and others, and report of Oct. 4, 1944, Harry Goodman MSS, London.

67. Buchman memos, Aug. 17 and 18, 1944, Genl. Turkey, JDC; Kotler-Kalmanowitz to Griffel, Aug. 16, 1944, Va'ad HaHatsala MSS, Yeshiva University, New York. Nothing came of the proposal, as the Swedish foreign office indicated that no such vessel would be available for at least two months. Olsen to Dexter, Aug. 14, 1944, Box 39, WRB.

68. Steinhardt to Pehle, June 14, 1944, Box 70, WRB; Hirschmann to Pehle, Aug. 19, 1944, Turkey Emerg., JDC; Jabotinsky memo, n.d., Box 6, Eri Jabotinsky MSS, Metsudat Ze'ev, Tel Aviv; Penkower, "Bergson Boys," pp. 299–306.

69. Pehle to Leavitt, Aug. 30, 1944, Box 40, WRB; conclusions of Sept. 21, 1944, Box 396, RG 165, War Dept. MSS, NA. For the Revisionist Zionist's erring partisan attack against the Jewish Agency for Joel Brand's arrest and the deportation of 400,000 Hungarian Jews, see Jabotinsky to Mirelman, July 31, 1944, Mayer-Musy file, Leo Baeck Institute, New York.

70. Ch. 7; Hirschmann to Pehle, Aug. 10, 1944, 76A, WJC; dispatch to Admiralty, July 17, 1944, FO 371/42809, PRO; Katzki to Hirschmann, Sept. 13, 1944, Box 45, WRB; Hirschmann, *Lifeline,* pp. 166–67; Hirschmann to Pehle, Sept. 19, 1944, Box 39, WRB.

71. Ueberall to Hirschmann, Sept. 30, 1944, Box 2, Hirschmann MSS; Hirschmann, *Lifeline,* pp. 168–71; Magnes et al. to Hirschmann, Oct. 11, 1944, Box 40, WRB; Schweitzer notes, Oct. 26, 1944, folder 13/22, HIAS-HICEM 1, ser. 18, YIVO Archives.

72. V[enya] to Chaverim, Jan. 23, 1945, Correspondence, BGA; Avriel, *Open,* pp. 190–93; Klarman interview; Steinhardt to board, Sept. 29, 1944, 76A, WJC.

73. Mason to Shertok, Sept. 25, 1944, FO 371/42817, PRO; Bader letter, Oct.

28, 1944, D.1.708, MA; Barlas to Goldmann, received Sept. 21, 1944, 264, WJC; Leavitt to Passman, Oct. 9, 1944, Box 39, WRB. Those arriving on the Mossad ships during these past eight months (given as 3,074 in a different calculation) constituted 77 percent of the total immigration exclusive of other Middle East countries to Palestine. In 1943, by contrast, illegals made up 46 percent of the total reaching Istanbul on the way to Palestine. 1943–Sept. 1, 1944 memo, Correspondence, BGA.

74. Ch. 7; Moyne to FO, Aug. 25, 1944, FO 371/42816, PRO; FO to Washington, Sept. 14, 1944, FO 371/40137, PRO; Shertok-Stanley talk, Sept. 14, 1944, CO 733/462/75872, PRO; Wasserstein, *Britain,* pp. 333–34, 340.

75. Leavitt report to JDC executive committee, Nov. 15, 1944, 268/87, WJC; Proskauer to secretary of state, Oct. 27, 1944, Rumania 1938–1944, AJC; Katzki memo, Nov. 19, 1944, Box 41, WRB; Tartakower memo, Oct. 31, 1944, 268/66, WJC.

76. Katzki to Pehle, Oct. 30, 1944, Box 37, WRB; Katzki to Pehle, Nov. 8, 1944, Box 40, WRB; Boswell to FO, Nov. 24, 1944, FO 371/42822, PRO; Petersen to FO, Dec. 5 and 6, 1944, FO 371/42823, PRO; Petersen to FO, Dec. 13, 1944, FO 371/42824, PRO. The Palestinians' figures were 539 on the *Salhattin* and 958 on the *Toros.* Memo, Dec. 24, 1944, Correspondence, BGA.

77. Gort to Stanley, Nov. 4, and Eastwood to Mason, Nov. 9, 1944, FO 371/42821, PRO; Wasserstein, *Britain,* pp. 340–41; Gort to Stanley, Dec. 10, and Le Rougetel to FO, Dec. 7 and 9, 1944, FO 371/42824, PRO.

78. Boswell to FO, Nov. 23, 1944, FO 371/42823, PRO; Avriel, *Open,* pp. 194–97; Katzki to Pehle, Dec. 12, 1944, Box 40, WRB; Ben Gurion to Bulgarian foreign minister, Dec. 6, 1944, Correspondence, BGA; JAEJ, Dec. 17, 1944, CZA.

79. FO to Ankara, Dec. 18, 1944, FO 371/42824, PRO.

80. Katzki to Pehle, Jan. 6, 1945; Katzki to Pehle, Dec. 25, 26, and 30, 1944; board to Katzki, Feb. 3, 1945, all in Box 39, WRB; Steinhardt to Katzki, Dec. 20, 1944, Box 41, WRB. The first two exchanges took place in Nov., 1942, and Jan., 1943. Chs. 3–4. For the third, see Behar memo, n.d., Z 4/15136, and L 15/116, CZA; p. 252 below. A final exchange in early 1945 brought 130 Jews from Bergen-Belsen, armed with South American passports, into Switzerland. MK (Kahany) memo, Jan. 22, 1945, L 22/92, CZA; Kubowitzki diary, Feb. 15, 1945, in Kubovy, *Ultimate Rescue Efforts, 1944,* vol. 3, YV.

81. Jabotinsky letter (excerpt), Nov. 20, 1944, Box 1-8, Emergency Committee MSS, Metsudat Ze'ev, Tel Aviv; Kook interview with the author, June 21, 1972; Katzki to Pehle, Dec. 16, 1944, Box 40, WRB.

82. Katzki to Pehle, Jan. 1, 1945, Box 40, WRB; Grew to Ehrhorn, Mar. 2, 1945, Joseph Grew MSS, Houghton Library, Harvard University, Cambridge, Mass.; *New York Post,* Mar. 2, 1945; *New York Herald Tribune,* Mar. 3, 1945.

83. Ben Gurion to Lourie, Oct. 10, 1944, Correspondence, BGA; Joseph conversation with board, Dec. 7, 1944, Z 5/379, CZA; Hirschmann, *Caution,* pp. 146–47; Boukstein to Jewish Agency, Mar. 9, 1945, Jewish Agency files, ZA; Boukstein interview with the author, Apr. 3, 1978.

84. Boukstein to Jewish Agency, Apr. 16, 1945, Jewish Agency files, ZA; Eastin to O'Dwyer, Feb. 9, 1945, Box 44, WRB; Trobe to Mayer, received Apr.

28, 1945, SM supplement-4, JDC. Seven hundred Hungarian refugees of the "Kastner train" from Bergen-Belsen, who refused to go to the UNRRA camp in Philippeville, departed for Palestine in late Aug., 1945. The last of the Mossad wartime ships, the *Smyrnie,* arrived in Palestine in 1946.

85. Grigg to Eden, Jan. 29, 1945, PREM 4, 52/3; Ben Gurion–Gort talk, Mar. 13, 1945, CO 733/462/75872, 26G; Gort to Stanley, Mar. 15, 17, and 20, 1945, CAB 95/14, all in PRO.

86. Ueberall to Meriminski, Feb. 14, 1945, Correspondence, BGA; Shertok to Weizmann to Ben Gurion, Apr. 5, 1945, caught in British censorship, CO 733/454/75113, PRO; Eastwood to Jewish Agency, May 7, 1945, FO 371/51118, PRO.

87. Moyne comment, Mar. 28, 1941, at War Cabinet meeting, FO 371/29162, PRO.

88. Hirschmann to Pehle, Mar. 6, 1944, vol. 703, MD; Steinhardt to State, Apr. 5, 1944, Box 37, WRB; Hull to Steinhardt, June 5, 1944, vol. 739, MD. The most detailed study of Turkish diplomacy during World War II omits reference to this sorry record. Edward Weisband, *Turkish Foreign Policy, 1943-1945* (Princeton, N.J., 1972).

89. Chs. 4, 5; State-FO representatives' talk, Apr. 24, 1944, FO 371/42725, PRO; Hirschmann, *Caution,* p. 159.

90. Max Lerner in *PM,* Apr. 24, 1944; Washington to Randall, May 30, 1944, FO 371/42730, PRO.

91. Bader, *Shlichuyot,* pp. 121–23. The Palestinians' ships brought 4,321 during 1944. Memo, Dec. 24, 1944, Correspondence, BGA.

92. Bauer, *Holocaust,* pp. 63–66. Ch. 7 indicates that Hungary's regent held similar views. Leon Poliakov and Josef Wulf estimate that 7,000 Bulgarian and 425,000 Rumanian Jews were murdered during the war, or 14 and 50 percent of their respective countries' Jewish populations as of September, 1939. Cited in Paul R. Mendes-Flohr and Jehuda Reinharz, eds., *The Jew in the Modern World: A Documentary History* (New York, 1980), p. 520. For some efforts by Jews in the free world to save their people in Bulgaria from deportation during Mar. and Apr. 1943, see Bader comment in *Peulot Hatsala Be Kushta,* p. 15; *Unity in Dispersion,* pp. 181–82; and Glanz report to Kubowitzki, July 15, 1946, 265, WJC.

93. Ben Gurion speech, Dec. 28, 1944, file 174a, Robert Szold MSS, ZA; Eden memo, Apr. 10, 1945, CAB 66, PRO; *FRUS, 1941,* 2:2–4. Emerson followed the Foreign Office line in opposing Palestine for large Jewish postwar settlement. Memo of talk, Apr. 25, 1944, Immigration 1940-1944, AJC; Herbert Emerson, "The Postwar Problems of Refugees," *Foreign Affairs* 21 (Jan., 1943):211–20.

94. Shertok to "Dear Brothers," Aug. 10, 1943, S 26/1235, CZA. *Tisha B'Av* marks the fast day in the Jewish calendar that commemorates the destruction of the Holy Temple in Jerusalem by Babylonians and Romans in 586 B.C.E. and 70 C.E. respectively.

Chapter 7—Auschwitz-Birkenau and the Martyrdom of Hungarian Jewry

1. Michoel Dov Weissmandel, *Min HaMeitsar* (New York, 1960), pp. 103–11.

A copy of the original, with Schwalb's name written on it, reached the headquarters of the World Jewish Congress in New York. 266, WJC.

2. Weissmandel, *Min Ha Meitsar;* Livia Rothkirchen, *Churban Yahadut Slovakia* (Jerusalem, 1961); Binyamin and Brudi Stern interview with the author, July 23, 1979; Weissmandel interview, Feb. 28, 1950, 266, WJC; Vagman-Eshkoli, "Emdat Ha Manhigut Ha Yehudit," pp. 97–115; Bauer, *American Jewry,* pp. 359–79; Nahum Goldmann's reservations, in a letter to the author, Nov. 22, 1978. For the WJC's reaction to the Allied financial blockade, see Ch. 5.

3. Weissmandel, *Min Ha Meitsar,* pp. 112–19; *Der Kastner Bericht* (Basel, 1946), p. 30; Jenö Levai, ed., *Eichmann in Hungary, Documents* (Budapest, 1961); statements by Stern, Petö, and Freudiger, in Randolph Braham, ed., *Hungarian-Jewish Studies,* 3 (New York: 1973):1–146; Yehuda Gutman, Bela Vago, and Livia Rothkirchen, eds., *Hanhagat Yehudei Hungaria Be Mivchan Ha Shoa* (Jerusalem, 1976).

4. Gideon Hausner, *Justice in Jerusalem* (New York, 1968), pp. 139–40; Rudolf Vrba and Alan Bastic, *I Cannot Forgive* (New York, 1964 ed.), pp. 212–46; Filip Müller, *Auschwitz Inferno: The Testimony of a Sonderkommando* (London, 1979), pp. 121–22; Erich Kulka, "Five Escapes from Auschwitz," in Yuri Suhl, ed., *They Fought Back* (New York, 1975 ed.), pp. 205–7; Oscar Karmil (Krasniansky) interview with Erich Kulka, June 8, 1964, Hebrew University, Jerusalem; Schwalb memo, "Tatsachenbericht ueber Auschwitz und Birkenau," May 17, 1944, SM–16, JDC; Weissmandel to Sternbuch, May 15, 1944, Box 62, WRB.

5. Kornianski, *Bishlichut Chalutzim,* pp. 186–89; Asher Cohen, "HeChalutz Underground in Hungary: March-August 1944 (Based on Testimony of Survivors)," *Yad Vashem Studies* 14 (1981):247–67; Bauer, *Holocaust,* pp. 103–4, 107–9; Mayer notes, May 15, 1944, SM–22, also SM–20, JDC; Schwalb to Neustadt, May 3, 1944, S26/1281, CZA.

6. Bauer, *Holocaust,* pp. 109–13; Kastner affidavit, Jan. 4, 1946, copy in 266, WJC, NG–2994, Nuremberg Documents, Columbia University Law Library, New York. For the Himmler–von Ribbentrop feud, see Paul Seabury, *The Wilhelmstrasse: A Study of German Diplomats under the Nazi Regime* (Berkeley, Calif., 1954), pp. 127–31.

7. Andre Biss, *A Million Jews to Save* (Cranbury, 1975 ed.), pp. 45–46; Alex Weissberg, *Desperate Mission* (New York, 1958), pp. 123–24; Bauer, *Holocaust,* pp. 113–19.

8. For Kastner's not informing Jews during a visit in early May to save family and friends in his hometown of Cluj, see Rosenfeld, *Tik P'lili 124,* and *Kastner Bericht,* pp. 35–36. The charge against the local Jewish leadership has been most recently advanced in Randolph L. Braham's *The Politics of Genocide: The Holocaust in Hungary,* 2 vols. (New York, 1981), 1:ch. 14, 2:chs. 23–29.

9. Kornianski, *Bishlichut Chalutzim,* ch. 3; Asher Cohen, "Hashpa'at HaPelitim Al Hithavut Ha Machteret HaChalutzit Be Hungaria," in *Dapim Le Cheker Tekufat HaShoa,* ser. 2 (Tel Aviv, 1981), pp. 121–49; Moshe Rosenberg testimony at the Eichmann trial, May 31, 1961 (copy in ZA); Weissberg, *Desperate Mission,* pp. 122–23n; Moses Weinberger-Carmilly, "The Tragedy of Transylvanian Jewry," *Yad Vashem Bulletin* 15 (Aug., 1964):12–27; Livia E. Bitton Jackson, *Elli: Coming of Age in the Holocaust* (New York, 1980), pp. 3–68;

Lavi, *Yahadut Rumania,* pp. 140–43. For the relation of this response to current scholarship on human behavior in *extremis,* see p. 290 below.

10. Hall to OSS director, Apr. 5, 1944, Office of the Chief, Box 2, RG 226, NA; Martin Gilbert, *Auschwitz and the Allies* (New York, 1981), p. 197; Bela Vago, "The British Government and the Fate of Hungarian Jewry in 1944," in Gutman and Zuroff, *Rescue Attempts,* p. 308. And reports reaching the OSS at the end of May, which "seem correct," spoke of the gassing of many Hungarian Jews in box cars en route to the Polish frontier. Hall to OSS director, May 25, 1944, Office of the Chief, Box 2, RG 226, NA.

11. MacMichael to CO, May 26, 1944, CAB 95/15, PRO; Bauer, *Holocaust,* pp. 119–32; Pomeraniec summary, May 25, 1944, JAEJ, CZA; Resnick report, June 6, 1944, 840.48 Refugees/6178, RG 59, SD; n. 18 below; Martin Gilbert in *Jerusalem Post,* Feb. 8 and 15, 1980, published later in pt. 3 of his *Auschwitz* (who thus errs in claiming that Brand, and therefore the West, did not know of the deportations and their fate until one month after his arrival); June 11, 1944, JAEJ, CZA; MacMichael to Shertok, quoted in Barlas, *Hatsala,* p. 125. I am persuaded by Yehuda Bauer's subtle analysis that Brand distorted certain facts to impress upon the West the significance and urgency of his mission. *Holocaust,* pp. 127–28.

12. *FRUS, 1944,* 1:1056–57; June 12, 1944, CAB 65, PRO.

13. Bauer, *Holocaust,* pp. 131, 134–35; Goldmann to Stettinius, June 7, 1944, 840.48 Refugees/6300, SD; Goldmann interview with the author, Nov. 7, 1976; Gilbert in *Jerusalem Post,* Feb. 15, 1980; memo of Brand-Shertok talk, June 11, 1944, Correspondence, BGA; Hirschmann interrogation of Brand and memo, June 22, 1944, Box 70, WRB; JAEJ, June 24, 1944, CZA; *FRUS, 1944,* 1:1074–75.

14. Biss, *Million Jews,* pp. 48–81; Gilbert in *Jerusalem Post,* Feb. 15, 1980; SM–20, JDC; NG–2260, Nuremberg Documents, Columbia University Law Library; Zvi Erez, "Shisha Yamim BeYuli 1944 BeHungaria," *Yalkut Moreshet* 20 (Dec., 1975):n. 23.

15. Betsalel Mordowicz, "Pa'amayim Yatsati Chai MeiAuschwitz," *Yalkut Moreshet* 9 (Oct., 1968):7–20; Kulka, "Five Escapes," pp. 208–9; Braham, *Politics,* 2:711–12.

16. Kornianski, *Bishlichut Chalutzim,* pp. 173–77; Asher Cohen, "LeDemuta Shel 'Va'adat HaEzra VeHaHatsala' BeBudapest BeReishit Darka," *Moreshet* 29, (May, 1980):143–60; Eugene Levai, *Black Book on the Martyrdom of Hungarian Jewry,* ed. Lawrence P. Davis (Zurich, 1948), pp. 275–76, 261; Chaim Pazner interviews with the author, July 14, 1978, and June 20, 1979.

17. Pazner interview, June 20, 1979; reports of Krausz to Pozner, June 19, 1944, and Krausz to Pazner, July 19, 1971, Chaim Pazner MSS, YV. Levai credits the receiver to Mantello, but the later forged his name for that of the Jewish Agency representative. (Ben Hecht's *Perfidy* (New York, 1961), p. 263, suggests, like Levai, that Pozner did nothing with the report.)

18. Herman Landau interview with the author, Dec. 1, 1980; Sternbuch to London Agudas Israel, Mar. 12, 1945, Isaac Sternbuch MSS, private collection of Avraham Sternbuch, London; Sternbuch to Goodman, July 18, 1944, Harry Goodman MSS, private collection of Victor Goodman, London; Weissmandel-

Fleischmann letter, May 22, 1944 (excerpts), in Kubovy, *Ultimate Rescue Efforts,* vol. 3, YV; Weissmandel cable, May 24, 1944, Box 62, WRB; Sternbuch to Union, June 2, 1944, Box 70, WRB. Sternbuch's activity further contradicts the claim (Gilbert, *Auschwitz,* p. 216) that Weissmandel's cables did not reach the West until June (and see n. 11 above). For Weissmandel's regular letters thereafter in this vein to Jewish rescue organizations in Switzerland, see Weissmandel, *Min HaMeitsar,* pp. 182–219.

19. Gruenbaum-Pinkerton talk, June 2, 1944, S44/471, CZA; Pinkerton to board, June 2, 1944, Box 30, WRB; Schwartz to Reiss, July 19, 1944, 264, WJC. This Weissmandel cable had come to Brand's attention prior to his departure for Aleppo. Gruenbaum's associates opposed death camp bombings at this time. JAEJ, June 11, 1944, CZA.

20. Pazner interview with the author, June 20, 1979; Pozner to Barlas, June 23, 25, and 29, July 1, 1944; Barlas to Pozner, June 24 and 27, 1944; Lichtheim to Dobkin, July 3, 1944, all in Pazner MSS, YV; Levai, *Eichmann in Hungary,* p. 118; Lichtheim to Gruenbaum, June 19, 1944, S 26/1281, CZA; Ch. 8; Kopecky to McClelland, June 19, 1944, and McClelland notes attached, Box 58, WRB; Gilbert, *Auschwitz,* pp. 232–34, 246, 248; FO 371/38941, PRO. The underground Jewish National Committee in Poland also knew of the Theresienstadt group's fate in Auschwitz. Cable, June 3, 1944, to Schwartzbart (London), in Kubovy, *Ultimate Rescue Efforts,* vol. 3. See, too, the cable sent on June 20, 1944, to London, in Stefan Korbonski, *Fighting Warsaw* (New York, 1968), p. 255.

21. McClelland to Pehle, June 24, 1944, Box 34, WRB; Norton to FO, June 26, 1944, FO 371/42807, PRO; Lichtheim to Gruenbaum, June 26, 1944, S26/1281, CZA. Schwalb had also supplied regular reports to McClelland, who in turn helped dispatch Mayer's funds to Schwalb's contacts in Hungary. Box 58, WRB. For the profound shock of even Allen Dulles, America's chief intelligence officer abroad, upon receiving a copy of the Auschwitz-Birkenau report from Garrett, see Laqueur, *Terrible Secret,* pp. 98–99.

22. David Wyman, "Why Auschwitz Was Never Bombed," *Commentary* 65 (May, 1978):38–39; John McCloy interview with the author, May 17, 1977. For that department's earlier discussion on rescuing Jews, see OPD 383.7 II, RG 165, War Dept. MSS, NA.

23. Bauer, *Holocaust,* pp. 137–38, 141; FO to DC, July 1, 1944, FO 371/42808, PRO. Already in March, U.S. military intelligence received a detailed Polish report about the mass gassing of Jews in Auschwitz-Birkenau. Berkeland to G-2, Mar. 17, 1944, Poland, RG 165, Federal Records Center, Suitland, Md. On June 26 the Foreign Office's Central Department received its first eyewitness report on the gassing of Jews there. Stockholm to London, June 18, 1944, FO 371/39451, PRO. Earlier British information about their fate was highly limited. Hinsley, *British Intelligence,* 2:673.

24. *PM,* July 6, 1944; Mallet to FO, July 2, and Ripka to Nichols, July 4, 1944, FO 371/42807, PRO; July 3, 1944, Cabinet conclusions, FO 371/42808, PRO; messages quoted in Gilbert in *Jerusalem Post,* Feb. 22, 1980; Kastner-Bader cables, June 29, July 2, 1944, Correspondence, BGA; Ch. 6, n. 52; July 6, 1944, minutes and *aide-mémoire,* FO 371/42808, PRO; Eden to Churchill,

July 6, 1944, FO 371/42809, PRO. Also see Ben Gurion to Goldmann, July 11, 1944, Mayer-Musy file, Leo Baeck Institute, New York.

25. Churchill to Eden, July 7 and 11, 1944, FO 371/42809, PRO. At the same time Churchill endorsed Eden's announcement in Commons (July 5) that a swift Allied victory was the "principal hope" for the Jews. Churchill to Melchett, July 13, 1944, PREM 4, 51/10, PRO.

26. Bauer, *Holocaust,* pp. 142, 135, 145–50, 152; Venya-Menachem to Pozner et al., July 21, 1944, Silberschein MSS, M20/36, YV; July–Aug., 1944, Correspondence, BGA. For Hull's cable, *FRUS, 1944,* 1:1089–91. Years later the British government defended this outright rejection as "inevitable." Henderson (quoting Prime Minister Harold MacMillan) to Easterman, Sept. 1, 1964, WJCL.

27. Hull to Tittman, May 26, 1944, Box 58, WRB; Livia Rothkirchen in Lavi, *Pinkas Hungaria,* p. 115; Kubowitzki to Office Committee, June 19, 1944, 264, WJC; *FRUS, 1944,* 1:1088–98; Chs. 8, 9; Petö in Braham, *Hungarian-Jewish Studies* 3:53–56; Barou-Easterman to Goldmann et al., received July 13, 1944, 178A, WJC. The Hungarian leaders were aware earlier of general Nazi intentions regarding the deportations. Braham, *Politics,* 2:716–17.

28. Hilberg, *Destruction,* pp. 548–49; Wagner to Kaltenbrunner, July 5, 1944, JM/2214, YV; Hausner, *Justice,* p. 142; Isaac Rosengarten, "Hungarian Jews Must Be Saved!" *Jewish Forum* 22 (May, 1944):2.

29. Hilberg, *Destruction,* p. 549.

30. Erez, "Shisha Yamim," pp. 154–61; Freudiger in Braham, *Hungarian-Jewish Studies,* 3:130, 57; Levai, *Eichmann in Hungary,* p. 123.

31. Levai, *Eichmann in Hungary,* p. 126; Sunderman conference, July 19, 1944, Box 58, WRB; Springer report, Aug. 1, 1944, Sternbuch MSS; Braham, *Eichmann,* p. 23.

32. Wasserstein, *Britain,* pp. 311–13. For earlier British deliberations regarding reprisal bombing against Germany, see Ibid., pp. 306–7.

33. Ibid., pp. 314–17. Churchill employed this decision in turning down a related request from the chief rabbi of the empire and some other Jews. Toward the end of July a cable from Weissmandel via Sternbuch and Hugo Donenbaum of Berne had reached Agudas Israel in London. The Slovak rabbi had asked on July 10 that his brother, David, and Solomon Schonfeld, a former student at the Neutra Yeshiva who became the son-in-law of Chief Rabbi Joseph Hertz and head of the latter's Religious Emergency Council, be notified that "already 60 per cent of the Jews from Hungary have been deported to Poland by railroad, Kosice-Presov." He urged that that line be bombed. According to Mr. "Ziggy" Stern, who had worked for the council, Rabbis Hertz and Schonfeld asked the prime minister for an airplane to bomb the tunnel on this route between Hungary and Poland, two Jewish RAF pilots having volunteered for the mission. Churchill replied that the quickest way to win the war was bombing on the priority of strategic war conditions, not human concerns. Sternbuch to Goodman, July 18, 1944, Harry Goodman MSS; copy from the Polish government-in-exile (Kozrebrodski) to Easterman, July 18, 1944, WJCL; "Ziggy" Stern interview with the author, July 19, 1979. Sternbuch had heard of the same response from the American air command in Bari. Sternbuch to McClelland, June 22, 1944, Box 62, WRB.

34. Akzin to Lesser, June 29, 1944, 204A, WJC; Kubowitzki to Pehle, July 1, and to Frischer, Aug. 2, 1944, 76A, WJC; reference to July 6, 1944, cable in Erich Kulka, "Teudot Amerika'iyot Al Haftsatsat Auschwitz-Birkenau," *Yalkut Moreshet* 16 (Apr., 1973):151-53; Schonfeld to State, July 5, 1944, Box 30, WRB; Pehle to Stettinius, July 13, 1944, Box 34, WRB.

35. Pehle memo to Morgenthau, Sept. 6, 1944, Box 34, WRB; McCloy to Kubowitzki, Aug. 14, 1944, 76A, WJC; McCloy interview, cited in Roger M. Williams, "Why Wasn't Auschwitz Bombed?" *Commonweal*, Nov. 24, 1978, p. 750.

36. Levai, *Eichmann*, p. 130; Braham, *Eichmann*, p. 30; Rosenfeld, *Tik P'lili 124*, pp. 167-69; Kahany to Schwarzenberg, July 24, 1944, Box 58, WRB. In receipt of this information, the Jewish rescue team in Istanbul did what it could to obtain boats for the projected exodus from Hungary. Letter from Kushta (Istanbul), July 30, 1944, D.1.722, MA. Also see Ch. 6.

37. Levai, *Eichmann*, p. 131; Hausner, *Justice*, p. 145.

38. Cables quoted in Gilbert, *Auschwitz*, pp. 287-92; Shertok to Randall, July 20, 1944, FO 371/42810, PRO, Penkower, "Bergson Boys," pp. 298-99, 302; Pchlc to Stettinius, July 27, 1944, 264, WJC; memo (n.d.), "Emergency Relief Shelters in Palestine," Box 70, WRB (with penciled notation, "wanted to present via Winant to Eden but no go").

39. Wasserstein, *Britain*, pp. 264-66; Friedman memos, Aug. 5 and 11, 1944, Box 70, WRB; DuBois to board, Aug. 17, 1944, vol. 763, MD; *FRUS, 1944*, 1:1120-23, 1125-27. For the British dominions' response, see Gilbert, *Auschwitz*, p. 300. The Canadian government did not even reply.

40. Quoted in Vago, "British Policy," p. 220; Pozner to Krausz, July 2, 1944; MK (Kahany) memo, July 3, 1944; Pozner to Perez, July 4 and 25, 1944, all in Pazner MSS, YV; Shertok to Randall, July 12, 1944, and Randall reply, Z4/14870, CZA; Wasserstein, *Britain*, pp. 267-69. For the first U.S. government knowledge of the Krausz idea in operation, see McClelland to Tait, June 27, 1944, Box 58, WRB.

41. Hugo Valentin, "Rescue and Relief Activities in Behalf of Jewish Victims of Nazism in Scandinavia," *YIVO Annual 8* (1953):240-41.

42. Eleanor Lester and Frederick E. Werbell, "The Lost Hero of the Holocaust: The Search for Sweden's Raoul Wallenberg," *New York Times Magazine*, Mar. 30, 1980, pp. 38-39; Braham, *Politics*, 2:1086; Morse, *While 6 Million Died*, p. 292; Johnson to State, July 15, 1944, vol. 749, MD.

43. Per Anger, *With Raoul Wallenberg in Budapest* (New York, 1981), pp. 46-51; Olsen to Pehle, Aug. 10 and 14, 1944, Box 72, WRB; Wallenberg reports, July 29, Sept. 29, 1944, 251/36, WJC; Frederick E. Werbell and Thurston Clarke, *Lost Hero: The Mystery of Raoul Wallenberg* (New York, 1982), chs. 2-3.

44. Lutz report, June 12, 1945, SM-39, JDC; Lutz's first collective pass, covering 967 human beings in July, 1944, Lutz MSS, P 19/10, YV; McClelland to Schwarzenberg, Sept. 15, 1944, Box 57, WRB; Gulden-LeClerc talk, Jan. 12, 1945, SM-39, JDC; Blet, *Actes et documents,* 10:390-91; Rafi Benshalom, *Ne'evaknu LeMa'an HaChayim* (Tel Aviv, 1977), pp. 170-75.

45. Biss, *A Million Jews,* pp. 82-99; Braham, *Politics*, 2:925-57; Dobkin to

Gruenbaum, July 14 and 27, 1944, Correspondence, BGA; Fülöp Freudiger interview (Yehuda Bauer), Mar., 1975, Institute for Contemporary Jewry, Hebrew University, Jerusalem; McClelland memo, July 21–22, 1944, Box 58, WRB. The transport experienced a great scare when the train made an unscheduled stop at Auspitz, near Brünn. The passengers, who by then knew about Auschwitz, understandably confused the names. Schwalb to McClelland, Aug. 14, 1944, Box 58, WRB.

46. Sternbuch to Mayer, July 4, 1944; McClelland to board, July 5, 1944; Kastner to Schwalb, July 15, 1944; Mayer memo to McClelland, July 19, 1944, all Box 58, WRB; Mayer-Pilpel telephone conversations, June 10 and July 5, 1944, SM-21-1, JDC; Isaac Lewin, "Attempts at Rescuing European Jews with the Help of Polish Diplomatic Missions during World War II: Part II," *Polish Review* 24 (1979):56–58; Kastner-Komoly to Schwalb, July 28, 1944, Box 58, WRB.

47. Ch. 9, n. 59; Reszoe (Kastner) cable, July 18, 1944, Correspondence, BGA; Yehuda Bauer, "The Negotiations between Saly Mayer and the Representatives of the SS in 1944–1945," in Gutman and Zuroff, *Rescue Attempts*, pp. 12–14; McClelland notes, July 26, June 30?, and Mayer's notes, Aug. 18, 1944, Box 58, WRB; Mayer-Schwartz telephone talk, Aug. 6, and Pilpel to Mayer, Aug. 11, 1944, SM-9, JDC; McClelland interview (with Yehuda Bauer), July 13, 1967, Institute for Contemporary Jewry.

48. Bauer, "Negotiations," pp. 14–17; Kastner-Mayer meeting, Aug. 21, 1944, SM-13, JDC; McClelland notes, Aug. 23, 1944, Box 58, WRB. Biss, *A Million Jews*, pp. 122–27, repeats the position taken in Kastner's postwar critique of Mayer regarding the negotiations. Neither man, however, was aware of the severe limits under which the Swiss Jew was then operating.

49. Bauer, "Negotiations," pp. 18–19; Mayer to Leavitt, Aug. 24, 1944, SM-13, JDC; Levai, *Eichmann*, pp. 136–42; McClelland, "Final Report," July 31, 1945, Box 43, WRB; Lichtheim to Linton, Aug. 18, 1944, C 11/13/23/4, BD; Hausner, *Justice*, p. 151.

50. McClelland notes, Aug. 23, 1944, Box 58, WRB; Bauer, "Negotiations," pp. 19–23; Mayer-Pilpel telephone talk, Sept. 13 and 26, 1944, SM-9, JDC; McClelland notes, Oct. 3, and Kastner to Mayer, Oct. 4, 1944, Box 57, WRB; McClelland to Pehle, Oct. 5, 1944, Box 71, WRB. For the end of Slovakian Jewry (which included the martyrdom of Mrs. Gisi Fleischmann and Weissmandel's escape from a deportation train heading for Auschwitz), see CIRC to Schwartz, Dec. 19, 1944, Czech Genl., JDC; Stern interview.

51. Kubowitzki to McCloy, Aug. 30, 1944, 76A, WJC; Schwartzbart to Mikolajczyk, Aug. 18, 1944, 264, WJC; McCloy to Kubowitzki, Sept. 3, 1944; Kubowitzki to Pehle, Oct. 1, 1944, and to Kapustin, same date, all 76A, WJC; Kubowitzki to McCloy, Sept. 25, 1944, 178A, WJC.

52. Sternbuch cable, Aug. 28, 1944, Box 34, WRB; Akzin to Pehle, Sept. 2, 1944, Box 35, WRB; meeting with Pehle, Aug. 16, and Hevesi to Slawson, Aug. 17, 1944, Foreign Countries, Hungary 1944, AJC; Morgenthau to Kalmanowitz, Aug. 25, 1944, 265, WJC. For the "free port" idea, wherein Jewish refugees were analogized to goods, see Feingold, *Politics*, pp. 260–65.

53. Wyman, "Auschwitz," pp. 40–41; Kirk to State, Sept. 15, 1944, 264, WJC;

McClelland to board, Sept. 15, 1944, Box 71, WRB; Gruenbaum to Shertok, Sept. 28, 1944, S 26/1235, CZA; Ch. 9, n. 25.

54. Wasserstein, *Britain,* p. 317; Gruenbaum to Shertok-Brodetsky, Sept. 13, 1944, WJCL. Nahum Goldmann's pleas notwithstanding, British General John Dill of the Allied high command refused to bomb the death camps on the grounds that the bombers were needed for military-industrial targets and that Jews would be killed in the operation. Goldmann to the author, Nov. 22, 1978.

55. Brotman-Mason talk, Oct. 12, 1944, C 11/7/1/6, BD; Eden memo, Sept. 15, 1944, CAB 95/14, PRO.

56. Braham, *Eichmann,* p. 33; Hausner, *Justice,* p. 152.

57. Levai, *Eichmann,* pp. 145–52; ICRC Budapest report (summary), Nov. 20, 1944, 251/32, WJC; Braham, *Eichmann,* pp. 34–35. For the immediate response of Jewish organizations in the free world, see Chs. 8, 9; AGB (Brotman)-Hall talk, Oct. 18, 1944, C 11/13/23/4, BD; office committee, Oct. 20, 1944, 2A, WJC.

58. Pozner to Krausz, Oct. 26, 1944; Krausz to Pozner, Oct. 30, 1944; Kahany memo, Nov. 16, 1944; Buchman to Pozner, Nov. 7, 1944, all Pazner MSS, YV; *aide-mémoire,* Oct. 27, 1944, P 19/9, YV; Pilet-Golaz to MacKillop, Nov. 7, 1944, Box 57, WRB; Werbell and Clarke, *Lost Hero,* pp. 74–78; Ch. 8; ICRC report, Nov. 15, 1944, WJCL. The State Department sought a papal broadcast to Hungary against the further "extermination" of the Jews—to no avail. Stettinius to Avnat, Oct. 25, 1944, vol. 768, MD.

59. Braham, *Eichmann,* p. 35; Levai, *Eichmann,* p. 175; Hausner, *Justice,* p. 153. For some pictures of the forced march, see McClelland to Pehle, Nov. 27, 1944, Box 57, WRB.

60. Werbell and Clarke, *Lost Hero,* pp. 86–116; "Missing Hero, Raoul Wallenberg" (BBC, 1981), John Bierman director; Philip Friedman, *Their Brothers' Keepers* (New York, 1978 ed.), p. 163; Morse, *While 6 Million Died,* pp. 296–97; Hausner, *Justice,* p. 154.

61. Friedman, *Brothers' Keepers,* p. 164; P 19/11, YV; Fishzohn to Passman, May 5, 1945, SM-39, JDC; Perez to Natan (Schwalb), Oct. 30, 1944, Box 57, WRB; Bauer, *American Jewry,* pp. 444–46. For JDC allotments in Hungary during the last six months of 1944, see Leavitt report, Feb. 21, 1945, Box 2, Jewish Welfare Board MSS, New York.

62. *FRUS, 1944,* 1:1174–75; Pehle to McCloy, Sept. 29, 1944, Box 72, WRB; Ullio to Rosenberg, Sept. 29, 1944, RG 107, Sec. of War MSS, 385.3, NA; SHAEF to War Department, Oct. 14, 1944, RG 107, 400.38 Germany, NA; McClelland to board, Oct. 26, 1944, 76A, WJC. "Jews" were also absent from a related Anglo-American statement (the Soviets did not reply to this request) on Oct. 10. Gilbert, *Auschwitz,* pp. 324–25.

63. Documents quoted in Kulka, "Teudot," pp. 151–54; Reiss, "Perakim MiPeulot," p. 34.

64. Quoted in Kulka, "Teudot," p. 155.

65. Pehle speech at McGill University Hillel Holocaust Conference, Oct. 22, 1975, American Jewish Archives, Cincinnati, Ohio; Joseph Borkin, *The Crime and Punishment of I. G. Farben* (New York, 1978), pp. 112–13; "German Extermination Camps Auschwitz and Birkenau" (Washington, D.C., 1944), and

WRB press release, Nov. 28, 1944, vol. 799, MD; *New York Times,* Nov. 26, 1944.

66. Biss, *A Million Jews,* pp. 179, 141; Livia Rothkirchen, "The 'Final Solution' in Its Last Stages," *Yad Vashem Studies* 8 (1970):21–22; Bauer, "Negotiations," pp. 24–27, 32–33; SM–16, JDC; Ch. 9; Ainsztein, *Resistance,* p. 816. On October 11 hundreds of Jewish teenage boys and some men were abruptly ordered to leave the anteroom of a gas chamber, quickly redress, and return to barracks. (Ultimately, however, all but about 50 were gassed.) A few days later "Angel of Death" Dr. Josef Mengele informed the remainder that the "selection" process had come to an end. Joseph Müller interview with the author, Apr. 1, 1983; TR–3/1649, YV. There is no evidence that the War Department predicated its mid-November decision upon knowledge of Himmler's order to halt the mass gassing of Jews. Moreover, thousands of additional Jews were killed by the SS from that point until V-E day without receiving any aid from the War Department.

67. Bauer, "Negotiations," pp. 30–31; memo, Nov. 4, 1944, of Becher-Mayer et al. talk, and Mayer's "12 points," Nov., 1944, Box 57, WRB; Wyler memo, June 15, 1945, SM–17; Thompson article and Mayer notes, Nov. 5, 1944, SM–14, all JDC.

68. McClelland to board, Nov. 16, 1944, Box 71, WRB. Biss, *A Million Jews,* pp. 159–61, overemphasized McClelland's role at Mayer's expense.

69. Bauer, "Negotiations," pp. 32–33; Mayer-Pilpel telephone talks, Nov. 18 and 20, 1944, SM–9, JDC; Schwalb memo, Dec. 4, 1944, and McClelland to Pehle, same date, Box 57, WRB; Biss, *A Million Jews,* pp. 176–79; eyewitness report, sent by McClelland to Pehle, Dec. 4, 1944, Box 31, RG 238, NA; Hausner, *Justice,* pp. 154–55.

70. McClelland to board, Nov. 16, 1944, Box 71, WRB (Bauer errs in stating in "Negotiations," p. 31, that McClelland took Mayer's side and "asked for the money"); Kettlitz to Mayer, Nov. 27, 1944, Box 57, WRB; Mayer draft to JDC, Dec. 1, 1944, SM–6, JDC.

71. Bauer, "Negotiations," pp. 33–35; Biss, *A Million Jews,* pp. 183–85. For their ultimate fate, see Ch. 6, n. 84. Eichmann did not permit Brand's family and a few others to leave Belsen, however. Another factor in the German calculations, noted by Bauer, "Negotiations," pp. 32–33, was the Rumanian government's interest in exchanging Jews from northern Transylvania for Germans from the Transnistria area. For Rumanian Zionists' efforts in this regard, see Lavi, *Yahadut Rumania,* pp. 184–88, and Bela Vago, "Peilut Politit VeDiplomatit LeHatsalat Yehudei Tsefon-Transylvania," *Yad Vashem Studies* 6 (1966):131–47. Also Gruenbaum to Goldmann, Nov. 24, 1944, Correspondence, BGA.

72. Biss, *A Million Jews,* pp. 191–97; Levai, *Eichmann,* pp. 175–76; Braham, *Eichmann,* p. 36.

73. Pehle to Wallenberg, Dec. 6, 1944, *Documents of the Swedish Foreign Ministry Regarding Raoul Wallenberg, 1944–1949* (Stockholm, 1980), vol. 3; Lester and Werbell, "Lost Hero," pp. 21, 28; London *Jewish Chronicle,* Mar. 23, 1945; *Dagens Nyheter,* Mar. 6, 1945, Box 36, WRB.

74. Benshalom, *Ne'evaknu Lema'an HaChayim;* S. J. Roth interview with the author, Nov. 7, 1979; Moshe Biederman, "Pirkei HaNoar HaTsiyoni BeHungaria," *Masua* 1 (1973):66–89; David Margalit, "Mivtsa'ei Hatsala BeHungaria," *Masua* 2 (1974):90–95; Elizabeth Eppler interview with the author, July 24,

1979. Some reports about this heroic effort, which requires a scholarly history beyond Gilles Lambert's *Operation Hazalah* (Indianapolis, 1974), reached McClelland via Schwalb. See Boxes 57-58, WRB.

75. Zvi Goldfarb, *Ad Kav HaKetz* (Tel Aviv, 1980), Biss, *A Million Jews*, pp. 200-201; Eppler interview. For the three young parachutists sent into Hungary by the Hagana of Palestine, Joel Nussbecher (Yoel Palgi), Peretz Goldstein, and Hannah Szenes, as well as for Kastner's role in their fate, see Yoel Palgi, *Ruach Gedola Ba'ah* (Tel Aviv, 1977 ed.); *Hannah Szenes, Her Life and Diary* (New York, 1972); Rosenfeld, *Tik P'lili 124*, pp. 122-63; Biss, *A Million Jews*, pp. 143-47; Wasserstein, *Britain*, pp. 289-95.

76. Bauer, "Negotiations," pp. 35-36; Biss, *A Million Jews*, p. 203; Mayer-Schwartz talk, Dec. 10, 1944, SM-14, JDC.

77. Biss, *A Million Jews*, pp. 206-12; Friedman, *Brothers' Keepers*, p. 165; Lester and Werbell, "Lost Hero," p. 28; Werbell and Clarke, *Lost Hero*, pp. 154-55. The *Wehrmacht* confiscated the trucks and Becher could not get them back. Unknown to McClelland and even Kastner, Mayer helped pay for Sternbuch's tractors and sent them to Germany. Bauer, "Negotiations," pp. 37, 34; Kastner-Trobe interview, June 13, 1945, SM-17, JDC.

78. Braham, *Eichmann*, p. 36; Hausner, *Justice*, p. 155; Weissberg, *Dangerous Mission*, p. 289; Ira Hirschmann address, Mar. 5, 1981, CUNY-Eisner Holocaust Institute, New York (author's notes); Biss, *A Million Jews*, pp. 216-17.

79. Anger, *With Wallenberg*, p. 86; Lester and Werbell, "Lost Hero," pp. 28-32; report on Hungary, Jan. 10, 1945, 251/35, WJC; Ainsztein, *Resistance*, p. 816; Lavi, et al., *Pinkas Hungaria*, p. 117.

80. Lavi, *Pinkas Hungaria*, p. 117.

81. Kastner to Mayer, Oct. 29, 1945, 184A, WJC; Ch. 9; Morgenstern, "Va'ad HaHatsala," p. 88; Eppler interview. For Gruenbaum's general perspective on the Yishuv and the Holocaust, see Yitzchak Gruenbaum, *BeYemai Churban VeShoa* (Tel Aviv, 1946), pp. 62-70. Even the far more prescient group of Palestinian Jewish emissaries in Istanbul asked about resistance. "Moladeti" (Pomeraniec) to Jewish Agency, Aug. 12, 1944, S 26/1428, CZA.

82. Wasserstein, *Britain*, p. 351; Eden minute, June 28, 1944, FO 371/42807, PRO; Mason to Linton, Oct. 27, 1944, C 11/13/23/4, BD. Postcards bearing the "Waldsee" address mark, written at times by inmates on arrival in Auschwitz-Birkenau, carried a standard message intended by the Nazis to calm Jews yet in Hungary: "I have arrived. Am Well." Levai, *Eichmann*, p. 187. And only in mid-December did British war intelligence possess a chemical analysis of Zyklon-B. Report, Dec. 17, 1944, WO 208/2169, PRO.

83. Bradley F. Smith, *The Road to Nuremberg* (New York, 1981), p. 94. Morgenthau and his Treasury staff, who championed the rescue of European Jewry during the Holocaust, took a far more stringent position on the prosecution of Nazi war criminals and Germany's postwar occupation. Smith, *Road*.

84. Bauer, "Negotiations," p. 36. For the last part of Mayer's discussions, see ibid., p. 40; Box 57, WRB; and SM-15, JDC. Mayer's estimate of the talks at this point (memo of Dec. 28, 1944, Box 43, WRB) was repeated by McClelland in his final report to Washington (July 31, 1945, ibid.). Discussions of Becher's activities between Dec., 1944, and the end of war can be found in Biss, *A Million Jews*, pp. 235-44; Rosenfeld, *Tik P'lili 124*, pp. 227-59; and SM-16, JDC.

85. Fleischmann to Silberschein, Sept. 6, 1943, quoted in Raul Hilberg, ed., *Documents of Destruction: Germany and Jewry, 1933–1945* (New York, 1971), p. 192; Gruenbaum at Jewish Agency Executive, Oct. 4, 1943, CZA; Kubowitzki to Weissman, Mar. 7, 1944, 265, WJC. It is most probable that Kubowitzki received this same information from Silberschein, who had directed RELICO with the aid of Gerhart Riegner in Switzerland since Sept., 1939. Ch. 8, n. 5. (It took four months on the average for Silberschein's letters to reach WJC headquarters in New York.) For Westerbork, see J. Presser, *The Destruction of the Dutch Jews,* trans. Arnold Pomerans (New York, 1969), ch. 7.

86. Wasserstein, *Britain,* p. 310.

87. Wyman, "Auschwitz," p. 42; Gilbert, *Auschwitz,* pp. 220–21, 238, 249; Dino A. Brugioni and Robert G. Poirer, *The Holocaust Revisited: A Retrospective Analysis of the Auschwitz-Birkenau Extermination Complex* (Washington, D.C., 1979), p. 3.

88. Wyman, "Auschwitz," p. 42; Brugioni and Poirer, *Holocaust Revisited,* pp. 9–12; Gilbert in *Jerusalem Post,* Mar. 7, 1980 (for photographic reproduction); Kulka, "Teudot," p. 150.

89. Wyman, "Auschwitz," pp. 43–44; Kulka, "Teudot," pp. 150–51.

90. Martin Gilbert, *Final Journey: The Fate of the Jews in Nazi Europe* (New York, 1979), pp. 155–56, 190; Friedman, *Roads,* p. 231; McClelland note, Aug. 30, 1944, Box 58, WRB; Loebel to editor, *Commentary* 66 (July, 1978):10.

91. Williams, "Why Wasn't Auschwitz Bombed?" pp. 750–51; Wyman, "Auschwitz," p. 44; Leopold Amery diaries, May 2, 1944 (courtesy of Julian Amery), London. Anne Frank died in Bergen-Belsen one month before its liberation.

92. Churchill, *Second World War: Triumph and Tragedy,* pp. 110–24; Poland—Aid to Warsaw file, Box 10, RG 218, NA; Wyman, "Auschwitz," p. 46.

93. Easterman-Zinchenko interview, Mar. 22, and Easterman to Gusev, Mar. 31, 1944, WJCL; Lester and Werbell, "Lost Hero," pp. 32, 62.

94. Werbell and Clarke, *Lost Hero,* pts. 3–4; Kaplan to editor, *New York Times Book Review,* Mar. 14, 1982; Ernie Mayer, "Family's Faith," *Jerusalem Post International Edition,* Jan. 27–Feb. 2, 1980; *New York Times,* Jan. 16, 1981; Anger, *With Wallenberg,* pp. 147–59.

95. Wyman, "Auschwitz," p. 46; Weizmann to Smuts (and copy to Churchill), June 19, 1944, WA. The Emergency Committee to Save the Jewish People of Europe also suggested the threat of poison gas (similar to Churchill's 1942 warning in this vein, which halted German use of gas on the Russian front) as a retaliatory measure against the Nazi gassing of European Jewry. Smertenko to Roosevelt, July 24, 1944, Box 1/12, Palestine Statehood Committee MSS, Sterling Library, Yale University. New Haven, Conn. The U.S. joint chiefs of staff decided—four months later—that the suggestion "does not come within their cognizance." Leahy to Hebrew Committee, Oct. 4, 1944, RG 218, Joint Chiefs of Staff MSS, NA.

96. Ainsztein, *Resistance,* pp. 782–88, 796–97, 800–804, 809–12; Halivni, "Birkenau Revolt," pp. 130–43; Isaac Kabeli, "The Resistance of the Greek Jews," *YIVO Annual* 8 (1953):287–88; Yuri Suhl, "Underground Assignment in Auschwitz," in Suhl, *They Fought Back,* pp. 189–94. For the tragic fate of a Jewish woman who tried to follow in the footsteps of Rosenberg and the other Jewish male escapees, see Gisza Weisblum, "The Escape and Death of the

'Runner' Mala Zimetbaum," in ibid., pp. 182-88; Wieslaw Kielar, *Anus Mundi, 1500 Days in Auschwitz/Birkenau,* trans. Susanne Flatauer (New York, 1980), pp. 224-55; Ber Mark, *Megilat Auschwitz* (Tel Aviv, 1978), pp. 106-113; Fania Fenelon, with Marcelle Routier, *Playing for Time* (New York, 1977), pp. 152-68.

97. Halivni, "Birkenau Revolt," pp. 143-44; Ainsztein, *Resistance,* pp. 812-15; Yuri Suhl, "Rosa Robota—Heroine of the Auschwitz Underground," in Suhl, *They Fought Back,* pp. 219-225; Müller, *Auschwitz Inferno,* pp. 143-60; Mark, *Megilat Auschwitz,* pp. 127-42.

98. "Autobiography of Rudolf Höss," in *KL Auschwitz Seen by the SS,* ed. Jadwiga Bezwińska and Danuta Czech (Krakow, 1978), p. 33. The commandant of Auschwitz, as his memoir (written shortly before his hanging on the grounds of Auschwitz on Apr. 16, 1947, by a Polish court) makes clear, continued to the end to think of Jews in the Nazi ideological framework.

99. Mark, *Megilat Auschwitz,* pp. 143-56, 181-269.

100. The chief SS medical officer of Auschwitz could not believe this order had been issued until, wishing to check for himself, he made a trip to Birkenau. Ainsztein, *Resistance,* pp. 790-97.

Chapter 8—The World Jewish Congress Confronts the International Red Cross

1. Gerhart M. Riegner interview with the author, Apr. 22, 1977; Riegner-Marc Dvorjetski interview, July 13, 1972, Riegner Archives, Geneva; Ch. 3; Harrison to State Department, Apr. 4, 1944, 840.48 Refugees/5542 CF, RG 59, SD; McClelland to board, June 24, 1944, vol. 747, MD. For the board's creation, see Ch. 5.

2. Ch. 7.

3. Ch. 7; *Unity in Dispersion,* p. 167; Riegner interview with the author, Oct. 19, 1977.

4. Grossman to Kubowitzki, Aug. 26, Dec. 28, 1943, 265, WJC; Jean S. Pictet, ed., *The Geneva Conventions of 12 August 1929* (Geneva, 1958), 4:3-5. It was considered "particularly inappropriate for the IRC to recommend including civilians in the 1929 Geneva convention," because the state of "general optimism which reigned at the time" led various representatives to conclude that such a resolution "would be regarded in international circles as almost equivalent to betraying the cause of peace." Ibid., p. 4.

5. Riegner memo, "One Year of RELICO," Nov., 1940; Guggenheim-Riegner-Davis talk, Nov. 4, 1939; Goldmann-Nicholson talk, Dec. 13, 1939, all in 265, WJC; Riegner interview with the author, Apr. 22, 1977.

6. Kubowitzki to Peter, Dec. 10, 1943, 264, WJC. The ICRC did pay one visit to the Theresienstadt ghetto in June, 1944, at the invitation of the German government, but refused to release its *favorable* report on the (correct) assumption that this "could be used to whitewash the [Nazi] treatment of Jews in general." McClelland to board, Sept. 15, 1944, 264, WJC.

7. J. Wise memo, "Relief Rendered to Jews in German-Occupied Poland," to Peter, n.d., 212/20, WJC; Wise to Tartakower, Aug. 31, 1942 (enclosing Peter's reply), 265, WJC; *Inter Arma Caritas, The Work of the International Red Cross during the Second World War* (Geneva, 1947), pp. 79-80. Despite the official WJC position, Silberschein and Riegner continued on their own to defy the

blockade. Ch. 5. The ICRC also refused, after months of delay, to send WJC supplies of worn clothes and shoes to the 522 Jewish refugees in a concentration camp in St. Giovanni, Rhodes, via a Red Cross ship. Bienenstock report, Jan., 1942, 212/20, WJC.

8. Davis to Wise, Sept. 19, 1942, and Tartakower to Kubowitzki, Feb. 9, 1943, 265, WJC; Tartakower to Wise et al., Feb. 19, 1943, U–134, WJC; Tartakower to Peter, Mar. 4, 1943; Tartakower to Peter, Apr. 12, 1943; Ryan to Tartakower, Apr. 25, 1943; Tartakower to Wise et al., Nov. 1, 1943, all in 265, WJC; Tartakower and Kubowitzki to Peter, Dec. 10, 1943, 264, WJC. The ICRC did not carry out an investigation of the Nazi murder of Jewry, despite a plea from Stephen Wise and Joseph Proskauer, presidents of the congress and the American Jewish Committee respectively (representing the Emergency Committee for European Jewish Affairs), that "the entire Jewish population of Hitler-occupied Europe may be destroyed within the near future" if this process continued unchecked. Wise-Proskauer to ICRC, June 15, 1943, 265, WJC.

9. Davis to Kantor, Oct. 20, 1943, 265, WJC; Peter to Tartakower-Kubowitzki, Dec. 17, 1943, 264, WJC. The American Red Cross was consistent. It had also not supported the proposal of Roosevelt's Presidential Advisory Committee on Political Refugees (PACPR) after *Kristallnacht* that 9,000 German-Jewish refugee children be given aid in Holland, and had refused (following the recommendation of anti-Zionists in the State Department) to give help to Palestinian Jewry after Tel Aviv had been bombed in Sept., 1940, by Italian airplanes. PACPR minutes, Nov. 21, Dec. 8 and 12, 1938, MKM 4–1, John Chamberlain MSS, YIVO Archives, New York; Montor memo, Oct. 8, 1940, 144, Robert Szold MSS.

10. Kurt Grossman, "An Unfulfilled Testament," *Congress Weekly* 10 (Nov. 12, 1943):10–11; Celler to Hull, Dec. 27, 1943, 265, WJC; *Unity in Dispersion*, p. 169; J. Wise memo, Jan. 10, 1944, 265, WJC; Joseph Tenenbaum, "Red Cross to the Rescue," *Yad Vashem Bulletin* 4/5 (Oct., 1959):7–8.

11. Goldmann-Long talk, Sept. 16, Oct. 28, 1943, 265, WJC; *FRUS, 1943*, I:356–57, 374–75, 379; J. Wise-Long talk, Dec. 3, and Goldmann-Long talk, Dec. 9, 1943, 264, WJC; *Unity in Dispersion*, pp. 176–77; Kubowitzki memo, June 6, 1944, 264, WJC.

12. Kubowitzki to Wise et al., Apr. 23, 1943; Kubowitzki-Peter talk, Jan. 5, 1944; WJC-ICRC representatives' talk, Jan. 27, 1944, all in 265, WJC; Kubowitzki memo to Wise, Apr. 5, and Kubowitzki memo, June 6, 1944, 264, WJC.

13. Tartakower-Kubowitzki to Peter, Dec. 10, 1943, 264, WJC; Goldmann-Kubowitzki to Riegner, Aug. 15, and Riegner to Kubowitzki, Oct. 10, 1944 (cited in Guggenheim to Stucki, Oct. 24, 1944), 265, WJC; WJC meeting, Oct. 17, 1944, Advisory Committee on European Jewish Affairs, 153, WJC. Quick results were forthcoming from the Swiss government. Stucki to Guggenheim, Nov. 10, and Riegner to Kubowitzki, Nov. 13, 1944, 265, WJC. For Wallenberg's herculean efforts, see Ch. 7.

14. Riegner interview with the author, Oct. 19, 1977; Carl Burckhardt, *Meine Danzig Mission, 1937–1939* (Munich, 1960); *Documents on German Foreign Policy*, 5: ch. 1; *Weiner Library Bulletin* 14 (1960):54.

15. Riegner-Dvorjetski interview; Ch. 3.

16. *Unity in Dispersion,* pp. 185–86; Harrison to State, July 24, 1944, Box 58, WRB; Riegner interview with the author, Oct. 19, 1977; Guggenheim-Riegner to ICRC, Aug. 22, and Huber to Guggenheim-Riegner, Oct. 2, 1944, with attached memo "Sur la Notion d'Internes Civils." 265, WJC. Also see Ch. 7 for the tragedy of Hungarian Jewry.

17. Riegner to Goldmann-Kubowitzki, Oct. 25, 1944, 265, WJC.

18. Riegner interview with the author, Apr. 22, 1977; Schirmer to ICRC, received July 31, 1944, Box 58, WRB; Grossman to WJC office committee, Jan. 8, 1945 (enclosing Riegner's report of Nov. 10, 1944), 265, WJC; Riegner report, Nov. 30, 1944, to congress, 251/32, WJC. For help from ICRC delegates in the Balkans and Slovakia, see Ch. 6 and Georges Dunand's *Ne perdez pas leur trace* (Neuchâtel, 1950). The ICRC's account of this issue is given in *Report of the ICRC,* 1:650–57, 3:336, 519–24.

19. Guggenheim-Riegner to Huber, Oct. 23, 1944, 265, WJC; Riegner interview with the author, Apr. 22, 1977.

20. Riegner interview with the author, Oct. 19, 1977; Bienenstock report, Jan., 1942, 212/20, WJC. On other Silberschein activities, see Nathan Eck, "The Rescue of Jews with the Aid of Passports and Citizenship Papers of Latin American States," *Yad Vashem Studies* 1 (1957):125–52.

21. Riegner interviews with the author, Oct. 19 and Nov. 7, 1977; Ch. 7; Livia Rothkirchen, "The Czechoslovak Government-in-Exile: Jewish and Palestinian Aspects in the Light of the Documents," *Yad Vashem Studies* 9 (1973):157–99; Ota Kraus and Erich Kulka, *The Death Factory: Document on Auschwitz,* ed. Stephen Jolly (London, 1966), pp. 167–81.

22. Riegner-Dvorjetski interview. Kastner, the Zionist spokesman from Hungary involved in the Gestapo's talks with Saly Mayer, managed to slip away and inform Riegner of the secret conversations. Since the cautious Mayer had avoided all contact with the congress in rescue matters, Riegner expected no support from Mayer and did not keep him informed of the *demarche.* Riegner interview with the author, Oct. 19, 1977, and Ch. 7. A fine analysis in this connection is Bauer's "Negotiations"; his speculation (pp. 40–44), however, that some connection may exist between Mayer's negotiations and those of Burckhardt is unfounded, as I shall show below.

23. Riegner interview with the author, Oct. 19, 1977; Kopecky to Riegner, Nov. 14, 1944, 264, WJC.

24. *FRUS, 1944,* 1:1174–75.

25. Riegner interview with the author, Oct. 19, 1977; minutes of meeting, Nov. 17, 1944, 264, WJC.

26. Kopecky to Riegner, Dec. 7, 1944, 264, WJC.

27. Bruggman to Wise, Nov. 15, 1944, 3a/1, WJC; Reading-Zelmanovits to Barou-Easterman, received Nov. 17, 1944, and Tartakower to WJC office committee, Nov. 21, 1944, 265, WJC. For Tartakower's previous efforts, see citations, n. 8 above.

28. Kubowitzki-Zelmanovits-Mann talk, Jan. 4, 1945; Kubowitzki-Zelmanovits-Hoehler-Cooley talk, Jan. 9, 1945; Kubowitzki-Reading-Emerson talk, Jan. 8, 1945; Kubowitzki-Zelmanovits-Cellerier talk, Jan. 12, 1945, all in 264, WJC; *Unity in Dispersion,* p. 189. Kubowitzki also found out that in Feb., 1944,

Emerson's second-in-command had brought back from Geneva a program prepared by the ICRC that relied on a credit basis. The British War Cabinet's committee on refugees considered the suggestions therein, and Emerson had left for America to gain support of the U.S. government for the proposal. The expenses involved, however, were such that the legislature would have had to be approached, and Roosevelt's available funds would not have sufficed to finance the project. Had the question been submitted to the U.S. Congress, its secret character would have been ruined. Consequently, it was decided to limit the financial scope of the project. Kubowitzki-Kullman talk, Jan. 17, 1945, 265, WJC. (The Intergovernmental Committee on Refugees, established as a result of the Evian conference of July, 1938, for rescue work, achieved minimal successes during the war.)

29. Kubowitzki-Grenfell-Rathbone et al. meeting, Jan. 17, 1945, and Kubowitzki-Frischer-Ripka talk, Jan. 19, 1945, 264, WJC.

30. Ch. 7; Stettinius to Huddle-McClelland, Jan. 8, 1945, Box 32, WRB; Grossman report, Jan. 17–18, 1945, 264, WJC; *History of the War Refugee Board with Selected Documents* (Washington, D.C., n.d.), 2:441; Huddle to State, Dec. 21, 1944, Box 63, WRB. The American secretary of state pressed the Swedish government concurrently to intervene with Berlin "in view of [the] well-known German practice of exterminating Jews surviving in any area previous to its evacuation." Stettinius to Johnson, Jan. 19, 1945, 840.48 Refugees CF/1–1945, SD.

31. Peter to Tartakower, Jan. 23, 1945 (replying to Tartakower et al. to Peter, Jan. 19, 1945); Tartakower to WJC office committee, Jan. 30, 1945; Hodel to Goldmann, Feb. 3, 1945 (enclosing Riegner's cable of Jan. 31, 1945), all in 265, WJC.

32. Grossman report, Mar., 1945, 264, WJC; Tartakower to WJC office committee, Feb. 6, 1945, 265, WJC.

33. Kubowitzki-Riegner-Burckhardt talk, Feb. 20, 1945, 264, WJC.

34. Riegner interview with the author, Oct. 19, 1977; Ch. 9.

35. Minutes of Feb. 26, 1945, meeting, and memo of Feb. 26, 1945, to Burckhardt (attached), 264, WJC; Riegner interview with the author, Oct. 19, 1977; McClelland to Huddle, Dec. 15, 1944, Box 63, WRB; McClelland to board, Feb. 24, 1945, 266, WJC. For copies of the six reports on Hungary issued by McClelland during June and July, 1944, to "swing Swiss public opinion in a favorable direction," see McClelland to Pehle, Dec. 19, 1944, RG 238, NA.

36. Kubowitzki-Steiger talk, Mar. 3, 1945, 265, WJC; Kubowitzki-Burckhardt talk, Mar., 1945, 264, WJC.

37. Burckhardt reply, quoted in meetings of Mar. 3 and 12, 1945, 264, WJC.

38. WJC news agency cable, received Mar. 15, 1945, 3a/1, WJC; McClelland to O'Dwyer, Mar. 22, 1945, 266, WJC; meeting, Mar. 26, 1945, 265, WJC.

39. John Toland, *The Last 100 Days* (New York, 1966 ed.), p. 233; Hilberg, *Destruction,* p. 128. Kaltenbrunner claimed at the Nuremberg trials that as, in his view, the Schellenberg-Himmler negotiations via Musy and the Va'ad HaHatsala were "tricks" which he discredited with Hitler as "demeaning to the cause and the Reich," he "forced Himmler to adopt a different attitude in this question by asking Burckhardt personally to visit these camps." *IMT,* 9:279–80.

Testimony on Burckhardt's negotiations and the subsequent ICRC-Gestapo talks can also be found in *IMT*, 40:306–25, and *Report of the ICRC*, 1:620–23. Also Ch. 9.

40. Minutes of meeting, Mar. 26, 1945, 265, WJC; Harrison to State, Apr. 13, 1945, 266, WJC.

41. Riegner interview with the author, Nov. 7, 1977; Ch. 9. It should be recalled that Himmler had given legal sanction to the Wannsee conference decisions on the implementation of the Final Solution to the new Reich minister of justice, Sept. 18, 1942, in asserting that Jews and some other minority groups were to be "worked to death." Cited in *Documents on International Affairs, 1939–1946* (Oxford, 1954), 2:13–15.

42. Stein memo to office committee, May 14, 1945, 265, WJC; Riegner interview with the author, Oct. 17, 1977. The first report of such segregation was actually publicized three years earlier, when Jewish soldiers in Soviet territory received separate treatment from the invading German army. *JTA*, Nov. 18, 1941, p. 2.

43. Riegner-Chenevière-Beck talk, Mar. 13, 1945, 265, WJC.

44. Burckhardt-Riegner et al. talk, June 11, 1941, 266, WJC; Lichtheim memo, June 12, 1941, L22/95, CZA; Riegner interview with the author, Apr. 22, 1977; Burckhardt quoted in Riegner-Guggenheim to Burckhardt, Mar. 29, 1945, 265, WJC. Also see Yoav Gelber, "Palestinian POWs in German Captivity," *Yad Vashem Studies* 14 (1981):132.

45. Riegner-Guggenheim to Burckhardt, Mar. 29, 1945, 265, WJC.

46. Burckhardt to Guggenheim-Riegner, Apr. 5, 1945, 265, WJC.

47. Guggenheim-Riegner-Burckhardt talk, Apr. 11, 1945, 265, WJC.

48. Minutes of meeting, Apr. 11, 1945, 265, WJC.

49. Aryeh Tartakower, "Where the International Red Cross Failed," *Congress Weekly* 13 (May 3, 1946):9–10. For the effort of some ICRC delegates to save Jews despite the Nazis' last-minute effort to carry out the Final Solution, see Ch. 9.

50. Riegner interview with the author, Oct. 17, 1977. For a judicious analysis of the Holocaust as "an absolute *novum*," see Jacob Katz, "Was the Holocaust Inevitable?" *Commentary* 59 (May, 1975):41–48. Meir Dworzecki's "The International Red Cross and Its Policy vis-à-vis the Jews in the Ghettos and Concentration Camps in Nazi-Occupied Europe," in Gutman and Zuroff, *Rescue Attempts*, pp. 71–110, provides additional information but neglects the subject of this study entirely.

51. Tartakower, "Where the Red Cross Failed," p. 9; *Inter Arma Caritas*, pp. 67–77. The ICRC's record of its dispersal in 1944 of $100,000 from the JDC can be found in Schwartz to JDC-NY, Dec. 27, 1944, Rumania Genl., JDC. Also see SM-23, JDC.

52. Riegner-Dvorjetski interview.

53. Minutes of ICRC-sponsored meeting, Mar. 3, 1947, 265, WJC; Riegner interview with the author, Oct. 19, 1977.

54. Riegner interview with the author, Oct. 19, 1977; minutes of ICRC-sponsored meeting, Mar. 3, 1947, 265, WJC.

55. Minutes of ICRC-sponsored meeting, Mar. 4, 1947, 265, WJC; Riegner

interview with the author, Oct. 19, 1977; Tartakower, "Where the Red Cross Failed," p. 9.

56. Kubowitzki statement, Mar. 4, 1947, and Moshe Glitkovsky article, July 21, 1947, 265, WJC; *Report on the Work of the Conference of Geneva Experts for the Study of the Conventions for the Protection of War Victims, April 14–26, 1947* (Geneva, 1947), pp. 269–329.

57. Riegner interview with the author, Oct. 19, 1977; *The Geneva Conventions of August 12, 1949: Analysis for the Use of National Red Cross Societies* (Geneva, 1950), 2:81. The 1948 gathering also received the ICRC's three-volume report about its relief and rescue activity in World War II, including its standard defense regarding the matter of aid extended to European Jewry during that time. *Report of the ICRC,* 1:642, 2:299–300, 3:513. A later IRC summary of its historical development has no mention of the organization's record regarding Jews during World War II. Henri Coursier, *The International Red Cross* (Geneva, 1961).

58. Riegner interview with the author, Oct. 19, 1977.

59. *FRUS, 1944,* 1:1021, 1039–40, 1147–48; Huber to Harrison, Apr. 21, 1944, Box 58, WRB; McClelland to board, July 18, and board to McClelland, Sept. 6, 1944, 264, WJC; see also n. 30 above. The board's official history neglects entirely the reasons for the IRC's shift in position toward the end of the War. *History of the War Refugee Board,* 1:346.

60. Riegner interview with the author, Oct. 19, 1977; WJC *passim,* especially files 264–65; Kubowitzki quoted in Levai, *Black Book,* Preface.

61. *Unity in Dispersion,* p. 168. For other WJC efforts during the Holocaust, see Chs. 3-7, 9, and Eppler, "Rescue Work," pp. 47-69.

Chapter 9—The Sternbuchs, Storch, and the *Reichsführer* SS

1. Pehle to Union of Orthodox Rabbis, Oct. 24, 1944, VH.

2. Efraim Zuroff, "Rescue Priority and Fund Raising as Issues during the Holocaust: A Case Study of the Relations between the Vaad Ha-Hatsala and the Joint, 1939-1941," *American Jewish History* 68 (Mar., 1979):305-8, 314.

3. Ibid., pp. 309-17, 324-26; Irving Bunim interview with the author, Jan. 3, 1977. For the background to the plight of these academies, see Efraim Zuroff, "Hatsalat Talmidei Yeshivot Polin Derech HaMizrach HaRachok BeTekufat HaShoa," *MiDor Dor* 1 (1979):49-76; Zuroff, "Attempts to Obtain Shanghai Permits in 1941: A Case of Rescue Priority during the Holocaust," *Yad Vashem Studies* 13 (1979):321-51. Their fate under Japanese control is thoroughly examined in David Kranzler, *Japanese, Nazis and Jews: The Jewish Refugee Community of Shanghai, 1938-1945* (New York, 1976).

4. Louis Septimus interview with the author, Jan. 24, 1981; "Report ... of Agudath Israel Youth," June, 1941, Tress MSS; Ch. 5, n. 6; Breckenridge Long diary, LC, Sept. 18, Dec. 12, and 23, 1940; Zuroff, "Rescue Priority," p. 317.

5. Rosenheim to McDonald, Oct. 27, 1941, PAC files, James McDonald MSS, Columbia University, New York; Wyman, *Paper Walls,* ch. 7; author's telephone conversation with Rabbi Simon Langer, New York, Sept. 30, 1980.

6. Eli Sternbuch interview with the author, Dec. 8, 1980; Recha Sternbuch interrogation, May 5, 1941, and Isaac Sternbuch to Min. of Justice, State of

Israel, Apr. 15, 1954, HIJEFS MSS, Agudath Israel of America Archives, New York; file 680, Righteous Gentiles dept., YV. Although "HIJEFS" continued unchanged, "Shanghai" was later dropped for "Ausland" (foreign territory).

7. Sternbuch interview; Seidman, *Yoman Ghetto Varsha,* pp. 113–16; Eck, "Rescue of Jews," pp. 125-52; G. Mantello memo, June 1, 1944, SM-5, JDC; Schwartzbaum, "Peulot Ezra," pp. 142-43; Kühl to the author, Aug. 18, 1981; Ch. 3. Kühl also obtained Nuncio Bernardini's aid for the release of Recha Sternbuch and of Jewish refugees who illegally crossed into Switzerland from occupied Europe. Julius Kühl interview with the author, Feb. 17, 1982.

8. Tress memo, Dec. 23, 1942, Tress MSS; Kranzler, *Japanese,* pp. 462, 468, 572; Lewin, "Attempts-II," pp. 48-49; Kühl interview; Rosenberg to Hertz, Feb. 18, and Celler to Rosenberg, Mar. 17, 1943, Hatzala MSS, Agudas HaRabbanim of America and Canada Archives, New York.

9. Rosenheim to McDonald, May 26, 1943, PAC files, McDonald MSS; Goodman report attached, in Rosenheim to Tress, June 11, and Peter to Rosenheim, Nov. 11, 1943, Tress MSS.

10. Chs. 3-5; Hull to Rosenberg, Aug. 13, 1943, VH; Aguda Political Report, July-Dec., 1943, Tress MSS.

11. Aguda Political Report, July-Dec., 1943, Tress to Daina, Jan. 26, and license, Jan. 22, 1944, Tress MSS; Schoen-Riegelman talk, Jan. 28, 1944, 840.48 Refugees/5077, RG 59, SD; financial statement ending Dec. 31, 1943, VH.

12. Long to Travers, Dec. 16, 1943, Box 202, Breckenridge Long MSS, LC; Rosenheim to Long, Dec. 23, 1943, 840.48 Refugees/5969, SD; Travers memo, Jan. 7, 1944, 840.48 Refugees/4934, SD; Yitschak Katznelson, *Vittel Diary* (Tel Aviv, 1964), pp. 25-26; Sternbuch interview; Abraham Shulman, *The Case of Hotel Polski* (New York, 1982); Apr. 7, 1944, vol. 717, MD; Shabse Frankel interview with the author, Dec. 28, 1981.

13. Hillel Seidman interview with the author, Dec. 1, 1980; Baruch Korff, *Flight from Fear* (New York, 1953), p. 44; Berne to State, Mar. 4, 1944, Box 32, WRB; Rosenheim to Pehle, Mar. 23, 1944, Tress MSS. Also in Vittel was Eli Sternbuch's fiancée, Guta Eisenzweig of Warsaw, who survived on a Paraguayan passport along with Hillel Seidman (the Warsaw journalist then using a similar document made out to another Eisenzweig). Notwithstanding possession of such documentation, I. M. Domb, an Orthodox Jew of Swiss parentage who had first informed Eli Sternbuch about the mass deportation of Warsaw Jewry, was shot in Vittel by the Germans. The State Department's interpretation of Domb's Sept. 4, 1942, coded postcard (repeated at the time in *Congress Weekly,* Dec. 4, 1942, and years later in Morse's *While 6 Million Died,* pp. 19-20) erred in translating "Miss Eisenzweig" as "ironworkers"; the reference was to Eli's future wife, while "Hügli" hinted at the Paraguayan consul in Berne. Sternbuch and Seidman interviews; Ch. 3, n. 38.

14. Pehle to Kalmanowitz, Apr. 4, 1944, VH; meetings, Apr. 6 and 7, 1944, vol. 718, MD; Frankel interview. Kalmanowitz did this on more than one occasion for the sake of rescue. Morgenthau's secretary, a Jewish woman whose knowledge of Yiddish enabled her to understand Kalmanowitz's discussions among his associates, only informed the Secretary of this tactic after the war. Henrietta Klotz interview with the author, Mar. 14, 1977.

15. Korff, *Flight,* pp. 45-48; Segal to Slawson, Apr. 20, 1944, Foreign Coun-

tries, AJC; Harrison to Hull, Apr. 13, 1944, vol. 720, MD; Hull to South Amern. embassies, Apr. 22, 1944, 840.48 Refugees/5850 CF, SD; Huddle to Lichtheim, Apr. 22, 1944, Lichtheim MSS, L22/92, CZA. For Hayes, see Ch. 4.

16. Isaac Lewin, "Attempts at Rescuing European Jews with the Help of Polish Diplomatic Missions during World War II," *Polish Review* 22 (1977):11–12.

17. Ch. 7; McClelland notation on Sternbuch cable to McClelland, July 20, 1944, Box 58, WRB; Ch. 6, n. 80; Springer to Vitturo, Aug. 21, 1944, Agudas Israel MSS, London; Saul Friedländer, *Pius XII and the Third Reich* (New York, 1966), pp. 223–35; memo, July 11, 1944, Box 241, Edward Stettinius, Jr., MSS, University of Virginia, Charlottesville; Kotler et al. to Herzog, July 7, 1944, VH; Kotler et al. to Stettinius, July 12, 1944, Tress MSS.

18. Tress memo, July 26, 1944; Berle memo to Pehle, May 31, 1944; Pehle to Berle, June 3, 1944, all in Box 71, WRB; Adolf A. Berle, Jr., diaries, Apr. 24, May 31, Aug. 5, Sept. 1, 1944, FDRL; Pehle to Va'ad HaHatsala, Aug. 29, 1944, VH.

19. Lewin, "Attempts," p. 12.

20. Receipt cables of June 12, July 28, and Sept. 7, 1944; Aguda Political report, Jan.-June, 1944; Childs to Reichmann, June 13, 1945, all in Tress MSS; Reichmann to Va'ad HaHatsala, Oct. 2, 1946; Karlinsky to Berger, Mar. 15, 1949; Sternbuch to Kalmanowitz, July 28, 1944, all in VH; Weissmandel quoted in Pehle to Kalmanowitz, June 12, 1944, 264, WJC. For Donati's plan to transfer 20,000 Jews to North Africa, frustrated by Anglo-American delays and those governments' premature publicity of the Italian armistice, see Zanvel Diamant, "Jewish Refugees of the French Riviera," *YIVO Annual* 8 (1953):279–80, and FO 371/36666, PRO.

21. Eli Sternbuch saw a copy of the letter by means of Paul Grüninger, the local police chief who aided Recha's effort until the Swiss authorities dismissed him from office without pension for this "illegal" activity. In 1969 Israel's Yad Vashem honored Grüninger with a tree along the Avenue of the Righteous of Nations (*"Chasidei Umot HaOlam"*) for saving Jews during the Holocaust. Sternbuch interview; Reuven Hecht testimony, June 24 and Aug. 15, 1954, "Kastner trial," HIJEFS MSS; Reuven Hecht interview with the author, Jan. 6–7, 1982; n. 6 above.

22. Bachman letter, May 5, 1944, MRD-1, 3/2, UJA; Kubowitzi to Office Committee, June 27, 1944, 264, WJC; Chs. 6, 7; Sternbuch to Va'ad, Aug. 28, 1944, Box 34, WRB.

23. Bauer, "Negotiations," p. 24; SM-27a, JDC; *Wiener Library Bulletin* 16 (Apr., 1962):32; McClelland memos, July 21–22 and 26, 1944, Box 58, WRB.

24. Bauer, "Negotiations," pp. 24–25; Mayer to McClelland, July 17, and McClelland-Mayer talks, Aug. 27 and 30, 1944, Box 58, WRB; Duft memo, Sept. 16, 1944, M 20/46, YV; Sternbuch to Va'ad, Sept. 26, 1944, VH. In the next few months Mayer paid almost another $75,000 for the tractors. SM-21-2, JDC.

25. Hecht interview; "Possibility of Rescue for the Hungarian Jews," Aug. 8, 1944, Reuven Hecht MSS, Haifa; Ch. 7; *JTA,* Sept. 6, 7, and 12, 1944; Seidman interview; Goodman to Walshe, Oct. 31, 1944, Harry Goodman MSS, London; Strakacz to Lewin, Sept. 25, 1944, Agudas HaRabbanim MSS; Kalmanowitz to Cicognani, Sept. 28, and reply, Oct. 3, 1944, VH; Sternbuch to Va'ad, Oct. 5,

1944, Tress MSS; Kotler-Kalmanowitz to Pehle, Oct. 15, 1944, Box 35, WRB. For a British propaganda official's concurrent anxiety about "signs of a Niebelung complex among Nazi leaders" leading to a mass slaughter of all Jews in Nazi hands, see Heathcote-Smith memo, Oct. 19, 1944, FO 898/422, PRO.

26. Memo on conversation with E. Roosevelt (which James McDonald arranged), Oct. 14, 1944, E. Roosevelt folder, Genl. Correspondence files, McDonald MSS. A warning was finally issued on Nov. 7, 1944, but the word "Jews" was specifically omitted. See Ch. 7, n. 62.

27. Herman Landau interview with the author, Dec. 1, 1980; Musy interrogation, Oct. 26, 1945, RG 238, War Department records, NA (hereafter Musy-1); Musy report dictated to son Benôit, June 9, 1954, HIJEFS MSS (hereafter Musy-2); #144403, report, Apr. 17, 1945, RG 319, Army Staff, ACSI Intelligence Documents, Federal Records Center, Suitland, Md.; Berne report, Sept. 17, 1945, XL20458, RG 226, NA.

28. Musy-1; "Vereinbarung," Oct. 18, 1944, HIJEFS MSS.

29. Musy-1; Sternbuch to Va'ad, Oct. 31, 1944, VH. Also see n. 69 below.

30. Summary of Schellenberg interrogation, Dec. ?, 1945, Box 16A, RG 238, NA (hereafter Schellenberg-1); Walter Schellenberg, *The Labyrinth: Memoirs,* trans. Louis Hagen (New York, 1956), ch. 34; Heinz Höhne, *The Order of the Death's Head,* trans. Richard Barry (London, 1965), ch. 17; Musy-2. A copy of excerpts from Schellenberg's diary for the war's last months, which he shared with the World Jewish Congress's Hilel Storch (June 9, 1945), is in 76A, WJC.

31. Musy-1 and 2; Bauer, "Negotiations," p. 26; Schellenberg, *Labyrinth,* p. 378. The figure of 600,000 is actually closer to the number of all concentration camp prisoners recorded in Germany as of early 1945 (see n. 38 below); a sociologist who worked with SHAEF on this subject later estimated that Jews made up some 75,000 of this total. Malcolm Proudfoot, *European Refugees* (New York, 1957), p. 306.

32. Musy-1; Musy to Himmler, Nov. 18, 1944, T 175, Roll 118, RG 242, NA (courtesy of Robert Wolfe); Sternbuch to Va'ad, received Nov. 20, 1944, VH; Lewin, "Attempts," pp. 17-18.

33. Wash. report, Nov. 27, 29, 1944, Tress MSS; Goodman to Mason, Dec. 1, 1944, and attached minutes, FO 371/32823, PRO; Bauer, "Negotiations," pp. 31-36; Kotler-Kalmanowitz to Sternbuch, Dec. 5, and Rosenheim to Jung, Dec. 10, 1944, VH.

34. Hecht testimony, June 24 and Aug. 15, 1954, and Sternbuch to Va'ad, Dec. 26, 1944, VH; Mayer-Kastner-Wyler talk, Dec. 26, 1944, SM-21-1, JDC; Musy-1.

35. Himmler memo, Jan. 18, 1945, T 175, Roll 118, RG 242, NA; Musy-1 and 2.

36. Musy-1 and 2; McClelland to State, Jan. 29, 1945, Box 71, WRB; Göring diary summary, 76A, WJC, and his Nuremberg statement, Feb. 24, 1948, P 13/148 YV. Widespread killing of Jewish survivors was taking place simultaneously. Several thousand in Stutthof, for example, met their deaths only days before that center's liberation on Jan. 25, 1945. Freidman, *Roads,* p. 232.

37. McClelland to State, Feb. 3 and 8, 1945, Box 71, WRB; McClelland note re Mayer talk, Feb. 7, and McClelland memo, Feb. 6, 1945, Box 57, WRB.

38. Rothkirchen, "'Final Solution,'" pp. 24-26; Göring diary; note on Good-

man lecture, Mar. 15, 1945, C 11/7/2/10/2, BD. A German historian estimates that the original Hitler directive on evacuation from the camps resulted in the deaths of at least one-third of the more than 700,000 inmates recorded in Jan., 1945. Hans Buchheim, in Helmut Krausnick et al., *Anatomy of the SS State* (New York, 1968), p. 504.

39. Goodman report, Mar. 15, 1945, 184A/99, WJC; Göring diary. Berlin's leading Reform rabbi, Leo Baeck, preferred to remain with his fellow Jews in the camp, while those among the 423 Danish Jews there refused to go since they could not depart together. They would later be rescued as a unit by Count Bernadotte. Leonard Baker, *Days of Sorrow and Pain: Leo Baeck and the Berlin Jews* (New York, 1978), pp. 314–15; Goodman note on Theresienstadt, received Mar. 15, 1945, Chatham House, Goodman MSS. Also see p. 280 above.

40. Hecht interview; Woods file, Hecht MSS; von Steiger-Hecht meeting, Feb. 7, 1945, HIJEFS MSS; Sternbuch to Va'ad, received Feb. 10, 1945, VH; Alfred Häsler, *The Lifeboat is Full* (New York, 1969), pp. 155–60, 175–78.

41. *Journal de Montreux* (among others), Feb. 8, 1945, Aguda London MSS; *New York Times,* Feb. 8, 1945; Sternbuch to union (two cables), Feb. 8, 1945, Isaac Sternbuch MSS, private collection of Abraham Sternbuch, London; Landau? to Va'ad, Feb. 16, and Sternbuch to Va'ad, Feb. 17, 1945, VH; McClelland to board, Feb. 17, 1945, Box 71, WRB. For Saly Mayer's unresolved doubts, particularly as Becher rushed to claim credit for Musy's success (meeting, Feb. 11, 1945, SM-15), see Mayer-Kastner talk, Feb. 14, 1945, SM-21-1, JDC.

42. McClelland to board, Feb. 17, 1945, Box 71, WRB; Sternbuch to McClelland, Feb. 19, 1945, Sternbuch MSS. For the British Foreign Office's opposition to the Dutch government's interest in ransom proposals via Musy, see FO 371/51112, PRO.

43. Wash. report, Dec. 28, 1944, Tress MSS; Bunim and Frankel interviews; Rosenheim to Goodman, Mar. 13, 1945, Aguda London MSS; Baerwald to Mayer, Apr. 30, 1945, SM-21-1, JDC; Warren to Grew, Feb. 15, 1945, 800.4016 DP/2-1545, SD; McClelland to secretary of state, Feb. 22, 1945, Box 1, Paul O'Dwyer MSS, Jewish Theological Seminary Archives, New York.

44. Meetings, Feb. 27, 1945, vol. 823, MD; meetings, Feb. 28, 1945, vol. 824, MD.

45. Landau interview; Sternbuch to Va'ad, Mar. 3, 1945, Tress MSS; Musy-2; McClelland to Sternbuch, Mar. 9, 1945, HIJEFS MSS.

46. Hecht testimony, Aug. 15, 1954; drafts of statement, Mar. 13, and Sternbuch to McClelland, Mar. 14, 1945, Sternbuch MSS; Goodman to editor, London *Jewish Chronicle,* Apr. 9, 1945, Aguda London MSS. Kühl joined Sternbuch as co-signer because the latter wished to be free from all possible suspicion. Kühl interview and Kühl MSS.

47. Memo of interview, Mar. 13, 1945, Box 71, WRB; Bunim interview (slightly different from his own taped interview, Dec. 12, 1976, copy of transcript in Agudath Israel of America Archives); Va'ad HaHatsala memo, Mar. 13, 1945, vol. 827, MD.

48. Kalmanowitz to Cicognani, Mar. 16, 1945, VH; Kotler et al. to Roosevelt, Mar. 16, 1945, OF-76-C, FDRL; Bunim self-interview. The Va'ad and the union had asked Roosevelt three months earlier for such a warning by the Big Three, a

declaration that Jews be considered prisoners of war, and that large sums be expended on rescue. There is no record of a reply. Memo to Roosevelt, Jan. 15, 1945, VH.

49. McClelland to board, Apr. 6, 1944, Box 71, WRB; Hecht to Sternbuch, Mar. 3, 1945; Hecht memo, Mar. 22, 1945; meeting with Musy, Mar. 25, 1945, all in Hecht MSS; Huddle to Sternbuch, Mar. 26, 1945, HIJEFS MSS.

50. Sternbuch to Va'ad, Mar. 26, 1945, HIJEFS MSS.

51. Kersten to Storch, Mar. 24, 1945, WJCL.

52. Adler-Rudel to Felner, May 24, 1943; Storch to Leavitt, Sept. 9 and 16, 1942; Storch to JDC, Nov. 15, 1942, all in Genl. Sweden, JDC; Valentin, "Rescue," pp. 224-27, 231-34; Leni Yahil, *The Rescue of Danish Jewry: Test of a Democracy* (Philadelphia, 1969), pp. 320-25. Ehrenpreis contributed to the rescue of Bulgarian Jewry during 1942, but was not helpful in confirming news during the fall of that year about the Final Solution. *Unity in Dispersion,* pp. 181-82, and p. 74 above.

53. Manfred Lehmann interview with the author, Aug. 26, 1980; Shlomo Wolbe interview, Dec. 1966, 03/3044, YV; Zuroff, "Hatsalat," p. 67; Valentin to Brodetsky, June 21, 1943, C 2/2/5/1, BD. (Lehmann's son, Manfred, then studying in New York, communicated with his father regarding the Va'ad's financial and visa programs.) The Orthodox group's conflict with Ehrenpreis continued after the war.

54. S. Adler-Rudel, "A Chronicle of Rescue Efforts," *Leo Baeck Institute Yearbook* 11 (1966):217-35; FO 371/36659-36665, PRO; Adler-Rudel to Warburg, May 18, and to Hyman, Oct 11, 1943, Genl. Sweden, JDC; memo, "Children from Occupied Areas into Sweden," Box 32, WRB. My focus on Allied responsibility disagrees with an evaluation critical of Adler-Rudel's superiors. See Beit-Tsvi, *HaTsiyonut HaPost-Ugandit,* pp. 335-37. The WRB would try (unsuccessfully) to revive the Adler-Rudel scheme one year later. Board to Amern. legation, Stockholm, Apr. 12, 1944, 840.48 Refugees/5167, SD.

55. Yahil, *Rescue,* pp. 326-33; memo, Feb. 22, 1944, Box 31, WRB; *Unity in Dispersion,* p. 183. For the switch in Sweden's rescue position as perceived by the *Wilhelmstrasse,* see Nuremberg Documents, NG-5217 and NG-5121, Columbia University Law Library, New York.

56. Yahil, *Rescue,* pp. 334-38; Fritz Hollander interview with the author, Apr. 9, 1979; Storch to the author, Feb. 27, 1979. Erlander, later Swedish prime minister, alluded to his regular contact with Storch in an address (copy courtesy of Hilel Storch) at the WJC Stockholm branch's 30th anniversary celebration of V-E day.

57. Valentin, "Rescue," pp. 240-41; Ch. 7; Storch memo, Apr.-Nov., 1944, Box 34, WRB.

58. Storch to the author, Feb. 27, 1979; Ehrenpreis to King's Chamber, June 29, 1944, *Documents Regarding Wallenberg,* vol. 1; Engzell to the author, Apr. 2, 1981; Mallet to FO, July 12, 1944, FO 371/42809, PRO; Johnson to State, July 6, 1944, vol. 750, MD; Ch. 7.

59. Johnson to State, June 28, July 3, 1944, History of the WRB, 2, Box 110, FDRL. According to Kleist's later remarks to Olsen, Boening had so blown up

their talk to "fantastic proportions" that it helped influence a decision made in Berlin during mid-1944 not to murder the remaining Jews outright. Olsen to O'Dwyer, June 15, 1945, Box 72, WRB.

60. WRB to Olsen, July 10, 1944, vol. 749, MD; FO 371/42867, PRO; Ch. 7; July 12, 1944, #39004, OSS reports, RG 226, NA; Peter Kleist, *The European Tragedy* (Isle of Man, 1965), pp. 139-71. Also see H. W. Koch, "The Spectre of a Separate Peace in the East: Russo-German 'Peace Feelers,' 1942-1944," *Journal of Contemporary History* 10 (July, 1975):531-49; Thompsen interrogation, #336875, RG 319, Army Staff, ACSI Intelligence Documents, Federal Records Center; and on peace feeler rumors, Boxes 1417, 1419, and 3481, RG 165, G-2 records, Federal Records Center.

61. Olsen to Pehle, Aug. 10, 1944, Box 72, WRB; Storch to author, Feb. 27 and June 28, 1979; Storch to Kubowitzki, Aug. 16, 1944, 178, WJC; Storch to author, May 2, 1981; Storch interview with author, Oct. 25, 1982.

62. Storch to author, May 2, 1981; Adler-Rudel, "Chronicle," pp. 237-38; Johnson to State, Oct. 14, 1944, Box 70, WRB. McClelland, interestingly enough, heard from Saly Mayer at the time that, according to an agent of Himmler emissary Becher, "B[echer] wishes to succeed where Ribbentrop failed." McClelland notes, Sept. 4, 1944, Box 57, WRB. For the Vilna ghetto's destruction, unlike that of its Kaunas (Kouno) and Siaulai (Shavli) counterparts, see Yitzhak Arad, *Ghetto in Flames* (New York, 1981).

63. Johnson to Hull, June 1, 1944, vol. 738, MD; *FRUS, 1944*, 1:1049n; Storch to author, June 28, 1979, and memo, May 2, 1981; report, July 22-Sept. 1, 1944, 228—Rescue II, WJC. Olsen had already received detailed reports, some from Storch, about the martyrdom of Baltic Jewry. See Box 31, RG 238, War Crimes Commission records, NA.

64. Ch. 8; Hollander interview; Storch to WJC, received Sept. 6, 1944, WJCL; Johnson to State, Oct. 14, 1944, 264, WJC; Mayer-Pilpel talk, Oct. 18, 1944, SM-9, JDC; Storch to Hollander, Apr. 19, 1956 (courtesy of Storch); Storch memo to author, May 2, 1981.

65. Margolis report, Nov., 1944, and Whister to Glaser, Jan. 13, 1945, Genl. Sweden, JDC; Storch to Zelmanovits, received Feb. 9, 1945; Zelmanovits to WJC NY, Nov. 10, 1944; receipts from Bergen-Belsen of Storch's packages, Jan. 11, Mar. 6, 1945; Zelmanovits to WJC British section, Apr. 10, 1945, all WJCL. These four exchanges, honoring British documents for prospective Palestine settlers, had initially been proposed by some Dutch Jewish representatives and the Jewish Agency's Chaim Pozner in Switzerland. See Ruth Zariz, "Hatsalat Yehudim MeHolland BeEmtsa'ut Ishurei Certifikatim," *Yalkut Moreshet* 23 (Apr., 1977):135-63; Gertrude van Tijn, "Contribution towards the History of the Jews of Holland" (Nahariya, 1944), pp. 42-43, Holland Genl., JDC; Kubowitzki report, Mar. 16, 1945, WJCL; Chaim Pazner interview with the author, June 20, 1979.

66. Ch. 8; Zelmanovits to Tartakower (quoting Storch), Feb. 26, 1945, WJCL; Swedish government White Paper, Apr. 25, 1956 (English summary), Bernadotte file, Wiener Library, London (hereafter Swedish White Paper); Leni Yahil, "Peulot Ezra VeHatsala BaMedinot HaScandinaviot Lema'an Asirei Machanot HaRikuz," *Yad Vashem Studies* 6 (1966):162-74; Folke Bernadotte,

The Curtain Falls: Last Days of the Third Reich (New York, 1945), pp. 8-22. The Swedish government sought a joint *demarche* to Berlin, urging that it not massacre Jews in concentration camps, but stopped when the Swiss minister in Berlin and the papal nuncio there would not cooperate. Mallet to FO, Feb. 8, 1945, FO 371/51113, PRO.

67. Fclix Kersten, *The Kersten Memoirs, 1940-1945*, ed. H. R. Trevor-Roper (New York, 1957); Storch taped intervicw, Dec. 11, 1978 (courtesy of F. Werbell); Storch interview with author.

68. *Kersten Memoirs*, pp. 11, 140-46, 187-97; file 15, Joseph Tenenbaum MSS, YIVO Archives, New York; Schellenberg-1; Donovan to Roosevelt, Mar. 20, 1944, Box 6, PSF OSS, FDRL; R. Harris Smith, *OSS* (Berkeley, Calif., 1972), pp. 215-16.

69. *Kersten Memoirs*, pp. 226-32, 203-5 (note the reference to Musy's intial conference with Himmler, first suggested in *The Memoirs of Doctor Felix Kersten*, ed. Herma Briffault (New York, 1947), pp. 218-19).

70. Schellenberg-1; Höhne, *Order of Death's Head*, pp. 556-58; *Kersten Memoirs*, pp. 11, 271, 276.

71. *Kersten Memoirs*, pp. 275-76; Storch memo, Mar. 2, 1945, WJCL.

72. Storch to Bernadotte, Feb. 23, and reply, Feb. 26, 1945; Storch to Wise, Oct. 15, 1947, all in WJCL; Storch to Posthmus, Aug. 1, 1955 (courtesy of H. Storch); Fritz Hesse, *Das Spiel um Deutschland* (Munich, 1955), pp. 399-414; Olsen to board, Mar. 7, 1945, WRB history, 2, Box 110, FDRL.

73. Hesse, *Das Spiel*, pp. 415-19; Johnson to State, Mar. 9, 1945, vol. 827, MD. For U.S. Army intelligence's later evaluation of Hesse's philosophy and politics, see report #139682, July 12, 1945, RG 226, NA.

74. Hesse, *Das Spiel*, pp. 420-31; *Final Entries, 1945: The Diaries of Joseph Goebbels*, ed. H. R. Trevor-Roper, (New York, 1978), p. 238. Also see Ch. 7, n. 6. General Wolff, present at the conference with von Ribbentrop and Hitler in early February, went on to finalize his talks with American intelligence director Allen Dulles in Switzerland. Toland, *100 Days*, pp. 73-74. Hesse's postwar account, *Das Spiel*, quotes Olsen (pp. 415-16) as saying that Roosevelt, now realizing "the danger that comes from the east," was prepared to negotiate over every point, the Allied unconditional surrender policy notwithstanding. Minister Johnson's cable (n. 73 above), which carries no such statement, has Olsen frequently interrupting Hesse's bitter comments regarding the Russians with the observation that the latter were not at all related to "this humanitarian discussion." The minister spccifically suggested that perhaps this talk should be brought to the Soviets' attention, and he concluded that Olsen's rescue underground operations in the Baltic, according to the latter, may have brought him "under a cloud" in local communist circles. A standard Soviet-line interpretation after the war of this and similar German-Western talks, allegedly seeking a separate peace while using the "Jewish question" as subterfuge, is A. Eisenbach, "Di Geheime Unterhandlugen fun di Mcrbedike Grossmachten mitn 'Dritten Reich' uhn der Goiral fuhr der Yiddische Befelkerung," *Bleter Fun Geshichte* 7 (Sept.-Dec., 1950), Jewish Historical Institute, Warsaw (copy, YIVO Library, New York).

75. *Kersten Memoirs*, pp. 276-78; Musy-2; memo signed by Kersten-Himmler, Mar. 12, 1945 (courtesy of Hilel Storch). A copy of Himmler's March 10, 1945,

letter to four SS officials, including Kaltenbrunner, regarding medical care for the typhus epidemic in Bergen-Belsen, is in WJCL. (Kersten later gave copies of this and related materials to Storch.)

76. *Kersten Memoirs,* pp. 278–82; Brandt to Kersten, Mar. 21, 1945, WJCL.

77. Himmler to Kersten, Mar. 21, 1945, WJCL; Roger Manvell and Heinrich Frankel, *Heinrich Himmler* (London, 1965), pp. 209–15. The 2,700 Jews cited by Himmler must have referred to the two Hungarian transports from Bergen-Belsen (Aug. and Dec., 1944) and the Musy transport of Feb., 1945.

78. Yahil, "Peulot Ezra," pp. 184–85; Swedish White Paper; Easterman to Mason, Apr. 3, and Storch to Mallet, Mar. 11, 1945, FO 371/51115, PRO; *Kersten Memoirs,* p. 283; Kersten to Storch, Mar. 21, 27, 29 and 31, and Storch to Kersten, Mar. 28, 1945, all WJCL; Storch to Posthmus, Apr. 18, 1956 (courtesy of Storch). For Zelmanovitz's talks in Sweden, see Mann to board, Mar. 28, and Zelmanovits to Easterman, Mar. 11, 1945, WJCL.

79. Mallet to FO, Feb. 25, and Watson to FO, Feb. 6, 1945, FO 371/48026, PRO; Mallet to FO, Mar. 26, 1945; Eden to Churchill, Apr. 1, 1945, and attached FO minutes; Churchill to Eden, Apr. 5, 1945, all in FO 371/51194, PRO; *Stalin's Correspondence with Churchill and Attlee, 1941–1945* (New York, 1965), pp. 188–89; FO to DC, Feb. 22, 25, 1945, FO 898/912, PRO; Ch. 7. Washington also received copies of the Kersten-Himmler correspondence at this time. Johnson to State, Apr. 3, 1945, 840.48 Refugees CF/4-345, SD.

80. Storch to Wise et al., Mar. 27, 1945 (courtesy of Storch); Yahil, "Peulot Ezra," p. 185n.

81. Schellenberg-1; Schellenberg, *Labyrinth,* pp. 386–87; Toland, *100 Days,* pp. 241–51; three articles in the Swiss *Die Woltwoche* (June, 1945), summarized in #019476, RG 319, Federal Records Center; Box 172, PSF OSS, FDRL; *Final Entries,* pp. 345–46.

82. Bernadotte, *Curtain Falls,* pp. 44–48; Swedish White Paper; Mallet to FO, Apr. 3, 1945, FO 371/46747, PRO. Also see Bernadotte's statement, May 17, 1946, regarding Schellenberg, P 13/148, YV.

83. Musy-2; Schellenberg, *Labyrinth,* pp. 379–80; Hecht to Sternbuch, Apr. 3, 1945, HIJEFS MSS; McClelland memo, Apr. 9–10, 1945, Box 71, WRB; HIJEFS executive meeting with Musy, May 1, 1945, HIJEFS MSS. The French legation in Berne informed the British of the German suggestion to Musy about such a blackmail trade (McClelland also heard this from Musy, see p. 260 above), which de Gaulle had advised turning down. The Free French leader did request ICRC president Carl Burckhardt at the same time to rescue French deportees, especially women and children, in probable return for the Allied promise not to bomb certain areas where German women and children would be concentrated. Holman to FO, Feb. 16, 1945, and Norton minute, Mar. 13, 1945, FO 371/46888, PRO.

84. HIJEFS executive meeting with Musy, Apr. 8, 1945, Hecht MSS; Musy-2; McClelland memo, Apr. 9–10, 1945, Box 71, WRB; Schellenberg, *Labyrinth,* p. 380. For Himmler's order about Ohrdruf, see Eugen Kogon, *The Theory and Practice of Hell: The German Concentration Camps and the System behind Them* (New York, 1950), p. 250.

85. Hecht to Sternbuch, Mar. 13, 20, 23 and 24, Apr. 9, 13, 15, and 16, 1945;

McClelland to Sternbuch, Apr. 4, 1945, all in HIJEFS MSS; Mayer-Lisbon talk, Apr. 5, 1945, SM-10, JDC; McClelland to board, Apr. 11, and Harrison to State, Apr. 13, 1945, 266, WJC. For Recha Sternbuch's trips into Germany to rescue Jews, see Lewin, "Attempts," p. 21, and Weingort-Sternbuch to Va'ad, May 2, 1945, VH. For more on Hans Eggen, the German contact whom she met, see Nuremberg Documents, NG-5498, Columbia University Law Library, New York. An attempt by Recha and Hecht to enter Germany in Musy's company did not obtain Nazi approval. Hecht memo, Apr. 20, 1945, Hecht MSS.

86. Musy-2; Göring diary; Schellenberg testimony, Jan. 4, 1946, *IMT,* 4:381–82. For Musy's contemporary evaluation of his mission, see HIJEFS-Musy meeting, May 1, 1945, Hecht MSS.

87. Musy-2; Göring diary.

88. Kersten to Storch, Apr. 3, 1945, and reply, same date; Kersten to Storch, Apr. 4, 1945, all in WJCL; Storch to Posthmus, Aug. 1, 1955 (courtesy of Storch); Storch to author, May 2, 1981.

89. Kersten to Storch, Apr. 10, 1945, WJCL; *Kersten Memoirs,* p. 284; Storch to author, Feb. 27, 1979; Kersten to Storch, Apr. 12, 1945, WJCL. A good part of Storch's parcels, held back by the Germans, would save Jewish inmates from starvation after Bergen-Belsen's liberation. *Outline of Activities,* p. 29. For a document conveying the German surrender of Bergen-Belsen to British forces on April 12, see Eberhard Kolb, *Bergen-Belsen* (Hanover, 1962), pp. 225–26. For the concurrent activities of Himmler emissary Kurt Becher in this regard, see the sources cited in Ch. 7, n. 84.

90. Yahil, "Peulot Ezra" pp. 185–86; Storch to author, Mar. 1, 1979; Mallet to FO, Mar. 27, Apr. 4, 1945, FO 371/51194, PRO. For more on Olsen's opposition to Storch and his intended trip, see Storch to Hollander, Apr. 19, 1956 (courtesy of Storch).

91. Schellenberg, *Labyrinth,* pp. 387–88; Schellenberg affidavit at Nuremberg, Nov. 10, 1945, *IMT Blue Series* (Nuremberg, 1948), 31:470–71; *Kersten Memoirs,* p. 288; Toland, *100 Days,* pp. 486–89. Himmler also ordered that Jewish camp inmates receive food packages and medical supplies through the IRC. Brandt to Kersten, Apr. 19, 1945, WJCL.

92. Engzell document, Apr. 16, 1945 (courtesy of Storch); Engzell to author, Apr. 2, 1981. Günther's legalistic approach to a Swedish passport for Storch had a parallel in foreign ministry caution regarding the last months of the war in Hungary. See Anger, *With Wallenberg,* pp. 109–12, 141–42.

93. Storch to Bernadotte, Apr. 11, 1945, and Bernadotte to Storch, Apr. 17, 1945, WJCL; Engzell memo, Apr. 25, 1945, file HP 21, I, vol. 1051 (courtesy of the Riksarkivet, Stockholm); Storch to the author, Feb. 27, June 28, 1979, May 2, 1981; Kersten to Masur, Apr. 17, 1955 (courtesy of Storch). For Kleist's version, see *European Tragedy,* p. 193.

94. Norbert Masur, *My Meeting with Heinrich Himmler* (1945), trans. M. Hurwitz, 76A, WJC; Hollander interview; Storch to Trevor-Roper, Apr. 18, 1956 (courtesy of Storch); *Kersten Memoirs,* pp. 284–85. A recent summary of Masur's trip makes no mention of Storch's prior key role. London *Jewish Chronicle,* Jan. 30, 1981, p. 20, repeated in *Jewish-Week Examiner* (New York), Mar. 1, 1981, p. 37.

95. *Kersten Memoirs,* pp. 284–85; Schellenberg pass, Apr. 19, 1945, WJCL; Manvell and Frankel, *Himmler,* pp. 226–27.

96. *Kersten Memoirs,* p. 285; Masur, *My Meeting;* Schellenberg, *Labyrinth,* pp. 391–93.

97. *Kersten Memoirs,* pp. 282–84, 286; *Memoirs of Doctor Kersten,* p. 284.

98. Masur, *My Meeting; Kersten Memoirs,* pp. 286–90; Kersten to Günther, Apr. 23, and Brandt to Kersten, Apr. 21, 1945, WJCL; Olsen to board, Apr. 23, 1945, WRB history, 2, Box 110, WRB. Curiously, the first searching look at the Wagnerian twilight of what he termed the Third Reich's "revolution of destruction" (a phrase first used by Herman Rauschning in 1938) erred in stating that Schellenberg told Himmler that he had been "negotiating with his friends of the International Red Cross about the Jewish question," and entirely omitted the Himmler-Masur meeting. Trevor-Roper, *Last Days of Hitler,* pp. 7, 115.

99. *Kersten Memoirs,* pp. 291–92. For this nihilist strain among Himmler's colleagues, see Trevor-Roper, *Last Days of Hitler,* pp. 47–51, 77, 82.

100. Brandt pass, Apr. 20, 1945, WJCL. According to Göring's contemporary account, he subsequently got Himmler via Brandt to cancel Kaltenbrunner's order that all 3,500 Jewish women in Ravensbrück be killed in favor of their evacuation to Sweden. They joined 450 Jewish women in Malchow, along with more than 1,500 French and Polish women (including Jews) from Newbrandenburg on a trip aboard Swedish Red Cross buses and one train to safety. A second train, composed of 950 Jewish, 250 French, and 750 Polish women from Neuengamme, arrived in Copenhagen. Benôit Musy, who accompanied Göring, arrived in Stockholm in mid-May. Göring diary; Musy-2.

101. Kersten to Günther, Apr. 23, 1945, WJCL; Masur to Günther, Apr. 26, 1945 (copy of Swedish original, courtesy of Wilhelm Carlgren, Swedish Foreign Office Archives, Stockholm), and translation in Mallet to FO, Apr. 26, 1945, FO 371/51194, PRO; *Kersten Memoirs,* p. 293; Kersten to Storch, Apr. 27, 1945, WJCL; Swedish White Paper; Yahil, "Peulot Ezra," p. 187.

102. Manvell and Frankel, *Himmler,* pp. 231–39; Schellenberg-1; Truman to Eleanor Roosevelt, May 10, 1945, Box 4560, E. Roosevelt MSS, FDRL; Toland, *100 Days,* pp. 527–43.

103. Rothkirchen, "'Final Solution,'" pp. 26–27; Kogon, *Theory and Practice of Hell,* pp. 251–57, confirmed in Christopher Burney, *The Dungeon Democracy* (New York, 1946), pp. 117–39 (where Kogon is given as Emil Kalman); Tooms report, Apr. 24, 1945, FO 371/46796, PRO; Michael Selzer, *Deliverance Day: The Last Hours at Dachau* (New York, 1978), pp. 41, 229–30, 88–89; Nora Levin, *The Holocaust: The Destruction of European Jewry, 1933–1945* (New York, 1973 ed.), p. 703; Gilbert, *Final Journey,* pp. 211–13; H. G. Adler, "Belsen," *Wiener Library Bulletin* 16 (July, 1962):44, 50. For Ravensbrück, see Whister to Johnson, Apr. 30, 1945, FO 371/51193, PRO.

104. Selzer, *Deliverance Day,* pp. 105, 112, 125, 238–39, 168–71, 204; Moscovoic report, May 29, 1945, WJCL; *JTA,* June 24, 1945; H. G. Adler, *Theresienstadt 1941–1945: Das Antlitzeiner Zwangsgemeinschaft* (Tubingen, 1960), pp. 161–75; Dunant report, Apr. 23, 1945, Hecht MSS; *Dansk Presstjänst,* Aug. 3, 1944, Box 32, WRB; p. 297 above; Graham broadcast, May 16, 1945, WJCL;

Baker, *Days of Sorrow and Pain,* pp. 316–18. For the possibility of a special Soviet effort to reach Theresienstadt because of Adler-Rudel's activities in Stockholm at the end of 1944, see Adler-Rudel, "Chronicle," pp. 239–41.

105. Rothkirchen, "Final Solution," p. 27; Becher interrogation at Nuremberg by U.S. military authorities, Mar. 27 and 28, 1946, Box 1, and July 7, 1947, Box 8, RG 238, NA; Rosenfeld, *Tik P'lili 124,* pp. 230–59; A. Deutschkorn and M. Oberbaum, "Halsh SheHitsil MiMavet 60 Elef Ish," *Ma'ariv,* Sept. 30, 1979; *Report of the ICRC,* 1:623–25.

106. Manvell and Frankel, *Himmler,* pp. 238–48. For one German scholar's final judgment on the SS, see Höhne, *Order of Death's Head,* pp. 580–83.

107. Pehle remarks, Dec. 17, 1945, Va'ad HaHatsala dinner, German Mission files, Box 66,058, UNRRA MSS, UN Archives, New York; Herman Landau interview. As for funds returned by the Va'ad to the JDC of the original $937,000, see JDC statement, Jan. 28, 1946, MRD-1,3/2, UJA, and Bunim taped interview. For Sternbuch's payments to Musy, see Sternbuch memo to Va'ad HaHatsala, Dec. 4, 1945, VH. Subsequent letters between Sternbuch and Musy's widow and son can be found in the HIJEFS MSS.

108. *Kersten Memoirs,* pp. 294–307, 160–64; Erich Goldhagen, "Albert Speer, Himmler, and the Secrecy of the Final Solution," *Midstream* (Oct., 1971):43–50; Robert L. Koehl, *RKFDV: German Resettlement and Population Policy 1939–1945* (Cambridge, 1957); Friedman, *Roads,* pp. 47, 62; Ihor Kamenetsky, *Secret Nazi Plans for Eastern Europe: A Study of Lebensraum Policies* (New York, 1961), p. 169; Hitler quoted in Mendes-Flohr and Reinharz, *Jew in the Modern World,* p. 484. For Himmler's attitude in 1938, see Karl A. Schleunes, *The Twisted Road to Auschwitz: Nazi Policy toward German Jews, 1933–1939* (Urbana, Ill., 1970), ch. 7; for the *Reichsführer*'s negotiations regarding Hungarian Jewry, see Ch. 7. A broad perspective on Himmler's approach is offered in Yehuda Bauer, *The Jewish Emergence from Powerlessness* (Toronto, 1979), pp. 7–25.

109. JCS memo, Mar. 20, 1945, OPD 000.5, Ref. folder Auschwitz, War Dept. records, NA; Bergson to Roosevelt, Apr. 1, 1945, 862.4016/4-2045, SD; Rosenheim to Truman, Apr. 26, 1945, 862.4016/ 4-2645, SD; Grossman report, May 1, 1945, 264, WJC. For Sweden's very limited response to the first news of the Final Solution, see Laqueur, *Terrible Secret,* pp. 49–53. British opposition to supporting elements of the German resistance in 1942 is discussed in "The Church and the Resistance Movement in Germany," *Wiener Library Bulletin* 11 (1957):21–23, and Peter Hoffmann, *The History of the German Resistance 1933–1945,* trans. Richard Barry (Cambridge, 1977), pp. 216–24.

110. Bauer, "Negotiations," p. 41; McClelland to board, Apr. 6, 1945, Box 71, WRB; Ch. 8, n. 39 for Kaltenbrunner's defense at Nuremberg of his torpedoing the Musy effort; Kersten to Günther, Apr. 23, 1945, WJCL; Engzell statement, July 11, 1938, *Evian Proceedings,* pp. 34–35, file 21, John Chamberlain MSS, YIVO Archives; Engzell to author, Apr. 2, 1981; Manès Sperber, *... than a tear in the sea* (New York, 1967). Rabbi Weissmandel, whose heroic rescue activities had few counterparts in the years of the Holocaust, exempted no Jewish organization. From the pages of a *Maharsha* Talmudic commentary printed in

Shanghai with Va'ad HaHatsala funds during World War II, he subsequently told a Yiddish journalist, "dripped the blood of Jewish children." Seidman interview.

111. Katzenelson, *Vittel Diary*, pp. 140, 36–38; Natan Eck, *HaToim BeDarkei HaMavet, Havai VeHagut BeYemai HaKilayon* (Jerusalem, 1960), pt. 3 and pp. 190–219; Yitschak Katzenelson, *The Song of the Murdered Jewish People* (Israel, 1981); *Final Entries,* p. 163. In a just irony of history, Storch got the WJC, with help from Skandinaviska Banken, the South African Jewish Board of Deputies, and DAIA in Argentina, to purchase part of the Swedish granite that Hitler had ordered for his victory monument and to then erect a memorial in Warsaw. On April 19, 1948, the fifth anniversary of the Warsaw ghetto uprising, this monument, executed by Nathan Rappaport, was unveiled in a square called "The Ghetto Heroes' Square." Storch to author, Mar. 1, 1979.

112. Grinberg address, May 27, 1945, Box 13/62, Sh'eirit HaPleita MSS, YIVO Archives; Leo Schwartz, *The Redeemers: A Saga of the Years, 1945–1952* (New York, 1953); Bartley C. Crum, *Behind the Silken Curtain* (New York, 1947), ch. 5. For some time after the war the Allies would continue to deny the reality of the Holocaust and its implications for these officially designated "displaced persons." The Jewish survivors, on the other hand, who insisted on maintaining their own identity, ultimately played a vital role in the establishment of the state of Israel three years later. For a poignant statement immediately after World War II of this pressing necessity, see Abba Kovner, "The Mission of the Survivors," July 17, 1945, address, reprinted in Yehuda Gutman and Livia Rothkirchen, eds., *The Catastrophe of European Jewry: Antecedents-History-Reflections* (Jerusalem, 1976), pp. 671–83.

Epilogue—"Believe the Unbelievable!"

1. Bruno Bettelheim, *The Informed Heart* (New York, 1960); Hannah Arendt, *Eichmann in Jerusalem: A Report on the Banality of Evil* (New York, 1964 ed.); Hilberg, *Destruction,* esp. pp. 14–19, 662–69; Edward Alexander, "The Incredibility of the Holocaust," *Midstream* 25 (Mar., 1979):49–58. This also leads to a reduction in death totals. See the incisive critique by David Luck, "Use and Abuse of Holocaust Documents: Reitlinger and 'How Many'?" *Jewish Social Studies* 41 (Spring, 1979):95–122, and n. 114 for other authors who exculpate the killers at the expense of the victims.

2. David Rousset, ... *L'univers concentrationnaire* (Paris, 1946). Bettelheim alone of those mentioned spent a year in Buchenwald and Dachau, but he left in 1939 for the United States—before the camps were turned into the "universe" Rousset and other survivors of the Holocaust have described. Jacob Robinson, *Psychoanalysis in a Vacuum: Bruno Bettelheim and the Holocaust* (New York, 1970).

3. Bauer, *Holocaust,* pp. 30–49; Leon Festinger, *A Theory of Cognitive Dissonance* (Stanford, Calif., 1957); Jack W. Brahm and Arthur R. Cohen, *Explorations in Cognitive Dissonance* (New York, 1962); Leon Festinger, *Decision and Dissonance* (Stanford, Calif., 1964).

4. Irving L. Janis, "Psychological Effects of Warnings," in George Baker and

Dwight Chapman, eds., *Man and Society in Disaster* (New York, 1962), pp. 55-92; Stephen B. Withey, "Reactions to Uncertain Threat," in ibid., pp. 93-123; Clars B. Bahnson, "Emotional Reactions to Internally and Externally Derived Threat of Annihilation," in George Grosser et al., *The Threat of Impending Disaster: Contributions to the Psychology of Stress* (Cambridge, 1964), pp. 251-80; Alexander Donat, *The Holocaust Kingdom* (New York, 1978 ed.), p. 104. Also see George M. Kren and Leon Rappoport, *The Holocaust and the Crisis of Human Behavior* (New York, 1980), p. 96, for related findings in this connection.

5. Jacob Robinson, *And the Crooked Shall Be Made Straight* (New York, 1965), pp. 148-50; Abba Kovner, "HaNes BaChildalon," in *Sefer HaShomer HaTsa'ir*, 1 (Merchavia, 1954):647; comments by M. Dworzecki and J. Robinson respectively in Moshe Kohn, ed., *Jewish Resistance during the Holocaust* (Jerusalem, 1971), pp. 375-76, 501; Lord Russell of Liverpool, *The Scourge of the Swastika* (London, 1954), pp. 23, 48-49, 59-62, 92-94, 105-11; James J. Weingartner, *Crossroads of Death, The Story of the Malmédy Massacre and Trial* (Berkeley, Calif., 1979). For the mass executions of Russian POWs, see Hans-Adolf Jacobsen, in Krausnick et al., *Anatomy of the SS State*, ch. 5.

6. Chaim Shamir, *BeTerem Shoa, Redifat Yehudei Germania VeDa'at HaKahal BeMa'arav Eiropa, 1933-1939* (Tel Aviv, 1974); Bauer, *Brother's Keeper;* Shlomo Shafir, "American Diplomats in Berlin [1933-1939] and Their Attitude to the Nazi Persecution of the Jews," *Yad Vashem Studies* 9 (1973):71-104.

7. Hilberg, *Destruction*. Representative documents can be essayed in Hilberg, *Documents;* Dawidowicz, *Holocaust Reader;* and Yitzhak Arad, Yisrael Gutman, and Abraham Margaliot, eds., *Documents on the Holocaust* (Jerusalem, 1981); Ben-Cion Pinchuk, "Soviet Media on the Fate of Jews in Nazi-Occupied Territory (1939-1941)," *Yad Vashem Studies* 11 (1976):221-33; Luck, "Use and Abuse," 107; Robinson, *Crooked*, pp. 205, 213; Jacob Celemenski, *Mitn Farshnitanem Folk* (New York, 1963); report, Dec. 10, 1941, SM-24, JDC; Mendes-Flohr and Reinharz, *The Jew in the Modern World*, p, 520.

8. Yehuda Bauer, "Genocide: Was It the Nazis' Original Plan?" *Annals of the American Academy of Political and Social Science* 450 (July, 1980):40-43; Yitschak Zuckerman, "25 Years after the Warsaw Ghetto Revolt," in Kohn, *Jewish Resistance*, pp. 24-34; Robinson, *Crooked*, pp. 188-98; Chaim Grade, *The Seven Little Lanes* (New York, 1972), pp. 72-73; Yosef (Kornianski) report, Jan. 27, 1944, Va'ad HaPoel minutes, Histadrut Archives, Tel Aviv; Friedman, *Roads*, pp. 34-58; Isaiah Trunk, *Judenrat: The Jewish Councils in Eastern Europe under Nazi Occupation* (New York, 1972); *Patterns of Jewish Leadership in Nazi Europe, 1933-1945* (Jerusalem, 1979).

9. George Steiner, *Language and Silence: Essays on Language, Literature and the Inhuman* (New York, 1967), pp. 95-109; Shaul Esh, "Words and Their Meaning; 25 Examples of Nazi Idiom," *Yad Vashem Studies* 5 (1963):113-68.

10. Alexander Donat, ed., *The Death Camp Treblinka: A Documentary* (New York, 1979); Nachman Blumenthal, "On the Nazi Vocabulary," *Yad Vashem Studies* 1 (1957):63-64; Fenelon, *Playing for Time*. And a last note, which reached Lodz ghetto workers cleaning clothes of the deported, read: "We arrived at the place after an extended journey, at the front of the entrance flies a sign

'bathhouse,' outside people receive soap and a towel, who knows what they will do with us?" 0 39/33, YV. For an insightful analysis of one cog in this totalitarian mass murder program, see the essay by Raul Hilberg, "German Railroads/Jewish Souls," *Society* 14 (Nov.-Dec., 1976):60-74.

11. Zvi Szner, "The Rabbi of Sanik," in *Extermination and Resistance,* 1 (Kibbutz Lochamei HaGetaot, 1958), pp. 105-6; the author's notes of Kovner remarks, May 14, 1979, Holocaust Seminar, National Jewish Conference Center, New York; Arad, *Ghetto in Flames,* chs. 14-15, 22-23. Also see *Wiener Library Bulletin* 13 (1959):16.

12. Evidence of Zivia Lubetkin-Zuckerman and Yitschak Zuckerman, Eichmann trial, May 3, 1961 (copy at the Zionist Library and Archives, New York); Eck, *HaTo'im BeDarkei HaMavet,* pp. 222-23; Nina Tannenbaum-Backer, *HaAdam VeHaLochem, Mordechai Tennenbaum Tamaroff, Gibor HaGetaot* (Jerusalem, 1974), pp. 102-4; Chaika Grossman, *Anshei HaMachtaret* (Merchavia, 1950), pp. 76-77, 88, 91; David Wdowinski, *And We Are Not Saved* (New York, 1963), pp. 53-55; Zivia Lubetkin, *BeYemei Kilayon VaMered* (HaKibbutz HaMeuchad, 1979), pp. 60-70 and *passim;* Fredka Mazia, *Rai'im BaSa'ar, Noar Tsiyoni BeMa'avak Im HaNatsim* (Jerusalem, 1964), pp. 84, 98-100, 102-3; Meyer Barkai, ed. and trans., *The Fighting Ghettos* (Philadelphia, 1962).

13. Chs. 6, 7, 9; Marrus and Paxton, *Vichy France,* pp. 346-56. For the similar response of native populations elsewhere in occupied Europe to Jewry's plight, see Helen Fein, *Accounting for Genocide: National Responses and Jewish Victimization during the Holocaust* (New York, 1979), chs. 3 and 5.

14. And in Sept., 1944, fellow passengers of Czeslaw Mordowicz, one of the four Jewish escapees from Auschwitz-Birkenau the previous April whose reports reached the West and the only one of his comrades to be deported back, thought his persistent warnings the concoctions of a trouble-maker. When he then tried to escape from the Auschwitz-bound cattlecar alone, the Bratislava Jews beat Mordowicz into near unconsciousness. Betsalel Mordowicz, "Pa'amayim Yatsati Chai MeiAuschwitz," *Yalkut Moreshet* 9 (Oct. 1968):7-20.

15. "Credit the fact" is Alexander's charge, in "Incredibility," p. 49; *The Shop on Main Street,* Ladislav Grossman original screenplay (Czechoslavakia, 1965); Bauer, *Holocaust,* pp. 36-37; *Notes from the Warsaw Ghetto: The Journal of Emmanuel Ringelblum,* ed. John Sloan (New York 1974 ed.), p. 300. For similar contemporary perceptions by Jews in Warsaw of their people's singular disaster, see Seidman, *Yoman Ghetto Varsha,* pp. 154-56, and especially *The Warsaw Diary of Chaim Kaplan,* ed. and trans. Abraham I. Katsch (New York, 1973 ed.).

16. Robinson, *Crooked,* pp. 178, 333 (n. 129); Friedman, *Roads,* chs. 12-14; Nachman Blumenthal, *Darko Shel Yudenrat, Te'udot MiGhetto Bialystok* (Jerusalem, 1962); Abba Kovner, "Shlichutam Shel HaAcharonim," *Yalkut Moreshet* 16 (Apr., 1973):39-40; Yisrael Gutman, "The Concept of Labor in Judenrat Policy," in *Patterns of Jewish Leadership,* pp. 172-73. Hope existed even in Auschwitz. Tadeusz Borowski, *This Way for the Gas, Ladies and Gentlemen* (New York, 1980 ed.), pp. 121-22.

17. Kovner, "Shlichutam," pp. 37-38; Salo Baron testimony at the Eichmann trial, Apr. 24, 1961; Donat, *Holocaust Kingdom,* p. 103; Nachman Blumenthal, "Kadosh Meuneh O Gibor? BeShulei Yomano Shel Adam Czerniakow," *Yad*

Vashem Studies 7 (1968):155–60; *Adam Czerniakow, Yoman Ghetto Varsha*, ed. Nachman Blumenthal et al. (Jerusalem, 1970), pp. 304–28.

18. Chs. 2, 5; H. Beeley memo, Jan. 1, 1942, FO 371/32680, PRO: James M. Read, *Atrocity Propaganda, 1914–1919* (New Haven, Conn., 1941), pp. 38–41; Roberta Wohlstetter, *Pearl Harbor: Warning and Decision* (Stanford, Calif. 1962).

19. Wasserstein, *Britain*, pp. 295–96, 310, 259, 178; Ch. 7; Alexander Werth, *Russia at War, 1941–1945* (New York, 1964), pp. 806–15; Kubovy, "Criminal State," p. 7; Natan Eck, "Mechkar Histori O Ketav Sitna? (Al HaSefer Shel R. Hilberg)," *Yad Vashem Studies* 6 (1966):360. Also see the reaction of the JDC's French representative after his country's liberation, cited in Bauer, *American Jewry*, p. 264.

20. Wasserstein, *Britain*, pp. 295–99; Alexander, "Incredibility," p. 52; Ch. 7; Stember, *Jews in the Mind of America*, p. 141; MacLaren to Calder, Jan. 3, and reply, Jan. 11, 1945, FO 898/422, PRO.

21. Zvi H. Zimmerman testimony at the Eichmann trial, June 1, 1961; Ch. 8, n. 6; Livia Rothkirchen, "The Zionist Character of the 'Self-Government' of Terezin (Theresienstadt)," *Yad Vashem Studies* 11 (1976):58; Louis de Jong. "The Netherlands and Auschwitz: Why Were the Reports of Mass Killings So Widely Disbelieved?" in *Imposed Jewish Governing Bodies under Nazi Rule, YIVO Colloquium, December 2–5, 1967* (New York, 1972), pp. 12–30; Elie Wiesel, *Night* (New York, 1969 ed.), p. 42.

22. Conference, Oct. 11, 1939, Minutes, BGA; Moshe Prager, *Yeven Metsula HaChadash, Yahadut Polanya BeTsipornei HaNatsim* (Tel Aviv, 1941); Yehuda Bauer, "When Did They Know?" *Midstream* 14 (Apr., 1968):51; A. Hartglass in *Davar*, Sept. 1, 1942; Chs. 2, 6, 7; Bauer, *Diplomacy*, p. 354; Lichtheim to Goldmann, Sept. 9, 1942, Correspondence, BGA; Dobkin remarks, Dec. 31, 1942, and Rubashov remarks, May 5–7, 1943, Va'ad HaPoel minutes, Histadrut Archives. Between Dec., 1942, and Feb., 1943, a noted literary critic penned his realization of the Holocaust's distinctive nature, but refrained from publishing it until many years later. Baruch Kurzweil, *HaNesia* (Tel Aviv, 1972).

23. Bauer, *Holocaust*, pp. 21–22, 24; Chs. 4, 5. For early manifestations of a lack of perception by otherwise astute Jewish observers, see e.g. Salo W. Baron, "Reflections on the Future of the Jews of Europe," *Contemporary Jewish Record* 3 (July-Aug., 1940):355–69; Benjamin Azkin, "The Jewish Question After the War," *Harper's* 183 (1941):430–40; Simon Segal, *The New Order in Poland* (New York, 1942), pp. 59–69.

24. Ch. 3, n. 94, and succeeding chapters. On the same grounds, the United Nations Commission for the Investigation of War Crimes refused to consider the specific murder of European Jewry. Still, its chief British delegate felt free to offer frank advice in early Aug., 1944, to the political secretary of the World Jewish Congress's London office: "People do not believe the facts as they are being presented by the press. They are too comfortable to let themselves be impressed by those stories about lethal chambers and such like. Therefore, the material you are going to present should be carefully sifted. More credence will be given to it, I think, if it is presented to the world at large as coming from non-Jewish sources." Easterman memo of talk, Aug. 2, 1944, WJCL.

25. Chs. 2, 4, 6, 8; Kohn to Shertok, July 29, 1943, Correspondence, BGA;

Friedman, *No Haven,* p. 196. For additional observations on Moscow's non-position, see Bauer, *Holocaust,* pp. 84–85, and Levin, "Attitude of the Soviet Union," pp. 225–36. And not long after the war Stalin suppressed publication of *The Black Book,* a documentary collection about the Nazi murder of 1.5 million Jews on occupied Soviet territory. A Russian-language edition of the original manuscript, compiled by Ilya Ehrenburg and Vasily Grossman in 1944–46, appeared in Israel in 1980, with an English translation the following year.

26. Chs. 1, 4, 5, 6; *New York Times,* Oct. 29, 1944. The director of the U.S. War Refugee Board gave an account of the Amiens raid to the under secretary of war in an effort to have the lines to Auschwitz-Birkenau bombed. See Ch. 7, n. 63.

27. Babylonian Talmud, *Sanhedrin,* 37a. For a good summary of the *Führer*'s views on the "Jewish question," see Eberhard Jäckel, *Hitler's Weltanschauung: A Blueprint for Power,* trans. Herbert Arnold (Middletown, 1972), ch. 2. Annihilation followed from the antisemitic illusion of international Jewish power out to destroy Germany, but so did efforts from mid-1944 onward to seek a separate peace against the Soviet Union by freeing Jews, who would later physically "contaminate" the West. See Chs. 7–9. The Nazi ideology has not disappeared with Germany's World War II defeat. See, for example, Bauer, *Holocaust,* pp. 38–40; Yehuda Bauer, "Whose Holocaust?" *Midstream* 26 (Nov., 1980):42–43; Edward Alexander, "Stealing the Holocaust," ibid., pp. 47–49.

28. Wasserstein, *Britain,* p. 344; *Atrocities and Other Conditions in Concentration Camps in Germany, Senate, 79th Congress, 1st Session, May 15, 1945* (Washington, D.C. 1945); *New York Times,* Oct. 18, 1977; Osborne to Eden, May 28, 1945, FO 371/46796, PRO; John S. D. Eisenhower, *Strictly Personal: A Memoir* (New York, 1974), p. 90; Yehuda Bauer, *Flight and Rescue: Brichah* (New York, 1970), p. 54. For a lengthier discussion, beyond the preceding chapters, of the pope's stance during the Holocaust, see my review essay of John Morley's *Vatican Diplomacy and the Jews during the Holocaust, 1939–1943,* in the *Association for Jewish Studies Newsletter* 29 (June, 1981):17–18.

29. Wasserstein, *Britain,* p. 344; Edgar Snow, "How the Nazi Butchers Wasted Nothing," *Saturday Evening Post* 217 (Oct. 28, 1944):19; *New York Times,* Nov. 16, 1980; Robert W. Ross, *So It Was True: The American Protestant Press and the Nazi Persecution of the Jews* (Minneapolis, 1980), pp. 228–57; Yaffa Eliach and Brana Gurewitsch, *The Liberators,* vol. 1 (New York, 1981). After graphic photographs in *Life* (May 7 and 14, 1945), the figures for those polled by George Gallup who had consistently disbelieved accounts of concentration camp atrocities plummeted to minute percentages. Hadley Cantril and Mildred Strunk, eds., *Public Opinion 1935–1946* (Princeton, N.J., 1951), pp. 1070–71. Yet also see Marie Syrkin, "On Hebrewcide," *Jewish Frontier,* July, 1945, pp. 10–12. The word "Holocaust" had not then been used in connection with the destruction of European Jewry. I subscribe to the argument that this term differs markedly from that of "genocide," the word coined during the war by the Jewish scholar of international relations Raphael Lemkin (*Axis-Rule in Occupied Europe* (Washington, D.C., 1944), pp. 79–95). For recent articulations of this point, which warn that the Jewish tragedy during World War II again faces different forms of depersonalization, see Bauer, "Whose Holocaust?," pp. 42–46; Alexander, "Steal-

ing the Holocaust," pp. 46–51; Uriel Tal, "On the Study of the Holocaust and Genocide," *Yad Vashem Studies* 13 (1979):7–52; and Lucy Dawidowicz, "Lies about the Holocaust," *Commentary* 70 (Dec., 1980):31–37, and *The Holocaust and the Historians* (Cambridge, 1981).

30. Oxford English Dictionary (Oxford, 1933), entry under "Holocaust"; I. Schwartzbart address at the WJC British section press conference, Dec. 1, 1942, 264, WJC, cited in Ch. 1, p. 82.

31. Andrew Sharf, *The British Press and Jews under Nazi Rule* (London, 1964), p. 71; John Winant quoted in *Wiener Library Bulletin* 2 (Jan.-Mar., 1948):7.

32. This significant aspect of Jewish behavior during the Holocaust, which truly deserves individual analysis, reflects an additional failure of imagination on the part of critics like Arendt and Hilberg. The interested reader might begin with the articles by S. Esh and M. Dworecki, in Gutman and Rothkirchen, *Catastrophe*, pp. 346–99; Dawidowicz, *War against the Jews*, pt. 2; Friedman, *Roads;* Isaiah Trunk, *Jewish Responses to Nazi Persecution* (New York, 1979); Yehoshua Eibschitz, *BeKedusha U'VeGevura* (Tel Aviv, 1976); Terence Des Pres, *The Survivor: An Anatomy of Life in the Death Camps* (New York, 1976).

33. Kovner comments (the author's notes), May 14, 1979, at the Holocaust Seminar, National Jewish Conference Center, New York; Emil Fackenheim, *The Jewish Return into History: Reflections in the Age of Auschwitz and a New Jerusalem* (New York, 1978); "The Lesson of the Murder Camps," London *Jewish Chronicle*, Apr. 27, 1945, p. 10. Persuasive in this connection is Helen Fein's stress (*Accounting for Genocide*, ch 3) on "a universe of obligation." I have expounded further upon this theme in "From Holocaust to Genocides" (paper delivered at the International Conference on the Holocaust and Genocide, June 23, 1982, Tel Aviv).

34. Albert Camus, *The Plague* (New York, 1960 ed., trans. Stuart Gilbert, © 1948 by Stuart Gilbert, reprinted by permission of Alfred A. Knopf, Inc.), p. 127. Chaim Weizmann made the same point in his address to the "Stop Hitler Now!" rally in Madison Square Garden: "At this moment, expressions of sympathy without accompanying attempt to launch acts of rescue, become a hollow mockery in the ears of the dying." *Congress Weekly*, Mar. 5, 1943, p. 4. For Camus's particular influence on Elie Wiesel, see Rosette C. Lamont, "Elie Wiesel: In Search of a Tongue," in Rosenfeld and Greenberg, *Confronting the Holocaust*, pp. 88–96.

Bibliography

Archives

Adler-Rudel, S., MSS, Leo Baeck Institute, New York.
Agudas HaRabbanim (Union of Orthdox Rabbis of the United States and Canada), Hatsala files, New York.
Agudas Israel Archives, London.
American Council for Judaism Archives, State Historical Society of Wisconsin, Madison.
American Jewish Committee Archives, New York.
American Jewish Congress Archives, New York.
American Jewish Joint Distribution Committee Archives, New York.
Amery, Leopold, diaries and MSS, London.
Baerwald, Paul, MSS, Herbert Lehman Archives, Columbia University, New York.
Baruch, Bernard, MSS, Firestone Library, Princeton, N.J.
Ben Gurion, David, Archives, Sde Boker, Israel.
——, MSS, Central Zionist Archives, Jerusalem.
Berle, Adolf, diaries, Franklin D. Roosevelt Library, Hyde Park, N.Y.
Board of Deputies of British Jews Archives, London.
Bowman, Isaiah, MSS, Johns Hopkins University, Baltimore, Mc'.
Breslau, Isidor, MSS, Washington, D.C.
Brodetsky, Selig, MSS, Mocatta Library, London.
Bund Archives, New York.
Celler, Emanuel, MSS, Manuscript Division, Library of Congress, Washington, D.C.
Central Zionist Archives, Jerusalem: Z 4, Z 5, S 5, S 25, L 15, Jewish Agency Executive Jerusalem, Minutes.
Chamberlain, John, MSS, YIVO Archives, New York.
Cohen, Israel, MSS, YIVO Archives, New York.
Davis, Norman, MSS, Manuscript Division, Library of Congress, Washington, D.C.
Federal Records Center, Suitland, Md.: RG 165 (G-2 records); RG 319 (Army Staff, ACSL, Intelligence Document files).
Frank, Jerome, MSS, Sterling Library, Yale University, New Haven, Conn.
Frankfurter, Felix, MSS, Manuscript Division, Library of Congress, Washington, D.C.
Gildersleeve, Virginia, MSS, Special Collections, Columbia University, New York.
Goldmann, Nahum, MSS, Central Zionist Archives, Jerusalem.
Goldstein, Israel, MSS, Jerusalem.
Goodman, Harry, MSS, London.
Grew, Joseph, MSS, Houghton Library, Harvard University, Cambridge, Mass.
Hadassah Archives, New York.

Hagana Archives, Bet Eliyahu, Tel Aviv.
Hecht, Reuven, MSS, Haifa.
HIAS-HICEM files, YIVO Archives, New York.
HIJEFS MSS, Agudath Israel of America Archives, New York.
Hirschmann, Ira A., MSS, Franklin D. Roosevelt Library, Hyde Park, N.Y.
Histadrut Archives, Tel Aviv.
Hull, Cordell, MSS, Manuscript Division, Library of Congress, Washington, D.C.
Ickes, Harold, diaries, Manuscript Division, Library of Congress, Washington, D.C.
Jacobs, Rose, MSS, Hadassah Archives, New York.
Jewish Frontier files, New York.
Jewish Labor Committee Archives, New York.
Jewish Welfare Board Archives, New York.
Kaplan, Eliezer, MSS, Zionist Archives and Library, New York.
Kühl, Julius, MSS, Miami Beach.
Labor Party Archives, Transport House, London.
Labor ZOA MSS, YIVO Archives, New York.
La Guardia, Fiorello, MSS, New York City Archives, New York.
Lazaron, Morris, MSS, American Jewish Archives, Hebrew Union College, Cincinnati, Ohio.
Lehman, Herbert, Archives, Columbia University, New York.
Lichtheim, Richard, MSS, Central Zionist Archives, Jerusalem.
Lipsky, Louis, MSS, New York.
Long, Breckenridge, MSS and diaries, Manuscript Division, Library of Congress, Washington, D.C.
Lutz, Charles, MSS, Yad Vashem Archives, Jerusalem.
Magnes, Judah, Archives, Hebrew University, Jerusalem.
Mayer, Saly, Archives, American Jewish Joint Distribution Committee Archives, New York.
Mayer-Musy file, Leo Baeck Institute, New York.
McDonald, James, MSS, Herbert Lehman Archives, Columbia University, New York.
Metsudat Ze'ev Archives, Tel Aviv.
Moreshet Archives, Givat Chaviva, Israel.
Morgenthau, Henry, Jr., diaries and presidential diaries, Franklin D. Roosevelt Library, Hyde Park, N.Y.
Mowshowitz, David, MSS, YIVO Archives, New York.
National Archives, Washington, D.C.: RG 59 (State Department Records)—867N.01, 848.48 Refugees, 740.0016 EW 1939, 862.4016, Harley Notter MSS, OSS R and A reports; RG 107 (Secretary of War files); RG 165 (War Department MSS); RG 218 (Modern Military Branch)—Joint Chiefs of Staff MSS, William Leahy MSS; RG 238 (United Nations War Crimes Commission MSS); RG 242 (Records of the *Reichsführer* SS)—T 175, Roll 118; RG 226 (OSS Records).
Neumann, Emanuel, MSS, New York.
O'Dwyer, Paul, MSS, Jewish Theological Seminary Archives, New York.
Palestine Statehood Committee MSS, Sterling Library, Yale University, New Haven, Conn.
Pazner, Chaim, MSS, Yad Vashem Archives, Jerusalem.
Public Record Office, Kew, England: Cabinet Papers—65, 66, 67, 95; Colonial Office Papers—733; Foreign Office Papers—371, 600, 800, 898; Premier (Prime Minister) Papers—3, 4, 5; War Office Papers—32.

Riegner, Gerhart M., Archives, Geneva (select documents from Dr. Riegner).
Roosevelt, Eleanor, MSS, Franklin D. Roosevelt Library, Hyde Park, N.Y.
Roosevelt, Franklin D., Library, Hyde Park, N.Y.: Map Room MSS, Official Files (OF), President's Personal Files (PPF), President's Secretary's Files (PSF), Press Conferences, Roosevelt-Churchill Correspondence.
Rosenberg, Israel, MSS, Jewish Theological Seminary Archives, New York.
Rosenman, Samuel, MSS, Franklin D. Roosevelt Library, Hyde Park, N.Y.
Sagalowitz, Benjamin, MSS, Yad Vashem Archives, Jerusalem.
Schwartzbart, Ignacy, MSS, Yad Vashem Archives, Jerusalem.
Sh'eirit HaPleita MSS, YIVO Archives, New York.
Silberschein, Alfred, MSS, Yad Vashem Archives, Jerusalem.
Silver, Abba Hillel, MSS, The Temple, Cleveland, Ohio.
Sternbuch, Isaac, MSS, London.
Stettinius, Edward, Jr., MSS, University of Virginia, Charlottesville.
Stimson, Henry, MSS and diaries, Sterling Library, Yale University, New Haven, Conn.
Swedish Foreign Ministry, select documents 1945 (courtesy of the Riksarkivet), Stockholm.
Szold, Henrietta, MSS, Hadassah Archives, New York.
Szold, Robert, MSS, Zionist Archives and Library, New York.
Taylor, Myron, MSS, Franklin D. Roosevelt Library, Hyde Park, N.Y.
Tenenbaum, Joseph, MSS, YIVO Archives, New York.
Thomas, Elbert, MSS, Franklin D. Roosevelt Library, Hyde Park, N.Y.
Tress, Michael, MSS, Agudath Israel of America Archives, New York.
United Jewish Appeal Archives, New York.
United Nations Archives, New York.
Va'ad HaHatsala MSS, Yeshiva University, New York.
Villard, Oswald G., MSS, Houghton Library, Harvard University, Cambridge, Mass.
Wadsworth, James, MSS, Manuscript Division, Library of Congress, Washington, D.C.
Wagner, Robert, MSS, Georgetown University, Washington, D.C.
Wallace, Henry, diaries, Special Collections, Columbia University, New York.
War Refugee Board MSS, Franklin D. Roosevelt Library, Hyde Park, N.Y.
Weizmann, Chaim, Archives, Rechovot, Israel.
Wiener Library, London (Bernadotte file).
Winant, John, MSS, Franklin D. Roosevelt Library, Hyde Park, N.Y.
Wise, Stephen, MSS, American Jewish Historical Society, Waltham, Mass.
Wolsey, Louis, MSS, American Jewish Archives, Cincinnati.
World Jewish Congress Archives, New York.
World Jewish Congress, British Section Archives, Institute of Jewish Affairs, London.
Yad Vashem Archives, Jerusalem.
Zionist Archives and Library, New York.

Interviews

Note—all interviews were conducted by the author, unless otherwise stated.

Akzin, Benjamin. July 7, 1972, and Aug. 19, 1976.
Avigur (Meyerov), Shaul. July 15, 1976.

——. Interview by Jordan S. Penkower, Nov. 19, 1977 (copy in author's possession).

Barlas, Chaim. July 15, 1976.

Begin, Menachem. Nov. 29, 1976.

Ben Ami, Yitshaq. Mar. 28, 1972.

Berlin, Isaiah. July 1, 1976.

Boukstein, Maurice. Apr. 3, 1978.

Bunim, Irving. Jan. 3, 1977.

——. Self-interview, Dec. 12, 1976. Transcript at Agudath Israel of America Archives, New York.

Celler, Emanuel. June 9 and 14, 1975.

Ciolkosz, Adam. Interview by Rabbi and Mrs. M. S. Penkower, Aug. 16, 1978 (copy in author's possession).

Cohn, Josef. June 8, 1976.

De Sola Pool, Tamar. Feb. 19, 1976.

Easterman, Alexander. Interview by Andrea P. Rosen, Oct. 25, 1977 (copy in author's possession).

. July 30, 1979.

Eppler, Elizabeth. July 24, 1979.

Freudiger, Fülöp (Philip). Interview by Prof. Yehuda Bauer, Mar., 1975. Transcript copy at the Institute for Contemporary Jewry, Hebrew University, Jerusalem.

Frankel, Shabse. Dec. 28, 1981.

Goldmann, Nahum. Mar. 14, 1974; Nov. 7, 1976; May 8, 1977.

Gurfein, Murray. June 7, 1979.

Hadari, Ze'ev (Venya). Jan. 18, 1982.

Handler, Milton. May 26, 1976.

Hecht, Reuven. Jan. 6–7, 1982.

Hirschmann, Ira. Address, Mar. 5, 1981, Eisner Institute for Holocaust Studies– City University Graduate Center, New York (notes by author).

Hollander, Fritz. Apr. 9, 1979.

Joseph, Bernard (Dov). June 21, 1972.

Karmil (Krasniansky), Oscar. Interview by Erich Kulka, June 8, 1964. Transcript at the Central Archives for the History of the Jewish People, Hebrew University, Jerusalem.

Karski, Jan. Address, Oct. 28, 1981, International Liberators' Conference 1981 of the U.S. Holocaust Memorial Council (notes by author).

Klarman, Joseph. Jan. 14, 1982.

Klotz, Henrietta. Mar. 14, 1977.

Kook, Hillel (Bergson, Peter). June 22, 1972.

——. Address, June 1, 1972, Hebrew University, Jerusalem (notes by author).

——. Interviews, 1968, at Institute for Contemporary Jewry, Hebrew University, Jerusalem.

Kovner, Abba. Address, May 14, 1979, Holocaust Seminar, National Jewish Resource Center, New York (notes by author).

Kühl, Julius. Feb. 17, 1982.

Landau, Herman. Dec. 1, 1980.

Langer, Simon. Telephone conversation, Sept. 30, 1980 (notes by author).

Lehmann, Manfred. Aug. 26, 1980.

Lerner, Max. May 7, 1979.

Levenberg, S. Aug. 2, 1979.
Lewin, Isaac. Oct. 5, 1979.
Margolis, Laura. Interview, Apr. 26, 1976. Transcript at United Jewish Appeal Archives, New York.
McClelland, Roswell. Interview by Prof. Yehuda Bauer, July 13, 1967. Transcript at Institute for Contemporary Jewry, Hebrew University, Jerusalem.
McCloy, John. May 17, 1977.
Merlin, Samuel. Mar. 27, 1972; Jan. 18, 1978.
——. Address, Dec. 5, 1974, Holocaust Seminar, Touro College (notes by author).
Miller, Irving. May 14, 1978.
Müller, Joseph. Apr. 1, 1983.
Netanyahu, Ben-Zion. Nov. 15, 1973; June 2, 1974.
Pazner, Chaim. July 14, 1978; June 20, 1979.
Pehle, John. Address, Oct. 22, 1975, McGill University Holocaust Conference. Transcript at American Jewish Archives, Cincinnati, Ohio.
Perlzweig, Maurice. Dec. 13, 1975; telephone conversation, May 3, 1981 (notes by author).
Polier, Justine. May 17, 1976.
——. Sept. 14, 1977. Eleanor Roosevelt Oral History Project, Franklin D. Roosevelt Library, Hyde Park, N.Y.
Rafaeli (Hadani,) Alexander. Aug. 15, 1976.
Riegner, Gerhart M. Apr. 22, Oct. 19, Nov. 7, 1977; Nov. 7, 1979.
——. Interview by Dr. Marc Dvorjetski, July 13, 1972 (courtesy of Dr. Riegner).
Roth, S. J. Nov. 7, 1979.
Schwartz, Joseph. Interview by Prof. Yehuda Bauer, June 14, 1968. Transcript at Institute for Contemporary Jewry, Hebrew University, Jerusalem.
Seidman, Hillel. Dec. 1, 1980.
Septimus, Louis. Jan. 24, 1981.
Stern, Binyamin Shlomo and Brudi. July 23, 1979.
Stern, Ziggy. July 19, 1979.
Sternbuch. Eli. Dec. 8, 1980.
Storch, Hilel. Oct. 25, 1982.
——. Dec. 11, 1978. Taped interview (courtesy of Frederick Werbell).
——. Interview in *Das Vort* (Munich), Nov. 17, 1947 (copy, YIVO Library, New York).
Tartakower, Aryeh. June 24, 1982.

                              Correspondence

Celler, Emanuel, to author, Jan. 26, 1977.
Engzell, Gösta, to author, Apr. 2, 1981.
Goldmann, Nahum, to author, Nov. 22, 1978.
Kühl, Julius, to author, Aug. 18, 1981.
McClelland to Bauer, Mar. 8, 1969 (courtesy of Prof. Yehuda Bauer). Copy at Institute for Contemporary Jewry, Hebrew University, Jerusalem.
Morgenthau to Klotz, Aug. 5, 1945 (courtesy of Henrietta Klotz, New York).
Pazner, Chaim, to author, Dec. 12, 1979.
Raczynski, Edward, to author, Dec. 12, 1979.
Rosenbloom, Herzl, to author, Mar. 1, 1978.
Speer, Albert, to author, Aug. 28, 1981.
Storch, Hilel, to author, Feb. 27, 1979; Mar. 1 and 6, 1979; June 23 and 28, 1979; July 9, 1979; May 2, 1981, and memo of same date.

Syrkin, Marie, to author, Jan. 19, 1980.
Tartakower, Aryeh, to author, Aug. 3, 1981; Apr. 7, 1982.

Books and Pamphlets

Abella, Irving, and Harold Troper. *None Is Too Many: Canada and the Jews of Europe, 1933-1948.* Toronto, 1982.
Ainsztein, Reuben. *Resistance in Nazi-Occupied Europe.* London, 1974.
Aliav (Kluger), Ruth, and Peggy Mann. *The Last Escape.* New York, 1973.
Anger, Per. *With Raoul Wallenberg in Budapest.* New York, 1981.
Arad, Yitzhak. *Ghetto in Flames: The Struggle and Destruction of the Jews in Vilna in the Holocaust.* New York, 1981.
——, Yisrael Gutman, and Abraham Margaliot, eds. *Documents on the Holocaust.* Jerusalem, 1981.
Arendt, Hannah. *Eichmann in Jerusalem: A Report on the Banality of Evil.* New York, 1964 ed.
Atrocities and Other Conditions in Concentration Camps in Germany, Senate, 79th Congress, 1st Session, May 15, 1945. Washington, D.C., 1945.
The Autobiography of Nahum Goldmann: Sixty Years of Jewish Life. New York, 1969.
Avigur, Shaul. *Im Dor HaHagana.* 2 vols. Tel Aviv, 1970 and 1977.
Avni, Chayim. *Sefarad VeHaYehudim BeYemei HaShoa VeHaEmantsipatsya.* HaKibbutz HaMeuchad, 1974.
Avni, S. *Ge'alani MiYad Tsar.* Tel Aviv, 1978.
Avon, Earl of. *The Eden Memoirs: The Reckoning.* London, 1965.
Avriel, Ehud. *Open the Gates!* New York, 1975.
Bader, Menachem. *Shlichuyot Atsuvot.* Merchavia, 1954.
Baker, Leonard. *Days of Sorrow and Pain: Leo Baeck and the Berlin Jews.* New York, 1978.
Barkai, Meyer, ed. and trans. *The Fighting Ghettos.* Philadelphia, 1962.
Barlas, Chaim. *Hatsala BeYemei Shoa.* Tel Aviv, 1975.
Bartoszewski, Wladyslaw. *Warsaw Death Ring, 1939-1944.* London, 1968.
——, and Zofia Lewin, eds. *Righteous among Nations: How Poles Helped the Jews, 1939-1945.* London, 1969.
Bar-Zohar, Michael. *Ben Gurion.* Vol. 1. Tel Aviv, 1975.
Bauer, Yehuda. *American Jewry and the Holocaust: The American Jewish Joint Distribution Committee, 1939-1945.* Detroit, 1981.
——. *Flight and Rescue: Brichah.* New York, 1970.
——. *From Diplomacy to Resistance: A History of Jewish Palestine, 1939-1945.* Philadelphia, 1970.
——. *The Holocaust in Historical Perspective.* Seattle, 1978.
——. *The Jewish Emergence from Powerlessness.* Toronto, 1979.
——. *My Brother's Keeper: A History of the American Jewish Joint Distribution Committee, 1929-1939.* Philadelphia, 1974.
Beit-Tsvi, S. B. *HaTsiyonut HaPost-Ugandit BeMashber HaShoa.* Tel Aviv, 1977.
Ben-Ami, Yitshaq. *Years of Wrath, Days of Glory.* New York, 1982.
Ben-Shachar, Malka. *Masa Tiger Hill.* Tel Aviv, 1980.
Benshalom, Rafi. *Ne'evaknu Lema'an HaChayim.* Tel Aviv, 1977.
Bernadotte, Folke. *The Curtain Falls: Last Days of the Third Reich.* New York, 1945.
Bettelheim, Bruno. *The Informed Heart: Autonomy in a Mass Age.* New York, 1960.

Biss, Andre. *A Million Jews to Save*. Cranbury, 1975 ed.

Bivrit HaHapala, April 23, 1941. Hagana Archives, Tel Aviv.

Blet, Pierre, et al. *Actes et documents du Saint-Seige relatifs à la Second Guerre Mondiale*. 10 vols. Vatican, Rome, 1974-80.

Blum, Howard. *Wanted! The Search for Nazis in America*. New York, 1977.

Blumenthal, Nachman. *Darko Shel Yudenrat: Te'udot MiGhetto Bialystok*. Jerusalem, 1962.

Borkin, Joseph. *The Crime and Punishment of I. G. Farben*. New York, 1978.

Borowski, Tadeusz, *This Way for the Gas, Ladies and Gentlemen*. Trans. Barbara Wedder. New York, 1980 ed.

Bracher, Karl D. *The German Dictatorship: The Origins, Structure and Effects of National Socialism*. New York, 1970.

Braginski, Yehuda. *Am Choter El Chof*. HaKibbutz HaMeuchad, 1965.

Braham, Randolph L. *Eichmann and the Destruction of Hungarian Jewry*. New York, 1961.

———. *The Politics of Genocide: The Holocaust in Hungary*. 2 vols. New York, 1981.

Brahm, Jack W., and Arthur R. Cohen. *Explorations in Cognitive Dissonance*. New York, 1962.

Browning, Christopher. *The Final Solution and the German Foreign Office*. New York, 1978.

Brugioni, Dino A., and Robert G. Poirer. *The Holocaust Revisited: A Retrospective Analysis of the Auschwitz-Birkenau Extermination Complex*. Washington, D.C., 1979.

Burckhardt, Carl. *Meine Danzig Mission, 1937-1939*. Munich, 1960.

Burney, Christopher. *The Dungeon Democracy*. New York, 1946.

Burns, James MacGregor. *Roosevelt: The Soldier of Freedom, 1940-1945*. New York, 1970.

Camus, Albert. *The Plague*. Trans. Stuart Gilbert. New York, 1960 ed.

Casey, Richard. *Personal Experience, 1939-1946*. New York, 1962.

Celemenski, Jacob. *Mitn Farshnitanem Folk*. New York, 1963. (English trans., courtesy of Chaim Ellenbogen, New York.)

Chary, Frederick, *The Bulgarian Jews and the Final Solution, 1940-1944*. Pittsburgh, 1972.

Churchill, Winston S. *The Second World War*. 6 vols. Boston, 1948-53.

Ciechanowski, Jan. *Defeat in Victory*. Garden City, New York, 1947.

Cohen, Gabriel. *Churchill U'Sheailat Eretz Yisrael, 1939-1942*. Jerusalem, 1976.

Cohen, Michael J. *Palestine: Retreat from the Mandate, the Making of British Policy, 1936-1945*. New York, 1978.

Congressional Record. Washington, D.C., 1939-45.

Coursier, Henri. *The International Red Cross*. Geneva, 1961.

Czerniakow, Adam. *Yoman Ghetto Varsha*. Ed. Nachman Blumenthal et al. Jerusalem, 1970.

Dalek, Robert. *Franklin D. Roosevelt and American Foreign Policy, 1932-1945*. New York, 1979.

Dawidowicz, Lucy S. *The Holocaust and the Historians*. Cambridge, 1981.

———. *The War against the Jews, 1933-1945*. New York, 1975.

———, ed. *A Holocaust Reader*. New York, 1976.

Dekel, Efraim. *Seridei Cherev: Hatsalat Yeladim BeShnot HaShoa U'LeAchareha*. 2 vols. Tel Aviv, 1963.

Des Pres, Terence. *The Survivor: An Anatomy of Life in the Death Camps*. New York, 1976.

Divrei Yemei Va'ad Hatsala. New York, 1957.
Documents of the Swedish Foreign Ministry Regarding Raoul Wallenberg, 1944-1949. 7 vols. Stockholm, 1980.
Documents on German Foreign Policy, 1918-1945. Series D. Washington, D.C., 1950-64.
Documents on International Affairs, 1939-1946. vol. 2. Oxford, 1954.
Donat, Alexander, ed. *The Death Camp Treblinka: A Documentary.* New York, 1979.
——. *The Holocaust Kindgom.* New York, 1978 ed.
DuBois, Josiah E., Jr. *The Devil's Chemists.* Boston, 1952.
Dunand, Georges. *Ne perdez pas leur trace.* Neuchâtel, 1950.
Eck, Natan. *HaTo'im BeDarkei HaMavet, Havei VeHagut BeYemai HaKilayon.* Jerusalem, 1960.
——. *Sho'at Ha'Am HaYehudi BeEiropa.* HaKibbutz HaMeuchad, 1975.
Ehrenburg, Ilya, and Vasily Grossman, eds. *The Black Book.* Trans. John Glad and James S. Levine. New York, 1981.
Eibschitz, Yehoshua. *BeKedusha U'VeGevura* Tel Aviv, 1976.
Eliach, Yaffa, and Brana Gurewitsch. *The Liberators.* Vol. 1. New York, 1981.
Fackenheim, Emil. *The Jewish Return into History: Reflections in the Age of Auschwitz and a New Jerusalem,* New York, 1978.
Fein, Helen. *Accounting for Genocide: National Responses and Jewish Victimization during the Holocaust.* New York, 1979.
Feingold, Henry. *The Politics of Rescue: The Roosevelt Administration and the Holocaust, 1938-1945.* New Brunswick, New Jersey, 1970.
Fenelon, Fania, with Marcelle Routier. *Playing for Time.* Trans. Judith Landry. New York, 1977.
Festinger, Leon. *Decision and Dissonance.* Stanford, Calif. 1964.
——. *A Theory of Cognitive Dissonance.* Stanford, Calif., 1957.
Final Entries, 1945: The Diaries of Joseph Goebbels. Ed. H. R. Trevor-Roper, New York, 1978.
Fisher, Julius S. *Transnistria, the Forgotten Cemetery.* New York, 1969.
Foreign Relations of the United States, 1939-1945. Washington, D.C., 1956-69.
Frank, Gerold. *The Deed.* New York, 1963.
Freier, Recha. *Let the Children Come.* London, 1961.
Friedländer, Saul. *Counterfeit Nazi: The Ambiguity of Good.* London, 1969.
——. *Pius XII and the Third Reich.* New York, 1966.
Friedman, Philip. *Roads to Extinction: Essays on the Holocaust.* Ed. Ada J. Friedman. New York and Philadephia, 1980.
——. *Their Brothers' Keepers.* New York, 1978 ed.
Friedman, Saul S. *No Haven for the Oppressed: United States Policy toward Jewish Refugees, 1938-1945.* Detroit, 1973.
Gelber, Yoav. *Toldot HaHitnadvut.* Vol. 1: *HaHitnadvut U'Mekoma BaMediniyut HaTsiyonit VeHaYishuvit, 1939-1945.* Jerusalem, 1979. Vol. 2: *HaMa'avak LeTsava Ivri.* Jerusalem, 1981.
The Geneva Conventions of August 12, 1949: Analysis for the Use of National Red Cross Societies. Vol. 2, Geneva, 1950.
Gilad, Zerubavel, ed. *Magen BeSeter.* Jerusalem, 1952.
Gilbert, Martin. *Auschwitz and the Allies.* New York, 1981.
——. *Exile and Return: The Struggle for a Jewish Homeland.* Philadelphia, 1978.
——. *Final Journey: The Fate of the Jews in Nazi Europe.* New York, 1979.
Goldfarb, Zvi. *Ad Kav HaKetz.* Tel Aviv, 1980.

Golomb, Eliyahu, *Chevyon Oz.* Vol. 2. Tel Aviv, 1955.

Gorni, Yosef. *Shutfut U'Ma'avak.* Tel Aviv, 1976.

Grade, Chaim. *The Seven Little Lanes.* Trans. Curt Leviant. New York, 1972.

Grossman, Chaika. *Anshei HaMachteret.* Merchavia, 1950.

Gruenbaum, Yitzchak. *BeYemei Churban VeShoa.* Tel Aviv, 1946.

——, and Livia Rothkirchen, eds. *The Catastrophe of European Jewry: Antecedents-History-Reflections.* Jerusalem, 1976.

——, Bela Vago, and Livia Rothkirchen, eds. *Hanhagut Yehudei Hungaria BeMivchan HaShoa.* Jerusalem, 1976.

Gutman, Yisrael. *Yehudei Varsha 1939–1943, Ghetto, Machteret, Mered.* Tel Aviv, 1977.

Habas, Bracha. *The Gate Breakers.* Trans. David Segal. New York, 1963.

Halperin, Samuel. *The Political World of American Zionism.* Detroit, 1961.

Hannah Szenes, Her Life and Diary. Trans. Marta Cohn. New York, 1972.

Häsler, Alfred A. *The Lifeboat Is Full.* New York, 1969.

Hassett, William D. *Off the Record with FDR, 1942–1945.* New Brunswick, N.J., 1958.

Hausner, Gideon. *Justice in Jerusalem.* New York, 1968.

Hearings, House Resolutions 350 and 352, 78th Congress, 1st Session. Reprinted in *Problems of World War II and Its Aftermath.* Washington, D.C., 1976.

Hecht, Ben. *A Book of Miracles.* New York, 1939.

——. *A Child of the Century.* New York, 1954.

——. *A Guide for the Bedevilled.* New York, 1945.

——. *Perfidy.* New York, 1961.

Hesse, Fritz. *Das Spiel um Deutschland.* Munich, 1955.

Hilberg, Raul. *The Destruction of the European Jews.* New York, 1973 ed.

——, ed. *Documents of Destruction.* Chicago, 1971.

Hinsley, F. H., et al. *British Intelligence in the Second World War: Its Influence on Strategy and Operations.* Vol. 2. London, 1981.

Hirschmann, Ira A. *Caution to the Winds.* New York, 1962.

——. *Lifeline to a Promised Land.* New York, 1946.

History of the War Refugee Board with Selected Documents. 2 vols. Washington, D.C., n.d.

Hoffmann, Peter, *The History of the German Resistance 1933–1945.* Trans. Richard Barry. Cambridge, 1977.

Höhne, Heinz. *The Order of the Death's Head.* Trans. Richard Barry. London, 1965.

Hull, Cordell. *Memoirs.* 2 vols. New York, 1948.

Hurewitz, J. C. *The Struggle for Palestine.* New York, 1950.

Ilan, Amitsur. *America, Britania, VeEretz-Yisrael, Raishita VeHitpatchuta Shel Meoravut Artsot HaBrit BaMediniyut HaBritit BeEretz-Yisrael.* Jerusalem, 1979.

Inter Arma Caritas: The Work of the International Red Cross during the Second World War. Geneva, 1947.

Iranek-Osmecki, Kazimierz. *He Who Saves One Life.* New York, 1971.

Jabotinsky, Eri. *Avi, Ze'ev Jabotinsky.* Tel Aviv, 1980.

Jabotinsky, Vladimir. *The Jewish War Front.* London, 1940. Reprinted as *The War and the Jews.* New York, 1942.

Jäckel, Eberhard. *Hitler's Weltanschauung: A Blueprint for Power.* Trans. Herbert Arnold. Middletown, 1972.

Jackson, Livia E. Bitton. *Elli: Coming of Age in the Holocaust.* New York, 1980.

Kamenetsky, Ihor. *Secret Nazi Plans for Eastern Europe: A Study of Lebensraum Policies.* New York, 1961.

Karski, Jan. *Story of a Secret State.* Boston, 1944.

Der Kastner Bericht. Basel, 1946.

Katzburg, Natan. *Mediniyut BeMavoch, Mediniyut Britania BeEretz Yisrael, 1940-1945.* Jerusalem, 1977.

Katzenelson, Yitschak. *The Song of the Murdered Jewish People.* Trans. Noam Rosenbloom. Bet Lochamei HaGetaot, 1980.

———. *Vittel Diary.* Trans. Myer Cohen. Tel Aviv, 1964.

Katznelson, Berl. *Kitvei Berl Katznelson.* Vol. 5. Tel Aviv, 1947.

Kersten, Felix. *The Kersten Memoirs, 1940-1945.* Trans. Constantine Fitzgibbon and James Oliver. New York, 1957.

Kielar, Wieslaw. *Anus Mundi: 1500 Days in Auschwitz/Birkenau.* Trans. Susanne Flatauer. New York, 1980.

Kirk, George. *The Middle East in the War.* London, 1952.

Klarsfeld, Serge, ed. *The Holocaust and the Neo-Nazi Mythomania.* New York, 1978.

Kleist, Peter. *The European Tragedy.* Isle of Man, 1965.

Koehl, Robert L. *RKFDV: German Resettlement and Population Policy 1939-1945.* Cambridge, 1957.

Kogon, Eugen. *The Theory and Practice of Hell: The German Concentration Camps and the System behind Them.* New York, 1950.

Kohn, Moshe, ed. *Jewish Resistance during the Holocaust.* Jerusalem, 1971.

Kolb, Eberhard. *Bergen-Belsen.* Hanover, 1962.

Kolko, Gabriel. *The Politics of War: The World and United States Foreign Policy, 1943-1945.* New York, 1968.

Korbonski, Stefan. *Fighting Warsaw: The Story of the Polish Underground State 1939-1945.* Trans. F. B. Czarnomski. New York, 1968.

Korff, Baruch, *Flight from Fear.* New York, 1953.

Kornianski, Yosef. *Bishlichut Chalutzim.* Haifa, 1979.

Kranzler, David. *Japanese, Nazis and Jews: The Jewish Refugee Community of Shanghai, 1938-1945.* New York, 1976.

Kraus, Ota, and Erich Kulka. *The Death Factory: Document on Auschwitz.* Ed. Stephen Jolly. London, 1966.

Krausnick, Helmut, et al. *Anatomy of the SS State.* New York, 1968.

Kren, George M., and Leon Rappoport. *The Holocaust and the Crisis of Human Behavior.* New York, 1980.

Kubowitzki (Kubovy), A. Leon. *Survey of the Rescue Activities of the World Jewish Congress, 1940-1944.* New York, 1944.

Kurzweil, Baruch. *HaNesia.* Tel Aviv, 1972.

Lambert, Gilles. *Operation Hazalah.* Indianapolis, 1974.

Lamdan, Yitschak, ed. *Sefer HaHitnadvut.* Jerusalem, 1949.

Laqueur, Walter. *The Terrible Secret: Suppression of the Truth about Hitler's "Final Solution."* Boston, 1980.

Lash, Joseph P. *Eleanor: The Years Alone.* New York, 1972.

Lavi, Teodor, et al., eds. *Pinkas HaKehilot, Hungaria.* Jerusalem, 1975.

———, et al., eds. *Pinkas HaKehilot, Rumania.* Vol. 1. Jerusalem, 1969.

———. *Yahadut Rumania BaMa'avak Al Hatsalata.* Tel Aviv, 1965.

Lazar, Chayim. *Af Al Pi, Sefer Aliya Bet.* Tel Aviv, 1957.

Lederer, Zdenek. *Ghetto Theresienstadt.* London, 1953.

Lemkin, Raphael. *Axis-Rule in Occupied Europe.* Washington, D.C., 1944.

Lengyel, Olga. *Five Chimneys: The Story of Auschwitz.* New York, 1947.

Levai, Eugene. *Black Book on the Martyrdom of Hungarian Jewry.* Ed. Lawrence P. Davis. Zurich, 1948.
——, [Jeno], ed. *Eichmann in Hungary: Documents.* Budapest, 1961.
Levin, Nora. *The Holocaust: The Destruction of European Jewry, 1933-1945.* New York, 1973 ed.
Lewin, Isaac. *Churban Eiropa.* New York, 1948.
——. *No'chen Churban.* New York, 1950.
Lifschitz, Jacob. *Sefer HaBrigada HaYehudit.* Tel Aviv, 1947.
Lowdermilk, Walter. *Palestine, Land of Promise.* New York, 1944.
Lowrie, Donald A. *The Hunted Children.* New York, 1963.
Lubetkin, Zivia. *BeYemei Kilayon VaMered.* HaKibbutz HaMeuchad, 1979.
MacLeod, Roderick, and Denis Kelly, eds. *The Ironside Diaries, 1937-1940.* London, 1962.
Malaparte, Curzo. *Kaputt.* Trans. Cesare Foligno. New York, 1946.
Manvell, Roger, and Heinrich Frankel. *Heinrich Himmler.* London, 1965.
Mardor, Munya. *Strictly Illegal.* London, 1964.
Mark, Ber. *Megilat Auschwitz.* Tel Aviv, 1978.
Marrus, Michael R., and Robert O. Paxton. *Vichy France and the Jews.* New York, 1981.
Masur, Norbert. *My Meeting with Heinrich Himmler.* Trans. M. Hurwitz. World Jewish Congress, 1945.
Mazia, Fredka. *Rai'im BaSa'ar, Noar Tsiyoni BaMa'avak Im HaNatsim.* Jerusalem, 1964.
Meinertzaghen, Richard. *Middle East Diary, 1917-1956.* London, 1959.
Meir, Golda. *My Life.* New York, 1975.
The Memoirs of Doctor Felix Kersten. Ed. Herma Briffault, trans. Ernst Morwitz. New York, 1947.
Memorandum of the Emergency Committee to Save the Jewish People of Europe, July 20 to 25th. New York, 1943.
Mendes-Flohr, Paul R., and Jehuda Reinharz, eds. *The Jew in the Modern World: A Documentary History.* New York, 1980.
Meridor, Ya'akov. *Aruka HaDerech LeCheirut.* Tel Aviv, 1975.
Moczarski, Kazimir Z. *Sichot Im Talyan.* Tel Aviv, 1979.
Morley, John F. *Vatican Diplomacy and the Jews during the Holocaust, 1939-1943.* New York, 1980.
Morse, Arthur. *While 6 Million Died: A Chronicle of American Apathy.* New York, 1967.
——. *VeHaOlam Shatak, Et Nispu Shisha Milyonim.* Intro. Shlomo Derech. Tel Aviv, 1972. (Hebrew ed.)
Mosley, Leonard. *Gideon Goes to War.* New York, 1955.
Müller, Filip. *Auschwitz Inferno: The Testimony of a Sonderkommando.* London, 1979.
Murphy, Robert. *Diplomat among Warriors.* New York, 1965 ed.
Navigating the Rapids, 1918-1971: From the Papers of Adolf A. Berle. Ed. Beatrice Berle and Travis Jacobs. New York, 1973.
Neuman, Oscar. *BeTsel HaMavet.* Tel Aviv, 1958.
——. *Gisi Fleischmann: The Story of a Heroic Woman.* Tel Aviv, 1970.
Neumann, Emanuel. *In the Arena, An Autobiographical Memoir.* New York, 1976.
Niv, David. *Ma'archot HaIrgun HaTsva'i HeLeumi.* Vol. 3. Tel Aviv, 1967.
Notes from the Warsaw Ghetto: The Journal of Emmanuel Ringelblum. Ed. Sloan. New York, 1974 ed.

Oren, Elchanan. *Hityashvut BeShnat Ma'avak, Istrategya Yishuvit BeTerem Medina, 1936-1947*. Jerusalem, 1978.

Palestine Royal Commission. *Minutes of Evidence Heard at Public Sessions*. London, 1937.

Palgi, Yoel. *Ruach Gedola Ba'ah*. Tel Aviv, 1977 ed.

Parliamentary Debates, 5th Series, Hansard. House of Commons and House of Lords. London, 1939-45.

Patterns of Jewish Leadership in Nazi Europe, 1933-1945. Yisrael Gutman and Cynthia J. Haft, eds. Jerusalem, 1979.

Perl, William R. *The Four-Front War: From the Holocaust to the Promised Land*. New York, 1979.

Peulot Hatsala BeKushta, 1940-1945. Jerusalem, 1969.

Philipp, Rudolph. *Raoul Wallenberg, Fighter for Humanity*. Stockholm, 1947.

Pictet, Jean S., ed. *The Geneva Conventions of 12 August 1929*. Vol. 4. Geneva, 1958.

Playfair, I. S. O. *The Mediterranean and the Middle East*. Vol. 2. London, 1956.

Political Report of the London Office of the Executive of the Jewish Agency, Submitted to the Twenty-Second Zionist Congress at Basle, Dec. 1946. London, 1946.

Prager, Moshe. *Yeven Metsula HaChadash, Yahudut Polanya BeTsipornei HaNatsim*. Tel Aviv, 1941.

Presser, J. *The Destruction of the Dutch Jews*. Trans. Arnold Pomerans. New York, 1969.

The Price of Vision: The Diary of Henry Wallace, 1942-1946. Ed. John Blum. Boston, 1973.

Proudfoot, Malcolm. *European Refugees*. New York, 1957.

Raczynski, Edward. *In Allied London*. London, 1962.

Reitlinger, Gerald. *The Final Solution: The Attempt to Exterminate the Jews of Europe, 1939-1945*. New York, 1961 ed.

Relief and Rescue of the Jews Threatened with Extermination by the Enemy, Submitted to the War Refugee Board by the World Jewish Congress. New York, 1944.

Report of the International Committee of the Red Cross on Its Activities during the Second World War (September 1, 1939-June 30, 1947). 3 vols. Geneva, 1948.

Report on the Work of the Conference of Geneva Experts for the Study of the Conventions for the Protection of War Victims, April 14-26, 1947. Geneva, 1947.

Reports of the Executives Submitted to the 22nd Zionist Congress at Basle, December 1946. Jerusalem, 1946.

Ringelblum, Emmanuel. *Polish-Jewish Relations during the Second World War*. Ed. Joseph Kermish and Shmuel Krakowski. Jerusalem, 1974.

Robinson, Jacob. *And the Crooked Shall Be Made Straight*. New York, 1965.

——. *Psychoanalysis in a Vacuum: Bruno Bettelheim and the Holocaust*. New York, 1970.

Rose, N. A., ed. *Baffy: The Diaries of Blanche Dugdale, 1936-1947*. London, 1973.

Rosenfeld, Alvin H., and Irving Greenberg, eds. *Confronting the Holocaust*. Bloomington, Ind., 1978.

Rosenfeld, Shalom. *Tik P'lili 124: Mishpat Gruenwald-Kastner*. Tel Aviv, 1955.

Ross, Robert. *So It Was True: The American Protestant Press and the Nazi Persecution of the Jews*. Minneapolis, 1980.

Rothkirchen, Livia. *Churban Yahadut Slovakia, Tai'ur Histori Be Teudot.* Jerusalem, 1961.

Rousset, David. ... *L'univers concentrationnaire.* Paris, 1946. Also as *The Other Kingdom.* Trans. Ramon Guthrie. New York, 1947.

Russell, Lord (of Liverpool). *The Scourge of the Swastika.* London, 1954.

Schechtman, Joseph B. *Fighter and Prophet: Vladimir Jabotinsky—The Last Years.* New York, 1961.

——. *The Mufti and the Fuehrer: The Rise and Fall of Haj Amin el-Husseini.* New York, 1965.

Schellenberg, Walter. *The Labyrinth: Memoirs.* Trans. Louis Hagen. New York, 1956.

Schleunes, Karl A. *The Twisted Road to Auschwitz: Nazi Policy toward German Jews, 1933-1939.* Urbana, Ill., 1970.

Schwartz, Leo. *The Redeemers: A Saga of the Years, 1945-1952.* New York, 1953.

Seabury, Paul. *The Wilhelmstrasse: A Study of German Diplomats under the Nazi Regime.* Berkeley, Calif., 1954.

Sefer Ha Ma'apilim. Ed. Moshe Basok. Jerusalem, 1947.

Segal, Simon. *The New Order in Poland.* New York, 1942.

Seidman, Hillel. *Yoman Ghetto Varsha.* New York, 1957.

Selzer, Michael. *Deliverance Day: The Last Hours at Dachau.* New York, 1978.

Sereny, Gitta. *Into That Darkness: From Mercy Killing to Mass Murder.* London, 1974.

Shamir, Chaim. *Be Terem Shoa, Redifat Yehudei Germania Ve Da'at Ha Kahal Be Ma'arav Eiropa, 1933-1939.* Tel Aviv, 1974.

Shapira, Anita. *Berl.* Vol. 2. Tel Aviv, 1980.

Sharett, Moshe. *Yoman Medini.* Vols. 4-5. Tel Aviv, 1974, 1979.

Sharf, Andrew. *The British Press and the Jews under Nazi Rule.* London, 1964.

Shazar, Zalman. *Tsiyon Va Tsedek.* Vol. 2. Tel Aviv, 1971.

Sherman, A. J. *Island Refuge: Britain and Refugees from the Third Reich, 1933-1939.* London, 1973.

Shirer, William L. *The Rise and Fall of the Third Reich.* New York, 1960 ed.

Shonfeld, Moshe. *The Holocaust Victims Accuse.* New York, 1977.

Shulman, Abraham. *The Case of Hotel Polski.* New York, 1982.

Slutsky, Yehuda. *Sefer Toldot Ha Hagana.* Vol. 3: *Mi Ma'arach Le Milchama.* Tel Aviv, 1972.

Smith, Bradley, F. *The Road to Nuremberg.* New York, 1981.

Smith, R. Harris. *OSS.* Berkeley, Calif., 1972.

Sperber, Manès. ... *than a tear in the sea.* Trans. Constantine Fitzgibbon. New York, 1967.

Stalin's Correspondence with Churchill and Attlee, 1941-1945. New York, 1965.

Steiner, George. *Language and Silence: Essays on Language, Literature and the Inhuman.* New York, 1967.

Steiner, Gershon A. *Patria.* Tel Aviv, 1964.

Steinert, Marlis G. *Hitler's War and the Germans.* Trans. Thomas E. J. De Witt. Athens, Ohio, 1977.

Stember, Charles H., et al. *Jews in the Mind of America.* New York, 1966.

Stephens, Robert. *Nasser: A Political Biography.* New York, 1971.

Stevenson, William. *A Man Called Intrepid: The Secret War.* New York, 1976.

Suhl, Yuri, ed. *They Fought Back.* New York, 1975 ed.

Sykes, Christopher, *Orde Wingate, a Biography.* Cleveland, 1959.

Tannenbaum-Backer, Nina. *Ha Adam Ve Ha Lochem, Mordechai Tennenbaum Tamaroff, Gibor Ha Getaot.* Jerusalem, 1974.

Teller, Judd. *Strangers and Natives: The Evolution of the American Jew from 1921 to the Present.* New York, 1966.

Toland, John. *The Last 100 Days.* New York, 1966 ed.

Trevor-Roper, H. R. *The Last Days of Hitler.* New York, 1947.

Trial of Adolf Eichmann. "Minutes of the Trial: Official Translation into English" (unrevised). Jerusalem, 1961.

Trial of the Major War Criminals before the International Military Tribunal. 42 vols. Nuremberg, 1947–49.

Trunk, Isaiah. *Jewish Responses to Nazi Persecution.* New York, 1979.

———. *Judenrat: The Jewish Councils in Eastern Europe under Nazi Occupation.* New York, 1972.

The 21st Zionist Congress (in Hebrew). Geneva, 1939.

The United Nations and the Jewish National Home In Palestine, American Palestine Committee Dinner, May 25, 1942, N.Y.

Unity in Dispersion: A History of the World Jewish Congress. New York, 1948.

Urofsky, Melvin I. *We Are One! American Jewry and Israel.* New York, 1978.

U.S. Military Tribunal. "Documents: Staff Evidence Analysis." Unnumbered vols. Law Library, Columbia University, New York.

Van Paassen, Pierre. *The Forgotten Ally.* New York, 1943.

Veisman, Yitschak. *Mul Aitanei HaResha.* Tel Aviv, 1968.

Vrba, Rudolf, and Alan Bestic. *I Cannot Forgive.* New York, 1964 ed.

The War Diary of Breckenridge Long. Ed. Fred L. Israel. Lincoln, Nebr., 1966.

The Warsaw Diary of Chaim Kaplan. Ed. and trans. Abraham I. Katsch. New York, 1973 ed.

Wasserstein, Bernard. *Britain and the Jews of Europe, 1939–1945.* Oxford, 1979.

Wdowinski, David. *And We Are Not Saved.* New York, 1963.

Weingartner, James. J. *Crossroads of Death: The Story of the Malmédy Massacre and Trial.* Berkeley, Calif., 1979.

Weisband, Edward. *Turkish Foreign Policy, 1943–1945.* Princeton, N.J., 1972.

Weissberg, Alex. *Desperate Mission.* New York, 1958.

Weissmandel, Michoel Dov. *Min HaMeitsar.* New York, 1960.

Weizmann, Chaim. *Trial and Error.* New York, 1949.

Werbell, Frederick E., and Thurston Clarke. *Lost Hero: The Mystery of Raoul Wallenberg.* New York, 1982.

Werth, Alexander. *Russia at War, 1941–1945.* New York, 1964.

Wiesel, Elie. *Night.* Trans. Stella Rodway. New York, 1969 ed.

———. *One Generation After.* New York, 1970.

Wise, Stephen. *Challenging Years: The Autobiography of Stephen Wise.* New York, 1949.

Wohlstetter, Roberta. *Pearl Harbor: Warning and Decision.* Stanford, Calif., 1962.

Woodward, Llewellyn. *British Foreign Policy in the Second World War.* London, 1962.

World Jewish Congress, British section. *Outline of Activities, 1936–1946.* London, 1948.

Wyman, David S. *Paper Walls: America and the Refugee Crisis, 1938–1941.* Boston, 1968.

Yahil, Leni. *The Rescue of Danish Jewry: Test of a Democracy.* Philadelphia, 1969.

Yelin-Mor, Natan. *Lochamei Cheirut Yisrael.* Jerusalem, 1975.

Zerubavel, [Gilad], ed. *Chantche VeFrumka, Michtavim VeDivrei Zikaron.* Tel Aviv, 1945.

Zygielbojm Buch. Ed. S. J. Hertz. New York, 1947.
Zygielbojm, Szmul, and Josiah Wedgwood. *Stop Them Now!* London, 1942.

Articles

Adler, H. G. "Belsen." *Wiener Library Bulletin* 16 (July, 1962):44, 50.
Adler-Rudel, S. "A Chronicle of Rescue Efforts." *Leo Baeck Institute Yearbook* 11 (1966):213–41.
Ainsztein, Reuben. "New Light on Szmul Zygielbojm's Suicide." *Yad Vashem Bulletin* 15 (Aug., 1964):8–12.
Akzin, Benjamin. "The Jewish Question after the War." *Harper's* 183 (1941):430–40.
Alexander, Edward. "The Incredibility of the Holocaust." *Midstream* 25 (Mar., 1979):49–58.
——. "Stealing the Holocaust." *Midstream* 26 (Nov., 1980):46–51.
The Answer (1943–46).
Artsi, Y. "BeRumania BeYemei HaShoa." *Masua* 1 (1973):104–50.
"Autobiography of Rudolf Höss." In Jadwiga Bezwínska and Danuta Czech, eds., *KL Auschwitz Seen by the SS.* Krakow, 1978, pp. 33–136.
Avital, Tsvi, "Yachaso Shel HaShilton HaPolani BaGola El HaSh'eila HaYehudit." *Yalkut Moreshet* 16 (Apr., 1973):133–46.
Avni, S. "Al Tochnit Transnistria." *Yalkut Moreshet* 30 (Nov., 1980):199–203.
Bahnson, Clars B. "Emotional Reactions to Internally and Externally Derived Threats of Annihilation." In George Grosser et al., *The Threat of Impending Disaster: Contributions to the Psychology of Stress.* Cambridge, 1964, pp. 251–80.
Ball-Kaduri, H. I. "HaAliya HaBilti-Chukit MeiGermania HaNatsit L'Eretz Yisrael." *Yalkut Moreshet* 8 (Mar., 1968):127–44.
Barlas, Chaim. "Mivtsa Aliyat Lita." In *Dapim LeChecker HaShoa VeHamered,* ser. 2a. HaKibbutz HaMeuchad, 1969, pp. 246–55.
——. "Pegishot BeKushta." *Masua* 4 (1976):125–33.
Baron, Salo W. "Reflections on the Future of the Jews of Europe." *Contemporary Jewish Record* 3 (July-Aug., 1940):355–69.
Bauer, Yehuda. "Genocide: Was It the Nazis' Original Plan?" *Annals of the American Academy of Political and Social Science* 450 (July, 1980):35–45.
——. "The Negotiations between Saly Mayer and the Representatives of the SS in 1944–1945." In Yisrael Gutman and Efraim Zuroff, eds., *Rescue Attempts during the Holocaust.* Jerusalem, 1977, pp. 5–45.
——. "When Did They Know?" *Midstream* 14 (Apr., 1968):51–56.
——. "Whose Holocaust?" *Midstream* 26 (Nov., 1980):42–46.
Ben Gurion, David. "Jewish Army." *New Judea,* Aug., 1940, pp. 122–24.
——. "Memoirs." *Jewish Observer and Middle East Review,* Aug. 30, 1963–May 22, 1964.
——. "To the Tribunal of Nations." *Palestine and Middle East* 17 (July, 1944):123–24.
——. "War and the [Jewish] People." *New Palestine,* Oct. 27, 1939, p. 5.
——. "Zionist Policy Today." *New Palestine,* Jan. 17, 1941, pp. 7–8.
Biederman, Moshe. "Pirkei HaNoar HaTsiyoni BeHungaria." *Masua* 1 (1973):66–89.
Blumenthal, Nachman. "Kadosh Meuneh O Gibor? BeShulei Yomano Shel Adam Czerniakow." *Yad Vashem Studies* 7 (1968):155–60.

——. "On the Nazi Vocabulary." *Yad Vashem Studies* 1 (1957):49–66.

Broszat, Martin. "Hitler and the Genesis of the 'Final Solution': An Assessment of David Irving's Theses." *Yad Vashem Studies* 13 (1979):73–126.

Carpi, Daniel. "The Diplomatic Negotiations over the Transfer of Jewish Children from Croatia to Turkey and Palestine in 1943." *Yad Vashem Studies* 12 (1977):109–21.

"The Church and the Resistance Movement in Hungary." *Wiener Library Bulletin* 11 (1957):21–23.

Ciolkosz, Adam. "In London mit Artur Zygielbojm." *Unzer Zeit,* May, 1965, pp. 23–24.

——. "Paminci Bohaterow Ghetta Warszawskiego." *Robotnik Polski* New York, May 18, 1958, pp. 1–5 (copy in the Bund Archives, courtesy of Hilel Kempinski).

——. "Torne-Crakow-London." *Unzer Zeit,* 11-12 (1957):75–78.

Cohen, Asher. "Hashpa'at HaPelitim Al Hithavut HaMachteret HaChalutzit BeHungaria." In *Dapim LeCheker Tekufat HaShoa,* ser. 2. Tel Aviv, 1981, pp. 121–49.

——. "HeChalutz Underground in Hungary: March-August 1944 (Based on Testimony of Survivors)." *Yad Vashem Studies* 14 (1981):247–67.

——. "LeDemuta Shel 'Va'adat HaEzra VeHaHatsala' BeBudapest BeReishit Darka." *Moreshet* 29 (May, 1980):143–60.

Cohen, Gabriel. "Churchill and the Establishment of the War Cabinet Committee on Palestine, April-July, 1943" (in Hebrew). *Zionism* 4 (1975):259–336.

Congress Weekly (1939–45).

Contemporary Jewish Record (1939–45).

Cruz, Ya'akov. "HaLaila Bo Tub'ah 'Mefkure'" *Yediot Aharonot,* Aug. 10, 1979.

Dawidowicz, Lucy S. "American Jews and the Holocaust," Apr. 18, 1982, *New York Times Magazine,* pp. 46ff.

——. "Lies about the Holocaust." *Commentary* 70 (Dec., 1980):31–37.

Deutschkorn, A., and W. Oberbaum. "HaIsh SheHitsil MiMavet 60 Elef Ish." *Ma'ariv,* Sept. 30, 1979.

Diamant, Zanvel. "Jewish Refugees of the French Riviera." *YIVO Annual* 8 (1953):264–80.

Dijour, Ilya. "The Preparations for the Bermuda Conference." *YIVO-Bleter* 21 (1943):5–19.

"Dossier Holocaust." *Schweizer Illustrierte,* May 7, 1979.

Dworzecki, Meir. "The International Red Cross and Its Policy vis-à-vis the Jews in the Ghettos and Concentration Camps in Nazi-Occupied Europe." In Yisrael Gutman and Efraim Zuroff, eds., *Rescue Attempts during the Holocaust.* Jerusalem, 1977, pp. 71–110.

Eban, Abba. "Tragedy and Triumph, 1939-1949." In Meyer Weisgal and Joel Carmichael, eds., *Chaim Weizmann: A Biography by Several Hands.* London, 1962, pp. 249–313.

Eck, Natan. "Mechkar Histori O Ketav Sitna? (Al HaSefer Shel R. Hilberg)." *Yad Vashem Studies* 6 (1966):343–81.

——. "The Rescue of Jews with the Aid of Passports and Citizenship Papers of Latin American States." *Yad Vashem Studies* 1 (1957):125–52.

——. "Yehudim Temurat Germanim." In *Dapim LeCheker HaShoa VeHamered,* ser. 2b. (Tel Aviv 1973), pp. 23–49.

Eisenbach, A[ron]. "Di Geheime Unterhandlugen fun di Merbedike Grossmachten mitn 'Dritten Reich' uhn der Goiral Fuhn der Yiddische Befelkerung." *Bleter fun Geshichte* 7 (Sept.-Dec., 1954):3–54.

Emerson, Herbert. "The Postwar Problems of Refugees." *Foreign Affairs* 21 (Jan., 1943):211–20.

Eppler, Elizabeth. "The Rescue Work of the World Jewish Congress." In Yisrael Gutman and Efraim Zuroff, eds., *Rescue Attempts during the Holocaust*. Jerusalem, 1977, pp. 47–69.

Erez, Zvi. "Shisha Yamim BeYuli 1944 BeHungaria." *Yalkut Moreshet* 20 (Dec., 1975):149–68.

Esh, Shaul. "Words and Their Meaning: 25 Examples of Nazi Idiom." *Yad Vashem Studies* 5 (1963):113–68.

"The Extermination of the Polish Jewry." *Polish Fortnightly Review*, Dec. 1, 1942.

Förster, Jürgen. "The Wehrmacht and the War of Extermination against the Soviet Union." *Yad Vashem Studies* 14 (1981):7–34.

Fox, John R. "The Jewish Factor in British War Crimes Policy in 1942." *English Historical Review* 92 (Jan., 1977):82–106.

Freudiger, Fülöp [Philip], et al. "Report on Hungary, March 19–August 9, 1944." In Randolph L. Braham, ed., *Hungarian Jewish Studies*. New York, 1973, 3:75–146.

Friedländer, Saul. "The Historical Significance of the Holocaust." *Jerusalem Quarterly* 1 (Fall, 1976):36–59.

Gelber, Yoav. "HaItonut HaIvrit BeEretz Yisrael Al Hashmadat Yehudei Eiropa." In *Dapim LeCheker HaShoa VeHaMered*, ser. 2a. Tel Aviv, 1969, pp. 30–58.

———. "Palestinian POWs in German Captivity." *Yad Vashem Studies* 14 (1981):89–137.

Genizi, Haim. "James McDonald and the Roosevelt Administration." In Pinchas Artsi, ed., *Bar-Ilan Studies in History*. Ramat Gan. 1978, pp. 285–306.

The Ghetto Speaks (1942–44).

Gilbert, Martin. Series on the Holocaust in Hungary in *Jerusalem Post*, Feb. 8–29, 1980.

Goldhagen, Erich. "Albert Speer, Himmler, and the Secrecy of the Final Solution." *Midstream* 17 (Oct., 1971):43–50.

Goldmann, Nahum. "The Influence of the Holocaust on the Change in the Attitude of World Jewry to Zionism and the State of Israel." In *Holocaust and Rebirth: A Symposium*. Jerusalem, 1974, pp. 77–103.

Greenberg, Hayim. "Bankrupt." *Yiddishe Kemfer*, Feb. 12, 1943. Reprinted in *Midstream* 10 (Mar., 1964):5–10.

———. "The Plan of Destruction." *Jewish Frontier*, Nov., 1942, p. 8.

Grobman, Alex. "What Did They Know? The American Jewish Press and the Holocaust, 1 Sept. 1939–17 Dec. 1942." *American Jewish History* 68 (Mar., 1979):327–52.

Grossman, Kurt. "An Unfulfilled Testament." *Congress Weekly* 10 (Nov. 12, 1943):10–11.

Gutman, Yisrael. "The Attitude of the Poles to the Mass Deportations of Jews from the Warsaw Ghetto in the Summer of 1942." In Yisrael Gutman and Efraim Zuroff, eds., *Rescue Attempts during the Holocaust*. Jerusalem, 1977, pp. 399–422.

———. "The Concept of Labor in Judenrat Policy." In *Patterns of Jewish Leadership in Nazi Europe 1933–1945*. Jerusalem, 1979, pp. 151–80.

Halivni, Tzipora Hager. "The Birkenau Revolt: Poles Prevent a Timely Insurrection." *Jewish Social Studies* 41 (Spring, 1979):123–54.

Hecht, Ben. "A Champion in Chains." *Esquire,* Oct., 1942, pp. 36, 168–69.
——. "Remember Us!" *Reader's Digest* 42 (Feb., 1943):107–10.
Hilberg, Raul. "German Railroads/Jewish Souls." *Society* 14 (Nov.-Dec., 1976):60–74.
Ilan, Amitzur. "HaMinimax VeOrmat HaHistoria." In Yosef Gorni and Gedalia Yogev, eds., *Medina'i Beltot Mashber, Darko Shel Chaim Weizmann BaTenua HaTsiyonit, 1900–1948.* Tel Aviv, 1977, pp. 103–19.
Janis, Irving L. "Psychological Effects of Warnings." In George Baker and Dwight Chapman, eds., *Man and Society in Disaster.* New York, 1962, pp. 59–92.
Jelinek, Y[eshayahu]. "The Vatican, the Catholic Church, the Catholics and the Persecution of the Jews during World War II: The Case of Slovakia." In Bela Vago and George L. Mosse, eds., *Jews and Non-Jews in Eastern Europe.* Jerusalem, 1974, pp. 221–55.
Jewish Affairs 1 (Oct.-Nov., 1947), World Jewish Congress, London.
Jewish Frontier (1939–45).
Jewish Telegraphic Agency Daily News Bulletin (JTA) (1939–45).
Jong, Louis de. "The Netherlands and Auschwitz: Why Were the Reports of Mass Killings So Widely Disbelieved?" In *Imposed Jewish Governing Bodies under Nazi Rule, YIVO Colloquium, December 2–5, 1967.* New York, 1972, pp. 12–30.
Kabeli, Isaac. "The Resistance of the Greek Jews." *YIVO Annual* 8 (1953):281–88.
Kaplan, Yonatan. "Peilut HaHatsala Shel Mishlachat HaEtzel BeArtsot HaBrit BeTekufat HaShoa (a)." *Yalkut Moreshet* 30 (Nov., 1980):115–38.
Katz, Jacob. "Was the Holocaust Inevitable?" *Commentary* 59 (May, 1975):41–48.
Katz, Shlomo Z. "Public Opinion in Western Europe and the Evian Conference of July 1938." *Yad Vashem Studies* 9 (1973):105–32.
Koch, H. W. "The Spectre of a Separate Peace in the East: Russo-German 'Peace Feelers,' 1942–1944." *Journal of Contemporary History* 10 (July, 1975):531–49.
Kovner, Abba. "HaNes BaChidalon." In *Sefer HaShomer HaTsa'ir.* Merchavia, 1956, 1:643–54.
——. "Nisayon Rishon LeHagid." *Yalkut Moreshet* 16 (Apr., 1973):7–23.
——. "Shlichutam Shel HaAcharonim." *Yalkut Moreshet* 16 (Apr., 1973): 35–42. Reprinted as "The Mission of the Survivors," in Yehuda Gutman and Livia Rothkirchen, eds., *The Catastrophe of European Jewry: Antecedents-History-Reflections.* Jerusalem, 1976, pp. 671–83.
Kubovy, Aryeh L. "Criminal State vs. Moral Society." *Yad Vashem Bulletin* 13 (Oct., 1963):3–11.
Kulka, Erich. "Teudot Amerika'iyot Al Haftsatsat Auschwitz-Birkenau." *Yalkut Moreshet* 16 (Apr., 1973):147–56.
——. "Five Escapes from Auschwitz." In Yuri Shul, ed., *They Fought Back.* New York, 1975 ed., pp. 196–218.
Lamont, Rosette C. "Elie Wiesel: In Search of a Tongue." In Alvin H. Rosenfeld and Irving Greenberg, eds., *Confronting the Holocaust.* Bloomington, Ind., 1978, pp. 88–96.
Laqueur, Walter. "The Mysterious Messenger and the Final Solution." *Commentary* 69 (Mar., 1980):54–64.
Lawrence, Boris. "Sipur Shel HaOniya Pencho, 1940–42." *Yalkut Moreshet* 20 (Dec., 1975):35–50.

Lenski, Mordecai. "Problems of Disease in the Warsaw Ghetto." *Yad Vashem Studies* 3 (1959):283–93.

Leshem, Perez. "Rescue Efforts in the Iberian Peninsula." *Leo Baeck Institute Yearbook* 14 (1969):231–56.

Lester, Eleanor, and Frederick E. Werbell. "The Lost Hero of the Holocaust: The Search for Sweden's Raoul Wallenberg." *New York Times Magazine*, Mar. 30, 1980, pp. 20ff.

Levin, Dov. "The Attitude of the Soviet Union to the Rescue of the Jews." In Yisrael Gutman and Efraim Zuroff, eds. *Rescue Attempts during the Holocaust*. Jerusalem, 1977, pp. 225–36.

Lewin, Isaac. "Attempts at Rescuing European Jews with the Help of Polish Diplomatic Missions during World War II." *Polish Review* 22 (1977):3–23.

——. "Attempts at Rescuing European Jews with the Help of Polish Diplomatic Missions during World War II: Part II." *Polish Review* 24 (1979):46–61.

Lowenstein, Sharon. "A New Deal for Refugees: The Promise and Reality of Oswego." *American Jewish History* 71 (Mar., 1982):325–41.

Luck, David. "Use and Abuse of Holocaust Documents: Reitlinger and 'How Many?'" *Jewish Social Studies* 41 (Spring, 1979):95–122.

Lurie, Jessie. "Guns in Palestine." *Nation*, Jan. 22, 1944, pp. 92–94.

Margalit, David. "Mivtsa'ei Hatsala BeHungaria." *Masua* 2 (1974):90–95.

McDonald, James G. "The Time for Discussion Is Past." *New Palestine* 33 (Mar. 19, 1943):5–7.

Meyer, Ernie. "Family's Faith." *Jerusalem Post* International Edition, Jan. 27–Feb. 2, 1980.

Michel, Henri. "Jewish Resistance and the European Resistance Movement." In *Jewish Resistance during the Holocaust*. Jerusalem, 1972, pp. 365–75.

Mordowicz, Betsalel. "Pa'amayim Yatsati Chai MeiAuschwitz." *Yalkut Moreshet* 9 (Oct., 1968):7–20.

Morgenstern, Aryeh. "Va'ad HaHatsala HaMeuchad SheLeYad HaSochnut HaYehudit U'Peulotav BaShanim 1943-1945." *Yalkut Moreshet* 13 (June, 1971):60–103.

Morgenthau, Henry, Jr. "The Morgenthau Diaries, VI—The Refugee Run-Around." *Colliers* 120 (Nov. 1, 1947):23ff.

Nation (1939–45).

New Judea (1939–45).

New Palestine (1939–45).

New Republic (1939–45).

Opinion (1939–45).

PM (1939–45).

Penkower, Monty N. "Ben Gurion, Silver, and the 1941 UPA National Conference for Palestine: A Turning Point in American Zionist History." *American Jewish History* 69 (Sept., 1979):66–78. Reprinted in Nathan Kaganoff, ed., *Solidarity and Kinship: Essays in American Zionism*. Waltham, Mass., 1980, pp. 88–100.

——. "In Dramatic Dissent: The Bergson Boys." *American Jewish History* 70 (Mar., 1981):281–309.

——. "The 1943 Joint Anglo-American Statement on Palestine." *Herzl Yearbook* 8 (1978):212–41.

——. Review essay on John Morley, *Vatican Diplomacy and the Jews during the Holocaust, 1939-1943. Association for Jewish Studies Newsletter* 29 (June, 1981):17–18.

Pinchuk, Ben-Cion. "Soviet Media on the Fate of Jews in Nazi-Occupied Territory (1939-1941)." *Yad Vashem Studies* 11 (1976):221-33.

Pomeraniec, Venya. "Kushta, Merkaz LePeulot Ezra VeHatsala." In Zerubavel Gilad, ed., *Magen BeSeter*. Jerusalem, 1952, pp. 197-204.

"Reflections on the Holocaust." Special issue, *Annals of the American Academy of Political and Social Science* 450 (July, 1980).

Reiss, A. "Perakim MiPeulot HaEzra VeHaHatsala." In *Dapim LeCheker HaShoa VeHaMered*, ser. 2a. HaKibbutz HaMeuchad, 1952, pp. 19-36.

"Remember the *Patria*." *Jerusalem Post*, Nov. 27, 1980.

Review of the Yiddish Press. American Jewish Committee, 1941-45.

Riegner, Gerhart. Interview in *Das Neue Israel (Zurich) 5 (Nov., 1968)*.

Rosenkranz, Herbert. "The Anschluss and the Tragedy of Austrian Jewry, 1938-1944." In Josef Fraenkel, ed., *The Jews of Austria: Essays on Their Life, History and Destruction*. London, 1967, pp. 479-546.

Rothkirchen, Livia. "The Czechoslovak Government-in-Exile: Jewish and Palestinian Aspects in the Light of the Documents." *Yad Vashem Studies* 9 (1973):157-99.

——. "The 'Final Solution' in Its Last Stages." *Yad Vashem Studies* 8 (1970):7-29.

——. "The Zionist Character of the 'Self-Government' of Terezín (Theresienstadt)." *Yad Vashem Studies* 11 (1976):56-90.

Rubin, Barry. "Ambassador Laurence A. Steinhardt: The Perils of a Jewish Diplomat, 1940-1945." *American Jewish History* 70 (Mar., 1981):331-46.

Salin, Edgar. "Über Artur Sommer, den Menschen und List-Forscher." *Mitteilungen der List Gesellschaft* (Basle) 6, nos. 4/5 (Nov. 30, 1967):81-90.

Schwartzbaum, Alf. "Peulot Ezra MiSchveits BaShanim, 1940-1945." *Masua* 2 (1974):138-46.

Shafir, Shlomo. "American Diplomats in Berlin [1933-39] and Their Attitude to the Nazi Persecution of the Jews." *Yad Vashem Studies* 9 (1973):71-104.

Silver, Abba H. "The Cause of Zionism Must Not be Minimized." *New Palestine*. Jan. 31, 1941, pp. 7-8, 25-27.

Slutsky, Yehuda. "The Palestine Jewish Community and Its Assistance to European Jewry in the Holocaust Years." In Moshe Kohn, ed., *Jewish Resistance during the Holocaust*. Jerusalem, 1971, pp. 414-25.

Snow, Edgar. "How the Nazi Butchers Wasted Nothing." *Saturday Evening Post* 217 (Oct. 28, 1944):18-19, 96.

Steiner, Erich. "Zwei Jahrzeite nach der 'Patria'" *Jedioth Chadashoth* (Hagana Archives, Tel Aviv).

Syrkin, Marie. "Letter to the Editor." *Midstream* 14 (May, 1968):62-63.

——. "On Hebrewcide." *Jewish Frontier*, July, 1945, pp. 10-12.

——. "What American Jews Did during the Holocaust," *Midstream* 28 (Oct., 1982):6-12.

Szner, Zvi. "The Rabbi of Sanik." In Zvi Szner, ed., *Historical Records and Source Material: Extermination and Resistance*. Kibbutz Lochamei HaGetaot, 1958, 1:103-9.

Tal, Uriel. "On the Study of the Holocaust and Genocide." *Yad Vashem Studies* 13 (1979):7-52.

Tartakower, Aryeh. "Where the International Red Cross Failed." *Congress Weekly* 13 (May 3, 1946):9-10

Tenenbaum, Joseph. "Red Cross to the Rescue." *Yad Vashem Bulletin* 4/5 (Oct., 1959):7-8.

Vago, Bela. "The British Government and the Fate of Hungarian Jewry in 1944." In Yisrael Gutman and Efraim Zuroff, eds. *Rescue Attempts during the Holocaust.* Jerusalem, 1977, pp. 205-33.

——. "The Intelligence Aspects of the Joel Brand Mission." *Yad Vashem Studies* 10 (1974):111-28.

——. "Peilut Politit VeDiplomatit LeHatsalat Yehudei Tsefon Transylvania." *Yad Vashem Studies* 6 (1966):131-47.

Valentin, Hugo. "Rescue and Relief Activities in Behalf of Jewish Victims of Nazism in Scandinavia." *YIVO Annual* 8 (1953):224-51.

Van Paassen, Pierre. "World Destiny Pivots on Palestine." *New Palestine,* Dec. 12, 1941, pp. 9-10.

Voice of the Unconquered (1943-45).

Von Weisl, Wolfgang. "Illegale Transporte." In Josef Fraenkel, *The Jews of Austria: Essays on Their Life, History and Destruction.* London, 1967, pp. 165-76.

Weinberger-Carmilly, Moses. "The Tragedy of Transylvanian Jewry." *Yad Vashem Bulletin* 15 (Aug., 1964):12-27.

Weisblum, Gisza. "The Escape and Death of the 'Runner' Mala Zimetbaum." In Yuri Suhl, ed., *They Fought Back.* New York, 1975 ed., pp. 182-88.

Weizmann, Chaim. "Palestine's Role in the Solution of the Jewish Problem." *Foreign Affairs* 20 (Jan., 1942):324-38.

Weyl, Nathaniel. "Israel and Francisco Franco." *Midstream* 28 (Feb., 1982):11-16.

Wiener Library Bulletin.

Wiesel, Elie. "Telling the Tale." *Dimensions in American Judaism* 2 (Spring, 1968):9-12.

Williams, Roger M. "Why Wasn't Auschwitz Bombed?" *Commonweal* Nov. 24, 1978, pp. 746-51.

Wilson, John P. "Carlton J. Hayes, Spain, and the Refugee Crisis, 1942-1945." *American Jewish Historical Quarterly* 62 (Dec., 1972):99-110.

Withey, Stephen B. "Reactions to Uncertain Threat." In George Baker and Dwight Chapman, eds., *Man and Society in Disaster.* New York, 1962, pp. 93-123.

Wyman, David. "Why Auschwitz Was Never Bombed." *Commentary* 65 (May, 1978):37-46.

Yad Vashem Bulletin (1957-68).

Yahil, Leni. "Madagascar Chazon Ta'atuim Shel Pitaron HaShe'ela HaYehudit." *Yalkut Moreshet* 19 (June, 1975):159-74.

——. "Mivchar Teudot Britiyot Al HaAliya HaBilti-Ligalit LeEretz Yisrael (1939-1940)." *Yad Vashem Studies* 10 (1974):183-208.

——. "Peulot Ezra VeHatsala BaMedinot HaScandinaviot Lema'an Asirei Machanot HaRikuz." *Yad Vashem Studies* 6 (1966):162-74.

Zariz, Ruth. "Hatsalat Yehudim MeiHolland BeEmtsa'ut Ishurei Certifkatim." *Yalkut Moreshet* 23 (Apr., 1977):135-63.

Zionews (1938-44).

Zuckerman, Yitschak. "25 Years after the Warsaw Ghetto Revolt." In Moshe Kohn, ed., *Jewish Resistance during the Holocaust.* Jerusalem, 1971, pp. 24-34.

Zuroff, E[fraim]. "Attempts to Obtain Shanghai Permits in 1941: A Case of Rescue Priority during the Holocaust." *Yad Vashem Studies* 13 (1979):321-51.

——. "Hatsalat Talmidei Yeshivot Polin Derech HaMizrach HaRachok BeTekufat HaShoa." *MiDor Dor* 1 (1979):49-76.

——. "Rescue Priority and Fund Raising as Issues during the Holocaust: A Case Study of the Relations between the Vaad HaHatsala and the Joint, 1939–1941." *American Jewish History* 68 (Mar., 1979):305–17, 324–26.

Zwergbaum, Aaron. "Parshat Mauritius." *Yad Vashem Studies* 4 (1960):191–247.

Zylberberg, Moshe. "Ketsad Nodah BeVarsha HaEmet Al Treblinka." *HaDoar* 20 (2 Iyar, 5743–Apr., 1983):325.

Note: Newspapers that have been used can be found in the notes.

Unpublished Studies and Miscellanea

Berman, Aaron. "The Hebrew Committee of National Liberation and the Rescue of the European Jews." Hampshire College Honors Paper, Apr., 1975 (courtesy of Mr. Berman).

Kubovy, Miryam. *Ultimate Rescue Efforts, the Year 1944*. 3 vols. (n.d.) (copy in Yad Vashem Archives, Jerusalem).

"Missing Hero: Raoul Wallenberg" (BBC, 1981), John Bierman, director.

Ofer, Dalya, "HaAliya-HaBilti Chukit LeEretz Yisrael BeTekufat Milchemet HaOlam HaShniya 1939–1942." Ph.D. dissertation, Hebrew University, 1981.

——. "Peulot Ezra VaHatsala Shel 'HaMishlachat HaEretz-Yisraelit' BeKushta 1943." M.A. thesis, Hebrew University, 1972 (copy in YIVO Library, New York).

Penkower, Monty N. "From Holocaust to Genocides." Paper presented at the International Conference on the Holocaust and Genocide, June 23, 1982, Tel Aviv.

——. "Oral Histories of the Holocaust: A Preliminary State of the Field." Paper submitted to the First Oral History Conference on the Holocaust, sponsored by the Holocaust Survivors' Memorial Foundation, Feb. 26, 1980, City University Graduate Center, New York.

"The Shop on Main Street" (Czechoslovakia, 1965), Ladislav Grossman, original screenplay.

Vagman-Eshkoli, Chava. "Emdat HaManhigut HaYehudit BeEretz Yisrael LeHatsalat Yehudei Eiropa, 1942–1944," M.A. thesis, Bar-Ilan University, 1977 (courtesy of Ms. Vagman-Eshkoli).

Van Tijn, Gertrude. "Contribution towards the History of the Jews in Holland from May 10, 1940, to June 1944." Nahariya, 1944. (Copy in the JDC Archives, New York).

"Who Shall Live and Who Shall Die?" (documentary film, 1981), Laurence Jarvik, director.

Index

A Note on the Author

MONTY NOAM PENKOWER, professor and chairman of the history department at Touro College, is the author of *The Federal Writers' Project: A Study in Government Patronage of the Arts* (University of Illinois Press, 1977) and has published extensively on American and modern Jewish history. He is a consultant to the U.S. Holocaust Memorial Council and a member of the Academic Council of the American Jewish Historical Society. Professor Penkower is currently completing research for a study of Anglo-American foreign relations regarding Palestine during World War II.